ECONOMICS HANDBOOK SERIES

Seymour E. Harris, *Editor*

International and Interregional Economics

ECONOMICS HANDBOOK SERIES

SEYMOUR E. HARRIS, *Editor*

ADVISORY COMMITTEE: Edward H. Chamberlain, Gottfried Haberler, Alvin H. Hansen, Edward S. Mason, and John H. Williams. *All of Harvard University.*

International and Interregional Economics

SEYMOUR E. HARRIS

Lucius N. Littauer Professor of Political Economy and
Chairman, Department of Economics
Harvard University

McGRAW-HILL BOOK COMPANY, INC.

New York   Toronto   London

1957

INTERNATIONAL AND INTERREGIONAL ECONOMICS

THE MAPLE PRESS COMPANY, YORK, PA.

Again
for
R. B. H.

Editor's Introduction

For years many teachers of economics and other professional economists have felt the need of a series of books on economic subjects which is not filled by the usual textbook, nor by the highly technical treatise.

This present series, published under the general title *The Economics Handbook Series,* was planned with these needs in mind. Designed first of all for students, the volumes are useful in the ever-growing field of adult education and also are of interest to the informed general reader.

The volumes present a distillate of accepted theory and practice, without the detailed approach of the technical treatise. Each volume is a unit, standing on its own.

The authors are scholars, each writing on an economic subject which he is an authority. In this series the author's first task was not to make important contributions to knowledge—although many of them do—but as to present his subject matter that his work as a scholar will carry its maximum influence outside as well as inside the classroom. The time has come to redress the balance between the energies spent on the creation of new ideas and on their dissemination. Economic ideas are unproductive if they do not spread beyond the world of scholars. Popularizers without technical competence, unqualified textbook writers, and sometimes even charlatans control too large a part of the market for economic ideas.

In the classroom *The Economics Handbook Series* will serve, it is hoped, as brief surveys in one-semester courses, as supplementary reading in introductory courses, and in other courses in which the subject is related.

SEYMOUR E. HARRIS

Preface

I should explain to the reader the evolution of this book. The original book was Part Five (Some Aspects of Adjustment in the Postwar Period), which includes about half the volume. But after writing it, I was dissatisfied. It seemed that it should be tied more to some general considerations. Hence Part Four (Adjustments in International Economics). These two parts of the book, covering almost three-quarters of the space, may be the more important part. But I still was not happy. It seemed that the material ought to be related more closely to the elements of the theory of trade and money. Hence Parts One to Three. The theory and its history in Part One are elementary and incomplete. I am sure it is too brief and may be unsatisfactory to many. I have relied heavily on the views as presented by the outstanding classical theorists and probably have undertreated the more modern advances and embellishments. Some may prefer to skip this part or run over it quickly. There is very little that is new in this relatively small part of the book (Part One). I hope that the reader who starts at the beginning will be patient when treatment seems inadequate; he will frequently find gaps filled and discussion extended in later parts. I have tried to warn the reader of future discussions that are relevant.

This book centers around problems of disequilibrium. We start with a discussion of classical and neoclassical theories of international, *and to some extent* interregional, economics. We integrate monetary and fiscal theory and policy, both past and present, with international economics. Then we consider institutional changes which, in fact, are or require deviations from the free market, e.g., economic development, abnormal restraints on trade, and therapeutic institutions—all of which reduce the relevance of classical economics. The final part of the book includes a fairly thorough study of the postwar disequilibrium in the first postwar decade. Dollar shortage is the central theme here, but it is related to such issues as restrictions on trade, capital exports and assistance, exchange rates, the price of gold, convertibility, and the change in trade patterns.

In the early part of the book I have relied to some extent upon quotations from the classical writers. The reader thus gets the flavor of the contributions of these superior minds. But of course, this is only to a very slight degree a book of readings.

Over a period of almost twenty years, Professor Haberler and I have shared a seminar in international economics in the Graduate School of Public Administration, where I have learned much from him and from the many experts from government and elsewhere who have been kind enough to share their *expertise* with us. I am sure, however, that both Professor Haberler and some of these experts will not approve of all that is in this book.

I owe much to the Graduate School of Public Administration for sponsoring this seminar and providing part of the expenses of research required for this book. Mr. Peter Kenen, of the Harvard Graduate School of Arts and Sciences, read a good part of the manuscript and made many helpful suggestions; Mr. Robert Haynes, assistant librarian of Harvard University, as usual helped me find materials; Mrs. Joan Eckstein contributed both editorial and research help; and my secretary, Mrs. Anna Thorpe, helped in various ways but most of all by her consistently good humor. I am greatly indebted to all of them.

SEYMOUR E. HARRIS

Acknowledgments

The Works and Correspondence of David Ricardo, edited by Piero Sraffa, proved invaluable to the author in writing the first part of this book, and he is greatly indebted to Mr. Sraffa and to the Royal Economic Society for permission to include a number of quotations from this collection.

The author is also indebted to the publishers and journals concerned for permission to quote from the following:

Gottfried Haberler, *The Theory of International Trade*, 1936 (William Hodge & Company, Edinburgh)

Jacob Viner, *Studies in the Theory of International Trade*, 1937 (Harper & Brothers, New York)

W. Randolph Burgess, *Interpretations of Federal Reserve Policy—Speeches and Writings of Benjamin Strong*, 1930 (Harper & Brothers, New York)

Helen Hill Miller, "Trade, Aid and the Shades of Smoot and Hawley," *The Reporter*, Mar. 31, 1953

J. R. Hicks, "An Inaugural Lecture," *Oxford Economic Papers*, June, 1953 (Oxford University Press, New York)

Sir Dennis Robertson, *Britain in the World Economy*, 1954 (George Allen & Unwin, Ltd., London)

W. Y. Elliott et al., *The Political Economy of American Foreign Policy*, 1955 (Henry Holt and Company, Inc., New York)

Bertil Ohlin, *Interregional and International Trade*, 1933 (Harvard University Press, Cambridge, Mass.)

Gottfried Haberler, *A Survey of International Trade Theory*, 1955 (Princeton University Press, Princeton, N.J.)

T. E. Gregory (ed.), *British Banking Statutes and Reports, 1832–1928*, 1929 (Oxford University Press, New York)

S. E. Harris, "Dollar Scarcity," *Economic Journal*, 1947

Francis Y. Edgeworth, *Papers Relating to Political Economy*, 1925 (published on behalf of the Royal Economic Society by Macmillan & Co., Ltd., London)

Alfred Marshall, *Money, Credit and Commerce*, 1923 (Macmillan & Co., Ltd., London)

Contents

PART ONE

The Distribution of Tasks among Nations:
Mainly Principles and History

Introduction

In this part of the book I am concerned primarily with the factors that determine the distribution of output among nations. I have depended to a substantial degree upon the British classical school, which contributed so much to the development of the theory of international trade. Because Smith, Ricardo, Mill, and the others present their views so much better than I can and because I should like to give the reader the flavor of their writings, I have in this part and to some extent in the next part quoted passages from the writings of the major figures. The reader should not, however, view this book as a book of readings, for actually only about 10 per cent of the book consists of quotations.

Part One includes seven chapters. The first is devoted primarily to a long excerpt from Adam Smith's *Wealth of Nations* (1776), for it was Adam Smith more than anyone else who put across the principles of free trade. Indeed the time was ripe, for the world was weary of the minute interferences of the mercantilist system, and Locke, Hume, and the Physiocrats, among others, had provided the philosophical foundations for a free system. The importance of Smith lies in still another direction; namely, he argued for free trade as a means of obtaining the best allocation of economic resources. He was at great pains to show that the individual secures a much more effective allocation of his resources than could be achieved through meddling by the State. Interference, moreover, would also reduce the gains to be associated with the distribution of resources and abilities among nations.

Early in the nineteenth century Ricardo, the successful stockbroker turned economist, the economist who alone impressed the brilliant essayist De Quincey as a first-rate mind among economists, and probably the most acute mind in the history of economics, contributed greatly to the acceptance of a modern theory of international trade. Some authors, Schumpeter, for example, tend to underestimate the contributions of Ricardo and to overestimate those of his predecessors. It is true that Torrens, before Ricardo, had introduced the theory of comparative costs. But Ricardo, more than anyone else, won acceptance for the theory of comparative costs, the foundation of the theory of international trade. Under the most simplified assumptions Ricardo showed that two coun-

3

tries, each producing two commodities, could each gain from trade if the relative costs of production of the commodities varied between the two countries and that this would be so even if the absolute costs of production were lower for both commodities in one of the countries. The theory of international trade for the next 125 years was concerned much less with overthrowing Ricardo's theory than with removing its unreal assumptions and bringing the model closer to reality. Ricardo had introduced money, exchange rates, and wage rates into his discussion of disequilibrium, but he put the pure theory of international trade into one compartment and the monetary treatment into another. This division of international-trade theory into two parts—the pure theory, which is part of general static-value theory, and the dynamic price and monetary theory—has continued into recent years. As Myrdal observes in his new book *The International Economy* (1956), "the classical theory of international trade was an adjunct to this doctrine of a free market economy."

There are few examples in economics of a fundamental theory (such as comparative costs) which has so well withstood the assaults of generations of critics. Chapter 2 presents Ricardo on the theory of comparative costs.

In 1830 Nassau Senior explained why wage rates were much higher in some countries than in others. His explanation was largely in terms of the higher productivity of labor in some countries than in others, whether due to more diligence, higher intelligence, or the greater contribution of capital. This was an important attempt to consider the relevance of differences in wage rates to the theory of comparative costs, in turn related to the cooperation of capital. Ricardo had discussed labor time, not wage rates. J. S. Mill and Cairnes also observed that wage rates could affect a country's competitive position in a particular industry. But it remained for a twentieth-century economist to elaborate further the effects of wage rates and also to consider the relevance of capital costs. Taussig allowed that wages may reflect institutional obstacles and hence that when particular classes of workers were lower paid in some countries than in others, the commodities produced by them would be relatively cheap in international markets. But it was Taussig's view that there were not large differences among countries in the relative rates of wages for different classes of wage earners.

Taussig also allowed that capital costs were a relevant consideration and that a country with much capital and low rates of interest would be at an advantage in producing commodities which required much capital. But Professor Viner, Taussig's outstanding student, in general seems to agree with him that serious modifications in the theory of comparative costs are not required when capital costs are considered. However, Taussig and Viner seem to exaggerate the importance of labor relative to all costs, and they tie capital costs to the rate of interest, whereas the availability of capital, the costs of replacement, and the management of capital are also relevant.

We should, perhaps, add that Taussig and Viner alone among the outstanding international-trade theorists have adhered to a real cost theory of international trade. They concentrate on the unpleasantness of labor and the abstinence costs of saving. As Professor Haberler observes, they assume that all inputs involve disutility and that their remuneration is proportionate to the disutility involved, or that the different types of labor and other inputs are employed in approximately the same proportions by all industries. These assumptions are far removed from the facts of the real world.[1]

In Chapter 3 we consider further the contributions of Senior, Taussig, and Viner in introducing a consideration of wages and capital costs into the theory of international trade.

Chapter 4 brings together some empirical materials, based on several studies, concerned with the factors determining the over-all competitive position of different countries and some of their industries. These studies underline the importance of such factors as the amount of horsepower used per worker, productivity and capital, the quality of management, the attitude of labor unions, tax systems, the size of the business unit, and external economies (e.g., availability of satellite industries) as variables which help to fix the relative competitive positions of countries and of their individual industries. It is found, for example, that there are large variations in the structure of wage rates in different countries and also that in the United States wages are only about 40 per cent of value added. Furthermore, the ratio of salaries to wages varies greatly, suggesting that the importance of management, research, and the like differs from country to country. It is also shown that manufacturing wages are a small part of the price of the finished product, so that the understanding of competitive position involves a consideration of selling costs, with all the. imperfections involved. Where the landed price is X but the final consumer price is $4X$ or $5X$, the theory of international trade leaves out much that is important when it concentrates on labor time in manufacturing exports or even on the corresponding wages.

Thus far, we have considered only the role of costs in the theory of international trade. We have, moreover, concentrated upon that line of reasoning which Ricardo first set forth and which received its fullest statement in the works of Taussig and Viner. It remains for us to examine in the remaining chapters of Part One the influence of demand upon the course of international trade and the writings of those

---

[1] G. Haberler, *A Survey of International Trade Theory*, 1955, p. 13.

economists, Marshall, Edgeworth, Ohlin, and Haberler, who substituted
for Ricardo's concentration upon labor time a consideration of *all* the
factors of production.

John Stuart Mill was the first economist to analyze in detail the influence of demand upon international trade. Mill sought a measure of
the gains from trade and the precise ratio at which goods would be
traded between countries. Ricardo's analysis gave no answer to these
questions; he had provided only the limits within which the terms of
trade must lie. It was among Mill's most original and permanent contributions to economics that he demonstrated the manner in which the
terms of trade are determined, invoking for this purpose and formulating
quite precisely what he called the "equation of international demand."

However, Mill's use of the terms of trade as a measure of the gains
from trade has been much criticized, and we shall have, in Chapter 5,
to present not only Mill's analysis of the determination of the terms of
trade but also a critique of his argument.

Whereas Senior, Taussig, and Viner have tried to amend the Ricardian
analysis, later economists have tried to build for the theory of comparative costs a broader foundation. In Chapter 6, we shall summarize
their efforts and consider the means by which they have joined the
theory of comparative costs to Mill's analysis of demand. Among the first
of the new analyses was that of Alfred Marshall. Marshall introduced
a composite commodity he called the bale, each bale being produced by
the same aggregate investment of labor (of various qualities) and of
capital.

Following closely upon Marshall, F. Y. Edgeworth carried even
further the analysis of the gains from trade and had much to say about
protection and the terms of trade.

But a more radical departure was that of Ohlin. He attempted to
treat all the relevant factors and, in so doing, to stress the impact upon
trade of international differences in factor endowments. Ohlin argues
that each country concentrates on the industries which use the relatively
plentiful factors. He also considers the role of demand, observing that
the prices of the factors of production depend upon demand conditions;
a country with much cheap labor tends, for example, to favor industries
using much low-priced labor, but the increased demand that results from
its low price will, in turn, raise the price of the relatively cheap factor
as well as the prices of factors that are complementary to the plentiful
factors. Ohlin's theory is, in short, an application of general-equilibrium
theory to the problems of international trade, as is the simpler model
constructed by Professor Haberler. The latter assumed for simplicity that
each country has a fixed and different supply of factors. Like Ohlin, he
then demonstrated the manner in which international differences in factor

endowments make for trade between countries. Professor Haberler rejected the classical equation of real with money costs.

The final chapter (Chapter 7) of Part One presents some general remarks concerning the theory of international trade and takes note of recent work in the field. It also contains some material relating to the actual international distribution of employments.

CHAPTER 1

Free Trade and the Origins of Classical Theory: The Views of Adam Smith

In classical economics the theory of international trade was linked with the issue of free trade and protectionism and, in fact, was developed in support of free trade. Adam Smith signalized the coming death of mercantilism by a vigorous assault upon government interference with the deployment of economic resources. In the passages below from the *Wealth of Nations* (1776) it will be noted that Smith supports free trade as promoting the division of labor and thereby raising revenue (income). Free trade promotes the division of labor because it causes each country to concentrate on those products which it can produce most cheaply. Smith takes great pains to show that losses are involved in producing, say, grapes in Scotland instead of importing grapes and paying for them with commodities that would have required less capital and industry than the producing of grapes. In a way Smith's support of the division of labor was an advanced view, since he stressed the resultant higher incomes. On several other issues Smith sounds modern. He accepts the defense argument for protection, the possibility of retaliatory duties being used as a weapon for imposing liberalization of trade abroad, and suggests the folly, where large vested interests are involved, of large and rapid reductions of tariff rates. Smith also recognized that transportation costs cut down trade, and hence argued that manufacturers gain much more from protection than do farmers. Agricultural goods are bulky and were expensive to transport; the consequent high transport costs were a natural obstacle to imports and reduced the need for tariffs to protect agriculture. Finally, note that Smith tended to underestimate the problem of adjustment in a free-trade economy, as many economists do today, but to appraise well the importance of pressure groups.[1]

Relevant passages from the *Wealth of Nations* follow.

[1] A. Smith, *Wealth of Nations* (E. Cannan, ed.; Lerner edition), 1937, book IV, chap. 2.

THE CASE FOR FREE TRADE

What is the species of domestic industry which his capital can employ, and of which the produce is likely to be of the greatest value, every individual, it is evident, can, in his local situation, judge much better than any statesman or lawgiver can do for him. The statesman, who should attempt to direct private people in what manner they ought to employ their capitals, would not only load himself with a most unnecessary attention, but assume an authority which could safely be trusted, not only to no single person, but to no council or senate whatever, and which would nowhere be so dangerous as in the hands of a man who had folly and presumption enough to fancy himself fit to exercise it.

To give the monopoly of the home-market to the produce of domestic industry, in any particular art or manufacture, is in some measure to direct private people in what manner they ought to employ their capitals, and must, in almost all cases, be either a useless or a hurtful regulation. If the produce of domestic can be brought there as cheap as that of foreign industry, the regulation is evidently useless. If it cannot, it must generally be hurtful. It is the maxim of every prudent master of a family, never to attempt to make at home what it will cost him more to make than to buy. The taylor does not attempt to make his own shoes, but buys them of the shoemaker. The shoemaker does not attempt to make his own clothes, but employs a taylor. The farmer attempts to make neither the one nor the other, but employs those different artificers. All of them find it for their interest to employ their whole industry in a way in which they have some advantage over their neighbours, and to purchase with a part of its produce, or what is the same thing, with the price of a part of it, whatever else they have occasion for.

What is prudence in the conduct of every private family, can scarce be folly in that of a great kingdom. If a foreign country can supply us with a commodity cheaper than we ourselves can make it, better buy it of them with some part of the produce of our own industry, employed in a way in which we have some advantage.[2]

The natural advantages which one country has over another in producing particular commodities are sometimes so great, that it is acknowledged by all the world to be in vain to struggle with them. By means of glasses, hotbeds, and hotwalls, very good grapes can be raised in Scotland, and very good wine too can be made of them at about thirty times the expence for which at least equally good can be brought from foreign countries. Would it be a reasonable law to prohibit the importation of all foreign wines, merely to encourage the making of claret and burgundy in Scotland? But if there would be a manifest absurdity in turning towards any employment, thirty times more of the capital and industry of the country, than would be necessary to purchase from foreign countries an equal quantity of the commodities wanted, there must be an absurdity, though not altogether so glaring, yet exactly of the same kind, in turning towards any such employment a thirtieth, or even a

2 *Ibid.,* pp. 423–425.

three hundredth part more of either. Whether the advantages which one country has over another, be natural or acquired, is in this respect of no consequence. As long as the one country has those advantages, and the other wants them, it will always be more advantageous for the latter, rather to buy of the former than to make. It is an acquired advantage only, which one artificer has over his neighbour, who exercises another trade; and yet they both find it more advantageous to buy of one another, than to make what does not belong to their particular trades.

Merchants and manufacturers are the people who derive the greatest advantage from this monopoly of the home-market. The prohibition of the importation of foreign cattle, and of salt provisions, together with the high duties upon foreign corn, which in times of moderate plenty amount to a prohibition, are not near so advantageous to the graziers and farmers of Great Britain, as other regulations of the same kind are to its merchants and manufacturers. Manufactures, those of the finer kind especially, are more easily transported from one country to another than corn or cattle. It is in the fetching and carrying manufactures, accordingly, that foreign trade is chiefly employed. In manufactures, a very small advantage will enable foreigners to undersell our own workmen, even in the home market. It will require a very great one to enable them to do so in the rude produce of the soil. If the free importation of foreign manufactures were permitted, several of the home manufactures would probably suffer, and some of them, perhaps, go to ruin altogether, and a considerable part of the stock and industry at present employed in them, would be forced to find out some other employment. But the freest importation of the rude produce of the soil could have no such effect upon the agriculture of the country.[3]

EXCEPTIONS TO FREE TRADE

There seem, however, to be two cases in which it will generally be advantageous to lay some burden upon foreign, for the encouragement of domestic industry.

The first is, when some particular sort of industry is necessary for the defence of the country. The defence of Great Britain, for example, depends very much upon the number of its sailors and shipping. The act of navigation, therefore, very properly endeavours to give the sailors and shipping of Great Britain the monopoly of the trade of their own country, in some cases, by absolute prohibitions, and in others by heavy burdens upon the shipping of foreign countries. The following are the principal dispositions of this act. . . .

The second case, in which it will generally be advantageous to lay some burden upon foreign for the encouragement of domestic industry, is, when some tax is imposed at home upon the produce of the latter. In this case, it seems reasonable that an equal tax should be imposed upon the like produce of the former. This would not give the monopoly of the home market to domestic industry, nor turn towards a particular employment a greater share of the stock and labour of the country, than what would naturally go to it. It would only hinder any part of what would naturally go to it from being

³ *Ibid.*, pp. 425–426.

turned away by the tax, into a less natural direction, and would leave the competition between foreign and domestic industry, after the tax, as nearly as possible upon the same footing as before it. In Great Britain, when any such tax is laid upon the produce of domestic industry, it is usual at the same time, in order to stop the clamorous complaints of our merchants and manufacturers, that they will be undersold at home, to lay a much heavier duty upon the importation of all foreign goods of the same kind.[4]

The case in which it may sometimes be a matter of deliberation how far it is proper to continue the free importation of certain foreign goods, is, when some foreign nation restrains by high duties or prohibitions the importation of some of our manufactures into their country. Revenge in this case naturally dictates retaliation, and that we should impose the like duties and prohibitions upon the importance of some or all of their manufactures into ours. Nations accordingly seldom fail to retaliate in this manner.[5]

There may be good policy in retaliations of this kind, when there is a probability that they will procure the repeal of the high duties or prohibitions complained of. The recovery of a great foreign market will generally more than compensate the transitory inconveniency of paying dearer during a short time for some sorts of goods. To judge whether such retaliations are likely to produce such an effect, does not, perhaps, belong so much to the science of a legislator, whose deliberations ought to be governed by general principles which are always the same, as to the skill of that insidious and crafty animal, vulgarly called a statesman or politician, whose councils are directed by the monetary fluctuations of affairs. When there is no probability that any such repeal can be procured, it seems a bad method of compensating the injury done to certain classes of our people, to do another injury ourselves, not only to those classes, but to almost all the other classes of them. When our neighbours prohibit some manufacture of ours, we generally prohibit, not only the same, for that alone would seldom affect them considerably, but some other manufacture of theirs. This may no doubt give encouragement to some particular class of workmen among ourselves, and by excluding some of their rivals, may enable them to raise their price in the home-market. Those workmen, however, who suffered by our neighbours' prohibition will not be benefited by ours. On the contrary, they and almost all the other classes of our citizens will thereby be obliged to pay dearer than before for certain goods. Every such law, therefore, imposes a real tax upon the whole country, not in favour of that particular class of workmen who were injured by our neighbours' prohibition, but of some other class.[6]

GRADUALNESS OF REMOVAL OF RESTRICTIONS AND TRANSFER OF WORKERS

The case in which it may sometimes be a matter of deliberation, how far, or in what manner, it is proper to restore the free importation of foreign goods, after it has been for some time interrupted, is, when particular manufactures,

---

[4] *Ibid.,* pp. 429–432.
[5] *Ibid.,* p. 434.
[6] *Ibid.,* p. 435.

by means of high duties or prohibitions upon all foreign goods which can come into competition with them, have been so far extended as to employ a great multitude of hands. Humanity may in this case require that the freedom of trade should be restored only by slow gradations, and with a good deal of reserve and circumspection. Were those high duties and prohibitions taken away all at once, cheaper foreign goods of the same kind might be poured so fast into the home market as to deprive all at once many thousands of our people of their ordinary employment and means of subsistence. The disorder which this would occasion might no doubt be very considerable. It would in all probability, however, be much less than is commonly imagined, for the two following reasons:

First, all those manufactures, of which any part is commonly exported to other European countries without a bounty, could be very little affected by the freest importation of foreign goods. Such manufactures must be sold as cheap abroad as any other foreign goods of the same quality and kind, and consequently must be sold cheaper at home. They would still, therefore, keep possession of the home market, and though a capricious man of fashion might sometimes prefer foreign wares, merely because they were foreign, to cheaper and better goods of the same kind that were made at home, this folly could, from the nature of things, extend to so few, that it could make no sensible impression upon the general employment of the people. But a great part of all the different branches of our woollen manufacture, of our tanned leather, and of our hard-ware, are annually exported to other European countries without any bounty, and these are the manufactures which employ the greatest number of hands. The silk, perhaps, is the manufacture which would suffer the most by this freedom of trade, and after it the linen, though the latter much less than the former.

Secondly, though a great number of people should, by thus restoring the freedom of trade, be thrown all at once out of their ordinary employment and common method of subsistence, it would by no means follow that they would thereby be deprived either of employment or subsistence. By the reduction of the army and navy at the end of the late war, more than a hundred thousand soldiers and seamen, a number equal to what is employed in the greatest manufactures, were all at once thrown out of their ordinary employment; but, though they no doubt suffered some inconveniency, they were not thereby deprived of all employment and subsistence. The greater part of the seamen, it is probable, gradually betook themselves to the merchant-service as they could find occasion, and in the meantime both they and the soldiers were absorbed in the great mass of the people, and employed in a great variety of occupations. Not only no great convulsion, but no sensible disorder arose from so great a change in the situation of more than a hundred thousand men, all accustomed to the use of arms, and many of them to rapine and plunder. The number of vagrants was scarce any-where sensibly increased by it, even the wages of labour were not reduced by it in any occupation, so far as I have been able to learn, except in that of seamen in the merchant-service. But if we compare together the habits of a soldier and of any sort of manufacturer, we shall find that those of the latter do not tend so much to disqualify him from being employed in a new trade, as those of the former from being employed in any. The manufacturer has always been accustomed to look for his subsistence from his labour only: the soldier to expect it from his pay. Application and industry have been familiar to the one; idleness and dissipation to the other. But it is surely much easier to change the direction of industry from one sort of labour to another, than to turn idleness and dissipation to any. To the greater part of manufactures besides, it has already been observed, there are other collateral manufactures of so similar a nature, that a workman can easily transfer his industry from one of them to another. The greater part of such workmen too are occasionally employed in country labour. The stock which employed them in a particular manufacture before, will still remain in the country to employ an equal number of people in some other way. The capital of the country remaining the same, the demand for labour will likewise be the same, or very nearly the same, though it may be exerted in different places and for different occupations. Soldiers and seamen, indeed, when discharged from the king's service, are at liberty to exercise any trade, within any town or place of Great Britain or Ireland. Let the same natural liberty of exercising what species of industry they please, be restored to all his majesty's subjects, in the same manner as to soldiers and seamen; that is, break down the exclusive privileges of corporations, and repeal the statute of apprenticeship, both which are real encroachments upon natural liberty, and add to these the repeal of the law of settlements, so that a poor workman, when thrown out of employment either in one trade or in one place, may seek for it in another trade or in another place, without the fear either of a prosecution or of removal, and neither the public nor the individuals will suffer much more than those who defend it with their blood, nor deserve to be treated with more delicacy.[7]

VESTED INTERESTS AND PROTECTION

To expect, indeed, that the freedom of trade should ever be entirely restored in Great Britain, is as absurd as to expect that an Oceana or Utopia should ever be established in it. Not only the prejudices of the public, but what is much more unconquerable, the private interests of many individuals, irresistibly oppose it. Were the officers of the army to oppose with the same zeal and unanimity any reduction in the number of forces, from which master manufacturers set themselves against every law that is likely to increase the number of their rivals in the home market; were the former to animate their soldiers, in the same manner as the latter enflame their workmen, to attack with violence and outrage the proposers of any such regulation; to attempt to reduce the army would be as dangerous as it has now become to attempt to diminish in any respect the monopoly which our manufacturers have obtained against us. This monopoly has so much increased the number of some particular tribes of them, that, like an overgrown standing army, they have become formidable to the government, and upon many occasions intimidate the legislature. The member of parliament who supports every proposal for strengthening this monopoly, is sure to acquire not only the reputation of

[7] *Ibid.*, pp. 435–437.

understanding trade, but great popularity and influence with an order of men whose numbers and wealth render them of great importance. If he opposes them, on the contrary, and still more if he has authority enough to be able to thwart them, neither the most acknowledged probity, nor the highest rank, nor the greatest public services, can protect him from the most infamous abuse and detraction, from personal insults, nor sometimes from real danger, arising from the insolent outrage of furious and disappointed monopolists.

The undertaker of a great manufacture, who, by the home markets being suddenly laid open to the competition of foreigners, should be obliged to abandon his trade, would no doubt suffer very considerably. That part of his capital which had usually been employed in purchasing materials and in paying his workmen, might, without much difficulty, perhaps, find another employment. But that part of it which was fixed in workhouses, and in the instruments of trade, could scarce be disposed of without considerable loss. The equitable regard, therefore, to his interest requires that changes of this kind should never be introduced suddenly, but slowly, gradually, and after a very long warning. The legislature, were it possible that its deliberations could be always directed, not by the clamorous importunity of partial interests, but by an extensive view of the general good, ought upon this very account, perhaps, to be particularly careful neither to establish any new monopolies of this kind, nor to extend further those which are already established. Every such regulation introduces some degree of real disorder into the constitution of the state, which it will be difficult afterwards to cure without occasioning another disorder.[8]

[8] *Ibid.*, pp. 437–439.

CHAPTER 2

Ricardo and Comparative Costs

Ricardo was the true author of the comparative-cost doctrine. As Alfred Marshall, the great British economist, wrote:[1]

Professor Hollander . . . has shown that nearly every part of Ricardo's doctrine was anticipated by some of his predecessors; but his masterly genius, like that of Adam Smith, was largely occupied with the supreme task of building up a number of fragmentary truths into coherent doctrine. Such a doctrine has constructive force, because it is an organic whole.

In presenting his theory of comparative costs, a theory which had been presented earlier but with less effectiveness by Torrens, Ricardo showed that trade would be profitably carried on between two countries even when one of them produced both commodities with less labor than another, provided its advantage was greater in the production of one commodity than in another.

This emphasis on comparative advantage as opposed to absolute advantage marks Ricardo's great advance over Adam Smith. Smith's presentation was couched entirely in terms of absolute advantage.

By way of illustration, Ricardo presents the famous case of trade in wine and cloth between Portugal and England. Trade is carried on to the profit of both countries even though Portugal requires less labor to produce both wine and cloth. Whereas Portugal has a comparative advantage in wine, England's lesser disadvantage is in cloth.[2]

England may be so circumstanced, that to produce the cloth may require the labour of 100 men for one year; and if she attempted to make the wine, it might require the labour of 120 men for the same time. England would therefore find it her interest to import wine, and to purchase it by the exportation of cloth.

To produce the wine in Portugal, might require only the labour of 80 men for one year, and to produce the cloth in the same country, might require

[1] A. Marshall, *Money, Credit and Commerce*, 1923, p. 41.
[2] *The Works and Correspondence of David Ricardo* (Sraffa, ed.), 1952, vol. I, pp. 135–136.

the labour of 90 men for the same time. It would therefore be advantageous for her to export wine in exchange for cloth. This exchange might even take place, notwithstanding that the commodity imported by Portugal could be produced there with less labour than in England. Though she could make the cloth with the labour of 90 men, she would import it from a country where it required the labour of 100 men to produce it, because it would be advantageous to her rather to employ her capital in the production of wine, for which she would obtain more cloth from England, than she could produce by diverting a portion of her capital from the cultivation of vines to the manufacture of cloth.

Thus England would give the produce of the labour of 100 men, for the produce of the labour of 80. Such an exchange could not take place between the individuals of the same country. The labour of 100 Englishmen cannot be given for that of 80 Englishmen, but the produce of the labour of 100 Englishmen may be given for the produce of the labour of 80 Portuguese, 60 Russians, or 120 East Indians. The difference in this respect, between a single country and many, is easily accounted for, by considering the difficulty with which capital moves from one country to another, to seek a more profitable employment, and the activity with which it invariably passes from one province to another in the same country.

Ricardo held that such exchanges would not be possible within a country, for capital and labor would move to the region where they were more productive. The contrast between international and inter-regional economics here is based on the assumption that capital and population move within a country but not from country to country.[3]

It would undoubtedly be advantageous to the capitalists of England, and to the consumers in both countries, that under such circumstances, the wine and the cloth should both be made in Portugal, and therefore that the capital and labour of England employed in making cloth, should be removed to Portugal for that purpose. In that case, the relative value of these commodities would be regulated by the same principle, as if one were the produce of Yorkshire, and the other of London: and in every other case, if capital freely flowed towards those countries where it could be most profitably employed, there could be no difference in the rate of profit, and no other difference in the real or labour price of commodities, than the additional quantity of labour required to convey them to the various markets where they were to be sold.

Experience, however, shows, that the fancied or real insecurity of capital, when not under the immediate control of its owner, together with the natural disinclination which every man has to quit the country of his birth and connexions, and intrust himself with all his habits fixed, to a strange government and new laws, check the emigration of capital. These feelings, which I should be sorry to see weakened, induce most men of property to be satisfied with a low rate of profits in their own country, rather than seek a more advantageous employment for their wealth in foreign nations.

[3] *Ibid.*, pp. 136–137.

Ricardo developed his theory of comparative costs on the assumption of two commodities, and though he did not insist (as some have implied) that population and capital never move across national frontiers, he certainly was aware that movements were less free than within a country. At the outset we should note that Ricardo did not entirely neglect the relevance of theory on the basis of more than two commodities. What is more, he was aware that the extension of analysis to more than two commodities meant that with a change in costs, the effects on gold movements and prices would be less because other commodities could move as well as the one export commodity assumed. That is to say, a country tending to lose gold could export not one, but many commodities as a substitute for gold.[4]

To simplify the question, I have been supposing the trade between two countries to be confined to two commodities—to wine and cloth; but it is well known that many and various articles enter into the list of exports and imports. By the abstraction of money from one country, and the accumulation of it in another, all commodities are affected in price, and consequently encouragement is given to the exportation of many more commodities besides money, which will therefore prevent so great an effect from taking place on the value of money in the two countries as might otherwise be expected.

John Stuart Mill, summarizing Ricardo's contribution, provides an excellent appraisal of its significance and its place in the history of economic thought.[5]

Of the truths with which political economy has been enriched by Mr. Ricardo, none has contributed more to give to that branch of knowledge the comparatively precise and scientific character which it at present bears, than the more accurate analysis which he performed of the nature of the advantage which nations derive from a mutual interchange of their productions. Previously to his time, the benefits of foreign trade were deemed, even by the most philosophical enquirers, to consist in affording a vent for surplus produce, or in enabling a portion of the national capital to replace itself with a profit. The futility of the theory implied in these and similar phrases, was an obvious consequence from the speculations of writers even anterior to Mr. Ricardo. But it was he who first, in the chapter on Foreign Trade, of his immortal *Principles of Political Economy and Taxation*, substituted for the former vague and unscientific, if not positively false, conceptions with regard to the advantage of trade, a philosophical exposition which explains, with strict precision, the nature of that advantage, and affords an accurate measure of its amount.

He showed, that the advantage of an interchange of commodities between nations consists simply and solely in this, that it enables each to obtain, with a given amount of labour and capital, a greater quantity of all commodities

[4] *Ibid.,* p. 141.
[5] J. S. Mill, *Essay on Some Unsettled Questions of Political Economy,* 1877, pp. 1–3.

taken together. This it accomplishes by enabling each, with a quantity of one commodity which has cost it so much labour and capital, to purchase a quantity of another commodity which, if produced at home, would have required labour and capital to a greater amount. To render the importation of an article more advantageous than its production, it is not necessary that the foreign country should be able to produce it with less labour and capital than ourselves. We may even have a positive advantage in its production; but, if we are so far favoured by circumstances as to have a still greater positive advantage in the production of some other article which is in demand in the foreign country, we may be able to obtain a greater return to our labour and capital by employing none of it in producing the article in which our advantage is least, but devoting it all to the production of that in which our advantage is greatest, and giving this to the foreign country in exchange for the other. It is not a difference in the *absolute* cost of production, which determines the interchange, but a difference in the *comparative* cost. It may be to our advantage to procure iron from Sweden in exchange for cottons, even although the mines of England as well as her manufactories should be more productive than those of Sweden; for if we have an advantage of one-half in cottons, and only an advantage of a quarter in iron, and could sell our cottons to Sweden at the price which Sweden must pay for them if she produced them herself, we should obtain our iron with an advantage of one-half, as well as our cottons. We may often, by trading with foreigners, obtain their commodities at a smaller expense of labour and capital than they cost to the foreigners themselves. The bargain is still advantageous to the foreigner, because the commodity which he receives in exchange, though it has cost us less, would have cost him more. As often as a country possesses two commodities, one of which it can produce with less labour, comparatively to what it would cost in a foreign country, than the other; so often it is the interest of the country to export the first mentioned commodity and to import the second; even though it might be able to produce both the one and the other at a less expense of labour than the foreign country can produce them, but not less in the same degree; or might be unable to produce either except at a greater expense, but not greater in the same degree.

On the contrary, if it produces both commodities with greater facility, or both with greater difficulty, and greater in exactly the same degree, there will be no motive to interchange.

Later Developments in the Theory

Ricardo had oversimplified the problem. As Professor Viner, the greatest living authority on classical economics, put it, Ricardo's theory was based on the following assumptions:[6]

. . . ample time for long-run adjustments; free competition; only two countries and only two commodities; constant labor cost as output is varied; and

---

[6] J. Viner, *Studies in the Theory of International Trade,* 1937, p. 444; also cf. F. W. Taussig, *Selected Readings in International Trade and Tariff Problems,* 1921, chaps. 2, 4, 5.

proportionality of both aggregate real costs and supply prices within each country to labor-time costs within that country.

Moreover, he left out of account demand conditions.

Marshall put Ricardo's assumptions as follows:[7]

. . . we may proceed on Ricardo's lines, and suppose that E and G are neighbouring islands which trade with one another, the goods being carried at public expense to the extent of one half by either island; and thus the cost of transport is eliminated from the trading account: the peoples, however, are supposed to be intolerant of one another's customs, and to refuse to migrate from one island to the other. The real cost of production of each commodity in each island is taken to be constant; though differences of soil, climate, agricultural and mineral resources cause many differences in the relative cost of various commodities in the two islands. Differences in the skill required for different occupations, and in the amount of capital by which each man's labour needs to be assisted, are neglected (or else the values of the several classes of labour and stocks of capital are expressed in terms of the value of labour of a standard efficiency), so that the real cost of production of any commodity in either island can be regarded as proportional to the amount of the standard labour of that island. Also, transport being gratuitous, the relative values of different things would of course remain generally the same in the two islands: if a quarter of oats and a hundred-weight of sugar were of equal value in one island, they would be of equal value also in the other.

[7] Marshall, *op. cit.*, pp. 322–323.

CHAPTER 3

The Elaboration of Ricardo's Model

Introduction[1]

Though he was aware that many elements enter into the cost of producing a commodity, Ricardo had tied his theory of international trade to labor costs or, more precisely, to labor time. Obviously, with the gradual abandonment of a labor-cost theory of value, the theory of international trade had to undergo surgery. But Ricardo's approach was not immediately cast aside. It was, instead, broadened and modified by his successors.

It was not long after Ricardo's work on international trade appeared that a brilliant classical economist introduced money wages into the theory of international trade. Nassau Senior, writing in 1830, stressed the relevance of labor's productivity—and the disagreeableness of certain occupations—as factors explaining differences in money wages. John Stuart Mill also revealed an awareness of the impact of money-wage differences upon the structure of export trade. In Senior's discussion, as in the further elaboration by Taussig almost one hundred years later, productivity in the export industries was given much attention; it was thought to be crucial to the determination of the structure of money wages in the economy. (I suspect that the influence of export productivity was overdone.)

In the 1870s the British economist Cairnes raised further objections to the simple labor theory of value. He pointed out that there might be restrictions on the movement of labor from place to place and from occupation to occupation and that one group protected by institutional barriers might receive higher rewards than another. Wages, therefore, would not correspond to labor time.

F. W. Taussig also drew attention to the effects of international differences in wage structure, the differences that Cairnes had explained by imperfections. He also called attention to the relevance of capital costs;

[1] For an excellent survey of the literature, see Professor Angell's classic volume *The Theory of International Prices*, 1926, especially pt. I.

differences in interest rates and in the amounts of capital used would yield a structure of trade different from that which the exclusive consideration of labor time would suggest.

Wages and Productivity in Export Industries

Nassau Senior, in lectures delivered in 1829 at Oxford, greatly advanced our understanding of the role of prices in international-trade theory.[2] Senior begins with a comparison of the cost (in silver) of labor in Hindustan, England, and America.[3]

The average annual wages of labor in Hindustan are from one to two pounds troy of silver a year. In England they are from nine to fifteen pounds troy. In Upper Canada and the United States of America, they are from twelve to twenty pounds troy. Within the same time the American laborer obtains twelve times and the English laborer nine times as much silver as the Hindu.

The difference in the cost of obtaining silver, or, in other words, in the wages of labor in silver, in different countries at the same period has attracted attention, though not perhaps so much as it deserves, and various theories have been proposed to account for it.

Then Senior refutes various "fallacious" explanations of the differences: greater densities of population in Hindustan, higher cost of living in the West, lower living standards in the East, differences in rates of profits, and variations in taxes.[4]

For Senior the explanation of the higher wages (in silver) in the West is as follows:[5]

. . . the diligence and skill with which English labour is applied enables the English labourer to produce in a year exportable commodities equal in value to those produced in a year by eight Hindoos; . . .

In fact the portableness of the precious metals and the universality of the demand for them render the whole commercial world one country, in which bullion is the money and the inhabitants of each nation form a distinct class of labourers. We know that in the small market of every district the remuneration paid to the producer is in proportion to the value produced. And consequently that if one man can by superior diligence, or superior skill, or by the assistance of a larger capital, or by deferring for a longer time his remuneration, or by any advantage natural or acquired, occasion a more valuable product, he will receive a higher reward. It is thus that a lawyer is better paid than a watchmaker, a watchmaker than a weaver, a first-rate than an ordinary workman. And for the same reason in the general market of the

[2] N. Senior, *Three Lectures on the Cost of Obtaining Money,* 1830.
[3] *Ibid.,* p. 1.
[4] *Ibid.,* pp. 2–10.
[5] *Ibid.,* pp. 11, 14.

world an Englishman is better paid than a Frenchman, a Frenchman than a Pole, and a Pole than a Hindoo.

Wages in export industries, according to Senior[6] (and Taussig), determine wages in other employments.

In the first place it follows that the amount of the income in money of each individual depends on the prosperity of our foreign commerce. If the worst land that can be profitably cultivated in England will produce per acre, at an average, two quarters of corn a-year, after deducting what must be reserved for seed, the proprietor of an estate of one hundred acres, producing at an average, after the deduction of seed, four quarters of corn per acre, is entitled to two hundred quarters as his rent. The value in money of those two hundred quarters must be the same as that of the two hundred quarters which the farmer retains and divides between himself and his labourers. The value of those two hundred quarters must be equal to the wages of the labourers after deducting the farmer's profit for having paid those wages in advance. And those wages, though not precisely the same as the wages of the labourers who produce commodities for exportation, must bear a certain proportion to those wages. If the toils undergone by the manufacturer are supposed to be more severe by one-third than those of the agriculturist, the agricultural labourer will at an average receive just two-thirds of the wages of the manufacturer. If the foreign demand for English manufactures be such as to occasion the manufacturer to receive 15s. or about three ounces of silver a week, the agriculturist will receive 10s. or about two ounces of silver a week.

Overemphasis on Export Industries

Taussig concurred in Senior's argument. He, too, believed that productivity in the export industries has a decisive influence upon wages. But both Senior and Taussig went too far. Why should the American wage level be determined by the productiveness of export industries, which account for but 5 per cent of the national income of the United States? Productivity in other industries will react on the export industries, helping to determine what is exported or imported, the amount of precious metals in the country, and to this extent the level of prices and money wages. It is not even clear that, as Taussig used to claim, the highest wage industries are necessarily the export industries. For example, wages have been at a record level in coal and railroads in the United States, and these are not ordinarily export industries; wages have been low in agriculture, one of our strongest export employments (see, however, Chapter 4).

Nor is it always clear that the export industries are the most productive. For example, medicine in the United States is a highly productive employment. In a sense it is an export industry, but its major market, surely more than 99 per cent, is at home.

[6] *Ibid.,* pp. 16–17.

The assumption of high productivity in the export industries is used by a group of experts to support the view that Western Europe must expand its trade; the alternative is the expansion of less productive industries that serve the home market.[7] But this position rests on another assumption: that as export output rises and exports are pressed on foreign markets, export prices will not greatly decline. Otherwise, the higher productivity of the export industries, as against domestic industries, may be more than offset by deterioration in the terms of trade.

Imperfections in Labor Markets and Export Prices

Ricardo had fully understood that the structure of trade is proximately governed by money costs and prices.[8] He assumed, however, that the prices and commodities would be proportional to the labor time embodied in them and could, in consequence, argue that the pattern of trade would ultimately be governed by the relative amounts of labor expended in production.

Before many years had passed, however, Senior was to point out that prices can deviate from those which would be given by the quantities of labor devoted to production. He emphasized the productivity of the labor used. A bit later, John Stuart Mill was to contend that the deviation of wages (and prices) from strict proportionality with labor time could influence the structure of trade.

Mill maintained that low wages would not enable one country to undersell another if they prevailed in all industries. But he was very careful to say that a country could obtain a competitive advantage in some industries by depressing the wages of workers employed in those industries, and he cited the United States production of cotton and tobacco with slave labor as an example. Mill's discussion has a modern ring. He properly considers the relation of wages to productivity and continues as follows: "We continually hear of the disadvantage under which the British producer labours, both in foreign markets and even in his own, through the lower wages paid by his foreign rivals."[9]

Both Senior and Mill were inclined to treat the deviations of price from labor time as relatively infrequent exceptions to the Ricardian principle. It remained for Cairnes to show that prices would not *in general* be proportionate to labor time because wage rates would differ from industry to industry and that the pattern of trade could stray substantially from the channel it would follow under Ricardo's assumptions.

[7] W. Y. Elliott et al., *The Political Economy of American Foreign Policy*, 1955, p. 63.

[8] *The Works and Correspondence of David Ricardo* (Sraffa, ed.), 1951–1952, vol. I, p. 137.

[9] J. S. Mill, *Principles of Political Economy* (Ashley, ed.), 1920, pp. 680–687.

Cairnes observed that there are obstacles to the spread of a wage increase or decrease, that the labor force is not homogeneous, and that wage rates are not determined by the competition of workers, each with all the others. He stressed the division of the labor force into a great number of "non-competing groups."[10]

What we find, in effect, is not a whole population competing indiscriminately for all occupations, but a series of industrial layers, superposed on one another, within each of which the various candidates for employment possess a real and effective power of selection, while those occupying the several strata are, for all purposes of effective competition, practically isolated from each other. . . . I am far from contending for the existence of any hard lines of demarkation between any categories of persons in this country. No doubt the various ranks and classes fade into each other by imperceptible gradations, and individuals from all classes are constantly passing up or dropping down; but while this is so, it is nevertheless true that the average workman, from whatever rank he may be taken, finds his power of competition limited for practical purposes to a certain range of occupations, so that, however high the rates of remuneration in those which lie beyond may rise, he is excluded from sharing them. We are thus compelled to recognize the existence of non-competing industrial groups as a feature of our social economy; . . .

By means of the concept of noncompeting groups Cairnes was enabled to make of Mill's exceptional case a very general phenomenon.[11]

Let me now state the point to which the general argument has been carried. I have endeavored to show that a rise or fall of wages in a country, so far forth as it is general, has no tendency to affect the course of foreign trade: a fall in the general rate does not tend to an extension of foreign trade, any more than a rise in that rate necessitates a contraction. On the other hand, I have pointed out that, where, owing to the existence of impediments to the action of free industrial competition, partial movements in the rate of wages occur, inasmuch as these issue in a change of relative prices, the course of foreign trade is in this case affected. . . .

The doctrine of noncompeting groups thus filled a gap in Mill's earlier analysis; it explained why a wage change in one industry might not become general and so could affect the course of trade.

Taussig gave extended consideration to Cairnes's criticism of the Ricardian model, but he was inclined to minimize its importance. Defending Ricardo's emphasis upon labor time, he argued that there are but slight differences as between countries in the structure of wage rates because each country has about the same sort of noncompeting groups.[12]

[10] J. E. Cairnes, *Some Leading Principles of Political Economy Newly Expounded,* 1874, pp. 66–68.
[11] *Ibid.,* p. 334.
[12] F. W. Taussig, *International Trade,* 1927, pp. 47–48, 56.

The general conclusion thus indicated is that the existence of non-competing groups within a country affects international trade only so far as the situation thus engendered is peculiar to that country. If the groups are in the same relative positions in the exchanging countries as regards wages—if the hierarchy, so to speak, is arranged on the same plan in each—trade takes place exactly as if it were governed by the strict and simple principle of comparative costs. If the rate of wages in a given occupation is particularly low in one country, this circumstance will affect international trade exactly as would a high effectiveness of labor in that country. But if in other countries also the same occupation has a particularly low rate of wages, international trade will not be affected. The coefficient to be allowed for will be the same all around, and no special influence on trade between the countries will be felt. Trade will develop as it would if prices within each country were governed by labor costs alone.

. . . Now, in the occidental countries—those of advanced civilization in the Western world—as a rule the stratification of industrial groups proceeds on the same lines. And it is between these countries that the principle of comparative costs is presumably of greatest importance. Since differences of climatic and physiographic character are less wide, divergences of absolute costs are less common and less great, and the limits within which the terms of exchange are confined not so far apart. And in the Western countries, to repeat, we find roughly the same social and industrial layers. The unskilled, by far the most numerous, get the lowest wages; the mechanics and well-trained stand distinctly higher; and so upward. This being the case, the differences in money costs *between* countries are mainly determined by differences in labor costs; even tho *within* each country this factor may be profoundly modified.

Trade and Capital Costs

Capital costs are also relevant, but Taussig minimizes the degree to which capital costs affect comparative costs. For him labor costs remain decisive.[13]

The general proposition to which this series of illustrative figures points is that interest on capital acts on international trade not in itself, but only in so far as it operates differently on different commodities. At the very start it is obvious that an interest charge, added uniformly to the expenses of production, brings no alteration in relative prices, since it acts equally on all commodities. Nor does an interest charge have an effect simply because it is at a different rate in the two countries—higher in one than in the other. If within each it acts uniformly thruout, it leaves the relations between the countries undisturbed. Further: an interest charge does not alter conditions for trade, even tho it act on one commodity only, provided it acts on that commodity in the same way in both countries. The same is true (illustration in figures may be spared) if the interest charge instead of being absent on one article while present on another, is merely greater on one than on another.

[13] *Ibid.*, chap. 7, p. 65.

If the difference is the same in both countries, international trade goes on in the same way as if this factor had not entered.

But the circumstance that the rate of interest is higher or lower in a country does have an effect when the needed capital equipment is greater for one commodity than for another. It bears *more* on those commodities which are made with much capital, making them relatively higher in price in the country where there is a higher rate of interest and a higher interest charge, lower in a country where there is a lower rate.

A low rate of return on capital, then, tends to give to a country a comparative advantage (i.e. the equivalent of one) for those goods which are made with much capital; these tend to be exported from it. A high rate of interest is correspondingly a handicap on the export of these same goods, a stimulus to their import. To put it in a more concrete way, a country in which capital has accumulated in large amounts and in which the investors are content with a low rate of return, tends to export articles which are made with much plant, and with raw materials which it takes *time* to produce and transport; whereas a country in which accumulation is smaller and the interest rate is higher, tends to import such articles. High or low interest does not in itself act as an independent factor; it exercises an influence of its own only so far as it enters to greater degree in one commodity than in another.[14]

The quantitative importance of the capital charge factor in international trade is probably not great. As the whole tenor of the preceding exposition indicates, the range of its influence is restricted to a special set of circumstances. Within that range, its influence is further limited by the absence of wide inequalities in the rate of return on capital. Interest, while it does vary somewhat from country to country, does not vary widely between the leading countries of western civilization; and it is in the trade between these, and in the competition between them for trade with other countries, that the interest factor is most likely to enter with its independent and special effects.[15]

The Degree of Modification of Labor-cost Theory

By taking into account money wages and capital costs as variables that affect the pattern of specialization and export and import trade and cause it to deviate from that suggested by a concentration on labor time, Taussig moved the theory of international trade closer to an acceptable explanation of the real world. But he underestimated the difference made, and I believe that even Professor Viner, in support of Taussig, similarly does not acknowledge the degree to which the labor-cost theory has been undermined.[16]

It would not be seriously contended by anyone today—if ever—that the doctrine of comparative costs in terms of labor costs lays down an exact and

---

[14] *Ibid.*, pp. 65–66.
[15] *Ibid.*, p. 67.
[16] J. Viner, *Studies in the Theory of International Trade*, 1937, pp. 512–514.

universally applicable rule of policy, any deviation from which necessarily involves national loss. It could still be held that the doctrine provides a generally valid rule of policy, to be departed from only upon clear demonstration in particular instances that there exist special circumstances which make the rule inapplicable in those circumstances, if for most products entering into foreign trade wages costs were so predominant a part of the total costs that the differences as between different products in the percentages of wages costs to total costs were narrowly limited in range. . . .

The plight of the comparative-cost doctrine appears still less serious, moreover, if it is granted, as I believe it must be, that a real-cost theory of value should provide for real capital costs as well as for labor costs. If interest charges are different fractions of total expenses in different industries, then if money costs were to be proportional to real costs they could not be proportional to labor costs alone. Specialization in accordance with money costs may still be in conformity with real costs if these include both labor and capital costs, even when it is clearly not in conformity with labor costs alone. The logical difficulty for the doctrine of comparative costs created by interest charges is not that they can be shown to result in a deviation of money costs from real costs, but rather that there is no satisfactory way of showing whether money costs which include both wages and interest costs do or do not conform to real costs.

CHAPTER 4

Empirical Aspects of Comparative Costs

Price competition is what counts in international trade. When Ricardo estimates what one day's labor will produce in units of wine or cloth, he omits consideration of many important variables.

What, for example, determines that product A rather than B becomes an export commodity? Certainly an answer cannot be given by the fact that one day's labor produces more of A than B. When Ricardo said that 80 days' labor in Portugal would produce X of wine and 90 days' labor Y of cloth and in England 120 and 100 days of labor, respectively, were required, he implicitly included capital costs as part of labor costs. Taussig admits that when an industry uses much capital and rates of interest are lower than abroad, then comparative costs are influenced. Despite the great authority of Viner's name in this field and his view to the contrary, I suggest that the amount of capital per worker varies greatly and is an important consideration.

Nor is the problem treated adequately when the costs of capital are reduced to interest charges. We must also consider the total cost of producing, of keeping up, and of replacing the capital as well as the power to use it. These costs are likely to be much more important than the rate of interest charged. What is also relevant is the availability of capital. What helps to account for high productivity in the United States is partly the consequence of an ample supply of capital.[1] For example, Rostas has found that for thirty-one sample industries, productivity in the United States (output per head) for the years 1935 to 1939 was 214 to 223 and per man-hour, 284 to 290 (United Kingdom = 100). These large differences in productivity (in 1939 the maximum was wireless sets, 348, and the minimum, cement, 101) are to be explained by such factors as (1) management, (2) extent of the market, (3) economies (e.g., satellite industries and responsive labor market), (4) size of the business unit or plant, (5) availability of external economies, (6) amount

[1] Cf. L. Rostas, *Comparative Productivity in British and American Industry*, 1948, pp. 2–4, 14–17.

of capital (inclusive of age of equipment) and effectiveness of use of capital (layout of plant, programming of output), (7) use of power, (8) economies in use of raw materials, (9) research, (10) institutional factors (e.g., taxation), (11) natural conditions (rich coal veins in the United States), and (12) standardization. These are all relevant, though Rostas has found that the correlations of horsepower used, size of plant, or size of market with differences in output per man are not so great as is generally assumed.[2]

Of these factors that account for differences in man-day or man-hour output, many might be subsumed under labor costs, but not labor time. But others, such as management, differences in the amount of capital used, and variations in resources, are not easily tied down to labor costs. Or to put it another way: When we include in labor costs the effects of management, of the use of capital, etc., on man-hour output, we are linking to labor cost much that is not properly associated with labor.

Graham Hutton has conducted a careful survey of productivity in the United States and the United Kingdom, based largely on the numerous studies of the Anglo-American Council on Productivity (AACP) under the sponsorship of the European Cooperation Administration (ECA). He concludes that the differing trends of productivity in the United Kingdom and the United States are the joint result of numerous factors, but he emphasizes especially management, the use of machinery, education, labor attitudes, and institutional factors (taxation, freedom of markets). There obviously is, in the United States, a greater amount of indirect labor used, much more emphasis on the contribution of management, a greater use of machinery and power. All these contributions are not adequately treated as labor costs.[3]

The position is summarized as follows.[4] Mr. Hutton finds:

1. *That there is no peculiarly American "secret" of high industrial productivity;*

2. *that the principles and practices behind it are familiar, but are carried out in better ways;*

3. *that they can be carried out just as productively in any other country with good management, good human work, and good equipment, but to produce finished goods which need not be like American goods; and*

4. *that the only real problem of productivity is that of securing the degree of "goodness" of management, human work, and equipment.*

An example of the influence of nonlabor costs on productivity is the British brickmaking industry. As Hutton describes the situation:[5]

[2] *Ibid.*, especially pp. 27–30 and chap. 5.
[3] G. Hutton, *We Too Can Prosper*, 1953.
[4] *Ibid.*, pp. 207–208.
[5] *Ibid.*, p. 214.

The brick-making industry in Britain has been short of labour for over ten years. In 1951 it reached a total output only five-sixths of its pre-war volume. But the London Brick Company—which is responsible for about 30% of the country's output of bricks—that year, on a number of days, managed to recapture its pre-war daily output with 800 fewer workers, and therefore with a gain of 17% in productivity over the 1938 figure. This was obtained by much more mechanization, especially of operations involving handling of bricks, which lightened the load of the labour employed. The increase in mechanization offset the reduction in human labour available.

Of course, productivity figures are one thing and prices another. One has to take into account differences in wage rates, imperfections in the market, and many other considerations if one is to reduce productivity totals to price comparisons. In an excellent survey of the relation of comparative costs, prices, and exports during the prewar period, Mac-Dougall showed that, in general, the relative command of export markets by British and American producers was what might be expected, considering the higher man-hour output in American factories and balancing it against the somewhat higher indirect labor costs of American industry, higher wages in the United States (2.0 to 2.2 times as high as in Britain), and restrictions on trade. He found that when output per worker was more than twice British output (as, for example, in tin cans and motor cars), the price of exports was lower in the United States and the volume of American exports ranged from 1.0 to 7.6 times that of the United Kingdom. But when United States output per worker was less than twice that of the United Kingdom (as, for example, in coke and woolens), the British prices were lower and United States exports ranged from $\frac{4}{10}$ of 1 per cent (woolen and worsted goods) to 47 per cent (cigarettes) of British exports. But especially significant is the fact that even in manufacturing, the variations in relative wages as between the two countries were large and hence greatly influenced the structure of export trade. These figures may, of course, reflect differences in the hierarchies of labor, in the structure of the labor force. In any case, they suggest that differences in wages affect comparative costs much more than suggested by Taussig or Viner.

Some of MacDougall's results are presented in Table 4-1. It will be noted that there is no clear correlation between high relative wages in the United States and large exports by the industry paying them. Taussig, it will be recalled, argued that the high-wage industries are generally export industries. Also note that the ratio of United States to United Kingdom wages (column 2) varied by as much as 75 per cent.[6]

In an important article, however, Professor Kravis showed that wages

[6] G. D. A. MacDougall, "British and American Exports: A Study Suggested by the Theory of Comparative Costs," *Economic Journal*, 1951, pt. I, especially pp. 697–720.

Table 4-1. Output, Wage Costs, and Exports, United States and United Kingdom, 1937–1938

	United States–United Kingdom ratio			
	Output per worker, prewar	Weekly dollar earnings, October, 1938	(2) ÷ (1) Wage costs per unit of output	Quantity of exports, 1937
	(1)	(2)	(3)	(4)
Pig iron....................	3.6	1.5	0.4	5.1
Motor cars.................	3.1	2.0	0.6	4.3
Machinery..................	2.7	1.9	0.7	1.5
Glass containers............	2.4	2.0	0.8	3.5
Paper......................	2.2	2.0	0.9	1.0
Cigarettes..................	1.7	1.5	0.9	0.47
Leather footwear............	1.4	1.5	1.1	0.32
Hosiery....................	1.8	1.9	1.1	0.30
Cotton spinning and weaving...	1.5	1.7	1.1	0.11
Beer.......................	2.0	2.6	1.3	0.056
Cement....................	1.1	1.7	1.5	0.091
Woolen and worsted..........	1.35	2.0	1.5	0.004
Men's and boys' outer clothing of wool..................	1.25	2.3	1.8	0.044

SOURCE: *Economic Journal*, 1951, p. 707.

tend to be higher in export than in all industries and than in import-competing industries. This study lends some support to the Senior-Taussig position, though it might be noted that the differences are not large in manufacturing and services are omitted. In part, the higher wages in export industries arise because exports come disproportionately from the highly productive durable-goods industries. It will be noted, for example, that whereas hourly wages in manufacturing in 1947 (weighted by man-hours) were $1.252, for leading export industries the figure was $1.290, for leading import-competing industries, $1.245, and for vulnerable (unweighted) industries, 8 cents below the general average. Leading export industries in mining paid $1.605 as against $1.395 for leading import-competing industries. The differences are significant in manufacturing, substantial in mining and all commodity-producing sectors, and not very significant in agriculture.[7]

In 1955, an American economist compared productivity in American and British industry—this time for the year 1947 in the United States and 1948 for the United Kingdom. His survey shows clearly how difficult

[7] I. B. Kravis, "Wages and Foreign Trade," *The Review of Economics and Statistics*, February, 1956, pp. 14–30

Table 4-2. Hourly Earnings in Various Groups of Manufacturing, Mining, and Agricultural Industries, 1947

Industry group	No. of industries	Average hourly earnings, dollars			
		Un-weighted	Weighted by		
			Man-hours	1947 trade	1952 trade
Manufacturing...................	328	1.216	1.252		
Leading export industries........	46	1.306	1.290	1.321	1.368
Secondary export leaders.........	54	1.256	1.257	1.283	
Leading import-competing industries......................	36	1.213	1.245	1.143	1.272
Vulnerable commodities..........	24	1.13	.....	1.16	1.15
Industries with highly dutiable imports.....................	21	1.123	.....	.....	1.163
Mineral........................	22				
Leading export industries........	3	1.591	1.605	1.614	1.615
Leading import-competing industries......................	7	1.277	1.395	1.310	1.331
Agricultural....................	15				
Leading export industries........	6	1.252	0.975	1.269	1.671
Leading import-competing industries......................	8	1.230	0.966	0.999	1.018
All commodity-producing sectors:					
All leading export industries......	55	1.327	1.177	1.330	1.457
All leading import-competing industries*....................	52	1.224	1.107	1.149	1.225

* Includes logging, which was not included in either manufacturing or agriculture.

it is to account for the variations in productivity. Among thirty industries, variations in man-hour output range from 4.97 for tin containers in the United States (Great Britain $= 1.00$) to 0.69 for manufactured ice. Differences in the relative availability of natural resources are noted, and variations in the size of market and in the size of plant are compared. But it is not easy to find a consistent relationship between, say, differences in productivity and the size of the market. It can be shown that great dependence on foreign markets, so often the case for British output, means less standardization and higher unit costs because output has to be geared to the differing tastes of several foreign markets. But plant size is very often as large in Great Britain as in the United States.

Table 4-3 suggests many of the problems.[8]

[8] M. Frankel, "Anglo-American Productivity Differences: Their Magnitude and Some Causes," *Proceedings of the American Economic Association,* 1955, p. 95; also see a discussion, pp. 96–112.

Table 4-3. Productivity in Thirty British and American Manufacturing Industries†

Industry	United States–Great Britain ratio				
	Physical output per worker	Physical output per man-hour	Size of market (physical output)	Size of establishment	
				By number of employees	By output
Tin containers................	4.96	4.97	9.49	1.04	5.43
Cardboard containers.......	4.20	4.24	11.75	0.94	4.59
Pig iron....................	4.17	4.91	5.78	0.80	3.42
Wool yarn..................	4.03	4.53	2.52	1.27	4.85
Radio receiving tubes.......	3.36	3.74	11.55	1.06	5.58
Cigarettes.................	3.25	3.63	3.80	2.77	16.96
Wool carpets and rugs.....	3.15	3.28	5.76	2.01	6.04
Glass containers...........	2.87	3.06	5.73	1.58	4.67
Soap......................	2.81	2.89	4.29	1.02	2.45
Paper sacks...............	2.71	2.77	10.61	1.81	5.05
Matches...................	2.48	2.59	5.53	2.86	7.06
Ice cream.................	2.11	2.14	28.24	0.73	1.43
Animal feeds..............	2.11	2.06	9.75	0.60	1.28
Biscuits...................	2.04	2.18	3.29	0.76	1.72
Malt liquors..............	1.98	1.98	2.13	1.53	2.40
Grain milling.............	1.94	1.86	2.59	0.82	1.64
Bicycles..................	1.80	1.88	1.37		
Rubber tires..............	1.76	2.03	6.98	1.39	2.64
Jute yarn.................	1.69	1.77			
Sugar:					
U.S. cane, G.B. beet.....	1.66	1.82	2.03	1.96	4.05
U.S. beet, G.B. beet.....	0.77	0.85	0.67	0.51	0.46
Building bricks...........	1.66	1.77	1.35	0.95	1.48
Paint brushes............	1.63	1.74	2.65		
Cotton piece goods........	1.62	1.78	6.32	4.56	7.64
Boots and shoes..........	1.51	1.67	4.30	1.42	2.96
Rope and twine..........	1.51	1.61	2.28	1.48	1.94
Margarine................	1.21	1.23	0.81	0.52	0.66
Cement...................	1.15	1.39	3.72	0.99	1.06
Razor blades.............	1.09	1.12	2.80		
Cured fish................	0.95	1.20	0.30	1.08	1.07
Manufactured ice..........	0.75	0.69	41.27	0.59	0.46

† For notes and sources, see original.

Anyone who has followed the controversy over tariffs will find that the issue frequently hinges on a comparison of greater American productivity with the percentage excess of American over foreign wage rates.[9] The industry which is subjected to high wages in this country and does not share its relatively high productivity gets into difficulties. This, for example, seems to be the problem confronting the bicycle industry in the United States, where high wages are not offset by an adequate superiority in productivity.

So far we have stressed the importance of costs that are not closely associated with labor time or even labor costs and yet greatly affect comparative costs. The contributions of management, of the amount of capital per worker, of the effectiveness with which capital is used, are of tremendous importance. It is not an adequate answer to say that as long as labor income is two-thirds of total income, the labor-cost version of comparative costs is adequate. It is essential not only to explain why, since World War II, an American factory worker earns $15 a day and a British worker only $5 or $6 but also to discover how this difference can be reconciled with lower unit costs in the United States. Here we must consider the contributions of capital, management, institutional factors, etc., which vary greatly among countries and, within countries, among the different industries.

Manufacturing Labor and Other Costs

Classical and neoclassical theory scarcely touches on some crucial aspects of the problem of comparative costs. It concentrates on *manufacturing labor* costs. Yet wages in manufacturing are less than 20 per cent of total export costs. Furthermore, the price to the consumer of an imported product may be from three to five times this export price. (The Swiss watchwork costing $4 sells in the American market for $25.) The major additions to price are selling costs.

To give some statistical meaning to these issues, Table 4-4 is presented.

The reader will note that wage costs are but 40 per cent of value added and a mere 16 per cent of the value of the product. By comparison, salaries are also of importance, though in varying degrees: 6 cents, or 7 per cent of wages, in liquors and 24.2 cents, or 27 per cent of wages, in the highly productive tire industry. Again, wages seem to be high when the proportion of salary costs per man-hour to wage costs tends to be large.

Even within the same industry, large differences emerge in important variables. Thus in motor vehicles hourly wages are 84 per cent above those in automobile trailers; cost of materials, two to three times as high; value added per man-hour, 81 per cent more; and electrical energy

[9] Cf. Chap. 16.

Table 4-4. Selected Industries: Various Costs, Value of Product, Value Added, Electrical Energy Used, and Horsepower per Wage Earner, 1939

Industry	Per wage-earner man-hour							Horse-power per wage earner
	Wage earnings, cents	Salary costs, cents	Cost of materials, dollars	Prime cost, dollars	Value, products, dollars	Value added, dollars	Electrical energy used, kwhr	
171 selected industries..........	61.2	14.1	2.23	3.09	3.88	1.55	6.01	7.66
Food industries.................	65.2	18.2	7.65	8.49	10.17	2.52	5.33	8.97
Feeds, prepared..............	50.9	24.3	10.02	10.77	13.11	3.09	6.27	17.44
Liquors, malt................	84.7	6.0	2.21	3.32	7.11	4.90	4.65	8.59
Textile-mills products..........	44.1	6.9	0.99	1.50	1.85	0.86	3.53	3.32
Rubber industries..............	73.0	19.9	2.25	3.18	4.08	1.83	7.25	7.96
Tires and inner tubes.........	93.3	24.2	3.64	4.81	6.04	2.40	11.12	9.77
Rubber boots and shoes.......	63.4	13.1	0.78	1.54	1.88	1.10	2.50	4.26
Iron and steel.................	82.4	13.5	2.68	3.64	4.39	1.71	12.79	22.52
Iron foundries.................	62.3	12.7	0.71	1.46	1.86	1.15	2.00	4.56
Motor vehicles and bodies, parts, etc.......................	90.0	15.8	3.81	4.86	5.63	1.83	3.48	5.61
Automobile trailers...........	49.0	11.4	1.59	2.20	2.61	1.02	0.38	1.12

SOURCE: Adapted from U.S. Census, "Man-hour Statistics for 171 Selected Industries," *Census of Manufacturing, 1939*, March, 1942.

used (kilowatthours) per man-hour, nine times as great. Obviously, effectiveness in international competition depends in no small part upon labor costs, but there are other important costs which affect the result, and labor costs in turn are to be explained by indirect labor used (salaries), the contribution of management and capital.

Wage rates, the cost of capital (rate of interest, depreciation, and amortization), and output per man-hour, influenced in turn by management and the contribution of capital, are not the only factors that determine what is exported or imported. A tax system, for example, may increase the costs of some otherwise exportable commodities more than it does others. In 1955, the British Government reduced its purchase tax on textiles in order to stimulate textile exports, which were confronted with increased competition abroad. In some countries, export taxes are levied to force the foreigner to pay a higher price, to discourage exports, or to absorb part of the gains of the domestic sellers. Or a government monopoly might be introduced to raise prices, as in the Argentine through the control of wheat prices in the postwar period. These policies obviously affect export structure.

Again, distribution costs, inclusive of markups, may vary. Whereas a consideration of production costs may point to exports of machine tools from Great Britain and only domestic sales of textiles, it is conceivable that distribution costs inclusive of margins may be so much higher on Great Britain's machine tools than the corresponding charges abroad that textiles rather than machine tools may be exported from Great Britain.[10]

This discriminatory application of commercial policy and of exchange control will also affect the pattern of trade. So will political and historic alliances. MacDougall points out that America exports less to the members of the British Commonwealth than might be expected on the basis of man-hour output and wage studies, and more to nonmembers. Some of this difference he attributes to the operations of imperial preference, the system of tariff concessions that members of the Commonwealth grant to one another and not to outsiders. But the greater part of the United States' disadvantage in Commonwealth markets he attributes to "commercial ties and other non-price factors" and to market imperfections.[11]

As this book goes to press, a recent article by Dr. Kravis comes to my attention. In this discussion Kravis contends that the composition of trade is not greatly influenced by varying wage structure, a study that lends some support to Taussig's position. For example, he compares the wages in twenty industries in Japan and the United States. In Table 4-5,

Table 4-5

Industry	Japan	United States
Textile and mill products.	4	5
Apparel.	1	3
Leather.	6	4
Lumber and wood.	2	2
Printing and publishing.	12	17
Chemicals.	17	13
Fabricated metals.	11	12
Machinery (except electrical).	13	16
Primary metals.	20	18

SOURCE: I. B. Kravis, "Influences on the Commodity Composition of Trade," *The Journal of Political Economy*, April, 1956, p. 145.

for example, are the rankings of hourly earnings (1 = lowest) for a number of crucial industries in Japan (1950–1951) and the United States (1950).

Kravis also casts doubt on Leontief's proposition that the United States is short of capital rather than labor. Leontief had shown that the labor content of United States exports is 7 per cent higher and capital content

[10] L. Tarshis, *Introduction to International Trade and Finance*, 1955, pp. 138–139.
[11] MacDougall, *op. cit.*, September, 1952, pt. II, p. 511.

18 per cent lower than for United States imports. In particular, Kravis notes the large amount of United States capital exported abroad, which provides foreign countries with goods equal to half the United States imports, and to a considerable extent this output is exported to the United States. These capital exports do not suggest a shortage of United States capital.

On the whole, Kravis suggests productivity (in relation to wage rates) and technological gains, inclusive of availability of new products, as the major determinants of the composition of exports. On the last, the relative growth of exports in categories 3 and 4 (in Table 4-6)

Table 4-6. Percentage of United States Exports, 1899, 1929, and 1952

	1899	1929	1952
1. Tobacco, textiles and apparel, leather and leather products	14.4	11.9	10.6
2. Miscellaneous, food and beverages, stone, clay, and paper..	43.7	19.5	13.2
3. Chemicals, rubber, metal machinery and instruments......	31.5	36.8	54.9
4. Printing, transportation equipment, and petroleum and coal	10.4	31.8	21.3

SOURCE: I. B. Kravis, "Influences on the Commodity Composition of Trade," *The Journal of Political Economy*, April, 1956, p. 152.

and declines in 1 and 2 are especially relevant, though there also were large gains in relative imports in categories 3 and 4 (from 21 to 44 and 1 to 6.3 per cent over the fifty-two years).[12]

[12] J. Tinbergen's excellent little book *International Economic Integration*, 1954, includes not only some useful simple models but also empirical data of relevance for problems discussed in this chapter.

CHAPTER 5

The Role of Demand, the Terms of Trade, and the Gains from Trade

Mill on the Role of Demand and the Terms of Trade

Our survey of the theory of international trade has thus far been concerned exclusively with the role of costs in setting the pattern of specialization and trade. We have now to examine the part which demand conditions have to play in the theory.

The classic approach to this problem is that of John Stuart Mill. Mill was concerned to discover the manner in which the terms of trade, the quantity of exports given for imports, are established. Neither Ricardo nor his immediate successors had dealt with this problem. They tried only to describe the conditions which give rise to trade, and their analysis was sufficient only to demonstrate the limits within which the terms of trade would lie; goods would be exchanged in a ratio somewhere between the pretrade cost ratios of the trading countries.

According to Mill, the exchange value of the two commodities traded will be so adjusted by the play of demand in both countries that the exports of each country will just pay for its imports.[1]

The value, then, in any country, of a foreign commodity, depends on the quantity of home produce which must be given to the foreign country in exchange for it. In other words, the values of foreign commodities depend on the terms of international exchange. What, then, do these depend upon? What is it which, in the case supposed, causes a pipe of wine from Spain to be exchanged with England for exactly that quantity of cloth? We have seen that it is not their cost of production. If the cloth and the wine were both made in Spain, they would exchange at their cost of production in Spain; if they were both made in England, they would exchange at their cost of production in England: but all the cloth being made in England, and all the wine in Spain, they are in circumstances to which we have already determined that the law of cost of production is not applicable. We must accordingly, as

---

[1] J. S. Mill, *Principles of Political Economy* (Ashley, ed.), 1920, chap. 18.

we have done before in a similar embarrassment, fall back upon an antecedent law, that of supply and demand: and in this we shall again find the solution of our difficulty.[2]

When the trade is established between the two countries, the two commodities will exchange for each other at the same rate of interchange in both countries—bating the cost of carriage, of which, for the present, it will be more convenient to omit the consideration. Supposing, therefore, for the sake of argument, that the carriage of the commodities from one country to the other could be effected without labour and without cost, no sooner would the trade be opened than the value of the two commodities, estimated in each other, would come to a level in both countries.

Suppose that 10 yards of broadcloth cost in England as much labour as 15 yards of linen, and in Germany as much as 20. In common with most of my predecessors, I find it advisable, in these intricate investigations, to give distinctness and fixity to the conception by numerical examples. These examples must sometimes, as in the present case, be purely supposititious. I should have preferred real ones; but all that is essential is, that the numbers should be such as admit of being easily followed through the subsequent combinations into which they enter.

This supposition then being made, it would be the interest of England to import linen from Germany, and of Germany to import cloth from England. When each country produced both commodities for itself, 10 yards of cloth exchanged for 15 yards of linen in England, and for 20 in Germany. They will now exchange for the same number of yards of linen in both. For what number? If for 15 yards, England will be just as she was, and Germany will gain all. If for 20 yards, Germany will be as before, and England will derive the whole of the benefit. If for any number intermediate between 15 and 20, the advantage will be shared between the two countries. If, for example, 10 yards of cloth exchange for 18 of linen, England will gain an advantage of 3 yards on every 15, Germany will save 2 out of every 20. The problem is, what are the causes which determine the proportion in which the cloth of England and the linen of Germany will exchange for each other.

As exchange value, in this case as in every other, is proverbially fluctuating, it does not matter what we suppose it to be when we begin: we shall soon see whether there be any fixed point above which it oscillates, which it has a tendency always to approach to, and to remain at. Let us suppose, then, that by the effect of what Adam Smith calls the higgling of the market, 10 yards of cloth in both countries exchange for 17 yards of linen.

The demand for a commodity, that is, the quantity of it which can find a purchaser, varies, as we have before remarked, according to the price. In Germany the price of 10 yards of cloth is now 17 yards of linen, or whatever quantity of money is equivalent in Germany to 17 yards of linen. Now, that being the price, there is some particular number of yards of cloth, which will be in demand, or will find purchasers, at that price. There is some given quantity of cloth, more than which could not be disposed of at that price;

² *Ibid.,* p. 584.

less than which, at that price, would not fully satisfy the demand. Let us suppose this quantity to be 1000 times 10 yards.

Let us now turn our attention to England. There, the price of 17 yards of linen is 10 yards of cloth, or whatever quantity of money is equivalent in England to 10 yards of cloth. There is some particular number of yards of linen which, at that price, will exactly satisfy the demand, and no more. Let us suppose that this number is 1000 times 17 yards.

As 17 yards of linen are to 10 yards of cloth, so are 1000 times 17 yards to 1000 times 10 yards. At the existing exchange value, the linen which England requires will exactly pay for the quantity of cloth which, on the same terms of interchange, Germany requires. The demand on each side is precisely sufficient to carry off the supply on the other. The conditions required by the principle of demand and supply are fulfilled, and the two commodities will continue to be interchanged, as we supposed them to be, in the ratio of 17 yards of linen for 10 yards of cloth.

But our suppositions might have been different. Suppose that, at the assumed rate of interchange, England has been disposed to consume no greater quantity of linen than 800 times 17 yards: it is evident that, at the rate supposed, this would not have sufficed to pay for the 1000 times 10 yards of cloth which we have supposed Germany to require at the assumed value. Germany would be able to procure no more than 800 times 10 yards at that price. To procure the remaining 200, which she would have no means of doing but by bidding higher for them, she would offer more than 17 yards of linen in exchange for 10 yards of cloth: let us suppose her to offer 18. At this price, perhaps, England would be inclined to purchase a greater quantity of linen. She would consume, possibly, at that price, 900 times 18 yards. On the other hand, cloth having risen in price, the demand of Germany for it would probably have diminished. If, instead of 1000 times 10 yards, she is now contented with 900 times 10 yards, these will exactly pay for the 900 times 18 yards of linen which England is willing to take at the altered price: the demand on each side will again exactly suffice to take off the corresponding supply; and 10 yards for 18 will be the rate at which, in both countries, cloth will exchange for linen.[3]

It may be considered, therefore, as established, that when two countries trade together in two commodities, the exchange value of these commodities relatively to each other will adjust itself to the inclinations and circumstances of the consumers on both sides, in such manner that the quantities required by each country, of the articles which it imports from its neighbour, shall be exactly sufficient to pay for one another. As the inclination and circumstances of consumers cannot be reduced to any rule, so neither can the proportions in which the two commodities will be interchanged. We know that the limits, within which the variation is confined, are the ratio between their costs of production in the one country, and the ratio between their costs of production in the other. Ten yards of cloth cannot exchange for more than 20 yards of linen, nor for less than 15. But they may exchange for any intermediate num-

³ *Ibid.*, pp. 584–586.

ber. The ratios, therefore, in which the advantage of the trade may be divided between the two nations are various. The circumstances on which the proportionate share of each country more remotely depends, admit only of a very general indication.

It is even possible to conceive an extreme case, in which the whole of the advantage resulting from the interchange would be reaped by one party, the other country gaining nothing at all. There is no absurdity in the hypothesis that, of some given commodity, a certain quantity is all that is wanted at any price; and that, when the quantity is obtained, no fall in the exchange value would induce other consumers to come forward, or those who are already supplied to take more.[4]

More Complex Cases

Mill also discusses the difference made by the cost of transportation and considers cases involving more than two commodities and more than two countries. He concludes that one cannot say how the costs of transportation will be distributed but adds that a country will export the commodities in which it has the largest advantage and import those in which it has the largest disadvantage; in between there are many commodities which will not be traded because the potential gain from trade would be absorbed by transportation costs.[5]

It is in his discussion of trade in more than two commodities that Mill especially stresses the relevance of reciprocal demand.[6]

If we now superadd coals or cottons on the side of England, and wine or corn, or timber, on the side of Germany, it will make no difference in the principle. The exports of each country must exactly pay for the imports; meaning now the aggregate exports and imports, not those of particular commodities taken singly. The produce of fifty days' English labour, whether in cloth, coals, iron, or any other exports, will exchange for the produce of forty, or fifty, or sixty days' German labour, in linen, wine, corn, or timber, according to the international demand. There is some proportion at which the demand of the two countries for each other's products will exactly correspond: so that the things supplied by England to Germany will be completely paid for, and no more, by those supplied by Germany to England. This accordingly will be the ratio in which the produce of English and the produce of German labour will exchange for one another.

If, therefore, it be asked what country draws to itself the greatest share of the advantage of any trade it carries on, the answer is, the country for whose productions there is in other countries the greatest demand, and a demand the most susceptible of increase from additional cheapness. In so far as the productions of any country possess this property, the country obtains all foreign commodities at less cost. It gets its imports cheaper, the greater the

[4] *Ibid.,* p. 587.
[5] *Ibid.,* pp. 588–589; for some reservations here see J. Viner, *Studies in the Theory of International Trade,* 1937, pp. 440–441.
[6] *Ibid.,* pp. 590–591.

intensity of the demand in foreign countries for its exports. It also gets its imports cheaper, the less the extent and intensity of its own demand for them. The market is cheapest to those whose demand is small. A country which desires few foreign productions, and only a limited quantity of them, while its own commodities are in great request in foreign countries, will obtain its limited imports at extremely small cost, that is, in exchange for the produce of a very small quantity of its labour and capital.

Mill was among the first to extend the theory of international trade to more than two countries, though many economists have since done so.[7] Mill shows that with the introduction of a third country interested in purchasing British exports, the terms of trade become more favorable to Great Britain, even if the third country does not produce commodities which the British want.[8]

Lastly, having introduced more than the original two commodities into the hypothesis, let us also introduce more than the original two countries. After the demand of England for the linen of Germany has raised the rate of interchange to 10 yards of cloth for 16 of linen, suppose a trade opened between England and some other country which also exports linen. And let us suppose that, if England had no trade but with the third country, the play of international demand would enable her to obtain from it, for 10 yards of cloth or its equivalent, 17 yards of linen. She evidently would not go on buying linen from Germany at the former rate: Germany would be undersold, and must consent to give 17 yards, like the other country. In this case, the circumstances of production and of demand in the third country are supposed to be in themselves more advantageous to England than the circumstances of Germany; but this supposition is not necessary: we might suppose that if the trade with Germany did not exist, England would be obliged to give to the other country the same advantageous terms which she gives to Germany; 10 yards of cloth for 16, or even less than 16, of linen. Even so, the opening of the third country makes a great difference in favour of England. There is now a double market for English export, while the demand of England for linen is only what it was before. This necessarily obtains for England more advantageous terms of interchange. The two countries, requiring much more of her produce than was required by either alone, must, in order to obtain it, force an increased demand for their exports, by offering them at a lower value.

It deserves notice, that this effect in favour of England from the opening of another market for her exports, will equally be produced even though the country from which the demand comes should have nothing to sell which England is willing to take. Suppose that the third country, though requiring cloth or iron from England, produces no linen, nor any other article which is in demand there. She however produces exportable articles, or she would have no means of paying for imports: her exports, though not suitable to the

[7] Cf. F. W. Taussig, *International Trade*, 1927, pp. 97–107; Viner, *op. cit.*, pp. 462–467.

[8] Mill, *op. cit.*, pp. 591–593.

English consumer, can find a market somewhere. As we are only supposing three countries, we must assume her to find this market in Germany, and to pay for what she imports from England by orders on her German customers. Germany, therefore, besides having to pay for her own imports, now owes a debt to England on account of the third country, and the means for both purposes must be derived from her exportable produce. She must therefore tender that produce to England on terms sufficiently favourable to force a demand equivalent to this double debt. Everything will take place precisely as if the third country had bought German produce with her own goods, and offered that produce to England in exchange for hers. There is an increased demand for English goods, for which German goods have to furnish the payment; and this can be done by forcing an increased demand for them in England, that is, by lowering their value. Thus an increase of demand for a country's exports in any foreign country enables her to obtain more cheaply even those imports which she procures from other quarters. And conversely, an increase of her own demand for any foreign commodity compels her, *ceteris paribus*, to pay dearer for all foreign commodities.

The law which we have now illustrated, may be appropriately named, the Equation of International Demand. It may be concisely stated as follows. The produce of a country exchanges for the produce of other countries, at such values as are required in order that the whole of her exports may exactly pay for the whole of her imports. This law of International Values is but an extension of the more general law of Value, which we called the Equation of Supply and Demand. We have seen that the value of a commodity always so adjusts itself as to bring the demand to the exact level of the supply. But all trade, either between nations or individuals, is an interchange of commodities, in which the things that they respectively have to sell constitute also their means of purchase: the supply brought by the one constitutes his demand for what is brought by the other. So that supply and demand are but another expression for reciprocal demand: and to say that value will adjust itself so as to equalize demand with supply, is in fact to say that it will adjust itself so as to equalize the demand on one side for the demand on the other.

Measuring the Gains from Trade

The reader will note that Mill measures the gain from trade by the extent to which the equilibrium terms of trade diverge from the domestic-cost ratio. He supposes that an increase in the difference between the terms of trade and the domestic-cost ratio implies an increase in the gains from trade and that its contrary implies a diminution of the gains from trade.

As the technique of making index numbers had not been greatly developed in the first half of the nineteenth century, Mill and the other classical economists did not compare the prices of all exports and imports as a measure of the gains from trade. But by concentrating on the quantities traded, they were, in fact, comparing variables that we study through a comparison of export and import prices.

It was to devise such a measure of the gains from trade that Mill first considered the role of demand. He sought to show how the gains from trade were divided between the trading countries by way of the effect of demand conditions on the terms of trade. But Mill's analysis, both of the determination of the terms of trade and of the gains from trade, was severely criticized.

Marshall pointed out that supply conditions also affect the terms of trade. He argued that " . . . the elasticity of her effective demand for foreign goods is governed not only by her wealth and the elasticity of the desires of her population for them; but also by her ability to adjust the supplies of her own goods of various kinds to the demands of foreign markets." He then went on to comment on Mill's point that large countries gain less from trade than poor countries because the demand of the former for foreign commodities is greater and hence the terms of exchange are modified to their disadvantage.[9] Agreeing that small countries, being most dependent on foreign trade, gain more for this reason, Marshall nevertheless observes that the rich country can pioneer in new goods, can profit from extensive and well-organized commercial relations, "need not push any one variety of any product on a market which shows signs of being glutted with that variety," and "has the better opportunities for adapting her output to the receptivity of various markets than the poor one is likely to have."[10] (This might have been written by one explaining the phenomenon of dollar shortage in 1955.)

It is practically certain that the demands of each of Ricardo's two countries for the goods in general of the other would have considerable elasticity *under modern industrial conditions*, even if E and G were single countries whose sole trade was with one another. And if we take E to be a large and rich commercial country, while G stands for all foreign countries, this certainty becomes absolute. For E is quite sure to export a great many things which some at least of the other countries could forego without much inconvenience: and which would be promptly refused if offered by her only on terms considerably less favourable to purchasers. And, on the other hand, E is quite sure to have exports which can find increased sales in some countries, at least, if she offers them on more favourable terms to purchasers. Therefore the world's demand for E's goods, which is practically unified by the machinery of modern commerce and the modern money market, is sure to rise largely if E offers her goods generally on terms more advantageous to purchasers; and to shrink largely if E endeavours to insist on terms more favourable to herself. And E, on her part, is sure on the one hand to import many things from various parts of the world, which she can easily forego, if the terms on which

[9] Nicholson and Graham later supported Mill's position. See F. D. Graham, "The Theory of International Values Reexamined," *Quarterly Journal of Economics*, 1923, and Viner, *op. cit.*, pp. 448–449.

[10] A. Marshall, *Money, Credit and Commerce*, 1923, pp. 167–169.

they are sold are raised against her; and on the other to be capable of turning to fairly good use many things which are offered to her from various parts of the world, if they were offered on terms rather more favourable to her than at present.

Also, those human resources of high energy and varied faculty, aided by a large supply of free capital, to which a great industrial country owes her prosperity, can be adapted and adjusted with comparative ease to a very large range of wants in various parts of the world: and, if she needs more imports, her demand for them can be quickly made effective by an increase of her exports, which will give her direct or indirect command over the things which she needs, without moving the terms of trade considerably against her. The fact that most of her products have to run the gauntlet of close competition before they can be sold at all, indicates that there is probably a large volume of foreign demand, which she can master, if her own demand for foreign goods rises. And, if, on the other hand, the reception of her exports by foreign markets should become less favourable to her, she has generally no very great difficulty in turning a part of the resources, with which she had produced her exports, to good account in meeting domestic demand for other products of like character.[11]

More than one way of measuring the terms of trade is possible. The simplest is to compare the prices of exports and imports. Another is to compare the total value of exports and imports. This latter comparison, proposed by Taussig and called by him the "gross barter" terms of trade, includes extraneous elements; a country exporting much capital will tend to show unfavorable terms of trade, for the capital exports would be reflected in additional exports. A third approach is one suggested by Viner but used by some of the older economists, namely, the double factoral terms of trade, which measure "the number of units of the productive services of the foreign country whose product exchanged for the product of one unit of the productive services of your own country."[12] Thus it is probably true that in 1955 United States exports cost less in labor, management, and capital relative to our imports than they did in, say, 1913. A unit of American resources commands in trade more foreign resources, so that our double factoral terms of trade have improved.

With Mill, many people assume that if a country's commodity terms of trade improve (export prices rise relative to import prices), the country gains more from trade. This is a great oversimplification, however, and may be misleading. One must take into account not only the commodity terms of trade but also the total volume of trade. It is possible for a country to achieve a great improvement in its terms of trade and

[11] *Ibid.*, pp. 171–172.
[12] See especially *ibid.*, chaps. 6–10; Taussig, *op. cit.*, chaps. 13, 21; G. Haberler, *The Theory of International Trade*, 1936, pp. 159–169; and Viner, *op. cit.*, pp. 319–322, 535–570.

yet to suffer large losses because it prices itself out of the market. In the interwar period the British improved their terms of trade greatly, in large part because of oversupply of exports of foods and raw materials from underdeveloped countries. The impoverished agricultural countries offered their goods at very low prices, but the result was that the British exports dropped drastically because the agricultural countries, her most important customers, had greatly to contract their imports. It is not at all clear that she made a net gain; she certainly did not make a gain proportionate to the increased cheapness of her imports. At times since World War II, the United Kingdom suffered a deterioration in her terms of trade, but a large part of the losses was recouped because customers in the outer sterling area could now buy more British goods. Again, by imposing restrictions on imports, a country can often improve her terms of trade, but any such success is to be put against the losses resulting from reduced trade and malallocation of the factors of production.

In all discussions of the gains of trade, it is necessary to consider also the causes of alterations in the commodity terms of trade. Thus the United States terms of trade may deteriorate because of large gains in productivity reflected in reduced export prices. (Actually the United States in the forties and fifties tended to absorb its gains in higher incomes rather than in reduced prices.) At any rate, a deterioration associated with increased productivity is to be differentiated from one caused by a loss of markets abroad, from one caused by increased import prices due to increasing unit costs abroad, or from one caused by a rise in the demand for imports.

The case for using Viner's double factoral terms of trade rests upon the relevance of costs as a measure of the terms of trade. In other words, when the loss in commodity terms is the result of increased productivity, the factoral terms of trade should not reveal a deterioration. Unfortunately the statistical problems raised in using this measure are almost insuperable.

Elsewhere, we discuss the problems of exchange depreciation. Here we should note that through exchange depreciation, authorities seek a balancing of international accounts and/or a rise of employment. Some deterioration in the terms of trade is likely to accompany depreciation. In the thirties the deterioration was substantial for countries depreciating but in the late forties and fifties much less.[13] With supply elasticities high in the depreciating country and demand elasticities high abroad, the required deterioration in the terms of trade should, *ceteris paribus*, be small. A small reduction in export prices would elicit a large response in sales abroad. This was suggested by Marshall in the passage quoted above. What is important to note here is that even if the terms

[13] See Chap. 15.

of trade deteriorate, it does not follow that the gains from trade are reduced: first, because the volume of trade may rise; second, because an improved balance of payments allows the authorities to relax monetary and fiscal restraints on domestic activity, demand increases, and employment and output rise.

A final point relates to the measurement of the terms of trade. Comparisons over long periods of time may be vitiated because of the difficulties inherent in measuring price changes when the basket of goods to be measured changes greatly. What, in the end, have we measured? To some extent this difficulty can be overcome by comparing prices two years at a time, changing weights gradually from year to year.

An instance of the difficulties involved is the common contention that over the last fifty to seventy-five years the terms of trade have improved for developed as against underdeveloped countries. The explanation of this deterioration has been held to be inelastic supply conditions in agricultural countries—they respond to reduced prices by producing more and offering more abroad—and an inelastic demand for raw materials and food in developed countries—they can cut output with relative ease and do without a substantial part of imports. In reply, others have stressed the difficulties of measuring price changes over so long a period.[14]

[14] United Nations, *Relative Prices of Exports and Imports of Under-developed Countries,* 1949; *Relative Prices of Primary Products and Manufactures in International Trade,* 1953; cf., however, *Commodity Trade and Economic Development,* 1953, pp. 11–12, and C. Kindleberger, "German Terms of Trade by Commodity Classes and Areas," *Review of Economics and Statistics,* May, 1954, pp. 167–174, and "Industrial Europe's Terms of Trade on Current Account, 1870–1953," *Economic Journal,* March, 1955, pp. 19–35; also see R. E. Baldwin, "Secular Movements in the Terms of Trade," *Papers and Proceedings of the American Economic Association,* 1955, pp. 259–269, for a discussion of the limited meaning of terms of trade measurement of welfare and some of the difficulties of measurement. Professor Kindleberger shows the relevance of prices of services and also the need for distinguishing among industrial countries.

CHAPTER 6

The Synthesis: International Trade and General Equilibrium

The Forerunners

While Taussig and, later, Viner were working to improve the Ricardian analysis, other economists had begun to shunt the theory of international trade onto a new track. Among the first of these was Alfred Marshall, who sought, first, to improve upon the classical use of labor time as a measure of costs and, second, to combine Mill's analysis of demand with the older analysis of supply.

Marshall, like Ricardo, was concerned to express the costs of production and the gains from trade in real terms, as effort and abstinence. It was for this reason that Ricardo had measured the value of commodities in terms of labor time. "But," wrote Marshall, "it seems better to suppose either country to make up her exports into representative bales; that is, bales each of which represents uniform aggregate investments of her labour (of various qualities) and of her capital."[1] As the bale corresponds to a fixed input of labor and capital, an increase in the effectiveness of either input or, in general, a reduction of costs would cause the size of the bale, reckoned in exportable goods, to expand.

To treat the exchange between two countries (E and G), Marshall had them exchange bales. He assumed that each country in turn would press the commodities in strongest demand abroad, relative to its costs of production, thus marketing to the best advantage. Beyond a certain point, it would become profitable to market a second commodity, and so on. Obviously the concept of the bale avoids one of the difficulties involved in two-commodity examples, that country E, say, could achieve better terms by substituting for the export good initially traded some other good or a combination of goods. By permitting the commodity composition of the bale to vary, as a result both of technological changes and of equilibrating adjustments, with individual goods shifting from

---

[1] A. Marshall, *Money, Credit and Commerce*, 1933, p. 157.

export to nonexport or import and vice versa, Marshall was able to treat complex phenomena quite simply.[2]

Marshall laid great stress upon the joint operation of supply and demand as the determinants of the structure of international trade.[3]

But in the general trade between two countries neither can be specially associated either with demand or with supply. The demand of each has its origin in the desires of her people to obtain certain goods from abroad; and her supply has its origin in her facilities for producing things which the people of other countries desire. But her demand is, in general, effective in causing trade, only in so far as it is backed by her supply of appropriate goods; and her supply is active, only in so far as she has a demand for foreign goods.

Marshall illustrates the trading possibilities by Table 6-1.[4]

Table 6-1

	Schedule of terms on which E is willing to trade		Schedule of terms on which G is willing to trade	
No. of E bales	No. of G bales per 100 E bales at which E will part with those in (1)	Total no. of G bales for which E is willing to part with those in (1)	No. of G bales per 100 E bales at which G will buy those in (1)	Total no. of G bales which G is willing to give for those in (1)
(1)	(2)	(3)	(4)	(5)
10,000	10	1,000	230	23,000
20,000	20	4,000	175	35,000
30,000	30	9,000	143	42,900
40,000	35	14,000	122	48,800
50,000	40	20,000	108	54,000
60,000	46	27,600	95	57,000
70,000	55	38,500	86	60,200
80,000	68	54,400	$82\frac{1}{2}$	66,000
90,000	78	70,200	78	70,200
100,000	83	83,000	76	76,000
110,000	86	94,600	$74\frac{1}{2}$	81,950
120,000	$88\frac{1}{2}$	106,200	$73\frac{3}{4}$	88,500

Consider the first row of the table. Country E is prepared to offer 10,000 E bales (column 1) for 1,000 G bales (column 3). But country G would be prepared to give 23,000 G bales for 10,000 E bales (column 5). The supply of G bales would be in excess of the demand. Consider now the final row of the table. Country E would be willing to offer 120,000 E bales for 106,200 G bales. But country G would be prepared

[2] G. Haberler, *The Theory of International Trade,* 1936, pp. 10–11.
[3] Marshall, *op. cit.,* pp. 157–161.
[4] *Ibid.,* p. 162.

to give only 88,500 G bales for 120,000 E bales. The demand for G bales would be in excess of the supply. When, however, country E is prepared to offer 90,000 E bales and to take in trade 70,200 G bales, an equilibrium will have been achieved, for country G is prepared to offer precisely 70,200 G bales for 90,000 E bales, so that the market for E bales and the market for G bales will be simultaneously cleared. The ratio of exchange (columns 2 and 4) will settle at 100 E for 78 G bales, terms of trade more favorable to E than those at the top of the table and less favorable than those toward the bottom.

The schedules given by Marshall are like ordinary supply-and-demand schedules. As the price of G bales in terms of E bales falls—as we travel down column 2—E's demand for G bales rises relative to the supply of G bales until, at the end of the column, it is in substantial excess of the supply. They are, in fact, reciprocal demand schedules and are frequently given graphic representation (and called "offer curves"). Like ordinary supply-and-demand curves, each point on these schedules is a point of potential equilibrium. But a movement along one of these curves presupposes that the economy of the relevant country has rearranged its internal trade to conform to the new equilibrium conditions.[5]

Marshall's offer curves were extensively employed by later economists, notably by Edgeworth, to examine problems in commercial policy. But they sometimes seemed to conceal more than they revealed. For one thing, there were subsumed under changes in the commodity composition of the representative bale complex changes in the structure of trade. To treat these changes explicitly, Edgeworth introduced still another measure of costs, the unit of productive forces, a combination of labor, capital, and other inputs that go into the production of a commodity. In a neat presentation based on earlier work by Mangoldt, Edgeworth then considered the bearing of costs on the composition of a country's exports. He was, of course, careful to point out that some commodities might be both produced at home and imported and that one must also consider the demand of each country for the different commodities to discover which would be exported.[6]

In his Appendix (*Anmerkung*) *On the Equation of International Trade* Mangoldt begins by following Mill's arrangement, dividing the subject according as the demand for a commodity is, or is not, inversely proportional to its price. Under the first head Mangoldt considers first the case of two variables, and deduces conclusions substantially identical with those of Mill, in usefully varied language. Mangoldt then goes on to the case of three or more variables. He discerns the general proposition that—cost of production being supposed constant irrespective of quantity, and abstraction being made of cost of transport—if trade is opened between two countries, the commodities previously

[5] Haberler, *loc. cit.*

[6] F. Y. Edgeworth, *Papers Relating to Political Economy*, 1925, vol. II, pp. 52–58.

produced in both countries will now fall into two groups, each produced altogether in one country; the rate of exchange between the members of each group *inter se* corresponding to the cost of production of each commodity (in the country in which it continues to be produced), and the relation between the two groups being determined by the rate of exchange between the produce of a unit of productive force in one country and that of a similarly defined unit in the other country. This simple truth Mangoldt complicates by positing a commodity as it were intermediate between the two groups, which may serve as a measure whereby to ascertain from which of the countries any particular commodity will be exported.

The following construction of our own seems to give the substance of Mangoldt's expositions; it being understood that the substance, as the metaphysicians say, is not a copy of its manifestations. Let us figure the relation between the costs of production of the set of commodities in Country No. I. by a series of points a, b, c, etc., on a line, any one of which a is obtained by measuring from a fixed origin o, a distance equal to the logarithm of the number of units of productive force which go to the production of a unit of that commodity in Country No. I. Let the natural values of the commodities in Country No. II. be similarly designated by the points a', b', c', etc., measured from o'; o' being taken so that oo' is the logarithm of the number of units of productive force in Country No. II. of which the produce is equivalent in the international market to the produce of a unit of productive force in Country No. I. ($\log v$, or $\log i/v$ in our notation). It appears at once from the figure that, when trade has been established, it is cheaper for Country No. I. to import a', b', and c' than to produce them; and to produce d and e than to export them.[7]

This theory brings into view an incident which is apt to be masked as long as we confine ourselves to the case of two commodities, the classical "cloth" and "linen"—namely, that it is not in general possible to determine *a priori*, from a mere observation of the costs of production in the respective countries before the opening of the trade, which commodities will be imported and which produced at home. "Comparative cost" cannot be ascertained by simply comparing the costs of different articles in the two countries. Thus if o' in the figure be pushed up a little, the distances $o'a'$, $o'b'$, etc., being preserved constant, C will become an export (from Country No. I.) instead of an import. But the position of o' depends not only on the cost of production in each country, but also on the law of demand in each country for the different commodities.[8]

International Trade and General-equilibrium Analysis

During the latter part of the nineteenth and into the twentieth century considerable interest in the theory of general equilibrium developed on the Continent of Europe. Most often, the theory of general equilibrium

[7] *Ibid.*, pp. 53–54.
[8] *Ibid.*, p. 55.

is given a complex mathematical statement; the economic system is described by an elaborate set of equations. But the fundamental point of general-equilibrium theory is quite simple. It is argued that each economic variable, be it a price or a quantity, is dependent upon all other variables in the economic system, that the prices and amounts of commodities, the rewards and the supplies of productive services are simultaneously determined.

That this proposition could be extended to an international economic system seems at once obvious, but its extension and development were tardy. Little work was done until after World War I. Then, in 1933, there appeared two works, by Bertil Ohlin and by Gottfried Haberler, that were, in essence, theories of international trade embedded in general-equilibrium systems.[9] Each had the virtue that it explicitly related international economic equilibrium to domestic economic conditions and was much more general than the labor-cost doctrine of the neoclassical theory.

Ohlin[10] lays much stress upon the similarities of interregional to international trade and ties the theory of international trade to a general-location theory.[11] He supposes each country (or region) to be endowed with a unique set of factors of production and argues that countries tend to concentrate on the industries using large amounts of the factors that are plentiful. Plentitude is, of course, a relative matter; a factor may be available in huge quantities, but the demand for its services may be even greater.

The extensive use of the cheap factors of production gives a country a comparative advantage in the production of certain types of commodities. Indeed, a country is supposed by Ohlin to export commodities that can be produced by its abundant factors of production and so will be relatively cheap. By thus relating costs to the supply of the factors and the effectiveness with which they are used, Ohlin provides a broader base for the theory of international trade than did the classical and neoclassical theories. He introduces all the factors and relates comparative costs to the price system, to factor supply and factor demand. Ohlin has no trouble dealing with noncompeting groups; he simply treats qualitatively different types of, say, labor as separate factors of production.

The structure of trade thus depends on international differences in the factor endowments, on the sizes of various national incomes, and on

[9] Pareto had dealt with the problem somewhat earlier but in no great detail, and there had appeared, in 1932, Yntema's *Mathematical Reformulation of the General Theory of International Trade*, another general-equilibrium analysis.

[10] B. Ohlin, *Interregional and International Trade*, 1933.

[11] Haberler observes that international-trade theory is of a higher order of abstraction than location theory. It treats separate countries or regions as spaceless points and abstracts from interregional transportation costs. Location theory emphasizes space and operates closer to reality. Haberler, *op. cit.*, p. 5.

the direction of demand. Once trade is opened between a country (or region) and the outside world, however, the initial system of internal prices will be modified. Ohlin, following an earlier treatment of this matter by Heckscher,[12] considered these modifications at length. He pointed out that foreign trade tends to raise the prices of factors that are relatively plentiful and to reduce those of the scarce factors.[13]

Let us take first a very abstract and simple case, where only two regions and two factors, which we may call labour and land, are considered. The region with an abundant supply of land but a scanty supply of labour finds it advantageous to import goods requiring much labour and to export goods requiring much land, as they can be more cheaply produced "abroad." Instead of producing goods of the former type, the industrial agents are directed toward industries producing the latter. Industries which use great quantities of labour are reduced or disappear, hence the demand for labour is diminished. Industries which use great quantities of land expand, therefore the demand for land is increased. Thus the scarcity of labour is reduced and that of land is increased. In the other region, which has an abundant supply of labour but little land, the concentration on industries that use much labour means greater relative scarcity of labour and lesser relative scarcity of land. In both regions, therefore, the factor which is relatively abundant becomes more in demand and fetches a higher price, whereas the factor that is scantily supplied becomes less in demand and gets a relatively lower reward than before. . . .

But this is only the immediate effect. It is necessary to take into account the response of factor supplies to the changed factor prices. If, for example, an increase in the exports of Japanese textiles, based in part upon large supplies of cheap labor, tends to raise the price of textile labor in Japan, a large increase may occur in the supply of labor, even in the short run, and the long-run increase in supply may be still greater. This increase in supply may arrest the rise in the price of labor and so diminish the change in relative factor rewards. In addition, and though they may already be in short supply, the factors that are complementary to labor in the production of textiles will also be demanded in greater quantity, and their prices may rise. Ohlin therefore concludes that though trade will tend to reduce international differences in the relative prices of the factors of production, factor prices will never be fully equalized. Commodity prices tend more toward international equality than factor prices.

There are special circumstances under which a complete equality of factor prices, both relative and absolute, will occur. Professor Samuelson has provided a proof but has had to assume free trade, no transporta-

[12] E. Heckscher, "The Effect of Foreign Trade on the Distribution of Income," *Ekonomisk Tidskrift*, 1919; translated by Laursen and reprinted in *Readings in the Theory of International Trade*, 1949.

[13] Ohlin, *op. cit.*, p. 35.

tion costs, pure competition in all markets, homogeneous production functions (no economies of scale), and the fact that all commodities are produced in both countries.[14] These are very restrictive assumptions.

Ohlin also gave considerable attention to the influence of transfer costs upon the location of industry, both within a region and as among regions. Of particular importance are the costs of transferring raw materials and finished products, but so are the transfer costs of labor and capital. Manufacturing, he argued, tends to be located where transportation costs are low and adequate supplies of labor are available. Thus, as the average haul of iron and steel is but 30 miles in the United Kingdom, 150 to 200 miles on the Continent, and 500 miles in the United States, Europe has some advantages in this industry. Similarly, the heavy haulage costs for a New England iron and steel industry barred the industry from New England despite the fairly favorable market conditions.

Institutional considerations, such as taxation and attitudes toward industry, seem to play a secondary part. But markets must be large enough to allow production on a large scale and, hence, at low costs. The indivisibility of some factors, as management, accounts in part for the importance of the size of the plant or business unit. For this reason international trade may diminish unit costs of production; foreign purchases allow production on a larger scale, and industry profits from both internal and external economies.

In many ways, Ohlin's (and Heckscher's) theory is a great improvement over the Ricardian approach, both because it properly emphasizes costs and prices and because it is a closer approximation to the facts. As Professor Viner contends, however, Ohlin may be unfair to the classicists, for Ohlin asserts that they did not consider the relevance of relative factor supplies. Viner clearly shows that some classicists were aware of this problem. He quotes passages from Adam Smith, Ricardo, Malthus, Longfield, McCulloch, and Cairnes to prove his point. Thus Malthus wrote:[15]

The lower value of money in England compared with the value of money in most of the states of Europe, has appeared to arise principally from the cheapness of our exportable manufactures, derived from our superior machinery, skill, and capital. The still lower value of money in the United States is occasioned by the cheapness and abundance of her raw products derived from the advantages of her soil, climate, and situation . . . neither the difference in profits, nor the difference in the price of labor, is such as to

[14] P. A. Samuelson, "International Trade and the Equalization of Factor Prices," *Economic Journal*, June, 1948, and "International Factor-price Equalization Once Again," *Economic Journal*, June, 1949.

[15] J. Viner, *Studies in the Theory of International Trade*, 1937, p. 505 (also cf. pp. 503–507), and T. Malthus, *Principles of Political Economy*, 2d ed., 1836, pp. 106–107.

counterbalance this facility of production, and prevent the abundance of exports.

I believe, however, that the classical *emphasis* was not on factor proportions, and Ohlin deserves the credit for having built factor endowments and location theory into a theory of international trade.

Still another approach to the theory of international trade by way of general-equilibrium analysis is the opportunity-cost doctrine of Professor Haberler.[16] He, too, emphasizes the role of differing factor endowments but assumes for simplicity that the factors available to a country are fixed in supply. They can, however, be used in several ways; some of the output of one commodity can be sacrificed to increase the output of another so that each country will be possessed of a set of production possibilities. In Professor Haberler's analysis, the costs of substituting one commodity for another take the place of labor costs; they are expressed in alternatives forgone.[17]

It is now obvious that we have no further need of the Labour Theory of Value. We can derive the conditions of substitution between the commodities, and express them in the form of a substitution-curve, when many different factors of production are available just as well as when there is only homogeneous labour. However many factors there may be, the relative prices of the two commodities will be determined (given the demand) by their costs—but we must now follow the Austrian school in measuring costs not by the absolute amount of labour required but by the alternatives forgone. Thus the marginal cost of a given quantity x of commodity A must be regarded as that quantity of commodity B which must be forgone in order that x, instead of $x - 1$, units of A can be produced. The exchange-ratio on the market between A and B must equal their costs in this sense of the term.

As the factor endowments of different countries are not the same, their substitution curves will be of different shapes. So, too, may be demand conditions. For the same reasons, then, as Ohlin had put forth, trade would be profitable for both countries.[18]

More recently, Professor Haberler has argued that his opportunity-cost analysis is a link between the classical theory of comparative costs and the full-blown general-equilibrium analysis involving variations in the amounts of factors of production.[19]

The Ricardian example of trade between England and Portugal can be interpreted in terms of the theory of opportunity cost without wrecking

---

[16] Haberler, *op. cit.*, chap. 12.

[17] *Ibid.*, p. 177.

[18] For a diagrammatic treatment of this argument cf. W. Leontief, "The Use of Indifference Curves in the Analysis of Foreign Trade," *Quarterly Journal of Economics*, May, 1933; reprinted in *Readings in the Theory of International Trade*, 1949.

[19] G. Haberler, *A Survey of International Trade Theory*, 1955, pp. 14–15.

Ricardo's reasoning and objectives. The explanatory function of the labor theory of value is to determine the price ratio, or, put in reciprocal terms, the exchange ratio between the two commodities. It also has the purpose of showing that the two commodities can be substituted for each other in proportion to their costs by means of a shift in production; that is, by a transfer of the means of production (labor). If it were possible to show, without making the unacceptable assumptions of the labor theory of value, that the exchange ratio (price ratio) in the market and the rate of substitution coincide, the conclusions of the classical writers regarding the advantages of international trade would remain intact. And it can indeed be proved that, under certain "ideal" conditions, even if we assume the existence of a large number of more or less immobile and specific factors of production, the exchange ratio will be equal to the marginal rate of substitution. These required conditions are identical to those which usually underlie general equilibrium theory: free competition in the commodity and product markets as well as the absence of so-called "external economies."

Professor Haberler places particular emphasis upon the degree to which factors of production are specific to one industry and of no use to others. When factors are specific, a change in demand or the opening of trade is likely to result in a greater change in internal prices than would otherwise occur.[20] He also gives detailed consideration to the problem of increasing cost, pointing out that the ease with which one commodity may be substituted for another may diminish as the output of the first is increased.[21] That production takes place under conditions of increasing cost helps explain why a country may depend upon its own production for part of its supplies and on foreign sources for the remainder. Thus in the United States we depend upon domestic sources of copper and wool for part of our requirements, but if we depended upon domestic sources for our entire supplies, a very large rise of prices would be involved, unless, of course, the government interfered with the free market, paid high-cost producers a premium, and then sold at prices below marginal costs.

Abandonment of the constant-cost assumption also raises some issues concerning the gains of specialization. Graham and others have pointed out that a country which tended to concentrate on industries subject to increasing costs and to import commodities subject to decreasing costs might well even lose as a result of trade.[22]

But increasing costs are not the only explanation of incomplete specialization. Another is differences in tastes. Even though most Americans

[20] Haberler, *The Theory of International Trade*, pp. 175, 182–189.
[21] *Ibid.*, pp. 176–177.
[22] For a full discussion, see Viner, *op. cit.*, pp. 470–482; also see Haberler, *The Theory of International Trade*, p. 144, where Professor Haberler greatly limits the area of decreasing costs and in particular rules out reductions in unit costs associated with such factors as technological change that tend to accompany rising output.

prefer American cars and even though this country can produce the cheapest cars of given quality, some Americans prefer British cars—just as some prefer French wines and Swiss watches to American wines and watches. Perhaps these patterns of production or sales should be interpreted, not as a division of markets, but rather as differentiation of products: the British car is one product; the American, another.

Space and Transport Costs

As late as 1950, Professor Metzler complained that the classical theory of international trade had seldom gone beyond two countries trading in two commodities, even in its latest refinements. (Cf. Mill and F. Graham, *International Values*, however.) In a provocative article, Professor Metzler attempts to deal with *n* countries, the income of which equals outlays on consumers and investment goods plus exports of goods and services and minus imports of goods and services. In equilibrium the output of each country equals the demand, and hence the income of each country is determined and imports are a function of income.

Professor Isard finds this approach especially helpful in contrast to the usual classical approach because it becomes easier to introduce problems of space and transport costs. (Smith, Mill, and Ohlin had, it will be recalled, dealt in varying degrees with transport problems.) "The impact of the distance variable may be implicitly contained in the different marginal propensities of nation I to spend in each of the other nations, this marginal propensity tending, *ceteris paribus*, to be low where the other nation is remote from nation I and high when contiguous to nation I."

In contrast to the international-trade theorist, who concentrates on aggregate exports, Isard stresses the contribution of the locational theorist, who would break down trade into industries, with the result that the relevance of transport costs would more effectively be examined. Allocation of resources can be understood only if input of distances is considered— whether it be in international or interregional relations. A breakdown of industrial structure would help not only because transportation costs could be taken into account relatively effectively but also because it would make it easier to understand the effects upon allocation of resources and trade of dynamic changes in the economy. Thus an increased demand for, say, copper would affect not only total income but also the supply of complementary agents and hence the total effects on income, and imports would be related to the industrial structure, elasticities of supplies in particular industries, etc. Hence, according to Isard both the Metzler approach and an input-output approach would be required for an understanding of these problems. "In brief, the multi-country framework involving aggregate propensities to import and the interregional input-output scheme which in essence represents in certain directions an extension and generalization of location analysis are to be viewed as complementary techniques for international analysis, rather than substitutes."

We have recently had a few empirical studies on the relation of transport costs and trade. Utilizing railroad shipments for interregional trade and a German study devoted to interregional trade, Isard finds an inverse correlation between distance and trade.

More important, Figure I . . . establishes without question the fact that the distance variable, or in dollar terms, the transport cost variable, shapes commodity flows in interregional trade in a very major way.

. . . Thus we can see how, once trade theory is extended to embrace realistic situations of commodities sensitive to differentials in transport cost, the distance variable can have a major influence on trade, as it does in fact.

Again, in a recent study Mr. Beckerman analyzed intra-European trade and showed that transportation costs play a significant part. It is not easy to eliminate other determinants of trade such as varying income levels, and the size of the countries involved (from which ports are commodities shipped?), the transport facilities, as well as distance, must be considered. The author finds a high correlation between distance and trade.[23]

[23] For the material in the last few pages, see especially L. G. Metzler, "A Multiple-region Theory of Income and Trade," *Econometrica*, October, 1953; W. Isard, *Location and Space-economy*, 1956; and W. Beckerman, "Distance and the Pattern of Intra-European Trade," *Review of Economics and Statistics*, February, 1956, pp. 31–40.

Later we discuss the relation of depressions in one country to movements abroad. For an able systematic treatment see J. J. Polak, *An International Economic System*, 1953.

CHAPTER 7

The Development of the Theory and Its Relevance

In medicine, there is a growing tendency to emphasize the study of health rather than disease. In fact, medical education begins with courses in anatomy and physiology and only afterward goes on to pathology. Despite the increased attention to the healthy patients, however, the medical profession still spends most of its time and investment on the ill. By contrast, the economist has tended to devote his energies primarily to the healthy economic organism, and nowhere is this more true than in international economics. Classical and even neoclassical economics allowed that temporary maladjustments might be forthcoming but argued that like the common cold, they would pass and there would be a return to normalcy, or, as the economist calls it, equilibrium. Little attention was paid to serious involvements or cumulative disequilibrating movements, which might be the counterpart of pneumonia, arthritis, cancer, or hardening of the arteries in the human body.

This book is concerned with economic disease as well as health. But to understand the causes of the diseases and the cure, it is important to understand the anatomy and physiology of international economics. For this reason we review the work of some of the distinguished economists—Hume, Smith, Ricardo, Senior, Thornton, Torrens, Mill, Marshall, Taussig, Viner, Ohlin, Haberler, Harrod, Meade, Leontief, Lerner, Samuelson, Machlup, and Metzler, among others—who performed brilliant and necessary tasks.

It is well to remind the reader that in the century following Ricardo's oversimplified and brilliant presentation, the task of the economists was to bring the theory closer to reality. It was necessary to consider costs other than labor, to allow for the varying effectiveness of the factors of production, to consider the difference made by the *prices* paid for factors, to extend the analysis to more than two commodities and more than two countries, and to analyze the impact of varying cost conditions and of imperfectly competitive conditions. The underlying assumption of full employment had to be removed, and that of perfect factor mobility within and immobility between countries modified. In a world of nationalism and underdeveloped economies, it was essential to implement the theory to meet the needs of a world with varying degrees of development and with institutions creating monopolies, rigidities, and restrictions.

Economists have advanced in many directions. Thus, not labor costs alone, but also material and capital costs are considered in analyzing the structure of trade and specialization. But despite the steady process of blowing up the theory to include all costs, there is still a striking tendency to concentrate on labor costs. The protectionists still stress differences in labor costs and, even more narrowly, differences in wages, and one of the most distinguished writers in international economics, Professor MacDougall, concentrates, not on labor costs in the large, but on labor costs *in manufacturing* in his analysis of British-American competition.

According to the modern theory, to what tasks will individual countries devote their resources? Obviously, if a country has large pools of labor, it tends to concentrate on industries that require much labor. What is more, such a country will tend to economize on capital, for capital is relatively expensive. However, competitive power depends not alone upon the supplies of factors but also on their prices. A country rich in labor may not concentrate on employments requiring much labor if wage rates are greatly inflated. At the very least the advantage of a rich labor supply may be partly lost, and industries requiring much labor may lose ground. Examples are France and Italy. It has been estimated that on top of the basic wage, French workers now receive about 30 to 35 per cent in fringe benefits and Italians even more. Such an increase in wage costs will injure especially the industries which use much labor. As payrolls rise, some of the industries using much labor and formerly producing for export might lose their export status. Concomitantly, industries with smaller relative labor costs and less affected by the inflation of wage costs may begin to sell abroad. *Relatively,* they become lower cost industries. In a similar manner, the price paid for raw materials, for capital, and for government services will variously affect the competitive position of industries according to the importance of each component.

What ultimately determines the competitive position of an industry is its capacity to price its products on international markets below the prices of competitors. Supplies of factors, their prices, the quality of the factors and the effectiveness with which they are used, the production function or method of combining the factors, the size of the plant and industry—these are all relevant.

Here I stress two aspects: first, the size of the unit. A country may gain a comparative advantage merely because it commands a large market. Here the United States, with a free market larger than Western Europe's twenty or so markets combined, has a great advantage. It can secure the low unit costs that may be provided by large plants and those that are conferred on an industry by the external economies associated with a large industry or a productive economy.

The huge American market explains the high productivity of the automobile industry in the United States. Though it is dependent almost exclusively on domestic sales, its costs are low; the size of the American market has made possible substantial subsidiary economies in the form of supplementary industries. The great advantage of the giant firm within this country also stems from its greater access to national advertising media, financial resources, and leadership in innovation. These help to explain the control of 95 per cent of the market by three companies by 1955.

Great Britain, with a national and overseas market for automobiles only one-tenth as large as that of the United States in 1954, may be under some disadvantage. But by producing a differentiated product, one tied especially to the needs of its export markets, the British (and more recently the Germans) have been able to gain a strong position in foreign markets—relatively much more favorable than the United States. One reason is that economies of scale may be achieved with an output of $800,000 cars, as in Britain, as well as with 8 million cars, as in this country, and part of the explanation lies in the discrimination against the dollar. But we cannot ignore the appeal of British industry to the interest of foreign buyers in the lightweight car which uses relatively little fuel (an important advantage abroad both because incomes are low and because gasoline prices are high) and costs less to operate generally than the heavy American car. Our comparative advantage is primarily in the heavy car, which is sought in the rich American market but is less suited to the needs of the European and Latin American.

The size of the market also seriously restricts the range of industries which can be introduced in underdeveloped countries and especially the small and impoverished ones. This consideration partly explains the increased demands for economic integration in both Europe and Latin America.

I wish, second, to stress the role of the production function. In this connection, attempts to study the relative productivity of the United States and Western Europe are of some interest. Again and again, the point has been made that an important part of the explanation of high American productivity is the greater use of capital in the United States, a practice verified by the amount of capital per employee or the machine power used.

Why less sweat for the American worker?

And the answer to that question is that they have, and use, more machines and more mechanical power per industrial worker: 8 h.p. is behind the elbow of each industrial worker; between 3 and 4 h.p. is the British figure; and 2½ h.p. for the average of Western European industrial workers. These figures for the non-human aid per worker go on diminishing country by country, down to the one man-power of the three quarters of all humanity who are not industrialized and whose standards of living are therefore lowest.[1]

. . . the universal availability in American industry of more and better tools, the extensive use of mechanical aids of all kinds, and the constant development of new methods involving greater use of mechanical power . . . machines doing all the lifting, moving, handling, packaging.[2]

Not only does this country use more capital, but its use of capital is more intensive. There is little wastage of capacity, partly because the equipment is more often worked by several shifts but also because this country replaces its machinery and equipment much sooner than other countries, thus ensuring the most modern machinery. Why is this so? Obviously, management is a factor; the cheapness and availability of capital is another and is in turn related to the profitability of industry.

But at times, it is easy to exaggerate the relevance of these considerations. First, one should compare industry with industry, not *all* employments as an aggregate. The British, perhaps, especially cultivate industries requiring less capital than the combination of industries in the United States, in part because labor is cheaper in the United Kingdom. (Wage rates are one-third to one-half those in the United States.) Second, attention should be paid to the kinds of commodities produced. Thus, the British textile industry favors specialized items that require more individual attention, that is, relatively more labor. Third, when labor is cheap and capital dear, it is sound economics to replace machinery less often than when labor is expensive and capital plentiful. American observers who are critical of British production methods do not always realize that a production plan appropriate in this country is not necessarily appropriate for the British, who have different relative supplies of factors of production.

Professors Heckscher and Ohlin advanced the theory of international trade well beyond the comparative-cost doctrine of Ricardo and his school, arguing that a country adapts its production to its endowment of the factors of production but taking into consideration demand as well as supply conditions. They showed why the United States concentrates

[1] G. Hutton, *We Too Can Prosper*, 1953, p. 61. Also see all of Chap. 3.
[2] *Ibid.*, p. 64.

on commodities requiring much capital, advanced technological skills, ample natural resources, and little labor, such goods as machine tools, automobiles, and cotton. The United States is apparently rich in the first three and is short of labor. They showed why the Argentine, in the absence of government interference, would produce meat, linseed oil, and wheat, both for domestic use and for export.

It should be observed, however, that rich natural resources may not facilitate large exports or even permit a high standard of living. As in many countries of Asia, large absolute supplies may be small relative to population and certain factors of production, complementary to those in ample supply, may be lacking.

And is the United States really rich in capital and poor in labor? The protectionists think so and complain that a scarcity of labor has driven up wages and jeopardized our competitive position. But Professor Leontief contends that the United States is rich in labor rather than in capital. He argues that the high quality of American management and the education and skills of our labor force make the United States worker more productive. Measured, then, in terms of its efficiency, labor in the United States is plentiful rather than scarce.

He finds, in fact, that the American export industries use more labor and less capital than do its import-competing industries. If, then, a country concentrates on commodities that use much of its plentiful factors, the United States must be rich in labor rather than rich in capital and short of labor.

Some questions can be raised concerning Leontief's analysis.[3] He does not compare the production functions of the United States with those of other countries but assumes them to be the same. Yet foreign countries may use different methods to produce their exports from the methods we use to produce import-competing goods. What must, then, be compared are the labor and capital requirements of America's export industries and those of foreign-export industries.

Professor Leontief ought also to explain the price of American labor relative to the price of American capital with the corresponding prices abroad. American labor is expensive,[4] but in terms of efficiency wages, American labor is cheap in many industries.

Professor Haberler has defended Professor Leontief against his critics in the following manner: The superiority of American labor, according to Leontief, is explained, not merely by superior intelligence, industry,

[3] Also see Chap. 4.
[4] W. Leontief, "Domestic Production and Foreign Trade: The American Capital Position Re-examined," *Proceedings of American Philosophical Society*, September, 1953, and cf. P. T. Ellsworth, "The Structure of American Foreign Trade: A New View Examined," *Review of Economics and Statistics*, August, 1954, pp. 279–285; also W. Leontief in *Review of Economics and Statistics*, November, 1956.

etc., but also by the greater contribution of "cooperating factors other than captial, namely: management, entrepreneurship and natural resources." Thus it is held that Leontief considers many factors, not merely two, and under these assumptions no sweeping generalizations are possible concerning relative factor scarcity. Considering more than two factors, Professor Haberler further suggests "import-competing industries in the United States are comparatively capital intensive because United States capital is a better substitute for foreign natural resources than United States labor."[5]

It is clear from the above that the theory of comparative costs is not adequate to explain the distribution of tasks among nations. It is necessary to take account of selling costs, geography, institutional arrangements like taxation and collective bargaining, controls, and, of course, cultural factors. The significance of the last becomes obvious in the discussion of economic development, for the structure of employment and production in underdeveloped countries is largely determined by non-economic factors, more so than in Western societies.

In a world where controls play a very important part we may even question the relevance of the comparative-cost analysis. Professor Viner, the leading neoclassicist writing in international trade, has said: "The world has changed greatly and is now a world of planned economies, of state trading, of substantially arbitrary and inflexible national price structures. . . . The Classical theory is not directly relevant for such a world, and it may be that for such a world there is and can be no relevant general theory."[6]

In conclusion, I submit that the Ricardian theory has been expanded over a period of more than a century into a helpful guide to the understanding of international economics. But the usual state of affairs is a divergence of prices from real or opportunity costs; hence the serious lacunae in Ricardo's theory. More important, as Professor Viner observes, the changes in the institutional setting have greatly reduced the value of classical trade theory. An increased emphasis on domestic stability and growth has, itself, diminished the importance of and interest in a theory which concentrates on the optimum allocation of factors.

[5] G. Haberler, *A Survey of International Trade Theory*, 1955, pp. 22–25; cf. S. Valavanis-Vail, "Leontief's Scarce Factor Paradox," *Journal of Political Economy*, December, 1954.

[6] J. Viner, *International Economics*, 1951, p. 16, and cf. Professor Haberler, who is not so pessimistic, in "The Relevance of the Classical Theory under Modern Conditions," *Papers and Proceedings of the American Economic Association*, 1954.

PART TWO

Money, Capital Movements, and the Balance of Payments

CHAPTER 8

Capital Movements and the Balance of Payments: International and Regional

The Balance of Payments

The emphasis in classical economics was on the export and import trade, and on the whole little attention was paid to capital movements. In part the explanation lies in the classical assumption that capital does not move across national boundaries or is transferred only with hesitation (see Adam Smith). But since World War I increased attention has been paid to this problem. In this chapter I shall discuss some general problems arising from capital movements and reserve discussion of other aspects of the problem for later chapters on economic development and loans and grants.

A word should be said at the outset concerning the balance of payments. In Table 8-1 I present a condensed balance of payments for the United States in the years 1947 to 1953. The major credit item is, of course, exports of goods and services (e.g., earnings on shipping, interest and profits on capital invested abroad), and the important debit item is imports of goods and services. In these years, it will be noted that exports exceeded imports by varying amounts, the difference being made up by (1) private unilateral grants (e.g., immigrant remittance) and by United States private capital net outflow (i.e., the excess of capital exported over capital imported, the latter, for example, including repayment of advances made by the United States in the past); (2) United States government credit and grants. For example, in 1951, the excess of exports of goods and services over imports was $3.6 billion. Foreigners obtained additional dollars as follows: (1) $0.5 billion from private unilateral transfers, (2) $1.1 billion from private net capital imports, (3) $3.1 billion from United States government credit and grants. The amount thus received exceeded the deficit on current account, and hence foreign countries were able to increase their gold and dollar balances by $0.4 billion. [Errors and omissions account for part of the excess of (1) to (3) over $3.6 billion.][1]

Before discussing the table further, I should say a word about capital movements and the meaning of the term "deficit" in the balance of payments.

Disequilibrium may result from excessive long-term capital movements, e.g., the British investor purchasing long-term Colonial bonds. Such problems as the failure of exports to respond to such capital movements and the ensuing attempts to stop outflows of gold through restrictive monetary policies troubled Keynes greatly in the interwar period.

But short-term capital movements are also troublesome. Investors tend to move their capital in response to returns offered. Hence one way of stopping a drain of gold is to raise rates on short-term money—then capital moves in or stops moving out. Such adjustments in rates were common in the nineteenth century and are a matter of discussion in assessing even the balance of 1956.

In the years since World War I, another kind of short-term capital movement has emerged which has greatly upset exchange markets— hot money. As financial crises and political uncertainties developed in the interwar period, movements of hot money became of increasing significance. A rise in the rate of interest would not stop these movements as a rule; yet large outflows might seriously disrupt the economy. Hence the increased recourse to exchange control as a means of stopping the outflow of capital. Indeed, exchange control is also used to treat outflows of other kinds of capital, short- and long-term, but particularly in relation to hot money is exchange control the only therapy of some effectiveness. A more stable economic and political world would, of course, reduce the supply of hot money.

Now a word about what is meant by a deficit in the international account. Often all that is meant is the differences between current credit items (e.g., exports, sales of services) and current debit items (e.g., imports, purchases of services). But for our purposes, this is inadequate. A country may have an adverse balance on current account of, say, $500 million, but if this country customarily borrows $800 million yearly, then the deficit is of limited significance. The country may actually be accumulating reserves. Indeed, if the inflow of capital is at a rate which cannot be maintained and financing will be impossible, then, of course, the current balance conceals an imbalance. Again, when the balancing is made possible by grants from foreign countries (e.g., Marshall Plan, Mutual Security) or abnormal purchases by foreigners

[1] *Economic Report of the President,* January, 1954, p. 219.

(e.g., American military purchases abroad), then the apparent balance may be deceiving unless it can be assumed that foreign government grants and the like are a more or less permanent condition.

A test of a balancing of accounts lies in the fluctuations of gold or, say, dollar reserves. When serious losses occur or when the gains are substantially less than government grants, abnormal capital inflows, and the like, or if the balancing of reserves is attained through restrictionist monetary and fiscal policies that impose unemployment, then maintenance or gains of reserves may not be evidence of a surplus in the international accounts.

Table 8-1. United States Balance of Payments, Excluding United States Government Grants of Military Goods and Services, 1947–1953
(In billions of dollars)

Area and type of transaction	1947	1948	1949	1950	1951	1952	1953
With the world:							
Exports of goods and services:							
Total..........................	19.8	17.0	16.0	14.4	20.2	20.6	21.4
Less unilateral military transfers...	0.1	0.4	0.2	0.6	1.5	2.6	4.7
Net total.....................	19.7	16.6	15.8	13.8	18.7	18.1	16.8
Imports of goods and services:							
Military........................	0.5	0.8	0.6	0.6	1.3	1.9	2.5
Other..........................	7.8	9.5	9.0	11.5	13.8	13.9	14.3
Total.........................	8.3	10.3	9.6	12.1	15.1	15.8	16.8
Unilateral transfers other than U.S. government grants [net outflow (−)]	−0.7	−0.7	−0.6	−0.6	−0.5	−0.6	−0.7
Balance on goods and services and unilateral transfers other than U.S. government grants [net outflow (−)]....	+10.7	+5.6	+5.5	+1.2	+3.2	+1.7	−0.7
U.S. private capital [net outflow (−)]..	−1.0	−0.9	−0.6	−1.3	−1.1	−1.1	−0.1
Errors and omissions.................	+1.0	+1.0	+0.8	+0.2	+0.5	+0.6	+0.3
Balance on goods and services and unilateral transfers other than U.S. government grants, U.S. private capital, and errors and omissions [net outflow (−)]..........................	+10.7	+5.8	+5.7	.....	+2.7	+1.2	−0.5
U.S. government credits and grants (excluding transfers of military goods and services)...................	−8.8	−4.6	−5.6	−3.6	−3.1	−2.4	−2.0
Increase (+) or decrease (−) in foreign gold and dollar assets through transactions with the United States......	−1.9	−1.2	−0.1	+3.6	+0.4	+1.2	+2.5

Table 8-1 reflects the fact that capital movements do not always respond to trade currents. Professor Taussig used to contend that trade adjusts to capital movements. After World War II the demand for

American commodities was strong and private capital movements small. The difference had to be made up primarily by government grants.

The classical economists tended to neglect capital movements; both Ricardo and Mill discussed payments of tribute. Ricardo, for example, held that primarily through adjustments of exchange rates (the currency of the paying country would depreciate slightly) and flows of gold, the tribute would ultimately be paid through a rise of exports by the paying country. In a letter to Malthus (December 22, 1811), he wrote:[2]

In my endeavors to trace the effects of a subsidy in forcing the exportation of commodities, I stated, if I recollect rightly that it would occasion, first, a demand for bills; secondly, an exportation of all those commodities the prices of which already differed so much, in the two countries, as to require only the trifling stimulus which the first fall in the exchange would afford; thirdly, a real alteration in the relative state of prices, viz. a rise in the exporting and a fall in the importing country,—in a degree to counterbalance the advantage from the unfavourable exchange; and lastly, a further fall of the exchange and a consequent exportation of an additional quantity of goods and then of money till the subsidy were paid. It appears, then, that if the subsidy were small it would be wholly paid by the exportation of commodities, as the fall in the exchange would be sufficient to encourage *their* exportation, but not sufficient to encourage the exportation of money. If the exportation of money were in the same proportion as the exportation of commodities, that is to say, supposing the commodities of a country to be equal to 100, and its money equal to 2, then if not less than one fiftieth of the exports in payment of the subsidy consisted of money, prices would after such payment be the same as before in both countries, and although the exchange must have fallen to that limit at which the exportation of money become profitable, it would immediately have a tendency to recover, and would shortly rise to par; but it is precisely because less than this proportion of money will be exported that the exchange will continue permanently unfavourable and will have no tendency to rise, more than it will have to fall.

Perhaps the explanation of the neglect of capital movements by the early classicists is to be associated with the smaller part played by these movements in the first part of the nineteenth century than in more recent times. Why, it may be asked, is capital transferred from one country to another? That is, why does, say, Mr. Jones convert his sterling into dollars? The answer may be that the returns abroad may be higher on capital allowing for risks taken than at home, and Cairncross has shown that this was generally the case when capital moved from Great Britain in the forty to fifty years before World War I. Again the failure of capital movements from this country to assume larger proportions after

[2] *The Works and Correspondence of David Ricardo* (Sraffa, ed.), 1951–1952, vol. VI, pp. 73–74.

World War II has been explained frequently by the high returns obtainable in the United States and the great risks of investing abroad. From a national viewpoint there may be additional gains, for example, as has been suggested by Cairncross and also by the Marxists: the availability of foreign outlets for savings contributed to increased demand for British exports and shorter depression periods for the British in the nineteenth century.

Whether or not higher returns are to be had abroad will depend, for example, upon the profits on investments abroad as compared with profits at home, the tax burden on these profits both at home and abroad, the freedom with which investors abroad are allowed to bring their profits home (a matter of increasing importance), the restrictions on repatriating capital, and, of course, on anticipated exchange rates. For example, if it is anticipated that the pound sterling is likely to depreciate, the exportation of capital becomes more profitable, for dollars may be purchased at, say, $4 per pound and each dollar may be brought back at twice as many pounds per dollar as the pound depreciates to $2; each dollar now purchases twice as much sterling.

The Transfer Problem

Keynes was not so sure as were Taussig and other neoclassicists that large sums could be transferred across national frontiers without serious effects on the paying country. His attention was first attracted to this problem by the large reparations demanded of Germany following World War I. In the interwar period he was also greatly impressed by the damage done to the British economy by unimpeded capital exports. In attacking both problems, Keynes stressed the difficulty of adapting trade to the required transfers. Among the obstacles to the achievement of an equilibrium position were the rigidity of costs and prices (the paying country seeks to expand exports), the low elasticity of demand for the products of the paying country (that is, a reduction in price does not yield a large rise of sales), the introduction of restrictionist programs by the receiving countries (i.e., their unwillingness to accept payment), and the failure of the receiving countries to put their newly acquired gold to use. (Keynes rather overemphasized this point as far as the United States was concerned, as one might gather from the vast expansion of bank deposits in the United States from 1914 to 1929.) The expansion may have been inadequate to relieve British monetary authorities of the fear of continued losses of reserves, but it was more than adequate to finance a great boom in the United States. (More on this later.) Although Keynes tended to emphasize the difficulties of price adjustments, he also underlined the relevance of reduced output, which resulted in fewer resources being available to the paying nation for producing export commodities. In postwar Germany the loss of territory, the reduced productivity associated with lower standards of living, and destruction of plant were relevant; in interwar Britain monetary stringency accompanying the excessive outflow of capital brought reduced output. Impressed by price rigidities, Keynes was hopeful that a depreciation of the exchanges might at least overcome the obstacle of price rigidities, for a depreciation would cut world prices of British exports through inflationary policies at home.[3]

By this we mean that in the wake of, say, British depreciation, prices in domestic currency tend to rise; e.g., per unit, imports cost more in domestic currency and exports rise in price in domestic currency. British products sold for dollars yield more pounds sterling per unit. Also the reduction of imports (foreign currencies cost more) and increase of exports (domestic currency costs less abroad) suggest reduced supplies and higher prices. Hence it is assumed that, say, the British pound sterling depreciates by 50 per cent in dollars but domestic prices in pounds sterling *rise* by 25 per cent; hence inflation at home and deflationary pressures abroad.[4]

Trade Adjusts to Capital Movements?

Whereas Keynes, relying largely on the classical theory of adjustments, emphasized the difficulties of achieving an equilibrium position and whereas Taussig, using the same approach, found that trade adjusted to capital or reparations payments as required by the theory, Ohlin, like Taussig, concluded that the adjustments would be made, but invoked as the equilibrating forces, not cost and price adjustments, but movements of purchasing power and income.[5]

Ohlin's attack can briefly be summarized as follows: A reduction of export prices in country B which lends to country A plays a relatively small part in the adjustment. What is crucial is that purchasing power in B is reduced and in A is increased. Hence it is to be expected that total spending will decline in B and rise in A. As part of the transfer problem B loses reserves and A gains; the reduction of purchasing power in B and rise in A as well as secondary effects on income will be related to the relative changes in reserves; and income being cut in B and increased in A will help move commodities from B to A and discourage

[3] See J. M. Keynes, *Economic Consequences of the Peace*, 1920; *Treatise on Money*, 1930, vol. I, chap. 21.

[4] This problem is discussed fully in Chap. 11.

[5] See the famous Keynes-Ohlin debate on reparations in the *Economic Journal*, 1928, and B. Ohlin, *Interregional and International Trade*, 1933, chaps. 19–22; also cf. A. K. Cairncross, *Home and Foreign Investment, 1870–1913*, 1953, pp. 196–197, 204. The author finds a marked causal relation between exports of commodities and those of capital.

movements from A to B. Obviously wrong-headed monetary policy in A may interfere with the expansion of purchasing power and money in A.

Writing in the late twenties, Ohlin did not introduce fiscal policy as an additional weapon that might have contributed toward the adjustment. A, for example, might have experienced a rise of government spending, and possibly in part loan financed, and hence eased the conversion of money into spending. It is of some significance that it was Ohlin, not Keynes, the later source of inspiration for the widespread recourse to income analysis, who in the late twenties appropriated the income approach.

Crucial in the Ohlin analysis is the contribution of sectional price movements toward a solution of the problem. In B (the lending nation), domestic commodities are subjected to a reduced demand. Hence their prices decline. In A, domestic commodities, confronted with increased demand, rise in price. Hence factors of production move out of domestic industries in B and into these industries in A. Since B has less purchasing power, her demand for her exportable commodities also falls, but this is made up in part by the increased demand for B's exports by A. In other words, though all prices may fall in B, domestic prices fall more than others. The larger the percentage of B's export commodities sold abroad, the less export prices would fall.

It has generally been assumed that B's export prices would fall relatively to A's. This does not necessarily follow, for it depends upon the pattern of spending of the purchasing power diverted to A (and any resultant increase of spending) as against the effects upon B's spending pattern resulting from the transfer of purchasing power from B. It is possible that demand may improve relatively for A's exports. Many years ago Wilson showed that the classical assumption of a deterioration in the terms of trade for the lending country would not *necessarily* follow.[6] The classical position is, however, the more likely one. Since domestic industries become less profitable in B (relatively) and more profitable in A, factors of production tend to move out of domestic into export industries in B and out of export into domestic industries in A. Hence, in response to the reduced purchasing power in B and the rise in A together with the movement of factors into and out of export industries in B and A, respectively, there should be a rise of exports and a reduction of imports for B and a reduction of exports and a rise of imports for A. In this manner, the required adjustments to capital movements are made: B pays by exporting more and importing less; A receives by exporting less and importing more.

In contrast to Keynes's position, Ohlin relies much less on the elasticity of demand for B's exports for bringing about the adjustments; instead,

[6] R. Wilson, *Capital Imports and Terms of Trade*, 1931.

he stresses the production and sale of new products by B and especially the effects of shifts of purchasing power and secondary effects on income in both countries.

Of course, in so far as factors do not move easily, the adjustment will be impeded: Profits will rise in export industries in B *relatively*, the output of export commodities will be relatively deficient and of domestic commodities excessive, and in A the shift to domestic industries will be slowed by immobility. It should be noted that where, as tends to be the case in underdeveloped countries, export and import industries are very loosely related, the effects of a rise in purchasing power are likely to be a large inflation in the domestic industries. This follows from the low elasticity of supply in underdeveloped countries and the sluggish movement of factors from one class of industry to another related to it.

In Professor Viner's classic study of Canadian borrowing in the early twentieth century, we have an estimate of sectional price movements.[7] It will be noted that Canadian prices rose much more than British (large loans were made from Great Britain to Canada) and that in Canada, prices of domestic commodities rose by 62 per cent as compared with an increase of but 14 per cent in import prices and 34 per cent in export prices. The domestic commodities especially felt the pressure of the additional purchasing power, and import prices rose relatively little because of the transfer of purchasing power from the exporting nations, the inflow of supplies associated with the importation of capital, and also the economies of scale in the production of import commodities.

In an able survey of the Canadian case, Professor Cairncross suggests that as investments and exports rise, incomes are driven up so that "the Canadians seek to make an exactly equal addition to their savings and expenditure on imports."[8] The rise of income is felt especially in the demand for factors in the construction industries, the result being a general upward pressure on domestic prices. Labor tends to move from consumption to construction industries and from foreign trade to domestic-goods industries. The last are the most profitable.

It is clear from Keynes's analysis in his *Treatise* that the thorny problem associated with capital movements revolves around the failure of trade to adjust to movements of capital. The neoclassical approach was to emphasize adjustments through gold movements, price declines, and reductions of wage rates in the lending country and opposite movements in the borrowing country. But in recent years emphasis has been put upon other attacks on the problem. An obvious approach is to raise the rate of interest in the lending country, thus attracting capital from abroad and discouraging the outflow. This particular attack had, how-

[7] J. Viner, *Canada's Balance of International Indebtedness, 1900–1913,* 1924.
[8] Cairncross, *op. cit.,* pp. 43–48.

Table 8-2. Price Indices, Wholesale, for Canada, United Kingdom, United States in Various Years, 1900 to 1913

Year	Canada weighted	World— Coats's Index (145 commodities)	Great Britain Labor Dept. Board of Trade weighted	United States un- weighted	Canada wholesale commodity prices		
					Domestic	Import	Export
1900	100.0	100.0	100.0	100.0	100.0	100.0	100.0
1904	104.5	100.9	98.2	102.2	119.1	94.0	104.0
1908	118.2	109.4	103.0	111.1	133.6	99.5	119.9
1912	136.0	122.6	114.9	120.9	161.8	113.1	138.8
1913	131.9	121.2	116.5	122.3	161.7	114.1	133.9

SOURCE: Adapted from Jacob Viner, *Canada's Balance of International Indebtedness, 1900–1913*, 1924, pp. 217–230. See original for notes and methods.

ever, become part of the classical literature by the second half of the nineteenth century. Its potency has been questioned on the grounds that the movement of capital is determined primarily by considerations other than the rate of interest, a point emphasized by the increased importance of movements of hot money. Yet as late as the 1920s the United States reduced its rate of interest as a means of stopping the inflow of capital into this country and encouraging the export to Europe, and even in 1955 the British have had recourse to higher rates of interest in order to attract capital. But this is a technique that can be used without serious danger only in periods of high or overhigh employment and then with caution, for the net effect may well be a deterioration of economic conditions. Reduced supplies of money and the higher rates of interest which tend to cut monetary supplies are likely to reduce output and increase unemployment.

The impotency and the costliness of this weapon explain in part the increased emphasis upon two other weapons, namely, adjustments in exchange rates and the use of controls. (I am not discussing the use of fiscal policy *here*, though this approach may be used; for example, higher taxes may reduce income in the exporting country and thus reduce savings and export of capital.) But here again one must be cautious lest in roasting the pig the house be burned down. It should be said of all these correctives, inclusive of price, wage, and exchange adjustments, that as a result of attempts to use them in order to bring an adjustment in trade to conform to capital movements, there is a great danger that the reductions in costs, wages, and exchange rates will be carried too far because of the time required to increase exports and reduce imports. There is, therefore, a case for the monetary authority interfering through the sale of dollars, say, in Great Britain in order to prevent excessive deterioration in the terms of trade and especially internal deflation.[9] This danger of excessive adjustments to a temporary situation is especially to be watched when the capital movements are of the hot-money variety, for example, movements in response to fears of devaluation or political and military events.

The use of controls has a special appeal because capital movements may require adjustments in the economy that are likely to be costly if minimum reserves are to be retained. There is today widespread agreement that the use of controls to stop or moderate the outflow of capital is frequently justified, but the case for interference of this kind is much stronger when the outward movement is hot capital. Even the more normal type of capital, however, may be exported excessively, given the rigidities in the economy, the needs of capital at home, and the costs involved in a deterioration in the terms of trade accompanying the free export of capital.

Perhaps a word should be said concerning actual experiences with adjustments. The Canadian case, in a general way, with some reservations about how purchasing power was transferred, seemed to lend support to the classical position, and sectional price movements conformed to Ohlin's expectations. But German reparations were never paid; new loans greatly exceeded reparation payments. Here there was no real opportunity to check the results. Post-World War II experience suggests that serious problems of adjustment may arise when a great burden is put on the adjustment process, and it may be said of this experience that what was required was a rise of capital exports by this country to finance the large demands for United States exports by dollar-short countries. This expansion of capital was not forthcoming.

Reconciliation of Internal and External Balance

Once the balance of payments becomes adverse, the authorities have to weigh the effects of any given policy upon the internal as well as the external balance. For example, country A may suffer from an adverse balance of payments as a result of depression abroad, with a resultant reduction of foreign sales. The classic method of correcting an adverse balance of payments is to reduce costs through a wage deflation or (later) through a depreciation of the exchanges. More recently the emphasis has been on income policy with the control of income through fiscal policy, for example, a rise of taxes or a reduction of public expenditures, and integrated with monetary policy, for example, reduced supplies of money and higher rates of interest. In the midst of an adverse balance of payments imports associated with the fall of incomes

[9] Cf. S. E. Harris, *Exchange Depreciation*, 1936, chap. 15.

contract. But in having recourse to financial policy,[10] the authorities must also consider the effects upon the internal balance. For example, a policy of contraction which might solve the problem of external balance for A may be the wrong policy if A is experiencing a condition of under-employment, for then employment would be further reduced.

The best systematic treatment of the issues raised when two countries are confronted with the problems of reconciling their internal and external balances (and discussed above) is to be found in Professor Meade's excellent treatment.[11] The Meade treatment is well summarized in Table 8-3.

Table 8-3. Conflicts of Criteria for Inflationary and Deflationary Financial Policies

National income in the surplus country	National income in the deficit country	In the interests of		
		external balance	internal balance in the surplus country	internal balance in the deficit country
is too low (L) or too high (H)		there should be an inflation (S+) or deflation (S−) of domestic expenditure in the surplus country and an inflation (D+) or deflation (D−) of domestic expenditure in the deficit country		
(*a*)	(*b*)	(*c*)	(*d*)	(*e*)
L	L	S+ D−	S+ D+	S+ D+ (1)
	H	S+ D−	S+ D+	S− D− (2)
H	L	S+ D−	S− D−	S+ D+ (3)
	H	S+ D−	S− D−	S− D− (4)

In this table it will be noted there are four rows, the first suggesting alternative policies to achieve internal and external balance when national income is too low in both countries. In other words, depression prevails everywhere. Obviously to achieve external balance the country

---

[10] A term used by Meade to include monetary and fiscal policies directed to influence domestic expenditures.

[11] J. E. Meade, *The Balance of Payments*, 1952, p. 117.

with a surplus in its international account must inflate its income, e.g., through deficit financing, and this policy by the surplus country would reduce or eliminate its surplus in the balance of payments, thus bringing both surplus and deficit countries closer to equilibrium in their international accounts. For the surplus country (S) the effect will be just what is wanted at home: increased income and employment and reduced unemployment. Hence, not only is S+ (inflation of domestic expenditures in the surplus country) correct policy for both internal and external balance and hence the S+ in 1c, 1d, and 1e, but there is a consistency of required policies for achieving external and internal balance for the surplus (S) country. In short, in the midst of a world depression the surplus country has special responsibilities to expand.

But what about the deficit country (D)? To move toward external balance, D must contract its income, the result being a reduction of income and of imports and hence a decline in the adverse balance. Unfortunately the proposed policy for external balance is exactly the wrong policy for bringing about internal balance. Obviously contraction is not the medicine when D is suffering from depression. Hence there is a serious conflict for D, and much therefore depends upon the correct policies of S, and failing to achieve internal and external equilibrium through the proper policies of S, then D would have to concentrate on the needs of her internal situation and depend on foreign loans and controls to keep the expansionist policy demanded by the internal situation from bringing about a catastrophic condition in her international accounts, for imports would tend to rise excessively.

The three other cases (i.e., low national income in S and high in D and high income in S with low and high income in D successively) also raise serious problems, but Meade finds that it is possible to reconcile internal and external requirements reasonably well in all instances but in row 3. This is the case where national income is high in S and low in D. To achieve *external* balance, again there should be an inflation of domestic expenditures in S and a deflation in D as in row 1. But to induce internal balance in S, both S and D should reduce domestic expenditures; for internal balance in the deficit country, which is an underemployed economy, both countries should inflate expenditures. Hence a correct policy for S's external needs is the wrong policy for her internal situation, for the rise of domestic expenditures which would correct the active balance would further inflate the internal situation and D would find that the reduction of domestic expenditures needed for external policy would further contract an already underemployed economy.

In a later chapter Professor Meade also considers the alternative policies in the same four cases when the authorities have at their disposal not only the modern weapon of variations in domestic expenditures through fiscal and monetary policies but also the price weapons, e.g., wage cutting and exchange depreciation. For the deficit country the way out of external imbalance through price measures is, of course, a reduction of wages or exchange depreciation, but again the conflict of external and internal objectives must be watched. It is possible to use financial policy for the preservation of internal balance and pricing policy for the preservation of external balance or vice versa.[12]

[12] See *ibid.*, especially pp. 156–162.

CHAPTER 9

Gold, Money, and Trade: Principles of the Bullion Report and the Bank Act of 1844

Introduction

The next four chapters are concerned with the relation of money and trade. The major problems are the part played by money in bringing about international adjustments related to such developments as changes in demand, real costs, and capital movements and the objectives of monetary policy in so far as they react upon international economic relations. The last is particularly important. Up until the last generation the primary, and frequently the only, objective of monetary policy was to achieve international equilibrium, but now other objectives are taking precedence—those of strengthening and expanding the domestic economy and particularly of increasing employment and output. This is, indeed, a revolution in policy. As part of the new policy there is an increased tendency to use fiscal policy as a major weapon in the determination of prices and output. The new emphasis on fiscal policy (i.e., controlling prices, output, and employment through government tax and spending policies) stems from dissatisfaction with the contribution of monetary policy, especially in periods of underemployment. In the underdeveloped countries, where well-organized money markets are not to be found, the appeal of fiscal policy is even greater than in the developed countries.

The Natural Distribution of the Precious Metals

At the outset I should say that the whole concept of monetary policy was, in a sense, foreign to classical economics. The general view was that economic analysis is first carried out under conditions of barter and then money is introduced. But the outcome is no different under a barter than under a money economy. No better statement of this view is to be found than in Mill's classic volume.[1]

[1] J. S. Mill, *Principles of Political Economy* (Ashley, ed.), 1920, pp. 619–621.

We shall not be surprised, therefore, if we find that international values also are determined by the same causes under a money and bill system, as they would be under a system of barter; and that money has little to do in the matter, except to furnish a convenient mode of comparing values.

All interchange is, in substance and effect, barter: whoever sells commodities for money, and with that money buys other goods, really buys those goods with his own commodities. And so of nations; their trade is a mere exchange of exports for imports; and whether money is employed or not, things are only in their permanent state when the exports and imports exactly pay for each other. When this is the case, equal sums of money are due from each country to the other, the debts are settled by bills, and there is no balance to be paid in the precious metals. The trade is in a state like that which is called in mechanics a condition of stable equilibrium. . . .

When, therefore, the state of prices is such that the equation of international demand cannot establish itself, the country requiring more imports than can be paid for by the exports; it is a sign that the country has more of the precious metals or their substitutes in circulation, than can permanently circulate, and must necessarily part with some of them before the balance can be restored. The currency is accordingly contracted: prices fall, and among the rest, the prices of exportable articles; for which, accordingly, there arises, in foreign countries, a greater demand: while imported commodities have possibly risen in price, from the influx of money into foreign countries, and at all events have not participated in the general fall. But until the increased cheapness of English goods induces foreign countries to take a greater pecuniary value, or until the increased dearness (positive or comparative) of foreign goods makes England take a less pecuniary value, the exports of England will be no nearer to paying for the imports than before, and the stream of the precious metals which had begun to flow out of England, will still flow on. This efflux will continue, until the fall of prices in England brings within reach of the foreign market some commodity which England did not previously send thither; or until the reduced prices of the things which she did send, has forced a demand abroad for a sufficient quantity to pay for the imports, aided, perhaps, by a reduction of the English demand for foreign goods, through their enhanced price, either positive or comparative.

Now this is the very process which took place on our original supposition of barter. Not only, therefore, does the trade between nations tend to the same equilibrium between exports and imports, whether money is employed or not, but the means by which this equilibrium is established are essentially the same. The country whose exports are not sufficient to pay for her imports, offers them on cheaper terms, until she succeeds in forcing the necessary demand: in other words, the Equation of International Demand, under a money system as well as under a barter system, is the law of international trade. Every country exports and imports the very same things, and in the very same quantity, under the one system as under the other. In a barter system, the trade gravitates to the point at which the sum of the imports exactly exchanges for the sum of the exports: in a money system, it gravitates to the point at which the sum of the imports and the sum of the exports exchange for the same quantity of money. And since things which are equal to the same thing are equal to one another, the exports and imports which are equal in money price would, if money were not used, precisely exchange for one another.

The latter part of this quotation suggests the manner in which through gold and price movements a position of disequilibrium is converted into one of equilibrium. This particular theory has had a long history and, subject to various reservations, still plays a crucial part in the theory of international trade. The classic statement goes back to Hume.[2]

Nothing can be more entertaining on this head than Dr. SWIFT; an author[2a] so quick in discerning the mistakes and absurdities of others. He says, in his *short view of the state of* IRELAND, that the whole cash of that kingdom formerly amounted but to 500,000 £.; that out of this the IRISH remitted every year a neat million to ENGLAND, and had scarcely any other source from which they could compensate themselves, and little other foreign trade than the importation of FRENCH wines, for which they paid ready money. The consequence of this situation, which must be owned to be disadvantageous, was, that, in a course of three years, the current money of IRELAND, from 500,000 £. was reduced to less than two. And at present, I suppose, in a course of 30 years it is absolutely nothing. Yet I know not how, that opinion of the advance of riches in IRELAND, which give the Doctor so much indignation, seems still to continue, and gain ground with everybody.

In short, this apprehension of the wrong balance of trade, appears of such a nature, that it discovers itself, wherever one is out of humour with the ministry, or is in low spirits; and as it can never be refuted by a particular detail of all the exports, which counterbalance the imports, it may here be proper to form a general argument, that they may prove the impossibility of this event, as long as we preserve our people and our industry.

Suppose four-fifths of all the money in GREAT BRITAIN to be annihilated in one night, and the nation reduced to the same condition, with regard to specie, as in the reigns of the HARRYS and EDWARDS, what would be the consequence? Must not the price of all labour and commodities sink in proportion, and everything be sold as cheap as they were in those ages? What nation could then dispute with us in any foreign market, or pretend to navigate or to sell manufactures at the same price, which to us would afford sufficient profit? In how little time, therefore, must this bring back the money which we had lost, and raise us to the level of all the neighbouring nations? Where, after we have arrived, we immediately lose the advantage of the cheapness of labour and commodities; and the farther flowing in of money is stopped by our fulness and repletion.

[2] David Hume, *Essays: Moral, Political and Literary* (Green and Gros, eds.), 1875, vol. I, pp. 332–333.

[2a] [Editions H and I read: An author, who has more humour than knowledge, more taste than judgment, and more spleen, prejudice, and passion than any of these qualities.]

Again, suppose, that all the money of GREAT BRITAIN were multiplied fivefold in a night, must not the contrary effect follow? Must not all labour and commodities rise to such an exorbitant height, that no neighbouring nations could afford to buy from us; while their commodities, on the other hand, became comparatively so cheap, that, in spite of all the laws which could be formed, they would be run in upon us, and our money flow out; till we fall to a level with foreigners, and lose that great superiority of riches, which had laid us under such disadvantages?

In classical theory, it was held that there was a natural distribution of the precious metals which was related to the economic strength of countries. Through monetary policy, it was held, this distribution could not be changed. The supply of precious metals held by a country and hence its price levels depend upon real factors, e.g., the products produced and demand for international commodities at home and abroad. Ricardo expressed the classical view as follows:[3]

The precious metals employed for circulating the commodities of the world, previously to the establishment of banks, have been supposed by the most approved writers on political economy to have been divided into certain proportions among the different civilized nations of the earth, according to the state of their commerce and wealth, and therefore according to the number and frequency of the payments which they had to perform. While so divided they preserved every where the same value, and as each country had an equal necessity for the quantity actually in use, there could be no temptation offered to either for their importation or exportation. . . .

If in the progress towards wealth, one nation advanced more rapidly than the others, that nation would require and obtain a greater proportion of the money of the world. Its commerce, its commodities, and its payments, would increase, and the general currency of the world would be divided according to the new proportions. All countries therefore would contribute their share to this effectual demand.

In stressing the natural distribution and the neutral effects of money, Ricardo and Mill reflected the strong reaction of classical economics against mercantilist economies of the sixteenth to eighteenth centuries which had stressed the large difference made by money in influencing prices, the rate of interest, employment, output, and trade. Devaluations, a mercantilist approach, as Hawtrey has shown, were a required technique to assure each country its fair share of the precious metals. It was only necessary to raise the mint price of an ounce of gold by X per cent for the British to attract an increased supply of gold, especially since commodity prices reacted slowly. The value of gold in Britain would rise greatly, for its price would rise more than prices of com-

[3] *The Works and Correspondence of David Ricardo* (Sraffa, ed.), 1951–1952, vol. III, pp. 52–53. (Hereafter referred to as *Ricardo*.)

modities for which it exchanged. In order to carry through more transactions with the rise of output under a monetary economy, it was essential to obtain more precious metals. A pound sterling had at one time been a pound of *silver*. The effects of successive devaluations is reflected in the fact that the pound sterling of 1955 is equal to but one two-hundredth of a pound of *gold*. In making devaluations much more fashionable and in stressing the relation of money to interest rates and output, monetary authorities today are to some extent embracing the mercantilist theories repudiated by the classical economists.

One may be sure that the theory of a natural distribution of the precious metals played a significant part in the theory and practice of money. Thus, Lord Overstone (then S. J. Loyd), the staunch supporter of rigid issues, testified as follows before a Select Committee of the House of Commons on Banks of Issue, 1840:[4]

Why do you not include deposits in your definition of circulation?—To answer that question, I believe I must be allowed to revert to first principles. The precious metals are distributed to the different countries of the world by the operation of particular laws, which have been investigated and are now well recognized. Those laws allot to each country a certain portion of the precious metals, which, whilst other things remain unchanged, remains itself unchanged. The precious metals, converted into coin, constitute the money of each country. That coin circulates sometimes in kind; but in highly advanced countries it is represented to a certain extent, by paper notes, promising to pay the coin to bearer on demand; these notes being of such a nature, in principle, that the increase of them supplants coin to an equal amount. Where those notes are in use, the metallic coin, together with those notes, constitutes the money or currency of that country. Now, this money is marked by certain distinguishing characteristics; first of all, that its amount is determined by the laws which apportion the precious metals to the different countries of the world; secondly, that it is in every country the common measure of the value of all other commodities, the standard by reference to which the value of every other commodity is ascertained, and every contract fulfilled; and thirdly, it becomes the common medium of exchange for the adjustment of all transactions, equally at all times, between all persons, and in all places. It has further the quality of discharging those functions in endless succession. Now, I conceive, that neither deposits nor bills of exchange in any way whatever possess those qualities. In the first place, the amount of them is not determined by the laws which determine the amount of the precious metals in each country; in the second place, they will in no respect serve as a common measure of value, or a standard by reference to which we can measure the relative values of all other things; and in the next place, they do not possess that power of universal exchangeability which belongs to the money of the country. . . .

[4] T. E. Gregory (ed.), *Select Statutes, Documents and Reports Relating to British Banking, 1832–1928*, 1929, vol. I, pp. 28–29.

The Gold Standard and the Currency School

From the classical theory of the distribution of the precious metals, it is not a long step to the gold standard, under which the monetary authority sets the price of an ounce of gold in its currency and other monetary authorities do likewise. Then if an ounce of gold is priced at £12 in Great Britain and fr. 12,000 in France, £1 = fr. 1,000. It should be observed, however, that in rigidly fixing the price of an ounce of gold, the government was in fact interfering with the freedom of the market (i.e., exchange rates are not allowed to fluctuate in response to supply and demand), and in this sense the gold standard is not compatible with the laissez-faire philosophy upon which classical economics was built.

In its early form the gold standard implied a circulation of gold only or else a circulation of gold and paper that would equal that of gold in the absence of paper money. With bank notes convertible into gold, it was expected that unfavorable balance of payments would not originate from excessive issue of Bank of England or other bank notes. The first great test occurred during the Napoleonic Wars, when great demands of the government forced upon the Bank of England inconvertibility of its bank notes and a premium on gold. In the famous *Bullion Report* of 1810, the premium on gold and the rise of prices were associated with the excessive issue of notes once the restraint imposed by convertibility had been removed. Ricardo had written: "I cannot help thinking that there is no unfavorable exchange which may not be corrected by a diminution in the amount of the currency, and I consider this to afford proof that the currency must be redundant for a time at least."[5]

Numerous witnesses before the Select Committee on the High Price of Bullion insisted that the cause of the fall of sterling lay in the large rise of imports. But the Committee answered that "the difference of exchange resulting from the state of trade and payments between two countries is limited by the expense of conveying and insuring the precious metals from one country to the other. . . . "[6] The Committee then went on to show that the depreciation greatly exceeded the expense of shipping gold (now referred to as the difference between par and the gold export point).[7]

Before its notes had been made inconvertible in 1797 by order of the government, the Bank would watch its loss of reserves and take corrective action. But now it was relieved of this responsibility:[8]

[5] *Ricardo's Letters to Malthus*, vol. XII.
[6] *The Paper Pound of 1797–1821: A Reprint of the Bullion Report* (Cannan, ed.), 1919, pp. 17–18, 24.
[7] *Ibid.*, especially pp. 31–32.
[8] *Ibid.*, p. 45.

It was a necessary consequence of the suspension of cash payments, to exempt the Bank from the drain of Gold, which, in former times, was sure to result from an unfavourable Exchange and a high price of Bullion. And the Directors, released from all fears of such a drain, and no longer feeling any inconvenience from such a state of things, have not been prompted to restore the Exchanges and the price of Gold to their proper level by a reduction of their advances and issues. The Directors, in former times, did not perhaps perceive and acknowledge the principle more distinctly than those of the present day, but they felt the inconvenience, and obeyed its impulse; which practically established a check and limitation to the issue of paper. In the present times, the inconvenience is not felt; and the check, accordingly, is no longer in force. But Your Committee beg leave to report it to the House as their most clear opinion, that so long as the suspension of Cash Payments is permitted to subsist, the price of Gold Bullion and the general Course of Exchange with Foreign Countries, taken for any considerable period of time, form the best general criterion from which any inference can be drawn, as to the sufficiency or excess of paper currency in circulation; and that the Bank of England cannot safely regulate the amount of its issues, without having reference to the criterion presented by these two circumstances.

Then the Committee contended that no officials could be trusted to provide the country with the amount of circulation needed by trade. The greater faith reposed in market forces than in human judgment is well put in the following passage:[9]

The most detailed knowledge of the actual trade of the Country, combined with the profound science in all the principles of Money and Circulation, would not enable any man or set of men to adjust, and keep always adjusted, the right proportion of circulating medium in a country to the wants of trade. When the currency consists entirely of precious metals, or of paper convertible at will into the precious metals, the natural process of commerce, by establishing Exchanges among all the different countries of the world, adjusts, in every particular country, the proportion of circulating medium to its actual occasions, according to that supply of the precious metals which the mines furnish to the general market of the world. The proportion, which is thus adjusted and maintained by the natural operation of commerce, cannot be adjusted by any human wisdom or skill. If the natural system of currency and circulation be abandoned, and a discretionary issue of paper money substituted in its stead, it is vain to think that any rules can be advised for the exact exercise of such a discretion; though some cautions may be pointed out to check and control its consequences, such as are indicated by the effect of an excessive issue upon Exchanges and the price of Gold.

In the deliberations recorded in the *Bullion Report* the simple quantity theory of money seemed to win wide acceptance, and the relation of excessive money supplies to the adverse foreign exchanges won wide acceptance. Yet in 1803 Henry Thornton had written a dis-

[9] *Ibid.,* pp. 52–53.

tinguished book in which he showed that no simple relation of money and prices prevailed, that the creation of money often was accompanied by a rise of output up to a point that offset the increase of money, that what was important was not the supply of money but the rate at which it circulated, and that an adverse balance of payments was an occasion for overissue as well as monetary policy at home.[10]

Parallels in the Post-World War I Period

One hundred years later, following World War I, similar issues arose. Again the responsibility was placed upon excessive short-term borrowing by the government, the resultant overissue, and the absence of the check of convertibility. Despite many vicissitudes following the Bank Act of 1844, which, in fact, was a rigid mechanism for restricting issues, and not alone through convertibility, the official commissions would not only reduce issues and thus raise the external value of the pound sterling but would provide for automatic reduction of issues through a sinking fund. The last would schedule repayments of public debt and concomitant destruction of notes—not a word concerning the effects of such repayments upon the economic situation.

The Cunliffe Committee put the matter as follows in 1918:[11]

The course of the war has, however, brought influences into play in consequence of which the gold standard has ceased to be effective. In view of the crisis which arose upon the outbreak of war it was considered necessary, not merely to authorise the suspension of the Act of 1844, but also to empower the Treasury to issue currency notes for one pound and for ten shillings as legal tender throughout the United Kingdom. . . .

It is not likely that the internal demand for legal tender currency which was anticipated at the beginning of August, 1914, would by itself have necessitated extensive recourse to these provisions. But the credits created by the Bank of England in favour of its depositors under the arrangements by which the Bank undertook to discount approved bills of exchange and other measures taken about the same time for the protection of credit caused a large increase in the deposits of the Bank. Further, the need of the Government for funds wherewith to finance the war in excess of the amounts raised by taxation and by loans from the public has made necessary the creation of credits in their favour with the Bank of England. Thus, the total amount of the Bank's deposits increased from, approximately, £56,000,000 in July, 1914, to £273,-000,000 on the 28th July, 1918, and, though a considerable reduction has since been effected, they now (15th August) stand as high as £171,870,000. The balances created by these operations passing by means of payments to contractors and others to the joint stock banks have formed the foundation

[10] H. Thornton, *An Enquiry into the Nature and Effects of the Paper Credit of Great Britain, 1802* (F. Hayek, ed.), 1939, pp. 96–99, 151, 225, 235–241.
[11] *Committee on Currency and Foreign Exchanges after the War, First Interim Report*, 1918, especially pars. 9–17.

of a great growth of their deposits, which have also been swelled by the creation of credits in connection with the subscriptions to the various War Loans. Under the operation of these causes the total deposits of the banks of the United Kingdom (other than the Bank of England) increased from £1,070,681,000 on the 31st December, 1913, to £1,742,902,000 on the 31st December, 1917.

The greatly increased volume of bank deposits, representing a corresponding increase of purchasing power and, therefore, leading in conjunction with other causes to a great rise of prices, has brought about a corresponding demand for legal tender currency which could not have been satisfied under the stringent provisions of the Act of 1844. Contractors are obliged to draw cheques against their accounts in order to discharge their wages bill—itself enhanced on account of the rise of prices. It is to provide this currency that the continually growing issues of Currency Notes have been made. The Banks instead of obtaining notes by way of advance under the arrangements described in paragraph 9 were able to pay for them outright by the transfer of the amount from their balances at the Bank of England to the credit of the Currency Note Account and the circulation of the notes continued to increase. The Government subsequently, by substituting their own securities for the cash balance so transferred to their credit, borrow that balance. In effect, the banks are in a position at will to convert their balances at the Bank of England enhanced in the manner indicated above into legal tender currency without causing notes to be drawn, as they would have been under the pre-war system, from the banking reserve of the Bank of England, and compelling the Bank to apply the normal safeguards against excessive expansion of credit. . . .

But it will be clear that the conditions necessary to the maintenance of an effective gold standard in this country no longer exist, and it is imperative that they should be restored without delay. After the war our gold holdings will no longer be protected by the submarine danger, and it will not be possible indefinitely to continue to support the exchanges with foreign countries by borrowing abroad. Unless the machinery which long experience has shown to be the only effective remedy for an adverse balance of trade and an undue growth of credit is once more brought into play, there will be very grave danger of a credit expansion in this country and a foreign drain of gold which might jeopardise the convertibility of our note issue and the international trade position of the country. The uncertainty of the monetary situation will handicap our industry, our position as an international financial centre will suffer and our general commercial status in the eyes of the world will be lowered. . . .

A primary condition of the restoration of a sound credit position is the repayment of a large portion of the enormous amount of Government securities now held by the Banks. It is essential that as soon as possible the State should not only live within its income but should begin to reduce its indebtedness. We accordingly recommend that at the earliest possible moment an adequate sinking fund should be provided out of revenue, so that there may be a regular annual reduction of capital liabilities, more especially those which constitute the floating debt. We should remark that it is of the utmost importance that such repayment of debt should not be offset by fresh borrowings for capital expenditure. . . . .

The Victory of the Restrictionists (the Currency School)

Beginning with the Napoleonic episode and continuing for more than a century until the Great Depression, a marathon debate has been carried on, often heatedly, concerning the principles of note issue and later of monetary policy generally. In simple terms two opposing schools evolved, one a banking school which insisted that as long as note issues were made in response to the needs of trade, there could be no excess. Among the supporters of this doctrine were Tooke, Fullarton, and Mill. The currency school, with Overstone, Norman, and Torrens prominently behind it, held that it was necessary to restrict the note issues of the Central Bank. Even Ricardo, who seemed to have some sympathy for the banking school, wrote in the midst of the Napoleonic War: "The argument that no more is issued than the wants of commerce require is of no weight, because the sum required for such purpose cannot be defined."[12]

The Bank Act of 1844, an epic in the history of money, marked a victory for the currency school. It was based on the theory that the circulation should fluctuate in the same manner as gold would circulate in the absence of a paper currency. That is to say, if under a pure metallic currency the British should lose £100 million of gold, then £100 million of bank notes should be withdrawn from circulation. A rise of notes in circulation should in turn rest upon a corresponding inflow of gold. Several, including Mill, had shown that actually the Bank Act of 1844 did not achieve what it intended, for actually much gold went out from hoards and not from circulation and hence notes were not required to be withdrawn but under the new legislation they would be withdrawn.[13]

Following serious speculative booms and later collapses in 1825 and 1837 in particular, Lord Overstone and his supporters would deal with further incipient booms by a rigid limitation on note issue. This they hoped to accomplish by limiting uncovered notes to a minimum amount which would always remain in circulation and tethering any further amounts to a 100 per cent coverage in gold. By dividing the Bank of England into note and banking departments, the sponsors of the Bank Act of 1844 would restrain the banking department from putting pres-

[12] "Reply to Bosanquet" in *Works* (McCulloch, ed.), 1846. For a fairly critical appraisal of the Bank's policies in the Napoleonic period and an excellent history over the period 1810 to 1865 see J. Viner, *Studies in the Theory of International Trade*, 1937, chaps. 3–5, especially pp. 165–170.

[13] Mill, *op. cit.,* pp. 664ff.

sure upon the note department as a means of obtaining cash and hence extending credit. In fact, by concentrating the gold reserves in the note department and limiting new issues severely, the authors of the Act of 1844 made the banking department *more* sensitive to even relatively small losses of reserves. In short, the Bank Act of 1844 put the British economy into a strait jacket on the theory that even convertible notes could be issued to excess and that this excess would bring speculations, panic, and a later bleeding of the economy, and the cure for excessive speculations, adverse balances of trade, and an ensuing deflation of the bubble was a rigid limitation of issues.

In this connection, it should be noted that the bank authorities time and again insisted that in the crises before 1844, large speculative booms followed because early contractions as required under the Bank Act of 1844 were not forthcoming.

Thus Lord Overstone said before the 1840 Committee:[14]

. . . my object in alluding to the drains of the four periods in question, namely, the drain terminating in the crisis of 1825, the drain which continued from the year 1830 to the year 1832, the third drain, which began in the end of the year 1833 and terminated in the year 1836, and the last drain, which began in 1838 and ended in the autumn of 1839, has been for this purpose; to show that of those four drains, three of them were not met by any contraction of the paper circulation of the country; and those three drains all terminated in a severe crisis, in a very exhausted state of bullion, in great commercial difficulties, and in a state of general alarm respecting the safety of our monetary system; but that the fourth drain, namely, that from 1830 to 1832, was met by a contraction on the part of the Bank of England, bearing about the same proportion to the amount of the bullion lost which the issues of the Bank of England bear to the aggregate paper issues of the country; the country issues at that particular period being under a legislative action which, no doubt, necessitated a reduction on their part; the result was, that the drain passed off, in the words of Mr. Horsley Palmer, "without discredit or distrust of any kind." It is also remarkable, with respect to those drains, that the three which terminated in a crisis, whilst they were not met by a contraction on the part of the Bank of England, were preceded in each case by an expansion of country issues from their lowest point to nearly their highest point; and it is also further remarkable that the drain of 1825, which terminated in the severest crisis of the four, and in which the bullion was reduced to much the lowest point, began upon a reserve of bullion considerably higher than that which any of the other crises began upon. The inferences from these facts seem to me to be so clear, that they do not require stating. . . .

What seemed a great advantage to the currency school had no such appeal to John Stuart Mill, who in 1857 pointed out to a Select Commit-

[14] Gregory, *op. cit.*, vol. I, pp. 32–33.

tee that excessive sensitiveness resulted from breaking up the reserves into two departments.[15]

Now every drain, as a general rule, is drawn from the deposits. Therefore, when the two departments are separated, the drain comes first on the deposits. . . . If, therefore, the Bank cannot help its banking department by sending notes or gold from its issue department, it must either keep in the banking department as great a reserve as it would otherwise be requisite to keep for both departments together; or if not, having a much smaller reserve available to meet the demands on the banking department, it must necessarily, the moment there is the smallest drain, contract its discounts and raise its rate of interest. It thus appears to me that the effect of the Act is, that whenever any drain, however small or temporary, commences, the Bank will be likely, with its present reserve in the banking department, at once to contract its discounts, or to sell securities, in a manner which, if the Act had not existed, it would only do in the case of a very considerable drain.

Members of the banking school had many other objections to the views of the currency school. They objected to issues on the basis of gold flows. Thus should gold flow in, then notes would be issued, and without additional trade needs, prices would rise and speculation grow. But when notes were issued according to the needs of trade, they would automatically be redeemed as trade contracted. Furthermore, as is suggested elsewhere, notes do not, in fact, circulate with gold as Overstone and his supporters contend. Thus, circulation is cut as the government accumulates funds for future dividend payments.[16]

Even the Bullionists during the Napoleonic Wars would not go so far as those responsible for the 1844 legislation. They did not ask that a severe limitation be put upon the issues of the Bank. Rather their complaint was that with the notes inconvertible, there was no adequate check on issues. The fact is that the Bullionists were supporters more of the banking than of the currency principle.[17]

The bank Directors, as well as some of the Merchants who have been examined shewed a great anxiety to state to Your Committee a doctrine, of the truth of which they professed themselves to be most thoroughly convinced, that there can be no possible excess in the issue of Bank of England paper, so long as the advances in which it is issued are made upon the principles which at present guide the conduct of the Directors, that is, so long as the discount of mercantile Bills is confined to paper of undoubted solidity, arising out of real commercial transactions, and payable at short and fixed periods. That the Discounts should be made only upon Bills growing out of real commercial transactions, and falling due in a fixed and short period, are sound

[15] Evidence of John Stuart Mill before the *Select Committee of the House of Commons on Bank Acts,* 1857, par. 2026.

[16] Gregory, *op. cit.,* especially pp. 73, 76, 81, 82, 90.

[17] Cannan, *op. cit.,* pp. 46–49.

and well-established principles. But that, while the Bank is restrained from paying in specie, there need be no other limit to the issue of their paper than what is fixed by such rules of discount, and that during the suspension of Cash payments the discount of good Bills falling due at short periods cannot lead to any excess in the amount of Bank paper in circulation, appears to Your Committee to be a doctrine wholly erroneous in principle, and pregnant with dangerous consequences in practice. . . .

Mr. Whitmore, the late Governor of the Bank, expressly states (*Min.* p. 91), "The Bank never force a Note in circulation, and there will not remain a Note in circulation more than the immediate wants of the public require; for no Banker, I presume, will keep a larger stock of Bank Notes by him than his immediate payments require, as he can at all times procure them." . . .

Your Committee cannot help again calling the attention of the House to the view which this Evidence presents, of the consequences which have resulted from the peculiar situation in which the Bank of England was placed by the suspension of Cash payments. So long as the paper of the Bank was convertible into specie at the will of the holder, it was enough, both for the safety of the Bank and for the public interest in what regarded its circulating medium, that the Directors attended only to the character and quality of the Bills discounted, as real ones and payable at fixed and short periods. They could not much exceed the proper bounds in respect of the quantity and amount of Bills discounted, so as thereby to produce an excess of their paper in circulation, without quickly finding that the surplus returned upon themselves in demand for specie. The private interest of the Bank to guard themselves against a continued demand of that nature, was a sufficient protection for the public against any such excess of Bank paper, as would occasion a material fall in the relative value of the circulating medium. The restriction of cash payments, as has already been shown, having rendered the same preventive policy no longer necessary to the Bank, has removed that check upon its issues which was the public security against an excess.

Ricardo and the Bank Act of 1844 and Policy over a Century

Ricardo had laid the groundwork for the Bank Act of 1844. Time and again he had upbraided the directors of the Bank for their excessive issues during the restriction period.[18]

If the Bank directors had kept the amount of their notes within reasonable bounds; *if they had acted up to the principle which they have avowed to have been that which regulated their issues when they were obliged to pay their notes in specie, namely, to limit their notes to that amount which should prevent the excess of the market above the mint price of gold, we should not have been exposed to all evils of a depreciated, and perpetually varying currency.*

. . . I do therefore acquit them of being influenced by interested motives, but their mistakes, if they are such, are in their effects quite as pernicious to the community.

[18] *Ricardo,* vol. III, pp. 95–96.

The extraordinary powers with which they are entrusted enable them to regulate at their pleasure the price at which those who are possessed of a particular kind of property, called money, shall dispose of it. The Bank directors have imposed upon these holders of money all the evils of a maximum. To-day it is their pleasure that 4£.10s. shall pass for 3£.17s.10½d., to-morrow they may degrade 4£.15s. to the same value, and in another year 10£. may not be worth more. By what an insecure tenure is property consisting of money or annuities paid in money held! What security has the public creditor that the interest on the public debt, which is now paid in a medium depreciated fifteen per cent., may not hereafter be paid in one degraded fifty per cent.? The injury to private creditors is not less serious. A debt contracted in 1797 may now be paid with eighty-five per cent. of its amount, and who shall say that the depreciation will go no further?

In his *Proposals for an Economical and Secure Currency* (1816), Ricardo requested that a check be put upon the Bank by requiring conversion of notes into bullion, the price of gold to be gradually reduced as the excess issues were withdrawn. This proposal would also be consistent with adequate accommodation of trade.[19]

Depreciation cannot be effectually checked by any other means than by depriving the Bank of the power which they at present possess of adding indefinitely to the amount of their notes. This might be done in a direct manner, by limiting the amount beyond which their paper should not be issued; but it has been plausibly urged against such a measure that occasions may arise in which sound policy may require a temporary augmentation of bank paper, and to deprive the Bank of the power of increasing their notes at such periods might be the cause of considerable distress and difficulty to the mercantile classes.

This argument does not appear to me to have as much weight as those who advance it imagine. The objection however may be obviated by the measure which I beg leave to recommend; it is simply to oblige the Bank to sell gold bullion to any purchaser of not less than 50, 100, or 200 ounces at a fixed price somewhere about the present market price,—such regulation to continue for six months.

This would secure the public against any further depreciation of Bank notes, as the Bank would be obliged for their own safety to keep the amount of their circulation within the present limits whilst commerce and credit continued in its present state, to prevent such a rise in the price of bullion as would make it profitable to individuals to purchase it of them for exportation;—and if a greater circulation were required from the operation either of increased commerce, or of embarrassed credit, the bank might augment their issues without producing any effect whatever on the price of bullion, and consequently without exposing the Bank to any inconvenience, or depriving the merchants of that increased accommodation, which might be essential to their operations.

[19] *Ibid.*, vol. IV, pp. 65–73, and vol. VI, pp. 67–68.

Ricardo was especially concerned that the notes of the Bank had depreciated in terms of gold, suggesting to him a moral bankruptcy. He was ready to admit that the standard itself might fluctuate in value. He distinguished the *value* of gold influenced by all kinds of fluctuations in the supply and demand for gold and the *price* of gold, the rise to be explained by excess issues of notes.[20]

Suppose the only currency in the country was a metallic one, and that, by clipping, it had lost 10 per cent of its weight; suppose, for instance, that the sovereign only retained 9-10ths of the metal which by law it should contain, and that, in consequence, gold bullion, in such a medium, should rise above its mint price, would not the money of the country be depreciated? He was quite sure the hon. alderman would admit the truth of this inference. It was quite possible however, that, notwithstanding this depreciation, some of those general causes which operate on the value of gold bullion, such as war, or the mines from which gold is annually supplied becoming less productive, that gold might be so enhanced in value, as to make the clipped sovereign comparatively of greater value in the market than it was before the reduction in its weight. Would it not then be true that we should possess a depreciated currency, although it should be increased in value? The great mistake committed on this subject was in confounding the words "depreciation" and "diminution in value." With reference to the currency, he had said, and he now repeated it, that the price of gold was the index of the depreciation of the currency, not the index of the value of the currency, and it was in this that he had been misunderstood. If, for instance, the standard of the currency remained at the same fixed value, and the coin were depreciated by clipping, or the paper money by the increase of its quantity, five per cent, a fall to that amount and no more, would take place in the price of commodities, as affected by the value of money. If the metal gold (the standard) continued of the same precise value, and it was required to restore the currency thus depreciated five per cent, to par, it would be necessary only to raise its value five per cent, and no greater than that proportionate fall could take place in the price of commodities. In these cases he had supposed gold always to remain at the same fixed value; but had he ever said that there were not many causes which might operate on the value of gold as well as on the value of all other commodities? No, he had not, but just the contrary. No country that used the precious metals as a standard, were exempted from variations in the prices of commodities, occasioned by a variation in the value of their standard. To such variations we had been subject before 1797, and must be subject to again, now that we have reverted to a metallic standard. In the plan which he had proposed, there was nothing which could cause a demand for gold, and therefore he had been justified in anticipating a variation in the price of commodities, from adopting it, of only five per cent, the then difference between the value of gold and of paper. If, indeed, it had been necessary to purchase gold in order to revert to a metallic standard, then he would allow that a greater difference than 5 per cent would take place in prices, but

[20] *Ibid.*, vol. V, pp. 203–205.

this was wholly unnecessary; because we had adopted a gold standard, were we therefore to be exempted from those variations in the prices of commodities which arose from the cheapness of their production at one period compared with another? Was the discovery of new improvements in machinery, or a superabundant harvest, or any of those general causes which operate to reduce price, to have no effect? Were the injudicious purchases of the Bank to have no effect on the value of gold? Did he deny that in the present state of the world, the occurrences in South America, might have impeded the regular supply of the precious metals to Europe, have enhanced their value and affected the prices of commodities all over the world?

But Ricardo did not seem to realize that the maximum depreciation of the notes of about 30 per cent might be explicable *at least in part* by what had happened to gold as well as to the overissue of paper. (Here one could compare the British advance with resumption after World War I as gold appreciated in 1920–1921.)

Indeed he seemed to see vaguely the case for a commodity standard, that is, a currency stabilized in term of commodities, but he envisaged serious practical difficulties in measuring prices of commodities and hence held out for a metallic standard.[21]

It has indeed been said that we might judge of its value by its relation, not to one, but to the mass of commodities. If it should be conceded, which it cannot be, that the issuers of paper money would be willing to regulate the amount of their circulation by such a test, they would have no means of so doing; for when we consider that commodities are continually varying in value, as compared with each other; and that when such variation takes place, it is impossible to ascertain which commodity has increased, which diminished in value, it must be allowed that such a test would be of no use whatever.

. . . To determine the value of a currency by the test proposed, it would be necessary to compare it successively with the thousands of commodities which are circulating in the community, allowing to each all the effects which may have been produced upon its value by the above causes. To do this is evidently impossible.

It was not, however, merely the policies of the Bank during the war that had upset the sensitive Ricardo; he was extremely hostile to the Bank, in part because it had not followed his advice in the steps taken to resume payments. As early as 1811 Ricardo had proposed a gradual resumption.[22]

The remedy which I propose for all the evils in our currency, is that the Bank should gradually decrease the amount of their notes in circulation until they shall have rendered the remainder of equal value with the coins which they represent, or, in other words, till the prices of gold and silver bullion shall be brought down to their mint price. I am well aware that the total

[21] *Ibid.*, vol. IV, pp. 55, 59–60.
[22] *Ibid.*, vol. III, p. 94.

failure of paper credit would be attended with the most disastrous consequences to the trade and commerce of the country, and even its sudden
limitation would occasion so much ruin and distress, that it would be highly
inexpedient to have recourse to it as the means of restoring our currency
to its just and equitable value.

If the Bank were possessed of more guineas than they had notes in circulation, they could not, without great injury to the country, pay their notes in
specie, while the price of gold bullion continued greatly above the mint price,
and the foreign exchange unfavourable to us. The excess of our currency
would be exchanged for guineas at the Bank and exported, and would be
suddenly withdrawn from circulation. Before therefore they can safely pay
in specie, the excess of notes must be gradually withdrawn from circulation.
If gradually done, little inconvenience would be felt; so that the principle
were fairly admitted, it would be for future consideration whether the object
should be accomplished in one year or in five. I am fully persuaded that
we shall never restore our currency to its equitable state, but by this preliminary step, or by the total overthrow of our paper credit.

He had even announced that he would not have been opposed to a
devaluation when the currency was greatly depreciated but, once the
currency had risen within 5 per cent of parity, he would not support a
devaluation.[23]

The time had then arrived [in 1819] for fixing a standard, and the only
consideration was as to the selection of the particular standard which ought
to be adopted. They had two courses of proceeding open to them on that
occasion; one was either to regulate the standard by the price of gold at
the moment, or to recur to the ancient standard of the country. If, in the
year 1819, the value of the currency has stood at 14s. for the pound note,
which was the case in the year 1813, he should have thought that upon a
balance of all the advantages and disadvantages of the case, it would have
been as well to fix the currency at the then value, according to which most
of the existing contracts had been made; but when the currency was within
5 per cent of its par value, the only consideration was, whether they should
fix the standard at 4£.2s., the then price of gold, or recur at once to the
old standard. Under all the circumstances, he thought they had made the best
selection in recurring to the old standard. The real evil was committed in
1797, and the opportunity of mitigating its consequences was lost by the conduct subsequently pursued by the Bank; for even after the first suspension,
they might, by proceeding upon right principles in managing their issues, by
keeping the value of the currency at or near par, have prevented the depreciation which followed. It might be asked how they could have done so?
His reply was, that *quantity regulated the value of every thing.*

Ricardo insisted that the Bank, instead of reducing her issues gradually, proceed rapidly and therefore bid strenuously for gold, which she
then put into circulation. As a result of the excessive enthusiasm for

[23] *Ibid.*, vol. V, pp. 208–209.

deflation at home and for accumulating gold from abroad as the price level declined in Britain and the value of gold rose, the economy suffered greatly, and Ricardo's name was widely associated with the ensuing distress.

His *Plan for the Establishment of a National Bank,* published posthumously in 1824, reflected his lack of faith in the directors of the Bank and became the inspiration of those who would greatly restrict the discretionary powers of the Bank. In fact, by the 1840s the directors of the Bank, fearful of the use of discretion themselves, urged the government to deprive them of the right to issue notes beyond a fixed limit except on the basis of gold.[24] In Ricardo's view the profits of note issue had been excessive and should go to the government, and he would entrust the right of issue to the public commissioners. It was his view also that the contribution of the Bank to the accommodation of the business of the country was not important and hence even liquidation of the Bank would not be costly.[25]

If the view which I have taken of this subject be a correct one, it appears that the commerce of the country would not be in the least impeded by depriving the Bank of England of the power of issuing paper money, provided an amount of such money, equal to the Bank circulation, was issued by Government: and that the sole effect of depriving the Bank of this privilege, would be to transfer the profit which accrues from the interest of the money so issued from the Bank, to Government.[26]

He would even make it impossible for the Treasury to borrow from the bank of issue.[27]

I ask then, whether the country would not possess a greater security against all such influence, over the minds of the issuers of paper, as would induce them [the directors] to swerve from the strict line of their duty, if the paper money of the country were issued by Commissioners, on the plan I have proposed, rather than by the Bank of England, as at present constituted? If Government wanted money, it should be obliged to raise it in the legitimate way; by taxing the people; by the issue and sale of exchequer bills, by funded loans, or by borrowing from any of the numerous banks which might exist in the country; but in no case should be allowed to borrow from those, who have the power of creating money.

It is clear that the separation of note issue from banking, as required by the Bank Act of 1844, stemmed from Ricardo's views concerning the dangers of leaving to the management of merchants, the directors of the

---

[24] *Papers in English Monetary History* (T. S. Ashton and R. S. Sayers, eds.), 1953, pp. 110–111.
[25] *Ricardo,* vol. IV, pp. 276–285, "Plan for a National Bank."
[26] *Ibid.,* vol. IV, p. 281.
[27] *Ibid.,* vol. IV, p. 283.

bank, the prerogative of determining the volume of notes instead of tying issues with gold supply. In one respect this conclusion was surprising, for on occasion Ricardo showed that the amount of currency required depended on such considerations as the amount of trade and the rate with which money was used—even as Thornton did.[28] In short, the ghost of Ricardo for more than a century ruled over monetary rules and administration in that the system was tied excessively to gold and little play was left for discretion by the managers of the system.

[28] *Ibid.*, vol. IV, pp. 57–58, and Ashton and Sayers, *op. cit.*, pp. 25–27.

CHAPTER 10

After 1844: *Gold, Bank Policy, and Instruments of Control*

Parallels in the Post-World War I Period

On the whole, the 1844 Act seems to have been foolish legislation. That it did not prove disastrous was the result of the willingness of the authorities in the midst of great crises (1847, 1857, 1866, 1914) to suspend the Act and thus allow additional uncovered issues. But much more important than the suspension of the Bank Act was the growing practice of deposit creation by commercial banks which had already achieved a large development by 1844 but apparently had largely escaped the attention of the monetary experts. Through the creation of bank deposits, the deposit banks were able, despite the restrictions on note issue, to provide the country with greatly increased supplies of money needed in a growing economy.

The folly of the Bank Act of 1844 did not prevent the British from committing another serious error in imposing upon the country the recommendations of the famous *Cunliffe Report* (1919), which proposed a great deflation through a limitation of note issue, and the policy enunciated in 1919 was confirmed in 1924. The resultant deflation in 1920 to 1925 proved to be costly.[1]

In considering the Bank Act of 1844 after World War I, the official committees and the government in general endorsed it. They wanted a separation of departments because thus the reserve against notes was strengthened; they wanted the protection of convertibility against excess and would have no truck with any kind of standard that would seek price stabilization; and they apparently wanted a highly sensitive system which operated through higher money rates on domestic prices and output and the flow of international capital.

---

[1] *Final Report of Committee on Currency and Foreign Exchanges,* Cmd. 464, 1918; *Report of the Committee on Currency and Bank of England Note Issues,* Cmd. 2392, 1924–1925; and S. E. Harris, *Monetary Problems of the British Empire,* 1931, bks. V, VI.

The Cunliffe Committee, in its preliminary report, concluded as follows:

32. Having regard to the foregoing considerations, we are of opinion that the principle of the Act of 1844, which has upon the whole been fully justified by experience, should be maintained, namely, that there should be a fixed fiduciary issue beyond which, subject to emergency arrangements which we recommend below, notes should only be issued in exchange for gold. It is noteworthy that from 1866 till the outbreak of the present war no suspension of the Act was ever necessary. We think that the stringent principles of the Act have often had the effect of preventing dangerous developments and the fact that they have had to be temporarily suspended on certain rare and exceptional occasions (and those limited to the earlier years of the Act's operation when experience of working the system was still immature) does not, in our opinion, invalidate this conclusion. We recommend, therefore, that the separation of the Issue and Banking Departments of the Bank of England should be maintained and that the Weekly Return should continue to be published in its present form.

The victorious adherents to the currency principle had oversimplified the problems of monetary management, and not merely because the problem of deposit creation had largely escaped them. There were other serious omissions. They tended to concentrate on the relation of gold inflows and outflows (the latter reflecting excessive issues) and to neglect the importance of internal drains and other changes in the requirements for money. Failing to allow for what Marshall called changes in the manner of doing business, as well as the factors mentioned above, they assumed a relation of gold and prices which was not to be found in the real world.

Tooke, Fullarton, and others had attracted attention to the growth and decline of monetary hoards.[2] Internal demand for increased hoards contributed importantly to the pressure on the Bank of England once there was cause for alarm, and a rise of rates in London proved to be an effective mechanism for reversing the movement as the higher returns to be had on money resulted in hoards flowing back to London. Jevons has estimated the monetary gold in the United Kingdom at £95 million in March, 1868, but with the gold of the Bank of England varying from £12 to £24 million sterling in the sixties, it amounted only to

[2] Thornton was one of the first, if not the first, to bring attention to the significance of monetary hoards, and in his early analysis he said: "The quantity of circulating paper, that is paper capable of circulation . . . may be great and yet the quantity of actual circulation may be small, or vice versa." His views of the use of money, rather modern in their approach, resulted in an emphasis on the point that "a state of distrust causes a slowness in the circulation of *guineas,* and that at such a time a greater quantity of money will be wanted in order to effect the same money payments. . . . " H. Thornton, *An Enquiry into the Nature and Effects of the Paper Credit of Great Britain, 1802* (F. Hayek, ed.), 1939, pp. 98–99.

one-third to one-sixth of the gold in circulation. These internal drains were often much more important than the external drains.[3]

Even the Bullion Committee was much more aware of the need of adapting currency to changing demand than was implied in the 1844 legislation (see quotation below). The Act of 1844 did not provide off-setting mechanisms to cover changes in hoards. Hence large losses of reserves of the Bank followed withdrawals of gold for internal hoards, and the Bank would react by deflating the economy as though inflation was being experienced and with inflation, an outflow of gold. It would be better to issue notes to satisfy the increased demands for liquidity.[4]

But Your Committee must not omit to state one very important principle, That the mere numerical return of the amount of Bank notes out in circulation, cannot be considered as at all deciding the question, whether such paper is or is not excessive. It is necessary to have recourse to other tests. The same amount of paper may at one time be less than enough, and at another time more. The quantity of currency required will vary in some degree with the extent of trade; and the increase of our trade, which has taken place since the suspension, must have occasioned some increase in the quantity of our currency. But the quantity of currency bears no fixed porportion to the quantity of commodities; and any inferences proceeding upon such a supposition would be entirely erroneous. The effective currency of the Country depends upon the quickness of circulation, and the number of exchanges performed in a given time, as well as upon its numerical amount; and all the circumstances, which have a tendency to quicken or to retard the rate of circulation, render the same amount of currency more or less adequate to the wants of trade. A much smaller amount is required in a high state of public credit than when alarms make individuals calls in their advances, and provide against accidents by hoarding; and in a period of commercial security and private confidence, than when mutual distrust discourages pecuniary arrangements for any distant time. But, above all, the same amount of currency will be more or less adequate in proportion to the skill which the great money-dealers possess in managing and economising the use of the circulating medium.

Testifying before an expert committee seventy-six years after the *Bullion Report* was published and forty-two years after the Bank Act of 1844, Marshall, severely critical of this legislation, was at pains to show that "changes in the method of business and the amounts of the commodities, or as we may say, changes in the commercial environment, have much greater effects in disturbing prices than changes in the supplies of the precious metals." In the early part of the nineteenth century, the supply of gold was relatively constant and fluctuations in

[3] See R. G. Hawtrey, *A Century of Bank Rate*, 1938, especially pp. 41, 48–52, 93–96, 281–300.

[4] *The Paper Pound of 1797–1821: A Reprint of the Bullion Report* (Cannan, ed.), 1919, pp. 57–58.

prices were violent, but from 1844 to 1886, the fluctuations in gold supplies were much greater and price fluctuations less. Marshall's position was much closer to that of the experts of 1810 than to that of the victors of 1844.[5]

Supporters of the currency school had also introduced an untenable theory, namely, that once the boom had been deflated, it was imperative to withhold additional supplies of money. But such practices would only multiply losses and bankruptcies. In fact, as Hawtrey shows, on one occasion before 1847 the Bank of England had refused to give credit in the midst of a crisis. In later years, the Bank became less restrictive; it would lend but at much higher rates of interest. The presently accepted view that once the bubble had burst or there were signs of impending declines, the rate of interest should be reduced was not clear to the British even as late as 1920–1921 and apparently not clear to many an authority in this country even as late as 1954.[6]

With a collapse, prices would fall, the rate of interest rise, and hence the outflow of gold would stop. More British exports and long-term securities would be purchased, for at higher rates of interest the prices of securities would be depressed. Indeed in a great decline, it may take much time and much money to induce purchases of securities. It is difficult, then, to justify the restrictions on issue even if they did contain the original cyclical rise. In a passage below, Mill expresses well the folly of rigid limitations on central bank issues, and in a later passage he insists upon the need for satisfying the liquidity preference of businessmen in a period of lack of confidence. (Here he sounds almost like a nineteenth-century Keynes.)[7]

In the first place, a large extension of credit by bankers, though most hurtful when, credit being already in an inflated state, it can only serve to retard and aggravate the collapse, is most salutary when the collapse has come, and when credit instead of being in excess is in distressing deficiency, and increased advances by bankers, instead of being an addition to the ordinary amount of floating credit, serve to replace a mass of other credit which has been suddenly destroyed. Antecedently to 1844, if the Bank of England occasionally aggravated the severity of a commercial revulsion by rendering the collapse of credit more tardy and hence more violent than necessary, it in return rendered invaluable services during the revulsion itself, by coming forward with advances to support solvent firms, at a time when all other paper and almost all mercantile credit had become comparatively valueless. This service was eminently conspicuous in the crisis of 1825–6, the severest probably

[5] *Official Papers of Alfred Marshall*, 1926, pp. 54–55, 111–112, and 140–141.

[6] Hawtrey, *op. cit.*, pp. 21–23, 133; and *United States Monetary Policy: Recent Thinking and Experience*, 1954, Hearings of the Joint Committee on the Economic Report, pp. 26–27.

[7] J. S. Mill, *Principles of Political Economy* (Ashley, ed.), 1920, pp. 662–664.

ever experienced; during which the Bank increased what is called its circulation by many millions, in advances to those mercantile firms of whose ultimate solvency it felt no doubt; advances which if it had been obliged to withhold, the severity of the crisis would have been still greater than it was.

What Mill knew in the middle of the nineteenth century was not known to many in authority in the twentieth century. I do not have in mind merely the British mistakes even as late as the 1920s. When the American economy collapsed in 1929 and remained dormant in the early thirties, the Secretary of the Treasury announced that we must liquidate labor, liquidate farmers, etc., and the President insisted that the way out was to increase taxes and reduce public expenditures (and thus reduce monetary supplies and increase bankruptcies), and even candidate Roosevelt would balance the budget in the midst of declining demand.

Central Bank Responsibility

Some of the points raised in the preceding sections suggest the need of a somewhat fuller discussion of the problem of central banking. Policy is virtually ruled out unless a country has a central monetary authority which assumes some responsibility for the public interest, however that is defined. It took a long time, however, before central banks acknowledged such responsibilities in an adequate manner.

Thus, in 1840, Lord Overstone, the greatest authority, commented as follows to an official committee: " . . . It seems to me that the whole doctrine of the duty of the Bank of England to support public credit (a doctrine strongly enforced by public opinion, . . . [is] I think, too readily acquiesced by the Bank itself. . . .)." At the 1857 hearings an ex-governor of the Bank of England, when questioned by Gladstone, then Chancellor of the Exchequer, concerning sales of securities by the Bank to restore its reserves, replied that securities were indeed sold but with the notes thus received discounts were increased. Imagine a central bank taking cash away from the public in the midst of a panic! "Both in 1847 and 1857 . . . the Bank directors contended that the Banking Department was quite safe though its reserve was nearly all gone, and that it could strengthen itself by selling securities and refusing to discount. . . . "[8] As late as 1857, Newmarch was complaining of the Bank of England's practice of reducing rates and competing with the market.[9]

By the time Bagehot wrote his book in 1873, he agreed that the Bank was taking its public responsibilities seriously but complained it was not ready to acknowledge them. The bank had in fact moved from a policy

---

[8] W. Bagehot, *Lombard Street, 1873* (H. Withers, ed.), 1915, p. 65, and T. E. Gregory (ed.), *Select Statutes, Documents and Reports Relating to British Banking, 1832–1928*, 1929, vol. II, p. 50.

[9] Gregory, *op. cit.*, vol. II, pp. 60–64.

of refusing to discount or restricting the period of discount in crisis periods, to one of making credit available but at much higher rates. As Bagehot put it, a panic, in a word, is a species of neuralgia, and according to the rules of sciences you must not starve it. " . . . In contrast to Ricardo, who had held that banks 'have no security on any system' under panicky conditions," Bagehot insisted "upon very large loans at very high rates of interest when a foreign drain is added to a domestic drain."[10]

We have indeed moved far from the views held by S. J. Loyd (then a banker in Manchester) when he testified as follows:[11]

The Act of 1844 was supposed to have released the Bank from any necessity of attending to the public interest, and it was supposed that the bank was at liberty practically to look to its own profits, and not to the general interest of the public; was that your impression of the operation of the Act?—In a certain sense of the word, I think that is correct; it is desirable so to organize all public institutions, that looking to their own interests wisely and discreetly, and taking a sufficiently comprehensive view of them, will be the best course not only for their own but for the public interest also. At the same time, the Bank, from the magnitude of its resources and transactions, stands in a peculiar position. The Bank, to whatever extremity it may allow its means to be reduced, can, by the very magnitude of its operations, in the last extremity make an effort which is almost sure to protect itself, but that effort will entail on the community very serious consequences and produce very great mischief; in that respect the Bank seems to me to differ considerably from all private concerns. If I mismanage my private bank, I am ruined but the public sustain little inconvenience; but if the Bank of England commits some great mistake, the Bank can save iteself, whilst it spreads extensive injury throughout the community; in that respect, I think it differs in an important sense from a private concern.

Management of Gold and the Bank Rate

It is widely thought (perhaps too widely) that the gold standard functioned reasonably well from the Napoleonic War to World War I, though not the gold standard as envisaged, say, by the adherents of the currency school. The gold standard gradually became a managed standard, with the primary objective being protection of gold reserves as the means of preventing large international disequilibria. Indeed, the management was often primitive and especially since such legislation as the Bank Act of 1844 tied the hands of the managers.

A major factor in the evolution of management has been the use of bank rate. Even in the 1830s, it was known that a rise in the bank rate by the Bank of England would discourage demand for credit and thus influence business activity. A governor of the Bank of England said

[10] Bagehot, *op. cit.*, pp. 48–65.
[11] Evidence of S. J. Loyd before the *Secret Committee on Commercial Distress*, May, 1848, par. 5192.

in 1848 that a high bank rate " . . . is extremely prejudicial to commerce, and that it is totally uncalled for when the exchanges are in favor of this country, which they must be at those times of commercial pressure." But with gold moving out, it was held necessary to protect the Bank, for rates would rise and the Bank, if it were not to be pressed too hard, must protect itself.

The view so well expressed by Ricardo in his essay on *The Higher Price of Bullion* (1810) continued to be the dominant one throughout the nineteenth and part of the twentieth centuries. It was not possible in his view to influence the rate of interest except temporarily through monetary creation. Wicksell and notably Keynes were to correct this view more than one hundred years after Ricardo. To accept the position of Ricardo (and Adam Smith) would be to deny that there can be any control over the rate of interest.[12]

To suppose that any increased issues of the Bank can have the effect of permanently lowering the rate of interest, and satisfying the demands of all borrowers, so that there will be none to apply for new loans, or that a productive gold or silver mine can have such an effect, is to attribute a power to the circulating medium which it can never possess. Banks would, if this were possible, become powerful engines indeed. By creating paper money, and lending it at three or two per cent. under the present market rate of interest, the Bank would reduce the profits on trade in the same proportion; and if they were sufficiently patriotic to lend their notes at an interest no higher than necessary to pay the expences of their establishment, profits would be still further reduced; no nation, but by similar means, could enter into competition with us, we should engross the trade of the world. To what absurdities would not such a theory lead us! Profits can only be lowered by a competition of capitals not consisting of circulating medium. As the increase of Bank-notes does not add to this species of capital, as it neither increases our exportable commodities, our machinery, or our raw materials, it cannot add to our profits nor lower interest.

Let us review the history of control through variations in the bank rate, that is, the rate charged by the central bank. As early as 1832, the governor of the Bank of England acknowledged that with a monopoly of free issue of currency notes, the Bank of England could set a rate above which other lenders could not lend. In 1857, the greater influence in rising than in declining periods was stressed.[13]

The 1832 pronouncement was as follows:[14]

The Bank, fixing a public rate of interest at which it may be willing to discount all approved bills of a given description, and being the only body issuing

[12] *Ricardo*, vol. III, p. 92.

[13] Gregory, *op. cit.*, vol. I, p. 15; vol. II, pp. 56–58.

[14] *Ibid.*, vol. I, p. 15; cf. also E. Wood, *English Theories of Central Banking Control, 1819–1858*, 1939, chaps. 4–5; and Tooke and Newmarch, *A History of Prices*, vol. III, pp. 109–113.

money *ad libitum,* within the sphere of the circulation of such bills, thereby fixes the *maximum* of the rate of interest during the existence of such notice, and consequently all persons having money already in existence to employ, must necessarily offer to lend it under the Bank's public rate, except in times of actual scarcity or deficiency of money currency. . . .

As more was learned about rate controls, changes in rates were used more frequently. Thus in the 1840s there were relatively few changes in rates. In 1873, the Bank of England revised its rates twenty-four times. After an exhaustive survey, Palgrave associated the increase of changes in rates with the small cash reserves relative to the rise in the supply of loanable capital.[15]

Throughout the nineteenth century, however, the orthodox view was that the Bank follows the market. At the hearings of the Select Committee of Banks of Issues in 1840, Lord Overstone put the usual view well:[16]

2794. Upon what do you conceive the rate of interest to depend; does it depend upon the amount of circulation?—The rate of interest may be temporarily affected during an increase or a diminution in the amount of paper circulation. I apprehend that the general range of the rate of interest is liable to be affected in varying degrees by many considerations; but it is correct to say generally, that it depends upon the proportion between the quantity of capital in the country and the demand for the employment of it.

2795. Does the Bank of England regulate it?—No. It cannot be said, in the proper meaning of the words, that the Bank regulates the rate of interest in this country, though she undoubtedly may exercise an influence over the temporary fluctuations in the rate of interest. During short periods, the Bank of England, being a very large and powerful body, with means and resources out of proportion to the mass of the community, may produce slight temporary oscillations in the rate of interest; but she cannot affect the general altitude of the rate of interest.

But somehow he did not see the contradiction between the above position and his insistence that higher rates by the Bank stop the outflow of gold and bring contraction.[17]

2839. What was the effect of the Bank raising the rate of interest in 1839?— I apprehend that the effect was extremely valuable; it was the one measure by which the Bank did any thing to meet the drain under which we were suffering. I think it is important to observe, that raising the rate of interest during an efflux of bullion is a measure strictly in conformity to what would be the course of things with a metallic circulation. If with a metallic circulation a drain took place, the circulation would, of course, be undergoing a con-

[15] R. H. I. Palgrave, *Bank Rate and the Money Market,* 1903, especially pp. 96–105.
[16] Gregory, *op. cit.,* vol. I, pp. 44–46.
[17] *Ibid.,* pp. 46–47.

traction; which contraction would necessarily produce a continuous tendency to a rise in the rate of interest; and the Bank administering a paper circulation is strictly conforming to the action of a metallic currency, when she raises the rate of interest during the export of bullion.

In 1857, a former governor of the Bank agreed that with a rise in the rate the market followed. But the ex-governor insisted that "it [the Bank] has no other power than what is given to it by the state of the floating capital of the country, and the portions which the Bank itself holds." He maintained that its influence is especially great when cash accumulates at the Bank in anticipation of Treasury disbursement of dividends.[18]

Bagehot, writing in 1873, also insisted upon limited control of money rates by the Bank, even when it had a monopoly of issue. "A bank with a monopoly of note issue has great sudden power in the money market, but no permanent power: it can affect the rate of discount at any particular moment, but it cannot affect the average rate."[19]

Even Marshall adhered to the conventional view, though he conceded that over short periods the discount rate could deviate from rates set by market forces, e.g., through the interaction of supply and demand for capital. Even as late as 1954, top management in the United States was insisting upon the hegemony of free-market forces even though the assets held by Reserve banks exceeded the total reserves of commercial banks (a rise of these assets increases reserves correspondingly, *ceteris paribus*) and even though over a preceding generation monetary expansion in the face of unprecedented demands for capital had reduced long-term rates from 4 to 2 per cent.[20]

Marshall was prophetic here: "The rate of discount, in my opinion, is merely the ripple of a wave on the surface, the average level is the rate of interest which can be got for the investment of capital and this is being lowered by the rapid and steady growth of capital. . . . I should not be at all surprised if a railway company could borrow on debentures, on even less than 2 per cent in the next century."[21]

But to return to the main theme. The orthodox view in the nineteenth century was far from the Keynesian one that through monetary policy the rate of interest could be influenced greatly and especially through the effects upon income and savings. It is now widely admitted that intervention by monetary authorities can greatly affect the rates.[22]

[18] *Ibid.*, vol. II, pp. 56–57.
[19] Bagehot, *op. cit.*, pp. 110–111.
[20] Hawtrey, *op. cit.*, pp. 27–28, 66–67; Marshall, *op. cit.*, pp. 130–131.
[21] Marshall, *op. cit.*, pp. 27, 49.
[22] J. M. Keynes, *The General Theory of Employment, Interest and Money*, 1936, chaps. 13, 14. But Keynes, with his emphasis on liquidity preference, was less optimistic than in 1930 of the capacity of the monetary authority to determine rates.

How is a rise of rates to reestablish equilibrium? On several occasions (e.g., 1857), the authorities of the Bank of England denied that higher rates attracted large amounts of capital from abroad.[23] (This view was held much more widely in the next seventy-five years.) Rather they tended to emphasize the effects of higher rates on domestic demand and, therefore, the conservation of central bank reserves. In his analysis of nineteenth-century policy, Hawtrey listed the effects of higher central bank rates in three stages: (1) an initial effect through inflows of capital, (2) the reduced demand for notes (and reserves) accompanying the deflation, and (3) the ultimate gain, namely, a return of notes from circulation in response to higher rates for all countries involved. Hawtrey insisted that obtaining gold at the expense of other countries was only a temporary solution. They, in turn, would adopt deflationary policies and attract back the gold previously lost. The competition for gold in the 1920s is a case in point. Here a deflation in the United States increased pressure on British reserves, and the British, in turn, introduced deflationary policies. Again in the late twenties the United States reduced rates as a means of easing pressures on British reserves.[24]

A central bank attempts to determine the amount of money outstanding by making its rates effective; that is to say, a rate of 6 per cent by the central bank is innocuous with market rates 4 per cent. To bring the market rate up to 6 per cent, the central bank must force the market to borrow from it. Hence, central banks have developed techniques for forcing the money market, inclusive of commercial banks, to borrow. Even in the latter part of the nineteenth century, the Bank of England had introduced open-market operations as an instrument for forcing the market to borrow—first by the sale of consols and then through borrowing on bills from the market.[25]

But before we discuss open-market operations at greater length, we should add a final word on bank rate. The discussions in the nineteenth century seem rather amateurish compared with the more sophisticated treatment of the post-World War I period. In the *Macmillan Report* or in the much more technical treatment in Keynes's *Treatise on Money*, one will find much on the relation of bank rates to market rates; on the relation of rates to the flow of capital and gold; on the effects of rates on costs, prices, cost-price ratios, and output; and finally, on the limitations of central-bank influences on money rates even when supplemented by open-market operations. These limitations spring in no small part from the bluntness of the instrument at all times, the possibility of misinter-

[23] But cf. Bagehot, *op. cit.*, p. 47.
[24] Hawtrey, *op. cit.*, especially p. 45 and chap. 4, and S. E. Harris, *Twenty Years of Federal Reserve Policy*, 1933, chap. 25.
[25] Cf. W. B. Smith, *Economic Aspects of the Second Bank of the United States*, 1953, p. 53. (Sporadic open-market operations are described.)

pretation by the business community of changes in rates, and the impotency of the instrument, especially in periods of depression.[26]

In Meade's more recent treatment, the reader will find an even more complex approach. Here it is shown, for example, that in response to a spontaneous increase of lending from A to B, corrective measures are taken under both a gold and a paper standard. Under the former, the rise of interest rates in A (and reduction in B) results in less lending by A and more by B; in response to higher rates and less money, in reduced domestic expenditures in A and hence reduced imports (and the opposite movements for B); and with appropriate marginal propensities to import in both countries, in a reduced demand for A's products and hence downward pressure on A's costs and prices. Under a paper standard, the initial depreciation induces an adjustment for A (less imports and more exports), but here again the rate of interest will play a part as a means of ensuring internal balance and offsetting the inflation associated with depreciation.[27]

A history of United States rate policy since 1913 also is not very reassuring. On the whole, the great hopes held out for the penalty rate (i.e., a rate in excess of the market and used as a depressant) have not been fulfilled. In crucial periods the reserve authorities have not used this weapon; frequently they were restrained by the availability of large liquid resources, by banks or their customers, and finally in the few instances when they had recourse to this weapon (e.g., 1953), the authorities revealed a high degree of ineptitude.[28]

Through open-market operations a central bank tries to influence the cash position of the money market. For example, it sells assets, and as the market buys them, the cash reserves of the market are reduced. But it should be noted that any accumulation of deposits by the Treasury at the central bank (other than through direct borrowing of the Treasury from the central bank) is at the expense of the money market and, therefore, deprives the market of cash. Such accumulations are then a variant of an open-market operation. Even in the 1830s the Bank of England had learned how to offset Treasury accumulations of cash in anticipation of payments of dividends on consols. " . . . The Bank has, within the last few years, resorted to a measure that has worked extremely well for the purpose of mitigating that difficulty, namely, that of making tem-

[26] See especially *Report of the Committee on Finance and Industry*, 1931, pt. I, chaps. 8–11, pt. II, pp. 94–99, and J. M. Keynes, *Treatise on Money*, 1930, chaps. 13, 30–38.

[27] J. E. Meade, *The Balance of Payments*, 1952, pp. 190–195.

[28] The author has discussed many of these issues in his *Twenty Years of Federal Reserve Policy*, vols. I and II, 1933, but also see the various hearings (several listed in this book) on monetary policy and more recently in Joint Committee on Economic Report, *Monetary Policy and the Management of the Public Debt*, 1952, and *United States Monetary Policy*, 1954.

porary advances during the month preceding the payment of the dividends, to be discharged during the month in which the dividends are coming due; and by that means an approach is made to an equalized state of the circulation."[29] In the later years of the nineteenth century (cf. Bagehot and Hawtrey), techniques improved for preventing a starvation of credit as the government absorbed cash, and the Bank had learned how to drive the market to the Bank through open-market operations in periods of excessive expansion.

The policy of the Bank of England in the first half of the nineteenth century might be compared with some early experience of the United States. In the years 1817 to 1835 the government repaid debt in almost every year. The effects on circulation were adverse, but the historian of the Second Bank of the United States welcomes the repayment as a check to inflationary forces. In the later years of the Second Bank, the government, in order to destroy the Bank, carried through an unusual policy, namely, large withdrawals of cash from the Bank and especially from the Northeastern centers.[30]

Open-market Operations

Even in the first half of the nineteenth century, there was evidence that banking authorities had some understanding of open-market operations, but the evidence is mixed. Indeed, in the late 1830s officials of the Bank denied that they varied their securities in response to favorable or unfavorable exchange conditions, but the explanation of inaction was that they felt no responsibility to interfere. On another occasion (1839) the Bank threatened to sell securities as a means of reducing the circulation in a period of external drain. This suggests a comprehension of the mechanics if not an awareness of the responsibility of a central bank. No central bank in modern times would be likely thus to impair confidence further. But interestingly enough Tooke criticized the Bank for not carrying out its threat.[31] Professor Elmer Wood, the careful historian of the period, tells us that in the second quarter of the nineteenth century there was an awareness of the relation of the Treasury bills held by the Bank and funds available to the market and that the market was aware it could replenish its funds by refusing to purchase Treasury bills.[32] Yet, according to Wood, the Bank authorities in the thirties apparently did not understand that sales of securities reduced the reserves of the market.

[29] Gregory, *op. cit.*, vol. I, p. 46. Cf. p. 76.
[30] Smith, *op. cit.*, pp. 65, 161–162.
[31] Tooke and Newmarch, *op. cit.*, pp. 88–89.
[32] Wood, *op. cit.*, pp. 68–69, 87.

Through open-market operations the monetary authority may seek much higher objectives, namely, reducing or increasing the cash reserves of the banks, the source of monetary expansion of banks. A purchase of securities would increase and a sale of securities would deplete reserves. But even as late as the 1920s the objective of the Federal Reserve Board was to force member banks into debt to the Reserve banks and thus through a dislike of indebtedness force the banks to contract their loans from the central bank. This theory was revived in the early fifties. In the Great Depression the Reserve banks tried to expand the total supply of money by trying to increase reserves of member banks through purchases of securities in the open market. But the rise of reserves of banks was disappointing, in part because they used the additional cash substantially to repay debts at Reserve banks.

Yet the history of the years 1930 to 1955 suggests that central banks now try to increase or reduce reserves of member banks, though any net effects are related to gold flows (an importation increases reserves), currency movement (an inflow increases reserves), and several other factors. What is more, the Reserve banks are prepared to treat reserves directly through changes in reserve requirements.[33]

Gold and Management

Aside from management, however, the gold standard underwent considerable change. The amount of money has not been rigidly tied to gold. In fact, the major fluctuations in currency supplies, as well as the major growth, occurred in bank deposits, often not closely tied to fluctuations in gold supplies.

That the gold standard functioned as well as it did in the nineteenth century is, then, to be associated with the new techniques of management, not only the use of the bank rate but, as noted, the beginnings of what has since come to be known as "open-market operations." Another weapon was developed in the later years, namely, small variations in the price of gold. Thus the Bank of England might stimulate an inflow of gold by varying (reducing) slightly the charge for coinage.

In addition to the factors mentioned, we shall comment on several additional points. One is that the management of the gold standard lay largely with the British in the nineteenth century, and the readiness of the British to convert sterling into gold and act as a short-term and long-term banker for the world provided the outside world with secondary reserves when a great inflation or a loss of exports threatened the external position of any of these countries. Moreover, the willingness of

[33] Hawtrey, *op. cit.*, pp. 68–71; E. A. Goldenweiser, *Monetary Management*, 1949, chap. 4; Harris, *Twenty Years of Federal Reserve Policy*, pts. 2, 7, 8.

the British in general to play the game of the gold standard (i.e., contract in periods of outflow and expand in those of inflow) helped sustain it and provide the necessary leadership. In these years, moreover, wages and prices had not assumed the rigidity which they were to experience in the twentieth century. Again, there were some fortuitous developments that were also helpful. Gold supplies would have been much less adequate to lubricate the economic machine after years of declining prices and assumption of the gold standard by many additional countries had not the great gold discoveries been made in the 1850s and at the end of the century. It is extremely doubtful that the price collapse of the 1840s and the last quarter of the nineteenth century would have been allowed to continue much longer. The cure would have been an abandonment of gold. What is more, in the years following these gold discoveries the great economic advances with increased needs for money provided a rise of demand to offset the increase of supply and thus excluded a major inflation. Throughout, the expansion of bank deposits helped solve the problem of monetary needs in a century of great development. All in all, except in wartime, oscillations in prices were moderate.

A Contrast of Positions on Gold, 1918, 1931, and 1946

Even as late as 1918, the Cunliffe Committee expressed strong approval of the gold standard. No question was raised concerning such problems as rigidities of costs as prices decline or the possibility that it might be preferable to stabilize commodity prices rather than gold or to seek higher output rather than protect reserves or that a policy which achieved equilibrium through contraction might unnecessarily damage the economy. Later on, these questions were to be raised by Keynes during his attack on gold, and some of them were even to be raised by the more moderate authors of the *Macmillan Report* of 1931. In this 1931 report the authors suggest the difficulties of reconciling domestic and international objectives as well as the obstacles to expanding purchasing power through central-bank policy. At this time, the emphasis had shifted to the problem of getting out of a depression, whereas the Cunliffe Committee had concentrated its attention on treating inflation.

In the Bretton Woods Agreements of 1946, the principles enunciated in 1931 were given the support of the signatory powers, for in these agreements it was acknowledged that the gold standard must be operated in a manner not to interfere with domestic objectives of employment and output, and revisions of exchange rates, inconsistent with the principle of gold, would be not only tolerated but encouraged.

Because it is an excellent statement of how gold is supposed to work, we give below the Cunliffe description of the gold standard. The advances over Hume's statement in the eighteenth century are limited to the greater scope given to management.[34]

When the exchanges were favourable, gold flowed freely into this country and an increase of legal tender money accompanied the development of trade. When the balance of trade was unfavourable and the exchanges were adverse, it became profitable to export gold. The would-be exporter bought his gold from the Bank of England and paid for it by a cheque on his account. The Bank obtained the gold from the Issue Department in exchange for notes taken out of its banking reserve, with the result that its liabilities to depositors and its banking reserve were reduced by an equal amount, and the ratio of reserve to liabilities consequently fell. If the process was repeated sufficiently often to reduce the ratio in a degree considered dangerous, the Bank raised its rate of discount. The raising of the discount rate had the immediate effect of retaining money here which would otherwise have been remitted abroad and of attracting remittances from abroad to take advantage of the higher rate, thus checking the outflow of gold and even reversing the stream.

If the adverse condition of the exchanges was due not merely to seasonal fluctuations, but to circumstances tending to create a permanently adverse trade balance, it is obvious that the procedure above described would not have been sufficient. It would have resulted in the creation of a volume of short-dated indebtedness to foreign countries which would have been in the end disastrous to our credit and the position of London as the financial centre of the world. But the raising of the Bank's discount rate and the steps taken to make it effective in the market necessarily led to a general rise of interest rates and a restriction of credit. New enterprises were therefore postponed and the demand for constructional materials and other capital goods was lessened. The consequent slackening of employment also diminished the demand for consumable goods, while holders of stocks of commodities carried largely with borrowed money, being confronted with an increase of interest charges, if not with actual difficulty in renewing loans, and with the prospect of falling prices, tended to press their goods on a weak market. The result was a decline in general prices in the home market which, by checking imports and stimulating exports, corrected the adverse trade balance which was the primary cause of the difficulty.

When, apart from a foreign drain of gold, credit at home threatened to become unduly expanded, the gold currency system tended to restrain the expansion and to prevent the consequent rise in domestic prices which ultimately causes such a drain. The expansion of credit, by forcing up prices, involves an increased demand for legal tender currency both from the banks in order to maintain their normal proportion of cash to liabilities and from the general public for the payment of wages and for retail transactions. In this case also, the demand for such currency fell upon the reserve of the Bank of England,

[34] *The Committee on Currency and Foreign Exchanges after the War*, 1918, pars. 4–7; also see *Report of Committee on Finance and Industry*, 1931, pp. 18–24; S. E. Harris, *Keynes: Economist and Policy Maker*, 1955, chap. 20 (and references there); and *Articles of Agreement, International Monetary Fund and International Bank for Reconstruction and Development*, 1944; cf. earlier treatment by Meade.

and the Bank was thereupon obliged to raise its rate of discount in order to prevent the fall in the proportion of that reserve to its liabilities. The same chain of consequences as we have just described followed and speculative trade activity was similarly restrained. There was therefore an automatic machinery by which the volume of purchasing power in this country was continuously adjusted to world prices of commodities in general. Domestic prices were automatically regulated so as to prevent excessive imports; and the creation of banking credit was so controlled that banking could be safely permitted a freedom from State interference which would not have been possible under a less rigid currency system.

Under these arrangements this country was provided with a complete and effective gold standard. The essence of such a standard is that notes must always stand at absolute parity with gold coins of equivalent face value, and that both notes and gold coins stand at absolute parity with gold bullion. When these conditions are fulfilled, the foreign exchange rates with all countries possessing an effective gold standard are maintained at or within the gold specie points.

Some Conclusions to Chapters 9 and 10

Ricardo's views on monetary policy greatly influenced the discretion or lack of it allowed the monetary authority and, of course, monetary policy. His influence was felt in the resumption of payments in the post-Napoleonic period, in the Bank Act of 1844, and in monetary regulations and policy in the century following 1844. But Keynes and the Great Depression greatly reduced the hold of the Ricardian ghost.

For Ricardo the task of the monetary authority was a distinctly limited one, for in his view, as in Adam Smith's, the distribution of precious metals was determined by fundamental forces, and therefore the supply of money, inclusive of paper money, had to be limited to the supply that would have been outstanding had only gold circulated. The central bank had only to redeem its notes at a fixed price in relation to gold, and it followed that should the foreign exchanges depreciate beyond a point given by the cost of shipping gold, the explanation could only be excessive issues brought on by the absence of the restraining influence of convertibility. Though Ricardo was aware that the value of gold itself might fluctuate and therefore was not an ideal standard, he nevertheless preferred it to a commodity standard, which he considered impractical. But despite his awarness of the deficiencies of gold, he nevertheless exaggerated the extent to which overissue of paper money accounted for the depreciation of the exchanges, and underestimated the contribution of the changing value of gold and the political and military events which Malthus stressed so much. Nor did he allow, as many of his contemporaries and later authorities had allowed, for the variations in the demand for money associated with increased drains from within, a movement in current terminology which might be subsumed under increased liquidity. Thornton, Fullarton, J. S. Mill, and Marshall all recognized the fact that the Ricardian system and the theory behind the Bank Act of 1844 could greatly damage the economic system in that money would be reduced as though gold were being exported when, in fact, more money was being absorbed in hoards or possibly to meet increased needs of trade.

The strait jacket imposed upon the economy by the Bank Act of 1844 would have done much more damage than it actually did had not an element of elasticity been injected by the rise of banking deposits, fortunate discoveries of gold, and suspension of the Act. Moreover, the system gradually emerged as a managed system, not the automatic one envisaged by Ricardo and Overstone, the joint parents of the Bank Act of 1844. Though for long periods disposed to act on behalf of their stockholders, the managers of the Bank gradually assumed responsibilities in the public interest. Confused for many years in their use of rate policy and especially of open-market policies, they gradually learned, however, to use these weapons as a means of averting speculative movements and providing help in periods of distress.

But fundamentally the principle of tying the hands of the authority prevailed throughout the nineteenth and early twentieth centuries, in part because of the fear of abuse and in part because of a persistent view that the issue of money could not influence the rate of interest in any significant sense. It is not surprising, then, that from the check of convertibility demanded by the Bullionists in the Napoleonic War, the system deteriorated to the one-third reserve rule of the 1830s and then to the system of rigid limitations imposed in 1844. Indeed, the system was relaxed to some extent through the suspension of the Bank Act in emergencies, in war through the issue of Treasury notes, and finally in recent years by more flexible limitations on fiduciary issues and a system of shielding the economy from external movements of reserves. But once the view is accepted that monetary and especially fiscal policy can influence the rate of interest in a fundamental sense, then the rigid monetary systems inherited from Ricardo and Overstone must give way to more elastic systems.

What is more, the much greater attention paid to domestic employment, growth, and balance, in contrast to the Ricardian concentration on the effects of domestic policy upon the foreign exchanges, suggests the need of adjusting monetary supplies to the needs of the domestic situation. Where the result is external imbalance, then, as we shall see, special measures must be taken to protect the external position, but not at the expense of substantial losses at home. Among these measures are controls, the use of exchange flexibility, and international cooperation in the form of credits, agreements on adjustments in exchanges, and reasonable commercial policies. How far we have moved from the Ricardian system is suggested by the fact that the United Kingdom could lose half of its gold reserves from the end of 1950 to the end of 1952, yet the total earning assets of the Bank of England increased as did the total supply of money in the country, and, of course, no serious decline in business activity occurred. Under the present British system the economy is protected against the effects of large losses of reserves in contrast to the 1844 system, under which they were purposely subjected to pressures with small losses of reserves.

Over a period of about 160 years we have moved from the view that monetary policy has a most restricted part to play in economic policy to one that stresses monetary policy and finally to one that in some circles emphasizes fiscal policy perhaps even more than monetary policy, although, of course, the two should be integrated. In order to give both monetary and fiscal policy greater scope, it is obviously necessary not to tie the monetary system to the supplies of gold available even in the more elastic relation that developed in the seventy-five years following the Act of 1844. The inadequacies of gold stand out the more the greater the emphasis put upon domestic objectives. More will be said about the interplay of monetary and fiscal policy in later chapters.

Finally an additional word should be said concerning the policy of neutralization sponsored by Keynes and carried out to some extent in the twenties and thirties. In World War I, Sweden had allowed her exchanges to appreciate as a means of insulating herself against worldwide inflation. In the twenties, the United States tried to reduce the magnetic inflow of gold by reducing its interest rate, thus easing the monetary situation for European countries embarrassed by outflows of gold, related in part to overvalued currencies. In the thirties, the problem was to escape from the worldwide forces of depression. One approach, frequently supported by smaller and especially agricultural countries, was to restrict output and exports as a means of improving the terms of trade, and these measures were often followed by exchange control as a means of restricting imports and conserving reserves. A common therapy was, of course, exchange depreciation. Here the objective was to insulate against the decline of prices of international commodities. A pound sterling reduced from $4.86 to $3.50 meant higher prices for imports and at least temporarily lower world prices for exports. The resultant gains of competitive position facilitated an expansion of monetary supplies at home and gave greater scope to deficit financing, for the adverse international effects would be blunted. Even general devaluations as one depreciation offset another would at least encourage monetary expansion everywhere. These experiences in the interwar period made easier a wide acceptance of monetary and fiscal policies that would stress objectives of high employment, domestic stability, and growth rather than rigidities of exchange rates.

Anyone who has followed the central banking theory and practice of the last one hundred years knows that much progress has been made. Though central banks even in the last generation have sometimes confused profit making with broader objectives, they, in general, pay little attention to the size of their profits. They operate on behalf of the public interest. Here, indeed, many disagreements arise. What should be their objectives? (More on this later.) Should they, as Keynes insisted, use all their reserves or put aside a large proportion never to be used? Do they behave with adequate courage (cf. Bagehot and Keynes) in such crises as those of 1914 or 1939? Have they paid excessive attention to the needs of the Treasury in the post-World War II period? Are they influenced too much by international objectives and interests?[35]

[35] For helpful fuller treatments of many of these issues, see *Report of Committee on Finance and Industry*, 1931, Cmd. 3897; R. G. Hawtrey, *The Art of Central Banking*, chap. 4, 1932; J. M. Keynes, *Treatise on Money*, 1930; Kisch and Elkins, *Central Banking*, 1928; cf. also the able treatment in E. Wood, *English Theories of Central Bank Control*, 1939.

CHAPTER 11

Trade under Gold and Variable Exchange Rates

Introduction

In this chapter, the objective is to discuss the relation of prices and foreign exchanges. In Chapter 10, we have presented a brief discussion of the adjustments under gold. The historical survey suggests that there are difficulties in obtaining an adjustment, that is, a stoppage of gold movements through effects of these flows upon prices. Hence, in this chapter we dwell in somewhat more detail on the obstacles to the achievements of equilibrium under gold. Then we turn to the relation of prices and exchange rates. Many of the issues involved were treated in Chapters 8 to 10. Here we concentrate largely on the difficulties of explaining exchange rates exclusively by fluctuations in money and prices, as was done, for example, during the Napoleonic Wars.

Then follows an analysis of the relation of exchange depreciation to the balance of trade and to prices. (In Chapter 15, we consider the reasons for adequate or inadequate recourse to exchange depreciation, and in Chapters 12 and 25 we go over some of the major experiences with depreciation.) The final bit is concerned with the contributions of the analysis of devaluation through the orthodox approach of movements in prices, costs, and elasticity as against that of incomes.

It is scarcely necessary to remind the reader that since World War I and especially since World War II, the recourse to fluctuating exchange rates or at least to occasional modification of rates has been much greater than in the pre-World War I period. In part, the explanation has been the pressure on government finance related to war; in part, dissatisfaction with the gold standard, which tended to impose a rigidity or deflation upon many countries. Depreciation of the exchanges offered an opportunity to expand monetary supplies and spending. In the absence of exchange control and other controls affecting international transactions, the recourse to exchange adjustments would have been even greater than they actually were after the Great Depression.

118

Adjustment under Gold

It will be remembered that the classical economists believed that automatic adjustments under gold would be made in the following manner:

A country with an unfavorable balance loses gold, so that prices fall, exports rise, imports fall, and the loss of gold stops. In other words, the country's industries become more competitive.

A country with a favorable balance gains gold, so that prices rise, exports fall, imports rise, and the flow of gold is stopped.

Those who were dependent on this mechanism to equilibrate the balance of payments today would, of course, be greatly disappointed. This simple theory is based on assumptions not verified in the actual world. Among these assumptions are the following:

First, the monetary authority will allow gold to flow. Actually central banks are disposed to tie up a large part of gold reserves which is then not available for use.

Second, a loss of gold brings a corresponding decline in the supply of money. In the modern world of credit and distaste for deflation, the association of gold exports and corresponding reductions in money is not to be expected. Even when an export of gold is allowed, the monetary authority may neutralize the effects on bank reserves by open-market operations, i.e., the purchase of government securities, which increases the reserves of the banks of the country concerned.

Third, there is much less confidence in the relation of monetary supplies and prices than there was in Hume's day or even in the nineteenth century. Hence we cannot be sure that a reduction in monetary supplies would yield a corresponding reduction of prices or even any decline of prices.[1]

Fourth, prices are much more rigid and subject to all kinds of imperfections than was assumed in the classical theory. With extensive cartelization of industry, for example, prices may not be cut in response to reduced supplies of money, and even if cut by exporters, they may be kept up by intermediaries selling the exported commodities abroad.

Fifth, it was assumed that costs would move with prices. Confronted with international competition and with reduced supplies of money, exporters in the first country may, indeed, reduce prices, but with large capital, tax, and other fixed charges and, possibly, intransigent trade unions which refuse to accept the brunt of the adjustment in a cut in money wage rates, the decline of prices may not be offset by a corresponding fall in costs. Hence the decline of prices does not solve the problem of maladjustment, for with business becoming increasingly un-

[1] Cf. fuller discussion in Chap. 12.

profitable, output and exports decline. In this context rigidities in the domestic industries received much attention in Great Britain in the interwar period. With wages and other costs fairly constant in these industries, in part because they were sheltered from foreign competition, it was not easy to cut them in the export (nonsheltered) industries. Thus unchanging wage rates in the major (i.e., the sheltered) industries aggravate the difficulties of cutting them in the nonsheltered industries.

Sixth, as prices of exports decline, it is assumed that (together with the reduction of imports) sales will rise sufficiently to balance the accounts. Obviously assumptions are made here concerning elasticities of demand for both exports and imports which, in fact, may not be realized. The response to a reduction in the price of exports may be small abroad, and the reduction in imports associated with an increase in price may also be inadequate. This is aside from the complications introduced when allowance is made (1) for other countries sharing this problem of adjustment and thus tending to cut elasticity of demand, which is assumed to be high in part because the country in trouble is presumed to capture part of the market of other countries, and (2) for the restrictions introduced by the countries being "flooded" with cheaper goods from abroad.

Seventh, no allowance is made for the effects on other items in the balance of payment, e.g., capital movements. In more refined versions of this theory, it was held that the loss of gold is accompanied by higher rates of interest and, hence, the adjustment is facilitated by an inflow of capital into the country losing gold, reducing monetary supplies, and experiencing higher interest rates. But in the last generation, we have also learned that outward flows of capital in the midst of gold losses may aggravate rather than ease the adjustment.

I shall not trouble the reader with an elaboration of the mistaken assumptions when considered in relation to developments in the receiving country.

In an interesting presentation Meade shows that the mechanism of adjustment is roughly the same whether the approach is through the gold standard or the variation in exchange rates. The treatment is given in Table 11-1.[2]

It will be noted that in both cases the emphasis is on the higher rates of interest, under gold because the loss of gold results in higher rates and under the paper or flexible exchange standard because the monetary authority treats the inflationary tendencies resulting from depreciation by an anti-inflationary policy at home. (But obviously failure to introduce anti-inflationary policies would mean that rates of interest would not rise.) Under gold the deflation of domestic expenditures re-

[2] J. E. Meade, *The Balance of Payments*, p. 192.

Table 11-1. The Operation of the Gold Standard and of Variable Exchange Rates with a Spontaneous Increase in Foreign Lending from A to B

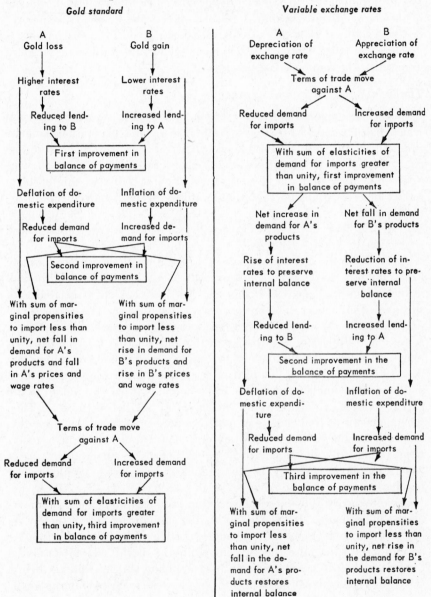

sults in reduced demand for imports; on the condition that the sum of marginal propensities to import is less than unity, a net fall in demand for A's products and a fall in prices and wages follow. The movement of the terms of trade against A further reduces the demand for imports, on the condition that the sum of elasticities of demand for imports is greater than unity. Similar developments follow under a flexible standard except that the sequence is different.

The Relation of Prices and Exchanges

Classical economists did not deal with an approach toward equilibrium which has received increasing attention in the last generation, namely, through adjustments in foreign-exchange rates. Their analysis of exchange rates was concentrated upon the relation of inflation in wartimes and fluctuations in the exchange rates. We discuss this problem briefly before turning to the equilibrating aspects of movements in exchange rates.

In World War I, Cassel, the Swedish economist, revived interest in a simple theory of the relation of prices and exchange rates. The reader will recall the discussion in Chapter 9 of the relation of excessive note issue, imports, and exchange depreciation. In World War I, the fall in the foreign exchanges of belligerents had been widely associated with speculative influences or, more narrowly, foreign plots. The emphasis by practical men during the Napoleonic period on excessive imports will be recalled. But according to Cassel, internal inflation was the explanation, exchange rates responding to changes in the relative purchasing power of two currencies. Thus, if prices in the United Kingdom doubled and remained unchanged in the United States, then the value of the pound sterling in dollars would decline from, say, $4.86 to $2.43. Then the dollar would buy twice as much in pounds sterling as previously, but each pound sterling would buy only half as much in British goods. Relative to 1913, the dollar then would buy as much in British as in American goods. Hence the new dollar-pound price would reflect purchasing-power parity.

Cassel's theory did not deal with the equilibrating effects of movements in exchange rates. He and other proponents tried merely to demonstrate that prices and exchange rates would be in equilibrium. As an antidote to the false theories circulating in World War I, the Cassel theory was helpful. But it was an oversimplified and misleading theory. Cassel did not make clear what price levels were relevant. International? Then why should they not be uniform the world over, with allowances for imperfections? (In fact, the early classicists and Ricardo in particular insisted that allowing for costs of transportation, tariffs, etc., prices of traded commodities were identical.) In this case the theory is, to say the least, not revolutionary. Domestic commodities? Why should exchange rates be expected to move in sympathy with changes in prices of domestic commodities, which are not subject to international competition?

Nor did Cassel allow for the changes in price levels that were to be associated with real, that is, nonmonetary, developments. For example, the British, losing markets and investments abroad in World War I, were confronted with a weakened economic position. They had to press their exports more strenuously to meet the new competition and offset the losses of foreign currencies resulting from the attrition of foreign investments. Their appropriate normal price vis-à-vis competitors had fallen. The issue is clarified by the following: Assume, as above, that prices rose by 100 per cent in the United Kingdom and remained unchanged in the United States. Then, if the United Kingdom wished to restore the pound sterling to $4.86 from the $2.43 level to which it had fallen, according to the purchasing-power-parity theory the British prices would have to fall from 200 to 100. (I assume no change in world prices.) But if account is taken also of the nonmonetary deterioration of the United Kingdom, then the normal price should be put at, say, 75, not 100, and hence the decline required for reestablishment of equilibrium would be from 200 to 75, not 200 to 100. The currency doctors who were traveling in Africa, Latin America, and Asia in the interwar period and basing their prescriptions on the Ricardo-Cassel diagnosis were applying a simplified theory to a complicated real world.

Finally, this theory underestimated the importance of speculative factors. There was not always, as Cassel assumed, the rebound from deviations of exchanges from purchasing-power parity caused by these factors. When in the early twenties the price of the dollar in marks rose by 1 billion times and commodity prices in Germany by but 100 million times (relative to price rises in the United States), it was possible to buy German commodities at 10 cents on the dollar. Each dollar purchased 1 billion times as many marks, and each mark $\frac{1}{100}$ million as much in goods. According to the simple theory, Germany's exports (a bargain) and their prices would have risen and imports (expensive) declined; exports from, say, the United States, then expensive, would have fallen, and their prices and United States imports risen until prices were again in equilibrium with the exchanges. Obviously, the mark would have risen in value as more marks were demanded to buy German goods and less dollars purchased with marks to buy American goods. But this theory leaves out of account that supplies of German goods were inadequate to offset the speculative purchases of dollars, which increased the more united was the opinion that the mark would continue to fall. Hence the dollar value of the mark fell progressively below that suggested by the purchasing-power-parity theory.

Ricardo indeed inspired the classical position that an overissue of currency was the explanation of a depreciation of the exchanges beyond the gold points, and hence anticipated Cassel's position. In the marathon correspondence with Malthus and in his many papers and speeches, Ricardo adhered to this position. In criticizing Thornton, he allowed that an unfavorable trade balance might bring about a depreciation, but not beyond the gold points. He did not seem to see, however, that once a depreciation had taken place, then the state of the balance of payments might greatly influence the degree of depreciation. On these matters, Malthus was much more realistic.[3]

Ricardo expressed himself thus:[4]

The supply of bills and the demand for them must depend on previous purchases and sales of goods in the two countries, and these are entirely influenced by relative prices. But relative prices are determined by relative value or quantity of currencies. Increase the quantity of currency in France, goods will rise in France, and will be exported thither from England. Bills on France will fall in England, bills on England will rise in France. The demand and supply will be strictly regulated by the relative value of the currencies of the two countries. Double the quantity of currency in England and commodities will rise to double their former price in England, and twice the quantity of the money of England will be given for the former quantity of the currency of France.

Malthus's views were as follows:[5]

It really appears that a desire to simplify, which has often led away the most scientific men, has induced you to ascribe to one cause phenomena that properly belong to two, and not to give sufficient weight to the facts which (to me at least) appear to make against your doctrine. I confess I am still of opinion that these facts are not all satisfactorily explicable upon your principles; and I never look over the tables of exchange without being more and more confirmed in the truth of what I stated in my first review, that "though the effects of a redundancy of currency upon the exchange are *sure*, they are slow compared with the effects of those mercantile or political transactions, not connected with the question of currency and while the former of these causes is proceeding with a steady and generally uniform pace, the more rapid move-

[3] *Ricardo*, vol. VI, pp. 82–83; cf. vol. III, p. 83.

[4] *Ibid.*, vol. VIII, p. 87. Note, however, that in 1802 Thornton anticipated Ricardo and presented a theory close to the modern purchasing-power parity. In his presentation, he showed that exchanges would respond to the relative movement of prices—the effects would be felt in the bill market, as the inflationary country would sell less and buy more. H. Thornton, *An Enquiry into the Nature and Effects of the Paper Credit of Great Britain, 1802* (F. Hayek, ed.), 1939, pp. 198–199.

[5] *Ibid.*, vol. VI, p. 82.

ments of the latter are opposing aggravating or modifying their operations in various ways, and producing all those complex and seemingly inconsistent appearances which are to be found in the computed exchange."

Flexible Rates and Equilibrium

Now we return to the use of flexible exchange rates as a means of equilibrating the balance of payments—in contrast to a theory which holds that exchange rates reflect relative purchasing powers of currencies. Impressed by the overwhelming difficulties of approaching equilibrium through the deflationary process at home, Keynes—according to Keynes nothing was so destructive of the capitalist process as the prospect of further declines in prices—in the twenties stressed a novel approach: deflate on world markets, and improve one's competitive position despite inflation in domestic prices. That is, what is required is a reduction in prices abroad for the country suffering from disequilibrium, and the way to achieve this, without introducing deflation at home, is through a depreciation of the exchanges. Thus allow the pound sterling to fall roughly 40 per cent from $4.86 to $2.90, and the pound sterling becomes cheaper in dollars, and as long as the price level in the United Kingdom does not rise vis-à-vis United States prices (here for purposes of simplification considered as world prices) in the proportion of 2.9 to 4.86, then British prices will fall on world markets. With dollars more expensive import prices would rise in sterling on the British market unless the depreciation were accompanied by a relative fall in world prices of British imports corresponding to the fall in the value of the pound sterling in dollars. As commodities are diverted to the more profitable world markets from the British domestic markets (assuming that output remains constant), and imports are discouraged because their prices in sterling rise, prices in the United Kingdom tend to rise. A unit of exports yields more pounds sterling per unit, and a unit of imports costs more per pound sterling. Hence the movements in exchange rates directly impinge on prices. But on top of that, prices rise in pounds sterling because less goods are available as exports rise and imports fall. (The latter requires correction in so far as the policy of depreciation, as in the thirties, raised output.)

How much the domestic prices in Great Britain will rise or British prices on world markets fall in response to the depreciation will depend on many factors. If the pound sterling falls 40 per cent in dollars (dollars rise by 67 per cent), the range of possibilities is a fall on world markets of British commodities by 40 per cent (with prices at home unchanged); or world prices of British exports unchanged and prices of export commodities in the United Kingdom up by 67 per cent; or something in between. Equality of prices on sterling and dollar markets with a 40 per cent fall in sterling is consistent with a 40 per cent decline on dollar markets and no rise in British markets or no fall of British export prices on world markets and a 67 per cent rise in pound markets. The more elastic supplies are at home, that is, in the United Kingdom, a country depressing its exchanges to treat a disequilibrium (e.g., with much unemployment or ease of movement of factors to export industries), the more world prices of these commodities will tend to fall and the less domestic prices will rise, for commodities then press on world markets in large quantities. Again, the more elastic is demand at home for British export commodities, the more world prices of British exports will tend to fall and the less sterling prices to rise. Here British purchasers of exports react to higher sterling prices (as each dollar buys more pounds sterling and hence each unit of export yields more pounds sterling and exports are diverted to foreign markets) by cutting purchases substantially. (For the problem of equilibrium, the reaction to higher sterling prices of imports is also relevant.) High elasticity of demand for imports would contribute further to balancing the pound-sterling account.

What of the relevance of foreign elasticities? The more inelastic foreign demand for the British commodities (assuming that the supply of these commodities is elastic), the greater the adjustment through a decline in world prices of British exports and hence the smaller the rise in pound-sterling prices of these commodities. Elasticity is likely to be low when British exports account for a large part of the foreign market or when competitors follow the pound sterling downward by depreciating their exchanges, and hence elasticity of demand is depressed because potential diversions of sales are thwarted by the competition in debasement. Much, of course, depends on the nature of commodities exported. Thus, demand for raw materials tends to be less elastic than for manufactured goods, but the demand is likely to be more elastic for a raw material from a country which provides a small part of the world's exports (e.g., Brazilian cotton) than for one where the contribution to world trade is large (e.g., Brazilian coffee).

Finally, there is the issue of elasticities of supply in the foreign country. Obviously when the depreciating country presses its exports on the United States, the extent of the depression of prices on world markets will be greater the more inelastic the supply conditions in the United States. Inelasticity of supply prevails when the foreign country (e.g., the United States) finds it difficult to cut output of commodities competing with the British exports or to divert them to domestic or third markets. Supply is likely to be especially inelastic in the foreign country when inventories of competing commodities are high, when demand conditions at home (the United States) or in third markets are unsatisfactory, when fixed charges are high and hence contraction of output costly, and when the rise of sales of the depreciating country (countries) is large relative to the domestic output and supplies of the competing commodities in the countries (e.g., the United States) confronted with the commodities of the depreciating countries.[6]

Table 11-2 sums up.

Table 11-2

	World prices tend to fall more and £ (domestic) prices to rise less when	World prices tend to fall less and £ (domestic) prices to rise more when
Elasticity of demand at home (U.K.) is....................	High	Low
Elasticity of supply at home (U.K.) is....................	High	Low
Elasticity of demand abroad is..	Low	High
Elasticity of supply abroad is....	Low	High

The following analysis is based on Mrs. Robinson's study[7] and is largely concerned with the effects of a fall in exchange rates upon the balance of trade. It should be noted, however, that the distinction is not always made between the effects on trade expressed in pounds sterling or in the foreign (i.e., dollar) currency. Under some conditions the balance in pounds sterling may improve but in dollars deteriorate.

Elasticity of Supply of Exports. Where supply conditions at home are *perfectly inelastic*, no change in supply results. Hence the value of exports in pounds would *rise* in proportion to the fall in exchange rates.

Where the supply conditions at home are *perfectly elastic* (home price constant), the decline of prices to foreigners would be in proportion to the fall in exchange rates.

Obviously under perfectly inelastic supply conditions, the country would not gain exchange and the exporters would obtain a windfall profit, with no advantage to the country other than a rise in prices. Under perfectly elastic supply conditions, the concessions in foreign prices would be made. Then foreign elasticity of demand would determine the net effects on, say, dollar supply.

Foreign Elasticity of Demand for Exports. When the foreign elasticity of demand is 1, expenditures are constant in terms of the foreign currency, the value of exports is independent of home elasticity of supply, and the value of exports rises in proportion to the fall in the exchanges.

[6] Cf. S. E. Harris, *Exchange Depreciation*, 1936, especially chaps. 1, 2, 4.
[7] Based on J. Robinson, *Essays in the Theory of Employment*, 1937, pp. 188–200.

When the foreign elasticity of demand is less than 1, the rise of export values (in pounds) is less, the less is the elasticity of supply. The minimum effect prevails when the foreign export demand has zero elasticity; the maximum effect, when foreign demand and domestic supply are perfectly elastic.

Imports (into the United Kingdom). When the foreign supply is perfectly elastic (prices constant), imports rise in proportion to the fall in the exchange rate. When the foreign supply is less than perfectly elastic (output is reduced or alternative markets are not adequate to offset unfavorable development in the United Kingdom), foreign prices fall and home prices rise less than in proportion to the fall in exchange rates. (The United Kingdom to this extent improves its terms of trade.)

Table 11-3

Exports:		
Elasticity of supply of exports	Perfectly inelastic (volume unchanged, foreign price unchanged)	Value of exports rises in proportion to fall in exchanges
	Perfectly elastic	Prices to foreigners reduced in proportion to reduction of exchanges
Foreign elasticity of demand	Unity (expenditures constant in foreign currency)	Value of exports (in pounds) rises in proportion to fall in exchanges
	<unity	Export values rise less the less is elasticity of supply
	0	Minimum effect
	Perfectly elastic	Maximum effect if supply perfectly elastic
Imports:		
Foreign supply	Perfectly elastic (foreign price of imports unchanged)	Import prices (in pounds) rise in proportion to fall in exchanges
Foreign supply	<perfectly elastic	Foreign prices minus and home prices plus with fall in exchanges*
Home elasticity of demand	<1	Value of imports rises more the greater the foreign elasticity of supply
	>1	Value of imports reduced more the greater the foreign elasticity of supply
Home demand	Perfectly inelastic	Maximum rise in import value
Home demand	Perfectly elastic and foreign supply perfectly elastic	Imports = 0

* But rise in domestic price less than fall in exchanges.

" . . . when the home demand has less than unit elasticity, the value of imports will rise by more, and when it has greater than unit elasticity, will fall by more, the greater is the foreign elasticity of supply." When home demand is perfectly inelastic, the fall in exchange rates results in the maximum rise in the value of imports; when home demand is perfectly elastic and foreign supply perfectly elastic, imports are reduced to zero.

Mrs. Robinson also considers the combined effects upon imports and exports. When home demand for imports has an elasticity greater than 1, then the trade balance must improve, for imports decline and exports, at worst, are constant. Even with elasticity of home demand less than 1, the balance will improve if the value of exports rises sufficiently. When elasticity of home demand for imports is very low and the rise of exports small, the balance will deteriorate. Also relevant is the relative value of exports and imports. Obviously if exports are three times as important as imports, then the net effect on the balance will depend much more on what happens to exports, and an equal proportionate rise of exports will count for much more than a similar proportionate rise in imports.

To summarize, see Table 11-3.

Adjustments through Elasticities and Income Movements

Although, as Meade shows, the adjustments under gold (fixed) and paper (flexible exchanges) are in many respects similar, nevertheless it is clear from experience that the treatment of an adverse balance under gold is much more difficult than under a paper standard or under a standard where the external value of the currency can be periodically adjusted (the adjusted-peg system). The explanation of this fact is, I believe, that under gold, though there is some reliance upon income changes, the major emphasis is on costs, prices, and elasticities (responses of sales to price movements). Under a flexible exchange system there is indeed also some dependence upon price and cost movements; for example, one of the objectives of a depreciation is clearly to reduce the price level in foreign markets for a country's exports and to raise prices or at least to stop or reduce the rate of decline at home. Moreover, the relative movements of prices of export and import-competing commodities and domestic commodities will influence the output of these commodities, and the effect of these price movements upon the value of exports and imports will depend upon the relevant elasticities.

Despite these considerations, however, the fact remains that under variable exchange movements the approach toward equilibrium depends especially upon income movements. In part this is true because where the more modern approach of exchange flexibility is used, there is likely to be greater recourse also to fiscal policy. But more important, the effects of, say, depreciation upon the supplies of money, upon the level of exports and imports, upon the price structure and the resultant structure of production, are likely also to have large effects upon income.

In a notable article Dr. Alexander stressed the importance of the income approach and the inadequacies of the relative-price approach. In criticism of the Alexander article Professor Machlup held that both the relative price and the income approach were necessary for an understanding of the effects of devaluation. Professor Morgan is also critical of the elasticity approach.[8]

. . . the theory of flexible exchanges is not a good subject for analysis in terms of elasticities and marginal propensities; the number of variables is too large and the functional relationships too complicated. It has only been handled in this way with tolerable simplicity by constructing models which leave out essential features of the adjustment mechanism, and the attempt to draw conclusions from such models is bound to be misleading.

In using the income approach, Alexander was inviting attention to the numerous causes and remedies of disequilibrium. A devaluation is considered relative to its effects on output, consumption, investment, and exports and imports. Where is the resultant change of income absorbed— in consumption, investment, imports? This approach is to be contrasted to the orthodox one which stresses price effects of devaluation.[9]

Conclusion

From Ricardo on, the tendency has been to stress the relations of money, prices, and foreign exchange and to underemphasize the relations of the balance of payments to exchange rates. Again the explanation in part rests on Ricardo's application of a theory, relatively defensible over the long run, to short-run problems.

With the failure of the gold standard to yield satisfactory adjustments, variable exchange rates under compulsion or choice became much more fashionable after World War I. The new standard has often been abused, e.g., to correct domestic inflationary situations resulting in external disequilibrium and to further beggar-my-neighbor policies. But as Morgan shows, there are important occasions when the flexible rate can bring external equilibrium along with high employment.[10] Much could

---

[8] S. S. Alexander, "The Effects of a Devaluation on a Trade Balance," *International Monetary Fund Staff Papers*, April, 1952, pp. 263–278; F. Machlup, "Relative Prices and Aggregate Spending in the Analysis of Devaluation," *The American Economic Review*, June, 1955, pp. 255–274; and E. V. Morgan, "The Theory of Flexible Exchange Rates," *The American Economic Review*, June, 1955, pp. 279–295, especially p. 295; also see Harris, *op. cit.*, pt. 1.

[9] Cf. E. Bernstein, *Strategic Factors in Balance of Payments Adjustment*, 1956 (mimeographed), pp. 13–14, and Harris, *op. cit.*, chap. 5.

[10] Morgan, *op. cit.*, pp. 290–295.

be said in support of its use in the thirties, when the relief of the restrictions of gold facilitated monetary expansion and appropriate fiscal
policies. In this chapter, we have analyzed the effects of a depreciation
upon prices, exports, and imports. Here a study of prices, costs, and
elasticities, that is, the orthodox approach, is relevant. But the direct
effects of depreciation and the ensuing change in the structure of prices
and output upon income, upon the distribution of income, and in turn
upon imports and fiscal policy are all relevant. Later we shall discuss
two important episodes of depreciation.

CHAPTER 12

New Objectives of Monetary Policy

Orthodoxy—Early Nineteenth Century

As has been observed above, the objective of monetary policy (in so far as any genuine policy was to be found) in the nineteenth century and most of the twentieth seemed to be the preservation of the gold standard and international equilibrium. It was assumed, of course, that tying monetary supplies to gold would eliminate or at least contain economic fluctuations. Even in the nineteenth century an occasional voice was raised against a policy which seemed to give excessive weight to the stabilization of the price of gold. Even the *Bullion Report* inveighed against a policy of excessive money and rising prices which would be unfair to many groups, but it associated excessive money with inconvertibility and did not see that with convertibility much injustice might be done.[1]

Your committee conceive that it would be superfluous to point out, in detail, the disadvantages which must result to the Country, from any such general excess of currency as lowers its relative value. The effect of such an augmentation of prices upon all money transactions for time; the unavoidable injury suffered by annuitants, and by creditors of every description, both private and public; the unintended advantage gained by Government and all other debtors; are consequences too obvious to require proof, and too repugnant to justice to be left without remedy. By far the most important portion of this effect appears to Your Committee to be that which is communicated to the wages of common country labour, the rate of which, it is well known, adapts itself more slowly to the changes which happen in the value of money, than the price of any other species of labour or commodity. And it is enough for Your Committee to allude to some classes of the public servants, whose pay, if once raised in consequence of a depreciation of money, cannot so conveniently be reduced again to its former rate, even after money shall have recovered its value. That future progress of these inconveniences and evils, if not checked, must, at no great distance of time, work a practical

[1] *The Paper Pound of 1797–1821: A Reprint of the Bullion Report* (Cannan, ed.), 1919, pp. 66–67.

conviction upon the minds of all those who may still doubt their existence; but even if their progressive increase were less probable than it appears to Your Committee, they cannot help expressing an opinion, that the integrity and honour of Parliament are concerned, not to authorize, longer than is required by imperious necessity, the continuance in this great commercial Country of a system of circulation, in which that natural check or control is absent which maintains the value of money, and by the permanency of that common standard of value, secure the substantial justice and faith of monied contracts and obligations between man and man.

In the debate over the resumption of cash payments after the Napoleonic Wars, the issue of the sanctity of gold over the welfare of the nation came to a head. The Bank demanded a rapid repayment of the government's debt to the Bank and a concomitant destruction of notes. A banker, Baring, surprisingly enough, took the modern view. A reduction of notes in circulation, he agreed, might bring gold into the country but not in sufficient amounts to ensure resumption of convertibility of paper into gold. But the reduction "must always be accompanied with some restraint and inconvenience to every branch of industry in the country; and that if it were forced . . . the injury would be intolerable. . . ."[2]

Tooke and Ricardo were much more optimistic concerning the effects of a reduction in the circulation in reducing the premium on gold and in attracting gold into the country. For Ricardo there was no limit to the fall in the price of gold that might be achieved by reducing the supply of paper money. When pushed, he admitted, however, that the cure might be worse than the disease and that the price of gold and its foreign exchange do not depend exclusively on the supply of bank notes outstanding. In the twentieth century, the bankers espoused Ricardo's position, whereas the economist Keynes took over the Baring position.[3]

The chairman of the Secret Committee made Ricardo retract on at least one occasion. The colloquy below is between Robert Peel, chairman of the Committee, and Ricardo.[4]

The following is an extract from a publication of yours:—"Why will not the bank try the experiment, by a reduction in the amount of their notes of two or three millions for the short period of three months? if no effects were produced on the price of bullion and the foreign exchanges, then might their friends boast, that the principles of the bullion committee were the wild dreams of speculative theorists;" do you still adhere to the opinion expressed in that extract? Yes, I do.

From July to December 1817, the average amount of bank of England

---

[2] *Second Report from the Secret Committee on the Expediency of the Bank Resuming Cash Payments,* 1819, p. 12.

[3] *Ibid.,* pp. 174–177, 193–209.

[4] *Ibid.,* p. 193.

notes in circulation, appears to have been 29,210,000 £; from July to December 1818, the amount appears to have been 26,487,000 £; in the latter period, the price of gold was higher than in the former, and the exchanges were more unfavourable to this country, so that the reduction in the issues, though carried to the extent of 3,000,000 £ produced no effect upon the exchange and on the price of gold; how do you reconcile these facts with the theory?— When I gave the opinion that has been stated, it was on the supposition, that no commercial causes were at that time to operate on the price of bullion or on the exchange, under those circumstances [a reduction of the circulation], would raise their value to any point which might be desired; I am fully aware that there are other causes, besides the quantity of bank notes, which operate upon the exchanges; but I am quite sure, that from whatever cause a bad exchange arises, it may be corrected by a reduction in the amount of the currency.

Then ought there not to have been an addition to the statement above referred to of words to the following effect; provided other causes do not counteract the effect of the reduction?—Clearly; I am speaking with respect to a given time; I did not mean to assert, that at all times and under all circumstances a reduction of bank notes would improve the exchange.

Unemployment and Policy

Just as in the first quarter of the nineteenth century, the authorities imposed a costly deflation on the country one hundred years later. This time there was an increased awareness of the damage done, and gold had lost much of its nineteenth-century prestige. It is worthwhile to consider the later period, for now it becomes clear that despite all the attacks on gold, an all-out struggle was required to dislodge it. In some respects the progress made after more than a century of debate was unsatisfactory.

The gold standard had not been working so smoothly as it had or as it was assumed to have done by those who were ignorant of theory or history. All kinds of explanations of the deterioration of the gold standard were offered: the increased rigidities of wages and prices, which ruled out the downward adjustments required when gold was going out; the increased importance of short-term capital movements, which increasingly tended to move in response to political expectations in an increasingly uneasy world (in the past, short-term capital movements had helped to stop gold flows, for capital would come in with losses of gold, but after World War I they tended to aggravate the drains); the failure of the credit or countries, notably France and the United States, to play the part that they were supposed to, namely, put the additional gold to use, so that their prices would rise, their imports increase, and their exports decrease; and mismanagement of the gold standard (e.g., the foolish British decision to deflate in the twenties, which involved a rise in the price of the pound from $3.50 to $4.86 at a time when the dollar was appreciating, the British were losing accustomed markets, and a wage deflation seemed out of the question).[5]

New ideas also helped to change established attitudes toward monetary policy. Fisher had discovered the compensated dollar, that is, a dollar stable in purchasing power. Keynes, in the twenties, convinced that the origins of cyclical instability lay in monetary events, published his famous *Tract on Monetary Reform,* in which he lent his great reputation and unusual persuasive powers to the view that it was more important to stabilize commodity prices than gold or foreign exchanges. A large brick in the new edifice was contributed by a respected economist, D. H. Robertson, who in 1926 wrote a distinguished and solid volume supporting inflationary monetary policy (yielding forced savings) as a means of supplementing savings in periods of rising activity.[6]

It was the economic difficulties of the British in the twenties and the Great Depression which invited careful reconsideration of monetary objectives. Some attention had also been paid to a policy of price stabilization in the United States in the twenties, a policy that Federal Reserve authorities were unwilling to acknowledge and, in fact, were at pains to deny on the grounds that they were incapable of stabilizing prices.[7] As we look back, it is clear that commodity prices were remarkably stable in the years 1923 to 1929, though on the basis of stock-market or real-estate prices or on that of the high commodity prices *relative* to costs of production, inflationary forces were operating. But despite this inflation, an inflow of gold embarrassed the American authorities, and they sought (in one of their rare attempts to seek international equilibrium) to counter the inflow by the introduction of cheap money rates, thus inviting capital exports. Here evolved a conflict between domestic and international needs; the lower rates helped stimulate speculation. Aside from this attempt of the central-bank authorities to influence the situation, it should be observed that net demand deposits had risen from $9 billion in 1913 to $15 billion in 1918 and $22.5 billion in 1930.

It is a striking fact that, unlike the twenties, in the great disequilibrium of 1945 to 1955 there was no serious discussion of the possibility of the United States reducing its money rates as a means of helping Western Europe reach international equilibrium. As a matter of fact, in 1951 right in the midst of a crisis in the dollar market, the American authorities embarked on their accord policy, which, in fact, was a policy of higher rates. How is one to explain this neglect of the use of monetary policy as a step toward international equilibrium? The answer

---

[5] For a further discussion of the breakdown of the gold standard, see Chap. 15.
[6] D. H. Robertson, *Banking Policy and the Price Level,* 1926.
[7] S. E. Harris, *Twenty Years of Federal Reserve Policy,* vol. I, pp. 86–90.

lies partly in the reduced prestige of monetary policy, partly in the low level of rates in the early postwar period in this country, in the substantial degree of disequilibrium, and in the availability of other therapeutic measures, e.g., grants, commercial policy, and revisions of exchange rates.

The effects of depression on attitudes toward monetary policy are evident in a comparison of two important official reports in the years 1925 and 1931. In the 1925 report, the possibility of a new standard was considered.[8]

. . . proposals for substituting the price level of commodities in general for gold as the regulating principle of the currency, has been fully and carefully explained in evidence before us. . . . We need only say that, as a practical present-day policy for this country, there is, in our opinion, no alternative comparable with a return to the former gold parity of the sovereign. In this conclusion we are supported by the overwhelming majority of opinion, both financial and industrial, represented in evidence before us.

In contrast, several years of unfavorable economic conditions are reflected in much stronger doubts concerning the gold standard as expressed in the *Macmillan Report*. Here emphasis is put upon the need of maintaining "the stability of international prices both over long periods and over short periods. . . , " of regulating "the volume and terms of credit as to maintain as much stability as possible in the rate of new investment and new enterprises generally, both at home and abroad," and "each central bank should undertake to do its best to avoid the importation of unwanted and unnecessary gold merely as a result of leaving natural forces to work themselves out unchecked."[9] In the report the problem of inadequacy of gold supplies, maldistribution, measures for economizing gold, the need of cooperation among central banks, the general consistency of domestic and international objectives— all these receive attention.

But to return to the sources of the new monetary policies. Large doses of unemployment were threatening capitalism in the early thirties. Many associated unemployment with restrictive monetary policies required under gold, for, as in the last quarter of the nineteenth century, a decline of prices in one large country could be met only by price deflation in others unless large excess reserves might offer a temporary respite. Failure to match deflation abroad would mean a loss of competitive power and hence of sales, for prices would be too high in the countries

[8] *Report of the Committee on the Currency and Bank of England Note Issues,* 1925, par. 8.

[9] *Report of Committee on Finance and Industry,* 1931, pp. 131–132; also pt. I, chap. 3, and pt. II, chaps. 2 and 3.

not deflating. Ultimately, the choice lay between deflation and abandonment of gold.

Abandon Gold?

How to deal with the ensuing unemployment? One approach was obviously to abandon gold. An epidemic of depreciation followed the collapse of 1929, with the result that when it was all over, the average devaluation in terms of gold of major currencies was 40 per cent. But there had been little gain of competitive power of one country against another. The main advantage was that having abandoned the promise to exchange gold for paper money and vice versa at fixed ratios, each country could with greater freedom create money to stop the great liquidations of the early thirties. For example, the United States, which on the whole was less embarrassed by shortages of gold than most, embarked on a policy through Reconstruction Finance Corporation financing of providing billions of dollars of aid to financial institutions as a means of unfreezing frozen dollars held by financial institutions.[10] Actually, the country gained gold net from 1929 through 1933, but the cause of embarrassment was a breakdown at home reminiscent of the internal drains in nineteenth-century Britain.

A country confronted with international disequilibrium, which, in turn, contributes toward monetary restraints and unemployment, may try to pull itself out of the quagmire of deflation and unemployment by depreciating its exchanges and gaining a competitive advantage. When the difficulties stem from a price-cost disparity, there is much to be said for such policies. But a country suffering from unemployment not traceable to overvalued currencies (and hence expensive exports) may also have recourse to competitive debasement, that is, may export its unemployment. Since this problem of depreciation is discussed fully in Chapters 15 and 27, and earlier, I shall not develop the theme further here.

I should note, however, that the use of exchange depreciation as an instrument for improving competitive position has become a serious subject of discussion among economists only in relatively recent times. Mill, for example, in the course of an extended discussion of exchange depreciation concluded: "It thus appears, that a depreciation of the currency does not affect the foreign trade of the country: this is carried on precisely as if the currency maintained its value."[11] There is no evidence in Mill's discussion that the prices of international commodities may not respond fully and immediately to the depreciation and hence that trade and gold movements may be affected.

[10] See S. E. Harris, *Exchange Depreciation*, for a full discussion of these issues.
[11] J. S. Mill, *Principles of Political Economy* (Ashley, ed.), 1920, p. 635.

In his classic volume on foreign exchanges (1861), Goschen's position was similar to Mill's, but there is at least limited recognition of the possibility of gains because of the uneven movements of prices.[12]

But in a certain sense these fluctuations are apparent, and do not involve the same gain or loss, the same difference in value, as those alluded to above. As the depreciation in currency affects, generally speaking, all prices alike, the fifteen florins bought by the Englishman for his sovereign are not worth more to him than the ten which he bought for the same money before. When the fluctuations were determined simply by the balance of trade, (within the limits of specie point upon either extreme,) the purchaser when he bought cheap—that is to say, when he obtained a greater sum than usual in foreign coin for his own money—secured an actual advantage; this greater sum of foreign coin had an actual greater purchasing power. But where the cheapness of the bills is caused by the depreciation of the foreign currency, he has no advantage; for the purchasing power of the nominally larger sum is not greater than that of the smaller.

. . . For instance, before any great fluctuation, he exported a certain quantity of sugar, and sold his drafts against this sugar for a certain price: let us suppose him to have sold the sugar for 10,000 florins, and to have sold these florins at the rate of ten to the pound. He would thus realize £1,000 for his sugar. A fluctuation of ten per cent now occurs, owing to an over-issue of paper in Austria. Prices generally rise 10 per cent., and the exchange rises also. The same foreign merchant now sells his sugar for 11,000 florins, but he must sell his florins at the rate of eleven to the pound, thus realizing £1,000, precisely as before. It is scarcely necessary to observe that in assuming a general equal rise in prices, it is not intended to express an opinion that such an event could actually occur. Some prices will rise much more than others, according to the well-known principles of political economy relative to this subject. In Austria the manufacturers insisted that they made considerable profits by the depreciation of the currency, as the cost of labour had not risen in the same proportion as the manufactured goods. The raw material being imported from abroad had risen to the full extent at once; and this enabled the manufacturers to increase the price paid for their products in the same ratio, though one element of production, labour, remained comparatively stationary. But this could only be temporary. The adjustment must take place sooner or later; and if the demand for labour had remained the same as before, wages would have risen till they commanded the same amount of the labourer's necessaries as before.

Keynes and New Policies

Keynes in particular, in endless articles, books, speeches, and government memorandums, insisted that the time had come for a radical change in the objectives of monetary policy. From an emphasis on price stabilization in his *Tract on Monetary Reform* (1924), he shifted in his

[12] V. Goschen, *The Theory of the Foreign Exchanges,* 3d ed., pp. 65–68.

Treatise on Money (1930) to the use of monetary policy to influence the rate of interest and through declines in the rate of interest, for example, to stimulate investment and reduce savings (holding that the excess of savings over investment was the cause of depression), and finally in his *General Theory of Employment, Interest and Money* (1936), though he still stressed the need of reduced rates of interest, he emphasized now the importance of public investments and programs to increase consumption as the means of solving the unemployment problem.[13]

But how, it may be asked, can a country indulge in expansionist policies without experiencing an unfavorable balance of payments? Once out of step, the expanding economy would then buy more abroad and sell less as its income and prices rose relatively if not absolutely. Keynes's answer to this dilemma was international cooperation so that all nations would expand together; the provision of large additional international reserves in order to protect countries that might, in an effort to stop a decline, expand more rapidly than their neighbors; and an increased responsibility upon creditor countries to import and lend. In the absence of such cooperation, the country bent on maximizing output and employment and seeking an escape from an international decline would have to balance its international accounts by restrictions on trade and foreign payments and by periodic recourse to exchange depreciation.

In presenting a plan for an International Clearing Union during the war, Keynes, the main author, clarified his views on monetary objectives and the means of achieving them.[14] In Keynes's views an *international* currency was needed "having general acceptability between nations, so that blocked balances and bilateral clearings are unnecessary." Again, "we need an orderly and agreed method of determining the relative exchange values of national currency units, so that unilateral action and competitive exchange depreciations are prevented."[14] This last quotation reminds us of a statement made by Marshall, Keynes's teacher, in the latter part of the nineteenth century: " . . . and I think the time will come at which it will be thought as unreasonable for any country to regulate its currency without reference to other countries as it will be to have signalling codes at sea which took no account of the signalling codes at sea of other countries."[15] I may add that even Keynes's more modest goal, in the light of the experience of the first ten years of the International Monetary Fund, still seems far off.

Keynes also wanted an international currency not determined "in an

[13] See J. M. Keynes, *The General Theory of Employment, Interest and Money; The New Economics* (S. E. Harris, ed.), 1947; and S. E. Harris, *John Maynard Keynes, Economist and Policy Maker*, 1955.
[14] *Proposals for an International Clearing Union*, republished (with some excisions) in Harris, *The New Economics*, pp. 322–341, especially pp. 325–326.
[15] *Official Papers of Alfred Marshall*, 1926, p. 135.

unpredictable and irrelevant manner, as, for example, by the technical progress of the gold industry, nor subject to large variations depending on the gold reserve policies of individual countries." The currency would be adjusted to world needs and would be capable of "deliberate expansion and contraction to offset deflationary and inflationary tendencies in effective world demand."

Fearful of the effects of external events on domestic output, Keynes would provide pressures on any country which through its behavior would bring substantial international disequilibrium for itself and unfortunate results for others. "More generally, we need a means of reassurance to a troubled world, by which any country whose own affairs are conducted with due prudence is relieved of anxiety for causes which are not of its own making, concerning its ability to meet its international liabilities. . . . "[16]

But despite the provisions for international cooperation, Keynes would not relieve each country of responsibilities to adjust its standard of living to its productive capacity. When wages and prices are too high, a corrective depreciation is necessary, but if the cause of disequilibrium is restrictions abroad, then the responsibility lies abroad.

Keynes was especially insistent that domestic policies should not be dictated from abroad. In a speech delivered before the House of Lords on May 23, 1944, on the International Monetary Fund, Keyes said:[17]

We are determined that, in future, the external value of sterling shall conform to its internal value as set by our own domestic policies, and not the other way round. Secondly, we intend to retain control of our domestic rate of interest, so that we can keep it as low as suits our own purposes, without interference from the ebb and flow of international capital movements or flights of hot money. Thirdly, whilst we intend to prevent inflation at home, we will not accept deflation at the dictate of influences from outside. In other words, we abjure the instruments of bank rate and credit contraction operating through the increase of unemployment as a means of forcing our domestic economy into line with external factors.

The gold standard was out. Keynes's proposal is that the external value "should be altered if necessary so as to conform to whatever *de facto* internal value results from domestic policies. . . . "[18]

The question, however, which has recently been given chief prominence is whether we are in any sense returning to the disabilities of the former gold

---

[16] Harris, *The New Economics*, p. 326.

[17] The speech is reprinted in *The New Economics*, pp. 369–379. The quoted passage is on p. 374.

[18] *Ibid.*, pp. 375–376. For the evolution of Keynes's views, see *ibid.*, especially chaps. 20–22.

standard, relief from which we have rightly learnt to prize so highly. If I have any authority to pronounce on what is and what is not the essence and meaning of a gold standard, I should say that this plan is the exact opposite of it. The plan in its relation to gold is, indeed, very close to proposals which I advocated in vain as the right alternative when I was bitterly opposing this country's return to gold. The gold standard, as I understand it, means a system under which the external value of a national currency is rigidly tied to a fixed quantity of gold which can only honorably be broken under *force majeure;* and it involves a financial policy which compels the internal value of the domestic currency to conform to this external value as fixed in terms of gold. On the other hand, the use of gold merely as a convenient common denominator by means of which the relative values of national currencies— these being free to change—are expressed from time to time, is obviously quite another matter.

Problems of Smaller Countries

One of the most interesting cases of economies expanding more rapidly than the outside world was that of Latin America from 1945 to 1953. These relatively small countries can pursue independent policies out of line with world movements only by introducing restrictions of all kinds. Freedom from external pressures is much more difficult to achieve than might be inferred from Keynes's views, which were more applicable to the larger countries. In these countries the problem was not to get out of a depression but rather to find productive work for many who were producing far below their potentials and also to stimulate a general shift to more productive industries. The gross national product of Latin American countries rose by 50 per cent in these eight years, or three times the increase for the United States in this period. As might be expected, there was much pressure on the exchange markets of these countries—and this despite substantial imports of capital. To keep their international accounts in balance the typical Latin American country controlled all demands for foreign exchange, artificially stimulated exports, and to some extent relied on exchange depreciation and trade restrictions.[19]

The small or the underdeveloped countries (a few of these are large) are then subject to special analysis. As has been suggested often and ably by Dr. Balogh and examined minutely by Dr. Bloomfield,[20] an expansion or a decline in the United States has important effects on the economic conditions of other countries. But expansion or decline in smaller countries does not greatly influence conditions abroad. A large

[19] I have discussed these episodes fully in a document for the Rio de Janeiro Conference of 1954: *Inter-American States, Measures for Increasing Latin American Trade.*

[20] See the excellent study of H. I. Bloomfield, *Capital Imports and the American Balance of Payments,* 1950, chap. 9.

rise in export prices in underdeveloped countries brings a boom, but the gains may largely be concentrated on a small group, and the effects on spending, prices, and incomes may be contained through large rises of hoards. This holds even if, as Dr. Wallich maintains, the main effects of expansion (or contraction) are felt through income rather than price movements.

In general, the underdeveloped or smaller countries have certain characteristics which must be noticed. Their exports are comparatively large (with some exceptions) relative to income as compared with investments or government outlays, that is, relative to the same relations for more advanced countries. The stimulus to increased activity tends to be felt through gains of reserves, soon converted into domestic currencies. But it should be noted that this is not always the case.[21] Note the large contribution of bank credit in Table 12-1 in the war period and in the postwar period.

Table 12-1. Percentage Contribution to Inflation, 1941 to 1945 and the Postwar Period 1946 to 1948 or 1946 to 1949

	1941–1945			1946–1948 or 1946–1949		
	Government debt	Bank credit	Foreign-exchange reserves	Government debt	Bank credit	Foreign-exchange reserves
Brazil	37	39	24	16*	61*	23*
Chile	23	61	16	−26	125	
Colombia	18	29	53	47	79	−25
Cuba	0	6	94	1	20	79
Mexico	12	65	22	65	118	−83
Peru	52	33	15	21	78	½
Arithmetic mean of six countries	24	39	37	21	80	−1

* 1946 only.

SOURCE: Calculated from materials in J. Keith Horsefield, "Inflation in Latin America," *International Monetary Fund Staff Papers*, September, 1950, pp. 175–202.

It is frequently held that the underdeveloped countries or the smaller countries also suffer from meager reserves. Table 12-2 suggests that this thesis can be supported by comparing the United States and other countries but not by comparing Western Europe and the other areas. Even allowing for the fact that the countries included in the other groups are of varying development, I still adhere to the general thesis that the underdeveloped or smaller countries are not clearly those with

[21] See the author's study for the Rio de Janeiro Conference, *Inter-American Trade: Measures for Its Expansion*, 1954, p. 76.

small reserves—their reserves may, however, be small given their large fluctuations in prices and trade.[22]

Table 12-2
(Figures for 1954)

Area	Imports, millions of dollars	Reserves, millions of dollars	% reserves to imports
United States..................	11,108	21,793	197
United Kingdom................	9,447	2,730	29
Continental EPU countries......	23,694	11,425	48
Latin American countries........	7,282	3,350	46
Other sterling countries.........	7,629	4,725	63
Rest of world*................	7,989	3,300	41

* As defined by the IMF does not include Western Europe, Iron Curtain countries, Canada, etc.

These smaller countries experience large doses of inflation for various reasons, not the least of which is pressure from the outside reflected in increased demands for exports and inflows of capital and the use of monetary expansion to exact savings. For example, the cost of living of eight Latin American countries rose by almost 500 per cent from 1937 to 1953, or about five times as much as prices rose in the United States. They frequently do not adjust their exchanges to the rise of prices, with the result that the exchanges tend to become overvalued. Thus from 1938 to 1947, on the basis of price movements, a depreciation of Latin American currencies of at least 50 per cent in terms of dollars might have been expected. Actually, the decline averaged about 10 per cent.[23] They then contend with overvaluation through restrictions on trade, inclusive of multiple exchanges and exchange control.

In general, it may be said that the smaller countries are more vulnerable to outside forces than larger countries, and their need for capital and their primitive monetary systems aggravate the inflationary effects of expansion induced from abroad.[24]

Monetary and Fiscal Policy

There is now a tendency to put more emphasis on fiscal policy than before World War II. Thus, if the British are unable to balance their accounts abroad, then one way out is to stimulate domestic investment.

[22] Cf. the penetrating article by H. C. Wallich, "Underdeveloped Countries and the International Monetary Mechanism," in *Money, Trade and Economic Growth*, 1951, pp. 15–32; *Economic Problems of Latin America* (S. E. Harris, ed.); and the author's two volumes for the Rio de Janeiro Conference (Harris, *op. cit.*, 1954, and *Inflation and Anti-inflationary Policies of American States*, 1951).

[23] Harris, *Inflationary and Anti-inflationary Policies of American States*, pp. 97–98.

[24] See above references.

To some extent, this is achieved through government subsidies and government direct investment. Hence, the unemployed in the export industries find jobs in the newly created employments. A substitution of high-cost domestic goods for goods previously imported may be costly, but the assumption is that the rise of costs thus incurred would be less than the gains from additional employment. The British in the post-World War II period have moved in this direction.

Other shifts of emphasis are to be noted. There is a tendency to concentrate much more attention on the direct repercussion of additional demand upon output and much less on the monetary contribution. In fact, the authorities emphasize monetary policy less because the stress is now put on spending and effective demand, not on increases in the supply of money. (In boom periods monetary policy may still act as a depressant.)[25]

Keynes and his followers also stress the relation of exports and imports rather than the optimum allocation of economic resources among countries which they assume to exist. A rise of exports relative to imports stimulates the economy through the resultant inflow of money and higher incomes. How much it does so depends on the export multiplier, that is, the ratio of the final rise of income to the initial one, a result, in turn, related to the leakages. The more the additional income in successive cycles of spending is hoarded or used to buy foreign goods, the greater the leakages and the smaller the multiplier.[26]

The modern theory shows how cycles are transmitted from one country to another. Thus income depends upon exports and other autonomous factors, and exports upon world trade and other autonomous factors. If spending declines in one country, the ultimate reduction of income in that country will be two to three times the original decline of income. In turn, imports will be reduced, the exact amount depending on the marginal propensity to import; that is, the exports of other countries will be reduced. A decline of exports brings an X drop of incomes (the export multiplier), and a reduction of income brings a Y decline of imports—given by the marginal propensity to import. Under the conditions of the 1930s, the net result might well be a world multiplier of about five; that is, a reduction of $1 billion of spending in country A would induce a $5 billion drop of world income. A figure of these proportions is suggested by estimating the marginal propensity to save in the thirties, for on a world-wide basis there is no leakage through imports, and hence the marginal propensity to save would yield the reduction of income. The world multiplier would be based on the reciprocal of the weighted average of propensities to save of all countries. These calculations suggest the danger of inaction in the midst of a world

[25] Cf. discussion in Chap. 16.
[26] Cf. F. Machlup, *International Trade and the National Income Multiplier*, 1943.

situation where spending is on the decline. The high multipliers are, of course, premised on the assumption of inaction.[27]

It may well be that the reaction against monetary policy has gone too far. Clearly in the fifties not alone in the United States but also in Western Europe, authorities once more turned to monetary policies as a major weapon. Indeed, the fact that in the struggle against inflation monetary policy is more potent than in the attack on deflation may partly explain the shift of emphasis. It is worthy of comment, however, that despite the strong statements made on behalf of its monetary policy, the governor of the Bank of England, early in 1955, following the most vigorous application of monetary policy in a generation, had to admit that monetary policy was not so potent as it used to be. The governor complained that monetary policy impinged on a smaller part of the economy than formerly and its impact can be outweighed by outlays and taxes of public authority.[28]

Undoubtedly it is necessary to use both monetary and fiscal policy, and the two must be integrated. An independent monetary authority, as proclaimed by President Eisenhower in 1956, is out of the question. It was unfortunate for the President to announce in the spring of 1954 that with inflation a threat, taxes could not be reduced even as the Federal Reserve was changing over from a policy of restraint to one of ease. In early 1956, a case could be made out for inflationary symptoms and hence for a mild anti-inflationary policy by the Federal Reserve, but it is unfortunate that the Federal Reserve, the Treasury, and the Council of Economic Advisors could not agree on the trends and produce a well-integrated monetary and fiscal policy. Disapproving of dear money, the Treasury might be forced into pushing for tax reduction.

In some instances less developed countries seem to rely more on an integrated monetary and fiscal policy than the more advanced countries. Possibly the less developed money markets put a greater strain on fiscal policy, but the relatively smaller revenues collected by the less developed and smaller countries may be a deterrent to effective use of fiscal policy. In some respects the smaller country faces a tougher problem, for excessive credit is reflected in a corresponding growth in the adverse balance of payments. A large country like the United States absorbs a substantial part of its excess in spending at home, not reflected in a corresponding rise of the external deficit. All this suggests both the greater task required of monetary policy for the smaller countries and also the pressure to use fiscal policy as well as controls.

[27] The fullest discussion of these issues is to be found in J. J. Polak, *An International Economic System*, 1953, and an able review of this book by A. C. Harberger in *The Review of Economics and Statistics*, November, 1956. Also see H. Neisser and F. Modigliani, *National Incomes and International Trade, A Quantitative Analysis*, 1953.

[28] International Monetary Fund, *Financial News Survey*, Oct. 14, 1955.

In 1954, the International Monetary Fund agreed to a devaluation of the Mexican peso and, in conjunction with this move, provided additional funds. The monetary and fiscal policies were well integrated, as can be gleaned from the following account:[29]

On the proposal of the Government of Mexico, in which the Fund concurred, the par value of the Mexican peso was changed on April 19, 1954 from 8.65 pesos to 12.50 pesos per U.S. dollar. The new par value represented a devaluation of 30.8 per cent from the previous rate, which had been in effect since July 17, 1949. At the same time, the Fund concluded a stand-by agreement under which Mexico may draw up to $50 million to serve as a second line of reserve during the period of adjustment to the new par value. The Government of Mexico proposed an exchange devaluation for several reasons. There had been a deterioration on ordinary balance of payments account, and a significant recovery was not considered likely in the absence of marked improvement in world demand and price conditions for many of Mexico's leading export products, especially minerals. Moreover, as export earnings declined, the business community became more cautious in its appraisal of future developments. The Mexican Government was determined to neutralize through compensatory fiscal policies the decline in private economic activity which had manifested itself before the devaluation. Without an exchange devaluation, such fiscal policies would have tended to place renewed pressure on the monetary system and on the country's balance of payments. Finally, the gradual reduction from 1951 onward of the gold and foreign exchange reserves of the Bank of Mexico had impaired its ability to cope with deficits on ordinary balance of payments account or with recurrent sizable outflows of short-term capital similar to the outflows in the middle of 1951 and the middle of 1952. A new wave of speculation against the peso developed in March 1954, when the period was approaching at which Mexico's exchange earnings are normally seasonally low. The Government, therefore, decided that it should act without delay in order to avoid a serious depletion of the international reserves of the Bank of Mexico. The devaluation of April 1954 was expected to restrain imports and to give a stimulus to foreign tourist receipts. At the same time the Government announced the imposition of higher export taxes, to absorb a large part of the profits that would otherwise accrue to exporters from devaluation. In spite of the increased public spending involved in the fiscal policies to which the Government of Mexico is for the time being committed, any considerable expansion in tax collections, mainly as a result of the new export taxes, was likely, also, to tend to insure a sounder fiscal position for the Federal Government.

Disregard of International Aspects in Postwar United States

In the postwar history of the United States, some aspects of the problems here under consideration are raised. A striking aspect of United States policy was the almost complete disregard of international reper-

[29] International Monetary Fund, *Annual Report*, 1954, pp. 84–85.

cussions in the discussion of monetary policy. The explanation was in part the fact that this country, with a strong dollar and about $24 billion of gold, or two-thirds of the world supply in the early fifties, could indulge in substantial inflationary and expansionist monetary policies without being excessively concerned about international reper- cussions. It might be held that the high wage policies in this country tended to correct the excessive strength of the dollar, that is, should bring higher costs and prices.[30] But rapid inflation abroad and the rapid rise of productivity here were offsetting factors. It is difficult to find, as noted above, any evidence that high wage policies or other inflationary policies in the United States were encouraged here in order to bring our international accounts closer to a balance. However, foreign aid was a facet of our international economic policies directed toward increasing the supply of dollars available to foreign countries, and there was some consideration given the possibility of raising the dollar price of gold, a policy that would have made more dollars available to foreigners.[31]

Then what was the major concern of United States policy? Un- doubtedly the authorities were anxious to keep the price of government securities up. Hence there was pressure to support the market for gov- ernment securities, a program fostered by Reserve bank purchases of government securities whenever they tended to fall substantially in price. In 1951, an agreement between the Reserve Board and the Treasury acknowledged that the objective of monetary policy should be the im- proved state of the economy. The result of the policies of supporting security prices was monetary expansion and hence upward movements in prices. No one justified this policy on the grounds of its contribution to international equilibrium. It should be noted, however, that the American policy prior to 1951 was one of supporting not only gov- ernment securities but all assets, that is, keeping a sufficient supply of money outstanding so that the price of all assets would be high or, in other words, the rate of interest low. The government had been mindful of the needs of the economy but may well have weighted the need of supporting government securities too heavily and hence have added to inflationary pressures.[32]

In 1953, the government attempted to modify past policies by raising the rate of interest through the issue of longer-term securities, and reduced support of the market. But the effects of higher rates of in- terest were a partial collapse of the government bond market and also some deterioration in the economic situation. Fortunately with unem- ployment rising to 3 million to 4 million in 1953–1954, the authorities

[30] Cf. J. M. Keynes's last article, "The Balance of Payments of the United States," *Economic Journal*, June, 1946, pp. 172–187.

[31] Discussed fully in Chap. 26.

[32] Cf. S. E. Harris, *The National Debt and the New Economics.*

reversed their monetary policies and also cut taxes, thus stimulating the economy. It was held by some that it had been unwise to increase rates of interest on the assumption that the country was suffering from inflation when, in fact, prices had been stable or falling for two years.[33]

Some Conclusions

In recent chapters, I have discussed problems of money, concentrating primarily on aspects of special significance for international trade and equilibrium, but to understand this relationship, one must pay some attention to alternative objectives of monetary policy.

Our modern monetary systems have evolved from a theory of money which emphasizes its unimportance and a theory of trade which stresses the point that trade theory is not modified by the introduction of money into the analysis. With an emphasis on the natural distribution of precious metals, there was little scope for management of the monetary system. Indeed, the banking school would tolerate management restricted by convertibility, but the currency school would impose upon the central bank a rigid restriction of issue, related to international gold flows. Hence the theory behind monetary systems during most of the one hundred years before World War I was that the objective was to preserve the gold standard, that is, a fixed price for gold and free exchange of gold for notes and vice versa at a fixed price. In order to ensure this kind of international system, it was held imperative to avoid excessive issues with resultant rise of prices and excess of imports. Hence the Bank Act of 1844, which forced on the central bank corrective measures upon the loss of relatively small amounts of gold abroad. The system failed to recognize the much greater significance of internal drains of gold and currency and did not provide the flexibility required to satisfy demands for increased liquidity.

Fortunately, despite the determination of the monetary theorists and practitioners to starve the economy, an element of growth and flexibility was introduced. New gold discoveries, the development of deposit banking, other economies in the use of money, and the suspension of the Bank Act helped greatly. Nevertheless, there was not enough money to go around. Even in the nineteenth and the early twentieth centuries, the gold standard was not a great success; after the Napoleonic War, in the last quarter of the nineteenth century, in the interwar period, the major countries competed for gold by depressing their price and even income levels. Even in the United States, where there was little indication of a monetary policy before 1913, the pressure of inadequate

[33] I have discussed this episode much more fully in a statement before a congressional committee: *United States Monetary Policy: Recent Thinking and Experience,* Hearings of the Joint Committee on the Economic Report, Subcommittee on Economic Stabilization, 1954, pp. 51–60.

supplies of money was felt in downward pressures on prices. That the gold standard performed as well as it did could be explained by economies in the use of gold adumbrated above, by the increased demand for money in the periods of large gold discoveries, and above all by the introduction of management by the Bank of England. The last responded to losses of gold with an increase of bank rates and to gains with a reduction of rates and learned about techniques to enforce rates. In the most recent failures of the gold standard, recourse was had to a series of devaluations.

After World War I, interest in a monetary policy that would stabilize prices and (later) maximize employment and output attracted increasing attention. Keynes, especially, laid the groundwork for the new policies. The major shift of emphasis was from a policy which seeks to preserve the gold standard to one that emphasizes the attainment of domestic objectives of high employment and output. It does not necessarily follow that the international system is then excluded. It is possible for each country to be guided largely by domestic objectives, and yet through international cooperation, with each country seeking expansion and the provision of adequate international reserves, the best points of a domestic and international system might be combined. But even under this kind of system periodic adjustments in exchange rates would have to be accepted as normal. Above all, this system would not subject economies to pressures from the outside which would deprive them of the supplies of money and the application of fiscal policies consistent with appropriate rates of interest and demand as required by domestic objectives.

In the absence of international cooperation, under the new monetary policies, each country would depend on exchange adjustments, restrictions on capital movements, and even other restrictions to ensure adequacy of demand in the face of noncooperative policies abroad.

In the modern approach to international equilibrium, much more attention is paid to income movements than in the past. In the discussion of dollar shortage in Chapters 16 and 20 to 24, we stress the relation of income movements and imports. Disequilibrium may arise because higher productivity in one country (despite accompanying increase of income and imports) yields gains in falling prices as well as higher incomes, and with a low propensity to import and inadequate increase of wages (and hence relatively low prices), the dollar market may become unbalanced. More on this later and more on the relation of prices and exchanges.

CHAPTER 13

A Brief Résumé of United States Monetary Policy

Introduction

In Chapters 9 to 12 I have treated the international aspects of monetary policy as well as other broad objectives primarily from the British viewpoint. This is understandable, since the major advances were made in Great Britain, but it is well to tie this analysis to the monetary history of the United States.

In this country, the monetary system before the Civil War was generally chaotic—if it could be called a system at all. The tie-in to gold was much less rigid than in the British system. In a growing country with little monetary organization and what seemed to be almost insatiable demands for cash, the fluctuations in supplies of money and prices were, indeed, of large proportions; and getting out of step with Europe in monetary creation, the authorities were confronted with drains of reserves and at times with great deflations.

In the post-Civil War period the monetary system was in some respects even more rigid than the British. The tie-in of money with the national debt contributed to a great deflation in the last quarter of the nineteenth century as debt was repaid, though in the face of great demands for additional supplies of money in a rapidly growing economy, means were found to expand the supplies of money but not adequately to stop the great deflation. Unorthodox proposals to expand the supply of money induced losses of confidence abroad, withdrawals of capital, and monetary crises.

In the post-1914 period, the attention given to international aspects of money was a minimum. A strong economy could attract gold from abroad and generally pursue domestic policies with little concern about losses of gold. The original objective of the Federal Reserve was to provide adequate supplies of money based on the needs of trade. The banking principle had emerged victorious in the United States, as it had not in Great Britain. Gradually this country created the weapons of monetary control which had been evolved much earlier in Great Britain. Later on this country also sought broader objectives of monetary policy as had the British. Political pressures often made these weapons innocuous. But above all, this country, in contrast to European countries, could pursue monetary policies with little thought to international repercussions.

Pre-Federal Reserve

Now I turn to United States monetary developments.[1] It was not until 1914 that this country established a central banking system. In the preceding century one crisis followed another. There was scarcely a genuine monetary policy. During a large part of the first half of the nineteenth century wildcat banks provided the country with a substantial part of the currency needed, but often the banks disappeared before the currency could be redeemed. Yet these issues probably did more good than harm. When Jackson destroyed the Second Bank of the United States, he left a hiatus in the monetary system, and the Sub-treasury system which followed greatly reduced the degree of monetary flexibility. (Wholesale prices declined by 40 per cent in the first half of the nineteenth century, and economic conditions improved little.)

Undoubtedly the Second Bank of the United States, operating for about twenty years after the War of 1812, provided the country with a modicum of leadership. The Bank transferred cash on behalf of the Treasury, a troublesome problem at this time; financed much domestic business; controlled issues of its branches in accordance with exchange movements, that is, with New Orleans exchange adverse, issues were reduced there; and controlled to some extent the issues of state banks. But even the Second Bank could not stop repayments of debt by the government and the accompanying contraction of currency, a process carried through with no thought to the effects on the domestic or international situation. It is rather surprising that Professor W. Smith should welcome this repayment of debt in every year from 1817 to 1833 as being anti-inflationary. Actually, wholesale prices declined by more than 25 per cent from the years 1817 to 1821 and 10 per cent further by 1830, and the cost of living also fell.[2]

---

[1] See especially D. Dewey, *Financial History of the United States;* "Federal Reserve System." (B. Hammond, historical introduction), in *Banking Studies,* 1941, pp. 5–38; A. Schlesinger, Jr., *The Age of Jackson,* on banking history; O. M. W. Sprague, *The National Banking System;* W. Smith, *Economic Aspects of the Second Bank of the United States,* 1953.

[2] U.S. Department of Commerce, *Historical Statistics of the United States, 1789–1945,* pp. 234–235; Smith, *op. cit.,* especially chaps. 3, 4, 8.

The gyrations of our monetary system may be gleaned from Table 13-1.[3]

Table 13-1
(In millions of dollars)
Circulation of State Banks

1829	48
1833	10

Circulation of the Second Bank of the United States

1817	1.9
1833	17.5
1836	23.0
1840	6.7

Fortunately by the latter part of the fifties the volume of deposits, growing rapidly, exceeded the notes outstanding.[4]

Finally, in the midst of the Civil War, the government established the national banking system, which virtually gave a monopoly of issue of bank notes to national banks, but the notes were to be covered by Federal securities. Again there was no central monetary authority. The folly of tying the currency system to government finance was revealed in the post-Civil War period, when national banks were forced to retire their notes. In the twenty-seven years 1866 to 1893 the government retired two-thirds of its national debt. Untutored in modern fiscal theories, the government repaid debt and destroyed money in the midst of a period of great expansion and even greater potential expansion. The result was great pressure on prices. Table 13-2 suggests the course of events. In this period of twenty-seven years, the country went through a record deflation wringer, with wholesale prices falling by 50 per cent. But even this deflation could not paralyze the country. The underlying conditions were so favorable that the national income rose by 100 per cent (200 per cent in stable wholesale prices). Fortunately, despite the repayment of debt, the national bank notes dropped by but one-third (the banks competed strenuously for outstanding bonds to serve as cover for notes). And in these years a moderate inflow of gold and the issue of silver money made possible a rise of money in circulation of two-thirds. On the basis of the rise of income (over our whole history the relative increase of money in circulation has greatly exceeded that of income), the expansion of monetary supplies was most inadequate, and the pressure felt by the debtor class in a period of falling prices was reflected in radical political movements springing from the West.

There is no doubt that the competition for gold among the leading

[3] *Historical Statistics of the United States, 1789–1945*, p. 261.
[4] Hammond, *op. cit.*, p. 13.

countries and especially Great Britain, the United States, France, and Germany had much to do with the pressure on prices. Time and again in the period between the Civil War and 1900 the British had to raise rates in order to protect their gold supplies. They suffered from falling prices, as did the United States. In this sense, the policy of debt contraction and accompanying reduction of bank notes may be said to have been consistent with the requirements of the gold standards, but it was not a healthy policy when viewed from the needs of the internal economy. That the government pursued the policy of debt reduction in order to obtain its share of world gold supplies through price reductions is not at all clear. The growth of the economy, despite the inadequacy of monetary supplies, was the explanation of revenue surpluses. An increase of gold supplies from $121 million in 1866 (when this country was off gold) to $502 million in 1893, however embarrassing to the British, was not enough to satisfy the needs of a dynamic American economy. To the accompaniment of reduced confidence in the dollar when this country experienced the great controversy over the introduction of bimetallism, the exports of gold (net) from the United States were no less than $323 million, or more than half of its accumulated stock. (Part was, however, from new production of gold.[5])

Table 13-2 suggests the main outlines of the developments from 1866 to 1893, but a word should be added concerning the resumption of pay-

Table 13-2. Economic Development: United States, 1866 to 1893

	1866	1893
National income, billions of dollars.....................	5.7	11.3
Wholesale prices (1926 = 100)........................	116	53
Cost of living (1913 = 100)...........................	103	75
Total money in circulation, millions of dollars...........	935	1,543
National bank notes in circulation, millions of dollars.....	276	175
National debt, millions of dollars......................	2,677	961

SOURCE: U.S. Department of Commerce, *Historical Statistics of the United States, 1789–1945.*

ments after the Civil War. Here the same issues were thrashed out as in Great Britain in the post-Napoleonic and post-World War I periods. Could this country by returning to the convertibility of currency into gold command enough gold to maintain convertibility? Would the resultant starvation of the currency damage the economy? In the course of official hearings in 1876, many warned the government that the effects would

---

[5] The contraction in the post-Civil War period is discussed more fully in S. E. Harris, *National Debt and the New Economics*, 1947, especially pp. 263–265; also see R. G. Hawtrey, *A Century of Bank Rate*, 1938, chap. 3.

be disastrous, but resumption was carried through despite the warnings of many and of the Monetary Committee:[6]

Those who now find themselves crushed beneath a load of debt through falling prices brought about by a contraction of the currency cannot be justly taunted with previous recklessness, because they transacted business in prices regulated by forces over which they had no control. . . .

A transition in this country from paper to coin involves a struggle for the needed coin with other countries, no one of which has any that is not all urgently needed for its own payments, prices and necessities. . . . It [the United States] can be successful [in obtaining gold] by a reduction of prices in this country, not merely to the present level of coin-prices throughout the world, but to the lower level to which they must descend under such a new and great demand for coin as the resumption of specie payment in this country would occasion. . . .

It is not surprising, then, that the government policy to resume was accompanied by a reduction of prices in excess of 25 per cent from 1872 to 1878 and beginning in 1877 a stoppage of the large outflow of gold which had persisted from 1873 to 1876. Nor are we surprised that the total supply of money actually declined in this period. The resumption of gold payments and the peculiar perversity of issues of bank notes resulting from debt repayments accounted for a monetary policy which could scarcely be supported by those in command of modern monetary theory.

Lack of a Policy and the Federal Reserve

In the hundred years before the founding of the Federal Reserve System there was then little evidence of a national monetary policy. This country shared the international crisis of Western Europe and, in addition, experienced additional years of crisis. So chaotic was the system that in the financial crisis of the 1890s, with the United States adherence to the gold standard threatened as a result of large outflows of gold, the government had to appeal to a private banking firm for help.

The Federal Reserve System was the answer for those who would introduce a central bank and control, if not eliminate, the periodic crisis last felt in 1907. As had been true in the past, little attention was paid to the international aspects of policy, though losses of gold were embarrassing, for if they had been considered adequately, a regional system of twelve Reserve banks might not have been established. In the course of development under the Federal Reserve System, despite the intentions of the founders, who were excessively frightened of Wall Street, the New York Bank has assumed a major responsibility for international equi-

[6] *The Report of the United States Monetary Commission,* 1877, vol. I, pp. 105, 106.

librium[7] (often sharing it with the Treasury) and a substantial control of the System.

At this point it may be useful to trace the main outlines of the development of the Federal Reserve System over a period of forty years. The System was established, not on the currency principle, the theoretical basis of the Bank of England, but rather on the banking principle: The Reserve banks were to rediscount paper based on commercial transactions, and the reserve against notes was to consist of gold and rediscounted commercial paper. The system was to be much less rigid than the British one. In part, the acceptability of the banking principle as well as the regional nature of the System can be explained by the greater importance of regional economics and the lesser significance of international economics for the United States than for Great Britain.

But the System did not develop as had been anticipated. The amount of commercial paper reaching the Reserve banks was much too small to provide the money needed by the country, especially in wartime. (Rediscounts of paper at the Reserve banks create cash reserves for the commercial banks.) The major contributions to the monetary supplies were provided through purchases of government securities by the Reserve banks (open-market operations, a technique most highly developed in this country), through gold inflows (offset by increased money in circulation), through reductions in reserve requirements for commercial banks, and through the purchase of government securities and other assets by the commercial banks. The significance of open-market operations (or direct purchases of securities by the Reserve banks from the Treasury) may be gleaned from the fact that Reserve bank holdings exceeded the reserves of member banks in the early fifties.

It will be noted from Table 13-3 that the major source of earning assets (the most important source of deposits) has been the purchase of government securities by commercial banks, which in turn obtained their cash through Reserve bank open-market operations and inflow of gold. (But the gains of gold were offset by losses of cash, as the banks had to convert reserves to pay for the rising stock of money required for circulation.)[8]

Fortunately, the monetary authority, even though concerned over increased monetary supplies, did not stifle the economy—with some notable exceptions —by excessive restrictions on monetary expansion. The reason was lack of

[7] An interesting analysis of the manner in which the New York Reserve Bank achieved much authority and the reasons for this "usurpation" of power will be found in G. L. Bach, *Federal Reserve Policy Making*, 1950, chap. 4.

[8] *Monetary Policy and the Management of the Public Debt*, Hearings of the Joint Committee on the Economic Report, March, 1952, pp. 380–389. The excerpt is from pp. 380–381.

authority and (later) lack of courage and popular support. The fact is that the country grew up to its monetary supplies. Indeed, there were periods, (e.g., the last quarter of the nineteenth century) when the monetary system was rigid and perverse in its behavior. Additional money was required not only to monetize the economy and finance the growth of the Nation, but also to provide the additional cash which the people want as their standards of living rise. Thus we can explain a rise of money greatly exceeding the increase of income. We should not forget, furthermore, that part of the added supplies of money financed inflationary episodes which are characteristic of economies with shortages of capital. In a developing economy, inflation serves a useful purpose, if not carried too far, in providing needed capital.

Had the traditionalists had their way (and these include even those who inspired the Federal Reserve System and were the precursors of the anti-monetization-of-debt school, Senator Glass, Professor Willis, and leading bankers), then the country would have been starved for money in the years since 1914. Only war and the growth of national debt vanquished these supporters of the theory that bank deposits must grow only with commercial loans. They failed to see that recourse to commercial lending does not necessarily give the country the money it needs.

Here are some rough figures for 1914 to 1951, inclusive. They show the importance of the monetization of the debt and the associated rise of deposits and of national income, the last only in small part reflecting inflation.

It will be observed that the major increase of assets (and especially proportionately) has been in securities, and that national income rose eight times as much as prices. (Cost-of-living figures are not too reliable for the earlier period but a rough estimate points to an increase of income of six times as much as in the cost of living.)

Table 13-3. All Commercial Banks: Deposits, Loans, Securities, and National Income, 1914 and June, 1951

	Rise, billions of dollars	Rise, no. of times
Deposits................	132	7.6
Loans..................	37	3.1
Securities...............	66	17.8
Prices, wholesale..........	...	1.1
National income..........	246	8.6

SOURCE: *Monetary Policy and the Management of the Public Debt*, Hearings before the Subcommittee on General Credit Control and Debt Management of the Joint Committee on the Economic Report, 82d Cong., pp. 380–381 (statement by S. E. Harris). Federal Reserve Board, *Banking and Monetary Statistics*, *Federal Reserve Bulletin*, *Historical Statistics of the United States, 1789–1945*, and the *Economic Report of the President*, Jan. 1, 1952.

In some respects the monetary history of the United States has been unusual. On the whole, little attention has been paid to international aspects of its policies, and this is especially true since 1914.[9] (In the occasional period—1924, 1927—when this country adapted its policy to the requirements of the international system, it was concluded that a great mistake had been made.[10]) The explanation of this fact is partly the *relative* unimportance of foreign trade for the United States and partly the strong international economic position of this country. As an indication of strength or else of overallegiance to orthodoxy, despite long periods of monetary scarcity, there had been no devaluation for a century previous to the 1934 devaluation. (See note at end of chapter.)

General Observations on the Federal Reserve

We have noted above that the Federal Reserve is not nearly so concerned with international aspects of policy as the Bank of England, that it has introduced a greater degree of flexibility and policy into the monetary arena, that it has used the important weapon of open-market operations, and that it has flirted with the problem of price stabilization. In this section, we shall comment on various aspects of Federal Reserve policy as suggested by its history. Benjamin Strong, the great figure in the Federal Reserve in the first fifteen years; E. A. Goldenweiser, the research director over a long period; and Randolph Burgess, a leading figure in the system, have all expressed their views in books, and these are helpful.[11]

First, the authorities have tended to minimize their control over member bank reserves, prices, and the credit policies of banks. Thus, though the Federal Reserve was established in part to control the *quality* as well as the quantity of banking, Benjamin Strong in 1922 said that the "eligible paper we discount is simply the vehicle through which the credit of the Reserve System is conveyed to members. But the definition of eligibility does not effect the slightest control over the use to which the proceeds are applied."[12] As late as 1928, Mr. Strong testified as follows before a congressional committee:[13]

Governor Strong. That question is really applicable to the last few questions in this questionnaire. Again getting back to the gold standard, the gold stand-

---

[9] How little part international considerations play in Federal Reserve policy is indicated by a perusal of Bach's comprehensive book *Federal Reserve Policy Making*. In 282 pages, the international problems receive much less than 10 pages. This should be contrasted to foreign interests of the Second United States Bank excellently treated in Smith, *op. cit.*, especially chap. 6.

[10] Cf. E. A. Goldenweiser, *Monetary Management*, 1949, pp. 52–53.

[11] W. R. Burgess (ed.), *Interpretations of Federal Reserve Policy in the Speeches and Writings of Benjamin Strong*, 1930; W. R. Burgess, *The Reserve Banks and the Money Market*, rev. ed., 1936; E. A. Goldenweiser, *op. cit.*, 1949. The author has also depended on his two volumes *Twenty Years of Federal Reserve Policy*, 1933.

[12] *Speeches and Writings of Benjamin Strong*, p. 184.

[13] *Ibid.*, pp. 330–331.

ard is a much more automatic check upon excesses in credit and currency than is a system where gold payment, if you please, is suspended and it is left to the human judgment of men to determine how much currency shall be issued which they do not need to redeem in gold—do you see the distinction? And when you speak of a gold standard, you are speaking of something where the limitation upon judgment is exact and precise and the penalty for bad judgment is immediate.

Where you are speaking of efforts simply to stabilize commerce, industry, agriculture, employment, and so on, without regard to the penalties of violation of the gold standard, you are talking about human judgment and the management of prices which I do not believe in at all. I do not think anybody should be given the power to say what the price of anything should be.

Mr. Wingo. Price fixing indirectly is just as vicious as price fixing directly.

Governor Strong. But if your system of price fixing is that which has been tested, so far as human society goes, by operation of the automatic system of gold payment and redemption of the notes of banks of issue, I think you minimize the possibilities of bad judgment or abuse of power by a better method than any that has yet been devised.

In 1928 Governor Strong repeated his objections to a bill which would impose upon the Federal Reserve the responsibility of stabilizing prices. At this time Strong again insisted that "a declaration as to the gold standard . . . might accomplish all of the purposes as to prices which are capable of being accomplished by monetary policy. . . . "[14]

In 1924 the Federal Reserve had given its official version of why it had introduced a policy of monetary ease. It is clear from this statement that the System was interested in the prevention of inflation as well as in helping Europe, but it was also aware that it did not want to assume any responsibilities for the stabilization of prices.[15]

1. To accelerate the process of debt repayment to the Federal reserve banks by the member banks, so as to relieve this weakening pressure for loan liquidation.

2. To give the Federal reserve banks an asset which would be automatically liquidated as the result of gold imports so that later, if inflation developed from excessive gold imports, it might at least be checked in part by selling these securities, thus forcing member banks again into debt to the reserve banks and making the reserve bank discount rate effective.

3. To facilitate a change in the interest relation between the New York and London markets, without inviting inflation, by establishing a somewhat lower level of interest rates in this country at a time when prices were falling generally and when the danger of a disorganizing price advance in commodities was at a minimum and remote.

[14] House Committee on Banking and Currency, *Hearings on Stabilization,* H.R. 11806, 1928, p. 13.

[15] *Hearings of the Subcommittee of the Committee on Banking and Currency, U.S. Senate, on S. Res. 71, Appendix,* pt. 6, p. 805.

4. By directing foreign borrowings to this market to create the credits which would be necessary to facilitate the export of commodities, especially farm produce.

5. To render what assistance was possible by our market policy toward the recovery of sterling and the resumption of gold payment by Great Britain.

6. To check the pressure on the banking situation in the West and North-west and the resulting failures and disasters.

In 1932 Governor Meyer of the Board continued to take the Strong position against assuming responsibility for price stabilization.[16] The reluctance to assume any responsibilities for price stabilization is no-where more evident than in the many statements of Adolph Miller, of the Federal Reserve Board, who agreed with the President in these matters. In hearings (May, 1932) in the midst of the greatest depression of modern times, Dr. Miller had this to say:[17]

You do not want to overload your firebox with coal. Others describe it as a process of over-feeding. You don't want to feed until your patient begins to spit up your food. You don't want in other words what is sometimes tech-nically described as "sloppy" money conditions. That in itself is disturbing. Our position is like that of the doctor who is alimenting a patient who, he feels, may not be too far removed from the point of convalescence. He will give him so many grains of this, that or the other tonic today and watch its effect; perhaps tomorrow he will hold off for two or three days. I think it is a well established principle in therapeutics that in all forms of artificial feed-ing, whether it is accomplished through chemical injection into the veinous system or otherwise, it is necessary to lay off from time to time. Even wise practitioners administering cod-liver oil through the stomach will lay off at the end of the month.

This is a remarkable statement coming in the midst of one of the greatest deflations of modern times. How could anyone have feared in-flation at such a time? But progress was being made. In 1937 Mr. Eccles, chairman of the Federal Reserve Board, also showed a reluctance to assume the responsibility for stabilizing prices, and in 1938 he was clear that price stability would not necessarily bring economic stability. He also insisted that there were distinct limitations to monetary control. But he added these significant words: "In the Board's view the essential ob-jective of monetary policy is to contribute to the maintenance of a flow of money and income through the channels of trade, industry, and agriculture that would tend to utilise to the full the country's human and material resources. . . . "[18]

[16] Senate Banking and Currency Committee, *Hearings on Restoring and Maintain-ing the Average Purchasing Power of the Dollar*, 1932, pp. 202–203.
[17] *Ibid.*, p. 237.
[18] House Banking and Currency Committee, *Hearings on Government Ownership of the Twelve Federal Reserve Banks*, 1938, pp. 444–446,

With a change in attitudes toward the responsibilities of government and hence of monetary policy following the depression, and especially in response to needling by Congress, the reserve authorities were prepared to move further. Thus Dr. Goldenweiser wrote in 1949: "The broad objective [of monetary policy] may be stated to be to contribute through the regulation of the volume, availability and cost of money to the maintenance of stable economic conditions and a rising level of economic well-being."[19] In a statement to the Joint Committee on the Economic Report (November 23, 1954), the Federal Reserve would provide a supply of money "which is neither so large that it will induce inflationary pressure nor so small that it will stifle initiative and growth . . . sufficient to facilitate outlays necessary to sustain a high level of production and employment."[20]

Second, as the problems of instability became increasingly complex, the Reserve banks sought or were required to use additional instruments. In the early 1920s open-market operations attracted much attention, not only as a basis of domestic expansion (through enabling member banks to repay debt) but also as a means of reducing rates to help Europe obtain capital and gold and also, even at this late date, to increase the profits of the central bank. In the late twenties, the approach was direct action, that is, attempts to control the types of assets purchased by member banks rather than high rates which might hurt legitimate business.

In the 1930s the Reserve authorities began to use a potent weapon: changes in reserve requirements. The effect might be a serious reduction of reserves and contraction without sales of public securities by the Reserve banks. Actually, its use was more likely to be to force member banks to borrow from the Reserve Banks, to cut excessive reserves of banks, or to provide banks with large additions of cash in periods of recession. The effects were most uneven.

Unfortunately, the Reserve authorities still lack the authority to deal with various intermediaries (e.g., insurance companies, government credit agencies, building and loan societies, business corporations), which can interfere with the achievements of important objectives. These intermediaries, with plenty of liquid resources, are able to lend to business even when the member banks are restrained by Federal Reserve policies. Thus in 1953, when the Federal Reserve was trying to impose some restraint, all banks increased their earning assets by $4 billion, or 3 per cent, but insurance companies and loan associations, by $9 billion, or almost 10 per cent.[21]

---

[19] Goldenweiser, *op. cit.*, p. 24.
[20] Joint Congressional Committee on Economic Report, *Recent Monetary and Fiscal Policies*, 1954.
[21] Figures from *Federal Reserve Bulletin*,

Third, the Federal Reserve clearly has helped to stabilize the money market. Even by the early twenties, the regional differences in rates on high-class paper had been reduced by two-thirds. The extreme fluctuations, seasonally and in panicky times, were also greatly cut. Here, through transferring cash from surplus to deficient regions and providing reserves in periods of stress, the Reserve authorities contributed greatly to stability. (Yet Strong would have the Federal Reserve exercise discretion lest, where rates were 10 to 12 per cent, the resources of the Reserve banks available at much lower rates would be used excessively.[22])

Fourth, we should stress again the fact that monetary policy, even though strengthened by all kinds of gadgets, is still subject to many infirmities. Freedom is restricted to some extent by international requirements, though, as has been contended, this has not generally been a serious deterrent for this country.[23] The availability of large liquid resources by nonbanking lenders is a problem of increasing importance. Again, in periods of unemployment, the expansion of monetary supplies, even if the Federal Reserve succeeds in increasing the supply, may influence interest rates a minimum and total investment inadequately. But here fiscal policy may contribute much, and the effective use of monetary policy awaits integrated monetary and fiscal policy. Finally, there are many institutional blocks, e.g., the opposition of those who habitually object to any exercise of monetary restraint (and resultant political pressures) and the fear of large monetary expansions even when prices are falling. Disagreements among the Treasury, the Reserve authorities, the Reserve Board, and the New York Reserve Bank are another important institutional block.

Postwar wage policies, associated with high employment and the increased strength of the trade unions, constitute another development of an institutional type which raises tough problems for the monetary authority. Indeed, it is conceivable, but not likely, that the monetary authority may thwart the trade unions by restrictionist policies. When the unions push money wages up, the result may well be, as Sir Dennis Robertson argues, an abandonment of a reasonable standard of value. A minimum amount of unemployment is another way out, for as Professor Haberler points out, this is a protection against inflationary wage demands. Keynes and Lerner have also offered fruitful suggestions for dealing with this problem. The international repercussions of high wage policies are also important, for example, as a contribution to the solution of the dollar problem.[24]

[22] F. R. Macaulay, *Bond Yields, Interest Rates and Stock Prices*, 1938, p. 216; Burgess, *op. cit.*, chap. 12.

[23] Cf. *Speeches and Writings of Benjamin Strong*, pp. 146–147, 256–259.

[24] D. H. Robertson, *Utility and All of That*, 1952; G. Haberler in *The Impact of the Union* (D. McC. Wright, ed.), 1951; J. M. Keynes, *Treatise on Money*, 1930; and A. Lerner, *The Theory of Employment*.

A Digression on the 1934 Devaluation

The devaluation of 1934 sprang much more from a desire to give the farmers a shot in the arm rather than any strong interest in re-establishing the competitive position of the United States following an epidemic of depreciations abroad. [A depreciation, as we have seen in Chapter 11, tends to improve the competitive position of the country depreciating its currency.] Apparently President Roosevelt had been impressed by a theory of Professor Warren's that commodity prices move with the price of gold. Hence, since in 1933 it was considered imperative to raise the price of farm products, the President supported a policy for increasing the price of gold in dollars. At first it was assumed purchases of domestic gold would be adequate to raise prices of domestic commodities, a theory ridiculous on the face of it: how could purchases of, say, a few hundred millions of gold raise prices substantially in a $40 billion economy which was suffering from large downward pressures on prices? Later, purchases from abroad were allowed.

Professor Warren did not explain the manner in which a rise in the price of gold would increase prices. Of course, the answer is that the additional sales of dollars in purchasing gold from abroad would depress the prices of the dollar on foreign exchange markets, as the sellers of gold in New York disposed of dollars. That process would go on until the price of gold would be no higher in the United States than elsewhere. Hence, should the price of gold rise from $20.67 to $35 (67 per cent), then this equality would be obtained once each dollar was reduced in value by 40 per cent (100 = 60 per cent of 167) in relation to (say) £ sterling, where the price of gold had not changed. Then there would be no advantage in selling gold in New York over London. In New York the price had gone up by 67 per cent. But when the dollars were converted into sterling, they yielded 40 per cent less in £ sterling. Of course, extra sales of dollars associated with extra purchases of gold or speculative sales of dollars based on anticipation of the depreciation of the dollar must be large enough relative to all sales on the exchange market to depress the dollar by 40 per cent. But even then prices of United States commodities would rise only insofar as export and import prices respond to the depreciation of the dollars (e.g., imports cost more in dollars). Since international trade is a small part of all trade, the increase in prices would be much less than the 67 per cent expected by Warren. In fact, it was not until 1947 that prices rose by 67 per cent; and it took about $250 billion of deficit financing to bring about a rise of these proportions.[25]

[25] The author has discussed this episode fully in D. V. Brown et al., *The Economics of the Recovery Program*, 1934, and S. E. Harris, *Exchange Depreciation*, 1936, chap. 9. Cf. Warren and Pearson, *Prices*, 1933.

PART THREE

Regional Economics

CHAPTER 14

Regional Economics

As noted in Chapter 8, in classical economics the emphasis has been on international, not on regional, trade. Indeed, Ohlin tried to increase the attention paid to regional trade. A curious fact is that a great British economist, lecturing in 1829, pointed out that regional trade in China and also in Great Britain was more important than international trade. His contention was, however, that this was so in Great Britain only because of obstacles put in the way of foreign trade.[1]

In China, a country comprising probably one-fifth of mankind, and separated from the rest of the civilized world by vast deserts, or ten thousand miles of sea, the internal trade is necessarily the principal one. It must also be the principal trade in those countries, which, though of moderate extent, and favourably situated for foreign commerce, perversely refuse her advantages; or, like Spain, submit to them only when inflicted by the smuggler. The home trade is also, at this instant, the principal trade of Great Britain; but whether necessarily, or naturally so, may be doubted.

As the British islands make but a small portion of the globe, and that portion is remarkably uniform in soil, climate, and produce, it might have been supposed that the market of the whole world would have been more extensive and more varied, than that of England, Ireland, and Scotland. The communication between the eastern and southern coasts of Great Britain, and the western coast of Europe, and that between the western coasts of England, Ireland, and Scotland, and the eastern coast of North America, is more easy than that between most of our counties which are not absolutely contiguous. The freight of a cask of wine from Oporto to London is rather less than the cost of its carriage from London to Oxford. It might have been supposed that the whole of our trade with those regions, so vast, so accessible, and so varied, producing so much that we want, and wanting so much that we produce, would be at least equal to the whole trade of our different provinces with one another. That it is not so, is to be attributed to war and mischievous legislation; or, in other words, to crime and to folly.

On the whole, the classicists contrasted regional with international trade, emphasizing the high mobility of factors in regional trade with the

[1] N. Senior, *The Cost of Obtaining Money*, 1830, pp. 30–32.

immobility in international trade. It is surprising that more attention
has not been given to regional trade. In the late eighteenth and nineteenth centuries, when the modern theory of international trade was
developing, the state of communication and transportation was such that
the *assumed* mobility of factors within a country was much greater
than the *actual* mobility. Mill pointed out that "if the north bank of the
Thames possessed an advantage over the south bank of the Thames in
the production of shoes, no shoes would be produced on the south
side; the shoemakers would remove themselves and their capitals to the
north bank. . . . " It should be said to Mill's credit, however, that he
concluded: " . . . *between distant places,* and especially between different countries [my italics], profits may continue different; because
persons do not usually remove themselves or their capitals to a distant
place without a very strong motive."[2] (He apparently was aware of immobilities within a country.)

James Mill, the father of J. S. Mill, was aware that there might be
substantial differences in prices within Great Britain: " . . . yet there
are places in Great Britain where a family can live at one half of the
expense at which it can live in some other places, the difference being
constituted entirely by the expense of carriage. . . . "[3]

A rise in circulation in London, not matched by a corresponding rise
in the country, Ricardo insisted, would result in higher prices in London,
purchases of commodities in the country, and eventually a return to the
former price relationship.[4]

But despite an occasional comment, regional economics was rather
neglected by the classicists.

No neoclassicist other than Ohlin attempted to deal with the problems
of interregional trade in the ample manner in which international trade
is discussed. Courses in international trade are to be found everywhere,
in regional trade almost nowhere. The explanation of this neglect may
be in part that in Great Britain, the source of modern theories of international trade, foreign trade is of great importance. But in many
countries (e.g., United States, U.S.S.R., China), it is interregional trade
that is of special importance. In this country regional trade is many
times as important as international trade. Indeed, in the last generation
with increased obstacles to international movements of factors and
greater ease of movement within countries, the facts of life conform
more to classical assumptions than they did during most of the period
during which classical theory was being formulated and extended. Yet
even in 1955, capital moved much more easily from New York to

---

[2] J. S. Mill, *Principles of Political Economy* (Ashley, ed.), 1920, p. 575.
[3] *Ricardo,* vol. VI, p. 57.
[4] *Ibid.,* pp. 11–13.

Montreal than from New York to Jackson, Mississippi, and income levels
in Ottawa are more nearly equal those of New York than are incomes in
Mississippi.

Location of Employments

In interregional as in international relations it is important to consider what determines the location of industry. According to a British
study the five primary considerations are (1) raw materials, (2) suitable
labor, (3) site and services, (4) access to market, and (5) finance.[5] In
some respects the problem is simple; thus employment in agriculture and
mining is determined by the location of the relevant resources. Again,
selling and many other services have to be near the purchaser. It is
especially in manufacturing that a careful appraisal is required. In his
excellent book, Dr. E. M. Hoover has written as follows:[6]

The profit-seeking individual enterprise responds to transfer costs by seeking to reduce them. Procurement costs can be lessened by moving to a point
with better access to materials, or distribution costs can be lessened by moving to a point with better access to markets. These two considerations are
quite likely to lead in different directions, so that the producer must strike a
balance of relative advantages in order to decide where best to locate along
the route connecting his materials source with his market.

Where processes result in a considerable loss of weight through
combustion or waste of part of the materials, as in the smelting of ores,
the tendency is to locate near the source of the raw material. Where
these raw materials are widely scattered and difficult to move, the industrial localization is widely scattered (bricks, cement products).
Where procurement costs are greater per ton-mile than distribution
costs, as in cotton ginning, the tendency is to locate near the raw materials. Again, when the product may spoil or the market varies according to location, production will be near markets, e.g., bread or news-
papers.

It should be noted, however, that there are some additional relevant
considerations. For example, peculiar institutional factors might influence
the location of early processing. Thus under the pressure of dollar
shortage the British after World War II encouraged the refining of oil
in the British Isles far away from the source of materials. Again through
manipulation of exchange rates the Uruguayan government made it
possible to process wool in the early stages at home and thus cut into
the business of the American woolen industry. Sellers of the processed
wool received an export bonus in exchanging dollars for local currency.

[5] Political and Economic Planning, *Report on the Location of Industry in Great
Britain,* 1939, p. 7.
[6] E. M. Hoover, *The Location of Economic Activity,* 1948, p. 29.

Perhaps more important in modern manufacturing, the tendency increasingly is to process more and more. For example, from 1939 to 1947 the increase of employment in apparels was five times as great as in textiles. What is more, in this country the manufacturing industry depends for four-fifths of its materials on other industries which have participated in the operation of processing. This fact perhaps explains in no small part the heavy concentration of manufacturing in the Northeast United States, far away from sources of raw materials. "In the Manufacturing Belt of the Northeastern United States, which occupies only a twelfth of the country, is concentrated half the entire national market, seventy per cent of the industrial labor force, and the sources of supplies of most materials and parts directly used in manufacturing."[7] The rise of manufacturing is related to the accessibility to markets, and industrial growth, in turn, increases the importance of nearby markets. When very large units are required to produce efficiently, concentration may also be required.

Dean Harris observes that the tying of industry to that of raw materials is on the wane and that a large part of manufacturing industry is not tied to local raw materials, local markets, or local differences in labor costs. Typical of these industries is the automobile industry, which is concentrated in areas having maximum accessibility to national or regional markets. Harris also observes that half the retail sales occur in a small belt in the Northeast extending from Boston to St. Louis. Again, the Eastern seaboard states from Massachusetts to Pennsylvania have a density of markets five to ten times the national average, whereas the Mountain states and the Dakotas have a density from a twentieth to a fourth of the national average. The New York metropolitan area has a market larger than all the Southern states on the Atlantic south of the Potomac, and in large part because of proximity to markets, 30 per cent of manufacturing employment in the country is to be found within 200 miles of New York City. The Middle Western part of the manufacturing belt has special advantages of access to the national markets and fair access to the South and West. Within the major manufacturing belt the New England industries, with transportation costs 10 to 20 per cent above those of the Central part, suffer a disadvantage in relation to those industries where transportation costs to market are an important factor. It is interesting that textiles in the South do not seem to have a transportation advantage over the New England industry.[8]

Harris's emphasis is clearly on the proximity to markets, and this is a very important factor. With the tremendous gains in transportation

---

[7] See the able analysis in Chauncey D. Harris, "The Market as a Factor in the Localization of Industry in the United States," *Annals of the Association of American Geographers*, 1954, especially p. 354.

[8] C. D. Harris, *op. cit.*, pp. 316–347.

over the last seventy-five or one hundred years, it should, of course, be of less importance than in the past. We note parenthetically that transportation developments have had the important effects in recent years of moving market and industry outside the large cities. Thus, as the automobile makes it possible for people to live in the country or the suburbs and yet be accessible to the city, there follow important savings in land values and in the cost of services, also in the availability of labor and improved living conditions.

Here we raise a number of locational factors that are rather neglected by Dean Harris, namely, the institutional factors. Included, for example, are such factors as taxation, community attitudes, the relation of capital and labor, government subsidies, financing, and the like. These considerations play a significant part in the movement of industry and the relative regional growth of industry. In France, for example, it has been held that there are strong institutional factors which tend to encourage the concentration of industry in the Paris area.[9]

Regional Income

In recent years there has been much discussion of the problem of what determines the income of a region. Much depends, of course, on how a region is defined. Obviously, the smaller a region, the greater the importance of its export base. The growth of a mill town like Lewiston, Maine, will depend very largely on its export base, but a region as large as the South will develop in substantial part because of the development of local or, as some regionalists call it, "residentiary" activities. Here the supply of factors and the effectiveness of their use, inclusive of transport costs, would be relevant, and the export base of the South would be influenced by the magnitude of its income (and imports), in turn related to the development of residentiary activities. Whether Lewiston, Maine, or the North American continent is considered a region —and there is little agreement among regionists as to what a region is, though in this book I assume that a region is part of the United States as given by the Census Bureau—will be relevant in the assessment of the importance of the export base.

In discussions by planners there seems to have been excessive emphasis on exports as a determinant of income. This can be understood in part because these planners frequently concentrate on the development of a city where the export base is of primary importance; yet it will be recalled that some of the classicists stressed the export base as

[9] On these issues see Hoover, *op. cit.*, especially chap. 15; United States National Resources Planning Board, *Industrial Location and National Resources*, 1943; Economic Commission for Europe, *Economic Survey of Europe in 1954*, pp. 179–180; S. E. Harris, *The Economics of New England*, 1952, especially chap. 19; and later in this chapter.

determining monetary supplies, prices, and economic well-being. The prosperous country was held not to be greatly dependent on foreign supplies and produced goods greatly in demand abroad and hence attracted a large part of the world's supply of precious metals.

In modern income analysis, exports, government deficits, and investment are the determinants of income. But even here assumptions are made concerning factor supply and the like. A country with a large export base may develop into a great economic area but not necessarily. It is interesting on this score to compare Great Britain and the United States; the latter has a much smaller export base. The growth of domestic investment and of governmental activity ("residentiary" factors) has played a much larger part in the growth of the United States than the export base. Obviously, however, the export base must be large enough to pay for the imports which are indispensable for the growth of the economy. Otherwise growth will be stunted—consider the British problem of the mid-1950s. But growth will be stunted even with a large export base when there is a dearth of labor and of natural resources and low productivity, and these deficiencies will react on the export base. And unwise monetary and fiscal policy, through effects on investment, may neutralize the contribution of large exports.[10]

Regional Interrelations

In recent years much more attention has been given to regional problems. In the application of the input-output analysis to interregional economics, Professors Leontief and Isard have been especially helpful in extending regional economics.[11] In this analysis they distinguish industries which are national in their scope, that is, those in which production and consumption are balanced on a national scale; industries which are regional, that is, consumption and production are balanced on a regional (and national) scale; and even subregional industries. For example, automobiles, with production substantially concentrated in one state and consumption widely distributed, are an excellent example of a national industry. Again, construction and eating and drinking places are considered regional or, better, subregional industries, with the balancing on a subregional basis. For an analysis of this problem Isard presents the sums for each industry without regard of sign of surpluses and deficits expressed as a percentage of national consumption by industries in each state. He finds that agricultural machinery, motor vehicles, and

[10] See especially Hildebrand and Mace, "The Employment Multiplier in an Expanding Industrial Market," *Review of Economics and Statistics*, August, 1950, and the reply of C. M. Tiebout and D. C. North, "Exports and Regional Economic Growth," *The Journal of Political Economy*, April, 1956.

[11] W. Leontief et al., *Studies in the Structure of the American Economy*, 1953, chaps. 4 and 5.

aircraft are the most heavily concentrated industries in the above sense, with total deviations of consumption (i.e., percentage less or more than production in each state) of 136, 122, and 122 per cent, respectively, and construction, households, and trade the most widely diffused and, hence, subregional industries with respective percentages of 4, 7, and 9.[12]

Disaggregation leads to regional breakdowns, and a theoretical formulation describes[13]

. . . the location of all the various branches of economic activity in its relation to their internal structure, on the one hand, and the balance requirements of the system as a whole, on the other. The regional balances of trade are accordingly explained in terms of the interregional distribution of industries and households. Applied to the actual regional distribution of all industries in the year 1939, this approach yields a detailed and consistent estimate of the regional balances of trade for the 48 separate states—an estimate which might be of some interest to the student of industrial location quite independent of its use in this particular investigation.

In short, we obtain, first, the geographic distribution of output of all nationally traded goods. From this we then derive the demand for the regionally balanced type of goods and from the latter the regional distribution of their total inputs. With the regional distribution of outputs obtained, then consumption figures are to be had from the input-output statistics for individual industries. A comparison of the output and consumption figures will yield the balance of exports and imports —for *regionally* balanced goods, there will be no balance. Obviously, allowance will have to be made also for input of government and diversion of output to foreign trade, government, and capital.[14]

Isard also estimates the effects of a 10 per cent rise in final demand for the output of each national industry upon the output of households and each industry of major regions and subregions. Under simplified assumptions and with substantial reservations concerning the estimates obtained, he also finds that a 10 per cent increase in final demand of agriculture and fishing would yield a rise in the national product of $74 million; the corresponding figure for automobiles is $100 million and for textile mill products, $15 million.

In these studies attention is paid then to the input and output of a region. Thus what is the relation of the various industries of a region or state and of all the regional employments to their external relations? What does the state of Utah buy from outside the state to produce its gross output? Or New England? What is the effect of reduction of demand for copper upon the income and employment of Utah? How

[12] *Ibid.*, p. 144.
[13] *Ibid.*, p. 15.
[14] *Ibid.*, p. 94.

much do the mineral and metal industries contribute toward total income and how much toward the total exports of Utah and similarly for textiles for New England? Again, how much does the Federal government pour into a state or region. And how much of the net flow is used to purchase within the region studied and how much outside? The net effect of a reduction of demand is likely to be a multiple of the original decline, but the multiplier is likely to be much less than for a country because dependence of the region and *a fortiori* for the state upon outside goods and services is much greater relatively than for the nation.[15]

In recent years one of the most interesting experiments has been TVA. The rise of income in the generation since 1933 in the TVA area has been surprisingly large, and many have held that the greater gains of income in that region are to be explained by the TVA policy. But as one writer has argued, the effects of this policy are not easily isolated from other policies and even events. Thus the whole South gained in these years from the industrialization, and much of the South gained little or nothing from the TVA. The higher prices for agricultural products; the fortunate combination of good water, water transportation, and power which stimulated the growth of the chemical industry only in part to be associated with the TVA; the technological revolution in agriculture which made much cheap labor available for industry—these and many other factors are relevant in explaining the high incomes in the South generally and in the TVA area in particular.[16]

For many years the State Department has tried to study the stake of regions in foreign trade, the motive being to show how much each region gains from international trade. These studies never seemed very helpful. However, recently a more successful attempt has been made to study this problem.[17] In this study the writer allocates export and import-competing trade by regions. The assumption is made that each region shares in the export trade as it shares in the value added for each industry in each region. Of course, this means that in so far as export-supporting industries account for the exports, then the final export industry receives excessive allowance for its contribution to the export industry. For example, the Connecticut spark plug is part of the automobile exported and credited to Michigan *in toto*. Hence if these

---

[15] See especially Leontief and Isard in Leontief, *op. cit.*, chaps. 4 and 5, and F. T. Moore and J. W. Peterson, "Regional Analysis: An Interindustry Model of Utah," *Review of Economics and Statistics*, August, 1955, and references given there.

[16] Cf. the discussion on regional economics by J. V. Krutilla and F. T. Moore in the *Proceedings of the American Economic Association*, 1955, pp. 120–155.

[17] P. J. Bourque, "The Domestic Importance of Foreign Trade of the United States, by Producing Regions, Manufacturing Sector, 1947," *Review of Economics and Statistics*, 1954, pp. 401–408.

exports are allocated entirely to the Central states, the New England contribution is underestimated. But there may be offsetting factors. Thus the export of textiles from New England may include the contribution of a machine manufactured in the Central states. Another factor not allowed for is cost of transportation. Thus the inclusion of transport costs would result in larger exports for regions near the ports of shipment.

With these reservations, what are the results? The Northeast exports less relative to value added than the South and West, and the latter seem to have much more to worry about when comparison is made of the competing imports and exports of the two sections. Import-competing goods are a much larger share of the nation's for the South and West than are their exports. The writer explains the disproportionate share of import-competing products on the ground that the products of the South and West are labor-intensive and hence highly competitive with foreign products, which are also labor-intensive.

Table 14-1. Shares of Competing Imports, Exports, and Value Added, Manufacturing Industries, by Area,† 1947
(In percentages)

Area	Estimated competing imports	Estimated exports	Value added
Northeast............	40.5	69.0	74.5
South and West........	59.5	31.0	25.5
U.S. total...........	100.0	100.0	100.0

† *Northeast* includes New England, Middle Atlantic, East North Central, and West North Central states; *South* includes South Atlantic, East South Central, and West South Central states; *West* includes Mountain and Pacific regions.

Finally, the increased concern with regional economics is suggested by a pioneering study by the Economic Commission for Europe.[18] In this study the authors note that there are vast differences of income within the various European countries, though the variations are greater within the poor than within the rich countries. For example, in the United Kingdom and Switzerland only a few per cent of the population is in regions with incomes less than two-thirds the average for the nation; in Italy, Turkey, and Spain, one-third. Underemployment and low productivity are the major explanation of low per capita incomes. In the periphery of Europe, incomes are low because of poor climate and disadvantages of transportation, both facets of low productivity. Development programs are not so helpful as they might be because, in the desire for quick returns, the tendency is to concentrate on the relatively well-to-do

[18] *Economic Survey of Europe in 1954*, pp. 136–171.

regions. This is aside from political obstacles which result from over-capacity in the developed regions or merely the exercise of much political influence by the wealthy regions. As some regions gain, others (notably in France) suffer from depopulation, and hence the greater need for government intervention. Thus in the Massif Central the population in 1950 was 65 (1851 = 100) but in the northeast and Paris region, 173.[19]

When economic development is not possible because of lack of capital or of government revenues or opposition from developed areas, another approach is special subsidies (e.g., in the form of agricultural support and financial transfers to the poor regions). This approach would not be so helpful as the provision of productive employment for the many unproductively employed in agriculture and service (tertiary) industries. Tertiary workers may be numerous in poor regions because there are no other opportunities, and large recourse to tertiary employment is not necessarily a sign of opulence, as C. Clark claims.

Frequently it does little good to pour capital into the poor regions which are impoverished not only in social capital but also in unutilized natural resources, for once new investments stop, income would fall back to the earlier level. Hence as the rest of the country profits from the expansion of the growing and dynamic industries, the result would be penetration of markets of the poor regions and serious balance-of-payments problems for these regions, nurtured only by part of the local market and limited exports of food and raw materials. Their survival would depend upon their sharing some of the growth in the dynamic industries.[20]

That more attention is being given to regional differences of capital and income is of great significance. The obstacles are many, but there is a growing realization that adequate policies at home directed toward raising the income of the submerged third or tenth, concentrated largely in impoverished regions, would emphasize national rather than international leadership and the national gains to be had by an attack on the economic position of the poor regions.

Regional Balance-of-payments Problems

Like countries, regions are confronted with balance-of-payments problems. Each region purchases from and sells to other regions and foreign countries. In addition, capital moves and the government transfers funds from one region to another. These transactions are consummated through checks drawn on commercial banks and in turn via the Reserve banks acting on behalf of the banks in their district, and the final credits and debits are transferred for the twelve Reserve banks at the Gold Settle-

---

[19] *Ibid.*, pp. 138–143.
[20] *Ibid.*, p. 158.

ment Fund in Washington. An increase in the price of meat ultimately *ceteris paribus* involves losses of deposits of, say, Northeastern banks (Middle Atlantic and New England) and losses of reserves of banks in these regions. (The banks pay the bills of their customers by drawing on their reserves.) Banks, of course, are compensated through a reduction of deposit liabilities, and there also follows a reduction of deposits and cash of the New York and Boston Reserve banks and gains by the Chicago, Omaha, etc., banks and the Chicago and Kansas City Reserve banks. The latter gain in the Gold Settlement Fund, and the former lose. That is, the Boston Reserve Bank pays for the National Shawmut Bank, say, and receives compensation through a reduction of its debt to the National Shawmut Bank.

To cite a few episodes: In the early years of the Great Depression, the prices of agricultural commodities and income of agricultural states tumbled and much more than did prices in the industrial states. Banks in these agricultural regions then lost deposits, reflecting an adverse balance of payments. With similar developments in agricultural countries, recourse is had to exchange depreciation and/or limitations on payments abroad. But within the United States there is little scope for a depreciation of the Kansas dollar against the Vermont dollar, and there is no mechanism for restricting payments short of a shutdown of banks. cash into the Chicago Reserve Bank district, or at least the latter might move into the regions short of capital. This is not, however, the major corrective. First, within a central banking system, the Reserve banks may redistribute their holdings of assets in such a manner as to help the capital-short regions. That is, the New York Reserve Bank might buy government securities held by the Chicago Reserve Bank and thus pump cash into the Chicago Reserve Bank district, or at least the latter might refrain from purchasing securities as current investments mature. Another important support is had by the United States Treasury shifting its deposits (commercial or Reserve bank) into the capital- or money-starved areas. The Treasury not only may transfer available supplies of cash but, through recourse to taxes or new borrowing, may transfer cash from relatively strong to relatively weak regions. That is, more funds may be collected in the East than are disbursed there. In this manner, a collapse may be averted or at least postponed. But there are limits of accomplishments here. With the underlying demand and price structure fundamentally unsound, the banks in the agricultural regions had to suspend payments in 1932–1933, a move that may be considered as equivalent to a 100 per cent depreciation of the, say, Illinois dollar. As the weakened states and regions withdraw their cash from correspondent banks in the financial centers, the search for liquidity results in a widespread suspension of payments.

The characteristics of regional payments are the close ties of regions, the unavailability of depreciation, restrictions on payments and other therapeutic measures available to countries, and the transfer of funds through Treasury and central-bank operations. (To some extent national corporations and commercial banks participate in these transfers.) The outcome is either continuance of free movements and a nondepreciated dollar or a complete cessation of payments and a disguised depreciation.[21]

In 1933 (see chap. 33 of my *Twenty Years of Federal Reserve Policy*) I discussed at length the Gold Settlement Fund and its significance for an understanding of the regional balance of payments. In 1956, twenty-three years later, three economists of the Federal Reserve (Bowsher, Einzig, and Doane, in a fruitful study, *Report on Interregional Flow of Funds and District Member Reserves*) suggested the need for a careful study of what is now called the Interdistrict Settlement Fund. In some interesting tables they show the clearings among districts for 1953, U.S. Treasury transactions (sources and uses of funds by districts), factors (e.g., currency movements, Treasury transactions, open-market operations, commercial and financial transactions) affecting member bank reserves by districts, sources and uses of Treasury deposits at Federal Reserve, and commercial and financial transactions by districts.

Obviously a study of these settlement funds will throw much light on the interregional balance of payments. Of course, these should be used with other approaches (e.g., trends in deposits, price and income movements, regional balance of payments, and input-output studies). Moreover, as I have suggested in my study of the New England balance for the Senate Banking and Currency Committee (*Flood Hearings,* November 9, 1955), the allocation of burdens of taxes and benefits of expenditures should be studied (they are examined in my study and also by Selma Mushkin in a study for the Public Health Service). The Federal Reserve would get along better if it could separate commodity from commodity and financial transactions.

Some other aspects of regional economics are brought out by an examination of some developments in the post-World War II period. Briefly, the South has moved ahead rapidly, in part at the expense of the North. The Northeast in particular has felt the impact of higher prices of food and raw materials and increased competition in markets of manufactured goods. As we shall see, government policies and the inflexibility of wages tended to aggravate the adjustment policies, and the newer industrial regions find it easier to raise man-hour output and adapt their plant and equipment to current market needs than do the older

[21] The author has discussed some of these issues more fully in his *Twenty Years of Federal Reserve Policy,* 1933, especially vol. II.

industrial regions. Capital and management move, but labor is relatively immobile.[22]

It might be expected that in view of these developments, the older regions would experience serious balance-of-payments problems. In a sense they have. This is evident in their gains of deposits being much smaller than in the country generally, in the tendency of their prices and wages to fall vis-à-vis the national level (and this despite the rigidities enforced by their greater degree of unionization), and in the losses of industries (reflecting reduced demand) to other regions. It is not surprising that though a generation ago New England was one of the highest wage areas, in the early fifties wages there were below the national level in almost every census industry. That the Northeast, despite outward drains through the Treasury, has not experienced the kind of crisis suffered by agricultural regions in their balance of payments in the thirties may be explained largely by the favorable balance of payments for the nation (with the Northeast profiting proportionately), by the reduced relative need for cash in view of the relative losses suffered by the Northeast, and at times by sales of capital assets by this region to other regions.[23]

Federal Transfers and the Balance of Payments

In international economic relations, the United States government has frequently intervened to balance the dollar account. Within this country, the transfers of cash from one region to another through tax, loan, and spending policies have at times tended to equilibrate interregional accounts, but often the transfers aggravate the balance-of-payments problems of some regions.

Money tends to flow into Southern states for various reasons, inclusive of Treasury transactions, and the inflow continues in part because (as noted) wages do not respond to increased supplies of money.[24] As the competitive position of Southern states has improved, as under govern-

[22] Cf. *Handbook of Regional Statistics, Materials Assembled for the Subcommittee on Unemployment of the Joint Committee on the Economic Report,* 1950, and U.S. Department of Commerce, *Economic Development Atlas,* 1950. Cf. statement by S. E. Harris before the U.S. Tariff Commission on behalf of the New England governors, *Tariffs and the New England Economy,* Dec. 14, 1954.

[23] For fuller discussion of these issues, see S. E. Harris, *The Economics of New England,* 1951, pt. II; his contributions to *The New England Economy, A Report to the President,* 1951, especially pt. III; and *The Report on the New England Textile Committee Appointed by the Conference of New England Governors, 1952,* especially the Research Report by S. E. Harris. Also see statement by S. E. Harris before the Senate Committee on Banking and Currency, *Hearings on Federal Disaster Insurance,* 1955, pp. 450–501, and *New England Textiles and the New England Economy, Report to New England Governors,* 1956, chap. 12 (by S. E. Harris).

[24] The author has discussed this problem fully before the Joint Committee on the Economic Report, February, 1955, and the Senate Labor and Welfare Committee on May 11, 1955.

ment guidance prices of agricultural products rose, as in response to more favorable economic conditions capital flowed in, and as the Federal government poured money into these states, the supply of money in the Southern states rose disproportionately. This inflow, evident in the deposits of member banks in the Reserve banks (the basis of monetary creation), helped sustain the rise of output but also increased pressure to raise prices and wages.

Table 14-2 suggests that the gains for the South were disproportionate, especially in the years 1941 to 1955. From 1914 to 1929, the South

Table 14-2. Member Bank Deposits at Reserve Banks, 1915, 1929, 1941, and February, 1955

(In millions of dollars)

Reserve District	1915	1929	1941	February, 1955
All................	401	2,355	12,450	18,562
Boston.............	28	142	569	743
New York..........	179	986	5,639	5,412
Richmond..........	11	65	452	768
Atlanta............	9	63	322	906
Dallas.............	10	64	307	1,027

SOURCE: Federal Reserve Board, *Banking and Monetary Statistics*, 1954, p. 339, and *Federal Reserve Bulletin*, March, 1955.

roughly maintained its relative position. But from 1929 to 1941, the rise for the three Southern Reserve Bank districts was 463 per cent as compared with 429 per cent for the nation and 300 per cent for New England (Boston). The Richmond Bank (the northern South) especially gained in this period. From 1941 to 1955, the respective gains for the nation, the South, and New England were 49, 150, and 31 per cent. In other words, the South's gains of cash reserves in these fourteen years were about three times as large as for the nation and almost five times as great as for Boston (New England). The gains in these later years were especially large for the Atlanta and Dallas districts.

That there were not greater degrees of wage inflation which might have slowed up the excessive migrations of industry may be explained by the inadequacies of minimum wages, the anti-trade-union policies of the South, and the effects of the new labor legislation.

That Federal tax and spending policies have contributed to the rise of monetary supplies in the South is evident from the following.

In 1951, the amount of Federal taxes paid (by "paid" I mean allowing for the incidence of taxes, that is, where the burden falls) in relation to income payments was as follows:

New England (Massachusetts, Rhode Island, Connecticut)...... 1.21
New York.. 1.24
Illinois and Michigan.. 1.04
Five Southern states (North Carolina, South Carolina, Alabama,
    Georgia, Tennessee)....................................... 0.74

Hence the proportions of payments relative to income were as follows:[25]

New England to South...................... 1.64
New York to South......................... 1.68
Illinois and Michigan to South............... 1.41

Of course, the net transfers are much greater than suggested by these
figures because the Northern states with much larger incomes pay more
relatively. The above figures merely indicate how much more they pay
in relation to their incomes.

For a comparison of all New England states, the Middle East, and the
Southeast, we find that the Federal tax incidence (allowing for incidence
of business taxes) as a percentage of adjusted income payments was as
follows (United States = 100):[26]

New England......................... 113
Middle East.......................... 111
Southeast............................ 83
New England to Southeast.............. 136
Middle East to Southeast.............. 134

In the years 1934 to 1951, the three large New England states received
$2,529 million from Federal disbursements and five major Southern
states (Alabama, Georgia, North Carolina, South Carolina, and Tennes-
see) received $5,841 million from the Federal government. Thus the
Southern states received two to three times as much as the three New
England states which account for about 85 per cent of the income of
the area. But it should be noted that the three New England states paid
in Federal taxes (allowing for passing on of taxes) $3,276 million and
the five Southern states paid in only $2,534 million.[27] If we apply the
percentage of Federal taxes paid by each group of states in 1951 (6.75
and 5.23) to the total Federal tax receipts in 1934 to 1951, then we obtain the following figures:

Taxes paid by three New England states.......... $31.9 billion
Taxes paid by five Southern states............... $24.7 billion

[25] Calculated from Mushkin and Crowther, *Federal Taxes and the Measurement
of State Capacity,* U.S. Department of Health, Education, and Welfare, Public
Health Service, May, 1954, p. 13.
[26] *Ibid.,* p. 30.
[27] Calculated from Committee on Nonessential Expenditures of the Federal Government, *Federal Grants-in-Aid, 1934–1951,* pp. 60–61, and Mushkin and Crowther,
op. cit., p. 13.

Whereas the three large New England states paid 29 per cent more into the Federal coffers, they received back only 44 per cent as much. In other words, on a pay vs. obtain basis the New England states vis-à-vis the South received only 34 per cent as much back for every dollar paid into the Federal treasury: $34 = {}^{44}/_{129}$.[28]

A Regional Balance of Payments

It is difficult to estimate the balance of payments of a region, in part because of the problems involved in measuring exports and imports. Below we give a balance for New England for the years 1929 to 1939, and this study, one of the best, is subject to many reservations. It suggests that New England imported much more than it exported of commodities and also of gold and paid for these deficits and transfers on Treasury account in a net export of services and imports of capital.[29]

Regional Problems of Adjustment

Above we have discussed briefly various problems that may be subsumed under regional economics: the location of economic activity, the effects of a development program (TVA), the input-output problem related to a state or region, the attack on impoverished regions in Europe, and regional problems of balance of payments. Here we turn to the

---

[28] The author applies the percentage of tax payments of 1951 to the 1934 to 1951 tax receipts on the assumption that tax structure and incidence do not vary greatly in 1934 to 1951 as compared with 1951. In fact, the application of this method suggests larger tax payments by the South for 1934 to 1951 than actually were made, since her taxes rose relatively in the later years. That the assumption of similar incidence and payments for 1934 to 1951 as for 1951 is justified is suggested by the following:

Per Cent of Federal Tax Receipts, 1934, 1940, 1951, 1934, to 1951

Year	Personal income	Corporation taxes	Indirect business	Social Security
1934	17	18	65	0
1940	16	31	31	22
1951	41	33	15	11
1934–1951	38	30	19	13

SOURCE: Calculated from *National Income*, 1954 ed.

Total Federal receipts............ $482 billion
Personal income................. 185
Corporation taxes............... 143
Indirect business................   93
Social Security..................   61

[29] P. Hartland, *Balance of Interregional Payments of New England*, 1950, p. 6.

Table 14-3. Balance of Interregional Payments of New England†
(In millions of dollars)

	1929	1931	1933	1935	1937	1939
Current account:						
Commodity trade...............	−1,032.1	−909.9	−871.3	−1,121.1	−1,329.8	−1,122.2
Freight and shipping............	−217.1	−164.8	−130.2	−141.9	−166.8	−184.4
Total balance of trade.........	−1,249.2	−1,074.7	−1,001.5	−1,263.0	−1,496.6	−1,306.6
Recreation.....................	+136.2	+52.4	−11.0	+60.7	+135.7	+95.8
Passenger transportation.........	−4.8	−3.5	−2.0	−1.6	−2.3	−2.5
Total travel account..........	+131.4	+48.9	−13.0	+59.1	+133.4	+93.3
Insurance.....................	+196.1	+160.8	+75.4	+260.1	+310.0	+297.1
Education.....................	+13.6	+11.8	+10.4	+9.9	+10.5	+9.9
Interest, dividends, net rents, and royalties.....................	+239.0	+609.0	+482.0	+493.0	+555.0	+502.0
Current account excluding balance of trade.....................	+580.1	+830.5	+554.8	+822.1	+1,008.9	+902.3
Net current account............	−669.1	−244.2	−446.7	−440.9	−487.7	−404.3
Gold and currency:						
Federal Reserve notes...........	+14.0	+13.9	+16.4	+11.5	+14.1	+12.0
Gold inflow due to commercial and financial transactions........	−95.2	−145.7	−182.6	−193.0	−177.9	−292.6
Gross gold movement.........	−81.2	−131.8	−166.2	−181.5	−163.8	−280.6
Gold outflow due to government account.....................	+49.7	+129.2	+171.3	+85.5	+214.0	+80.0
Net gold movement............	−31.5	−2.6	+5.1	−96.0	+50.2	−200.6
Capital account and residual:						
Interbank deposits..............	+18.1	−46.2	−14.2	−36.1	−2.1	−15.0
Federal Reserve foreign account..	−0.1	+4.7	−1.3	+0.7	+5.3	+14.9
Treasury transfers..............	−49.7	−129.2	−171.3	−85.5	−214.0	−80.0
Gross capital movement and residual.....................	+732.3	+417.5	+628.4	+657.8	+648.3	+685.0
Net capital account and residual..	+700.6	+246.8	+441.6	+536.9	+437.5	+604.9

† A plus sign indicates a net export; a minus sign a net import. To avoid confusion, it should be stressed that a plus or minus sign indicates the direction of the flow of *funds* resulting from any given transaction. Thus, a plus sign indicates that funds are moving into New England (as a result of transactions in insurance, for example, or as a result of capital movements); a minus sign, that funds are moving out of the region (for imports of commodities, in general also to pay for imports of gold). Thus, an "import" of capital (borrowing, say, to a greater extent than lending) has a plus sign, since it results in funds moving into the region as a result of capital transactions. Similarly, a capital "export" would imply an excess of lending, causing an outward movement of funds; hence, it would be indicated by a minus sign.

peculiar problems confronting an older industrial region when faced with the intense competition of newer industrial regions.

Above, we observed that there are regional balance-of-payments problems, and analyzed methods of easing the adjustments and settling accounts. New England, for example (I shall frequently refer to New England, since I have intensively studied this region), produces only 3 per cent of its income from agriculture (10 per cent for the nation) and hence has to import its major foods and raw materials, paying for them primarily through exports of manufactures and secondarily through exports of services. The region also pays for its agricultural and mining products through receipts on income from past investments abroad or in other regions. A great manufacturing region tends to export most of its manufacturing product—obviously if it accounts for 6 per cent of the national consumption, and if its total manufacture of textiles is 25 per cent of the nation's, it will export some textiles and import others, yet its net exports will be several times its consumption.

A region, like a nation, is concerned with the problem of paying its bills. If the prices of its imports rise vis-à-vis those of its exports, the balancing of accounts may cause difficulties. For example, because of both natural forces and also the intervention of government (raising agricultural prices and through its tariff policy depressing relatively prices of industrial products), the terms of trade of industrial regions have tended to deteriorate relative to agricultural regions in the years 1933 to 1955. Hence the balance of payments of the industrial regions has become precarious; this has been especially true of certain old industrial regions whose competitive position has been weakened by the pressure from newer industrial regions.

Industrial nations face similar problems, e.g., Great Britain since World War I; but there are special issues raised for the regional economies. A nation confronted with an adverse balance of payments would be under great pressure to reduce costs, though British experience in the interwar period showed that sheltered domestic industries, under no such pressure to reduce costs, tend to accentuate the difficulties of the nonsheltered (international) industries. If 75 per cent of the employments in sheltered industries maintain wages, then it becomes more difficult to cut wages (or labor costs) in the 25 per cent nonsheltered employments.

A region may well experience even greater difficulties than a nation. A large part of labor in manufacturing is organized on a national basis, and therefore wages are set on a national wage level; this is true of the steel and automobile industries, for example. Hence, should the Middle West lose ground in iron and steel to the South, it cannot easily recoup its loss by cutting wages. Even when trade unions are of unequal strength in different regions or do not set wages on a national basis, adjustments may be greatly impeded. For example, according to one estimate, the percentage of workers unionized in eleven Southern states was 25 per cent of the national level in apparel and 43 per cent in textiles.[30] Hence, wage rates are likely to be lower in the South in these industries. Here is a peculiar situation. Wages generally are higher in the North than in the South. Hence it is very difficult for trade-union leaders in the North to

[30] F. T. DeVyver, "Labor Factors in Industrial Development of the South," *Southern Economic Journal*, October, 1951, p. 194.

accept cuts in wages in industries suffering losses in the North, for the wage level is set to some extent by the high-wage industries. If the unions do not agree to wage levels (and labor costs) commensurate with those in the South, however, unemployment in these industries rises.

Here we may all agree that the adjustment to an unfavorable balance of payments, whether the occasion is a deterioration in the terms of trade or loss of competitive position, is beset with difficulties. Nevertheless, there is evidence of adjustments. For example, whereas textile wages were about 50 per cent higher in New England than in the South early in the century, fifty years later they were around 10 per cent higher. These adjustments result from the pressure of unemployment in the regions losing cash as their competitive position suffers, and even the rigidities introduced by institutional factors yield to some extent. Other evidence of adjustment is to be found in net income payments. Thus, from 1929 to 1948, per capita income payments in New England rose by 79 per cent, in the seven most industrialized states outside New England by 99 per cent, and in the five most important industrialized states in the South by 197 per cent.[31]

Rigidities in wage rates, related to some extent to the policies of labor unions operating nationally, do, indeed, interfere with adjustments, but the problem of regions suffering competitive losses may also be aggravated by government policies. Thus the Federal government, through its agricultural policies, raises prices of raw materials and foods for the industrial regions, provides power and tax subsidies for the newly industrialized regions, and introduces social-security programs which put a greater burden on old than on new industrial regions. For all these reasons, the competitive position of the South as against the North improves. Ultimately, of course, the pressure of demand for labor and other factors should increase costs in the South and retard the influx of industries, but the large reservoir of labor being squeezed out of the farms by technological gains greatly slows up the upward pressure on costs. Compare the New England situation, where immigration as a source of labor is no longer available and where there is virtually no reservoir on the farm.

Not only Federal government but also state and local governments influence the competitive power of regions. In the fierce competition to hold or attract industries, state and local governments avoid new taxes and economize on school, health, and relief programs. Where incomes (notably wages) are lower and services less advanced, industry tends to move. The Southern authorities in particular tend to keep costs down. Not only do they keep costs down, but they provide tax systems that hit

[31] *The New England Economy: A Report to the President by the Committee on the New England Economy,* July, 1951, p. 31.

consumers rather than business, and they use taxes disproportionately to subsidize those industries which they seek to import.

Obviously with costs much lower in the South and with a relatively free flow of management and capital, the South tends to gain at the expense of the North. The lower wages in the South are not primarily the result of lower cost of living. Variations in the cost of living in the country seem to be about one-third as great as those in wage rates. In fact, when budgets applicable to each region are studied, it is found that the annual cost in a recent year for a family budget for ten Southern cities was only 1½ per cent less than for three New England cities. But the differences are larger when consideration is given to the fact that a new industrial area tends to establish itself in the smaller cities disproportionately—where costs are low. Thus in a recent year 30 per cent of the nation's population was in North Atlantic states and 28 per cent in Southern states, but the former accounted for 34 per cent of the 199 largest cities and the latter only 19, and similarly for other categories of large cities.[32]

The reader will find statistical material on regional variations in costs (inclusive of payroll taxes), all taxes, hydroelectric power, relative supplies of labor, etc., in the *Report on the New England Textile Industry*.[33]

In this discussion I have concentrated largely on North-South regional relations, but there are, of course, serious problems that arise in other contexts. For example, coal is a depressed industry in the United States because of the competition of oil. This competition, together with the high wage policies of a powerful trade union, rapid mechanization, and insufficient alternative opportunities, raises serious problems for the regions and states dependent on the coal industry. (Apparently the union protects the position of the miners even though a greater flexibility of wages might increase the number of jobs available to new entrants.)

The problem for a state like West Virginia, which is heavily dependent on its coal mines, is almost insoluble. Coal miners do not move easily; the resources of the state are limited. As the industry suffers reverses, unemployment grows and the state, short of revenues, is forced to reduce its services, inclusive of welfare programs. Its balance-of-payments problems become serious, for it suffers large losses in its major export industry. In one year in the forties, mining accounted for 28 per cent of all

[32] See *Handbook of Labor Statistics*, 1950, pp. 121–122, and *Bureau of Labor Statistics Serial 2*, 1909. Calculated from the *City Worker's Family and Budget*, 1948, p. 22.

[33] By the committee appointed by the conference of New England governors, 1952. Also see S. E. Harris, *Economics of New England*, 1952; *The New England Economy: A Report to the President by the Committee on the New England Economy*, 1951, and S. E. Harris, *New England Textiles and the New England Economy: Report to the Conference of New England Governors*, 1956.

employment in West Virginia and, in 1953, for 17.1 per cent of income (the average for the nation for this year was 1.4 per cent). From 1948 to 1954, nonagricultural employment in West Virginia declined by 70,000, or 13 per cent, and employment in bituminous coal in 1954 was roughly equal to that in the worst year of the depression. With great dependence on coal mining (inclusive of secondary effects, one-third to one-half of the economy is supported by coal), it is not surprising that the pressure is evident in a low per capita income in West Virginia (63 per cent of that for the Middle East in 1953) and the beginnings of substantial outward migration and population losses.[34]

Governmental activities, then, tend to influence the location of industry and in the United States, at least, to favor new industrial regions. In international relations, no government would allow a foreign nation to capture its markets at a rate, say, that the South has captured some of the Northern markets. Governments would interpose obstacles to trade. But in the United States not only have the Federal government and other governments not intervened but they have tended to accelerate the movement. (The welfare assumptions relevant here will be noted later.) There is one notable exception, however. By setting minimum wages (both on a general level and on an industry basis), the Federal government has tended to deprive the South to some extent of one of its most important competitive assets—plentiful supply of labor and low wages. But because of both the level at which minimum wages have been set and the administrative weakness, the effects of minimum wages have not been large.

South-North competition raises difficult problems. Without question, the South has important advantages and is bound to develop into a great industrial region. Proximity to rich raw materials and markets; a dedication on the part of labor, management, and the community to attract industry; the large supplies of labor—these are among the great advantages. With these great advantages, capital and management move easily into the South. The only question that can be raised is a noneconomic one. Should a region with these great advantages also be encouraged to depress standards of living, of government services, etc., below a level deemed desirable by the nation? In other words, on top of the great advantages of markets and of resources, should the South also through governmental measures be allowed to obtain additional advantages at the expense of Northern rivals, e.g., through an excess of Federal spending over receipts? The question may even be raised if Northern wages should be depressed relatively in response to wages set

[34] Figures from Joint Committee on Economic Report, *Handbook of Regional Statistics*, 1950, and *Survey of Current Business*, August, 1954; also see Hearings of the Joint Committee on the *Economic Report of the President, January, 1955*, 1955, pp. 263–265, 292–303.

by the large supplies of labor in the South, not held in check by strong trade unionism. The real issue comes down to the rate at which the South should be allowed to gain through governmental actions and depressions of standards, not whether she gains or not.

According to the theory of international trade, a country (or region) that loses ground in some industries then moves on to other industries. This will involve, of course, changes in occupations of workers and often of movement to other locations, investments in other industries, etc. All kinds of difficulties arise. Workers often do not want to write off skills acquired in an industry, and there is great reluctance on the part of management and investors to move into regions or localities which have suffered from economic dislocations. When there is much unemployment, the movement into new industries faces additional obstacles—as British experience in the interwar period showed. When economic conditions are improving and especially when overfull employment prevails, the adjustments are made more easily—as United States and British experience in the forties shows, though even in this period, part of the success stemmed from special measures taken by government and enterprise to implement the free-market forces. Even in the prosperous forties and fifties, many coal and textile towns have continued to experience large and long-continued spells of unemployment.

Outlets for the Displaced

That the problem of adjustment can be serious is suggested by the fact that the outlets for the unemployed (say in textiles, shoes, or apparel in the Northeast and in coal in Pennsylvania and West Virginia) are distinctly limited, though in a growing economy some of the slack may be taken up. This follows because most employments are necessarily restricted to given localities, and hence a region suffering from unemployment cannot easily capture employment from other regions.

I have discussed this problem more fully in another study from which several paragraphs are quoted below. The major conclusion to be drawn is that losses can be recouped only out of a limited area of economic activity.[35]

The major competition faced by American industry is interregional, not international. For example, exports out of the country are but 4–5 per cent of the gross national product. Obviously, most sales are at home. In fact, a large part of all sales are within the region or even city of production. This is perhaps even more true of services than of movable goods. A large part of our

[35] S. E. Harris, "Interregional Competition: With Particular Reference to North-South Competition," *Proceedings of the American Economic Association*, 1954, pp. 370–372.

services are almost exclusively free of interregional competition—medical, local and state government, public utilities, domestic service, local transport, public education, etc. Here competition outside the city or region is distinctly limited. This point is of importance because it underlines the limited area within which adjustments in response to losses in interregional competitive position must be made.

It is well to remember that manufacturing income in 1952 accounted for but 31 per cent of all income. The major adjustments in the competitive position of a region have to be concentrated to a considerable extent on this part of the economy. Hence, large losses in interregional competition, say in textiles and shoes, if they are to be made good in substitute exports, must largely be made good in improvements in manufacturing "export" industries. Agriculture, forestry, fisheries, and mining account for but 9 per cent of the national income. Here competition is relevant but the limits of adaptability are determined largely by the resources available.

An estimate of approximately forty items included in service employments and accounting for 60 per cent of all income suggests that only about 10 per cent of all income and corresponding employments included here are largely subject to interregional competition. Thus for retail trade, public utilities, transportation, telephone services, most services (education, religion, cinema, private households), local and state government, and a large part of federal government, the location of activities for the most part is determined by the present distribution of population and income. Only as population and income are redistributed will the services be redistributed. They are determinates, not determinants. Substantial parts of wholesale trade and of insurance are examples of services subject to interregional competition. (See *Survey of Current Business*, July, 1953, page 16.) . . .

An indication of the areas of competition is given by the distribution of various types of incomes by regions. . . . We compare for each region the percentage of incomes earned by different employments relative to the region's share of the nation's income. Thus in the seven regions of the country, for 1952, the average percentage of trade and service income to the region's total income payments varied only from 24.1 to 28.0 per cent (the U.S. average was 25.6). In construction, the range was from 3.4 per cent (New England) to 5.0 per cent (Southeast). Here the differences are explained largely by the slow advance of New England and the rapid industrial growth of the South—not by the South selling construction services to other regions. Where the percentage of income accruing to particular employments does not vary much from region to region, it may be assumed that competition is distinctly limited. In some instances, where percentage of employment varies generally, e.g., transportation, the explanation may well be that differences reflect geography rather than interregional competition. Heavy concentration of population explains a low proportion of employment in transportation in New England and Central States, and large distances explain high relative employment in transportation in the South, Northwest, and Far West. Differences in the proportion of service income may also reflect variations in spending patterns in part: the rich Northeast spends more on services than the poor South.

For agriculture, government, and manufacturing, the minimum and maximum figures (taken from the *Survey of Current Business,* August, 1953, page 9) were as shown in [Table 14-4].

Table 14-4

	National average	Minimum	Maximum
Agriculture (income)...........	6.7	Middle East, 1.5	Northeast, 20.3
Government (income payments)	15.9	Central, 12.5	Southeast, 20.3
Manufacturing (payrolls).......	24.5	Northwest, 10.6	New England, 32.9

If a manufacturing region loses heavily in exports, its losses must be recouped largely in manufactures, with some help from services. Yet even in manufactures there are segments where adjustments are not easily made. For example, in 1951, the distribution of manufacturing employment was as follows:

1. Seven industries with location predominantly determined by access to raw materials (and to some extent to proximity to markets) accounted for 35 per cent of the value added in 1951.

2. The location of seven industries accounting for 46 per cent of the value added was determined to a substantial degree by the need of being near the raw materials.

3. The other five industries (textiles, apparel and related, printing and publishing, leather and leather products, instruments and related products) accounting for 19 per cent of value added were industries which might be located largely independently of the proximity to the sources of the raw materials.

The last group would especially be subject to pressures for any adjustments that have to be made.

Regional Variations in Income

Ricardo's theory of international trade was based on the assumption that labor and capital do not move across national frontiers and that there are no impediments to movements within a country. On both assumptions Ricardo was wrong. In the nineteenth and early twentieth centuries, both capital and labor moved across national frontiers in large amounts and numbers. Relatively speaking, these movements have become a trickle since 1914. Across state or regional boundaries, movements are not so unrestricted as Ricardo assumed. Indeed, there are no immigration laws to contend with or exchange control or discrimination against foreigners. Yet it is interesting that in 1948, for example, per capita income in Mississippi was $758 as compared with $1,891 in New York State, $1,817 in Illinois, and $1,651 in California, or 40, 42, and 45 per cent of the per capita income in these states.

The most common explanation (e.g., by Colin Clark and L. Bean) of differences of income is variations in employment structure, but this is not always convincing. One state with large agricultural employment may have a per capita income one and one-half times as much as another with the same proportion of agricultural jobs. Dr. Perloff has presented the information in Table 14-5.

Table 14-5. States with Similar Sector-employment Patterns but Widely Different Per Capita Incomes, 1950†

State	Percentage of employed persons in			Per capita income, 1950†
	Agriculture, etc.	Manufacturing, etc.	Services	
Iowa............	29	21	50	$1,413
Georgia..........	22	30	48	967
Delaware........	9	42	49	1,956
Maine...........	11	40	48	1,157
Nevada..........	11	19	70	1,882
Florida..........	13	21	66	1,201
Connecticut......	3	49	48	1,789
New Hampshire..	7	47	46	1,310

† There are, of course, other cases in which the parallelism is striking, for example:

Tennessee........	22	30	48	$967
Georgia..........	22	30	48	967

SOURCE: H. S. Perloff, "Interrelations of State Income and Industrial Structure," *Review of Economics and Statistics*, 1957.

How can one explain the persistence of such large variations of per capita income within a country? To some extent these may be explained by statistical incomparability. Mississippi has more children relative to total population, more agricultural workers (low income), more Negroes (low income), lower cost of living, and hence smaller real differences; but genuine differences still remain. Yet why do not the agricultural workers and particularly the Negroes move to higher-income occupations and states? Indeed, there is movement from farm to city, from South to North, from North to West, and a net movement from South to West. For example, from 1929 to 1948, whereas the population of New England, the Middle Eastern states, and the Pacific Northwest rose 1.1, 1.2, and 4.3 times as much as the natural increase, in the Southeast and West North Central states, the percentages were 0.5 and 0.6.[36] And as has been noted earlier, per capita incomes rose much more in the South than in the North. That the rise of per capita income has been dis-

[36] U.S. Department of Commerce, *Economic Development Atlas*, 1950.

appointing in the Far West (108 and 77 per cent in the Pacific Northwest and Pacific Southwest, respectively, as compared with 107 per cent in the country and 179 per cent in the Southeast) is to be explained by the large influx of people into the Far West.

But why have differences not associated with equalizing factors (e.g., number of children) not been eliminated? Ignorance, lack of resources required for movement, noneconomic factors (e.g., a preference for living in Mississippi to living in California)—these are among the explanations. The sluggishness of movement relates especially to labor and to some extent to management. But, as noted earlier, capital moves with great ease across regional frontiers. Under modern corporate enterprise with more than 90 per cent of capital of corporations obtained without appeals to the market, the corporation allocates its capital on the basis of returns to be expected. A Northern steel or textile firm compares costs of producing and selling North and South, East and West, and on the basis of estimated returns the corporation then invests. With large supplies of labor available, rich resources, and proximity to rich markets in the South, the steel company will divert some of its capital to that region. With capital so mobile and labor considerably less mobile, labor in the regions experiencing competitive losses suffers the more because it loses so easily its complementary agent, capital.

Obviously a region that has a disproportionate investment in industries that are losing ground must find outlets elsewhere and for the reasons given is likely to lose ground. Table 14-6, for example, shows the trend of various industries:

Table 14-6. Percentage of Employment

	1899	1939	1951
Textiles, apparels, and shoes.........................	28.5	20.7	19.4
Chemicals, petroleum, and rubber...................	4.6	6.6	7.5
Primary metals......................................	....	8.6	8.6
Metals, machinery, instruments, etc. (five major industries)...	....	24.0	33.1

SOURCE: *U.S. Census of Manufactures,* 1947, II, various pages; and *1951 Annual Survey of Manufactures,* Advance Report, Series MAS 5/24, Mar. 11, 1953, p. 7.

Again, here is a comparison of employments in three rather weak manufacturing industries (textiles, apparels, and leather and products of leather) with eight relatively strong industries (chemicals and allied products; rubber products; primary metal industries; fabricated metal; electrical machinery; other machinery; transportation equipment; instruments and related products). The 1947 Census gave the following percentages of employment in the three weak to the eight strong industries: South Atlantic, 204; East South Central, 89; New England, 83; Middle Atlantic, 62; West North Central, 40; West South Central, 32; Pacific, 19; Mountain, 12; and East North Central, 10. It would be expected that Northern states with high wages and a substantial percentage of employment in the three weak industries would experience difficulties and that Southern states would also not grow so rapidly as other regions given the distribution of their industries, although this factor may be offset by their low costs.

An examination of employment trends over twenty years (1929 to 1949) shows that New England's gains in manufacturing have been small. For the whole country the relative proportion of manufacturing employment had risen by 1.84 per cent; for New England, only 0.31 per cent; for the Central states, 4.03 per cent; Southeast, 3.77 per cent; Middle East, 2.77 per cent. Nor do gains in non-commodity-producing industries (tertiary) necessarily accrue to the high-income regions. The South has a larger percentage than New England, and the high-income industrial Central states have but 46.22 per cent of employment in these industries as compared with 61.25 per cent in the Far West and 56.60 per cent in the Middle East. Among these industries, government, trade, and miscellaneous gained especially, and by comparison transportation, finance, industry, and real estate have lost considerable ground.[37]

The trend continued in later years. From 1947 to 1954, factory jobs in the country rose by 5 per cent; in New England they declined by 9 per cent. In the years 1947 to 1953, however, New England's manufacturing employment rose by 7.7 per cent but only 40 per cent as much as in the nation. That New England's value added in manufacturing rose about 70 per cent as much as the nation's reflects movements into high-valued (advanced) industries at a greater rate than in the nation.[38]

In summary, factor movements tend to bring about an equalization of income among regions. The equalization may be quickened by government aid for the regions gaining ground (though it should be noted that government operations may also prevent or slow up losses for low-income regions, as, for example, in the attempts in the thirties to keep incomes in agricultural regions from declining precipitously). For the regions losing ground, the intervention of the government on behalf of low-income (newly industrialized) regions may aggravate the problems of adjustment. Without the usual obstacles to trade or movement of capital and labor prevailing among countries, the losses of some

[37] These figures are all based on U.S. *Department of Commerce, Regional Trends in the United States,* 1953.

[38] S. E. Harris, *New England Textiles and the New England Economy, Report to the Conference of New England Governors,* 1956, pp. 40, 49.

regions and gains of others may be at an uncomfortable rate. The outlets for capital and labor displaced in the losing regions are limited, though the seriousness of the situation may be concealed by large government outlays and resultant high levels of employment. Under these conditions, mobility improves. No serious obstacles to trade prevail, although factor movements are large. Among countries with factor movements greatly restricted and hence the gains of trade correspondingly increased, trade restrictions are manifold.

It has been suggested to me that I should state the appropriate welfare assumptions in analyzing Federal policies that raise the economic level of some regions in part at the expense of others. Clearly a national objective is to raise the average income of the low-income states. That was what President Roosevelt was saying when he referred to the South as the No. 1 economic problem of the country. Hence the policies of social security, resource development, progressive taxation, and price supports for agriculture, which were bound to raise the economic status of the underprivileged areas and the underprivileged everywhere.

What can the spokesman for the richer regions say in reply? We should know the facts. Irrespective of objectives, it is important to estimate the magnitude of the transfers. In this connection, the author studied the extent of the transfers over a period of twenty years. The major Southern industrial states, for example, receive back three times as much compared with the Federal taxes borne by them than does New England and a fortiori vis-à-vis New York. New England receives about one-sixth as much government financing as might be expected from her economic importance. The transfers are then large.[39]

At what rate should these transfers be made? To what extent should the migration of industry, which raises problems of adjustment for the North, be considered in determining the rate of build-up of the South and West? What is the responsibility of the Federal government in helping bring about adjustments in the North required as a result of Federal policies favoring other regions? To what extent should the pace of these transfers be modified according to the over-all economic situation? (Here it may be assumed that adjustments are easier in periods of full or overfull employment, for new jobs are more easily found in the North. But this is just the period when Federal spending is to be discouraged.) Above all, should not the various programs be assessed as a whole and both constructive effects in the South and West and adjustment problems in the North be assessed? A loss of a million jobs is likely to be more costly in the North than a gain of a million jobs in the South and West.

[39] These issues are explored in a substantial study, *ibid.*, pp. 110–164.

PART FOUR

Some Aspects of Adjustment

CHAPTER 15

Problems of International Adjustment

Introduction

In the century before 1914, international trade was carried on with a minimum of restrictions and upheavals. Of course, all major countries did not stay on gold continuously, for there were periods of international panic—e.g., consider the gold shortage in the United States in the 1890s —and there were periods of restrictions on gold payments on the Continent. But in general gold was supreme. The price of gold was fixed in terms of the domestic currency; devaluations were rare. (The United States had experienced but one devaluation before that of 1933–1934.) Dollar shortages, exchange depreciation, exchange control, inconvertibility, multiple exchange rates, quotas, and a host of other problems that plague the world today were virtually unknown.

Why did the system work, even if not perfectly, in the period between the Napoleonic Wars and World War I?[1] Undoubtedly, British leadership contributed toward its smoothly functioning system. The British found it to their interest to support free trade and the allocation of resources on the principle of comparative advantage. According to the relative plenitude of supplies of factors and their quality (coal, steel, high skills in manufacturing, large savings), the British could deploy their resources in the most effective manner. Their major strength lay in manufacturing and their objective to export British manufactures in exchange for foreign food and raw materials.

British savings were large; the world relatively peaceful. It was in the interest of the British to export part of their savings in order to exploit the resources of underdeveloped countries, inclusive of the United States. Here the interests of the private investor and the nation were one: higher returns for the former and cheaper food and raw materials for the nation. Furthermore, the large outflow of capital, far greater relative to income than capital outflow and aid relative to

---

[1] Cf. Chap. 10, where this issue is considered at greater length.

United States income since World War I, financed the excess of imports of these countries without great disturbances.

Where some countries tended to expand too rapidly with the resultant rise of imports and decline of exports, gold flowed out with corrective effects on prices and incomes: reduced prices and incomes for the country losing gold and the reverse for those gaining gold. At least this is the simple theory, and events did not seem to deviate too far from those suggested by it.

Chaos since 1913

What has happened since 1913 to bring chaos into international economic relations? First, there has emerged a division of authority. France and the United States began to challenge Britain's hegemony in international economic relations. These countries might prefer to hoard gold and thus upset the equilibrating influence of gold movements and embarrass the rest of the world, which would then have to deflate its economies. (It is not, however, clear that the hoarding propensities of this country were always as great as Keynes, for example, sometimes claimed.)

Second, the new power in international economic relations (latterly the United States) might not assume the responsibilities generally associated with a creditor country. Her tariff policy might discourage the imports required to liquidate debt or at least ensure adequate financing. The exportation of capital might not be on the scale required of the creditor nation, or at the very least the flow might be most uneven and erratic. But the United States is sometimes unfairly charged with irresponsible behavior here. For example, in the thirties, the uneasy political situation in Europe accounted for a perverse movement of capital into the United States, and the epidemic of defaults with the Great Depression and the rise of nationalism since naturally discouraged exports of capital by private investors in the United States.

Third, the trouble lay in part with the countries embarrassed by unfavorable balances of payments. In such advanced countries as Great Britain and France, a kind of economic arteriosclerosis had set in. Their costs had become rigid; when, as in the British case, they pursued wrongheaded monetary policies which required declines in money costs, rigidities became an almost insuperable obstacle. Although there was a tendency to move into industries experiencing rising demand, often the movements were sluggish.

It would, however, be a mistake to conclude that progress has not been substantial. The shift has been from the weak to the strong industries. Some figures for the United Kingdom for 1901 to 1952 are shown in Table 15-1. Whereas there was a loss of 299,000 jobs in textiles,

Table 15-1. Changes in Employment, Percentage, 1901 to 1952

Coal mining.............................	−4
Cotton manufacture.....................	−49
Woolen manufacture....................	−20
Agriculture and fishing..................	−17
Building and contracting.................	+34
Chemicals..............................	+366
Metal goods and engineering.............	+185

there was a gain of 376,000 in chemicals and 2,675,000 in metal goods and engineering. What is more, real national income had risen by 97 per cent in fifty years (stable prices) and per capita income by 60 per cent (primarily since 1910).[2]

Despite these gains, however, there has been plenty of trouble for the older industrial nations. When confronted with international disequilibrium, they tended to protect themselves in ways contrary to nineteenth-century principles. Economists for years have been saying that a country in a strong bargaining position might improve its terms of trade by introducing protectionism. As the largest free-trade market, the British might force concessions by introducing protectionist devices: tariffs or exchange depreciation. The British embarked on protectionism after World War I not only as a means of controlling imports when exports were being threatened and as a means for improving its terms of trade, but also, again under Keynes's persuasive powers, in order to restrict capital exports that could not easily be balanced by exports.

Fourth, and probably most important, there have been the effects of two major wars, the cold war, and the political upheavals associated with these events. The result has been a tremendous burden on the adjustment mechanism. The loss of output, particularly in war zones; the diversion to war uses; the pressure to expand domestic investment in the post-World War II period because of war losses and great political uncertainties; in the struggle against communism the need of maintaining consumption standards inclusive of fringe payments, which greatly increase and rigidify costs; the loss of important markets related to the cold war; the reduced relative prices and incomes for gold-producing countries and economies related to them; the reduced income from invisible items (e.g., foreign investments); the tendency of underdeveloped countries in response to the rising nationalism to become more self-sufficient in manufactures and to discourage agricultural output, with reduced imports from older industrial nations and less favorable terms of trade for Europe compared with prewar years—these are among the concatenation of factors which greatly weakened the international posi-

[2] British Information Service, "Fifty Years of Progress in British Factories," *Labour and Industry*, September, 1953, pp. 114–115.

tion of the European nations in particular and, to some extent, of Asiatic countries.

One aspect of this problem should not go unnoticed. In the years since 1929, there has been much greater emphasis upon domestic economic conditions and less on international equilibrium than there was at least in the century preceding 1929. This shift of emphasis is to be associated at least in part with the lessons of Keynesian economics and in part with the substantial problems of unemployment. Whereas British economic policy (and to some degree American policy) had rested on the assumed need of moving toward equilibrium in the balance of payments (note the unwise and devastating monetary policies of the British in the 1920s and the foolish policies of repayment of debt and related contraction of monetary supplies of the United States in the last quarter of the nineteenth century), since 1929 the emphasis has been shifted to the primacy of domestic objectives: full employment and with it a growing economy. Once the countries relatively more affected in their international economic positions by the results of the wars and political upheavals and uncertainties concentrate their attention on such problems as full employment, redistribution of income, public consumption, etc., they increase the strain on the balance of payments. They not only divert resources from exports to domestic investment and consumption but also tend to stimulate imports, which are encouraged by the general rise of investment as well as the high-income and high-employment policies. These programs also tend to raise prices and costs and to this extent also to discourage exports and stimulate imports.

Exchange Depreciation: A Mixed Blessing

It is clear that there were strong forces at work operating to disequilibrate the balance of payments of many countries, but it has often been suggested that the countries suffering from pressure on their balance of payments could have solved their problems if they had cut imports or raised exports sufficiently. However, soon after World War II, when the excess of imports into Western Europe reached $10 billion to $11 billion a year, or perhaps 10 per cent of its national income, this would have been a difficult task. The economic sacrifices involved would have jeopardized many governments already in a precarious position. But the case could be argued with greater strength when this deficit had been cut to, say, 3 per cent of national income. (The deficit is higher if allowance is made for the repressed imports associated with abnormal restraints on imports from dollar countries and the stimulation of European export trade to dollar countries not associated with the free market.)

The charge has been made, particularly by Professors Viner and Friedman, that governments have not resorted to variations in exchange rates often enough. Failure to have recourse to depreciation is, indeed, an interesting subject for investigation. In the thirties, there had been an epidemic of revisions of exchange rates. Why had not similar policies been followed in the forties and early fifties? Perhaps one reason was a dissatisfaction with the results in the thirties or else the changed situation after World War II. In the Great Depression, exchange depreciation served the useful purpose of freeing countries from the restrictionist monetary policies necessary under gold. Once it was admitted that gold parities did not have to be maintained, then each country could pursue expansionist monetary and fiscal policies without excessive concern over international repercussions. This was undoubtedly the major gain of the epidemic of devaluations of currencies in the thirties. The response of exports and imports was not what might have been expected for the following reasons: First, devaluation by one country became a signal for similar practices by other countries. Hence *competitive* gains were not made—virtually every country ultimately followed the British in their descent, and even the United States, which could not defend devaluation on grounds of international disequilibrium but might support it on the grounds of disequilibrium for an important economic and political group. Second, with the accompanying rise of income (absolute or relative), there was a response of imports (absolute or relative). I remind the reader, however, of the *relative* monetary and income expansion accompanying devaluation.

This experience in the thirties undoubtedly influenced later policy makers. They had learned that the net results of a depreciation were uncertain because there was uncertainty concerning the exchange behavior of competitors. In the forties and fifties, however, this concern over the potential depreciation of competitors should not have been so great as in the thirties, for it was not likely that the United States would follow devaluations abroad. Hence a competitive gain might be made vis-à-vis the United States. But it should not be forgotten that there were serious competitive problems among countries for the available supply of dollars and even for other currencies. With, say, $10 billion to $12 billion made available each year, the British were much more interested in the dollars they could get at the expense of others than in an increased pool of dollars, for the major gains would be at the expense of others rather than out of additional dollars produced by a devaluation. (I shall comment on this point further.) Once devaluation was allowed in 1949, the British soon discovered that (as in the thirties) the major potential gains were lost because most countries followed sterling and partly lost because inflationary pressures associated with depreciation were not adequately checked. Moreover, neither the British nor many other countries could count upon a large gain resulting from a reduction of imports associated with an increased price for the dollar. They had learned how to deal with imports through quotas, exchange control, etc. The restrictionist effects on imports had been largely achieved before depreciation had been introduced. Finally, the fear of inflation dulled the enthusiasm for exchange depreciation.

I can list many other reasons for a lack of enthusiasm for exchange depreciation, but before I list any, may I add that in Chapter 25 I deal with the devaluations of the thirties and the depreciation of 1949, and some problems skipped over lightly here are discussed more fully there. Many countries were fearful of the effects of a deterioration in their terms of trade, though by 1950 their major concern was excessive imports rather than terms of trade. Effects on the terms of trade had been a concern of Keynes as early as 1929, when he could envisage depreciation as a means of increasing dollar receipts through a reduction of costs in world markets. But he was concerned over both the resultant deterioration in the terms of trade and the low elasticity of demand for exports. Again, countries with staple crops for which the demand was highly inelastic preferred to maintain the value of their currency, thus assuring themselves high dollar proceeds for their exports. When the general situation suggested an overvalued currency, they preferred to combine some control of imports and multiple exchange rates. When there was a substantial elasticity of supply at home and high elasticity of demand abroad and hence the stimulus of exchange of many units of domestic currency for a dollar, say, prevailed, the exporter of a commodity (e.g., meat) was allowed many units of local currencies for a dollar, but when supplies were inelastic and the demand inelastic (e.g., coffee), the price offered in domestic currencies was low. In this manner, the currency might be depreciated but in a way which reduced the terms of trade to a minimum. In similar fashion, petroleum- or copper-exporting nations might offer companies exporting coffee or petroleum and requiring domestic currency relatively few units of local currencies in exhange for dollars. In this manner, the country not only maintained the exchange value of its currency for exports of commodities subject to inelastic demand but also secured an effective method of taxation from the groups most able to pay taxes.

The multiple-exchange-rate system was one under which the authorities tended to set a different rate according to need. When a depreciation from 50 to 25 cents would greatly reduce the returns in local currency and mean a large deterioration in the terms of trade not offset by an adequate expansion of exports, the authorities might set a rate of, say, 40 cents. Differential rates both for exports and for imports (e.g., a 50-cent rate for purchase of necessaries) would mean that a depreciation of X percentage would be more effective than an across-the-board decline.

A country faced with an imbalance in its international accounts will consider a revision of exchange rates as an easy way of solving its problem of imbalance. But it first must be prepared to make the necessary sacrifices: more exports and/or less imports. Politically there may be serious difficulties, and the economist should not leave the political problems out of consideration. Furthermore, the authorities will not be certain of the appropriate rate at the time of the change, and besides, a successful revision awaits complementary policies. In the British experience of 1949, for example, the British had to estimate (1) the effects of speculation on the rate, both in depressing the rate in anticipation of depreciation and in raising it once the rate had fallen; (2) the appropriate price and wage policy which would support a reduced price of British commodities abroad; (3) the price elasticity of demand for British exports as well as any changes in the state of demand. Failure to anticipate the Korean War weakened the British international position following depreciation, for prices of imports rose spectacularly, and the resultant rise of demand and income abroad pointed to reductions in world prices brought on by depreciation which were not required. On the other hand wages and prices rose in the United Kingdom with a result that the competitive gains were to a considerable extent wiped out.

I am not sure that I agree fully with Professor Hicks that the British worker would not make the sacrifices—and hence the failure of the devaluation. British wages actually became cheaper in dollars. In the years 1950 to 1953 weekly wages had risen by but 15 per cent (average of four years) and the price of the dollar by 43 per cent. Even in 1953 wages were up only two-thirds as much as the dollar.[3]

It may be added that devaluation would have been a greater failure had not the British used planned techniques for stimulating exports and discouraging imports. Only thus and because of the rising incomes everywhere can we explain a much greater rise of exports in the years 1950 to 1952 than in the thirties, and this despite the fact that the 1949 devaluation sprang from a full-employment economy and the 1931 one from a heavily depressed economy. In 1931, devaluation had the great merit of containing the progress of deflation; in 1949, the demerit of strengthening the forces of inflation.

It has been held by Professor Viner and others that the failure to adopt exchange depreciation quite frequently was based on inaccurate estimates of the price elasticity of demand for exports. Beginning with Keynes, estimates of price elasticity of demand for exports have been

[3] This episode is discussed fully in Chap. 25.

low. Obviously, it would be foolish to allow exchanges to depreciate, say, by one-half if the net effect was to be a substantial fall in the dollar receipts (inclusive of savings on imports as dollar prices rose), as export prices on world markets declined greatly and sales responded inadequately.

In the last few years, Orcutt, Viner, Machlup, Adler, and others have contended that price elasticities are much higher than they so far have seemed to be. Among the reasons adduced in support of the high elasticity in recent studies as compared with earlier ones are the following: the importance of elasticity after the passage of sufficient time to allow the build-up of new markets at the reduced prices (earlier studies had measured elasticity within a brief span of time following the drop of price); past studies which concentrated too much on raw materials for which demand is inelastic; a failure to eliminate the effects of cyclical movements, that is, a decline in prices is accompanied by a reduction of income abroad which conceals the high price elasticity (but note that in the postwar period, the decline of prices following devaluation was accompanied by a rise of income); and the interdependence of supply and demand, that is, elasticity of demand is higher than it seems to be because the reduction of world price (and the rise of price in domestic currencies) results in an expansion of supply for export markets.

Yet admitting all of this, I am not convinced that pessimistic estimates by economists of the price elasticity of demand for exports were the major explanation of exchange-rate policy. I shall suggest below that there have, in fact, been many changes in rates. But aside from this, the exchange-rate policy was determined by other considerations. Ignorance of the real elasticities of demand was probably more important than underestimation. We are still in the dark on this matter. In order to measure real elasticities, the country considering depreciation must consider the behavior of its competitors and chief suppliers. Here is a large element of uncertainty. The British gained less in 1949 because many competitors followed sterling down. Demand for British manufactures may be highly elastic in the United States, as Adler claims, but it is less in so far as competitors, inclusive of United States competitors, meet British concessions. Even those with optimistic estimates frequently fail to take into account such factors as the following: the high price to the American consumer compared with the price of the export content and hence the much smaller elasticity for the foreign items derived from the *small* percentage concession to the *ultimate* buyer compared with the large relative concession made by the *exporter*. They do not always take into account the effect on elasticities of the product of one country of concomitant depreciation of other countries, nor do they consider retaliatory behavior on the part of countries confronted with more aggressive competition. United States protectionism in the fifties stems in part from the fears engendered by the series of devaluations in recent years.

Another uncertainty revolves around the state of demand abroad. In the early postwar period with large deficiencies of traded goods, a country resorting to depreciation was offering a concession in prices that was not required under the favorable demand conditions then current. A related uncertainty was the response of supplies for exports as foreign buyers reacted to reduced prices. Here again, great pressures on resources for government, for investment, for the backlog of consumer demand, are relevant. Again, in view of the difficulties of containing inflation, few countries wanted to introduce an additional force (i.e., depreciation) tending to strengthen inflationary tendencies.

I am not convinced that the studies by economists on the price elasticity of demand for exports have discouraged recourse to exchange depreciation in any substantial way. I have discussed earlier the broader issue of the adequacy of price elasticities as against income effects in dealing with the problem of variations in exchange rate, and one should recall Morgan's skepticism concerning the usefulness of studies of elasticities for measuring the effects of revisions in exchange rates.[4] Aside from the many points made above, authorities had learned how to deal with disequilibrium in other ways. They had to introduce exchange control in order to deal with troublesome capital movements; and with serious shortages prevailing after the war, they found it convenient to use exchange control to keep nonessential imports out in order to mobilize all foreign exchange for the most effective use given the over-all objectives of the nation. These measures did not exclude depreciation but integrated exchange-rate policies with the over-all objectives. The greater the scarcities, the more the temptation to divide up the market for foreign exchange, and the more the market was divided up on the basis of elasticities of supply and demand, the less the average depreciation required to achieve a rise of exports and/or a reduction of imports. With exchange control widely used, the authorities, of course, depended more on exclusion of imports and control of exports to achieve a manner of balance and depended less on the price mechanism (e.g., depreciation). But it should be noted that most of these countries used a combination of market control (exchange control) and the price mechanism (both varying exchange rates for different markets and changes in the over-all rates either by modifying the rates or by changing applicable rates for different transactions). On the whole, the poorer countries with adequate administrative machinery tended to favor the more complicated rate structures and controls.

[4] E. V. Morgan, "The Analysis of Deflation," *The American Economic Review,* June, 1955, especially p. 295.

Frequent Use of Exchange Depreciation

Never have trading nations resorted to exchange depreciation to the
extent that they have since the outbreak of World War I and especially
since World War II. It is entirely wrong to assume that in recent years
governments resorted to exchange control and only to exchange control.

From 1938 to 1954, there were seven countries with exchange statistics
available which had no recourse to depreciation, but these were dollar
countries accounting for only 2 per cent of the world's export trade.
Switzerland, with 1.5 per cent of world trade, and Canada, with 6.5 per
cent, actually raised the value of their currencies vis-à-vis the United
States dollar. But for other countries the price of the dollar rose as shown
in Table 15-2 from 1938 to 1954.

Table 15-2

Percentage rise in price of dollars	*No. of countries*
1–25	6
26–50	5
51–75	14
76–200	3
201–300	5
301–26,000	8

SOURCE: Material computed from *International Financial Statistics*, April, 1954.
Estimates of depreciation are rough because of the frequent use of more than one
rate, especially by the smaller countries.

A rough weighting by export trade of the countries accounting for
close to two-thirds of export trade which depreciated their currencies
vis-à-vis the dollar (and generally there was more than one drop) reveals
that the *rise* in price of the dollar weighted by trade in each instance
was no less than 673 per cent. That is to say, these forty-one currencies
depreciated on the average by 87 per cent, a much greater depreciation
even than in the Great Depression.[5]

The calculation in Table 15-3 is based on a weighting by 1952 export
trade. I have also weighted by 1938 export trade, a weighting which
yields a rise in the price of the dollar of 1,014 per cent, or a depreciation
of nondollar currencies (exclusive of the Iron Curtain countries) of 91

[5] These are rough estimates. The dependencies of the United Kingdom and Continental dependencies were classified with their mother country. The large rise in
the price of the dollar is explained by phenomenal depreciation of some major
countries with appreciable amounts of trade: The price of the dollar in Japanese
yen rose by 97 times; in French francs, more than 8 times; in Italian lire, 32 times;
in Greek drachmas, 255 times. We do not consider Iron Curtain countries here.
The rise of the price of the dollar in Hungarian pengos had risen by 10^{17}, surely a
world's record.

Table 15-3. Percentage Rise in Price of Dollar and Depreciation of Forty-one Nondollar Currencies

1938 weighting		1952 weighting	
Rise price of dollar	Depreciation of nondollar currencies	Rise price of dollar	Depreciation of nondollar currencies
1,014	91	673	87

Average of two = 89 per cent

per cent. Hence an average of the two weightings yields a rise in the price of the dollar of 843 per cent and an average depreciation of the nondollar currencies of 89 per cent—this depreciation applies to countries accounting for about two-thirds of the world's trade. A greater depreciation on the basis of 1938 weights would be expected, since the countries with the greatest degree of depreciation have lost ground in trade and therefore a weighting by 1952 trade shows less depreciation than the 1938 weighting. In general, this might suggest that depreciation does not solve the fundamental problems of disequilibrium, but we certainly do not hold that these countries would have been better off had they refrained from large devaluations.

The Dollar Problem

As has been said earlier, a shortage of foreign currencies is an old disease, but never before has the shortage been concentrated on one currency for so long a period and in such large amounts. Moreover, the actual shortage has been concealed to a considerable degree by the diabolical devices used to keep out goods from dollar countries.

We have already listed many of the factors that help to explain the dollar shortage and shall consider these further in the next chapter and especially in Part Five. Here I would like to comment briefly on the issue of the relative gains of productivity in the United States, which have been denied.

Of the greater rise of productivity of the United States, there can be little doubt. Over a long period man-hour output has tended to rise by $2\frac{1}{2}$ per cent each year. From 1929 to 1952, the gain of output per man-hour was 80 per cent.[6] The comparable figure in Great Britain is much less; for example, *over fifty years*, the *total* rise of per capita real income

[6] K. W. Kapp and L. L. Kapp, *A Graphic Approach to Economics*, 1951, p. 21; also cf. Harold Barger, *Distribution's Place in the American Economy since 1869*, 1955, chap. 3; but cf. article by Sir Donald MacDougall in *Review of Economics and Statistics*, May, 1956.

was but 60 per cent, or less than 1 per cent per year.[7] United States gains are measured not only by the improvement in per man-hour output but also by the large gains in the growing industries possibly not adequately measured by index numbers, and by the large issue of new products. Since so many of the technical changes have been capital-saving in the United States, it may be claimed that the productivity gains were even larger relatively than suggested by man-hour output. (We assume, of course, that the gains in *all* countries are reduced below the amounts given by man-hour output in so far as input of capital and management is increased.)

The interesting question relates to the issue of the repercussions of rising productivity upon the balance of payments. In the next chapter I discuss this problem further. Here I note that a disequilibrium may well be consistent with classical theory. Just as the movement of gold or changes in exchange rates tend to close the dollar gap, another rise of United States productivity or production of new products reopens the gap once more. This may, indeed, be a continuous problem in a dynamic economy. Hence the gap is never closed. Even the reader who denies the validity of this position will have to admit that continued gains of productivity in the United States, considered in conjunction with all the other disequilibrating factors felt by nondollar countries and related to war, political uncertainties, and growing nationalism everywhere, might put too great a strain on the adjustment mechanism.

In this connection, the following is of special importance. The area within which adjustments can be made has been greatly reduced. Thus if the United States exports of machinery rise and imports of textiles decline, nondollar countries experience difficulty in substituting other exports for textiles. Among the factors responsible for these difficulties are the following: the increased importance in the economies of *domestic* services, including military, welfare, and government outlays generally; the growing popularity of industrialization in underdeveloped countries, with resultant narrowing of markets; and the wide recourse to exchange control and quotas, not only limiting the area within which exports of dollar-short countries may move but also slowing up adjustments.

Unfortunately for the countries short of dollars, the substitution of exchange flexibility for gold movements as the instrument of adjustment has not been used with maximum effectiveness. Indeed, the problem would have been much more serious had not the United States absorbed its gains of productivity primarily in higher incomes rather than in lower prices. Taking the gains of increased productivity in reduced prices would have embarrased foreign countries much more than taking

[7] British Information Service, *loc. cit.*

these gains in higher incomes, for reduced prices mean increased competition. Professor Hicks is of a similar view.

One final point: As a result of the loss of markets in the Western Hemisphere following World War II, the position of Western Europe has been further weakened. Here the United States has gained a comparative advantage. Over the years, trade connections have been strengthened *within* the Hemisphere, the United States has tended to cultivate tastes of the Western Hemisphere countries, and our neighbors, embarrassed by the loss of accustomed sources of imports, are more inclined to trade with this country.

CHAPTER 16

The Pathology of International Economics

The Dollar Gap: Definition and Measurement

Unfortunately the orthodox theory of international trade is inadequate to explain developments in international economic relations since the twenties. Nowhere is this failure more evident than in an examination of the range of problems generally referred to as the dollar gap, dollar shortage, or dollar famine. Some of the problems of adjustment were discussed in the preceding chapter. Now we concentrate on dollar shortage.

Under classical economics, disequilibrium over a generation or longer was not envisaged. Temporary disequilibrium is treated through the appropriate movements in gold, money, prices, costs, exports, and imports. In more refined versions the neoclassicist adds exchange depreciation and introduces adjustments in purchasing power or income.

What is this dollar gap which has attracted so much attention over a generation? Simply stated, the nondollar world imports more goods and services than it can pay for through exports of goods and services plus capital obtained through the usual incentives of a capitalist system. Indeed, as Robbins suggests, it is possible to eliminate a dollar shortage in the market sense through operating on domestic monetary supplies or income or through revisions of exchange rates, exchange control, etc.[1] It should be observed here that once abnormal controls are used, however, balance in the market sense is not attained. Furthermore, in the actual world, political and other institutional factors have to be considered. A reduction of imports and/or rise of exports adequate to balance the accounts in a period of stress may involve such political risks as to rule out the balancing of the dollar account as practical policy.

Later (Chapter 21) we examine the excess of exports of goods and services from the United States of $125 billion over forty years, a rough measure of the dollar shortage. This total includes both capital exports later repudiated and those still being financed. (Obviously part of the latter should be deducted from the $125 billion.) It includes gold im-

[1] Cf. L. Robbins, *The Economist in the Twentieth Century*, 1954, pp. 42–45.

208

ported, both gold from excess reserves abroad and gold that could not be spared if foreign economies were to function effectively.[2] This total of $125 billion might also be corrected (reduced) for the increase of imports from dollar countries associated with dollar shortage, that is, encouraged by the availability of dollar aid, and corrected (increased) for the potential imports from dollar countries eliminated by abnormal trade restrictions and discrimination against the dollar as well as for the excess of exports (properly adjusted) of dollar countries other than the United States.

Incidentally, the inflow of short-term capital and especially hot money raises difficult problems. Thus in the thirties, the inflow of hot money into the United States accounted for a large part of the inflow of gold. Since abnormal losses of gold abroad are considered to be one measure of dollar scarcity, it might then be held that capital imports may account in part for the dollar shortage. Of course, these movements are reversible. At any rate, the $125 billion estimate includes *net* capital exports and hence allows for the inflow of capital. I am not sympathetic with the position taken by Sir Donald MacDougall and Dr. Lederer that most of the period since 1914 has been abnormal and hence is not relevant as evidence of dollar shortage. It may well be that the seven normal (?) years (1927–1929 and 1952–1955) are abnormal.

We might assume that the amount of foreign aid by the United States government is a crude measure of dollar shortage. This approach is helpful even if it is allowed, as Robbins claims, that this leaves out of account the measures that would have been taken had aid not been made available.[3] To this might be added expenditures by the United States military abroad (inclusive of outlays by personnel), as well as United States gold imports out of normal reserves. But with the continuance of the cold war or another hot war, foreign aid may in time become a normal part of the balance of payments, a kind of redistribution of income among friendly nations, a merging and consolidation of military operations. The time may then come when foreign aid would no more be a measure of the dollar shortage than private capital movements or private unilateral transfers (e.g., immigrant remittances). But the international redistribution of income on anything like the scale within a country (e.g., in 1952 New England transferred through the United States Treasury $1.3 billion, or 7 per cent, out of an $18 billion income) is not as yet likely. Regional distribution within a country may involve as much as transfers of 10 per cent of incomes from one region to another; a corresponding amount internationally from the United

[2] W. Lederer, "Major Developments Affecting the United States Balance of International Payments," *Review of Economics and Statistics*, May, 1956.
[3] Robbins, *op. cit.*, pp. 45–46.

States to foreign countries would amount to $40 billion annually. In view of the gradual decline of economic aid and continued scrutiny of military aid, the exclusion of aid from measures of the dollar shortage is a matter for the future.

It is wrong to assume that if the dollar account is in balance in any one or even two or three years, and without aid, the dollar gap has been closed. Thus, in 1953–1954, there was a great narrowing of the gap. But a turn in the terms of trade in favor of Western Europe, the great and continued prosperity in the United States (and hence large imports), the continued aid *and* outlays by the United States military abroad, and the discrimination against the dollar—all these raise doubts that the dollar problem had been definitely solved. As MacDougall well observes, with $2 billion of United States grants and loans, $2.5 billion of United States military expenditures abroad, and $4 billion of free military goods, one should not assume that the dollar problem has been solved. In 1953 and 1954, United States government loans and grants were $5.6 billion and $5.1 billion, or 28 and 26 per cent of United States expenditures abroad. For fiscal year 1957, the Congress appropriated $3,804 million for grants and loans, and the President's recommendation is $4,400 million for fiscal year 1958. The mean of these figures is about 16 or 17 per cent of United States foreign payments in 1956.[4]

Yet this is an oversimplification of the problems involved. Should military aid of the United States be reduced, then also certain subsidies (e.g., agricultural and shipping) given to United States exporters would be reduced or become less effective, and Western Europe, with some delay, would reduce military outlays and divert into export industries factors going into defense industries. Nevertheless, the aid and abnormal military expenditures abroad by the United States, though not an accurate measure of dollar shortage, should not by any means be written off as a measure.[5]

Skepticism Concerning the Dollar Gap

It might well be expected that since the dollar shortage clashes with the trade theory as developed before World War II, some economists would deny the reality of this phenomenon. Even Roy Harrod, in his brilliant pamphlet *Are These Hardships Necessary?* wrote:[6]

This [dollar famine] is one of the most absurd phrases ever coined. . . . They propound this doctrine with all seriousness, as though the dollar famine

[4] D. MacDougall, "A Lecture on the Dollar Problem," *Economica*, 1954, p. 187; Lederer, *op. cit.*, p. 184; *U.S. Budget*, 1958, p. M-35; *Survey of Current Business*, December, 1956, p. 5.

[5] Cf. R. Triffin, "International Currency and Reserve Plans," in *Policies to Combat Depressions*, 1956, pp. 395–396.

[6] R. Harrod, *Are These Hardships Necessary?* 1947, pp. 42–43.

were some kind of new disease. . . . In fact it is no more than the young man going forward and living beyond his resources without leave. . . . This allegation of a "world dollar shortage" is surely one of the most brazen pieces of collective effrontery that has ever been uttered. . . .

In a later book, however, Harrod seemed more receptive to the idea of a dollar shortage. He complained of the clumsy use of devaluation and proposed both a rise in the price of gold (more on this in a later chapter) and limited discrimination of imports.[7]

Professor Haberler was skeptical; holding that the classical inflation theory of dollar shortage is substantially correct (that is, the dollar shortage is explicable by the inflationary policies of the nondollar countries and continuance of overvalued currencies), he would attack the problem through stopping inflation and adjusting exchange rates. He admits that where substantial sacrifices would be involved, there would be some practical difficulties. But he is critical of the economists

who use the term [dollar shortage] with the more or less explicit allegation that it is a novel phenomenon which has never been contemplated in international trade theory and requires some new, unorthodox explanation. . . . They wish to imply that there is a persistent balance-of-payments problem which is not curable by orthodox measures, that is, by changes in prices or exchange rates, or that such a cure would have intolerable consequences. Only a balance of payments disequilibrium of a high degree of malignancy deserves to be called a dollar shortage in the strict sense. . . .

Haberler then goes on to stress the unwillingness of many countries to live within their means. The dollar shortage reflects the inflationary policies of countries that spend too much and save too little.[8]

On the whole, Professor Viner seems to support a position similar to Professor Haberler's, though not quite so extreme:[9]

Dollar scarcity can be "cured" by refusal or failure of the U.S. Government to finance any dollar deficits *ex ante* or *ex post*. It can be "cured" by the use of the deficit country of such methods as will either bring its current balance into equilibrium or will enable it to get regular and long-term financing in advance for its excess of exports. Such methods may be: deflation or disinflation, import restrictions, stimulus to exports, exchange depreciation, flotation of loans abroad or attraction of direct investment.

Is the dollar shortage the result of pressures from the outside to which the nondollar countries fail to adjust? Or is it the result of weak monetary and fiscal policies in the dollar-short countries? Both explanations are relevant for Professor Robbins. He is most critical of the British for pursuing a passive monetary policy, that is, for failing to adjust monetary

[7] R. Harrod, *The Dollar*, 1954, chap. 4.
[8] G. Haberler, "Dollar Shortage," in *Foreign Economic Policy for the United States* (S. E. Harris, ed.), especially pp. 426–427, 438–439, 444–445.
[9] J. Viner, *International Trade and Economic Development*, 1952, pp. 78–79.

policy to external shocks—aside from disequilibrium associated with inflationary monetary and fiscal policies initiated at home. At a fixed rate of exchange, Robbins insists that there must be a level of prices and incomes which would yield a position of equilibrium. It is not fair to blame the hills and curves, says Robbins, using the analogy of the automobile, when the car does not reach its destination. In the same manner, external forces should not be blamed because monetary policy has been wrong-headed or sterile. Too great a burden has been put on fiscal policy.[10]

In a somewhat similar view, Dr. Bernstein warns that there are limitations to the use of devaluation. When the disequilibrium is the result of persistent inflation, devaluation is no cure. Devaluation will not then correct the disequilibrium. When structural maladjustments are involved, e.g., shifts in demand for imports and exports, loss of foreign earnings, then shifts of resources are required. A devaluation may, however, cure a price-cost disparity.[11] Dollar shortage may be related to inappropriate use of devaluation or deflation.

Dollar shortage is, of course, a matter of definition. Where, for example, countries balance their dollar account only by introducing abnormal restraints on trade such as quotas, exchange control, and even discrimination against purchases in dollar markets and special subsidies for dollar sales, under such conditions even an apparent balancing of the dollar account conceals a genuine shortage of dollars.[12]

In an able presentation of the problem, Dr. Bernstein, director of research of the International Monetary Fund, raises additional questions concerning dollar shortage.[13] He would reserve the term for a shortage resulting from United States policy, e.g., a cut in imports following a recession here or new commercial policies. I do not see why the concept should be narrowed in this manner. The dollar shortage is just as real whether the occasion is what happens in the United States or abroad, and its persistence is to be associated with developments both at home and abroad. In reply to the argument that the dollar shortage stems from a greater rise of productivity in the United States than elsewhere, Dr. Bernstein contends that there is some doubt about the facts of productivity and also that the theory of international trade does not rule out uneven movements of productivity. *But there may be difficulties of adjustment*, Dr. Bernstein admits. Is this not all that is required in order

[10] L. Robbins, *The Balance of Payments*, 1951, especially pp. 13–21; and cf. J. Polk, *Sterling: Its Meaning in World Finance*, 1956, p. 209.

[11] E. Bernstein, *Strategic Factors in Balance of Payments Adjustments*, 1956, pp. 8–11 (mimeographed).

[12] See National Foreign Trade Council, *European Export Trade Promotion*, 1954, for a catalogue of these practices.

[13] E. Bernstein, "American Productivity and the Dollar Payments Problem," *Review of Economics and Statistics*, May, 1955, pp. 101–109.

to experience a long-continued shortage of dollars? It is, indeed, correct to argue, as Bernstein does, that different countries will be affected in varying degrees, depending upon the industries subject to large gains in the United States through improved productivity, disposal of new products, or discovery of substitutes for commodities previously imported (e.g., synthetic fabrics for silk). A deficit of $5 billion is a real dollar deficit even if one country out of eighty has a credit of $200 million and another a billion-dollar deficit. The net result will depend, as Bernstein well shows, upon the direction of the changes, upon relative gains in productivity here and abroad, upon the manner in which the gains are taken (a rise of wages or a fall in prices), upon the marginal propensity to import in both countries, etc. Thus, all countries (on the average) would experience a shortage of dollars should, as incomes rise in the United States, large relative gains in man-hour output in the United States be accompanied by a decline of prices here, a *small* rise of wages, and a low marginal propensity to import in the United States. Should the increase of imports from Great Britain be relatively small and the loss of markets in the United States great (because of the substitution of synthetic rubber for rubber and of synthetic fibers for wool), then Great Britain's relative loss of dollars would be severe.

Varying rates of pressure on different exchange markets do not rule out dollar shortage as a relevant factor. The experience of the United Kingdom in 1955 vis-à-vis the rest of the world may still suggest dollar shortage when British losses of reserves are considered as well as the world gains of reserves, the latter more than offset by abnormal outlays of the United States abroad and discrimination against dollar imports.

Or consider the varying gains of reserves since 1928 and 1938. From Table 16-1 it will be noted that in relation to 1928, reserves of countries outside the United States in 1953 were 300 per cent of the 1928 level, 190 per cent of the 1938 level, and 143 per cent of the 1948 level. But the variations are large. Thus in 1953 the percentage of reserves to 1938 varied from 35 per cent in France and 104 per cent for the sterling area to 138 per cent for Continental Western Europe, 380 per cent for Latin America, and 610 per cent for Canada. These movements point to large variations in trends of international competitive strength as compared with the prewar period.[14]

Dr. Harry Johnson's penetrating article in the *Economic Journal* also deals with the importance of relative productivity and the relative price changes that accompany the improvements in productivity. The emphasis is on the point that productivity gains are reflected not only in reductions of prices but also in rises of income, the latter in turn tending to bring an adverse balance of payments for the country (e.g., the United States)

[14] Triffin, *op. cit.*, p. 391.

with a high relative gain in productivity. It does not necessarily follow that the country with high relative gains in productivity will suffer from an adverse balance of payments. Here the elasticities of demand for its exports as compared with its elasticities of demand for imports are relevant. But Johnson argues that if the country gaining in productivity brings prices down and thus improves its balance of payments (with a tendency toward chronic dollar shortage), then the movement can be reversed, for this is the equivalent of an appreciation of the exchanges for the nondollar countries. Then why cannot these countries reverse the movement by depreciating their exchanges and thus cutting their imports and increasing their exports?

Table 16-1. Estimated Gold Reserves and Dollar Holdings of
Foreign Countries
(In billions of dollars)

	1928	1938	1948	1953	1953 as per cent of		
					1928	1938	1948
Continental Western Europe	$4.8	$7.3	$5.8	$10.1	207	138	172
France	2.0	3.0	0.8	1.1	52	35	132
Switzerland	0.2	0.9	1.9	2.1	1,080	235	112
Other	2.6	3.4	3.1	6.9	265	203	220
Sterling area	1.4	3.9	2.9	4.0	288	104	138
Canada	0.4	0.4	1.2	2.4	580	610	198
Latin America	1.1	0.9	2.7	3.6	320	380	132
All other foreign countries	1.0	1.3	2.3	2.9	300	225	126
International organizations	....	.....	3.4	3.3	.....	...	99
Total outside United States*	$8.7	$13.8	$18.4	$26.4	300	190	143

* Details may not add to totals because of rounding.
SOURCE: *Federal Reserve Bulletin*, March, 1954, p. 245. (Taken from *Policies to Combat Depression*, a conference of the Universities–National Bureau Committee for Economic Research, p. 391.)

Dr. Johnson's analysis raises a few questions. It should be noted that what he suggests is that the British, for example, could correct a dollar shortage associated with rising productivity and declining export prices in the United States with a depreciation of the pound sterling. But note, first, that this amounts to saying that the British should treat a rise of productivity in the United States with a deterioration in British commodity terms of trade. Hence, the British would give more without producing more. Is this a feasible program over the years? Second, this is wasteful and costly in another sense, namely, that the British would offer all export goods at reduced prices even when, given demand conditions, the concessions would be excessive. (Broader considerations are relevant here, e.g., welfare aspects of free vs. controlled markets.) The United States limits its concessions to goods being produced more effectively. Third, there is also the problem if, given the institutional difficulties, it is possible to improve the competitive position substantially through depreciation. The possible gains are absorbed in no small part in increased costs.

The Dollar Gap Is Real in the Views of Many

Dollar scarcity has attracted attention especially because of the degree of involvement and the duration of the disease, but currency scarcity is not exactly new. Mercantilism was based in part on inadequacies, real or mythical, of international currencies. United States experience in the 1890s is also relevant. As early as 1921, Keynes[15] had seen the coming struggle for the dollar.[16]

This forecast of 1945 might well be compared with one made in his *Revision of the Treaty* (1921), when Keynes at this very early date sensed the seriousness of the dollar shortage problem. He anticipated that it would be necessary for the United States to advance 2 billion dollars a year in order to balance her account; but he also noted that this only postponed the solution, for interest would accumulate and Europe had no resources from which to pay. The United States would try to solve the problem by maintaining exports and cutting imports; but this obviously is no solution. The United States might scrap its export industries, Keynes continued, an outcome that would be too costly and not practical; and even large rises of imports to cover payment of debt would be too costly to special interests. Industries would be permanently destroyed to solve temporary disequilibrium. A rise of United States prices or (and) a fall in European prices seemed to him the only permanent way out; and of course an inevitable cancellation of interallied debts.

In a survey of the history of the problem, Professor Kindleberger in his excellent book found the first use of the term "dollar scarcity" in an article in the London *Economist* in 1940. In 1943, economists of the U.S. Department of Commerce in a famous study had written as follows: "At times, sharp strains may develop in the relationship between these concurrent two-way flows [dollars made available and dollars required], when the movement in one direction unduly rises or falls out of proportion to the other."[17] In 1943, apparently neglecting the applicability of the theory of comparative advantage, the London *Economist* wrote that one country "needs so little from the rest of the world, while

[15] J. M. Keynes, *Economic Consequences of the Peace*, 1920, pp. 227–231. Also see his *Revision of the Treaty*, 1921, pp. 159–162; *Essays in Persuasion*, 1930, pp. 292–293; *Treatise on Money*, vol. I, p. 347.
[16] S. E. Harris, *John Maynard Keynes*, 1955, p. 180.
[17] U.S. Department of Commerce, *The United States in the World Economy*, 1943, p. 1.

the rest of the world requires so much from it, that an equilibrium of accounts can be brought about by no means available to a free, or even a tolerably free, market."[18]

The dollar shortage was an old problem for Keynes. Not only had he foreseen it in 1919, but throughout a good part of the twenties and thirties he had been troubled by the shortage not only of dollars but also of francs. In his view the United States and France were in part responsible for the shortages, since they had failed to assume the responsibilities of creditor nations. They had not built an adequate superstructure of money on the gold received and thus encouraged imports and discouraged exports and had not lent adequately and removed barriers to trade.

In a speech before the House of Lords, delivered on December 18, 1945 (and in a posthumous article in the *Economic Journal*), Keynes once more addressed himself to the problem of dollar scarcity. He was optimistic and counted especially on the classical adjustments through increases in wages and liberal commercial policies in the United States, and he emphasized the importance for the British of obtaining dollars through expansion of export trade in third countries. For once, Keynes's prophetic powers had deserted him. Even with $50 billion of aid, the problem ten years later had not been solved. The help expected from inflation in the United States (Keynes had failed to stipulate relative inflation) and from liberal commercial policies was not forthcoming.[19]

Indeed, if in the next five or ten years the dollar turns out to be a scarce currency, seldom will so many people have been right. . . . Our exports are not, and are not likely to be, as large as our direct imports from the United States. The object of the multilateral system is to enable us to pay the United States by exporting to any part of the world. . . . For the first time in modern history the United States is going to exert its full powerful influence in the direction of reduction of tariffs, not only of itself but by all others.

. . . this is a problem of which today every economist and publicist in the United States is acutely conscious. Books on economics are scarcely written about anything else. They would regard it as their fault, not ours, if they failed to solve it. . . . the United States is rapidly becoming a high living and a high-cost country. . . .

In a comment on Keynes's last article, I had this to say:[20]

In an important sense, the persistence of dollar scarcity is inconsistent with the classical theory of international trade adjustments. An excess of credits on

[18] *Economist*, Dec. 4, 1943, and C. Kindleberger, *The Dollar Shortage*, 1950, chap. 1.

[19] "The Anglo-American Financial Arrangements," reproduced in *The New Economics* (S. E. Harris, ed.), 1947, especially pp. 392–395.

[20] S. E. Harris, "Dollar Scarcity: Some Remarks Inspired by Lord Keynes' Last Article," *Economic Journal*, 1947, pp. 166–167, 169–170.

current account should not persistently prevail: the inflow of gold or appreciation of the exchanges should raise costs and prices for the United States, and the loss of gold or depreciation of exchanges reduce costs and prices *on world markets* for the rest of the world to a degree which would once more re-establish equilibrium. Unfortunately, the required adjustments in wages, other costs and prices were not forthcoming; and, besides, elasticity of demand was not so great as was assumed in classical theory (e.g., Marshall), and (or) through the introduction of trade restrictions the significance of elasticity of demand was reduced: prices of foreign goods were not allowed to fall on the American market *pari passu* with the fall in costs. Since the adjustments required and the elasticity assumed did not prevail, classical theory was not very helpful in explaining the actual state of affairs—as Keynes so eloquently and so often argued in the inter-war period.

This brings me to the main theme. Is scarcity of the dollar an ephemeral phenomenon or are there long-run forces that tend to make dollars scarce? In his stimulating article in the June 1946 issue of the *Economic Journal*, Lord Keynes seemed dubious of the theory of dollar scarcity, and expressed the view that dollars in the coming years would be plentiful and, therefore, that gold might flow out of the United States rather than in.

At the outset we should draw some conclusions from the experience in the twenty-five years 1914–1939. Adjustments as assumed in classical economics did not take place. Changes in underlying economic and political conditions tended to prevent the required adjustments in wages, prices, etc., from occurring. Apparently the rapid relative reduction of costs and the steady gains in rate of offer of new American products greatly in demand tended to give strength to the dollar, and despite monopolistic pricing in many markets and despite the pressure of inward movements of gold and expansion of deposits, the competitive position of the United States tended to improve. On top of this, demand for United States products improved because of the shortages engendered abroad by one major war and preparation for another. So long as the gains in the competitive position of the United States (e.g., reduced relative costs and prices, offer of new products) continue at a rate rapid enough to more than neutralise the corrective effects of gold or exchange movements, so long will the dollar remain scarce. So long as the political situation deteriorates abroad, and so long, therefore, as capital moves into this country or the outflow is discouraged, the dollar will tend to be strong.

In this article, I also expressed some doubts concerning Keynes's contention that wage inflation in the United States would contribute importantly toward a solution of the problem of dollar scarcity. Keynes had concentrated on the difference in wage rates but had failed to compare relative *movements* in wage rates and productivity in both countries with adjustments for changes in exchange rates.[21]

In 1946, Balogh also had stressed the continued disequilibrium, pointing to the relevance of *uneven* technological changes.[22]

[21] *Ibid.*, pp. 172–175.
[22] *Ibid.*, p. 178.

Since writing this paper, an article by Dr. Balogh covering similar ground has appeared (T. Balogh, "The United States and the World Economy," *Institute of Statistics,* Oxford, October 1946, pp. 309–323.) Dr. Balogh is not nearly so optimistic as Keynes was that the dollar problem is about to be solved. Anticipating a serious depression in the United States from which other countries cannot be shielded both because of the dominant economic position of the United States and the restrictive measures likely to follow in the United States, Dr. Balogh forecasts a continued shortage of dollars. In fact, the developments since 1939, in his view, will make the situation worse. Dr. Balogh envisages two alternatives. The United States may continue to make vast investments, in which case her competitive position will continue to improve; or saving will be dissipated and the United States will lead the world into depression. External investments by the United States on a scale adequate to deal with excess savings is, in his view, out of the question.[23]

Balogh especially emphasized the danger of cyclical or secular instability in this country as a disequilibrating force. Possibly writing in 1955, his views would be different here. Dr. Lederer notes that for several reasons he would expect less international instability to result from United States policies, e.g., the large part played by relatively stable government issues of dollars for foreign use.[24]

In a brilliant essay written in 1953, Professor Hicks accepted the thesis of a dollar shortage.[25]

Once we assume (and such facts as are readily available offer . . . confirmation of the assumption) that nineteenth-century improvements were mainly export-biased, while those of our day have a predominant bias in the other direction, the whole story begins to make sense. And the dollar problem fits into its place as an episode, albeit a critical episode, in a wider evolution.

It is true that the forms in which the dollar problem has actually appeared have constantly tempted us to regard it as something much less deep-rooted. In the nineteen-twenties it was entangled with war debts; in the nineteen-thirties with world depression and the flight of capital before Hitler; in the nineteen-forties with war damage, more war debts, and the Cold War in international trade. A special explanation of the difficulties which were being experienced by European countries in settling their dollar debts could always be found. But the continuance of the same consequence, the same dollar shortage, as the result of these various "causes," has by now become very striking. That there is some general influence underlying these particular manifestations can now no longer be doubted. It is hard to see that there is

[23] For a fuller treatment by Balogh, one which repudiates devaluation as the way out for dollar-short countries and finds hope in the imposition of controls, see T. Balogh, *Dollar Crisis: Causes and Cure,* 1949.

[24] Lederer, *op. cit.,* pp. 190–191.

[25] J. R. Hicks, "An Inaugural Lecture," *Oxford Economic Papers,* June, 1953, pp. 117–135, especially pp. 130–131.

any other general force which would account for what has been happening than the disparity in growth of productivity which we have been discussing.

The main theme presented by Professor Hicks was that trade develops at first through rises of productivity in the strongest industries, that is, the export industries. Gradually the older industrial countries begin to feel the competition of the newer industrial nations. Thus in the twenties the British were increasingly embarrassed by the greater rise of productivity of the United States, but their losses were offset by continued gains in agriculture and hence increased cheapness of imported foods and raw materials. The crisis comes once the gains in productivity are made mainly in import-competing industries and the rise of productivity in agriculture ceases or becomes much smaller. Then the British can compete only through great rises in productivity or acceptance of cuts in real wages, enabling them to compete with the United States in third markets. In Hicks's view, the devaluation of 1949 had failed because British workers had refused to accept a cut in their real wages; in other words, money wages rose with the rise in the price of imports. But as MacDougall and Machlup note, only a moderation in the rise of real wages is required.[26]

I raise but one point here. Is it clear that improvements are now made primarily in the import-competing industries? Whatever figures are available in the United States do not support this view, and in fact, since 1939, man-hour output in agriculture in this country seems to have risen more than in manufacturing. There has been a veritable revolution in the use of fertilizers, insecticides, machinery, and farm practice. Thus, from 1939 to 1953, farm output in the United States rose by 36 per cent, man-hours of farm work declined by 18 per cent, and output per man-hour rose by 65 per cent. From 1941 to 1953, the number of tractors on farms rose from 1,675,000 to 4,400,000; the fertilizers used rose by 250 per cent from the prewar years to 1952.[27] In support of Mr. Hicks, it should be added that in the underdeveloped countries, the movement increasingly is toward development of industry and neglect of agriculture (though the largest gains in productivity may still be made in agriculture). Western Europe may, however, suffer from the relative gains of output in industry as against agriculture. The disequilibrating effects here may be felt in less favorable terms of trade related to the reduced *availability* of agricultural products, even though technical gains continue. Keynes's fears expressed in 1919 that with the great rise of

[26] F. Machlup, "Dollar Shortage and Disparities in the Growth of Productivity," *Scottish Journal of Political Economy*, October, 1954, pp. 264–267, and MacDougall, *op. cit.*, pp. 191–192.

[27] U.S. Department of Agriculture, *Agricultural Outlook Charts*, 1954, pp. 32–36. Dr. Bernstein also develops this point in the International Monetary Fund publication *The Revival of Monetary Policy*, p. 1.

population in agricultural countries and hence reduced availabilities of food for export, Western Europe would suffer—these fears are not without basis. Hence I conclude that there is some evidence supporting Hicks's position here and some casting doubts upon it.

But the crucial point in Hicks's presentation is that the dollar shortage is not a temporary phenomenon and that failure of the older countries to adapt their economies to the new alignments as required by the theory of comparative costs is the source of the trouble. These countries do not adequately cut their costs and standards of living (at least relatively) in relation to the steady rise of productivity in competing countries and the slowing up of gains of productivity (or as Hicks would add, reduced relative supplies of agricultural products) in the agricultural countries.

In a comment on Hicks, Sir Donald MacDougall, in an interesting article, criticizes Hicks's position. MacDougall is not at all certain that productivity rises more rapidly in the United States than in Europe. (But note that he eliminates war periods and examines productivity of agriculture in the United States by comparing output and population, not output and numbers working on the farm.)[28] On the productivity issue, note Table 16-2.[29]

Table 16-2. Rise of Production per Man-Hour, 1937–1938 to 1954

% rise

United Kingdom....... 28
United States.......... 41

Professor John Williams, in his able Stamp Memorial Lecture delivered on November 11, 1952, also envisaged the dollar problem as something more than a mirage: "My own view, however, has been that the wars hastened processes of change already under way, and that the successive short-run crises have been primarily the symptoms of longer-run and deeper-seated maladjustments in international relationships that go back for at least three-quarters of a century." Like Hicks, Williams emphasizes the competition of the newer industrial regions:[30]

The great size of the United States relative to most other Western countries, its large home market, its diversified resources, its comparative self-sufficiency, its high productivity and rapid technological progress have introduced a tendency away from, rather than toward, equilibrium in world trade. . . .

Meanwhile the rest of the world has become increasingly dependent upon the United States, and demand for its goods has persistently outrun ability to pay with exports. This is the "chronic dollar shortage". . . . But over time,

[28] MacDougall, *op. cit.*, especially pp. 191–194; cf. "Does Productivity Rise Faster in the United States?" *Review of Economics and Statistics,* May, 1956, pp. 155–176.
[29] United Kingdom, *Labour and Industry,* March, 1955, p. 61.
[30] J. H. Williams, *Trade Not Aid: A Program for World Stability,* 1953, pp. 9–14.

if there are divergent rates of growth of productivity, the trade will be progressively less favorable to the countries less rapidly advancing in productivity. . . .

In *The Dollar Shortage* (1950), Professor Kindleberger exhaustively analyzed the problem.[31] From almost every angle, the evidence points to a serious and long-continued maladjustment. Building on Keynesian economics, Kindleberger contends that the major cause of dollar shortage lies in the tendency toward depression and even stagnation in the United States and inflation and overexpansion in the older ("senescent") countries and the young ones (developing). Whereas in the United States savings tend to go to waste, in the other two groups of countries investments tend to exceed available savings, with inflationary results. A contributory factor to dollar shortage is the failure of deficit countries to adapt to structural changes, e.g., those brought on by war or technical changes.

Inflation in some countries and deflation in others would not be an adequate explanation, for the classical medicine of movements of gold and/or of exchange, with some help from capital movements, should correct the disequilibrium. But Kindleberger finds that there are all kinds of obstacles. Thus exchange depreciation not only may be unwise, for it may be used to treat a temporary disequilibrium and hence require movements of factors that otherwise would not be required, but, if used, may not remove a genuine disequilibrium. He seems to agree at least in part with Dr. Polak that exchange depreciation can treat only disequilibrium associated with monetary factors and cannot treat structural disequilibrium. In response to higher domestic prices in the depreciating countries, contends Kindleberger, supply conditions may be inelastic in these countries, and hence the gains from high elasticities of demand abroad may be small. Actually, both price and income elasticities of demand for imports abroad are low. (I think recent evidence might suggest to Professor Kindleberger that he is a little on the pessimistic side, especially on income elasticities.)[32] Following Professor Samuelson and others, he agrees that elasticity of demand for the products of dollar-short countries is low. According to Professor Samuelson,[33]

. . . if the U.S. export surplus is equal to about one-half of our total exports, minor exchange rate variations of not more than 10 per cent could only wipe out the surplus if the net elasticity of reciprocal demand were very great indeed. A net demand elasticity of 2.0 or 3.0 [relatively high] would require

[31] The major points are to be found throughout this volume, but see especially pp. 120–144 and 180–189.

[32] J. Polak in *Review of Economics and Statistics*, 1947.

[33] P. A. Samuelson, "Disparity in Postwar Exchange Rates," in *Foreign Economic Policy for the United States* (S. E. Harris, ed.), 1948, p. 399.

a tremendous relative exchange rate and price change to wipe out the enormous postwar imbalances.

In addition, Kindleberger stresses the inelasticity of supply in the dollar countries, e.g., the obstacles to allowing the liquidation of the textile industry (or any other industry vulnerable to foreign competition) in the United States when intervention by government may save it.

Especially prominent is the development of the Keynesian income and trade analysis, which has had careful treatment by Professor Metzler and more recently by Professor Kindleberger. The first cousin to Say's law (supply begets its own demand) is Hume's law (exports beget imports). In his first attack on free trade, Keynes in 1930–1931 had contended that protection was justified in Great Britain because imports had not called forth the required volume of exports. Hence he argued at that time against Lord (then Sir William) Beveridge and his co-authors (*Tariffs: The Case Examined,* 1931) that the usual free-trade argument—a cut in imports reduces exports correspondingly—was not germane, for British exports had already been cut.

Now Kindleberger (as had Metzler before him) developed a similar line of argument; with the Keynesian system available he tethered it to income analysis. Thus assume that from a position of disequilibrium the United States develops an export surplus and therefore a rise of income, as suggested by the export multiplier. Trouble arises because the United States does not expand its imports sufficiently to balance the rise of exports.

In this connection, Kindleberger ingeniously notes that tariff reduction may not be so effective as it otherwise might seem to be, because it is necessary to take account of the income effects. Thus, income will rise in the exporting nations as they expand markets in response to lifting of trade restrictions and fall in the importing nations as competitors capture their markets. (Of course, in highly inflationary periods this result may not occur in the importing nations, though allowance must be made for unemployment in injured industries even in the midst of general excess demand.) In the exporting nations, the resultant rise of imports with higher money incomes and, in the importing nations, the reduction of imports associated with a loss of income may well reduce, if not neutralize, the effects of the tariff cut in reducing the dollar gap.[34]

The Crux of the Matter

Acceptance of the dollar-shortage thesis does not necessarily imply a refutation of the comparative-cost analysis, but it does suggest that this

---

[34] Kindleberger, *op. cit.,* pp. 188–189; "The Propensity to Import and the Balance of Payments," *American Economic Review,* March, 1949, pp. 491–494; and L. Metzler, "Transfer Problem Reconsidered," *Journal of Political Economy,* 1942, in *Survey of Contemporary Economics,* p. 215.

theory has to be implemented. The dollar problem arises because in a dynamic world there are institutional factors that prevent the adjustments from taking place that would yield the distribution of tasks required by the static theory of comparative costs.[35]

Professor Haberler, the most persistent critic of those who support a theory of dollar shortage, though willing to admit to transitional difficulties, does not give us an adequate answer:[36]

Suppose, however, for argument's sake, that in the United States progress is faster than elsewhere. It is, of course, entirely fallacious to say that this will lead to a continuously underselling the rest of the world by the United States. What it means, is, first, that the comparative cost situation changes *and that a new equilibrium must emerge.* [My italics.]

In 1954, my distinguished colleague repeats the position he had taken in 1948. Admitting that countries, advancing more slowly may, but need not, be hurt by their trade partners, he sees at worst a painful adjustment when the trading partners advance, especially in import-competing industries (substitution of rayon and nylon for silk or natural rubber for synthetic). But proper monetary and exchange policies will solve these problems.[37]

One may agree that a rise of productivity in A may temporarily embarrass B, but B will make the necessary adjustments. These adjustments take time, however, and therefore the transitional difficulties may persist for generations if one development adverse to B is followed by another before B has adjusted to the first, and so on.

Monetary and Fiscal Policy

At this point, it would be helpful to discuss briefly the many variables that have contributed to the dollar shortage (also see Chapter 15). The orthodox view seems to be that an appropriate monetary, exchange, and fiscal policy would solve the problem. Of course, most orthodox economists agree that in the early postwar years, the imposition of appropriate policies in these areas would have required great sacrifices in numerous countries. For Professor Graham, writing in 1949, the dollar crisis was "solely a matter of discrepancy between the controlled external . . . value of the pound sterling and other European currencies and their . . . internal value."[38] (Cf. Robbins's view, pages 211–212.)

Classical theory was based on the assumption that automatic adjustments would take place through gold movements, etc. Later the relevance of the behavior of the monetary authority was at least recognized.

---

[35] Polk, *op. cit.*, pp. 211–214, and H. S. Ellis, *The Economics of Freedom,* 1950, p. 71. Ellis is skeptical of differential productivity as being relevant.

[36] Haberler, *op. cit.*, p. 438.

[37] G. Haberler, *Currency Convertibility,* 1954, especially pp. 29–30, 42–43.

[38] Kindleberger, *op. cit.*, p. 153.

Why, it may be asked, has monetary and fiscal policy been inadequate? Before tackling that problem, I would note that the supporters of appropriate monetary and fiscal policies are also those who insist (and rightly) that trade is governed by the principle of *comparative* costs. It is difficult to find an explanation of why deflation or disinflation should affect comparative costs so as to bring about equilibrium. The answer must lie in the fact that as prices decline, commodities just too high-priced to be exported become exportable and commodities that are barely importable lose their markets as competing commodities at home are depressed in price. It is not stressed sufficiently, however, that pressure to reduce prices at home may well mean a contraction of output (though not strictly relevant in the peculiar conditions after World War II) and hence less goods become available for export.

In general, I agree that anti-inflationary policies tend to improve the balance of payments. I am convinced, for example, that the flattening out of the European price rise in the years 1952 to 1954, as compared with 1945 to 1951, contributed toward an improvement in the European balance of payments vis-à-vis dollar countries. The relative inflation had been almost completely eliminated.

Table 16-3. Average Annual Percentage Rise of Wholesale Prices

	1945–1951	1951–1953
United Kingdom	16	1
France	62	0
Western Germany	Not available	0
Italy	45	−1
Weighted average*	40	<1
United States	9	−2

* The weighting is by Gross National Product. The three countries (1945 to 1951) account for about 60 per cent of Western Europe's GNP; the four countries, for 80 per cent.

SOURCE: Based on material in International Monetary Fund, *International Monetary Statistics*.

Undoubtedly, monetary policy can make a contribution to the solution of the balance-of-payments problem. Elementary economics teaches that inflation tends to weaken a country's competitive position, increase imports, and reduce exports. Easy-money policies invoked during the war were undoubtedly carried over too long by some countries in the postwar period. The supply of money was out of line with prices and foreign exchanges and kept out of line through controls. The rise in imports, loan- or aid-financed, into countries suffering from excessive inflation and balance-of-payments problems was helpful in the sense that it tended to offset an inflationary excess of investment over savings at home. (A rise in imports is the equivalent of a rise in savings.) But the rise was not equal to countering the continued inflationary pressures.

In this connection, the International Monetary Fund makes a strong case for the revival of monetary policy, showing that the rise of reserves by nondollar countries and the flattening out of price rises were associated with improved monetary restraints and the gains in international reserves were larger when these restraints were exercised. The favorable experience of Germany in the early fifties is contrasted to the unfavorable one of France and more recently (1955–1956) of Britain. Indeed, the IMF may go too far in attributing to inflation the disequilibrium of the postwar period. But Dr. Bernstein wisely ends the IMF survey as follows:[39]

> Monetary policy cannot, by itself, solve problems which have their origin in other forces affecting the international economic position of a country. It cannot solve payments problems arising from a loss of export markets. It cannot solve payments problems arising from the loss of major import sources. These are problems that require fundamental changes in the structure of the world economy and the pattern of world trade. . . .

Yet despite this improvement, it is well to stress the great obstacles confronting monetary and Treasury authorities in the postwar world. The pressures for higher money wages are almost irresistible, being tied to the improved organization of labor, high employment, the quest for social security (here the increased rigidity of wages in the form of social security is especially important), and the struggle against communism, with resultant pressure on government budgets. Here are strong inflationary factors. That these pressures prevail weakens the case for exchange depreciation, for depreciation will not improve competitive position if domestic factors obtain increased rewards which raise prices at home *pari passu* with the rise in the price of foreign currencies.

Again, destruction caused by war and the demands for rising productivity further strengthen the pressure to increase government expenditures and the supply of money and to keep the rate of interest down. The scope for monetary policy becomes increasingly restricted as the effects upon the growing government-bond market are considered. A rise of rates may endanger that market, a risk not easily taken. The long-run way out is higher productivity; but for many years excessive investment, given the current balance of payments, means the strengthening of inflationary forces. Higher productivity itself may not solve the problem even if the gains of higher productivity are taken excessively

[39] International Monetary Fund, *The Revival of Monetary Policy*, 1953, p. 16.

in higher incomes (accompanied by higher imports). Earlier we discussed the relation of *relative* gains of productivities and the extent to which these gains are absorbed in higher incomes or reduced prices. Nor, as we shall see later (Chapters 20 and 25), is it easy to correct the overvaluation of European currencies through exchange adjustments.[40]

All this points to one major consideration, namely, the increased tendency to stress domestic against international objectives. In the classical theory of international trade, it was assumed that the required adjustments to the balance of payments would be made. In the modern world, not only are there great obstacles to these adjustments, but as a result of the Keynesian revolution and political upheavals there is an increased tendency to sacrifice objectives of international equilibria to the requirements of full employment and growth, a better distribution of income, improved plant and equipment, and higher productivity. Hence, here we stress not only the greater obstacles to international equilibrium but a change of values.

Limitations on monetary and fiscal policy undoubtedly strengthen the forces that make for the dollar shortage. Orthodox economists are justified in stressing this point, but it is also relevant that these adjustments are not automatic, and it is not at all clear that their unimpeded use would solve the problem of the dollar shortage. The reason for this is that an excessive strain is being put upon the mechanism.

In part this strain stems from political and economic conditions associated with the war and its aftermath. A large rise of population, a highly liquid position, backlogs of investment, full-employment objectives, increase of welfare outlays which strengthen inflationary pressures, the rise of military outlays—these are all relevant. In the face of these demands, it is not easy to accommodate fiscal policy to the requirements of a balanced dollar market, and even if it were, the accommodation of monetary policy would not be easy, to say the least.[41]

In the British crisis of 1955–1956, the authorities relied heavily on monetary policy, bringing the Bank Rate up to 5½ per cent. What is more, this policy was strengthened by the use of large direct pressures on banks and borrowers. Yet the Governor of the Bank of England, in an unprecedented statement, complained that the scope of monetary policy in the post-war had been greatly restricted. In the view of the Governor, the direct impact of monetary policy falls on a smaller proportion of the economy than formerly and the impact on borrowing and spending can be outweighed by Public Authority and the impact on consumption offset by the level of earnings and fiscal policy. Moreover, higher taxes also dull the effects of monetary policy.

[40] S. E. Harris, *European Recovery Program,* chap. 5.
[41] International Monetary Fund, *International News Survey,* Oct. 14, 1955; cf. *The Economist,* Jan. 10 and Apr. 14, 1956.

In this connection note what the New York Reserve Bank has to say:[42]

The present-day economic setting, however, imposes various limitations on the effectiveness of the discount rate weapon abroad. In certain countries, the growth of nationalized industries and other officially controlled enterprises has largely insulated major sectors of the economy against changes in the cost and availability of credit. Moreover, private demand for bank credit seems to be responding less readily to interest changes because of the higher levels of taxation, the widespread practice of financing investment by ploughing back profits, and the reduced importance of the commercial bill. Still another limitation on discount policy in certain countries is the great liquidity of their banking systems, which results in central bank accommodation being little used and the discount rate being out of touch with the market. Moreover, some foreign central banks have still not gained full control over the cash base of the banking system, since they continue to allow free access to their credit facilities through a "back door" at a low rate (often by standing ready to purchase Treasury bills at a pegged rate) rather than through the discount window. Furthermore, even in countries with relatively developed money markets the relationship between the money market and the capital market is often such that impulses imparted to short-term rates by discount rate changes are not necessarily reflected in long-term rates. Finally, international capital movements are less free than before the war and less sensitive to interest rate changes.

Pressures on the Balance of Payments

However, these are not the only pressures put upon the monetary and fiscal system. In many years the terms of trade have been adverse for Western Europe. Even a deterioration of 10 per cent in the terms of trade would cost Western Europe $3 billion per year in the middle fifties. Moreover, gains resulting in the postwar years from better terms of trade for overseas countries had not been made available to Western Europe in increased dollar receipts, as had been the case before the war.

Europe's dollar problem arose in part from the reduced receipts from property income, the fixed price for gold in a period of rising prices and trade, the increased responsibilities for spending abroad (e.g., military), and the financing of new loans abroad by Europe. The Economic Commission for Europe estimated that in 1950–1951 the additional burden for Western Europe vis-à-vis the 1938 volume of exports could be measured in the following way:

As a result of a decline of property income, this income yielded in 1950–1951 but 9 per cent of the receipts from the 1938 balance of exports as compared with 32 per cent in 1938. There was no improvement from 1950 to 1952 if we limit our study to the United Kingdom, by far the most important earner of foreign income. For Western Europe,

---

[42] *Monthly Review of Federal Reserve Bank of New York*, June, 1956, pp. 80–81.

Table 16-4 is relevant for 1950–1951 (also see the deterioration of the British capital position from 1938 to 1955).

Table 16-4

% of 1938 *volume of imports*

Cost of financing new borrowings............................... 7
Increased cost of adverse movement in terms of trade since 1938 (assuming middle of 1950 is normal)............................ 44
Overseas expenditures additional............................... 6

The significance of the fixed price of gold is suggested by the fact that gold production in 1937 and 1938 was 5 per cent of world trade; in 1952 and 1953, but 1 per cent. In the two years preceding the war, the United States purchased $6 billion of gold (these were, of course, abnormal years); in the seven years 1948 to 1955, she disposed of $2.6 billion; and even from 1946 to 1955, her net gains were but $1.1 billion. In 1955, gold held outside the United States, Canada, and the IMF was roughly equal to the value held just before the war but the amount of export trade was 3¾ times as high. Obviously, the nondollar world had to find substitutes for large absolute and relative reductions in sales of gold in dollar markets, losses which were consistent with a large reduction in relative reserves for nondollar countries.[43]

These are not the only adverse factors in the balance of payments. The breakdown of trade with Eastern Europe was serious. Western Europe had to find substitute imports of $2,300 million (all figures in 1938 prices) and export outlets of $900 million.

Table 16-5. Western European Trade with Eastern Europe
[In millions of dollars (1938 prices)]

	1938	1951
Imports.......	3,150	850
Exports.......	1,600	700

SOURCE: *Economic Survey of Europe since the War,* 1953, pp. 86, 100.

The loss of Eastern Europe as a source of supplies and markets was matched also by serious setbacks in Asia as a result of war and political upheavals and in the Americas as a result of closer ties among Western Hemisphere countries associated in part with the failures to sell and buy for Western Europe in World War II. Dollar countries have improved

[43] Figures from International Monetary Fund, *International Trade Statistics;* Economic Commission for Europe, *Economic Survey of Europe since the War,* 1953, pp. 11–13; and His Majesty's Stationery Office, *United Kingdom Balance of Payments 1946 to 1953,* pp. 6–7.

their competitive position as they adapted their products to the requirements of the Western Hemisphere markets and as these countries increasingly were prepared to favor exports from countries which were more likely to deliver.

Here we have, then, a listing of the factors (not by any means complete) that tended to weaken the position of Western Europe and to some extent of Asia. The latter's deterioration of a few billion dollars in exports vis-à-vis imports, of course, further jeopardized the position of Western Europe, for Europe could no longer depend upon the excess of exports from these countries and others to provide the dollars (through an excess of European exports over imports to these third countries) to finance Western Europe's excess of imports from dollar countries. In general, it may be said that one of the most troublesome problems for Western Europe has been its inability to find products from third countries that might be substituted for dollar products and to obtain dollars from third countries.

In the light of these adverse factors in her balance of payments, Europe had to press exports and discourage imports. Hence to balance their accounts countries had to expand exports relative to imports and, therefore, to sacrifice goods. The pressure to sell more tended to turn the terms of trade against these countries, and hence they would suffer an additional loss.

Whatever statistical material is available points to progress toward dollar equilibrium in the first ten postwar years. From a substantial excess of imports in the prewar period, the United Kingdom by 1953 had raised exports to an equality with imports, and a further improvement followed in 1954. Of course, exports rose much more than imports (70 and 45 per cent, respectively, from 1946 to 1953), though the rise was roughly equal in the years 1948 to 1953. For France the gains of exports, relatively speaking, were even more spectacular: from 1946 to 1953, a rise of exports of 371 per cent and of imports of but 17 per cent. It should be observed, however, that exports were at an especially low level in France at the end of the war. In Western Germany, the expansion of exports was also spectacular and especially from 1948 to 1953. By 1953, the volume of export trade in Western Europe seemed to have risen by more than 70 per cent above prewar levels.[44] According to the UN *Economic Bulletin* for November, 1956, in 1954 and 1955 exports of Western Europe to the outside world rose by 9 and 8 per cent, respectively.

Apparently the trade balance was being treated effectively, but it

[44] Estimated from International Bank for Reconstruction and Development, *Seventh Annual Meeting, Summary of Proceedings,* December, 1952, p. 53; and International Monetary Fund, *International Trade Statistics,* June, 1954.

should also be observed that the medicine was not by any means restricted to the classical prescription. The British depended in part upon planning and controls to divert resources to exports and to limit imports. In fact, most European countries used abnormal trade restrictions, inclusive of licensing of imports, exchange control, government trading, and other nonpricing and discriminatory measures. Moreover, the improvement in the export-import balance did not measure a corresponding gain in the dollar-trade balance, despite special measures to stimulate exports to dollar countries and discourage imports from these countries. For example, from 1946 to 1948 inclusive, the United Kingdom's adverse balance on current account averaged £280 million; from 1949 to 1953 inclusive, the total balance had been converted to an average credit balance of £47 million; for the dollar account, the corresponding figures were £254 million (adverse) to £241 million (adverse).[45] Relaxation of controls and expansionist policies were accompanied by a dollar crisis for the British from 1954 to 1956.

Conclusions

It is evident that there are two schools of thought on dollar shortage. The orthodox school, including, for example, Professors Graham, Viner, Haberler, Robbins, and Friedman, insists that appropriate monetary and fiscal policy could eliminate the dollar shortage. It is only necessary for the debtor countries to live within their means, and appropriate fiscal and monetary policies would help. Even the later Keynes might be classified as orthodox in this connection, for his approach was to treat the dollar shortage through reduced tariffs in the United States, changes in exchange rates, and wage inflation in the United States. Perhaps he was less orthodox when, in his discussions of the twenties, he was skeptical of the efficacy of price and exchange movements and would treat the disequilibrium through cancellation of reparations and debts.

Sir Dennis Robertson has expressed the orthodox view well:[46]

. . . the more fully developed countries of the Eastern Hemisphere have clung tenaciously to ways of life and standards of consumption which they could no longer afford; the less developed ones have aimed at a pace of advance which they had no possible means of implementing. Balance could have been attained by now if the former had shaken off their crippling rigidities and the latter had toned down the exuberance of their visions. . . . balance always *can* be attained between any two trading areas, however great the gap between them in productive power, provided that the less richly endowed area accepts the standard of living to which its relative efficiency entitles it, and does not keep kicking against the pricks by adhering obstinately to occu-

---

[45] Calculated from *United Kingdom Balance of Payments 1946 to 1953,* table 2.
[46] Sir Dennis H. Robertson, *Britain in the World Economy,* 1953, pp. 55–56.

pational immobility and utopian social policy, buttressed by monetary inflation and an over-valued exchange.

But Robertson also adds a very important reservation which to me seems to be the most vital aspect of the problem.[47]

. . . it [the comparative-cost presentation] is essentially a static picture. What is to happen if Country A is not only better endowed than country B, but if the disparity of endowment between them is continually increasing through the cumulative mutual interaction of capital accumulation and technical progress? . . . the task of attaining it [a distribution of functions in the best interests of both] and then of abandoning it almost immediately for a new one, may surpass the human capacity for adjustment in what is, *ex hypothesi*, the weaker country. . . .

To this orthodox school belong Viner, Haberler, Friedman, and many others. For example, Robbins is a member of this school. In the absence of deflation in the United States, it should have been relatively easy to bring about[48]

the positive contraction of costs and prices. . . . I am arguing in effect that while there were profound real influences tending to cause disequilibrium in the balance of payments of the non-dollar powers, the persistence of these influences is to be attributed in a very substantial manner to monetary influences operating on the same side—to the unwillingness of the deficit countries to curb their local inflation.

In similar vein, Machlup contended that the dollar-short countries were unwilling to live within their means. Their rise of productivity exceeded their losses in terms of trade, and hence with rising per capita real incomes there was little excuse for living beyond their means.[49]

Those who tended to stress the inadequacies of monetary and fiscal policies in the dollar-short countries were also inclined to raise questions concerning the thesis of relative productivity gains of the United States as the explanation of dollar shortage. There are numerous variations of this theme: For Johnson, the issue is largely the rise of income accompanying higher productivity for the United States and hence the tendency to increase imports; for Bernstein, the point was that productivity gains for the United States vis-à-vis other countries would be uneven and these should not bring long-term imbalances (MacDougall also noted that many poor countries were in balance on dollar account); for Lederer, the danger of increased productivity would be real only if, with the rise of productivity and lower prices, elasticity would be high enough to raise dollar payments or if higher productivity were not offset

[47] *Ibid.*, p. 58.
[48] Robbins, *op. cit.*, pp. 54–55; cf. p. 53.
[49] Machlup, *op. cit.*, p. 267.

by increased leisure or a corresponding rise of income (and hence United States prices would fall greatly in response to higher productivity). Lederer was also sanguine that Europe's productivity was on the rise. The European countries increasingly have a comparative advantage in manufactured products with limited markets or diverse markets and are much more alerted to innovation than before World War II. The large rise of manufactured imports into the United States is relevant.[50]

The adherents of the dollar shortage, however, dubious of therapy through monetary and fiscal policy, were especially impressed by the structural changes which were not adequately subject to monetary or fiscal treatment. This in a sense was Hicks's position and Williams's. It was also the position of those who stressed the great and persistent demand for American products (an aspect of productivity), the increased independence of America from foreign products with, for example, the advances of chemistry. The skeptics of the dollar shortage, on the other hand, pointed to the increased need of foreign food and raw materials by the United States. Polak had shown the limitations of monetary policies in treating structural changes. In a survey of United States economic policies, by a distinguished group of political economists, the following appeared:[51]

In principle, therefore, it can always be overcome by monetary and financial means—e.g., by some combination of deflation in, and devaluation by, the deficit countries—regardless of the "real" trading relations. But, in the case of Western Europe's and Japan's postwar dollar shortage, the economic cost of so doing would have been far too high to be politically acceptable in these countries. The reason it would be so high is, precisely, that the causes of Western Europe's and Japan's heavy dependence on North American primary products, and of their weak competitive position relative to the United States, are structural—that is, these causes are relatively unresponsive to changes in the internal monetary conditions, the export prices, and the terms of trade of the dollar-short industrial countries. Thus, the causes of lagging agricultural production outside North America will be affected relatively little by a further increase in agricultural prices and a further deterioration in Europe's and Japan's terms of trade. The most important causes of Western Europe's relatively weak competitive position (especially in Western Hemisphere markets) are in large part of a non-price and non-monetary character. They will, therefore, be offset to only a limited degree by export price-cutting (e.g., through devaluation) or by internal monetary restriction in Europe and Japan. In short, neither the rate of growth of the supply of primary products imported by Western Europe and Japan, nor the supply of their own manufactured exports, nor the demand of other countries for those exports, are likely to be sufficiently responsive to price and monetary changes.

[50] Lederer, *op. cit.*, p. 183.
[51] W. Y. Elliott et al., *The Political Economy of American Foreign Policy*, 1955, p. 92.

For the unorthodox school, then, the malady is chronic. Monetary and fiscal policies will not correct the situation, though obviously they may help. Neither the creditor nor debtor countries are free. In Mr. Crosland's view, devaluation, disinflation, and tinkering with interest rates will not suffice.[52]

For the origins of the problem are . . . in a major revolution of the kind that occurs perhaps once or twice in a century, in world economic relationships Britain has lost her industrial leadership to the United States, and that country now bestrides the world in so colossal a position that the dollar and non-dollar worlds can reach no proper balance.

As Professor Samuelson expresses it:[53]

If the authorities of both the debtor or credit countries are free to pursue any cooperative policies, and if they wish to end the chronic dollar shortage, there is much they can do about it. But they are not free. And the measures they take to "correct" the situation will have repercussions (*a*) on unemployment, (*b*) on inflation, (*c*) on terms of trade, (*d*) on an available national output, and (*e*) on relative exchange rates. . . .

What is the cause of the chronic dollar shortage? According to Kindleberger, it is the tendency toward depression and stagnation in the United States (excess of savings) with relative inflation (excess of investment) in other countries; according to Williams, it is the size of the United States, its strong and improving competitive position, its relative independence of imports; according to Hicks, it is the varying rate of gains of productivity, and particularly in import-competing industries in the non-dollar-short countries; according to Balogh, it is the greater technical gains in the United States and the propensity to depression if savings are not invested in the United States and to great gains in productivity if they are; according to Nurkse, it is the tendency of countries with lower standards of living to emulate the consumption standards of the United States, with unfortunate effects on savings and the balance of payments; according to Samuelson, it is natural for poor countries to receive aid or borrow from rich countries and then repudiate.

These, then, are fundamental forces that make for dollar shortage, and they are strengthened by wars and political upheavals, which help to explain a deterioration in the terms of trade for Western Europe, loss of property and income abroad by Western Europe, loss of markets, and diversion of trade away from channels suggested by relative costs. These also contribute to the dollar shortage, though to some extent losses are recouped as the effects of the hot war wear off. But there is a residue

[52] C. A. R. Crosland, *Britain's Economic Problem,* 1953, p. 202.
[53] Samuelson, *op. cit.,* p. 408.

here which tends to strengthen the forces making for the dollar shortage, e.g., a tendency toward excessive industrialization in agricultural countries, losses of property income abroad by Western Europe, greater emphasis on high employment and improved distribution of income at home, the new structure of trade with East-West trade largely cut and inter-American ties greatly strengthened, the effects of inflation upon the contributions of gold sales, etc.

Obviously, large sacrifices are involved if the dollar account is to be balanced, not only those measured by the current disequilibrium but increased sacrifices if the forces listed continue to operate, and on top of that the cost of a deterioration in the terms of trade as vast exports are pressed by nondollar countries. Shutting out imports means an additional loss involved in obtaining supplies under high-cost conditions. Moreover, with the rise of nationalism, the pressure of exports from countries short of dollars is confronted with protective measures abroad, and hence to achieve a given result even increased concessions in price are required. The struggle for dollars among the nondollar countries, which may be treated with a return to convertibility, aggravates the problem because it becomes more difficult to obtain dollars through sales in third markets.

All these obstacles to balancing the dollar account might not be decisive in the views of many if the dollar-short countries could cut imports and raise exports through appropriate exchange policies. This is aside from the question that they may be unwilling or that it would be dangerous from a political angle to make the sacrifices subsumed under exchange adjustments. But here there are all kinds of difficulties. With a delicate balancing of interests, recourse to exchange flexibility is always difficult. Some lose (e.g., importers), and others gain (e.g., exporters), and the question is raised of imposing mobility that may not be required in the long run. But the crucial point is that, even if used, the effects are not likely to be adequate, and I assume away the tough problem raised by further gains of productivity in dollar countries or higher prices for food and raw materials as successive adjustments in exchange rates are made.

At what exchange rates would equilibrium be achieved? It is a common view that under inelastic supply conditions of the early fifties at home and inelastic demand conditions abroad, it would not be possible to increase dollar receipts greatly through recourse to exchange depreciation. (By 1955 elasticities had undoubtedly increased.) Even at moderate rates of depreciation, inflationary forces would be greatly strengthened—not only because of the direct effects of depreciation on export and import prices but also because in democratic countries and especially those subject to Communist pressures, it is virtually impossible to force upon large segments of the population the sacrifices involved. Labor demands adjustments in wages to the higher cost of living, and all groups demand a continuance of investment programs that presumably will ultimately raise standards of living. What government fails to do directly through tax policy (e.g., increasing savings and cutting expenditures) or through reduced public expenditures or through controls, the public refuses to accept indirectly through exchange depreciation, which in no small part is a device for imposing a cut in the standard of living and the level of investment. In fact, depreciation requires a movement of factors, especially into export and import-competing industries, and some inflation is a condition for achieving this movement. It may even be said that inflation in moderate degree is a price that has to be paid for high levels of output. To this extent any anti-inflationary policy may be more costly through its direct effects on exports than helpful in reducing prices.

From all this I do not conclude that nothing can be done to solve the dollar problem. The most obvious source of gain would be an improvement in international political relations. Other fruitful sources would be strong antidepression policies in the United States, a more liberal trade policy in dollar countries, a *moderate* rise in the price of gold, increases of savings in nondollar countries (directly or through government action), investment policies geared more to the requirements of the international economic situation (as both Harrod and Robertson have eloquently contended), revitalization of the international capital market, more moderate industrialization policies abroad, and measures to increase the productivity of nondollar countries. As has been noted above, some progress has been made, especially in monetary and fiscal policies. As output and savings rise, it becomes easier for nondollar countries to make sacrifices which would tend to narrow the gap. But there still remain elements of incapacity, of unwillingness to make sacrifice, and of excessive pressures on the adjustment machinery. These pressures are the greater in so far as productivity (inclusive of improved demand for United States products) *continues* to gain here relatively and with prices, income, elasticities, and hence exports and imports moving in a manner to weaken the average dollar value of all foreign currencies, e.g., Europe in 1946 to 1953 and Asia in 1953.

A young economist and student, Peter Kenen, serving as a guinea pig, complained after reading this manuscript that Professor Haberler and the author, who discussed these issues in our seminars over the years, were in fundamental agreement on the theory of dollar shortage but disagreed on what could be done through monetary and fiscal policy. However, I believe our difficulties are more fundamental. Hence I make another attempt to classify writers. It is not easy to reconcile the various views further than has already been done. Many hold that the dollar-short countries insist upon living beyond their means. Haberler, Harrod (at one point), Viner, Machlup, Robbins, and Robertson, among others, fall into this category. The adherents to the position incline toward a view that adequate monetary or monetary and fiscal policies would solve the problem of the dollar-short countries. They tend to underestimate the institutional obstacles to proposed policies.

Others, skeptical of the dollar shortage, deny the relative gains of productivity of the United States, as an explanation of dollar shortage. Thus, MacDougall does not find that productivity rises faster in the United States; Lederer points to the gains of productivity elsewhere; Bernstein denies gains of the United States in relation to all countries; others (Lederer and Johnson) stress the relation of productivity to income and hence increased imports for the United States, the inference being that relative gains of productivity should not increase the scarcity of dollars.

On the other side of the fence will be found Balogh, Harris, Hicks, Keynes (the early one), Kindleberger, Nurkse, Robertson (at one point), Samuelson, and Williams. In such issues as the greater economic strength of the United States, the persistent tendency of relative deflation in the United States and inflation elsewhere, the steady relative gains of productivity here before adjustment can be made to earlier gains, the tendency for productivity to rise in import-competing industries in the dollar countries—in these and other explanations they find support of a long-continued shortage of dollars.

Writers in this category also tend to question the potency of monetary, fiscal, and wage- and exchange-rate policies as correctives of dollar famine. These policies may be invoked and may be helpful, but in the light of the restricted field of operation of these policies, the great burden put upon them by these fundamental trends, and the institutional blocks to effective use of these policies, the dollar shortage may continue for long periods of time.

I need scarcely add that the writers included in the latter category do not agree in all explanations of the dollar shortage or on the measurement of therapeutic effects.

No one can say how long the dollar problem will be with us, for so much depends on political, economic, and other institutional developments. There is much to be said for a position taken by Sir Donald MacDougall in an article written in 1954. We just do not know.[54] As we shall see in a later part of this book (Part Five), the dollar problem can be treated by tariff policy in the United States, loans and grants by

[54] Cf. MacDougall, *op. cit.*, pp. 185–200.

this country, and also surrender of export markets. Our great and increasing dependence on raw materials and food, as is evident from the *Paley Report*, also may contribute toward a solution over the next ten to twenty-five years. MacDougall notes, however, that the increased pressure on agricultural markets resulting from the rise of purchases by the United States may turn the terms of trade against the United Kingdom.

Interestingly enough, as I read these final proofs in March, 1957, the U.S. Department of Commerce announces for the last quarter of 1956 the first serious loss of gold and dollar reserves by foreign countries in several years.

CHAPTER 17

Trade and Restraints

Declining Significance of Trade

Classical economics stressed the advantage of the division of labor and hence the gains to be had from international trade. It was assumed in most instances that gains accrued not only to the world but also to each country. Even if one country introduced restrictions, another following this lead would only inflict damage on itself. As Mrs. Joan Robinson expressed it, these free traders would contend that it was stupid to drop boulders in a harbor merely because the people of another country had dropped them in their ports. Furthermore, the general position was that no distributive share (e.g., labor, capital) would gain as a result of the introduction of protectionism. This position is not unexpected when it is considered that only in relatively recent years has the theory of international trade explicitly encompassed more than one factor of production. Obviously, on the assumption of one factor, the substitution of one for another is out of the question—yet protectionism generally involves some substitution of one factor of production for another.

But here is what Malthus had to say in a letter to Ricardo in 1815:[1]

. . . and I am very far from agreeing with you in thinking, that high relative prices, with regard to other countries arise solely from the real difficulty of production. They may indeed, and do arise from the high price of the materials of capital, but by no means always from the greater quantity of labor required. . . .

It is necessary to consider restrictions on trade in the light of a fully developed theory of international trade and in the kind of world we have had in the last generation and are likely to have in the next: in this world we have planned, as well as relatively free, economies; developed economies short of international reserves and others with plenty of

[1] *Ricardo*, vol. VI, p. 256.

reserves; underdeveloped economies impatient to develop and indus-
trialize; a resurgence of nationalism and increased insecurity which
greatly affect trade policies and reduce capital movements as an equilibrating force; and with all these the evolution of the most devilish
techniques for restricting trade which were virtually unknown even
fifty years ago.

As early as 1919, Keynes, impressed by the increased population and
industrialization overseas and hence the higher costs of food and raw
materials for Europe, had argued that the advantages of trade were not
so great as had generally been assumed. In later years he and others
were to elaborate this position. In so far as the comparative advantage is
narrowed, then the pressure to restrict trade increases: first, because the
losses resulting are reduced, and, second, because with small differences
in comparative advantages the instability of trade is revealed (e.g.,
nonimports more easily become imports) and even increased, and hence
the advantages of trade seem less.

What are the factors that tend to make international trade less important? First, there is the rise of insecurity and hence the need of
ensuring self-sufficiency. As the Communist world grows, this aspect of
the problem becomes more important. The U.S.S.R.'s trade with the outside world over a period of forty years (aside from gifts) was probably
less than 1 per cent of her income. In the United States, even industries
like textiles clamor for protection on the grounds of security. Second, as
the rest of the world industrializes, the range of industries where differences in comparative costs are large is reduced. Most countries, once
they have gone through the learning stage, are capable of producing
commodities processed out of local materials at unit costs not greatly
out of line with costs in highly industrialized countries. Once the importation of capital goods goes through the early stages of industrialization—and here the gap of comparative costs is large and hence the
gains of trade large—then nondurable goods, where gaps of costs are
less, become significant. Third, even when manufactured goods can be
produced only at a great disadvantage, noneconomic considerations, e.g.,
national pride or militarism, drive countries toward industrialization.
Fourth (related), the general tendency is to import raw materials (low-
valued) increasingly and manufactured goods (high-valued) less. The
gains of technology are relevant here also, for, as noted, even materials
may be kept out. Fifth, the movement of population inland tends to
cut the ratio of trade to income. (Transportation costs become a greater
deterrent.) Sixth, science tends to narrow the gap of comparative advantage. Thus the development of electricity and atomic energy reduces
the advantage of location close to coal; the advance of synthetics in
rubber, nitrates, fabrics, and plastics cuts the gains from the exchange

between industrial and raw-material countries. Seventh, with advancing standards of living, spending patterns change and services account for a larger part of the consumer's dollar. These services include medicine, education, distribution, travel, etc., largely domestic commodities. Hence for this reason trade tends to fall relative to income. Eighth, in a world of increased nationalism, capital moves less easily and hence export (and later import) trade suffers, for part of the trade is tied to capital movements. (As is noted elsewhere, however, we should observe that with movements of factors more restricted, trade tends to expand.) Furthermore, in the nationalistic world, repayments of capital are more likely to be made by reduced imports by the debtor nation rather than through increased exports. Ninth, much of the trade is based on the exploitation of natural resources which cannot be permanent and which is subject to control by the underdeveloped countries. Venezuela will be unable permanently to export oil to pay for most of its imports, and Brazil refuses to allow the exploitation of its oil resources. The mines of Bolivia and Chile by the 1950s revealed serious depletions, while the gold of South Africa was mined at higher and higher costs.

This point might be elaborated. Venezuela finds the export of oil profitable on obvious comparative-cost principles. But would she find this profitable if a longer view were taken? Or would foreigners find the trade so profitable if the price charged included an adequate allowance for capital depletion?[2] Finally, as Robertson has noted, once the gap in comparative costs is greatly narrowed, the gains of trade are greatly reduced, and small relative shifts of costs bring large shifts in exports and hence point up instability and stimulate the use of protective devices.

The issue of the future of trade can be pointed up in a discussion of British history. In post-World War II Britain, a strong case can be made for restrictions on trade. British imports have been a large part of British income, a ratio explained by Britain's ability in the nineteenth century to command a large part of the world's output and exports of manufactures. But with increased industrialization abroad, the corresponding relative reduction of agricultural output, and the greater ease of imitation of new techniques, the British have found it increasingly difficult to pay for their imports, primarily food and raw materials. Mr. Austin Robinson shows, for example, that British imports relatively are much higher than German imports. Confronted with increased obstacles in selling abroad, the British must make great sacrifices in their terms of

---

[2] See especially D. H. Robertson, "The Future of International Trade," *Economic Journal*, 1938, pp. 1–14 (here Robertson throws an illuminating light on these problems, though he wrongly anticipates population trends), and J. M. Keynes, *Treatise on Money*, vol. II, p. 189, and *New Statesman and Nation*, Mar. 21, 1931.

trade (reduced prices for exports) and then not be sure of obtaining adequate foreign currency to pay for essential imports or produce more at home as substitutes for imports. There is no long-run solution other than a rise of exports or a decline of imports. The structural adjustments may come through unemployment (in response to loss of reserves) or through restrictions on imports, which, of course, may also cut productivity. In the last fifty years, the transfer from textiles to metal trades and chemicals has helped but has been inadequate to solve Britain's problems, especially in view of her large losses of income on capital invested abroad and other invisible income. In theory and practice the solution of Britain's weakened competitive position must lie in part in a relative rise of domestic activity. The resultant losses of uneconomic allocation of factors has to be put, in the absence of greater domestic activity, against those associated with deteriorated terms of trade and unemployment.[3] Indeed the trend toward advanced industries helps, but both the shifts and the needed exploitation of foreign markets advance too slowly.

The figures in Table 17-1 indicate the developments in the United Kingdom.

Table 17-1. Output, Imports, and Exports by Classes and Relation of Imports to Income, United Kingdom, Various Years, 1850 to 1953

	1850	1913	1933	1953
Imports, % national income...............	18	28	...	26
% distribution of occupied population:				
Agriculture and fishing..................	21.4*	7.8†	...	4.7‡
Manufacturing.........................	32.9*	29.9†	...	34.1‡
Textiles and clothing.................	22.2*	13.7†	...	7.7‡
Metals and machinery, etc............	6.1*	9.8†	...	17.5‡
Various services.......................	26.8*	39.6†	...	37.2‡
Exports, % manufacturing...............	93	79	...	88‡
Textiles..............................	63	34	...	19‡
Metal and engineering..................	18	27	...	49‡
Imports:				
% food and livestock...................	34	37	46	
% raw materials.......................	60	43	41	

* 1851.
† 1911.
‡ 1951.
SOURCE: E. A. G. Robinson, "The Changing Structure of the British Economy," *Economic Journal*, September, 1954, pp. 458–461.

So far we have tried to explain why trade is less important than it used to be. One explanation is the growth of restrictions. Then we dis-

[3] See especially E. A. G. Robinson, "The Changing Structure of the British Economy," *Economic Journal*, September, 1954, pp. 443–461.

cussed one aspect of the restrictions on trade—why under special conditions it may pay a country to restrict trade—and the relevant issue of retaliation. Then we discuss restrictive techniques.

Restrictions on Trade and Terms of Trade

In his famous *Memorandum on the Fiscal Policy of International Trade* (1903), Marshall demonstrated that A in imposing a 50 per cent tariff on the goods of B might force B to pay the tax, a result which in current language would suggest improved terms of trade for A.[4]

The burden of these taxes will be thrown mainly on B in the exceptional case in which B's demand for A's goods is very urgent (inelastic), while A's demand for B's goods is not. For then the tax will raise the price of B's goods in A; secondly, diminish their sales there a little; thirdly, lessen the supply of A's goods in B a little; and since B's demand is inelastic, the small check to their supply will cause each of these goods to be disposed of for a much greater quantity of the labour and of general commodities of B than before.

As a result of the tariff, gold would then flow from B to A, A's prices would rise, and B's prices fall. Hence B's commodities in A would sell for twice the price they would sell at home; yet they would represent not much more effort and possibly no more. In B, prices would fall and the cost of A's goods in B would be greatly increased.

But Marshall hastens to add that in a world of many countries and many commodities the possibility of putting much of the burden of the tariff on the foreigner is greatly reduced. A does not generally have a monopoly of a product, and even if it does, the effect of a tariff in A would be for B, C., etc., to purchase the monopoly item but cut other purchases. In the real world, moreover, B could seek sales in C, . . . , N and thus not be dependent on A's markets as assumed above. But Marshall points out that the British, with a monopoly of wool in the Middle Ages and with a monopoly in manufactures in the first half of the nineteenth century, might have forced the foreigner to pay a large part of any import taxes levied.

Marshall's position at the turn of the century is still the accepted one. For example, Haberler concludes: "In the long run such a shifting of duty very seldom occurs to any significant extent." In his analysis, Haberler considers, as did Marshall, the elasticity of supply and demand in both the exporting and importing countries. He notes the relevance of changes in unit costs associated with the new tariff (e.g., if less units are exported, do unit costs rise?) and also the relation of the bargaining power of the country imposing the tax, the freight costs to this country as against alternative markets, and finally the changes in the pattern of

[4] *Official Papers of Alfred Marshall,* 1926, especially pp. 370–377.

spending resulting from the new tax; e.g., is the additional income of A spent on domestic or import commodities?[5]

Ohlin in general also accepts the Marshallian position. A is the country imposing the tax; B is the country exporting the taxed commodities. When A imposes the tariff, its income rises. A substantial gain in A's terms of trade would require that (1) foreign countries have an insistent demand for A's products as prices of her exports rise; (2) supplies of third countries competitive with A's exports are inelastic (increases bring large rises in costs); (3) foreign countries reduce their prices for A as A imposes a tariff, because A's market is so important and her demand is elastic; and (4) A's demand for nonprotected goods is not much increased when A's income rises and these goods become cheaper. In general, domestic prices rise in A for both domestic and international goods and decline in B. In his analysis, Ohlin also distinguishes between immediate gains in terms of trade and those remaining after adjustments are made. Thus with income rising in A, exports will suffer, though the rise of prices and income should attract additional factors and moderate the rise of prices; in B, prices will fall and factors be released from the production of items protected in A; and generally with reduced incomes, prices in B would fall. But this decline is stopped and perhaps reversed as factors move into the more profitable industries not subject to new taxes, though movement is not always possible.[6]

Most economists today would agree that a country might improve its terms of trade by introducing restrictions on trade. How much would depend on the elasticities of supply and demand. Thus if demand in the country imposing the tariff is highly elastic for imports and the supply of the relevant exports abroad highly inelastic, the imposition of a tariff may greatly improve the terms of trade of A, the country imposing restrictions. Under these conditions the consumers in A would greatly cut demand as prices tend to rise in proportion to the new tariff, and foreigners confronted with a resultant reduced demand and unable to find substitute markets, to hoard commodities, or to cut output would react by continuing to sell in the British market, say, but at substantially lower prices. Thus the former price might be £1 a unit, a price inclusive of tariff. The final price,

$$15s. + 7s. 6d. (50 \text{ per cent tariff}) = £1 2s. 6d.$$

Hence the foreigner is forced to pay part of the tax.

Actually the British were in an unusually strong position in the

[5] G. Haberler, *International Trade*, 1936, pp. 290–295.

[6] B. Ohlin, *Interregional and International Trade*, 1933, especially pp. 473–489. Cf. also Sir William Beveridge and Committee of Economists, *Tariffs: The Case Examined*, 1931, pp. 35–36.

early thirties to force the foreigner to offer commodities at reduced world prices. British import trade was a large part of total world trade, with the British one of the few relatively free markets; British imports were predominantly raw materials and foods from countries suffering greatly from reduced foreign demand and finding alternative uses of resources most difficult. British price history in the thirties, following the British devaluation of 1931, suggests that the Beveridge group (*Tariffs: The Case Examined*, 1931) was wrong, for British terms of trade improved in relation to the predevaluation situation.

We do not mean to infer that any country can improve its terms of trade greatly by introducing restrictions on trade. Much depends upon the importance of a country's imports, both relative to all imports and relative to the imports of particular countries and groups of countries, and, of course, upon the nature of imports. Can the selling country dispose elsewhere or restrict output? Can the protectionist country do without the imports and/or find substitutes? The country imposing a tariff will gain less if the seller can dispose elsewhere or easily restrict output of the commodity now taxed and if substitutes are not easily procured at home.

Even the United States in 1954 accounted for only about 20 per cent of world imports; the comparable figures for the United Kingdom were 18 per cent in 1937 and 10 per cent in 1954.[7] Indeed, 75 per cent of Latin American exports were to the United States as compared with about 18 per cent of Europe's exports to the United States. It might then be assumed that through restrictive practices the United States could force Latin American countries to depress their prices and this country would improve its terms of trade vis-à-vis Latin America but not greatly vis-à-vis Europe. As one British economist observed, the countries (e.g., the United States) which could gain the most from large restrictions on trade would find it most difficult to justify such restrictions. But one may exaggerate the likely gains. Even relative to Latin America, the United States is not in such a good bargaining position as at first glance it seems to be. The imports are largely raw materials and foodstuffs, for which demand is highly inelastic relative to prices though highly elastic relative to income. Indeed, this country could embarrass Latin America if it imposed heavy tariffs on her products but allowed imports of rival countries in without payment of duty. Under discriminatory practices of this kind, the Latin American countries would compete more strenuously in third markets and also be forced to depress their export prices in our markets.

Professor Viner agrees that through an increase in protectionism a country can gain in terms of trade, but he concludes that "no economist,

[7] Figures from International Monetary Fund, *International Financial Statistics*.

so far as I know, has ever maintained that the gain to any country from the favorable shift in the terms of trade due to protection are ever likely, under conceivable circumstances, to equal her loss from the uneconomic reallocation of her productive resources." But this leaves out of account the possibility that the resultant higher prices, which Viner concedes, might contribute to reduced unemployment. Viner admits later, however, that employment might rise as protection raises prices without a corresponding increase of wages, but he also suggests that once having given up free trade, the British might well find it difficult to return and hence losses of malallocation are continued.[8]

The Issue of Retaliation

Obviously if one country introduces trade restrictions, its imports will fall. Hence it will achieve a favorable balance relative to the previous situation. When the net effect is the elimination or reduction of an adverse balance on current account, no retaliation may result. In fact, many were inclined to support British restrictive policies in the interwar period on the grounds that the move was imperative as a neutralizer of earlier restrictive measures elsewhere. In other words, obstacles to British exports must be offset by obstacles to British imports.

But retaliation is the usual course. It might be assumed that each country, before embarking on a program which, in effect, would yield that country an increased share of the gains of trade, would consider both the effects on total trade, that is, total gains, and also the likelihood of reprisal on the part of others. On the basis of the history of commercial policy since World War I, we may draw the following conclusions:

First, the introduction of restrictions is often explained by the pressure of the domestic industries to obtain protection in their domestic market. As a result, the possibility of countermeasures abroad is given inadequate attention.[9]

Second, when a country (A) considers the likelihood of similar measures by other countries (in the same manner as an oligopolist ex-

[8] J. Viner, *International Economics*, 1951, especially pp. 109–117.
[9] For a broader discussion of the trade policies of countries, one should consult a penetrating discussion by A. O. Hirschman, *National Power and the Structure of Foreign Trade*, 1945, especially chaps. 1 and 2. Here Dr. Hirschman discusses the broad objectives of trade policy and in particular the gains of trade; the use of trade policy to strengthen national power; the degree to which country A may press countries B, C, D, E, etc., in turn related to the total gains from trade of B, C, D, etc., from their trade with A; the length and painfulness of the adjustment process which A may impose on the others and the strength of the vested interests built up in B, D, C, etc., as a result of A's trade; and especially, following Marshall, the tendency of A, a rich country, to expand its trade through penetrating poorer countries rather than pressing the rich ones.

amines the probable price behavior of competitors should he consider capturing an increased share of the market through a cut in prices), A may well still increase restrictions. A's position may be that of a country accounting for a small part of world trade or the trade of particular countries, so that it may with immunity further shut out foreign goods. (In 1953, more than 100 countries were listed by the International Monetary Fund as sharing $75 billion of export trade.) Under these conditions, A's anticipation is that B, . . . , N would not introduce reprisals against A. In fact the general situation may be explained by the following reasoning by A's officials: We shall introduce new restrictions. Our gains in improved terms of trade will exceed our losses spread over the world resulting from reduced trade *associated with new restrictions*. A (and others) will then continue to seek a larger share of the gains of trade (or a correction of an adverse balance of payments) even as the total declines. Obviously under these conditions, though A's gains from its own restrictive practices may exceed its losses from reduced trade associated directly with its restrictions, its gains may be less than the losses from reduced trade associated both with its direct contribution toward a cut in trade and with the contributions of others toward less trade as they react to A's policies.

Policy decisions generally are not determined in the manner suggested above. A small country will almost certainly introduce obstacles without much thought given to the effects of its restraints on trade upon other countries. In fact, its policies may not greatly influence those of other countries, but the restrictions may tend to snowball. As A gains, B, C, and D follow, and finally a point is reached when no country can afford not to act. Balances of payments become more and more troublesome for those that do not seek reprisals. In this manner, we may explain, for example, the epidemic of bilateral agreements of Latin American countries in the late forties and early fifties. In 1953, Latin American countries were partners to 135 bilateral agreements, mainly with Western Europe. These agreements covered about one-third of Latin America's trade, with the largest proportion of the trade of Argentina and Brazil thus being covered.[10]

In these agreements, one discovers the tendency of the restrictive process to spread even among smaller countries. Shut off from much of European trade, in part as a result of the dollar problem and United States aid to Europe (and hence closer economic ties between Europe and the United States), Latin American countries, one by one, tried to retrieve past losses. Once the Argentine, say, made an agree-

---

[10] Department of State, "Bilateral Agreements in International Trade," *Intelligence Report* 6110R1, April, 1954, p. 4, and cf. the very helpful analysis and compilation of Trued and Mikesell, *Postwar Bilateral Payments Agreements*, 1955.

ment with France to exchange Argentine wheat, linseed oil, and meat for French machinery, Uruguay would seek such a treaty on penalty of loss of French markets, and similarly with Belgium and other European manufacturers. Bilateral agreements are particularly effective, as Professor Ellis has ably and eloquently argued, in forcing a deterioration of terms of trade upon trading partners, restricting the amount of trade, and driving trade into uneconomic channels (a debtor country may force concessions, or a country in a strong bargaining position as a seller or market may do so).[11]

One peculiarity of the bilateral agreements after the last war was the manner in which their field of operations was circumscribed. An important reason for this was that the United States and several other countries held out for multilateralism. In view of the dollar-shortage problem, the United States could still afford to stand by as other countries tended to squeeze her exports out of markets through the spread of bilateralism. What the United States lost through these closed markets she gained in the aid she saved as other countries saved dollars through bilateral trading but paid the penalty of higher costs for imports.

Whereas the Latin American country with an average export trade of about $350 million in 1953 could impose restrictions without concerning itself much with reprisals, the major trading countries, e.g., United States ($15.8 billion), United Kingdom ($7.5 billion), Canada ($4.6 billion), Germany ($4.4 billion), and France ($3.8 billion), would, of course, have to consider the effects of restrictive policies upon the behavior of competing countries. In particular, creditor countries (United States) would be likely to be confronted with restrictive and discriminatory policies abroad should they increase obstacles to trade.[12]

An Analysis of Restrictive Techniques

In classical economics tariffs were the almost exclusive mechanism in the analysis of trade restrictions, and stressing the advantages of the division of labor and the comparative-cost principle, developed in large part to support free-trade principles, the classicist concluded that tariffs were against national and world interests. But the problem is much more complicated in the modern world, in part because all kinds of techniques are used and in part because modern economics stresses employment as well as the allocation of economic resources.

Let us consider the various techniques and their relevance. Among those to be considered are tariffs, quotas, export subsidies, exchange

[11] H. S. Ellis, "Bilateralism and the Future of International Trade," *Essays in International Finance,* summer, 1945.

[12] For a penetrating discussion of some of these issues, see T. DeScitovsky, "A Reconsideration of the Theory of Tariffs," *Review of Economic Studies,* 1942, pp. 58–73.

depreciation, and exchange control. The objective of the restraints may be to protect domestic producers against foreign competition in their own market or give them special advantages in foreign markets.

How effective is each obstacle to trade in achieving improved terms of trade? The tariff is one of the most effective on this score, though, as has been noted, the large country is more likely to gain or to gain more than small countries but also to invite reprisals. Exchange depreciation may result in an improvement in the terms of trade, but this is unlikely. (For further discussion, see Chapters 11, 20, 25.) Exchange control may be as effective as tariffs or even more so, for by operating on total demand for foreign exchange, exchange control forces the foreigner to press his commodities on the markets of the country introducing exchange control even more than under a tariff policy.[13] The foreign countries must make up not only for the reduced exchange associated with the restrictions on its exports but also for losses from sales of services and reduced capital imports.

Restrictions of imports by quantity below what they would otherwise be may result in a deterioration in the terms of trade or not, depending on the techniques used. Obviously, if the supplies imported are reduced, then the price at home rises relatively to the foreign price in the absence of this interference. A tariff clearly means a higher price, but the government receives the additional revenue. When the monetary authority uses a multiple exchange rate, it can appropriate the difference between the import price in the absence of restrictions and the imported price of a reduced quantity by raising the price of the required foreign exchange correspondingly. Here again, the government absorbs the windfall gain. But under simple exchange control or quotas which limit the import of a commodity, the gains may accrue to the foreigner or the domestic seller. Should the government impose a tax on the sales of the item at home, then once more the government may absorb the gains. It is possible, however, that the importer or middleman or partly one or the other would absorb the windfall. Then the terms of trade do not deteriorate, but the consumer pays the higher price. When the foreign seller is in a strong position—elastic supply conditions and inelastic demand in the country of import—he may then obtain the windfall in a higher price per unit.

As Meade shows, results will vary when, instead of quantitative restrictions, the limits are put on the values to be imported. Here much depends upon the manner in which the market is organized and the competitive or monopolistic nature of the market. For example, if importers are allowed to import until the value quota is reached, those who come first would gain the windfall. But if the license is issued to ex-

[13] Cf. W. Thorpe, *Trade, Aid or What?* 1954, for a defense of exchange control.

porters, then the foreigner gains and terms of trade deteriorate. When demand is highly inelastic, the resultant rise of price may be large. The gains in the balance of trade may (when the rise in price accrues to the foreign seller) be had at the expense of a large deterioration in the terms of trade.[14]

In general, adverse effects of restrictive policies on the terms of trade are most likely under exchange depreciation, and favorable effects most likely under tariffs or the use of multiple exchange rates (without average depreciation). Under exchange control and quotas a country may improve its terms of trade, though much depends on the mechanisms used to restrict and the nature of the markets.

Perhaps a word should be said of export bounties. Here the objective is to depress export prices, and hence it is not surprising that the terms of trade deteriorate. The effects on the balance of payments are similar to those of a tariff: In one instance exports rise; in the other imports decline (though with low elasticities of foreign demand, export receipts for the commodity subject to an export bounty may actually fall). Export bounties are generally frowned upon because they suggest dumping, e.g., sales on foreign markets at prices lower than in the domestic market or lower than in the major foreign markets. For many years the United States has indulged in export bounties on agricultural products, but in one sense these are not export bounties. First the government raises prices of agricultural commodities above the world level through the imposition of support programs. Then the government sponsors sales abroad at reduced prices, that is, prices below those paid by the government or other domestic buyers. But only in so far as prices fall below the level given in the absence of government interference through agricultural policies can the resulting price be held to reflect an export subsidy.[15]

The effectiveness of restrictive policies rests not only on their influence on the terms of trade but also on another criterion. Whether the objective of these policies is to protect domestic industries or to improve the balance of payments, the net effect of alternative policies will depend also upon how much costs rise as domestic output expands. Obviously the rise will be less the greater the response of supplies of all factors to increased demand (e.g., the greater the unemployment and the less troublesome the bottlenecks), the greater the mobility of factors, and

[14] Cf. especially J. E. Meade, *The Balance of Payments,* chap. 21.
[15] Cf. National Foreign Trade Council, *European Export Trade Promotion,* April, 1954, for a discussion of the various types of export subsidies: remission of taxes, research help, special access to raw materials and credits, sales promotion, export credits, and guarantees.

the less the specificity in their use. But at any level of employment, the rise of costs will vary according to the choice of restrictive policies. The crucial test is how great is the concentration of employments affected directly by the policies.

Thus a restrictive policy of a general type (e.g., exchange depreciation or exchange control) is likely to put less pressure on the available supply of factors than is a restrictive policy that affects only a limited number of markets (e.g., tariffs or quotas). With exchange depreciation, for example, the incentive to expand is felt by all industries that compete with all imports, for all imports now presumably become more expensive. Hence the upward pressure on costs and hence the rise of costs per unit of additional employment are less when the increased pressure on output is widely distributed than when, as under a tariff, only a limited number of industries which yield similar products as those competitive with imports are shut off by tariffs or quotas. The analysis of exchange depreciation applies also for exchange control, except that under control authorities may conceivably discriminate among markets, for example, cutting the allocation of exchange for purchase of some imports where, for example, supply conditions in domestic markets are relatively elastic.

In choosing particular techniques, an intelligent administration will then consider both the effects on the terms of trade and the rise of domestic costs as output expands in response to both less imports and more exports. Thus, a tariff rates high on improvements of terms of trade but low on the relatively great tendency for costs to rise. Quotas *may* receive low ratings on both counts; exchange depreciation, low rating on terms of trade and a high one on costs.[16]

Restrictions, Balance of Payments, and Employment

In recent years much emphasis has been put upon the contribution of restrictive measures, such as those just discussed, toward improving the balance of payments. Countries faced with deficits in their balance of payments and loss of reserves followed by restrictive monetary policies and pressure on costs and prices are likely to recall the unemployment associated with adverse balance of payments in the interwar period. Hence the urge to adopt tariffs, quotas, exchange depreciation, etc., measures which Mrs. Joan Robinson refers to as "beggar-my-neighbor" remedies. As the balance of payments responds to the therapy, it becomes possible to expand monetary supplies, depress the rate of interest, and, with reduced rates, stimulate investment. In fact, the improvement in the export balance (excess of exports over imports) is similar in its effects to

[16] For a penetrating discussion of some of these issues, see J. Robinson, *Essays on the Theory of Employment*, 1937, pp. 210–228.

a rise of investment relative to savings. An initial rise of X dollars of income through secondary (multiplier) effects may be converted into a rise of 2X to 3X dollars, or an initial rise of X employment may expand to a gain of 2X to 3X over the original increase of employment. How much the employment multiplier would rise would depend upon the amount of unemployment at the outset of the introduction of the "beggar-my-neighbor" remedies and upon the extent to which additional income is used to pay off debts, to hoard, or to purchase abroad. In particular, if the marginal propensity to import (i.e., the rise of imports with a given rise of income) is high, the multiplier tends to be low. For example, when the export balance of Latin American countries tends to rise, the response in increased imports is large, the explanation in part being a strong tendency to follow consumption patterns of richer nations.

An improvement in the export balance, once it is achieved, tends to be reduced as incomes rise. With higher incomes, imports increase and exports tend to fall. Even though the output of export commodities may well respond to the increased demand, it is probable that exports will fall. On the average, exports are only about 10 per cent of national income, and except in countries producing a few raw materials or food for exports, the consumption of export commodities at home tends greatly to exceed sales of these commodities abroad—in part because foreign countries suffer from the restrictive measures imposed by their trading partners. Even when the concentration is on one or a few staple exports (e.g., coffee in Colombia or tin in Bolivia), the response of output to increased demand is slow. Hence in general with reduced exports and increased imports, the newly acquired export balance is gradually whittled down. Under rather restricted assumptions. Professor Metzler has shown, however, that the adjustment does not fully work itself out.[17]

In an early analysis of similar problems, Mr. F. W. Paish showed that with a decline of income (for the country affected adversely by beggar-my-neighbor measures), the response of a cut in imports is likely to be great for industrial countries importing luxuries and raw materials but slow and inadequate for the raw-material countries.[18]

In her pioneering work in the application of Keynesian economics to international economics, Mrs. Robinson has stressed the greater effectiveness of policies stimulating investment at home over the beggar-my-neighbor remedies, which only redistribute unemployment and then only temporarily. If Metzler is right, the redistribution may be more sustained than Mrs. Robinson suggests.

[17] L. A. Metzler, "The Transfer Problem Reconsidered," *Journal of Political Economy*, 1942, pp. 397–414.
[18] F. W. Paish, "Banking Policy and the Balance of International Payments," *Economica*, 1936; republished in *Readings in the Theory of International Trade*, 1949, pp. 45–46.

Tariffs and Employment

Perhaps a word should be added here concerning the relation of tariffs and employment. (Further consideration is given this problem in Chapter 22.) Obviously, if there is unemployment, it is possible to put some of the unemployed to work through the introduction of trade restrictions. The unemployed then move into the industries newly protected from foreign competition. This, of course, assumes an adequate degree of mobility, and obviously if the cause of unemployment is immobility, it would be wrong to assume that mobility prevails in the case of import-competing industries favored now by restrictive measures but otherwise does not prevail. This latter argument is irrelevant, however, if the causes of unemployment do not lie primarily in immobility. Under conditions of substantial unemployment, the additional employment in the import-competing industries is not necessarily and not likely to be at the expense of those employed elsewhere. Hence the interest in this solution. In 1905, Schuller, the German economist, had stressed the relevance of unemployed resources as well as the ineffective use of some factors. Not only might they be employed more effectively, but the amount of employment might rise. Hence he supported protectionism.[19]

The argument that domestic production is not susceptible of diminution by means of importation, owing to the fact that the total productive activity of every state represents a fixed quantity determined by the existing productive forces, and that the productive factors displaced from one branch of industry are merely diverted to another, still represents one of the main contentions of the advocates of free trade. It is opposed, however, by the fact that the productive forces of a state are exploited in very different degrees—or not at all. . . .

Obviously, the object of using trade restrictions is to increase demand. In the early thirties, Keynes, interested primarily in employment, embraced protectionism. Earlier he had written: "Is there anything that a tariff could do which an earthquake could not do better?" But the pound sterling was now overvalued, the proposal to correct disequilibrium through a depreciation of the exchanges or adequate checks on outward capital movements had not been accepted, and a direct assault on wages was not practical. Indeed, Keynes admitted that depreciation or tariffs might be a means of adjusting wages downward in export industries.

Neoclassical economists could envisage the possibility of protectionism increasing employment,[20] but they were dubious that any help could be

[19] F. W. Taussig, *Selected Readings in International Trade and Tariff Policies*, 1921, especially pp. 371–386.
[20] Cf. Haberler, *op. cit.*, pp. 259–268, and Ohlin, *op. cit.*, pp. 491–498.

rendered except for short periods. For Haberler, writing in the early thirties, the solution for permanent unemployment was a reduction of real wages. (Haberler probably would not take this position except for export industries in the 1950s.) Ohlin observed that idle capacity might be cut and savings on the whole obtained through tariffs. (As employment rose, the costs of supporting the unemployed would fall.) But Ohlin contended that with international payments in balance prior to the introduction of the restrictive measures, the country involved (say A) would export capital equal to the improved balance associated with reduced imports; that is, exports, despite the decline in imports, would be sustained. But how, asks Ohlin, would this movement continue without a decline in the rate of interest? (Actually with higher incomes and savings we might, unlike Ohlin, expect a reduction in the rate of interest.) Besides, adds Ohlin, the restrictive measures would interfere with the structural adjustments that would otherwise take place. In classical studies there is also a tendency to argue that the decline of imports would be offset by a reduction of exports. But note Keynes's reply:[21]

It [a corresponding fall of exports] would only be true in a hypothetical economic system possessing such inherent capacity for stable equilibrium, that not only were both the initial and the final positions in equilibrium but the elasticity of the system was such that any disturbance was responded to so immediately that the system was incapable of ever departing appreciably from equilibrium.

In short, restrictive measures might for many years increase employment, especially if, with increased demand, mobility improves. But several other aspects of these problems must be noted. As I contended in *Exchange Depreciation* (1936),[22] the major gains of the depreciation were not competitive, but rather their contribution was toward an easing of the restraints on monetary and fiscal policies associated with the depreciation. It now became possible to convert a deflationary into an inflationary trend or at the very least to moderate the decline of prices relative to costs. Another aspect of these beggar-my-neighbor measures should be noted. Often they are required in order to correct a genuine disequilibrium. Indeed, the British devaluation of 1949 might be considered a beggar-my-neighbor measure, for it improved the British competitive position, though not so much as was hoped. But though it might be interpreted by its results to be a means of redistributing employment, actually its major effect was to help reestablish equilibrium in the dollar market. Since employment was high in most countries, its

[21] *New Statesman and Nation*, Apr. 4, 1931.
[22] Cf. this book, Chaps. 11 and 25.

effects were felt primarily in improving the dollar position of nondollar countries.[23] It is scarcely necessary to add that any favorable effects on prices and employment from restrictions must be weighed against the increased malallocation of resources.

Restrictions and Income Redistribution

Protectionism is often defended on other grounds, namely, that through recourse to restrictions the distribution of income can be improved, that is, say, labor or agriculture and the low-income groups would improve their position. It is not the task of the economist *qua* economist to say that a more equitable income distribution should be the objective of policy, but the economist can analyze the effects of tariffs on distribution. Since World War I much emphasis has been put upon the use of restrictive devices to modify the distribution of income. Thus in the United States, farm policy is oriented toward raising farm incomes through government-support programs which send farm prices above world levels. In order to maintain these high prices and preclude the purchase of foreign agricultural commodities at prices above world levels, the government imposes tariffs and quotas on agricultural imports. The government goes even further: Agricultural commodities are sold abroad at below domestic prices, though not necessarily at prices below what they would have been in the absence of government-support programs. The defense for these policies lies largely in the assumed need of raising farmers' incomes, in the slow and inadequate response of farm output to price declines, and in the weak bargaining position of the farmers, largely unorganized, vis-à-vis industry. The result of this protectionism is the improved relative position of American agriculture but also an uneconomic production of, say, sugar, wool, and wheat. On comparative-cost principles the United States would produce less of these products and more of manufactured products.

But the losses associated with a violation of comparative-cost principles are not so large as they at first seem for the following reasons: First, the transfer of income to farmers, a low-income group, probably increases the total outlays for consumption and investment. Except in inflationary periods, the results of increased spending, and hence a rise of demand relative to supply, are likely to be increased output, which helps to offset the uneconomic allocation of factors of production. Second, the assumption implicitly made by those who are critical of the farm policies is that labor and management on the farms "unproductively" employed would move into the manufacturing and service employments. But it is

[23] J. Robinson, *op. cit.* Mrs. Robinson compares the effects both on terms of trade and on costs of alternative programs: wage cutting, exchange depreciation, export bounties, tariffs, and quotas.

well known that the migration is sluggish, as is evident, for example, in an average income on the farms in the United States of $1,546 in 1952 as compared with $3,833 in manufacturing.[24] Hence it may be held that even in the absence of price supports and protectionist policies, much uneconomic output in agriculture would have been sustained. Hence the contribution of the government to uneconomic production is not so great as it seems to be.

It is also possible to introduce protectionism in order to improve the relative position of labor. In fact, it has often been noted that protectionism in the nineteenth century in the United States had increased the relative proportion of labor income. Obviously, if labor is the scarce factor and trade is cut off, then the competition of foreign labor is reduced and American labor profits. In the absence of this protectionism, the American market would sell the products of foreign textile workers as well as American textile workers.

In an interesting study of the Australian tariff, an official committee (1929) concluded:[25]

The advantage of protection is in the maintenance of a larger population than could have been expected at the same standard of living without the protective tariff. It is not an advantage to every part of the population, nor has it produced the maximum of income per head. But given the basic Australian objective of seeking the largest white population at the highest standard of living, we consider that the protective tariff has been an effective means of securing it. The practical conclusion is that having established this population it would be disastrous to abandon the policy which has made it possible.

An expert committee supported the Australian tariff primarily on the grounds that without the tariff the national income would have been maintained but with a population at least 230,000 smaller. Hence the inference can be drawn, as it has been by Professor Viner, that a larger income would have been achieved under free trade. The Australian case rests on the *redistributive* effects of the tariff: It makes possible a larger income for the working classes at the expense of the landlords. This is not necessarily the most effective, though it may be the most practical, method of redistribution. Manufacturing, with large demands for labor, is encouraged at the expense of agriculture. The gain for workers is made in part because it is assumed that the worker is protected against rising prices by escalator clauses and the like, but little is said concerning other determinants of real wages. Had protection not been maintained, higher income, according to the Committee, would have gone to the landlords. Among the unfortunate effects of the tariff are

[24] *Survey of Current Business,* July, 1953, p. 20.
[25] *The Australian Tariff: An Economic Enquiry,* 2d ed., 1929, p. 141.

higher costs and prices, which, of course, discourage exports. But should protection be lifted even if, as estimated, costs should drop by 8 per cent, both the rise of unit cost of additional output of wheat and wool and the pressure on restricted world markets of additional sales of these products would result in a rise of incomes considerably less than the £47 million lost in protected industries through the introduction of free trade. Though the Committee approves the current level of protection, it is aware of much waste and hence sets up criteria to determine the distribution of protectionist favors: the size of the market, the possibility of producing in large plants at low unit costs, the amount of employment per pound of additional costs, and the effects on prices and export costs. "We have . . . good reason to believe that the extra costs of protected products range from a negligible amount up to over 40 per cent of their value, and that the costs of the more expensive are about twice as high as the average for the same benefits as measured by employment given."[26]

Since the classical theory of international trade assumed only one factor, labor, there was no question raised concerning the substitution of one factor for another. But once it is assumed that there are several factors of production (e.g., by Heckscher), it becomes evident that trade policy may influence the relative scarcities of factors. Once it is evident that the relative supplies of factors vary from country to country and that they are combined in the production of commodities in varying proportions (as would be expected as a result of differences in relative supplies not offset by differences in demand), then the gains of trade emerge. And once trade is opened, the scarce factors become less scarce and the plentiful factors less plentiful (commodities from abroad are imported into A which use *relatively* much of the factors scarce in A, and commodities are exported from A which use much of the plentiful factor in A). Therefore, with the expansion of trade in the United States in the nineteenth century, the shortage of the scarce factor, labor, was reduced (as manufactures were imported) and land, the plentiful factor, became less abundant (as wheat and cotton were exported). But with the introduction of protectionism, both labor and capital would move from, say, wheat into textiles. Since relatively little labor is used in wheat farming and much in textile production, the net effect would be a new structure of industry under which, though the proportion of labor and capital was unchanged, the demand for labor would rise vis-à-vis capital (and land) because of the changed structure of employment. Applying this type of analysis but restricting it to two factors and assuming that

[26] *Ibid.*, p. 141; also see especially pp. 3–6 and pts. III–VII, IX; and J. Viner, *International Economics*, pp. 86–93.

the supply of factors is fixed, Stolper and Samuelson, in an important article, showed that labor might increase not only its relative share of the national income but also its *absolute* share. Some of the neoclassicists —and notably Viner—had agreed that the *relative* share of a particular group might be improved.

Emphasizing the gains resulting from trade, the classicists did not pay sufficient attention to the redistributive effects of protectionism. Marshall, for example, stressed the point that despite great gains in efficiency, German real wages had declined while British real wages had gone up. Prices of necessaries had risen in Germany, while they had declined in Great Britain. No hint of the possibility of gains of labor at the expense of other groups. " . . . I believe it to be true that real wages of the Germans are increasing less rapidly than those of the Englishmen; and that if Germany abandons protection, which has no considerable service to render her, the wages of Germany would rise a great deal. To hazard a guess, I should expect them to rise by about a fifth."[27] As has been noted, a theory of international trade which deals with only one factor of production necessarily would not allow the gains of one factor against another. But even when the treatment relates to more than one factor, the possibility of gains through a redistribution of demand associated with protectionism was minimized against those associated with optimum allocation of factors of production. Thus Professor Taussig, who was one of the pioneers in extending the theory of international trade to a consideration of several factors, wrote:[28]

Wages at large, and the prosperity of the laboring class as a whole and so of the country as a whole, are not kept high by protection. . . . But none the less it is untrue that high wages in general have been caused by protection, or are now made possible only by protection. They rest not on that feeble prop but on the solid foundation of general effectiveness of industry—on the resources of the country and the genius of the people.

Later writers, e.g., Haberler and especially Viner, envisaged the possibility that labor might gain at the expense of other groups through the introduction of restrictive measures, but Haberler at least tended to emphasize the greater gains from a division of labor as against an improved distribution for labor under protectionism. First Heckscher and then Ohlin made it possible to analyze the redistributive effects on income among factors related to change in commercial policy. Indeed, Heckscher contended that if A (e.g., labor) gained, then against A's gains must be put the losses associated with malallocation of resources under restrictionism, and for B, C, etc., losses accrue because of both

---

[27] *Memorandum on the Fiscal Policy of International Trade*, 1903, pp. 423–424.
[28] F. W. Taussig, *Free Trade, the Tariff and Reciprocity*, 1920, p. 69.

the redistribution and the uneconomic use of factors. Finally, of course, Stolper and Samuelson suggested the possibility of relative and absolute gains for the scarce factor following the introduction of protectionism.[29]

These studies of the effects of restrictions upon the distribution of income are generally based on the assumption of fixed supplies of factors of production. Increased trade is a substitute for the movements of factors across national frontiers. Some factors cannot be moved (e.g., land), and others move sluggishly or encounter obstacles (e.g., immigration laws or discrimination against foreign capital). Since trade tends to make scarce factors less scarce and plentiful factors less plentiful, trade is a substitute for the movement of factors. Should factors be perfectly mobile, so that (aside from differences in unit cost resulting from the size of the business unit) the relative supplies of factors would be the same everywhere and similarly for the production function, then trade would not be required. But with protectionism on the increase and movement of factors reduced in the second half of the twentieth century, the tendency toward equalization of income among countries, which is strengthened by factor movements or trade, is reversed. These tendencies may largely explain the increased differences of income for countries richly endowed with capital, techniques, and other resources compared with poorer countries with little capital and large population relative to resources.

Trade and Unemployment

These discussions of the relation of commercial policy and the distribution of income do not treat the problem of unemployment. Obviously if protectionism increases employment, then it further affects the relative shares of labor, landlords, capitalists, etc. In general, the Keynesians, despite their emphasis on the relation of the export balance and unemployment, tended to minimize the contribution of trade restrictions to employment. Thus a committee of economists commented in 1931 as follows on Keynes:[30]

Though Mr. Keynes claims some direct increase of employment through the protective operation of the tariff that he proposes, this is for him only a subsidiary gain. His object is primarily the use of the tariff as an instrument of international equilibrium; he knows, it may be suggested, too much about the actual facts of British unemployment to make for his or any tariff proposals the extravagant claims of most protectionists.

[29] E. Heckscher, "The Effect of Foreign Trade on the Distribution of Income," 1919, reproduced in *Readings on the Theory of International Trade*, 1949, pp. 272–300; W. F. Stolper and P. A. Samuelson, *Review of Economic Studies*, 1941, reproduced in *ibid.*, pp. 333–357.

[30] *Tariffs: The Case Examined*, by a committee of economists under the chairmanship of Sir William Beveridge, 1931, p. 57.

It will also be recalled that Mrs. Robinson, in her emphasis on the beggar-my-neighbor aspects of restrictive policies, contended that any gains in the balance of payments and hence in the export balance and employment would be only temporary. What I would like to stress here is that countries suffering much unemployment, open or disguised, might easily increase the total amount of employment on a permanent basis. A gain may reflect a reduced propensity to import, either because of a revised pattern of spending at higher incomes or because of the introduction of controls which reduce imports or select imports that tend to sustain the export balance. Such effects are the more likely to follow if other countries do not counter with retaliatory control policies. The experience of underdeveloped countries points to the genuine possibilities here (see Chapter 19).

In summary, this chapter is concerned with the problems of restrictions on trade and their repercussions. Why does trade tend to become less important? How do tariffs affect the terms of trade? In what manner does retaliation reduce the gains of restrictionism? What are the most effective techniques for restricting trade when viewed through their effects on terms of trade and on real costs? How do restraints affect employment and the distribution of income?

In later chapters (22 and 23) we shall discuss fully the special problems of protectionism that have arisen in the post-World War II period.

CHAPTER 18

New Institutions and Disequilibrium

The Problem of International Equilibrium

First a word about disequilibrium, a term that has been used frequently in this book. The problem, as outlined in Mill's discussion of the gains of trade, was relatively simple. The terms of trade will settle at a point where the value of imports exactly equals that of exports. Indeed, there may be a temporary disequilibrium, e.g., an excess of imports, but this would be corrected in monetary economies by gold movements and the accompanying price adjustments. Hence it might be assumed that when gold flows out (in) or exchanges depreciate (appreciate), a temporary disequilibrium has emerged. In recent years there has also been much discussion concerning equilibrium rates of foreign exchange, that is, the exchange rate which is consistent with a balancing of accounts without abnormal capital movements. I discuss this problem in Chapters 11 and 25. Here let us note that some economists have held that there are times when no exchange rate yields an equilibrium position.

Since the war, there has been a tendency to redefine international equilibrium. It has been held by Professor Hansen, for example, that even with exchanges stable and gold flows relatively unimportant, a condition of disequilibrium prevails when the apparent balance is achieved by a repressive monetary (and fiscal) policy with an accompanying distortion of prices relative to costs, in turn reflected in a substantial amount of unemployment.[1] In other words, unemployment associated with policies forced upon a country because it seeks stable

[1] A. Hansen, "Fundamental Disequilibrium," in *Foreign Economic Policy for the United States* (S. E. Harris, ed.), pp. 379–383. Cf. also G. Haberler, "Currency Depreciation and the International Monetary Fund," in *ibid.*, pp. 384–396, where Professor Haberler is critical of Hansen's position, and also R. Nurkse, *International Currency Experience: Lessons of the Inter-war Period*, 1944. Cf. also H. S. Ellis, "The Equilibrium Rate of Exchange," and S. E. Harris, "Measures of Currency Overvaluation and Stabilization," in *Exploration in Economics: Essays in Honor of F. W. Taussig*, 1936.

exchanges and preservation of its reserves is an indication of disequilibrium. (British conditions in the late 1920s are an example.)

We can go further. Even when a country maintains its reserves and stability of exchanges and a high level of employment, international disequilibrium may still be found. Thus when the *apparent* equilibrium is achieved through abnormal capital imports (not likely to be financed) and/or grants and/or through the imposition of abnormal restrictions on trade such as exchange control, multiple exchange rates, quotas, numerous export subsidies, and other measures favoring exports, then it can scarcely be claimed that equilibrium prevails. (Equilibrium is a concept that applies to relatively free markets.) The indices of an apparent equilibrium (maintenance of reserves, exchange stability, high levels of employment) are then attained through the abandonment of the free market and an unusual degree of uneconomic production.

Keynes has put some of the issues well:[2]

We have to consider, on the one hand, a country's balance of payments on income account on the basis of the existing natural resources, equipment, technique and costs (especially wage costs) at home and abroad, a normal level of employment, and those tariffs, etc., which are a permanent feature of national policies; and, on the other hand, the probable readiness and ability of the country in question to borrow or lend abroad on long-term (or, perhaps, repay or accept repayment of old loans), on the average of the next few years. A set of rates of exchange which can be established without undue strain on either side and without large movements of gold (on a balance of transactions), will satisfy our condition of equilibrium.

How far considerations of employment enter into the issue of international economic policy is revealed by the *Havana Charter for an International Trade Organization* (ITO). Here the objective of full and productive employment is recognized at the outset. Furthermore, a responsibility is put upon each country to pursue these objectives, and that means also not to pursue a policy which makes it impossible for those seeking full employment to achieve it without imposing abnormal obstacles to imports. In other words, the implication is a call for expansionist policies everywhere.[3]

ARTICLE 2
IMPORTANCE OF EMPLOYMENT, PRODUCTION AND DEMAND IN RELATION TO THE PURPOSE OF THIS CHARTER

1. The Members recognize that the avoidance of unemployment or under-employment, through the achievement and maintenance in each country of useful employment opportunities for those able and willing to work and of a

---

[2] *Lloyd's Bank Review*, October, 1935, p. 528.
[3] *Havana Charter for an International Trade Organization*, 1948, p. 6.

large and steadily growing volume of production and effective demand for goods and services, is not of domestic concern alone, but is also a necessary condition for the achievement of the general purpose and the objectives set forth in Article 1, including the expansion of international trade, and thus for the well-being of all other countries.

2. The Members recognize that, while the avoidance of unemployment or underemployment must depend primarily on internal measures taken by individual countries, such measures should be supplemented by concerted action under the sponsorship of the Economic and Social Council of the United Nations in collaboration with the appropriate inter-governmental organizations, each of these bodies acting within its respective sphere and consistently with the terms and purposes of its basic instrument.

3. The Members recognize that the regular exchange of information and views among Members is indispensable for successful co-operation in the field of employment and economic activity and should be facilitated by the Organization.

ARTICLE 3
MAINTENANCE OF DOMESTIC EMPLOYMENT

Each Member shall take action designed to achieve and maintain full and productive employment and large and steadily growing demand within its own territory through measures appropriate to its political, economic and social institutions. . . .

Measures to sustain employment, production and demand shall be consistent with the other objectives and provisions of this Charter. Members shall seek to avoid measures which would have the effect of creating balance-of-payments difficulties for other countries.

ARTICLE 4
REMOVAL OF MALADJUSTMENTS WITHIN THE BALANCE OF PAYMENTS

1. In the event that a persistent maladjustment within a Member's balance of payments is a major factor in a situation in which other Members are involved in balance-of payments difficulties which handicap them in carrying out the provisions of Article 3 without resort to trade restrictions, the Member shall make its full contribution, while appropriate action shall be taken by the other Members concerned, towards correcting the situation.

2. Action in accordance with the Article shall be taken with due regard to the desirability of employing methods which expand rather than contract international trade.

Even the proposed (1955) charter of the Organization for Trade Cooperation (OTC), an organization proposed to administer the General Agreement on Tariffs and Trade (GATT), now modified in the light of experience, includes the following:[4]

---

[4] *General Agreement on Tariffs and Trade*, 1955, p. 22. Also see *The Agreement on the Organization for Trade Cooperation*, H.R. 5550, etc., 1956, p. 54.

The contracting parties recognize that, as a result of domestic policies directed towards the achievement and maintenance of full and productive employment or towards the development of economic resources, a contracting party may experience a high level of demand for imports involving a threat to its monetary reserves. . . . Accordingly a contracting party otherwise complying with the provisions of this article shall not be required to withdraw or modify restrictions on the ground that a change in those policies would render unnecessary restrictions which it is applying under this article.

New Institutions[5]

Since the war, nations have spawned numerous international institutions to deal with the growing problems of international disequilibrium. In organizing these institutions, governments acknowledge the persistency of disequilibria.

These institutions reflect the shortage of dollars and the widespread desire to expand trade and to slow up and even reverse the tendency to divert trade to uneconomic channels. Among their objectives are "realistic" exchange rates and the discouragement of abnormal restrictions on trade and, as conditions for these policies, adequate provision of additional capital, reserves, and liquidity.

By establishing these international institutions, the creators recognize the invalidity of the classical assumptions of adequate flexibility to achieve full employment after temporary disequilibrium. Provision is, therefore, made for sacrifices of liberalization of trade when the objective of high or full employment should take precedence, and it is recognized that depression, in turn, may reduce trade and frighten nations away from plans for liberalization. Provisions in the charters of these organizations reflect other doubts concerning the classical theory of trade; e.g., given inelastic demand abroad a reduction of prices under depression conditions may well mark a step away from equilibrium, and *private* capital movements cannot be depended upon to offset deficits in the balance of payments.

The Relevance of the Dollar Shortage

The specter of the dollar shortage is revealed in the charters and operations of most of these organizations. Thus, consider the International Monetary Fund (IMF), which was to play a vital part in the transitional years after the war. In theory, countries short of gold or foreign currencies should tap their own reserves first; then rely on the IMF for help to tide them over temporary deficits; then, if this proves inadequate, have recourse to exchange adjustments. The final step is to make structural changes within the country.

[5] Professor Hansen in *The United States and the World Economy* analyzes these institutions well.

But the IMF in some respects has been a disappointment. First, resources have been inadequate, in part because of the failure of Iron Curtain countries to participate; in part because of the inflation, rise of income, and the accompanying increase of trade (with trade in 1954 greatly in excess of 1938 or 1945, when the charter was being considered); in part because of the scramble for the dollar, with most other currencies not in great demand. Thus, from 1947 to March 31, 1955, member countries of this organization purchased $1,198 million of currencies from the IMF. Members repaid $807 million of the currencies; hence net sales outstanding were $390 million. The total net funds made available were an insignificant part of world trade. Though the quotas (amounts callable in gold or domestic currency and the determinant of borrowing rights) amounted to $8,732 million in 1955, the IMF had at its disposal, as of March 31, 1955, only $1,609 million in gold and $2,287 million in dollars.[6] (Subscriptions in gold are limited to 25 per cent of quotas or even less if reserves are low.) With quotas equal to about 10 per cent of imports and borrowings limited in any one year to 25 per cent of quotas, the members at most could obtain aid equal to but 2 to 3 per cent of import trade in any one year. Obviously greater resources were required.

Second, disappointment with the contributions of the IMF is tied to the failure of exchange adjustments to bring about equilibrium conditions. Behind the IMF is the theory that exchange rates related to the requirements of the international balance would bring equilibrium or at the very least make an important contribution to it. Here the unwillingness of some countries to adapt their exchanges to the international situation is relevant. For example, the IMF had to accept the rates in effect at the end of 1946, even though these were clearly overvalued generally vis-à-vis the dollar. But uncooperative attitudes, including refusals to yield on sovereignty (e.g., the French refusal in 1948 to devaluate on a nondiscriminatory basis and the British confronting the IMF with a precise devaluation in 1949), were not the decisive factors. Even when devaluation was used, and frequently it was, its effectiveness was not great (as we shall see).

Third, and perhaps most important, the transitional problems were much more serious than had been anticipated. The disequilibrium was one that had to be treated with much larger resources than the IMF had available and with vigorous policies to deal with structural maladjustments, both long- and short-term. Fourth, unfortunately, the IMF was distinctly limited in the manner in which it could control domestic policies. Members were free to pursue policies based on fundamental social and political objectives, and the IMF could not refuse a member's

[6] All figures from International Monetary Fund, *International Financial Statistics;* also see United Nations Monetary and Financial Conference, Bretton Woods, N.H., July, 1944, *Final Act and Related Documents.*

proposal for a revision of exchange rates on grounds of disapproval of policies related to these objectives. Indeed, as a condition for purchase of a country's currency (generally for dollars), the IMF might urge modification in domestic policies, but there is little evidence that the IMF had much influence.[7]

The failure of the IMF stems in part from the difficulty of eliminating exchange control and multiple exchange rates. Here again the dollar shortage and the chaotic conditions in the postwar period are relevant. The major task of the IMF was to help restore multilateralism through operating as a limited supercentral bank and inducing appropriate rates of exchange. The world was still far from multilateralism even as late as 1955 to 1957.

It is only necessary to list the purposes of the IMF as agreed to at Bretton Woods in 1944 to realize that all important objectives had not been attained even by 1957. This is aside from the pledge under Section 4: "Each member undertakes to collaborate with the Fund to promote exchange stability, to maintain orderly exchange arrangements with other members, and to avoid competitive exchange alterations."[8]

The purposes of the IMF are:

(i) To promote international monetary cooperation through a permanent institution which provides the machinery for consultation and collaboration on international monetary problems.

(ii) To facilitate the expansion and balanced growth of international trade, and to contribute thereby to the promotion and maintenance of high levels of employment and real income and to the development of the productive resources of all members as primary objectives of economic policy.

(iii) To promote exchange stability, to maintain orderly system of payments in respect of current transactions between members and in the elimination of foreign exchange restrictions which hamper the growth of world trade.

(iv) To assist in the establishment of a multilateral system of payments in respect of current transactions between members and in the elimination of foreign exchange restrictions which hamper the growth of world trade.

(v) To give confidence to members by making the Fund's resources available to them under adequate safeguards, thus providing them with opportunity to correct maladjustments in their balance of payments without resorting to measures destructive of national or international prosperity.

(vi) In accordance with the above, to shorten the duration and lessen the degree of disequilibrium in the international balances of payments of members.

In an address at the annual meeting of the IMF and the International Bank, the chairman of the latter appraised the accomplishments of the

[7] See also the able presentation in chap. 9 in R. Mikesell, *United States Economic Policy and International Relations*, 1951; Hansen, *op. cit.;* and Robert Triffin's provocative comments in scattered writings.

[8] United Nations Monetary and Financial Conference, Bretton Woods, *op. cit.,* pp. 28, 31.

IMF over the transitional period through 1954. Its accomplishments were, according to Mr. van de Kieft, to "lay the foundations of an orderly, stable, and multilateral system of payments" and contribute to the expansion of trade through a policy of fixed rates of exchange. But in the "maintenance of orderly exchange arrangements, and the avoidance of competitive devaluation, the Fund has met [only] with a fair measure of success." Competitive debasements have not been a source of trouble; rather the failure lay in inadequate devaluations and in recourse to controls. "It is in the realization of its fourth purpose, the establishment of a multilateral system of payments, that the Fund so far has been least able to achieve positive results," though some discouragement of the use of exchange restrictions is granted. Above all the abuse of Article XIV, which allows continuance and extension of the exchange control, must be watched.[9]

By the early 1950s there was much dissatisfaction with the operations of the IMF. It was, for example, apparent to many that the occasional revision of exchange rates with approval by the IMF was often not practical. The possibility of such decisions in itself brought much speculation which might drive a currency down far below the level considered appropriate. Recently a preference has been expressed for floating exchange rates:[10] The country would agree to hold rates within set limits. Hence there would not be once for all changes in exchange rates.

Another complaint registered against the IMF has been its niggardly lending policies. In the early fifties the IMF tried to improve its lending policies by providing stand-by credits, by giving special access to the Fund up to the limit of gold subscriptions, and by allowing withdrawals in a short period (e.g., a year) in excess of those ordinarily allowed under the charter. In 1953–1954 the Fund made available credits in dollars to several countries which in agreement with the Fund devalued their currencies (in the Mexican case in part to promote a fiscal expansionist policy) and in some instances (Chile) consolidated several rates.[11]

Even as late as the latter part of 1955 the managing director of the IMF could only raise the question if Article XIV, the article providing for *transitional* privileges for restricting trade, might not be deleted and Article VIII, which provides that discrimination and multiple exchange would be subject to IMF approval, substituted.[12]

[9] International Monetary Fund, *International Financial News Survey*, Oct. 1, 1954, pp. 105–108.

[10] Discussed more fully in Chaps. 25 and 27.

[11] See especially *International Monetary Fund Annual Report*, 1954, pp. 82–88, 131–136.

[12] International Monetary Fund, *International Financial News Survey*, Sept. 23, 1955.

Dollar shortage is a matter of concern for other institutions also. The charter of the International Trade Organization (ITO), which experienced a still birth, and General Agreement on Trade and Tariffs (GATT) had been very much concerned with the dollar shortage or more generally with all currency shortages. A crucial provision in the ITO charter is that a country faced with a balance-of-payments crisis can introduce restrictive trade policies, inclusive of quotas and discrimination. Ordinarily the charter precludes quotas and discrimination, though many exceptions are made.[13]

Members are permitted to impose quotas to the extent necessary to forestall an imminent threat of, or to stop, a serious decline in their monetary reserves. . . .

Members which are applying quotas on imports for balance-of-payments reasons under Article 21 are permitted by Article 23 to impose certain discriminations. The provisions of Article 23 are in broad measure parallel to the relevant provisions of the International Monetary Fund agreements regarding discriminations in the imposition of exchange controls.

Indeed, Secretary Dulles, in introducing the Administration bill in support of the OTC in 1956, could claim that the objectives of GATT had been narrowed so as to exclude the objectives of full employment. Nevertheless, the proposed GATT which the OTC was to administer allows countries to impose restrictions when "as a result of domestic policies directed towards the achievement and maintenance of full and productive employment, or towards the development of economic resources, a contracting party may experience a high level of demand for imports involving a threat to its monetary reserves. . . . "[14]

Even the Food and Agricultural Organization (FAO) proposed restrictive and stabilization policies in part because drastic declines of agricultural prices raise serious balance-of-payments problems for agricultural countries.[15] The International Bank for Reconstruction and Development (IBRD) provides dollars primarily to cover capital needed to finance purchases abroad and occasionally to cover an adverse balance related indirectly to expansion accompanying development. With a widespread demand for dollars, the IBRD has had to provide about two-thirds of its resources in dollars (or gold). Of $1,614 million dis-

---

[13] U.S. Tariff Commission, *Report on the Havana Charter for an International Trade Organization*, 1949, pp. 34, 37; also Department of State, *Analysis of General Agreement on Tariffs and Trade, Signed at Geneva, October 30, 1947*, 1947.

[14] *The Agreement on the Organization for Trade Cooperation*, H.R. 5550, for House Ways and Means Committee, 1956, p. 54; and *Department of State Press Release 107*, Mar. 1, 1956.

[15] See, for example, Cale and Zaglits, "Intergovernmental Agreements Approach to the Problems of Agricultural Surpluses," in *Readings on Agricultural Policy*, 1949, especially pp. 319–320.

bursed by April 30, 1955, $1,310 million was in dollars and $153 million in pounds sterling. Net loans outstanding amounted to $1,287 million.[16] Again, limited capacity to lend has been the result *in part* of a concentration of demands for dollars.

Even the operations of the European Payments Union (EPU), formed largely to facilitate trade and payments among Western European countries (and their dependencies), reflected the dollar problem. It was necessary to increase intra-European trade in part because in this manner Europe would become less dependent on supplies from dollar countries and hence would save dollars.

The Trade Problem

The international agencies have been formed with the objective in part of restoring trade to a multilateral basis and increasing the total amount of trade. Member nations are to be discouraged from distorting free-market forces to their advantage. Multilateralism is defended on the grounds that under multilateral arrangements each country purchases in the cheapest markets and credits and debits are pooled in a manner so that country A, for example, purchasing more from B, M, and P than it sells to these countries, can use cash received from an excess of sales to F, N, and R to liquidate its debts to B, M, and P. What is more, under multilateralism all countries are treated without discrimination. Hence, as much as with the amount of trade, the concern is with the misdirection of trade and uneconomic allocation of factors of production. Quotas, exchange control, multiple exchange rates, bulk buying, customs unions, export subsidies—these all tend to distort the pattern of trade. Apparently to restore trade to the channels dictated by comparative costs requires *intervention* by international agencies once the misdirection has assumed serious proportions; dependence on free-market forces to restore trade more nearly in accord with comparative costs will not be adequate. It is necessary, as a condition for removing abnormal interferences with trade, to provide not only liquidity (reserves) to the participating countries but additional capital, which would enable the dollar-short countries to raise output (and particularly on comparative-cost principles) so that they would be able primarily to increase their exports and secondarily to become *relatively* less dependent on imports.

So much is said about the restriction of trade that it is often forgotten that the volume of trade has risen greatly since before the war. In dollar value, world exports rose from $21 billion in 1938 to $84 billion in 1955, or a rise of much more than one-half after an allowance is made for price rise. Even when the real rise of trade is compared with that in total output, there has been an improvement. It is striking that despite

[16] International Monetary Fund, *International Financial Statistics,* June, 1955.

the spread of all kinds of abnormal interferences with trade, world trade expanded more than world output from 1938 to 1954. Undoubtedly, part of the explanation is prosperity (trade tends to rise relatively with increasing income); part of the explanation is the intensification of demand for raw materials and to some extent food, which is related to the more rapid rise of industrialization and population than of production of raw materials and food; part of the explanation lies in the structural damage done by war and political chaos [the need for trade then increases, even on comparative-costs principles (when many coal mines are shut down in Europe, the gains of importing coal increase greatly)]; part is the result of the stimulus of foreign aid; and, finally, the misdirection of trade (i.e., the higher costs) may be reflected in a rise of total trade. The last should, however, be reflected in dollar rather than volume terms.

The ITO in particular was concerned with the reduction of trade barriers and the rise of trade. But this organization had a still birth. A skeleton institution, GATT, made possible multilateral agreements to reduce tariff obstacles. In 1955, the OTC, based on the original ITO charter but with some modifications, was to assume the responsibilities formerly entrusted to the ITO and the GATT. But in 1957, approval by governments of the OTC was still awaited.

The ITO charter provided facilities and pressures for negotiations to reduce trade barriers; it insisted upon representation of consumers when commodity agreements are made for allotting quotas and fixing prices; it inveighed against certain business practices (e.g., cartels) "which restrain competition, limit access to markets, or foster monopolistic control, whenever such practices have harmful effects on the expansion of production or trade and interfere with the other objectives of the charter";[17] it ruled out export subsidies, quotas, discrimination in trade, internal taxes invoked for protective purposes, mixing arrangements for protection (though the United States' requirements for mixing X of synthetic rubber with Y of crude imported are exempt from this prohibition); and it objected to protectionist devices introduced through state trading (e.g., selling foreign commodities by state brokers at artificially high prices).

Unfortunately, many of these provisions had no teeth in them or were so surrounded by reservations as to be of limited effectiveness. For example, special restrictive privileges were given to countries bent on development. Quotas were excluded, but they were allowed *inter alia* when they were required in support of certain domestic agricultural policies or developments or to protect against serious adverse balance

[17] *Report on the Havana Charter for an International Trade Organization*, p. 64.

of payments. The charter included a general escape clause which might be invoked if imports were increased "in such relatively increased quantities and under such conditions as to cause or threaten serious injuries to domestic industries."[18] Discrimination was out, but special concessions were made for developing economies and for existing customs unions. And so it goes.

Even provisions not restricted by exemptions frequently were not enforceable. The attack on business restrictive practices was a case in point.

Even the section on commodity agreements did not promise effective enforcement:[19]

The commodity control agreements authorized by the Charter are to be resorted to only when the labor and resources devoted to the production of particular goods provide, or are capable of providing, outputs greatly in excess of the quantities that can be marketed at reasonable prices. Moreover, even in such cases control agreements are to be applied only if other employments for the labor and resources concerned are not available and are not likely to become available until after long and serious hardships have been experienced by large numbers of people. Such control agreements are not designed to deal with conditions of widespread under-utilization of productive capacities such as appear during periods of general industrial depression. Rather they are intended to be confined to situations in industries wherein shifts in demand or changes in techniques of production or other developments result in either (1) the persistent appearance of large surpluses of a commodity, or (2) large number of unemployed workers who cannot readily find employment in other industries.

The above quotation raises some questions. In practice, is it going to be easy to differentiate between cases where large surpluses persist or large numbers of unemployed for long periods are involved and instances of *cyclical* underutilization? Hence, this provision might not be workable. The problem of commodity agreements also focuses attention on the issue of classical adjustments. This provision in the ITO charter rests on the assumption that a fall in prices confronted with inelastic demand may induce movements away from, not toward, equilibrium, for with lower prices, despite rises in output, receipts in foreign currencies may decline. Hence, the classical assumption of price reductions as the road to balancing accounts may not hold. In other words, the charter is based here on some questions concerning assumptions of classical economics: elasticity and mobility.

We turn to the issue of mobility. In the classical assumptions it is contended that movements into other employments follow the reduced

[18] *Ibid.*, p. 10.
[19] *Ibid.*, p. 70.

profitability in the older employments. Even in highly developed economies, mobility is often low. In economies where standards of transportation, communication, and education are low, the problem of shifts is much more serious. One of the objectives of commodity agreements is to establish quotas and impose a price range: a minimum to protect producers and a maximum to protect consumers. This, of course, is interference with the market mechanism. Keeping prices higher through stabilization programs impedes the outward movements from depressed employments, and yet if other employments are available, mobility should be underwritten rather than impeded. The FAO tries to reconcile these policies, i.e., stability to avoid the high costs of concentrated losses and price adjustments to achieve a distribution of employment suggested by relative costs and demand, by insisting on *long-run* declines in the occupations with overproduction.

The ITO charter has been a charter and little else, and now even that is dead. But in 1947 countries accounting for about 80 per cent of world trade formed a body known as the General Agreement on Tariffs and Trade (GATT). In the intervening years this organization was a clearinghouse for tariff reductions. While awaiting action on the ITO, through the instrumentality of the GATT, these countries succeeded in substantially reducing tariff rates. (More than one congressman refuses to acknowledge the legality of cuts engineered under the auspices of the GATT even though the cuts do not exceed the limits allowed under the Trade Agreements Act.) Under the GATT, the negotiating agents agreed on multilateral extension of concessions, and it is probable that the general reductions were larger than they would have been in the absence of the GATT.

Mr. Vernon, a former member of the State Department who operated at a high level in the area of trade agreements, reported that by 1955, 60,000 tariffs "affecting perhaps 60 per cent of the world's trade, were the subject of these tariff concessions. By 1954 and 1955, this policy of tariff reductions was obviously producing tangible dividends for this country." In addition, Vernon stressed reductions of quotas, following pressure from the United States, and the large rise of imports from the United States. (Perhaps he neglects the relevance of higher incomes in Europe for the gains of imports.)[20]

But it should be observed that the GATT did not extend its trade umbrella beyond tariffs (see above, however). Quotas, the proper valuation of imports, the reduction of domestic taxes that discriminated against imports, etc., received some attention but little action other than the formulation of codes, etc. It remained for the Organization for

[20] *Hearings of Subcommittee of Joint Committee on the Economic Report on Foreign Economic Policy*, 1955, p. 415.

European Economic Cooperation (OEEC) and its offspring, the European Payments Union (EPU), to deal with the problems of quantitative restrictions. In a later section, some further details are given concerning the EPU. "By January, 1954 the OEEC was able to report that the percentage of intra-European trade on private account freed from all quantitative restrictions had reached 75.7 per cent for the member countries as a whole compared with 71 in June, 1953. At the beginning of April 1954 this percentage stood at 76.7."[21] (In 1955, the figure was 90.)

One of the interesting aspects of the tendency to form regional trading, and especially payment, organizations has been a large increase in the percentage of intraregional trade. These results are also related, of course, to the dollar shortage, with a resultant tendency to divert trade to nondollar countries. The final outcome may well *in part* be an uneconomic alignment of trade, not supported by comparative costs. But it should be observed that the appropriate allocation of employments among countries may be different in an age of insecurity (e.g., requiring increased trade among the inter-American states) than in the pre-1914 or pre-1939 days. Furthermore, the changed conditions may also bring an increased tendency for countries within a regional group to adapt their output and exports to the needs of the other members of the group, and thus increased trade within these regions is to some extent consistent with comparative-cost principles.

Hence we may be overhasty in drawing conclusions concerning the new pattern of trade. Here are some comments by the GATT on this issue.[22] (Some further statistics are presented in a later section.)

The increased regionalization of trade is distinctly a postwar phenomenon which has its obvious roots in the monetary disorganization of the earlier postwar years. In 1937 and 1938, the total value of commercial transactions within the regions that now comprise the dollar area, the sterling area and the combined continental OEEC countries and their dependencies accounted for 33 and 35 per cent of world exports, respectively, in those two years. Significantly, even in that period of comparative stability in monetary relations,

[21] General Agreement on Tariffs and Trade, *International Trade*, 1593, June, 1954, p. 100.

[22] For further discussion of GATT and ITO, in addition to references already given, see the frequent *Hearings before the House Ways and Means and Senate Finance Committee on Reciprocal Trade Agreements;* W. G. Brown, "General Agreements on Tariffs and Trade," and H. C. Hawkins, "Problems Raised by International Trade Organization," both in *Foreign Economic Policy for the United States* (S. E. Harris, ed.), 1948, pp. 254–286; R. Vernon, "America's Foreign Trade Policy and the GATT," in *Essays in International Finance*, October, 1954; W. Diebold, "End of ITO," in *ibid.*, 1952; *Commission on Foreign Policy Staff Papers*, 1954; various reports of U.S. Tariff Commission; and U.S. Council of the International Chamber of Commerce, *GATT: An Analysis and Appraisal of the General Agreement on Tariffs and Trade*, 1955; W. A. Brown, Jr., *The United States and the Restoration of World Trade*, 1950.

the decline in international trade from 1937 to 1938 gave rise to an increase in the share of intra-regional trade.

Since the war this ratio has been rising from 39 per cent in 1948 to 46 per cent in 1953, with only a minor interruption in 1951. . . . Although the comparison between prewar and postwar years is subject to a number of reservations, it may nevertheless be said that the progress of regionalization has affected the trade in manufactures more profoundly than trade in primary products.

In recent discussions concerning regionalism, that is, agreements among countries to increase trade within the regional bloc and at the same time, therefore, to discriminate against others, the economists have tended to support these agreements, at least in regard to the European agreements. Professor Viner holds that the effects of Western European agreements have been to increase trade; Professor Haberler, that these agreements are to be preferred to preferential agreements and that Europe is moving in the direction of reduced discrimination against the United States. For Professor Cairncross, the gains are much more trade for Europe, with comparatively small cost to the United States, which exports relatively little to these countries. In the view of Professor Kindleberger, the European trade agreements stopped the downward spiraling of trade and were especially successful because of the large amount of intra-European trade.[23]

But let us return to the trade organizations and their objectives. The 1955 proposed charter of the new Organization for Trade Cooperation (OTC) deals with the same range of problems as the original ITO, but it is a less complicated document. It does not, however, seem to have advanced much beyond the ITO in its treatment of troublesome problems. For example, the special exceptions made to many countries to use quotas in order to protect a weak balance of payments are still there. The tendency in the past has been to seek protection in this provision, and in no small part on the grounds that the fault lay abroad rather than, as was often the case, in the expansive policies at home. In the past also there has been a tendency for the IMF and the GATT to fail to integrate their policies, with, for example, the former granting exceptions under the balance-of-payments clause which, in fact, were protectionist exceptions. This integration between the two organizations still remains to be worked out. The contracting parties can still have recourse to these restrictions, and they are still sovereign in their control of domestic policies. The major change seems to be that once the new agreement goes into effect, the restrictions will be examined and then reviewed each year.[24]

[23] *Hearings of the Subcommittee of the Joint Committee on the Economic Report on Foreign Economic Policy*, 1955, pp. 169–170, 506–510, 609–610.
[24] *Department of State Press Release* 155, 1955, p. 2.

In connection with the review of the balance of payments provision of the GATT, it was recognized that some countries might experience severe difficulties in certain of their industries or branches of agriculture if what they referred to as their hard core import controls were eliminated too abruptly. These are controls which, while originally imposed for balance of payments reasons, provided incidental protection to certain industries. Their sudden removal could create severe economic and social problems for particular countries. Accordingly it was decided at Geneva that requests from these countries for a temporary waiver from the obligations to eliminate quantitative restrictions when the balance of payments justification for them no longer existed would receive sympathetic consideration on a case-by-case basis.

Numerous headaches continue to trouble the contracting parties. The underdeveloped countries still are entitled to special privileges, though there is now a greater determination to exclude from this rubric some of the richer nations such as Australia. Export subsidies are still allowed, though the wish is stated that countries indulging in this pastime should not seek an excessive share of the market, and new subsidies in non-agricultural commodities are not to be tolerated.

In general there has been some but not much progress. The underdeveloped countries seek special treatment so that they can move in the general direction of industrialization; the United States wants the discontinuance of discrimination, especially against the dollar, but seeks special concessions to impose agricultural quotas and dump agricultural products abroad; the British are fearful of making large inroads on imperial preference; and the Continental countries are fearful of the effects of the removal of bilateralism. It is no wonder, then, that with these problems still troubling the countries and with most of them still concerned with their dollar accounts and especially in view of the possibility of convertibility, the resulting document is necessarily one full of compromises. The possible conflict of domestic and international objectives further waters down the document. Perhaps this is the greatest obstacle to a trade document with teeth in it.

Undoubtedly the GATT contributed to a substantial lowering of trade barriers, particularly as a mechanism for extending concessions initiated by two countries to all participating countries. According to one estimate, agreements were made as listed in Table 18-1.[25]

Despite these advances, there was still in 1956 much opposition to the GATT and its proposed administrative agency. The United States government had assured Congress that the OTC would be only an administrative agency, facilitating trade talks and releases from obligations,

[25] Committee for National Trade Policy, *Trade Cooperation or Trade Warfare: The Choice before Us*, 1956, pp. 4–5.

Table 18-1

Year	No. of countries	No. of rates
1947	19	45,000
1949	28	50,000
1951	34	58,000
1955	35	60,000

obtaining information, and handling disputes. The OTC, in the view of the Secretary of State, would not reduce the authority of Congress to determine tariff policy, nor would it administer a GATT with such broad objectives as full employment, fair labor standards, and the like provided in the Havana Conference for the ITO. Furthermore, Secretary Dulles insisted that the charter of the OTC could not be changed without congressional approval. Much was also made of the contribution of the GATT to reducing discrimination against dollar imports. Nevertheless, there remains much opposition, in part because the net effect of the GATT has been to cut tariffs, and many are fearful of the effects of negotiation upon the condition of particular industries.[26]

Trade and Agricultural Policies

American agricultural policy is directed toward guaranteeing farmers reasonable prices and incomes. In order to provide minimum prices and income, the government offers nonrecourse loans (the farmer is guaranteed a minimum price through a loan and can redeem his crops if prices rise above the loan value) and purchases farm commodities for storage or sales in order to maintain prices. A condition for farmers sharing in benefits is frequently agreement to cut acreage or sales.[27]

One result of these policies is higher prices at home and a divergence between domestic and foreign prices. Hence American farm policy rests on the assumption that domestic prices will exceed foreign prices, and in order to maintain these differences, it obviously becomes necessary to keep foreign agricultural products out. The most effective means is the import quota. Otherwise, the United States policy would become one of raising world prices at a tremendous cost to taxpayers. With prices higher in the United States than abroad, the agricultural policy also is

[26] *The Agreement on the Organization for Trade Cooperation,* H.R. 5550; United Nations, *The Quest for Free Trade,* 1955, pp. 9–13, 44–45; U.S. Tariff Commission, *Operations of Trade Agreements Program,* 8th Report, pp. 36–45; *Department of State Press Release* 107, Mar. 1, 1956.

[27] See especially U.S. Council of the International Chamber of Commerce, *General Agreement on Tariffs and Trade; The Economist,* Nov. 24, 1953; Jan. 23, 1954; Dec. 21, 1954.

based on the premise that commodities will be disposed of abroad at a loss. These losses may be incurred through government selling out of stocks at prices below purchase or through "give-away" programs, e.g., the European Recovery Program.

These requirements of the United States farm policy, of course, are reflected in the charter provisions of the ITO.[28]

So far as imports into the United States are concerned, the most important exception to the prohibition of quotas is paragraph (c) of Article 20. This permits import quotas on agricultural or fisheries products if they are necessary to the enforcement of governmental programs which operate effectively to restrict the quantities of like (or directly substitutable) domestic products permitted to be marketed or produced, or to remove a temporary surplus of the domestic products by making the surplus available to certain groups of domestic consumers free of charge or at prices below the current market level.

Though the ITO charter contained provisions condemning export subsidies or other measures which operate directly or indirectly to expand exports or reduce imports, the charter also offered relief to a member whose interests "would be seriously prejudiced by the foregoing of an export subsidy on any primary commodity. . . . "[29]

Here is an international agency which recognized the need for special stimulation of domestic farm production and support of farm income. Obviously without these supports, the exodus from farms would be accelerated in accordance with the principles of comparative advantage. The charter offered protection for the American farm program. The defense must lie at least in part in the great costs involved in a hasty migration from the farms (offsetting the ultimate gains in an improved distribution of employment). Toleration of export subsidies, we should add, is in a sense not special treatment in so far as the difference between foreign and domestic selling price is offset by the rise of domestic prices related to the restrictionist policies.

It is difficult to envisage a satisfactory reconciliation of farm and trade policy. More emphasis on increased consumption of farm products (a likely trend with a rise in population of 25 per cent in twenty-five years in this country and even larger in the world); special incentives to get farmers off submarginal farms; an improved storage program; a program for *future* prices based to some extent on expected supply-and-demand conditions; provision of alternative employments in farm communities, in part through government spending and direction (e.g., the industrialization movement in the South); the use of direct subsidies to farmers

[28] U.S. Council of the International Chamber of Commerce, *op. cit.*, p. 3.
[29] *Ibid.*, pp. 44–45.

rather than quotas, for example, the provision of income subsidies rather than price guarantees (and hence with lower prices reduced need for trade restrictions, for the difference between domestic and foreign prices would be treated)—all these (though to some extent these proposals are not compatible one with the other) may reduce the dependence on trade restrictions and particularly quotas on farm products.

A concentration on income stability would involve a radical departure in farm policy and would arouse much objection in part because of its tie to the Brannan Plan. On the whole this plan had more merits than were generally ascribed to it, not the least of which was to give the consumer the advantage of plentiful supplies and to extend the program to perishable commodities. One of the problems of an income-stability plan is to get any precise estimate of costs. For years also there has been a struggle between the adherents of a fixed and of a flexible parity. The advantage given for the latter is that as prices fall in response to excessive supplies, the government would reduce support prices, thus encouraging a decline in output. But many are of the view that agricultural output does not respond to price movements in the anticipated manner.[30]

In numerous instances the United States has violated the spirit of these international-trade charters by imposing quotas even when no restrictions on production were imposed within the country. Under these conditions, quotas are frowned upon because they then are not part of a farm policy and are pure restrictionism in trade, e.g., quotas on butter, cheese, and dry milk. In view of the strong views held by American protectionists on Section 22 of the Agricultural Adjustment Act (import restrictions on agricultural products) even under the proposed OTC (1955), the successor to the ITO, "by separate decision a waiver was granted which makes it possible for the United States to apply import restrictions required under Section 22 of the Agricultural Adjustment Act, as amended, notwithstanding certain provisions of the Agreement."[31] In the words of a congressional group, by ensuring continuance in the GATT, we "open the door to international meddling and obstructive tactics in other legislation passed by the Congress, namely, the Agricultural Adjustment Act."[32]

[30] Cf. T. W. Schultz, *Agriculture in an Unstable Economy*, 1945, especially chaps. 7, 10, 12; D. G. Johnson, *Trade and Agriculture*, 1950; D. G. Johnson, *Agricultural Price Policy and International Trade*, 1954 (Essays in International Finance), and *Readings on Agricultural Policy*, pt. III; and S. E. Harris, Letter to *The Economist* on Stevenson's Sioux City speech, October, 1954.

[31] State Department, *Press Release* 155, Mar. 21, 1955, on *The Agreement on the Organization for Trade Cooperation and Amendments to the General Agreements on Tariffs and Trade*, p. 3.

[32] "Trade Agreements Extension Act of 1955," *Senate Report* 232, p. 27.

Trade and Regional Unions

Another approach to the expansion of trade is through currency or payments unions. The sterling area is one such union, and the European Payments Union (EPU) another.[33] Through organizations of this type an approach toward multilateralism is achieved. One member of the EPU can offset an adverse balance with another by a favorable balance with a third. The relative ease of achieving balances in this manner as compared with the stringency in dollar markets tends to divert trade to the countries participating in these unions. In a sense this means an uneconomic realignment of trade, for A, say, now buys some commodities from C, a member of the EPU, whereas previously she purchased from B (a dollar country), and presumably B was the cheapest market. But it should be observed that A is unable to pay B. By cutting prices greatly, she might be able to obtain B's currency and purchase in B. Her losses in purchasing from C are offset in whole or in part by averting losses in terms of trade with B had she pressed her commodities on B as required to maintain her trade with B.

There has certainly been a tendency to expand trade within the unions. In the EPU the payments agreements were implemented by agreements concerning trade policies, and to some extent, the EPU even influenced other internal policies.[34] A country with a favorable balance is under some obligation to reduce the percentage of trade subject to quotas, and the debtor countries can support recourse to increased quotas. In the early history of the EPU, Germany, with a large adverse balance, undertook a corrective monetary and fiscal policy, and numerous revisions of quota policy have occurred as a result of growth of deficits and credits.

In view of the shortages of supplies in nondollar vis-à-vis dollar countries, it might have been expected that trade within the payments union as a percentage of members' total trade would decline. Actually, for reasons suggested above, this trade tended to rise.

In general the results are about as might be expected: a tendency for trade relatively to rise within the payments or currency unions. But there are important exceptions. For example, the proportion of trade of the EPU countries with the United Kingdom declined. One explanation is undoubtedly a large drop in the proportion of United Kingdom trade to world trade; another is that the United Kingdom trade was pulled by the sterling bloc as well as by EPU. Again, though the proportion of *United Kingdom exports* to the other sterling countries rose, the propor-

---

[33] Also see Chaps. 26 and 27.
[34] Cf. the able analysis by Prof. L. Gordon, "The Organization for European Economic Cooperation," *International Organization*, 1956, vol. 10, no. 1.

Table 18-2. Percentage of Trade among Members of Payments Unions, 1937, 1950 to 1953

	Exports, % trade		Imports, % trade	
	1937	Avg. 1950–1953	1937	Avg. 1950–1953
A. Continental EPU countries, trade with:				
Other Continental EPU countries........	43	45+	36	39−
United Kingdom......................	14	10½	9	9−
B. United Kingdom, trade with:				
United Kingdom dependencies...........	9	14+	7	16
Other sterling countries................	30	33−	24	24
C. United Kingdom dependencies, trade with:				
United Kingdom......................	20	28+	27	27½
Other sterling countries................	7	9	7	11−
United Kingdom dependencies........	5	7	5	7½
D. Other sterling countries, trade with:				
United Kingdom.................... ..	45	34−	38	36+
Other sterling countries........... ..	12	13+	13	13+
United Kingdom dependencies..........	4	8	15	12

SOURCE: Calculated from International Monetary Fund, *International Financial Statistics.*

tion of United Kingdom imports from these countries did not rise. Perhaps a decline in Britain's competitive position is suggested by the failure of the proportion of *United Kingdom dependency imports* from the United Kingdom to rise substantially. A similar generalization may be relevant for the reduction of imports by *other sterling countries* from the United Kingdom, and the large relative decline of exports from other sterling countries to the United Kingdom may be explained in part by the intense demand and the availability of foreign currencies in the United States.[35]

The method of balancing accounts of the EPU is given well in a summary by the IMF. Through provision of credits by the United States and by individual members and provision of dollars and gold by debtors, the accounts are balanced.[36] It will be noted that Germany, Belgium, Luxemburg, and Switzerland were the large creditors and France, Italy, Turkey, Greece, and the United Kingdom, the largest debtors. The situation was roughly similar in April, 1955, though the cumulative deficit and surplus had risen to almost $2,900 million.

[35] The reader should note that the losses of the United Kingdom seem greater when trade is viewed from the outside (e.g., other sterling countries) than when the comparison is made from the viewpoint of the United Kingdom. The explanation of this fact lies in the reduced relative importance of United Kingdom trade.

[36] International Monetary Fund, *International Financial Statistics,* June, 1954.

Table 18-3. European Payments Union

Settlement of Net Surpluses and Deficits of Member Countries *

(In millions of United States dollars)

Members	April, 1954 Quota	Net surplus or deficit (−)	Cumulative net surplus or deficit (−)	Use of "Existing resources" (net)	Use of "Initial balances"	Use of "Special resources"	Cumulative accounting position Total	Settled by Credit	Settled by Gold
Austria	70	5.2	−6.4	15.8	80.0	45.0	118.6	66.3	52.3
Belgium-Luxemburg	360	−13.0	711.9	−29.4	.....	.....	385.5	228.7	156.7
Denmark	195	−16.0	−99.5	−5.0	.....	.....	−104.5	−78.3	−26.2
France	520	−26.1	−983.2	12.9	.....	.....	−881.4	−312.0	−569.4
Germany	500	44.4	1,022.7	11.9	.....	89.0	1,034.6	567.3	467.3
Greece	45	−7.4	−275.5	1.1	115.0	152.7	−6.6	.....	−6.6
Iceland	15	−1.3	−21.8	.....	4.0	11.2	−6.7	−5.2	−1.5
Italy	205	−28.7	−234.9	42.5	.....	.....	−192.5	−113.1	−79.4
Netherlands	355	−11.0	−299.9	.....	30.0	.....	−329.9	200.5	129.5
Norway	200	−4.8	−182.7	0.4	60.0	.....	−122.3	−89.2	−33.2
Portugal	70	−0.7	56.8	.....	.....	.....	53.8	33.9	19.9
Sweden	260	−8.7	162.7	15.4	−9.6	.....	168.5	110.2	58.2
Switzerland	250	10.9	317.2	.....	.....	.....	317.3	172.2	145.1
Turkey	50	21.7	−298.1	−1.9	−25.0	68.9	−206.2	−30.0	−176.2
United Kingdom and Ireland	1,060	78.9	−469.7	−93.1	−150.0	.....	−712.8	−504.8	−208.0
Totals	4,155	139.4 / −139.4	2,571.7 / −2,571.8	100 / −100	314.0 / −189.0	366.8	2,408.0 / −2,232.9	1,379.1 / −1,132.6	1,028.9 / −1,100.4

Balance Sheet

(In millions of United States dollars, after completion of operations for the month indicated)

Assets	December, 1951	March, 1954
Liquid resources	216.8	500.0
1. Amount obligated by the United States	111.9	123.5
2. Gold in bars	100.3	153.0
3. Dollar balances	4.6	22.4
4. United States Treasury bills, at cost	.....	201.0
Credits granted under quotas	808.5	1,146.2
Loans to Norway and Turkey under initial credit balances (amounts utilized)	35.0	35.0
	1,060.3	1,681.1

Liabilities	December, 1951	March, 1954
Capital fund	271.6	271.6
Credits received under quotas	617.3	1,048.1
Special credit from:		
Austria	.....	21.7
Belgium-Luxemburg	140.0	33.9
Germany	.....	245.1
Italy	16.3	.....
Netherlands	.....	.....
Portugal	14.9	.....
Switzerland	.....	16.8
Special funded loan from Belgium-Luxemburg	.....	40.0
Miscellaneous	0.2	4.0
	1,060.3	1,681.1

* Net deficits or surpluses are settled in the following ways: (1) Through the use of "existing resources," representing bilateral debts outstanding as of June 30, 1950, for which no specific amortization plan has been agreed on bilaterally. "Existing resources" may ordinarily be used by the holding country to settle a net deficit. (2) Through the use of "initial credit or debit balances." For the first year of the EPU operations, certain prospective debtors were allotted "initial credit" for which they received an equivalent amount of conditional ECA aid. (3) Through the use of "special resources." Beginning with the second year of operations, certain chronic debtors are allotted "special resources" by the United States government to cover deficits with the Union. As these "special resources" are used, equal amounts in dollars are paid to the Union by the United States government. (4) Through the use of credit and gold payments. The net surplus or deficit, adjusted by the amounts of "existing resources," "initial balances," or "special resources" used (accounting surplus or deficit), is settled by gold payments and/or credit extended to or by the EPU. For the purpose of determining the maximum cumulative accounting surplus or deficit that can be settled in this way, the member countries have been assigned quotas. The following schedule, as revised on July 1, 1952, shows how the monthly accounting surpluses and deficits, falling within the quota, are settled by gold and credit (all figures in per cent):

When cumulative accounting surplus or deficit equals	Monthly accounting surplus or deficit is settled			
	For cumulative creditors		For cumulative debtors	
	By credit to or from EPU	By gold payments to or from EPU	By credit to or from EPU	By gold payments to or from EPU
First 10 per cent of quota..........	100	0	100	0
Second 10 per cent of quota..........	100	0	80	20
Second 20 per cent of quota..........	50	50	70	30
Third 20 per cent of quota..........	50	50	60	40
Fourth 20 per cent of quota..........	50	50	50	50
Fifth 20 per cent of quota..........	50	50	30	70

A deficit in excess of the assigned quota shall be settled in gold unless the OEEC decides otherwise. An obligation to pay gold by a member or by the Union may be discharged by payment in United States dollars.

The United States government undertook the obligation of making available an amount of not less than $350 million so that the Union might meet any excess in gold and dollar out-payments.

The EPU keeps its accounts and makes the calculations for its operations in terms of a unit of account equal to 0.88867 gram of fine gold, the equivalent of the United States dollar.

281

In the spring of 1954, it was agreed that the EPU would be extended until June, 1956; provisions were made for settling outstanding debts, for providing credits in the future, for changing the proportions paid by debtors in gold from 50 to 60 per cent, for a 20 per cent rise of quotas, and for preparations for a new organization to serve under convertibility.[37]

Again in July, 1955, a new accord was reached. In addition to $261 million available to the Fund, the contracting parties were to make $328 million additional available. This agreement was based on the theory that multilateralism was on its way and that credits should be available to bolster members once convertibility was attained.[38]

Considering that, in order to maintain a high and stable level of trade and liberalization between the contracting parties as well as of employment in their respective countries—bearing in mind the need for their internal financial stability—while facilitating a return to full multilateral trade and convertibility, it is desirable that upon the termination of the Agreement for the Establishment of a European Payments Union a source of credit should be established which could be called upon by all contracting parties.

In 1954 and 1955, the growth of intra-European trade, both relatively and absolutely, continued. In part this was the result of liberalization of imports under the guidance of the OEEC and the EPU. It is hoped that, when convertibility comes, this liberalization will continue and that any restrictions required by countries with convertible currency will not be followed by restrictions elsewhere. The convertibility issue is discussed in a later chapter. But here note that the EPU or the proposed European Monetary Agreement of 1955 (EMA) would restrain competitive restrictions even as progress was made toward the goal of convertibility.[39]

The International Bank for Reconstruction and Development (IBRD) and Expansion of Trade

How is trade to be expanded? The IBRD was supposed to promote expansion, but it has failed to do so. Its total loans outstanding after almost ten years of operation amounted to only $1.5 billion, a very small percentage of trade during these years. Here again inadequacy of resources was of importance. The manner of operation of the Bank is also of some significance. The IBRD sets certain criteria before making a loan. Is the loan likely to be repaid? Are local resources being exploited

[37] International Monetary Fund, *International Financial News Survey*, July 16, 1954, pp. 18–19.

[38] Organization for European Economic Cooperation, *European Monetary Agreement*, August, 1955, p. 5.

[39] Seventh Report of the OEEC, *Economic Expansion and Its Problems*, 1956, pp. 45–48.

adequately? Have alternative sources of capital been adequately considered? Is the proposed project one that is sufficiently high on the scale of needs of the borrowing country? And is it one that can be carried through? The IBRD also seems hostile to government enterprise and is not in favor of social-service loans.[40]

In considering these criteria, the officials of the Bank take into account the effects of the loan on the balance of payments, for the financing of the loan generally requires the payment of dollars. When loans are made to the Netherlands to purchase airplanes, then the gain in dollars can easily be estimated, but when the funds are used to improve the roads of Colombia, the relation to exports and imports is much more difficult to estimate. Aware that monetary and fiscal policies may also affect the balance of payments, the IBRD is likely to suggest appropriate policies in these areas or even to reject applications for loans when it seems that domestic policies are likely to result in international disequilibrium.

Adequate financing of loans involves an assurance not only that the project would yield appropriate returns at home but also that transfers of, say, pesos into dollars could be consummated. For example, in the consideration of domestic profitability, the IBRD time and again urged upon governments adequate public-utility rates which would ensure the amortization of public-utility loans. The Bank even proposed that rates be high enough so that in this manner much of the required capital be obtained from users of the services through high prices. But high proceeds at home are not enough. It is also important to consider the probable trend in the balance of payments and the effects of the contemplated loans on this balance.

It is not the policy of the IBRD to insist upon loans which *directly* yield the dollars required for financing. For the Bank generally seems to realize that even if a loan (say to exploit copper mines) yields additional exports, the resultant flow of dollars might be squandered in increased imports of luxuries. It is understandable, then, why the Bank lends a large part of its reserves for power and transportation facilities though the direct effect on exports or imports is not ascertainable. But it is assumed that the gains of productivity will yield a larger output of export commodities and reduced imports. Here, however, it is necessary to take account of the effects of higher incomes on imports and also on the increased output at home which absorbs part of the additional purchasing power (the latter an anti-inflationary factor), and it is difficult to make such estimates.

Once having embarked on a lending policy largely to official agencies or through government-guaranteed loans, the IBRD, controlled to a

[40] An official history is *The International Bank for Reconstruction and Development, 1946–53*, 1954, especially chap. 5.

considerable extent by the United States, has found it necessary to sponsor a degree of planning of investment and allocation of economic resources that would not be tolerated in this country.[41] Here again the intervention of an international agency modifies the employment structure as compared with that in the absence of international lending agencies.

Below I quote an official statement on the policies of the IBRD.[42]

There is one last question, and by far not the least, and that is the relationship between the types of investment to be encouraged and the balance of payments. It has been assumed at the outset that the purpose of any development is to improve, in the end, the standard of living in the country and that could best be done by increased investment. However, it is not enough to increase production by relying on foreign resources. It is important that the servicing of this investment be made possible. It is not necessary to establish a close relationship between an individual investment itself and its foreign exchange proceeds, but it is important that the investment program as a whole should, in the end, not only benefit internal production but also, to an extent, ultimately benefit the balance of payments. It is not possible to over-emphasize the fact that increased national income and improvement in balance of payments are not synonymous. The necessity to balance, in an investment program, its effect on production and its effect on the balance of payment is fundamental. The immediate effect of an increased investment program on the balance of payments is a deficit. It may even be said, with only slight exaggeration, that the definition of a development loan, from the International Bank point of view, would be one where the borrowing member could voluntarily be prepared to incur a deficit on its balance of payments in order to satisfy its investment needs. This may go on for a number of years, and it may go on for a series of projects, but it is quite important that in the end the resulting benefit in the aggregate should favorably affect the balance of payments as well as over-all production.

In short, the main purpose of any investment program is, as has been assumed, to increase the standard of living, but in order that this may be realized it is necessary that the program be balanced. Balanced development would be development which does not endanger financial equilibrium; which does not entail depressing consumption from its existing level; which efficiently carries out several purposes at once and does not merely benefit one field at the expense of others; which achieves the desired results without over-burdening the government by its cost; which looks several years ahead, and

[41] See especially E. R. Black (president of IBRD): "Policies and Operations of the World Bank," *Lloyd's Bank Review*, July, 1953, and "The World Bank at Work," *Foreign Affairs*, April, 1952; International Bank for Reconstruction and Development, *Eighth and Ninth Annual Reports*, 1952–1953 and 1953–1954; and *Summary of Proceedings, Annual Meeting of the Board of Governors of the International Bank for Reconstruction and Development*, 1951, 1952, 1953.

[42] International Bank for Reconstruction and Development, *Fifth Annual Meeting of the Board of Governors*, September, 1950, p. 8.

not merely in short periods takes advantage of temporary market conditions, prices or restrictions; and finally, which gives proper attention to the need for improving the balance of payments at the same time as to the need for increased production.

Concentration on High-employment Objectives

In our discussion above, we noted that under the ITO charter commodity agreements would be supported if substantial amounts of unemployment threatened in the absence of such agreements. It is no exaggeration to say that the objective of full or high employment is generally given precedence over liberalization of trade. It is one thing to assume no conflict between these objectives, but it is another when, in fact, there may be conflicts. With an *assumption* of full employment and hence concentration on the most effective use of the factors of production, the classical economists could more easily embrace free trade than economists who remove this assumption, recognize unemployment, and make high employment an objective.

Charters of international agencies reflect an awareness of the problems of employment. Thus we can explain the provision in the Bretton Woods Agreements which excludes, as a condition for accepting proposed revisions of exchange rates, pressures to introduce policies at odds with the social and political objectives of a nation. The British in particular made it clear that they were not going to sacrifice internal stability or growth to any international agreements. Thus we can account in part for the special privilege given to underdeveloped nations in the ITO and OTC charters: They need help to put to work the unemployed and the underemployed. Thus we can also explain the responsibilities assumed by all contracting nations to ensure favorable economic conditions at home. But the trade charters also stress the point that depression tends to destroy markets and hence to discourage trade-liberalization programs. Here the two objectives are compatible.[43]

It [Article 2] states that members accept the view that avoidance of unemployment and maintenance of a large and increasing volume of production and effective demand for goods and services in each country is not of domestic concern alone, but is of concern to and will benefit all other countries. It further states, however, that the attainment of this objective must depend primarily on internal measures taken by the individual countries. . . .
As to the commitments regarding the achievement and maintenance of full and productive employment, it is made clear in Article 3 itself that measures to be taken by a given country in fulfillment of its commitments are to be such as it considers appropriate to its political, economic, and social institutions. . . .

[43] *Report on the Havana Charter for an International Trade Organization*, pp. 58–59.

In the pressure to obtain congressional approval of the OTC, the Eisenhower administration stressed the point that this agency could not administer a GATT which, as proposed under the ITO charter, would put full employment as one of its objectives. Here the ideology of the Republican party seeking support for the OTC as against that of the Democratic party seeking support for the ITO is relevant. The Republican party is less concerned with full employment. But despite the avowal of Secretary Dulles that full employment is not an objective of the GATT, there is a provision allowing abnormal restrictions on trade which follow expansionist policies at home and accompanying rises of imports.

CHAPTER 19

Economic Development and the Theory
of International Trade

The Larger Issues

Adam Smith had written: "Little else is requisite to carry a state to the highest degree of opulence from the lowest barbarism, but peace, easy taxes and a tolerable administration of justice; all the rest being brought about by the natural course of things."[1] This was the general view of classicists, though Malthus added the importance of demand, a theme considered further in recent literature. Baster summarizes the views of the leading classicist Viner as follows: The "general conclusion is therefore not essentially dissimilar from the classical position that 'good government' should provide a suitable framework within which the natural desires of individuals to better themselves should have maximum place."[2] But while we are on the classical approach, Ricardo's views are of some interest. The reader will note that he held views on the association of manufacturing and high incomes that anticipated Bean[3] and the position of many of the underdeveloped nations.[4]

Every research into this subject convinces me that trade should be left perfectly free, and that taxation should be so managed as to interfere with that freedom as little as possible. Manufactures and trade are alternately the cause and effect of wealth. An agricultural nation without trade and manufactures cannot be rich, because neither an individual or a nation can be said to be rich, if it have only food to eat. An agricultural nation might however have the command of a great quantity of labour besides that employed on the land, which it might expend on war, or in supporting the rude ostentation and magnificence conferred by a great number of retainers. Such a nation would

[1] J. Baster, "Recent Literature on the Economic Development of Backward Areas," *Quarterly Journal of Economics*, 1954, p. 590.

[2] *Ibid.*, p. 591.

[3] Bean had stressed the large gains resulting from a shift to manufacturing. See L. Bean, "International Industrialization and Per Capita Income," in National Bureau of Economic Research, *Studies in Income and Wealth* 8, 1946, pp. 122–139.

[4] *Ricardo*, vol. VIII, pp. 102–103.

have powerful resources, and would I think be more than a match for a country of the same extent and fertility which was also a manufacturing country. Why have we not heard of any such Agricultural nation? because none ever persevere in the course from which they commence—they prefer manufactures to menial servants—instead of a great man having a thousand persons about him ready to obey his mandates, they are accumulated in workshops manufacturing his lace, his china and his furniture, or they are digging the earth for the purpose of obtaining the precious metals of which he is so greedy. Give a country wealth, or let it acquire wealth, and it ceases to be purely agricultural, not because there is any thing which necessarily obliges it to be any thing else, but because with wealth a desire for manufactures is excited, and this desire becomes a powerful stimulus to the accumulation of capital, in order that the desire may be gratified. Even with this desire for manufactures, a country might continue to be purely agricultural, if by means of trade, she could in exchange for a portion of her agricultural produce obtain a larger quantity of manufactured goods, than, with the capital employed on the production of such portion of agricultural produce as she exported, she could manufacture at home.

It is the accumulation of wealth from Agriculture which first gives the notion and the means of establishing Manufactures. Manufactures in their turn become the cause of new accumulations of capital which tend to produce a fresh demand for labour, an increased population, and a greater consumption of agricultural produce. Thus Agriculture is alternately the cause and effect of manufacturing industry.

Many of the neoclassicists tend to minimize the advantages of industrialization. It is well to recall Ricardo's views. It is also well to be reminded by Gunnar Myrdal, a distinguished economic theorist and practitioner, that "to apply a general, and basically static, equilibrium theory of international trade to these countries without taking into consideration their actual estate of underdevelopment, amounts very nearly to scientific fraud."[5]

The objective of economic development is generally not only to raise the real per capita income of the population but to do so in a much shorter time than would be possible under the free-market system. Hence it would follow that the classical theory of international trade would be inadequate to deal with the problems raised by these development programs. The fact that the government has a large part to play is, in itself, of crucial importance, for the greater the part played by the government, the less the reliance on the pricing system. Indeed there are differences of opinion concerning the desirable contribution of the government. At one extreme there are the views of such writers as Frankel, who would give the government a most limited role, to those of Buchanan and Ellis and officers of the International Bank, who would

---

[5] G. Myrdal, *The International Economy*, 1956, chap. 13 (prepublication proofs).

depend largely on the price mechanism and yet would entrust to government responsibility for appropriate monetary and fiscal policy, the provision of adequate savings at home, and even some responsibility for feeder industries and social services, and finally to the view of the experts of the UN, who would demand of the authorities adequate *controls* to ensure allocations of scarce resources which would yield a balancing on international accounts, the required volume of savings and investments, and indeed the channeling of the investments in employments consistent with the broad objectives of the government.[6]

It is only necessary to catalogue the problems facing a country indulging in a substantial program to realize the extent of the intervention required by government. A large program means increased savings and investments, for if inflation is to be avoided, investments must not get too far out of line with savings. Therefore, measures must be taken to increase savings, obtain capital and imports from abroad (the latter an anti-inflationary measure), and make sure that the savings obtained are not offset by additions to consumption resulting from higher incomes. As a rule, because of the primitive state of the capital market, the government must provide a substantial part of the savings through the use of its tax powers.

In view of the almost inevitable inflationary pressures associated with these programs inclusive of the rise of real income, the authorities are faced with serious balance-of-payments problems. The pressure to conserve foreign exchange and to maximize receipts from foreign sales is usual, and in turn, the need of protecting the infant industries from foreign competition brings restrictions on trade which also help solve the general problem of the balance of payments. But the problem for these governments is not merely one of controlling domestic inflation and guarding the limited foreign exchange, but the much more difficult one of integrating these policies. It does little good to conserve foreign exchange by restricting imports of luxuries if through the absence of an adequate savings and tax program at home the money that otherwise would have been spent on foreign luxuries is spent instead on domestic consumption.

Many other reasons can be adduced for an absorbing interest of government in the development programs. Just because they are being telescoped into a relatively few years, the effects on the cultural pattern

[6] The International Bank seems especially reluctant to encourage government enterprise in underdeveloped countries. First, there is the fear of bringing about instability if development proceeds too rapidly. Second, there is the danger that with the government operating enterprises they would cut essential services. Hence the IBRD would restrict governmental enterprise to economies where capital and management otherwise would not be available. International Monetary Fund, *International Financial News Survey*, Sept. 23, 1955.

have to be watched carefully. Involved may be public outlays for social services, increased interest in population problems, measures to ensure that the workers are not being exploited by their new employers, assurances generally that the gains are not being excessively concentrated on a relatively few occupations or a relatively small part of the population, and above all a control of the rate of movement that takes account of the noneconomic costs of development.

It is, of course, obvious that in the light of the degree of impairment of the free pricing system, allocation on the basis of comparative costs would be of only limited usefulness. For example, this is a theory that assumes full employment, mobility of factors of production, and responses of demand to price cuts; but taking account of underemployment, immobilities and inelastic supply, and demand conditions for the products of underdeveloped countries requires a theoretical framework extending beyond the theory of comparative costs.

Again, the relative absence of external economies for the underdeveloped countries further restricts the usefulness of the orthodox theory. In various forms, Singer, Scitovsky, and Nurkse in recent years have dealt with this aspect of the problem. The underdeveloped countries cannot go very far unless they can build up the many industries which will make it possible to achieve some of the external economies of more advanced countries. They are dependent on a concomitant growth of industries to profit from new techniques and also to obtain the markets and the rise of investment which accompanies a simultaneous growth of industries and the rise of reciprocal demand that will make possible competitive unit costs. Here the public authorities have a special responsibility to stimulate the concomitant growth of industries. More on this later.

This brings us to a more general issue, namely, the inadequacies of static theory for the solution of the problems of underdeveloped economies. The marginal analysis is unsatisfactory, for many things are changing at once. Hence it is helpful to depend on linear programming. Professor Chenery in a stimulating paper has expressed the issues as follows:[7]

The main problem lies in evaluating the amount of scarce resources which will be actually required by alternative types of production. For a number of reasons, the price system, which makes this evaluation fairly accurate in highly developed economies, is often a rather unreliable guide to the desirability of investment of an underdeveloped economy. Even when corrections have been made for the more obvious defects in prices, such as tariffs and subsidies, there remain two sets of factors which make a partial equilibrium

[7] H. B. Chenery, "Development Policy in Underdeveloped Countries," *Papers and Proceedings of the American Economic Society*, 1955, p. 40.

analysis based on existing prices very difficult: (1) the existence of structural disequilibrium in the use of factors of production, with labor commonly under-employed and capital and foreign exchange rationed; and (2) the intercon-nectedness of productive sectors, as a result of which investment in one may make investment in others more profitable—often called "external economies."

In his study of the Italian experience Chenery has presented a model in which among other things he considers the available resources, proj-ects ranked according to their marginal productivities, returns on invest-ments, the effects on final demand resulting from the increase of invest-ment and income, and a comparison of the required output in each sector of industry based on the final demand and the estimated use from pre-ceding calculations.

The resultant calculations are not simple, but nevertheless Dr. Hagen points out that the model is of limited usefulness for the real world. Chenery limits his objective to raising income but does not consider alternative objectives such as distribution. Moreover, he limits his dis-cussion to only fourteen sectors of the economy, and his linear program-ming approach neglects the possibility of a varying production function except in so far as changes in the commodities produced affect the use of factors. Nor is any attention paid to the social cost of the program.[8]

Indeed, the linear programming approach, which allows consideration of many of the relevant variables and the effects of one upon the other as they move, is a helpful attack. Yet I have grave doubts that the model that considers alternative objectives and many more factors than Chenery found it convenient to deal with, even granting that the re-quired facts become available, will prove of great help to the countries that are embarking upon development programs. I have in mind such countries as Indonesia, Pakistan, and Chile. The models will be alto-gether too complicated; the authorities will be unable to understand them and will certainly not be willing to take the word of the technical experts. In the foreseeable future they will have to be content with much simpler analyses for determining the most effective and least disturbing use of their limited resources.

Comparative Costs and the Case for Development

Since World War II, interest in economic development, which we may define crudely and inadequately as a program for increasing the standard of living in underdeveloped countries within a *relatively* short time, has quickened. This concentration on economic development raises many questions not easily related to the orthodox theory of international trade.

[8] *Ibid.*, pp. 40–57, and E. E. Hagen, *Papers and Proceedings of the American Economic Society*, 1955, pp. 74–77.

According to this theory each country should favor employments for exports in which it has a comparative advantage. In general, then, the underdeveloped countries should favor the exploitation of natural resources, and the developed countries manufacturing. In exporting capital to the underdeveloped countries, the developed countries tend to stimulate the exploitation of natural resources and, at least until recent years, not to nurture manufacturing industries.

But it has been recognized for a long time even in classical economics that some countries gain an advantage in some industries merely because they develop these industries at an early stage. Hence a potential competitor seeks aid through tariffs, subsidies, etc., in order to overcome the advantage held by older countries by virtue of their primacy. It is not at all clear, for example, that if we were starting *de novo,* New England would harbor the textile industry. Yet its early establishment in New England has enabled this region to maintain a leading position for a century.

Professor Nurkse, in an excellent volume on underdeveloped economies, has contended that protection of the domestic industries will do little good. The difficulties of these countries lie in low productivity, inadequate capital, and impoverished markets. But surely there are many industries where a competitive position may be established even with only moderate markets; once the industry is given an opportunity to advance, capital will move in. This argument may, of course, be carried too far when markets are small and large producing units are required.[9] The test comes later when the crutch of restrictionism is removed.

The postulates of nineteenth-century economics no longer hold. There is no gold standard generally, movements of exchange rates are used to influence economic activity, resources move with difficulty, and there are numerous currency blocs. A United Nations study includes the following:[10]

Egyptian experience points to several tests of sound tariff policy. The first is that duties should be imposed selectively rather than generally, to provide relief from competition only to those industries which show prospects of ultimately being able to surmount the obstacles keeping their average costs high or otherwise retarding their development. Where there are idle factors of production, however, the case for protection becomes stronger. If, for example, because of the existence of under-employed manpower in the rural areas, the real cost to the community of increasing industrial output were relatively low and in consequence the ratio between money cost and real

[9] R. Nurkse, *Problems of Capital Formation in Underdeveloped Countries,* 1953, pp. 107–109.
[10] United Nations, *Processes and Problems of Industrialization in Under-developed Countries,* 1955, p. 66.

cost appreciably higher in industry than in agriculture, a uniform degree of customs protection accorded to all secondary industries that revealed potentialities for development would probably lead to a better utilization of domestic resources without any undue interference with the international division of labour. In terms of the principle of comparative costs, moreover, the extremely low marginal productivity of labour in agriculture tends to make it advantageous for such a country to divert resources to other activities, including secondary industry, even in the relatively inefficient form of handicraft production, which might require a fairly high degree of protection from the competition of more highly mechanised concerns in industrial countries.[11]

Planners in underdeveloped countries are impressed by arguments of this kind on behalf of protectionism. But even more, they are intent upon development, especially in manufacturing, because they are dependent upon a few products for a large part of their income. In 1951 to 1953, more than 95 per cent of Venezuela's exports was in petroleum products, 83 per cent of Colombia's in coffee, 66 per cent of Brazil's in coffee, 63 per cent of Bolivia's in tin.[12] Most of the underdeveloped countries are greatly dependent on trade not only for employment but also for the acquisition of essential raw materials, foods, capital goods, and services. The danger of relying upon a few products for a substantial part of their income and tax receipts and for the acquisition of dollars or gold and hence of imports lies in the fact that risks are too concentrated, especially when export values are very sensitive to income movements abroad. For example, in the early fifties Latin America depended upon the United States and Canada for the purchase of 60 to 70 per cent of her exports. In the thirties, Latin America suffered from a decline of prices of primary products in the United States of 55 per cent. Hence the effects of a substantial depression in the United States could easily be envisaged. According to a UN study, from 1922 to 1948 annual fluctuations of import prices into the United States varied from 10 to 20 per cent per year, that is, *from* year to year. The variations in import prices averaged 27 per cent within the year in the fifty years 1901 to 1950.[13]

It is, however, not only instability that interests the underdeveloped countries. They are also concerned with the low average income of their people. According to Spengler, the rates of income per capita of the richest countries had risen from five times over that of the least advanced countries before 1800 to perhaps forty times today.[14] Myrdal

---

[11] For other defenses of protective measures, see Myrdal, *loc. cit.*, and Professor Triffin in *Hearings of the Subcommittee of Joint Committee on Economic Report on Foreign Policy*, 1955, p. 134.

[12] From International Monetary Fund, *International Financial Statistics*.

[13] United Nations, *Commodity Trade and Development*, pp. 7–14.

[14] In Williamson and Buttrick, *Economic Development*, 1954, p. 102.

points out that despite more favorable terms of trade, productivity has
risen more in developed than in underdeveloped countries. He also notes
that the large rise in food production since the prewar period has been
in North America and the major industrial gains have also occurred in
the West. In fact, despite the large gains of the West, the average standard of living in the world is lower than in 1900.[15] According to an official estimate, the prewar per capita annual income in developed countries was $461; in intermediate countries, $154; and in underdeveloped
countries, $41.[16] As of 1949, the high-income countries with $915 of income per head accounted for 67 per cent of the world's income and but
18 per cent of the population. The 67 per cent of the population in low-
income countries had a per capita income only 6 per cent of that of high-
income countries and but 15 per cent of world income.[17]

With the great advances of communication, the peoples of the impoverished countries are conscious of their relatively low standards and
impatient to bridge the gap between their standards and others. There
is great pressure to raise consumption standards. The low-income countries try to emulate the high-income group in their command of medicine (the expectation of life is sixty-three years for the developed countries and forty years for the others), of durable consumers' goods (111
motor vehicles per 1,000 as against 1 for the underdeveloped countries),
etc.[18] Authorities in these countries have been fed many statistics showing that those countries with a large percentage of their population in
agriculture have low incomes and those with a large percentage in
industry have high incomes. Thus in a well-publicized estimate, Dr. Bean
contended that if the agricultural working population were reduced
from 60 to 40 percentage points in twenty countries with excess agricultural population, their per capita income of $70 from 1925 to 1934
would be raised by 170 per cent, or to $190.[19]

Some Gains and Losses

It is possible to be overimpressed by the association of a high percentage of workers in manufacturing and high average incomes. Professor Viner has argued eloquently that the difference in incomes
between agricultural and industrial countries may be explained by underestimates of income in the former (e.g., services received and not
included in income estimates) and especially by the greater over-all
productivity in countries concentrating on manufacturing—their high pro-

[15] Myrdal, *op. cit.*, chaps. 1, 11, and 13.

[16] Department of State, *Point Four*, 1949, pp. 17, 86–109.

[17] *National and Per Capita Incomes in 70 Countries*, 1949 (quoted by Nurkse,
op. cit., p. 63).

[18] Department of State, *op. cit.*

[19] Bean, *op. cit.*, pp. 123, 141–143.

ductivity prevails also in agriculture.[20] Buchanan and Ellis have argued along the same lines against Bean. The low incomes of agricultural countries are due to many factors inclusive of low productivity, they hold, and the low proportion of industrial workers may stem mainly from low productivity instead of vice versa.[21]

But the answer is not so simple as the one implied by these authorities. It is important to take into account aggregate employment and its structure. Orthodox economics, with its emphasis on the allocation of economic factors, did not allow for the effects of given policies on employment. It may well be that the developed countries have higher incomes in part because, through manufacturing and associated service industries, they absorb excess labor from agriculture. In one underdeveloped country, it has been estimated that 25 per cent of the labor force could be removed from agriculture without any reduction of output. Obviously, if the displaced labor could be absorbed in manufacturing and services, incomes would rise. Many of the underdeveloped countries suffer from much unemployment and from the low incomes of many workers who contribute little to output (disguised unemployment). Hence, if through a program of development and industrialization, productivity increases in agriculture and mining so that additional workers are released and employment in industry rises, there would be a net gain of income. (Techniques improve, and the less productive rural workers are released.) It is probably true, as has been argued, that with no excess of labor in agriculture, the improvements must come first in agriculture. When excess labor is to be found in agriculture, industrialization must attract the excess of labor from agriculture. As employment rises in the new or growing industries, they purchase from one another and thus increase the market. Over a period of eight years in Latin America (1945 to 1953), the gross national output rose in stable dollars by more than 50 per cent. The major part of the increase was accounted for by a rise of employment in manufacturing and related industries of somewhat less than 20 per cent, and these were the high-paying industries. What is more, the largest gains occurred in the countries with ambitious development programs.[22]

From this, it follows that a protectionist policy may be advocated for an underdeveloped country which introduces protection in order to increase employment, general demand, and a shift of employment to more productive industries and hence greater development. Of course, the penalty is incurred of increasing costs (temporarily at least) over those of alternative products that otherwise would have been imported.

[20] J. Viner, *International Trade and Economic Development*, 1952, pp. 63–70.
[21] Buchanan and Ellis, *Approaches to Economic Development*, 1955, pp. 260–261.
[22] United Nations, *Economic Survey of Latin America, 1953*, p. 23.

Against this additional cost, we weight the increase of income associated with a rise of employment, the higher average income of each employed worker, and the gains of diversification and stability. These are, of course, not the only costs of the development program. Frequently and even typically these programs involve an expansion at a rate beyond that given by available savings. Again using Latin America as an example, domestic savings over the years 1945 to 1953 seemed to equal only 30 to 40 per cent of the value of investments. Development programs, let us note, require large investments, because the emphasis is on new industries and often those that require much capital. This excess of investment over available savings is inflationary. The resultant inflation is costly, bringing as it does reduced voluntary savings, excessive diversions of capital to unproductive employments and unfortunate effects on distribution.

Inflation spawns uncertainty and increased risks and hence stimulates investments in real estate and inventories, in domestic industries, where price competition is less severe than in export industries, and in industries not vulnerable to inflation, such as those with large fixed plant, and in general discourages such risky investments as new industrial plants. Furthermore, in so far as the unorganized many are squeezed by inflation, the marginal consumption industries are discouraged.[23]

Both the inflation and the rapid expansion of income also raise serious problems in the balance of payments. Thus in the years 1945 to 1953, the gross national product (GNP) rose three times as much in Latin America as in the United States, and on top of that Latin America had experienced a rise of prices of more than 500 per cent from 1938 to 1953 (each country's prices weighted by GNP), or seven to eight times as much as its chief trading partner, the United States. In these circumstances, the effects on the balance of payments are likely to be serious. With relatively higher real incomes the underdeveloped countries tend to increase purchases abroad and sell less. If the monetary inflation had been offset by a corresponding depreciation of the exchanges, then the deterioration in international accounts associated with inflation might have been greatly reduced, if not eliminated. But in major countries with prices up four to twelve times as much as in the United States, the average price of the dollar rose by 100 per cent or less.[24]

In the process of industrializing, aside from the increase of income, the pressure on imports tends to rise. The secondary industries compete for factors of production, credit, etc., while exports consist largely of

[23] United Nations, *Processes and Problems of Industrialization in Under-developed Countries,* p. 54.

[24] Cf. S. E. Harris, *Inter-American Trade: Measures for Its Expansion,* for the meeting of the Organization of American States, Rio de Janeiro, 1954, pp. 70–72, 87–89.

primary products. With the manufacturing industries favored and the export industries facing new competition and suffering from discrimination and, even if in an expansive state, subject to inelastic demand, the effects on the balance of payments are likely to be adverse.

Economic Development and Factor Movements

Programs for economic development arise as a result of large differences in standards of living between developed and underdeveloped countries. Classical theory recognized these differences and, emphasizing the sluggish movement of capital and labor among countries, accepted the fact of varying standards of living. The movement of commodities was held to be a substitute for that of factors of production. But in the nineteenth century large movements of capital and population occurred, in this manner tending to reduce the differences in standards. In the first half of the twentieth century, however, the equalizing tendencies were obstructed by the reduced flow of capital and labor. Restrictions on migration in Western Europe and severe restrictions on immigration into the Americas as well as a tendency for capital movements in the second quarter of the twentieth century to become less important —these contributed to the widening gap in standards of living. Another factor of great importance was the rapid rise of population in some of the underdeveloped regions. Thus the annual increase for the world was 9 per thousand from 1920 to 1950. But in Latin America the figure was 19, in Japan 14, in Africa 13, and Southeast Asia 11.[25] By World War II the United States had become the great creditor nation, but in eight postwar years her private credits amounted only to one-tenth to one-fifteenth, relative to income, of those given by the United Kingdom from 1905 to 1913. Finally, trade tended to be increasingly restricted and to that extent tended to aggravate differences of income levels.

Perhaps an additional comment should be made about the population problem. Fertility rates are high in the underdeveloped countries, and one of the first effects of development is likely to be a reduction in death rates. At best it takes time to reduce the fertility rates, and the institutional difficulties are serious indeed. Large population increases mean that the development programs are spent primarily in taking care of more people, not in raising standards of living. Competent medical opinion seems to hold that there is no known, "harmless, simple or low cost method today [1 to 5 cents per week] with which we can apply fertility control." After a review of the problem, Buchanan and Ellis conclude: "All these considerations suggest a moderately pessimistic conclusion as to the probable relation between the output potential and

[25] J. S. Spengler, "Demographic Patterns," in Williamson and Buttrick, *op. cit.,* p. 88.

the population potential in the underdeveloped areas over the near future."[26]

According to Myrdal, in parts of Asia and Africa, the death rate has fallen by one-half since the prewar period. With a slow response of birth rates, a catastrophic result can be averted only through rapid economic development. The Western nations were fortunate in experiencing a fall in death rate prior to the major industrialization.[27]

With such rapid rises in population, with severe immigration laws in Western countries and deficient capital movements, the net result is a tendency for the standard of living to fall relatively and at times absolutely in the underdeveloped countries.

In the nineteenth century capital exports were devoted primarily to stimulating the exploitation of natural resources. That is to say, the British wanted cheap food and raw materials, and British investments paid a large social dividend in that the British profited from cheaper imports. What is more, the effectiveness of the movements was strengthened by the concomitant migration of people, often with the same social and cultural patterns. Alongside the highly productive export industries in underdeveloped countries made possible by foreign capital, other employments often continued scarcely touched by the productive export industries. In this instance the interest of the British private investors, who sought the highest return and found it in investing in the exploitation of natural resources with guaranteed markets in the developed countries, was one with the British national interest. But this was not the pattern of investment necessarily desired by the capital-importing nations. Furthermore, once British investments became excessive in that trade did not accommodate itself to the export of capital and hence restrictive monetary policies and unemployment followed, Keynes protested vigorously, and increasingly the United Kingdom and other countries checked the outflow.[28]

Let us return to the underdeveloped countries of today. The occasion for investing in them and the gains to be had are different from those in the pre-World War I period.

By undertaking vast development programs, the underdeveloped countries were modifying the comparative-cost structure and also disregarding it. In order to develop, it was necessary to increase investments greatly, for development meant new industries, more productive old industries, and shifts of population from the farms to the cities. In turn

---

[26] Buchanan and Ellis, *op. cit.,* p. 16; cf. pp. 92–116. Cf. S. Raushenbush, *People, Food, Machines,* 1950.

[27] Myrdal, *op. cit.,* chap. 12.

[28] See especially J. M. Keynes, *Treatise on Money,* 1930, vol. I, chap. 21; *Essays in Persuasion,* 1931, pp. 253–257; and *Macmillan Report,* 1931.

this meant large outlays for economic overhead, e.g., power and transportation, and also for social overhead, e.g., education and health. Aside from the overhead outlays, it was necessary to provide capital for the new workers in the factories and to increase productivity directly in old employments.

Emphasis was put especially on the provision of capital. But private capital sent to underdeveloped countries in the first ten postwar years did not greatly exceed $1 billion a year. Estimates of the annual amount of foreign capital needed (admittedly the most provisional estimate) varied from $13.9 billion by a group of UN experts to $4.1 billion by a Food and Agricultural Organization group, and another estimate based on the need of reducing agricultural employment in underdeveloped areas by 20 percentage points over a period of fifty years reveals an annual requirement of $7 billion of foreign capital in early years.[29]

Against annual outflows of $1 billion to underdeveloped countries, the Committee on Economic Development suggested that from $0.5 billion to $1.5 billion additional was required each year, the money to be channeled to transportation and other areas where private capital was not disposed to go. Dr. Thorpe, former State Department aide, would depend largely on public grants and criticized Secretary Humphrey for claiming that private capital could do the job.[30] Myrdal notes that $10 billion of aid would equal less than 15 per cent of the defense budgets of developed countries and that a United Nations fund of $3 billion, which had been proposed, would amount to less than 1 per cent of the income of the advanced nations. But these countries were not prepared to contribute $250 million.[31]

However, we should not underestimate the obstacles to investing in poorer countries. It is difficult to measure costs, prices, and markets. Entrepreneurship is often not a highly valued activity. External economies, e.g., transportation, may not be available. Markets may be too small. With a limited number of exports, risks are large. Domestic savings are limited. Monetary systems are unstable. In addition, many obstacles are introduced by relevant governments.[32]

In an interesting paper, Dr. Aubrey lists high costs, limited markets, tariffs and malallocation, lack of innovating entrepreneurs and skilled

[29] United Nations, *Measures for Financing Economic Development of Underdeveloped Countries*, 1951, pp. 52–76; and S. E. Harris, *Foreign Aid and Our Economy*, pp. 40–41.

[30] Committee on Economic Development, *Economic Development Abroad and the Role of American Foreign Investment*, February, 1956, p. 31, and *Senate Hearings on Technical Assistance*, 1955, pp. 167–170.

[31] Myrdal, *op. cit.*, chap. 9.

[32] See the interesting discussion by G. Aubrey, "Investment Decisions in Underdeveloped Countries," in *Capital Formation and Economic Growth*, 1955, pp. 397–440.

labor, and the use of high-cost methods as obstacles to capital formation in underdeveloped countries. The United States government also stresses the great difficulties involved in obtaining an adequate number of technicians.[33]

An official commission estimated that in order to maintain a rate of growth of 3.3 per cent in average real per capita income in Latin America (the rate achieved from 1946 to 1953), gross annual investments of 20 per cent of income would be required, but in 1953 savings were only 14 per cent of income. Hence capital equal to 6 per cent of income, or $2.8 billion yearly, should be obtained abroad. In four recent years, however, Latin America obtained only $600 million annually from abroad, mostly from the United States.[34]

Under the Colombo Plan, which includes Ceylon, India, Burma, Pakistan, Malaya, and British Borneo, or about one-third of Asia's population, the six-year project for economic development was to cost $5.2 billion. Approximately 60 per cent was to be financed from external funds. According to the governor of the Bank of Pakistan, this program, largely used to develop agriculture (one-third), transportation and communications (one-third), social services (one-sixth), and the remainder for fuel, power, mining, and industry, was not a large expansion over previous development, nor is the program excessive relative to absorptive capacities. On this basis, it might be agreed that a development program of several billion dollars annually might not be excessive once the plans were worked out sufficiently. The contribution of the developed countries might ultimately be $2 billion to $4 billion annually.[35]

Early in 1955 the British government announced that £120 million annually would be available to colonial governments for financing developments in the next five years. About two-thirds of the money in earlier years was raised locally, and about one-half was used for social services inclusive of education.[36] *Private* overseas investment by the British from 1952 to 1955 equaled 1 per cent of income, by the United States only ¼ of 1 per cent.[37]

In a general way much progress was made, e.g., new irrigated land in Ceylon, India, and Malaya; doubling of electric power in Pakistan; 1 million miles of irrigation canals reconstructed in Indonesia. Nevertheless in 1953–1954 backward steps had to be taken to conserve foreign

[33] Aubrey, *op. cit.*, and *Senate Hearings on Technical Assistance*, Subcommittee on Foreign Relations, February–March, 1955, pp. 30–31.

[34] International Monetary Fund, *International Financial News Survey*, Nov. 12, 1954, p. 157.

[35] Cf. International Bank for Reconstruction and Development, *Seventh Annual Meeting, Proceedings*, 1952, pp. 47–49, and "Colombo Plan," *Midland Bank Review*, May, 1955.

[36] Cmd. 9375.

[37] *British Record*, May 23, 1956.

exchanges. Thus imports were restricted, wage subsidies cut, factors moved from export to local industries, and the gap between resources available and needed for development tended to increase.[38]

Estimates of need and absorptive power vary greatly, as these estimates suggest. In the early postwar period there was a tendency to exaggerate the amount of capital that should be exported to underdeveloped countries, for inadequate attention was paid to the absorptive powers. With experience, it was discovered that in the absence of adequate plans and trained personnel much of the capital could be dissipated. Hence the need of *gradual* increases of exports of capital to underdeveloped countries. That profits were high in the leading countries and that the most profitable investments in underdeveloped countries had been made reduced the flow of capital from abroad and increased the pressure for grants.

Official Provision of Capital, Controls, and Deployment of Resources

With relatively small amounts of capital sent either by private investors or through government assistance, the underdeveloped countries had to prune their programs and depend heavily on tax revenues and the inflationary process. In Latin America governments accounted for one-third of total investment in the early fifties.[39] This emphasis on investment tended, of course, to favor industries requiring capital. In other words, direct investment and indirect investment, through the inflationary process which was stimulated or concurred in by government and which tended to reduce consumption relatively, resulted in an expansion of industries requiring much capital that would not have occurred in the absence of this interference. Thus in Latin America, where reasonably adequate figures are available, investments rose from 12 per cent of gross national product (GNP) in 1945 to 19 per cent in 1951 and 1952 and 17 per cent in 1953, but consumption declined from 87.5 per cent of GNP in 1945 to 82 per cent in 1948 and 1949 and 83 per cent in 1953. Between 1945 and 1951, per capita consumption rose at an annual rate of 4.5 per cent while per capita investment expanded at the annual rate of 9.1 per cent.[40]

As an aside we might point out here that there is considerable debate on the issue of whether development should proceed with an emphasis on capital-intensive industries or labor-intensive ones. In practice the emphasis has generally been on the former. But since capital is scarce,

[38] International Monetary Fund, *International Financial News Survey*, Jan. 21, 1953; *British Record*, Apr. 30, 1954.
[39] Calculated from United Nations, *Economic Survey of Latin America*, 1953; cf. Buchanan and Ellis, *op. cit.*, p. 311.
[40] *Ibid.*, pp. 8, 21.

it might be assumed that the desirable approach would be to economize on capital. The argument for recourse to capital-intensive industries and employments rests in part on the large proportion of the increased income that, with a concentration on these industries, goes into savings rather than consumption. In other words, the social marginal product may, in some instances, be greater over a long period of time if the capital-intensive industries are favored.[41] In general, however, the presumption is, given the shortage of capital, that industries requiring little capital would be encouraged. On this point there is large agreement. Buchanan and Ellis have even gone so far as to contend that the low income of underdeveloped countries is associated largely with the imperfect substitutability of factors, that is, the difficulty of substituting cheap labor when neither capital nor rich natural resources are available.[42] Hence the primary bottleneck for them is labor.

Professor Schultz has argued that too much emphasis is put upon capital needs: " . . . too much emphasis is being placed upon increasing the stock of reproducible capital. . . . They are expecting too much and thinking too much in terms of capital . . . the plants, roads, railroads, and not putting enough capital and effort into bringing people up and to increasing the arts with which one produces."[43]

To get back to the main theme, in various ways the governments of underdeveloped countries have accelerated the growth of employments which required much capital. The resultant expansion of employment and real per capita income has been consistent with a substantial rise of absolute and even per capita consumption and an even greater increase of investment: the latter's share of GNP has increased and the former's declined. There seems to be an incentive to move into industry; this is suggested by the higher pay and the increase in real per capita pay. One effect of the development program seems to have been, however, a greater rise in gross product per active person in agriculture and mining than in industry and building: a rise of 24, 83, and 17 per cent, respectively, for Latin America from 1945 to 1953.[44] In part the explanation lies in increased productivity, in the exploitation of natural resources (inclusive of improved demand), and in part the explanation lies in the tendency to stimulate the growth of industry and the workers' desertion of the farms and mines.

In general the development programs result in increased growth of

[41] Cf. W. Galenson, "The Problem of Industrial Productivity in Backward Areas," in *Labor, Management, and Economic Growth,* Proceedings of a Conference on Underdeveloped Countries, 1954, pp. 43–49.

[42] Buchanan and Ellis, *op. cit.,* pp. 42, 64–65; and United Nations, *Processes and Problems of Industrialization in Underdeveloped Countries,* pp. 48–49.

[43] *Hearings of the Subcommittee of Joint Committee on the Economic Report on Foreign Economic Policy,* 1955, p. 580.

[44] United Nations, *Economic Survey of Latin America,* 1953, p. 23.

employments requiring more capital and technical aid than would have otherwise been available. Factors now move not merely in response to pecuniary motivation but also in response to nonpecuniary motivation. Hence the structure of employment and the timing of new employments are affected.

In general, though there are large variations by countries and regions, the development programs have tended to increase the output of industry more than of agriculture. This might well be expected for reasons given above, inclusive of the fact that a large rise in the amount of capital available would favor industry more than agriculture because capital is a larger ingredient in industry than in the agriculture of underdeveloped countries. Thus in Latin America from 1945 to 1953, the rise of agricultural output was 4.4 per cent per year (cumulatively); of industrial output, 5.4 per cent; and of all output, 5.4 per cent.[45]

Not alone through the introduction of plans, provision of capital, voluntary and forced, and some control of private borrowing do the underdeveloped countries determine the allocation of resources and achieve a structure of output vastly different from what would have occurred without official interference. In fact, foreign governments and international agencies providing capital through the governments of the underdeveloped countries also determine the new pattern of employment to some extent. But aside from the provision of capital, what else do the governments of underdeveloped countries do? They give the favored industries priorities in the allocation of raw materials, power, foreign exchange, and bank credit; they give them special tax favors inclusive of exchange of many units of local currencies for dollars received from exports. In this manner, the new industries or the old ones specially favored are stimulated because they both buy cheaply (high priorities mean the acquisition of necessary supplies and services at prices below those that would have held in the free market) and sell dearly. Of course, the government may depress sales by allowing prices to rise too much, or if prices are raised, then the rest of the economy may suffer; e.g., the Argentine government soon after the war depressed prices received by farmers and used the differences between purchase and high sale prices in part to stimulate industry and pay higher factory wages. But the effects on agricultural output were disastrous, with the industrial and agricultural segments getting much out of balance.[46]

Government influenced the distribution of employment not only through depressing prices of raw materials and capital, giving special tax favors, and making available a disproportionate share of scarce items,

[45] *Ibid.*, p. 10.
[46] For examples of measures used, see United Nations, *Economic Development in Selected Countries*, pp. 31–35, 95–96.

all of which may be related to a policy of reducing costs for the favored employments, but also through setting higher prices for the products of the subsidized employments. When prices are raised above world levels, then, of course, the government provides protection against outside competition. Through tariffs and especially quotas, exchange depreciation, and exchange control, governments provide the necessary protection. In countries nurturing new industries one will find the most extreme forms of protectionism. Even tariffs, upon which these countries rely relatively little unless their administrative machinery is not equal to more complicated controls, are likely to be high. Thus, according to one study, six of the eight countries with highest average tariffs were Latin American countries.[47]

On one point there is much controversy, namely, the use of exchange control and quotas by underdeveloped countries. In Chapter 17, we discussed alternative restrictionist practices. Exchange control, in particular, can be complicated and troublesome, especially when combined with multiple rates, and it can clearly be used for protectionist purposes; it is a powerful weapon of the planning authority for determining the allocation of economic resources and will, of course, result in uneconomic production. Obviously the supporters of the free-market system as the mechanism for allocating resources find exchange control objectionable. It should be stressed, however, that once the free-market system has broken down—and often it does because of mistaken expansionist policies by underdeveloped countries—these controls may have to be invoked. Furthermore, it is well to remember that with relatively weak instruments to achieve monetary and fiscal policies, the underdeveloped countries are more dependent on exchange control than the others. Many faults can be found with exchange control, but for the countries faced with an inflationary situation not easily treated, given the political and economic milieu, exchange control often enables them to remove some of the objectionable features of distribution under inflation, helps them avert costly devaluations, and keeps the international account balanced, albeit artificially balanced.[48]

The Supply of Complementary Factors

Interference by government is not limited to the provision of additional capital or subsidies in the purchase of raw materials or equipment. The authorities in underdeveloped countries are also confronted with the problem of obtaining adequate supplies of labor, unskilled and skilled, as well as entrepreneurial ability. In this connection, it is of im-

[47] The American Tariff League, *Strength at Home*, 1954, pp. 36–37.

[48] For two rather contrasting views on this issue, see United Nations, *Processes and Problems of Industrialization in Under-developed Countries*, pp. 61–62, and Buchanan and Ellis, *op. cit.*, pp. 321–322, 401–405.

portance to realize that the underdeveloped countries have available about 36 per cent of their potential labor force (working age) as compared with 50 per cent for some European countries and about 40 per cent for the United States. The low proportions for the underdeveloped countries are explained by the large number of young (offset to some extent by smaller proportion of old) and hence the relatively small number of women available for the labor market because of the need of taking care of large numbers of young.[49] When much excess labor is to be found in agriculture, it may be relatively easy to provide the labor required. When these governments support the simplest kind of industries, which at first require little skilled labor, the problems will not be formidable. In fact, it is important at first to encourage industries that can use available supplies of labor. But even here there may be serious problems, for the industrialization of a country plays havoc with cultural patterns: The agricultural laborer finds the discipline of the factory hard to take; the movement to the cities means a break with family and other institutions. The process of mobilizing workers may be eased in so far as the workers are helped to aspire to higher standards of living and in so far as the additional rewards are high enough to justify the sacrifices involved in the migration of the workers. The use of employment exchanges, the provision of housing and expenses of moving, and an educational campaign may all help. Of course, education and training are crucial for the more advanced occupations.

The provision of entrepreneurial ability is even more difficult. Much will depend upon the system of land tenure (does it allow the farmers to make decisions?), upon the restrictions on movement into higher positions (are certain groups denied access to higher positions as in some parts of Africa?), upon the incentives allowed (does taxation favor risk-taking? and does the government protect the property of management?).[50]

Choice of Employments

What industries or employments are to be encouraged? Especially important would be those which can exploit raw materials nearby and are close to markets. Such considerations will explain, for example, why early industries in underdeveloped countries are so often those which use cotton, lumber, and food. These industries (e.g., beer, paper manu-

[49] F. Lorimer, "Demographic Trends," in *Labor, Management and Economic Growth*, 1954, pp. 11–13. Once fertility declines in these regions, a larger proportion of working population will become available.

[50] On these issues see especially Y. Borzen, "Entrepreneurship and Technological Change," and F. L. Hsu, "Cultural Patterns," both in Williamson and Buttrick, *op. cit.*, 1954, and especially M. G. Levy, Jr., "Some Social Obstacles to Capital Formation in Underdeveloped Areas," in *Capital Formation and Economic Growth*, 1955, pp. 441–500.

facture) generally do not require unusual skills, and the cost of transportation of the raw materials gives producers near at hand an advantage. Since capital scarcity is one of the bottlenecks, the favored industries are not likely to be those requiring much capital (though it is interesting that one study reveals that the relation of capital and output, i.e., the capital coefficient, is no so much out of line in underdeveloped countries as compared with these coefficients in developed countries[51]).

Dr. Bohr has made an interesting study of industries according to the total requirement of fixed capital, machinery equipment, skilled-labor requirements, degree of localization, and prevalent size. On the basis of these characteristics of industries in developed countries, some guidance may be given to underdeveloped countries in their programs of development. Obviously, they seek industries that have relatively small need of fixed capital, machinery and equipment, and skilled labor and that tend to be dispersed (that is, those where transportation costs tend to be large and hence imports costly) and finally those industries consisting in part at least of small plants. On the basis of these criteria, the authorities would select industries for special treatment. Even an industry which requires large investments per worker (e.g., cement products and meat packing) may attract the planners because of other advantages, e.g., large savings on transfers, and some industries that require little capital (e.g., rubber goods and electrical machinery) are ruled out because they require large plants to keep unit costs down (and hence large markets). Others requiring little capital (e.g., electrical machinery and ready-made clothing) are excluded because of the large needs of skilled labor.[52]

This is one attack on the problem of choice of employments. Another popular one has been on the basis of the effects of a deployment of resources upon the international position of a country. Foreign lenders are especially inclined to consider the feasibility of a loan upon the basis of whether or not it will increase exports sufficiently or reduce imports to ensure the acquisition of enough dollars or gold to finance the loan, that is, to ensure transfer of the required purchasing power. On this criterion, loans to exploit Venezuelan oil are especially popular because even if each year it becomes necessary to transfer 10 to 20 per cent of the original investment, the problem seems relatively simple, for most

[51] V. V. Bhatt, "Capital Output Ratios of Certain Industries," *Review of Economics and Statistics,* August, 1954, pp. 309–319, and cf. R. N. Grosse, "A Note on Capital Output Ratios," *Review of Economics and Statistics,* August, 1955, p. 305.

[52] K. A. Bohr, "Investment Criteria for Manufacturing Industries in Underdeveloped Countries," *Review of Economics and Statistics,* May, 1954, pp. 157–166. Cf. p. 159 for a table giving priorities of industries for underdeveloped countries on the basis of these criteria.

sales are made in dollars. Nevertheless, authorities, both creditors and debtors, tend to put excessive emphasis on the direct relation of loans and exchange earning potential, and this charge can occasionally be leveled against the International Bank for Reconstruction and Development.[53] New capital may be put into export industries, but the potential exchange earnings may be absorbed in increased sales at home and a large rise of imports associated with rising incomes. The serious exchange problems of Latin America and parts of Asia in the postwar period arose because, with rising incomes and inflation associated with development, exports generally tended to be reduced and imports stimulated. It is also possible to put capital into domestic industries or services, e.g., transportation, power, education, or health, which might reduce costs greatly and bring expenses of many industries down sufficiently to put their products on an exportable level.

The ultimate effects on the balance of payments will depend, for example, on monetary and fiscal policy, on exchange-rate policy, on (and related to the above) the proportion of additional income spent on investment and consumption, and on the mobility of the factors of production. Thus, if resources are put into the most productive employments (the maximum marginal productivity of new increments of capital) without paying special attention to direct effects on exports and imports, then the capital might go predominantly to agriculture, the products of which are consumed primarily at home. But if labor then transfers to export industries or import-competing industries, the secondary effects on the balance of payments would be favorable.[54] As Nurkse puts it, the country should invest in the enterprise that yields the highest returns. Transfer of interest through the exportation of goods is "determined by the scale of comparative costs in international trade (though this scale need not be regarded as fixed and may well change as a result of the investment itself)." Kahn added that against a rise of imports associated with higher incomes resulting from the import of capital is to be put the increased domestic noninflationary output which saves imports.

In an important article, Dr. Polak has considered the relation of foreign investment and international equilibrium.[55] If the marginal propensity to consume is one (e.g., no excess capacity in the borrowing country), then all the money put into circulation as a result of foreign loans would be drawn away in payment for imports. In general the net

---

[53] Cf. Chap. 18.

[54] See especially Nurkse, *op. cit.*, pp. 136–139; J. J. Polak, "Balance of Payments Problems of Countries Reconstructing with the Help of Foreign Loans," *Quarterly Journal of Economics*, February, 1943, pp. 208–240; A. E. Kahn, "Investment Criteria in Development Programs," *Quarterly Journal of Economics*, February, 1951, pp. 38–61; and N. S. Buchanan, *International and Domestic Welfare*, 1945.

[55] Polak, *loc. cit.*

effects would depend on both the marginal propensity to import and the marginal propensity to consume. The higher the former, the more any rise of income resulting from an inflow of investments would be dissipated in increased imports. The higher the latter, the less would any rise of income result in increased investments. Polak assumes a marginal propensity to consume of 75 per cent and to import of 25 per cent; and on these assumptions he finds an expansion rate (the rate of capital investment to capital inflow) of 1½ to 2.

A crucial issue is the form which the additional output takes. (1) Does it provide additional exports or substitutes for commodities or services previously imported? (2) Is it a substitute of one type of export for another or a substitution of one type of output for domestic use for another? (3) Does it result in a rise of goods sold in the home market in excess of amounts previously sold (e.g., on credit)? Obviously the larger is (1), the more favorable the effect on the balance of payments, and the larger is (3), the less favorable. Production of type (3) means higher incomes and pressure on import markets. Polak also suggests that there are dangers inherent in the banks expanding to the limit of their reserves (e.g., four dollars of expansion per dollar of reserves), for this is likely to result in an adverse balance of payments. Another crucial factor is the rate of flow of new capital. Even if the flow of capital declines, no crisis need result if the export balance is adequate to finance loans of the past.

Obviously, if so much depends on the allocation of the funds among the three classes of output enumerated above, it would not be adequate to control foreign borrowing or what is done with foreign funds. The foreign-exchange balance will depend on the marginal propensities to import and to consume, the expansion rates, the ratio of turnover to capital (the larger the ratio the less the service burden), the allocation of investment among the three types mentioned, the service charge as a percentage of capital imports, the annual rate of change of capital flow, and the lag of payments for imports in months. Polak shows that even changes of 10 per cent in these coefficients exercise considerable influence on foreign balances; hence the difficulty of estimating the effects of capital imports and the need of frequent adjustments of lending policy.

Control of Consumption

Imports of capital or foreign grants are not enough. It is also essential to make certain that the capital imported is not absorbed entirely in increased consumption. Through restrictions on imports of luxuries, through increased taxes and public investment, and even through some encouragement of inflation governments of underdeveloped countries seek a conversion of imports of capital into a corresponding volume of savings. In so far as restrictions on luxury imports result in corresponding increases in consumption of domestic commodities, the government may be thwarted. But it is likely that at least part of the cash that would have been converted into imported refrigerators, automobiles, textiles, etc., would be added to cash hoards or put into investment goods. Again, in so far as added taxes used for investment purposes are at the expense of domestic savings, then again the government has failed in its objective. But tax systems of underdeveloped countries are largely regressive (e.g., on commodities), and for this reason it may be assumed that a substantial part of the additional taxes will come out of consumption. It should be added, however, that with underdeveloped countries not generally taking more than roughly 10 per cent of income in taxes, the amount available for public investment and for taxes would be limited. (In Latin America public investment in the years 1945 to 1953 seemed to account for about one-third of all investment, but this came in substantial part out of deficit financing.) Finally, even when the government or the monetary authority through inflation ensures a conversion of foreign capital at least in part into domestic investment, it must be remembered that there are distinct limits of the part of national income that can be diverted into savings through inflation. The effects of inflation on malallocation of resources and hence on income and savings and the adverse effect of rising prices on saving should be considered.[56]

It is especially in underdeveloped countries that fiscal policy may be used effectively to influence the structure of employment. Thus special tax concessions may be made on behalf of secondary industries but only on the condition that they are likely to pay their own way (inclusive of higher taxes later) in a reasonable period of time. The reduced taxes should stimulate investment in secondary (i.e., manufacturing and construction) industries, discourage speculation, and contribute to higher productivity of the relevant factors. Other criteria should be considered also, for example, the extent to which the industry directly or indirectly is likely to affect the balance of payment.[57]

Net Effects upon Structure of Employment and Trade

Economic development, then, involves a reallocation of economic factors of production, with some factors becoming more plentiful relative to demand and others less so. Comparative costs of some products

---

[56] For an estimate of the limits of the contribution of inflation to savings, see S. H. Axelrod, "Inflation and the Development of Underdeveloped Areas," *Review of Economics and Statistics*, 1954, pp. 334–337.

[57] Cf. United Nations, *Processes and Problems of Industrialization in Under-developed Countries*, pp. 52–53, and *The Effects of Taxation on Foreign Trade and Investment*, 1950.

then rise and others fall in response to variations in the supply of factors. On top of this the authorities manipulate prices of factors, below or above the price determined by supply and demand, already influenced by government intervention—in favor of some employments and against others. What happens is consistent with a full-blown theory of comparative costs, except that the assumptions of full employment are removed and the distribution of factors of production is determined not primarily by free-market forces but by decisions of planning authorities. It is necessary to take account not only of unemployment and partial unemployment, as affected by a development program, but also of the proportion of the population on a labor market. A vigorous development program may well increase the proportion greatly as it did in the United States and as it did in Latin America after the war.

Aside from influencing relative prices and availabilities of the factors of production, the authorities flout the law of comparative costs by extending sales, even though, on the basis of comparative costs, the market would be closed. This is done either by putting the costs of higher prices (through taxation) on other segments of the economy or through protectionist measures which exclude foreign sellers. We should add here a reference to our earlier discussion on the inadequacy of a static analysis.

It is generally assumed that capital is invested in accordance with marginal productivities; that is, capital goes where it makes the largest gains. Hence in the nineteenth century there was much interest in exploiting natural resources where capital was highly productive and especially because foreign markets were large. The contribution of foreign capital in producing large quantities of goods at greatly reduced costs for rich markets was very large. But under development programs, much less attention is paid to the scale of marginal productivities. Much capital goes into fundamental industries which will help sustain other industries and especially to overhead industries, such as power and transportation, and to social employments, such as education and health. Many of these industries or employments would attract little capital if the exclusive criterion were returns in that employment, but now government considers not only the direct earnings of these investments but the effects on the whole economy. More education may increase productivity and output in all industries. In view of the political pressures and the need for quick results, investments are not determined merely by a scale of marginal productivities.[58]

In a stimulating essay, Professor Scitovsky has touched on some issues that are relevant here. His argument is that in an industrial economy, a

[58] Cf. Buchanan and Ellis, *op. cit.*, p. 274.

new firm contributes toward external economies, e.g., training of workers, research activities, and stimulating subsidiary industries. The new firm will also profit from the external economies contributed by others. In an agricultural community, however, the new industrial firm gives but does not receive. Hence the case for protection or subsidies for the new firm.[59]

All this does not mean that the comparative-cost principle is now discarded, but it does mean that the structure of employment has been greatly changed as a result of government intervention in the capital market. The most effective industries as viewed from comparative costs may still be the export industries. But by "effectiveness" we mean here capacity to compete pricewise on foreign markets, and this capacity has been influenced by governmental international and domestic policies in determining where foreign and domestic capital goes. These policies include all kinds of subsidy programs (discussed elsewhere) which influence relative costs and prices. Whereas under classical theory it is assumed that capital moves into fields where prospective returns are a maximum, under a development program the flow is determined to a considerable degree by expectations concerning the effects on *total* national income and on the desired deployment of resources given national objectives.

In so far as the program of development succeeds, incomes rise. As incomes rise, capital inflows respond. In other words, instead of capital movements being excluded from consideration as they were in nineteenth-century classical theory, and instead of capital movements being autonomous or accommodating, that is, tied to exports of goods as suggested in neoclassical theory (cf. Machlup), capital movements now are associated with rising incomes in the underdeveloped countries. The resultant inflow of capital in itself brings about a changed deployment of factors and output and hence some changes in exports and imports, not alone through effects on costs either. With higher incomes, the pattern of spending changes also: more imports, an increased tendency to purchase luxury goods, and some diversion of potential exports to domestic markets.

In this discussion, I have neglected the political aspects of economic development. They are, however, of great importance, and some brief comments are required. The case for economic development has been built up in part upon the premise that it is a responsibility of the developed nations to help the underdeveloped ones and in part because, unless standards of the impoverished nations rise, they become more

[59] T. De Scitovsky, "A Reconsideration of the Theory of Tariffs," in *Readings in the Theory of International Trade*, 1949, pp. 386–388.

vulnerable to Communist overtures. Much of United States aid policy springs from considerations of this kind. Thus one official stated that United States aid to ten countries with United States defense alliances received twelve times as much aid per capita as eleven countries that did not sign such agreements.

This approach has had unfortunate repercussions, however; the mixing of political objectives with foreign aid has displeased the recipients of aid. Most do not wish to be lined up on the democratic or Communist side. They want aid without strings attached. Again many of them resent aid as a disguise for dumping of agricultural products.

Beginning in 1955, the whole concept of foreign aid has had to be reexamined. United States authorities are still reluctant to advance funds to neutralists, and they are fearful of international agencies dispensing funds. Yet it is worth noting that the Russians, with much smaller funds, by relying on loans rather than grants, by purchasing rice and cotton rather than dumping, and by accepting payment of interest in local currencies, have been much more successful than the United States. Yet the United States in approximately $10\frac{1}{2}$ years to the end of 1955 gave $53 billion of aid, of which Asia and the Middle East, largely underdeveloped, received in excess of $15 billion. Part of this aid was for military purposes. The U.S.S.R., with loans of much less than $1 billion without strings in these non-Communist areas, seems to have accomplished much more than the United States with $15 billion of grants. Hence the frequent demands that this country overhaul its aid program to underdeveloped countries.[60]

Development and Trade

Even though they raise incomes of the developed countries, the effect of development programs, in so far as they depend upon restrictive policies, may result in a reduction of trade. Alfred Marshall, concentrating on British-German relations, was inclined to argue that the effects would be favorable: With higher incomes, more would be purchased by the newly developed regions. But when Marshall wrote, modern restrictionism was in its infancy. In this connection, a study by Dr. Dominquez, which shows over a long period of time that trade among developed nations has tended to become much less important than that between developed nations on the one hand and underdeveloped on the other, is of some significance. Developed countries were selling no more in dollars

[60] See International Review Service, *Aid for the Economic Development of Underdeveloped Countries*, 1956; *Senate Hearings on Technical Assistance*, February–March, 1955; Milliken and Rostow, *A Proposal; Key to an Effective Foreign Policy*, 1957; and U.S. Department of Commerce, *Foreign Grants and Credits by the United States Government*, December, 1955, table 3.

of constant purchasing power to one another in 1951 than in 1900, but nine nonindustrial countries had expanded their trade from 6.7 per cent of world trade in 1880 to 20.8 per cent in 1951.[61]

Various Approaches to Development

Finally, it should be noted that there are all kinds of ways to bring about economic development. In Britain and the United States development was allowed to take place without much interference or leadership by government. In Britain in the first half of the nineteenth century and in the United States even longer, private enterprise was allowed freedom—with some exploitation of workers, the creating of inflationary credit, and serious breakdowns from time to time. Germany and especially Japan were able to telescope their economic development into shorter periods by profiting from British and American experience and enlisting the interest of government, of the military, and even of leading families. In Japan, through heavy taxes the government enforced savings on the community. Perhaps the most accelerated program has been the Russian, with its recourse to regimentation and complete control of the economy and its primary objective, investment, especially on behalf of the heavy industries. Development programs in the post-World War II period fall in between the laissez-faire approach of the Anglo-Saxon countries and the controlled approach of the U.S.S.R. The pace is less rapid in the underdeveloped countries of Asia, Africa, and Latin America than in the U.S.S.R., the recourse to free-market forces is greater, and a larger part of the gains goes to current consumption (in the Russian case it is dubious that any of the gains in the first twenty-five years went to consumers except in that more consumers had to be fed and clad). But the annual gains of productivity from 1928 to 1939 were 6 per cent in the U.S.S.R. as compared with 2 per cent in the United States from 1899 to 1939, 1.4 per cent in Great Britain from 1907 to 1937, and 3.3 per cent for Latin America in recent years (1945 to 1953).

Development under democratic procedures and at least with substantial recourse to free markets on the one hand and development under compulsion on the other are illustrated in the recent programs of India and China. In China, the objective is rapid industrialization and the use of regimentation to keep consumption down. Both countries started with little industry and large populations with inadequate natural resources. The Chinese have succeeded in expanding investment and industry much more under their governmental controls and central planning than India

[61] Pan-American Union, *International Trade, Industrialization and Economic Growth*, pp. 64–71; cf. League of Nations, *Industrialization and Trade*, pp. 93, 95, for a contrary view; also see A. J. Brown, *Industrialization and Trade*.

has through her planning with cooperation of states and people. In her five-year plan (1951–1956), India was to spend $4.4 billion, with industry receiving 8.4 per cent. In China, the plans for 1953 to 1957 call for outlays of $32.6 billion, with industry receiving 58.2 per cent of expenditures.[62]

Development and Welfare

Some economists (e.g., Professor Frankel and Professor Viner, though to a lesser degree) have been extremely critical of the development programs. Professor Frankel, for example, in opposition to the views expressed by Pigou, contends that an increase in the standard of living cannot be held to imply a gain in welfare. Professor Viner writes:[63]

Let us suppose, for instance, that a country which has embarked on a program of economic development engages in periodic stock-taking of its progress, and finds not only that aggregate wealth, aggregate income, total population, total production, are all increasing, but that per capita wealth, income, production, are also increasing. All of these are favorable indices, but even in combination they do not suffice to show that there has been "economic progress," an increase in economic welfare, rather than retrogression.

Viner's complaint is that the test of success of these programs has been in terms of average increases of income, with no consideration of unfavorable effect on distribution. Indeed, it is essential that the effects on distribution be considered. Excessive inflation, for example, with unfortunate effects on distribution is a relevant consideration. Yet I would contend that the best available statistics show that the gains of development have often percolated to the lowest income groups. In some experiences, e.g., Argentina, the cause of later difficulties has been excessive wage increases. In the Russian program, however, the net results have largely been much more work combined with a standard of living which on the average scarcely rose at all in the first twenty-five years of economic development.[64]

In an interesting paper before the American Economic Association, Professor Nicholls also raised the question of the distributive objectives and effects of a development program. In his view, the gains of the farm program were excessively appropriated by a relatively small group of

[62] United Nations, *Economic Survey of Latin America*, 1953, p. 10; W. Galenson, *op. cit.*, p. 49; and J. Chapman, "Real Wages in the Soviet Union, 1928–52," *Review of Economics and Statistics*, May, 1954; for a full survey, see Buchanan and Ellis, *op. cit.*, pt. II, *Economic Development in India and Communist China*, Staff Study no. 6, Senate Subcommittee of Foreign Relations on Technical Assistance Programs (Senate Committee on Technical Assistance Programs), June, 1956, pp. 45–51.

[63] Viner, *op. cit.*, 1952, p. 126.

[64] United Nations, *Economic Survey of Latin America*, 1953, especially pp. 23–25, and Chapman, *loc. cit.*

wheat and cotton farmers, and it would be much better, especially when mechanization is not justified, to concentrate on increased productivity of the small farmers, improvements of marketing, and finding means of occupying profitably the otherwise idle time of village people.[65]

Professor Frankel's position may be summarized as follows:[66] Comparisons of per capita income of developed and underdeveloped countries are devoid of meaning. The $1,000 per capita income buys one basket of goods in the developed countries, and the $50 to $100 per capita income in the underdeveloped country yields an entirely different basket of goods and services. And nonmonetary income may be of greater significance in underdeveloped countries. It is wrong to suggest that the citizen of the developed country is twenty times as well off as the one from the other countries or even necessarily better off. The intelligent Bushman from Africa finds his welfare in hunting, and he cannot be pushed into seeking Western standards of living. Should the Westerner succeed in imposing his concept of welfare upon members of these societies, even then the higher income yielded would not necessarily mean a gain in welfare. The cost of uprooting people, the loss of advantages of past institutional arrangements now abandoned and of revision of living standards—these may well exceed the apparent gains in a higher (?) standard of living as measured by the Western accounting symbolism of national income, which is largely irrelevant in these societies. The planners in Western states, moreover, err in forcing capital on these countries. They do not need much capital, as they are rich in numbers; the successful investment of capital depends on the availability of complementary factors and the integration of investment with the institutional and cultural patterns in these societies; the experience with the nineteenth-century migration of capital, labor, and management, all integrated to the Western cultural pattern, is of little significance for modern development programs. Holding that much of private investment proved unwise and unprofitable, Frankel is especially critical of investments abroad by public bodies. In his view, they do not know how much capital is needed or where it should go. Moreover, the investments are wasteful in a world short of savings, in part because they discourage the contribution otherwise made locally.

Undoubtedly some of Professor Frankel's points can be supported. We tend too easily to associate economic gains with an improvement in welfare; we accept uncritically estimates of capital needs; we too readily assume that incomes can be measured accurately and are comparable without reservations. Nevertheless, in the author's view, Frankel greatly

[65] W. H. Nicholls, "Investment in Agriculture in Underdeveloped Countries," *Papers and Proceedings of the American Economic Society*, 1955, pp. 70–73.

[66] S. H. Frankel, *The Economic Impact of Underdeveloped Societies*, 1953, especially pt. I.

overstates his case and in no small part because he assumes that the East African case, say, is typical of all underdeveloped areas. The comparison of income of Latin America and the United States does have some meaning; the desire for development is one that is participated in by governments of underdeveloped countries and a large part of their citizens (a high official of Indonesia tells me that the government has 2 million applications for participation in three development programs though there are less than 100,000 vacancies per year); the impetus does not arise primarily from Western nations insisting on impoverished nations' accepting Western funds; and though the cultural pattern may greatly slow up absorption of capital, changes in these patterns do occur. It is not at all clear that the patterns of investment can safely be left entirely to private initiative. Without public intervention, the investment in overhead and social services is inadequate, and hence the whole process of development is excessively slowed down. In this connection, Dr. Lorimer has well observed that unless there is an intensity of capital formation and technological development, the dynamic part of the economy, which for underdeveloped countries accounts for, say, 25 per cent of the labor component, will not adequately absorb the excess population and hence the objective of higher per capita incomes will not be achieved.[67] Besides, a rise in the social dividend for both lending and borrowing nations can be had when governments assume leadership. These gains are not possible when the entire task is left to profit motivation—here note the political gains associated with making a country less vulnerable to Communist pressures when development brings higher standards. Both the Russian and Japanese experience showed that government aid can greatly accelerate development, though the costs of regimentation in the Russian experience should not be underestimated. Despite all the mistakes made by public lenders and borrowers and by government planning organizations, the fact remains that in many of the underdeveloped countries the standard of living has risen greatly and national income even more, and often the gains have gone largely to the low-income groups.

This does not mean that gains in national income are the only measure of economic welfare—the level of employment and the distribution of income are competing objectives. Nor need we assume that higher money or real incomes imply higher welfare attainments. But we can assume that it is possible to measure consumption standards (though there are statistical difficulties) and to conclude that country A has a higher or lower standard than B. We may even grant, as Marshall has,

---

[67] F. Lorimer, "Demographic Trends," in *Labor, Management and Economic Growth*, 1954, pp. 16–17. Cf. United Nations, *Processes and Problems of Industrialization in Under-developed Countries*, 1955, pp. 31–38.

that welfare is not necessarily increased *pari passu* with increased wants.[68]

In every civilised country there have been some followers of the Buddhistic doctrine that a placid serenity is the highest ideal of life; that it is part of the wise man to root out of his nature as many wants and desires as he can; that real riches consist not in the abundance of goods but the paucity of wants.

Finally, it is possible to compare national income across national borders. Nonmonetary transactions can be excluded in both developed and underdeveloped countries, and incidentally it is not always clear that they are a larger part of income of the latter countries. The developed countries obtain more relatively from the income not included in estimates of income from durable goods than do the underdeveloped countries, but if the former's incomes are underestimated on this account, the economic welfare reflected by income figures for developed countries may well be inflated relatively to that of underdeveloped countries when allowance is made for including in the income of developed economies a high proportion of governmental services, conventional goods, and income representing costs of a highly industrialized society. Greater need for housing and clothing in the developed countries is also relevant, and to that extent comparisons of income overstate the economic advantages of the industrialized nations.[69]

From all this we should not conclude that the social structure of underdeveloped countries does not hamper development programs. It does. In a well-balanced statement Professor Moore, an eminent sociologist, has shown that there is a contrast of views between economists who minimize these matters and anthropologists who are deeply concerned; e.g., note the various conflicts of kinship and movement of peoples required by development, cooperation of the village and the individualism of the factory, general values of the primitive society and the allocations, pecuniary motivation, etc., in the developing economy. Nor should we leave out of account the problems raised in the new industrial cities of Asia, where industrialization is being telescoped into a relatively few years as compared with the Western movement, which required centuries and involved relatively small numbers. The shattering of old values is multiplied by the pace of the modern movements and the numbers involved.[70]

[68] A. Marshall, *Principles of Economics*, 8th ed., p. 136.

[69] For a full discussion of these issues, see especially *International Association for Research in Income and Wealth*, 1953, papers by F. Benham, V. K. R. V. Rao, and D. Creamer; cf. S. Kuznets, quoted in Buchanan and Ellis, *op. cit.*, p. 15.

[70] W. E. Moore, "Labor Attitudes towards Industrialization in Underdeveloped Countries," *Papers and Proceedings of the American Economic Society*, 1955, pp. 156–165, and United Nations, *Processes and Problems of Industrialization in Underdeveloped Countries*, pp. 119–126.

Some Conclusions

Through economic-development programs, underdeveloped countries seek an increase in their standard of living, especially through the importation of capital. They thus tend to increase the international movement of factors of production, the slowing down of which in the last generation has tended to increase income differentials between developed and underdeveloped countries. The borrowing countries seek capital especially under the auspices of foreign governments or international agencies, in part because much of the capital needed will not move in response to pecuniary motivation, e.g., capital required for health facilities or for road building.

One effect of the development programs is to introduce a deployment of resources that would not have prevailed under free markets. Through control of capital movements and through exchange, wage, price, and allocation controls, governments shift the allocation of resources from a free-market pattern. They also have recourse to all kinds of protectionist devices in an effort to control allocations. The resultant rise of employment as well as the effects on prices and income in turn influence both the distribution of productive resources and the balance of payments. In general, there is some flouting of the law of comparative advantage, though to some extent what seems to be a violation of the principles of comparative advantages really takes a long view of the effective allocation of resources and also substitutes national objectives of over-all policy, both economic and noneconomic, for the allocations given by exclusive consideration of relative (and short-run) productivities in different employments. It is scarcely necessary to add that the "artificially" induced importation of capital, since it stimulates employments in industries requiring much capital, also tends to modify the pattern of production.

Finally, there is the problem of the relation of capital inflows, the gains of income and investment for the borrowing countries, and the effects on the foreign-exchange situation. Here especially significant are the marginal propensities to import and to consume and the types of commodities produced as a result of the inflow of capital. Obviously, the exchange problem would be eased the lower these marginal propensities and in so far as the additionally produced commodities contribute toward a rise of exports or replace previously imported goods; conversely exchange problems would be heightened in so far as the net effect is a rise of goods sold in domestic markets in response to increases in such variables as consumer credit.

In this discussion I have glossed over the problem of population growth, which increases the difficulties of putting over an adequate development program. "By the end of the Century the world's population is expected to increase from 2.4 to 4 billions. As compared to 1920, the population to date has grown by 76% in Latin America, 46% in Africa, 44% in the United States and Canada, 28% in Asia and 22% in Europe."[71] Unless this rise can be checked—and there are often serious institutional and economic barriers—the gains of productivity are likely to be consumed primarily in taking care of larger populations. The increased capital will be allocated over many more people and prove much less productive.[72]

As this book was ready to go to press, I had an opportunity to read the proofs of Gunnar Myrdal's important book on *The International Economy.* Here is presented the most forceful case for economic development that has yet appeared. Economic development "is a living, political force of immense and irresistible power in our contemporary world." Advanced nations have failed to send the required capital to underdeveloped nations, a source of gain to both developed and underdeveloped countries. Government planning is necessary, because the allocation of resources under a free economy would not yield the resources required for education, transportation, power, a rise in the standards, etc., and in the absence of controls of spending, the resources might largely be dissipated. The free-market approach is not appropriate for the underdeveloped countries, and it is imperative that they obtain a larger part of the gains of progress—in the past their gains have been inadequate. The gap between *haves* and *have-nots* widens. The Communists capitalize on these trends.

[71] International Bank for Reconstruction and Development, *Seventh Annual Meeting, Proceedings,* 1952, p. 3.

[72] Cf. W. S. Thompson, *Population Problems,* 1942, 3d ed., pp. 248–254, and S. E. Harris, *Foreign Aid and Our Economy,* 1950, p. 56; cf. Buchanan and Ellis, *op cit.,* chap. 5.

PART FIVE

Some Aspects of Adjustment in the Postwar Period

Introduction

In earlier parts of this book our attention has been concentrated primarily on the theory of international and interregional economics. We have traced the evolution of the classical theory and have considered relevant aspects of money. In this early part of the book, there were also chapters on economic development, restraints on trade, adjustments, and international institutions and also a chapter on the theory of the dollar gap. In other words, we have superimposed on the theory largely directed toward a study of equilibrium conditions a consideration of the modifications or additions required to deal with the problems of the real world, where economic development is uneven, where adherence to an international system may involve a country in output below its capabilities, where disequilibrium may be sustained for long periods.

This last part of the book is concerned largely with the major disequilibrium problems since World War I, namely, the range of problems subsumed under the generic term "dollar shortage." Hence, we discuss the origin and the extent of the dollar shortage, but the reader is referred back to Chapters 15 to 18 of the book. In discussing a solution to the dollar problem, we concentrate on tariffs (cf. the earlier chapter on restraints), foreign investment and aid (cf. the earlier chapters on balance of payments and economic development), and variations in the price of gold (cf. the earlier chapters on money). In the next to the last chapter, the issue of a return to multilateralism and convertibility is raised, inclusive of fundamental questions of comparative costs, restraints on trade, equilibrium rates of exchange, etc. The statistics of trade, a dull matter indeed, is relegated to the end. The first chapter of Part Five summarizes the issues discussed in the remainder of the book.

CHAPTER 20

The Issues

The Dollar Gap, 1914 to 1953

Over a period of forty years, exports of goods and services of the United States exceeded imports by $125 billion. This is a *rough* measure of the disequilibrating pressure on the balance of payments. (Allowance should be made for the relatively small part of *loans* financed.) The amounts have been especially large since 1940 and particularly in wartime and during the aftermath, but even in the prosperous twenties and the depressed thirties, the problem was serious. A measure of the concern felt by Western Europe is the amount of space given to this problem by Keynes in the twenties and thirties, who probably devoted as much attention to this problem as any other.

How, it may be asked, have the accounts been balanced? About two-thirds through unilateral transfers, almost one-quarter by capital exports from the United States (in part, as far as loans were repudiated, these might also be classified as unilateral transfers), the remainder through imports of gold by the United States. In Chapter 21 (The Size of the Dollar Gap), the reader will find a breakdown by six periods of the deficits and how they were covered. Over this period of forty years, imports amounted to 3.8 per cent of the nation's income, and the excess of exports of goods and services to 73 per cent of United States imports of goods and services. Imports would have had to rise by 75 per cent in these forty years to eliminate the gap. In these forty years, the gap equaled 2.8 per cent of the national income of the United States, and unilateral transfers (exclusive of loans repudiated), 1.9 per cent of national income.

Tariffs and International Equilibrium

In general, too much attention has been given to United States tariff policy as the explanation of disequilibrium in the dollar market. In part, the explanation of this emphasis is an excessive disposition on the part of foreign authorities to criticize our policies, and to some extent

American economists have been "taken in" by wrong analysis. Surely wrong-headed monetary and fiscal policies, cartelization, high-cost policies, failure to seek markets abroad aggressively, the unfortunate introduction of incentives that militate against exports to dollar countries and to all countries—these European policies all help explain the losses in foreign markets and especially in the dollar markets. Nor is it entirely irrelevant to suggest that restrictionist policies are prevalent in a much greater degree in nondollar than in dollar countries. The supporting evidence for these statements will be found in Chapters 22 and 23.

A dollar gap has plagued the world for more than a generation. True, the gap appeared to close in the years 1953 to 1955 following improved terms of trade for Europe and associated with continued foreign aid inclusive of offshore procurement, a spectacular improvement of economic conditions in the United States (and hence more imports), extended restrictions and discriminations against dollar imports in nondollar countries, and special incentives for exports to the United States. But a closing of the gap under these circumstances should not be taken as evidence that the dollar problem has been solved—far from it, especially under present-day conditions when changes in the political or military or economic situation may almost overnight raise the dollar deficit by several billion dollars at an annual rate. The real test will come when the nondollar world balances its accounts without the help of about $4 billion to $8 billion of United States government aid, United States military outlay abroad, and expenditures by United States personnel abroad and also without recourse to abnormal restrictions on trade inclusive of discrimination against the dollar.

In these chapters, the crucial issue discussed is what contribution can tariff policy, as against alternative measures, make toward closing the dollar gap as well as increasing trade. I believe that an attempt should be made to close the gap *primarily* through the United States' yielding of export markets in third countries and reliance on a generous lending and aid program by this country in the next ten years at any rate rather than through liberalizing trade.

My reasons for this position are numerous. Thus, many overestimate the effects of tariff reduction upon United States imports. Here I show that the more important association is between United States income and imports rather than between prices of imports (e.g., as affected by tariffs) and the value of imports. This position is sound even if it is granted that there is a substantial elasticity of demand for some imports, e.g., British manufactures. But for the solution of these problems what is relevant is the elasticity of demand for all United States imports and the difference between the elasticity of demand for the *export* part of the final commodity and the *final* commodity, e.g., a cut in price of exported Scotch, say, from $2 to $1 (50 per cent) is a cut in fact from, say, $7 to $6—14 per cent—for the final consumer.

Studies which purport to show a high inverse correlation between tariff cuts and imports are not convincing. The manner of obtaining the elasticities is subject to serious criticism, and inadequate attention is given to the imperfections of the market which seriously interfere with import responses to reduced prices.

A second reason for doubting the efficacy of tariff cuts in achieving equilibrium lies in the practical difficulties involved. These are considerations that a political economist should not shove aside as being irrelevant or as the problems of another discipline. It is necessary to consider the costs of adjustment as tariffs are reduced and the effects of liberalization of trade upon agricultural policies, widely supported in this country, which require implementation by trade policy. It is necessary to consider these trade restrictions, not as one problem independent of others, but as one facet of government intervention which must be related to other areas of government policies. Thus, if one industry or region suffers through government fiscal or (even) agricultural policy, it may have a special claim for consideration when the government determines its trade policy. These are not separate policies.

From all this, I do not draw the conclusion that tariff policy should not contribute toward a solution of the dollar problem. It may and should, but only in conjunction with other suggested policies. On grounds of neither economic analysis nor equity should the burden of achieving dollar equilibrium be put exclusively on import-competing industries, especially since export industries have received record help through $125 billion of "subsidies" the last forty years. Moreover, not merely tariff rates but quotas and customs administration should be reconsidered.

The uncertainty of our tariff policy is another obstacle. Here some gains may be made in customs simplification and administration, but it is probably going too far to demand that these measures be used to conceal a reduction of tariffs or that the escape clause be revoked. Surely both workers and employers with a vested interest in current trade policy should not be subject, without right of appeal, to decisions taken by government negotiators. In fact, the applications under the escape clause at least until 1956 touched a small part of trade, and as long as injury is defined in a sensible way, e.g., not in terms of a loss of the proportion of sales in this country, the continuance of this provision is not a matter for serious doubt. The treatment of the escape clause under H.R. I in 1955 may, however, greatly increase the recourse to its use.

While we are on this subject, we should stress the point that however justifiable the reciprocal trade agreements, with their emphasis on increased imports through concessions to purchase our exports, may have been in 1933 when unemployment was the disease of our economy, the whole program should be reconsidered now that the objective is more imports, not more imports *and* more exports. We must cure the dollar disease and expand trade.

In discussing the tariff issue, I cannot refrain from commenting on the dubious argument of the Randall Commission when it lists the number of jobs dependent on export industries as an argument for the reduction of tariffs. Against these jobs, the Commission ought to put the additional jobs that would accrue should imports be eliminated. The fact is that there would probably be more jobs as import-competing industries take over the tasks formerly performed by foreign-export industries. The argument for free trade is not more jobs, but more income as we produce in the most efficient manner. (This criticism of the Randall Commission is aside from some questions concerning the validity of the figures used.)

Another argument used by those who would minimize problems of adjustment related to trade liberalization is that in an expanding economy, some industries and regions decline and others grow and the net effect is favorable. The price of progress must be paid. The carriage manufacturers suffered, but note the much greater gains in the automobile industry. It is, however, easy to underestimate the cost of adjustment, and a case may be made out for public measures to slow up the rate of change rather than accelerate it. In my studies of the New England region, I have been convinced that on economic and other grounds, there was much to be gained by a slowing up of the rate of change in some sectors of our economy. At the very least, we should not expect government to accelerate the rate of change and telescope adjustments in altogether too short a time—as it is sometimes asked to do through tariff and trade policy. The fact is that movements of capital and management toward depressed regions and industries are sluggish, in part because of the higher tax costs, the labor-capital friction, and the depressed atmosphere of the high-unemployment places. In other words, unemployment related to tariff cuts or other variables is not so quickly erased through factor movements as is often claimed in the theory of trade. Furthermore, labor tends to stick rather than move out, even in periods of high employment.[1]

I hasten to add that the arguments used by protectionists are often

[1] Cf. S. E. Harris, *Economics of New England*, 1952; *Report of the New England Textile Industry by the Committee Appointed by the Conference of New England Governors*, 1953, S. E. Harris, chairman; "Interregional Competition: With Particular Reference to North-South Competition," *American Economic Association Proceedings*, 1954; and especially W. H. Miernyk, *Inter-industry Labor Mobility: The Case of the Displaced Textile Worker*, 1955.

faulty. It is not easy to defend their most popular argument for protection, namely, lower wages abroad not compensated by higher productivity at home. Should this argument be accepted, then the whole foundation for international trade is removed. In their increasing support of the defense argument, they are on safer ground. But the costs of protectionism should be carefully weighed, and that means there are limits concerning how far this argument can be carried. The further it is pressed, the greater the costs to the economy and the larger the present burden on the economy. In shipping, the argument carries much weight; in watches, less weight; in textiles, still less weight.

The dollar problem can be solved, though the ease with which it can be attacked depends on the political and military situation. We must use all approaches: trade policy, increased access to third markets by nondollar countries, United States loans and grants. As we argue fully later, we can expect substantial aid from increased outlays on tourism abroad, the greater access of foreign countries to our $50 billion government market (purchases from business in 1953), the expected rise of imports of raw materials and food in the next generation, and the continued rise, absolutely and relatively, in our national income. Some countries will gain less than others from these forces, and those that will not gain enough, in particular Western Europe, will have to depend to some extent on foreign aid, on penetration of third markets, and on strong measures generally to keep costs down.

The Contribution of Loans and Grants

Since trade policy will not solve the problems of imbalance, it is necessary to rely on other measures also. Loans and grants provide dollars for foreign interests. Hence if foreign countries cannot increase their sales in the dollar markets adequately, it is possible to finance the deficiency through the provision of dollars on a loan or gift basis.

In the postwar period, United States private loans have been at a disappointing level: about one-tenth to one-fifteenth of the ratio to income of British loans in the great period of British lending and a fraction of the ratio in this country to income in the twenties. For many reasons, we should not expect the United States to contribute in the proportions of the British before 1913, e.g., the greater gains from capital exports obtained by the British, the early saturation if the British ratio to United States gross national product were maintained, the chaotic conditions of today. But larger loans than in recent years might well be expected.

Offshore procurement, that is, use of dollars to buy goods and services in foreign countries for the use of our allies, is one approach to this problem. The amounts involved are substantial, though the gestation period is long. These purchases contribute toward a solution of the dollar problem, however, only to the extent that, say, the purchase of planes in France with dollars for the use of the European army does not reduce exports to dollar countries or increase imports. Had the planes not been produced, the exports might have been larger and imports smaller.

All kinds of suggestions, which are summarized in Chapter 24, have been made for accelerating the rate of private investments, but there are serious obstacles. Some countries prefer public loans or grants, in part because in their view private lending is unstable and badly allocated among countries and industries. (Public lending shares these weaknesses to some extent.) The profit motive does not always yield the borrowing country or the world the allocation of investment funds deemed consistent with national and free-world interests. The effect of tax concessions and guarantees against loss of principal as weapons for stimulating foreign investment, limited by considerations of equity and protection of the national budget, is not likely to be great.

In one sense, loans and even grants may not help greatly. If they are matched by a corresponding increase of imports by the favored country, then the pressure on the dollar market is not relieved. Ultimately a rise of productivity, and hence more exports and less imports associated with the inflow of funds, may, however, be significant.[2]

Loans and grants merely put off the day of reckoning unless the effect is to provide the basis of more exports and/or less imports for the recipient countries. The main advantages of this approach are that the transitional effects of a relative rise of imports for the United States is spread over a much longer time than if adjustment were to be made by relaxation of trade barriers, and the costs of the adjustment are spread more widely. In so far as the effects are to build up the economies of the borrowing countries in the manner suggested in Chapter 24, then the burden is reduced *pari passu* with the rise of their income and the disturbing effects of more imports for the United States economy are reduced with our rise of income (again see Chapter 24).

It is easy to exaggerate the economic gains for the countries receiving foreign assistance, especially if it is assumed too readily that industrialization always brings higher incomes. In many instances, the quest for industrialization goes too far, and the effects may often be reduced, rather than increased, income. On the other hand, many countries would gain through more productive agriculture as capital comes in and more secondary and tertiary employment absorbs the working population released from the farms; but the estimates of gains may be excessive.

It should not readily be assumed that the underdeveloped countries

[2] See the interesting paper by E. Nevin, "U.S. Foreign Investments and Dollar Shortage: A Comment," *Review of Economics and Statistics,* November, 1954.

can absorb unlimited sums of money. There must be years and even decades of preparation. Some hypothetical figures appear in Chapter 24. The amount made available will depend also upon other demands on the *developed* countries inclusive of military, their state of employment (the more unemployment, the greater the income offsets to lending or giving), the profitability of their domestic investments, the treatment of foreign capital abroad, etc. It should be noted, however, that the treatment of cyclical or even secular unemployment in developed countries through foreign assistance or loans might require a different timing of dollar aid than that which is required for the solution of the dollar shortage.

How effective loan programs will be depends also upon the conditions of financing. When, for example, as in our direct investments in the first postwar decade returns come to 15 per cent a year, within less than a decade, repayments on the assumption of a steady flow of X loans per year will exceed the new investment to be made. (Reinvestment abroad will ease the situation to some extent.) It makes a tremendous difference whether the return is 6 or 2 per cent, whether there is a provision for amortization or there is not. With high returns and amortization in, say, twenty years, a long-term lending program is not likely to be practical.

Finally, we shall note that the substitution of loans or grants for tariff liberalization is subject to this reservation. It may not be possible to pinpoint this kind of aid to the countries that might profit from tariff-liberalization measures, though the nearer to convertibility, the easier the spreading of the advantages of loans or grants to all countries.

Free Exchange Rates

One approach toward balancing the dollar account is a reduction of costs and prices by nondollar countries and hence more exports and less imports. The reasons for the failures to adjust under gold are given in Chapters 9 to 12 and need not be repeated here.

Disappointment with the workings of gold accounts in part for the more recent emphasis on flexible exchanges. Why not cut the value of the pound sterling? Would not prices of British exports on export markets fall and of imports rise in pounds sterling? Would not British exports rise and imports fall? Many insist that with appropriate movements of exchange rates, the problem of dollar disequilibrium would be solved. The International Monetary Fund operates largely on this premise. The pitfalls of adjustment through exchange rates are suggested in Chapter 11 (also cf. Chapter 18).

The British experience since 1949 discussed in Chapter 25 reveals that with inflationary pressure extant, it is not easy to keep export prices from rising as much as the price of dollars, and hence the world price does not fall vis-à-vis prices of competitors. In fact, though the pound sterling declined by 44 per cent in terms of the dollar from 1937 to 1952 and all nondollar currencies (except Iron Curtain countries) by about 90 per cent, the dollar problem is far from solved. The competitive position of the United States has actually improved, as is apparent from an examination of trade and gold-reserve figures. Although British manufacturing wage rates corrected for exchange movements reveal a large competitive gain for the British, they do not when these figures are corrected for *all* wage rates and for the relative rise of productivity in the United States. Export prices on world markets of British goods have not fallen vis-à-vis those of the United States, despite the much smaller rise of manufacturing wages in Great Britain and the 44 per cent depreciation.[3]

In the Great Depression, exchange depreciation seemed to help those countries that embraced it. But the situation was different from that in the post-World War II period. The problem, then, was not only balancing accounts as in the earlier period but primarily treating unemployment. Hence, with deflation rampant and with inflation not threatening, prices in depreciated currencies did not rise so much as the price of gold, and hence depreciation really cut world prices as it did not in the years from 1939 to 1952. Conditions were also conducive to an expansion of goods for export markets. The slower rate of growth of exports than in the post-World War II period is explicable by the depressed state of demand in the thirties, not by low elasticity of supply. The depreciation was effective in still another way in the thirties: The cost of imports in domestic currencies rose greatly, and, therefore, not only were imports reduced but import-competing industries were stimulated. In the later period, exchange depreciation could contribute little toward restricting imports, for these had already been rationed by licensing, and despite depreciation the outbreak of the Korean War resulted in a greater rise of imports than exports. In fact, all sterling countries, despite their substantial depreciation since 1949, suffered a relative deterioration in their proportion of world trade in the next few years—not so the rest of Western Europe.

Too much should not then be expected from flexible exchanges, though appropriate exchange rates may reduce the extent of imbalance. With a very large imbalance, with serious shortages at home, a large depreciation may still fall far short of balancing accounts. Is not the experience of 1938 to 1952 for all nondollar countries decisive on this point? The commodities may not be available for the export market, and if they are made available, serious effects on motivation and on political

[3] Cf. Chap. 25 for a more extended discussion.

stability associated with the ensuing sacrifices at home may follow, especially if imports are drastically cut. I need not discuss again all the obstacles to a large rise of exports following a depreciation.[4]

Adequacy of Reserves and the Price of Gold

In the 1930s, devaluation was widespread, and when it was all over, the price of gold on the average had risen about two-thirds in terms of domestic currencies. The result was a stimulation in the output of gold and a large increase in the value of gold reserves both on absolute terms and in relation to total trade and production. But from 1936 to 1955, wholesale prices in dollars rose by at least 100 per cent (international commodities even more) while the price of gold remained unchanged. Moreover, both the production of goods and services and trade have risen greatly since the thirties. It is not surprising, then, that there is much discussion of the need of a rise in the price of gold. That the non-dollar countries would especially profit from an increase in the price of gold adds weight to the arguments adduced. Mr. Roy Harrod has even gone so far as to contend that a rise in the price of gold equal to that in the prices of international commodities would erase the dollar gap.

The United States has a special interest in the determination of the appropriate price of gold. (Under the charter of the International Monetary Fund, the price of gold may be changed, but it would require approval of the United States.) Our special interest stems from the fact that this country is the primary purchaser of gold, and in exchange we give our goods, services, and property rights. A higher price would mean more goods at the expense of the American economy—at least until prices had responded to the rise in the price of gold. In making a decision, we would be influenced by two other considerations:

1. Goods would be given away on the basis of availability of gold abroad and not necessarily in accordance with this country's political objectives.

2. A doubling in the price of gold (a frequent proposal) would endanger the stability of our price level. With gold value increased by $22 billion, the government might indeed solve its budgetary problems temporarily (in fact, this is one of the strong appeals of revaluation of gold: foreign aid without a cost to the taxpayer), but it would have to take drastic measures to offset the effects of a rise in its deposits of $22 billion. Should the money be spent, bank reserves would be increased by an equal amount, thus providing a foundation for about $100 billion of additional money. Even if securities held by the banks and public were redeemed, the effects would be inflationary: Reserves of banks would rise. Only if the additional cash were used to purchase securities

[4] Cf. Chaps. 11, 16, and 25.

held by the Reserve banks would the potential inflationary effects be offset. Could we count on such a courageous attack? It is not likely, as the 1933–1934 episode suggests. Incidentally, one serious count against revaluation rests on the fact that whereas revaluation might be strongly supported in a great deflation, it is more difficult to support a rise in the price of gold when inflation has been the great threat.

A revaluation of gold raises many complex problems. What is the appropriate rise? Should the required supply of gold reserves be related to trade or prices? To what base year should the ratio of gold to trade or prices be tied? To 1938, when gold was more than adequate partly because trade was low, or 1928, when gold may have been somewhat deficient? How is allowance made for the economies of gold related to the flow into reserves since the twenties and even thirties, for the greater use of controls of trade and capital and hence smaller dependence on gold movements, for greater readiness to use exchange flexibility and hence less dependence on gold? Is adequacy measured by the total amount of gold? Or is maldistribution considered? Is the measure of adequacy given by gold availability, or gold and exchange? (On these issues, see Chapter 26.) Can we be certain that a rise in the price of gold, say, by 100 per cent will provide a corresponding amount of dollars? Obviously, much will depend on the rise of gold output and the use to which the dollars are put (to buy more dollar goods by gold countries or more goods in nondollar countries or to build up reserves or hoards?).

Convertibility

It is not likely that free convertibility, that is, the freedom to exchange one currency for another, a privilege withheld in most countries as late as 1957, will contribute toward a solution of the dollar problem. In fact, inconvertibility is a measure taken in large part to conserve dollars. Hence convertibility awaits a solution of the imbalance in international accounts—whether the attack is through United States liberalization of trade, rising incomes in the United States, increased capital exports and/or assistance from the United States, improved competitive position inclusive of appropriate monetary and fiscal policies for nondollar countries, and recourse to exchange flexibility by countries faced with adverse balances. It follows that a return to convertibility through recourse to increased restrictions on trade or a rise in dependence on foreign aid would constitute a sham victory.

From all this it is suggested that convertibility is the last step in a return to international relations primarily based on adjustments of the free market. That does not mean that no steps toward convertibility should be taken until all abnormal restraints on trade are removed, but it does seem sensible not to embark on convertibility at least until substantial progress has been made toward a balancing in the dollar account without recourse to large programs of unorthodox restrictions on trade. A premature return is likely to result in increased pressures to introduce restrictive measures as a means of preserving convertibility.

Convertibility is not a step toward the solution of the dollar problem. It, in fact, should reflect a return to more normal relations on international markets. Its objective is to reduce uneconomic purchases and production among countries. In Chapter 27, I dwell at some length on the extent of these uneconomic diversions of trade.

One of the crucial issues upon which decisions on convertibility must be made is the adequacy of reserves for the countries returning to convertibility. In Chapter 26, I discuss this issue: estimates depend so much upon the ratio of reserves to trade, the distribution of these reserves, the base year with which comparison is made, and many other factors. In 1938, reserves were large. On one estimate, it would require additions of more than $20 billion of reserves for nondollar countries to reestablish 1938 relationships. But on the basis of 1928, the required additions would be much smaller. In addition, it is well to remember that less reserves are needed because of the control of capital exports, the greater recourse to exchange movement to hasten adjustments, the availability of international agencies for temporary help, the greater awareness of the relation of domestic policies and international disequilibrium, and the more potent weapons available. In some other respects, the situation may be less favorable. In particular, chaotic political conditions and volatile changes in the terms of trade are relevant.

Should convertibility be a decision for the United Kingdom alone or for all European Payments Union (EPU) countries? Obviously there are dangers that other EPU countries might use the United Kingdom as a channel for draining dollars should the latter resume convertibility without association with the EPU countries or at least without agreements concerning purchases and sales in the United Kingdom (balances could be built up by buying less and selling more in the United Kingdom) and without agreements concerning the treatment of large credits built up by these countries. It might be necessary to limit convertibility of sterling thus acquired by Continental countries at least temporarily.

Some Aspects of Trade and the Dollar Shortage

On the whole, the newer countries tend to expand their trade much more rapidly than the older ones. With some major countries expanding their proportions of world trade by 50 per cent since before the war and others losing heavily, it might be expected that this symptom of greater growth and increased competitive position for some would embarrass the countries losing ground relatively or absolutely—at least for a time.

To some extent the countries suffering from a shortage of dollars try to protect themselves by introducing preferential arrangements (e.g., EPU and sterling convertibility), thus drawing trade into noneconomic channels although increasing trade, and also by discrimination against exports from the dollar countries in other ways. Thus, we can explain the large contribution toward closing the dollar gap made by reductions of imports from dollar countries. But it should be observed that closing the dollar gap in this manner is not a genuine approach toward equilibrium, for what is involved is the imposition of controls restricting trade and uneconomic production—not adjustments of a free market. In the later years of the first postwar decade, Western Europe gained also in her sales to dollar countries.

Despite the heroic measures taken, however, Western Europe and other countries continued to suffer from an imbalance in the dollar market during the 1950s. A major explanation has been the inadequate contribution made by third countries toward solving Western Europe's problems and the deterioration in the terms of trade (especially in the case of the United Kingdom). There is some evidence also that European economies, especially the United Kingdom, have been tethered excessively to industries that are not expanding and even declining.

The fact that third countries made such a small contribution had serious effects. Had Europe been able to obtain supplies from third countries as anticipated and to capture a substantial part of these third markets from the United States (aside from unrequited exports financed by loans from Western Europe) and had the third countries used increased supplies of dollars to purchase goods from Western Europe as anticipated (or at least to a greater extent than they actually did), then the problems would have been much less serious. Indeed, in the early fifties some progress had been made by Europe in relying more relatively on nondollar sources of supplies.

Unfortunately the nondollar overseas countries, especially other sterling countries and European dependencies, greatly increased their adverse balance on dollar account, using dollar balances disproportionately to buy dollar goods. A number of factors were responsible: Capital imports from the United States tended to encourage imports of goods from the United States, and this country so often had the goods wanted; war and political chaos have changed the pattern of world trade, although as international conditions improve (if they do), the old relationships will tend to be reestablished. As Mr. Lubell observed in a stimulating little volume, part of Europe's troubles, in the midst of a changing pattern of objectives of overseas countries, lay in her failure to produce the goods wanted by the outside world.[5] Again there is every indication that a residue of lost competitive power will be felt by Europe and parts of Asia as the United States adapts its output to Latin American wants and these third markets increasingly realize that in a troubled world there is an advantage in maintaining trade relations with neighboring countries—and often even when on the basis of simple comparative-advantage principles, it might seem preferable for Latin America, say, to buy from Europe or Asia.

These remarks apply generally to the first postwar decade, but they require some modification in view of the developments in 1953 to 1956. In these years, the nondollar world gained vis-à-vis the United States. Indeed, the gains were unevenly divided because the decline in the prices of agricultural products and especially of raw materials was reflected in gains for the nondollar *industrial* countries especially, and the gains are associated with the rise in military aid which accounted for 10, 17, 26, 20, and 15 per cent of exports of the United States in 1950, 1951, 1952, 1953, and 1954.

In the years 1953 and 1954, the gains of the nondollar world are evident, for example, in a decline of United States exports by $100 million from 1952 to 1954 as compared with a rise for the world of $3.5 billion and a decline of imports by the United States of $500 million as compared with one of $900 million for the world.[6] In 1955, this trend continued. The Continental EPU countries notably expanded their exports to the United States and reduced their dependence on United States imports. In other words, Western Europe was becoming less dependent on the United States sources for their imports and were beginning to capture third markets from the United States. On the latter, the General Agreement on Tariffs and Trade has commented as follows:[7]

As regards trade with the industrial world the largest change occurred in North America's surplus on account of primary products in its trade with Western Europe. At the same time, North America in 1953 had further increased its net imports of manufactured goods from other industrial areas. The total change in North America's trade balance vis-à-vis the industrial world between 1951 and 1953 nearly reached $1,500 million, and it was due not only to a large reduction in supplies of primary products to other industrial destinations but also, to the extent of nearly $400 million, to increased imports of manufactures.

[5] S. Lubell, *The Revolution in World Trade*, 1955, pp. 80–81.
[6] Figures from International Monetary Fund, *International Financial Statistics*, June, 1955.
[7] General Agreement on Tariffs and Trade, *International Trade*, especially pp. 15–16.

The report goes on to comment on the large reductions of sales of manufactured goods of North America to primary producing regions.

Along similar lines, the International Monetary Fund shows that the United States exports to regions other than Canada declined by $1,156 million in 1953, with Western Europe accounting for more than 40 per cent, Latin America less than 40 per cent, and other areas 22 per cent. The major losses were in grains and preparations ($420 million), in cotton ($350 million), and in coal, iron and steel products, and petroleum ($310 million).[8]

From 1953 to 1955–1956 the United States generally lost ground relative to the world level of exports although she rebounded in 1956. In 1954 to 1956, moreover, exports to the Western Hemisphere and other areas continued to rise, for on the basis of the first nine months of 1956 all exports were up by more than $4 billion, or one-third, compared with 1950 to 1953.[9]

[8] *International Monetary Fund Annual Report,* 1954, p. 20.
[9] *Survey of Current Business,* December, 1956, and *International Financial Statistics,* January, 1957.

CHAPTER 21

The Size of the Dollar Gap

A General Picture, 1913 to 1953

Over a period of forty years, the United States exports of goods and services have exceeded imports by more than $125 billion. (This is exclusive of shipments to service United States military forces abroad.) These summary figures suggest the magnitude of the dollar problem. For the purposes of this discussion, I define the dollar gap as the difference between exports and imports of goods and services. Over a period of a few years this definition would be inadequate.

How were foreigners able to obtain the dollars required to cover this deficit and thus pay for their excess of imports of goods and services? The major contributions to cover a deficit in excess of $125 billion through 1953 were as shown in Table 21-1.

1. *Unilateral transfers,* which are primarily grants by the United States government, were substantial contributions. Approximately $85 billion, or roughly two-thirds of the total (68 per cent), was met by unilateral transfers, or "gift" dollars.

2. Almost $29 billion, or 23 per cent, was covered by movements of capital, that is, by purchases of securities from foreigners or direct investments abroad by Americans. This total includes also repurchases of United States securities or properties by Americans and, of course, the short-term capital movements.[1] From these totals are deducted capital imports into the United States.

Elsewhere we shall deal with the problem of losses involved in capital movements. A dollar of capital movement should not be treated in the same manner as a dollar of unilateral grant. Returns on the investment are obtained, and presumably an asset is acquired. (But note that despite $29 billion of investment abroad since 1914, the *net* investments abroad of this country were only $15.7 billion in 1951. Some investments

[1] For example, deposits of foreigners in American banks, or purchases of short-term Treasury bills minus deposits abroad, etc., by Americans.

Table 21-1. Dollar Gap and Coverage, 1914 to 1953
(In billions of dollars)

Year	Deficit of dollars, current account	Unilateral transfers	Capital[a] (net outflow)	Gold (net purchases, U.S.)	Errors, omissions, transfers, etc.
1914–1918	10.8	0.4	11.4	1.0	2.1
1919–1920	8.3	1.7	3.7	0.2	3.2
1921–1930	11.8	3.7	5.4	1.8	1.1
1931–1939	4.6	1.8	5.0[b]	10.5	2.5
1940–1945	40.6	41.8	1.6[b]	2.3	1.5
1946–1953[c]	49.5	35.6	15.0[d]	0.2[e]	3.7[f]
	125.6	85.0	28.9	15.6	

[a] Includes government capital.

[b] Net inward movement of capital.

[c] 1953, based on figure for nine months (Since adjusted).

[d] The Randall Commission gives long-term *private* investments as $9.0 billion from 1944 to 1952, but this includes $5.5 billion of reinvested earnings. These, of course, do not provide dollars. In the five years 1948 to 1952, government investments were $2.3 billion additional. *Randall Commission Staff Papers*, pp. 80–81.

[e] Net loss of gold.

[f] For 1946 to 1951 only.

SOURCES: 1914–1920, U.S. Census, *Historical Statistics of the U.S., 1789–1945;* 1921–1939, U.S. Department of Commerce, *The United States in the World Economy*, 1943; 1940–1945, U.S. Department of Commerce, *The Balance of Payments, 1940–1945;* 1946–1951, U.S. Department of Commerce, *The Balance of Payments, 1946–1948*, and *The Balance of Payments, 1949–1951;* 1952, 1953, *Survey of Current Business*, December, 1953, and *Bell Report*.

were lost, and foreigners had invested here.[2]) An estimate for investments abroad at the end of 1952 was $23.1 billion of private investment and $14.4 billion of government investment.[3] By 1953, net income on investments was $1,899 million, and net payments, $448 million.[4] In fact, the dollar problem is aggravated because in 1952 United States income receipts from foreign investment were $1,819 million. The pressure on the dollar market would have been much greater had not $861 million of $2,680 million of total earnings been retained abroad.[5]

3. An inflow of gold accounted for $15 billion, or 12 per cent of the total. I would be inclined to classify gold receipts in the same manner as unilateral receipts. In exchange we gave goods and services. We

[2] U.S. Department of Commerce, *Balance of Payments of the United States, 1949–1951*, p. 162.

[3] *Randall Commission Staff Papers*, p. 79.

[4] *Survey of Current Business*, March, 1954, pp. 22–23.

[5] "Income on United States Foreign Investments," *Survey of Current Business*, December, 1955, pp. 8ff.

could well dispense with much of this; it is not likely that much of it will go out in the visible future in payment for goods and/or services. Foreign nations want food, raw materials, and machinery. Indeed, they would accept some gold to strengthen their reserves, but not substantially in place of commodities and services they need. The accumulation of reserves in 1952 to 1956 by foreign countries shows that they are ready to substitute gold and dollars for goods and services to some extent. The accumulation of dollars cuts our reserves.

4. Errors, omissions, etc., are a substantial item. To a considerable degree, they may be short-term capital movements.

World War I and Aftermath

The contribution of these three factors varied in different periods. Thus, in World War I, capital movements exceeded the adverse balance of $10.8 billion, and besides these loans, the United States purchased more than $1 billion of gold. Of course, these capital exports were primarily government loans, never to be repaid, and hence, in fact, were a form of unilateral transfers. Estimates for this period are only roughly accurate. Errors, omissions, etc., amounted to more than $2 billion.

In the two postwar years (1919–1920), the shortage of dollars was $8.3 billion. In this period, the facts are rather obscure. Unilateral transfers accounted for $1.72 billion (21 per cent); capital movements, $3.71 billion (45 per cent); gold, $234 million (3 per cent); and errors and omissions are a large item.

The Twenties

The outside world, with an adverse balance of $11.8 billion, continued to experience difficulties in the twenties. Capital exports by this country ($5.4 billion) and unilateral (primarily private) transfers ($3.7 billion), purchases of gold here ($1.8 billion), and errors and omissions ($1.1 billion) account for the adverse balance. This was the period of great prosperity in this country reflected in exports of capital, inadequate imports in part as a result of tariff policy, and large gains of productivity here. Europe felt the pressure in reduced reserves. The failure of prices to rise adequately here, despite the inflow of gold, prevented the required rise of imports or retardation of exports.

The Thirties

What of the dismal thirties? Indeed, the adverse balance of the outside world on current account was cut to $4.64 billion, or by more than 60 per cent—a smaller cut if allowance is made for the decline in prices. But the dollar problem was even more serious than in the prosperous twenties. Gold purchases by the United States were no less than $10.5 billion net, or more than twice the deficit on current account. In this way, the world paid for $5 billion of capital *shipped to this country* and $4.6 billion adverse balance on current account. Despite depression and reduced income here, fears of war and depression abroad accounted for the net movement of capital from the impoverished world to the United States, which was still the richest nation on earth.

World War II

In the war years 1940 to 1945, the dollar shortage amounted to more than $40 billion, and, of course, unilateral transfers (Lend-Lease primarily) provided foreign nations with the dollars to cover these demands. Capital movements (a net inflow) and gold inflow (more than $2 billion) were relatively unimportant.

1946 *to* 1953

In the eight postwar years 1946 to 1953 the deficit in the dollar account was almost $50 billion, or $9 billion in excess of the six-year wartime deficit (in dollars of reduced value, however). Unilateral grants (primarily public) provided more than two-thirds, and capital movements (public and private) accounted for less than one-third. Gold movements were relatively unimportant for the period as a whole, though transfers, omissions, errors, etc., were equal to almost 10 per cent of the total.

In relation to national income and imports, the gap has been significant. For the forty years 1914 to 1953, the gap amounted to $126 billion, or 2.8 per cent of the $4,476 billion of national income and 73 per cent of the $172 billion of our imports.[6] Unilateral transfers of $85 billion amounted to 1.9 per cent of the national income. Imports, in turn, amounted to 3.8 per cent of the national income. In general, the gap tends to be large relative to income in wartimes (4.9 and 5.4 per cent in World War I and World War II) and to decline in times of peace. (But note that in 1919–1920 the gap was 5.4 per cent of incomes as against 2.1 per cent in 1946 to 1953.) As a percentage of imports, the gap was 97 per cent in World War I and 151 per cent in World War II, and for the forty years involved, 73 per cent of imports. In other words, imports would have had to rise by three-quarters to eliminate the gap (by 150 per cent in World War II and by 60 per cent in 1946 to 1953). Yet the tendency has been for imports to decline as a percentage of

---

[6] Possibly about $15 billion accumulated in dollars by foreign central banks should be deducted, and note that military exports (grants) are included.

national income, though by 1953 imports had reached 4 per cent of national income. These over-all figures point to the importance of the gap and the vast improvement in imports which would be required if the gap were to be eliminated in this manner. In 1955 and 1956 the excess of exports was roughly 1 and 1.5 per cent of national income, a substantially smaller figure than for the preceding period of forty years.

For the purpose of this discussion, I have defined the gap as the excess of United States exports of goods and services over imports of goods and services. Some may prefer to measure the gap by the amount of

Table 21-2. Dollar Gap, Unilateral Transfers, Imports, and National Income, 1914 to 1953 and by Shorter Periods
(In percentages)

Period	Imports to U.S. national income	Dollar gap to U.S. national income	Dollar gap to U.S. imports	Unilateral transfers to imports
1914*–1918	5.0	4.9	97	3.6
1919–1920	6.1	5.4	89	18.4
1921–1930	4.8	1.3	31	9.7
1931–1939	3.7	0.9	24	9.2
1940–1945	3.1	4.7	151	156
1946–1953	3.5	2.1	59	38
1914–1953	3.8	2.8	73	49

* July 1, 1914.

SOURCE: See Table 21-1. National-income figures for private income, 1914 to 1928, from *Historical Statistics of the United States, 1789–1945*, p. 14 (adjusted on the basis of 1929 to 1938 figures of private income and Department of Commerce figures for 1929 to 1938).

unilateral transfers ($85 billion, or two-thirds of the $125.6 billion excess of exports). Unilateral transfers were much larger relatively after 1940 than in the years 1914 to 1920, but it should be noted that most of the capital loans of $12 million in World War I were repudiated. Unilateral transfers understate the gap, because they exclude capital loans which proved to be unilateral transfers, gold shipped here which the rest of the world could not spare, and no allowance is made for *abnormal* restrictions on United States imports, without which imports would have been much larger.

This survey of the balance of payments shows that the world has been short of dollars since 1913 at any rate. Undoubtedly, an important part of the explanation is the burden put upon the dollar market by the two great wars, but it is also significant that in the prosperous twenties and the depressed thirties, the dollar problem was still acute. In the twenties, it was generally held that the return to gold by the British (with an accompanying loss of competitive power, as costs did not fall with a higher-valued pound sterling) and the pressure of reparations payments strengthened dollar disequilibrium. But substantial outward capital movements from this country relieved the strain. In the thirties, the situation became more serious despite an epidemic of devaluations abroad. The strain upon the dollar market became unbearable as capital fled Europe and prices of food and raw materials of the underdeveloped countries tumbled. Europe gained directly from lower prices of imports but lost as the banker of underdeveloped countries and the seller of goods to these countries. Devaluation was not equal to the task imposed upon it: Gold poured into the United States.

In the fourteen years 1940 to 1953, the average dollar deficit was $6.5 billion, a deficit financed largely by United States government aid. The shortage was as serious in the postwar as in the war period, though when allowance is made for changes in the value of the dollar and also for rising average real income in this country and the dollar gains in world trade, the dollar gap might be considered less serious than in the war period. The reader is also reminded of some comments in the preceding discussion which suggest that there was some improvement in 1953 to 1956 over the preceding years.

In 1954, the dollar problem was still troublesome. After showing that in the 2¾ years terminating in the third quarter of 1954 the United States had made $7.8 billion available through military grants, military expenditures, and offshore purchases (the last 2½ years), the Economic Commission for Europe concluded as follows: "Clearly, therefore, the 'dollar' gap as such has not yet disappeared; in the absence of these extraordinary disbursements of dollars Western Europe would have had either to pay out gold and dollars to the United States in each period to the extent shown in the table, or to make other painful adjustments."[7]

In 1954, the United States excess of exports of goods and services was $4,938 million ($4,841 million in 1953); unilateral transfers, $5,274 million ($6,707 million in 1953); United States capital net outflow, $1,437 million ($597 million in 1953); gold sales, $298 million ($1,163 million in 1953). The dollar market improved to some extent in 1954, in part because of increased capital exports from the United States and in part because foreign countries took less gold.

However, there was still a dollar problem in 1954 and to all accounts in 1955 and 1956. In the first nine months of 1955, the United States excess of exports (annual rate) was $3,936 million; unilateral transfers

[7] Economic Commission for Europe, *Economic Survey of Europe*, 1954, p. 107.

(annual rate), $4 billion; United States capital outflow (annual rate), $1,236 million. In the years 1953 to 1955 the outside world was absorbing its gains in part by shipments of capital here: $1,106 million and $1,438 million in 1953 and 1954, respectively, and $1,184 million in the first nine months of 1955.[8] On the basis of the first nine months of 1956, the excess of exports was around $4.5 billion.[9]

[8] *Survey of Current Business,* June and December, 1955.
[9] *Op. cit.,* December, 1956.

CHAPTER 22

Tariffs and the Dollar Gap: I

The Tariff vs. Other Solutions

In recent years, our tariff has been attributed with a determining influence on the pattern of world trade and the dollar gap that it does not possess. Neither the large rise of tariffs in the pre-New Deal days nor a reduction in rates of three-quarters, associated partly with the Trade Agreements Program and partly with the rise of prices and accompanying reduction of protection where specific rates are applicable (e.g., the rate of 10 cents per yard becomes less restrictive when the price rises from 50 cents to 1 dollar per yard), has been so potent in reducing trade in the earlier years or in increasing trade in the later years as is frequently assumed.[1]

Time and again it has been shown (see also Chapters 23 and 28) that income is the crucial factor in determining imports, particularly in the United States, where a large proportion of imports consists of raw materials, the imports of which are tied to output, and luxuries and service—luxuries are also highly sensitive to income changes. The decline of income in the thirties and the rise since have been far more decisive in determining the level of imports than have tariff changes. That imports are largely agricultural and nondurable manufactured products, that tariffs (specific) are rigid, and that inventories fluctuate greatly with cyclical conditions explain the large movements of imports with cyclical changes. A depression, for example, brings large declines in imports of agricultural products and concessions in prices of domestically produced nondurables.[2]

In the twenties, there was much discussion of United States tariff policy as a deterrent to the collection of debts: Europe could not ship

[1] See U.S. Tariff Commission, *Operation of the Trade Agreements Program*, Fifth Report, July, 1951, to June, 1952, pp. 151, 159, 167. C. Kindleberger (*Dollar Shortage, passim*) also has some relevant remarks on the overemphasis of the effects of the tariff. D. D. Humphrey (*American Imports*, 1955, pp. 72–73, 84) also suggests that the tariff has not greatly reduced trade.

[2] See Humphrey, *op. cit.*, especially chap. 3.

345

commodities in payment unless the United States would accept them. Even in this period, however, unwise monetary and fiscal policies abroad, an unwillingness to pay past debts, the reluctance of this country to pursue appropriate monetary and fiscal policies that would stimulate imports—these were much more important than tariff policy.

Similarly, in recent years, the concentration on tariff policy tends to obscure the importance of monetary and fiscal policy abroad, other aspects of competitiveness of foreign producers, the limited elasticity of supplies for the export market in the context of full employment and large welfare programs abroad, the relevance of income policy in the United States, and the contribution that can be made toward solving the problems of the dollar gap through roads alternative to a rise of imports, namely, a reduction of United States exports or an adequate level of foreign loans or grants.

I would especially emphasize the last point. The dollar problem is a world-wide problem, a problem that is associated in large part with the political and economic disorganization associated with two world wars and the cold war; the solution of the problem rests on all nations and on all segments of this country.

It is unfair to concentrate the costs of the adjustment upon any one group. The industries that are vulnerable to foreign competition will undoubtedly have to share in the costs of adjustment, but why should not part of the costs be put upon the taxpayer through guarantees of private loans or through the provision of grants? And why should not the exporters, through losses of markets abroad, pay part of the bills? It is too easily forgotten that exports in the postwar period have been at an inflated level. "To take the exports of the 1950–52 period as the measure of our need to export is an unsound basis for any United States trade policy, since these exports never were a measure of the world's normal dependence on United States production."[3] Any contribution through private lending, which in a sense postpones the problem, would also be welcome, though the general view is that this contribution would not be large. Furthermore, more imports into the United States at the expense of nations often impoverished may not be a healthy solution. That is to say, one should consider the *deprivations* involved for exporting nations against the gains of more imports by these countries. Additional imports mean much to the relatively impoverished nations, and in the face of liberalization of trade by the United States, they would export more, that is, have less goods. It may be better to postpone the rise of exports for these countries.

It is not true that in the years 1913 to 1953 and particularly the years

[3] S. Lubell, *The Revolution in World Trade*, 1955, p. 91.

1940 to 1955, the exporters, who now have become the most vocal of all free traders, have profited immensely from $125 billion of subsidies in forty years, paid for primarily by the taxpayer in the form of unilateral transfers and secondarily by the whole economy through yielding goods for exports paid for by inflows of gold and loans later to be repudiated? The exporters do not have a strong case when, as a means of maintaining their exports, they insist upon a rise of imports to balance the present level of aid and grants. We should not support a policy which concentrates the cost of adjustment on our weaker industries and sacrifices them to an inflated level of exports. Of course, in the long run the weaker industries must yield, but there are issues of justice here and of time required to make the necessary adjustments.

It is an interesting point that economists are becoming increasingly aware of the adjustment problems. Questions are being raised concerning imports of agricultural products at a time when agricultural income continues to decline. The outward movement from the farms is apparently too slow. In his important book, Professor Humphrey stresses the concentration of losses from reduced tariffs on nondurable goods and particularly on the New England economy; the capacity of large-scale, many-product corporations, not too price-competitive, to take reduced tariffs in their stride; and the difficulties confronting the weak, many-unit industries, with declining or slowly growing markets, when faced with reduced tariffs.[4]

After a provocative discussion of the effects of reduced tariffs on imports, exports, and employment, which on the whole minimizes the damage done by reduced tariffs, Walter Salant nevertheless emphasizes the need of allocating tariff cuts with a consideration of the trends of industries, expected mobility (related to alternative opportunities for jobs), employment levels in affected regions, etc. Obviously tariff cuts should, *ceteris paribus*, be imposed on the growing, highly profitable industries and the growing regions.[5]

The following passage, though rather an extreme statement by a protectionist, nevertheless is of some interest:[6]

The giant mass-production industries, such as automobile manufacturers, producers of steel, mass-produced electrical equipment, rubber tires, office machinery, petroleum (the large international elements), etc., form yet another group. Since the turn of the century, because of their vastly increased output, these industries have spilled over the domestic market, even though it is the largest and richest in the world. As already indicated, they form a

[4] Humphrey, *op. cit.*, pp. 246–255, 363, 398–399, 413–415.
[5] *Hearings of the Subcommittee of Joint Committee on the Economic Report on Foreign Economic Policy*, 1955, pp. 238–249; also cf. Committee on Economic Development, *United States Tariff Policy*, 1954, p. 7.
[6] O. R. Strackbein, *Free Trade: A Form of Economic Pacificism*, 1953, pp. 5–6.

new group with growing free-trade tendencies. Although they already enjoy all the economic benefits of a mass market without exporting, in recent years they have been found more and more frequently in company (figuratively) with their old opponents and detractors, the free-trade advocates. This strange bedfellowship led in recent years to a wedding of convenience. We now see the northern political liberal standing hand in hand with the southern "Bourbons" of the cotton and tobacco interests, along with the northern wheat and flour interests, on one side of him, and the erstwhile "trusts" and "bloated plutocrats," the old "sinister interests" of the financial centers of the East, on his other side, singing the praises of free trade.

The issue is not merely one of justice. It is also the practical one of how the equilibrium can be achieved. Of course, much depends upon the size of the dollar gap. (This does not mean that the closing of the dollar gap is the only issue, for there were problems of trade long before the dollar gap confronted us. But this is the crucial problem that must be solved before we tackle broader problems.) In the postwar years, the gap has averaged at least $5 billion. How much it is in the middle fifties depends in part upon how the gap is defined.[7] It would be a mistake to assume a temporary balance achieved with improved terms of trade for Europe, with a great economic expansion in the United States, with widespread discrimination against dollar imports, with use of controls abroad to stimulate exports to dollar countries, with large offshore purchases by the United States in support of military programs abroad, with a few billion dollars yearly of United States military expenditures abroad (inclusive of outlays of personnel abroad) —that these mean a genuine balancing of the dollar account is far from supportable. It would be a mistake to assume that a dollar gap of several billion dollars a year would not prevail for many years.

It would be well, therefore, to consider the various alternatives for dealing with a dollar gap of, say, from $4 billion to $8 billion a year. Should the gap be reduced, then the recourse to each program could be reduced correspondingly. I should like to see the maintenance of reserves by the nondollar world for several years, the removal of discrimination against the dollar, the termination of about $4 billion of United States aid and $5 billion of United States military outlays and outlays abroad by military personnel (offset in the years 1953 and 1954 by a growth of reserves of $2.5 billion of gold and $5.5 billion of gold and foreign exchange)—all of these before the end of the dollar problem could be safely assumed. However, by the 1960s we may agree that large aid and military expenditures by United States forces are normal and hence should not be cited as evidence of dollar shortage. We are not, however, as yet prepared to take this position. But first I turn to

[7] Cf. Chaps. 16 and 21.

some analysis of what might be achieved through attacks on United States (and Canadian) restrictions.

In the 1950s the problem of tariff cutting as the solution of the problem of the dollar gap has especially interested management and labor in industries subject to serious competition as well as the regions harboring these industries. In the debate, the point has been made that tariffs are one form of interference with the free market, and in the determination of national policy, this interference should be considered alongside other interventions. Hence an industry or region adversely affected by government transfers of cash, through tax exemptions (building of plants in competing areas stimulated through tax favors), may have a special case when the government determines the allocation of tariff cuts. Its case may be even stronger if consideration is paid to large spells of unemployment, a loss of jobs in its major industry (textiles) of 40 per cent in a period of 7½ years, a high degree of immobility of labor, and hence heavily concentrated and long-continued unemployment. Surely under these conditions, it becomes difficult to support large cuts in tariffs on textiles. The weak industries may have to go nevertheless, but it is not practical or judicious to impose additional hardships upon such industries or regions. Growing industries and regions can much more easily absorb the increase of imports and competition for markets than the declining industries and declining (relatively) regions. The result may be a somewhat slower rate of progress, but also there will be much smaller costs of adjustment and improved distribution of the costs.[8]

The Level of the Tariff and Trade Restrictions

Since the Trade Agreements Program (referred to as TAP) was introduced in 1934, the United States tariff on dutiable imports had been reduced from 48.2 (based on 1939 values) to 12 per cent by early 1951. About half the reduction is to be associated with the rise of prices, for

[8] The author has argued this case fully before the Interdepartmental Committee on Reciprocity and the United States Tariff Commission (December, 1954), the Joint Congressional Committee on the Economic Report (*Hearings on the Problem of Older Economic Regions*, Jan. 27, 1955), and the House Ways and Means Committee (*Tariffs, the New England Economy and Textiles: Statement on Behalf of the Six New England Governors*, Feb. 1, 1955); Senate Finance Committee, Mar. 11, 1955, and Senate Labor and Welfare Committee, May 11, 1955; also see W. H. Miernyk, *Inter-industry Labor Mobility*, November, 1954, and S. E. Harris, *New England Textiles and the New England Economy: Report to Conference of New England Governors*, 1956, and the 1957 Report.

Senator Kennedy has proposed that problems of this kind be dealt with through special aids in the areas affected for the industries damaged and the workers injured (release of Senator Kennedy's office, Jan. 26, 1955). A group from Rhode Island insisted that in making tariff concessions, the Congress should consider the fact that about one-half of the manufacturing workers in that state are concentrated in two vulnerable industries: textiles and jewelry. [*Trade Agreements Extension, Hearings before the Senate Finance Committee* (H.R. 1), 1955, vol. II, p. 1023.]

without any change in rates, the tariff was reduced by one-half, the result of the effect that 76.2 per cent (by value of imports in 1949) was subject to specific duties. A specific rate, say, of 20 cents per pound for an item costing $1 yields a 20 per cent rate, but if the price rises to $2, the rate falls to 10 per cent. As a result of reduction in duties under the TAP, the average rate, by January 1, 1952, had been reduced from 25.8 to 13.3 per cent. Hence the total reduction was almost three-quarters.[9]

A large sweep is given by Table 22-1. Note the large decline from 1930 to 1933.

Table 22-1

Period or year	Average rates of duty on	
	Dutiable imports, %	Free and dutiable imports combined, %
1913–1933, Underwood Law..........................	27	9
1922–1930, Fordney-McCumber Law................	38	14
1930–1933, Hawley-Smoot Law (to adoption of Trade Agreements Act)................................	53	18
1939 (representative prewar year, after the Trade Agreements Act)................................	37	14
1947 (most recent year, preliminary)................	19	8
1947 (calculated on basis of reductions made by Geneva Agreement).....................................	15	6

Another approach to the problem is presented in a study by Dr. Coulter for the American Tariff League. Here the comparison is of the ratio of customs duties collected to total value of imports. In 1937, the percentage was 15.8 for the United States, or the tenth lowest rate among thirty-eight countries. By 1951, the percentage for the United States had been reduced to 5.1 per cent, eighth from the lowest, the reduction being 68 per cent, or the ninth largest decline.

Much criticism has been directed against estimates of this type. A comparison of duties collected and total imports is of limited significance, because a large (and varying) part of customs duties may be collected for revenue purposes only, e.g., customs on tobacco and wines in England. The British Ambassador expressed this criticism well:[10]

We often see statistics about the average level of national tariffs. But these are misleading, because no one has yet devised a technique which effectively

[9] Figures from U.S. Tariff Commission, *op. cit.*, Fifth Report, July, 1951, to June, 1952, pp. 151, 159, 167.

[10] British Information Service, Sir Roger Makin's address, *Freer Trade and Freer Currencies*, Nov. 18, 1953.

measures the average level of a country's tariff. Most people nowadays recognize that average figures of this kind merely measure the protective effect of the tariff, on those goods which are not completely excluded by it. They do not always achieve even this modest objective. In the case of my own country, for example, it has been claimed that we have an average tariff of about 25 per cent, and that this average figure is about 25 per cent higher than the comparable figure of 1937.

In fact, we have not increased the level of our tariff since before World War II. If we excluded from the calculations (as we obviously should) revenue duties which apply to domestically produced goods, as well as to imports, which have no protective purpose, the figure of 25 per cent for the average tariff which has had some publicity, is seen in effect to be less than 3 per cent.

The ratio of customs collected to *dutiable* imports has also been the subject of attack by the Economic Commission for Europe, which holds that these figures[11]

are of little relevance as a measure either of the restrictive effect of the tariff or of the extent to which it has been reduced by comparison with earlier periods. To put the case in an extreme form, the ratio so computed and the total volume of imports could both be reduced if duties were raised on goods for which sales are very responsive to price changes and lowered on goods for which sales are not responsive. Detailed studies suggest that in fact rates are relatively high on goods for which sales are very responsive to price changes and lower on goods for which sales are not responsive.

The Bell Committee also noted that the ratio of duty to dutiable commodities imported[12]

is misleading because a major share of imports into this country are raw materials and foodstuffs not produced here and on which there is no duty at all. The very high duties on many manufactures which limit severely or exclude entirely their importation are also not reflected in this ratio. Neither are the quotas which set positive limits on the imports of certain agricultural goods.

Undoubtedly, measures of tariff levels should be used with great caution. Nevertheless, the evidence points strongly toward a substantial *reduction* of trade restrictions in the United States compared with other countries. Surely, the decline in rates associated with the inflation (and hence lower percentage rates for specific duties) was not a selective decline tending (as has been claimed) to favor reductions which would not result in additional imports, and it is hard to believe that the negotiations under the TAP, undertaken by those favoring free trade and based on bargaining with foreign countries, concentrated on reductions which would not result in substantial rises in imports. Such a result would

[11] United Nations, *Economic Survey of Europe since the War,* 1953, p. 107.
[12] *A Trade and Tariff Policy in the National Interest: A Report to the President by the Public Advisory Board for National Security,* 1953, p. 4 (The Bell Report).

imply that foreign negotiators were duped by the Americans. Usually the opposite charge is made. In fact, many studies of United States government agencies have shown a high correlation between tariff reductions under the TAP and the rise of trade. An example is fisheries with an average tariff rate in 1952 of 9 per cent, and this rate had been reduced by 38 per cent under the TAP. Few who have experienced the angry denunciations of the TAP by the fisheries industry would contend that reductions were made only when there was not much opposition. And what of Swiss watch works, with both sides of the controversy agreeing that rates were at one time slashed from 82 per cent of value to 37 per cent?

A more reasonable attack on the TAP program is that the theory upon which it was based, i.e., a reduction of tariffs in the United States, should be matched by corresponding reductions abroad. This theory is not defensible. In so far as this was the procedure, the net result was a rise not only of imports but also of exports for this country. Hence exports were kept at a higher level than was necessary, with the result that to this extent the dollar shortage was not treated. What was required was more imports, not more imports *and* more exports. Even the Randall Commission falls into this trap.

Undoubtedly, the charge is justified that these studies sometimes ascribe to tariff cuts a greater significance than they have in fact. Of course, they do not measure commodities excluded altogether by tariffs; of course, trade restrictions are not limited to tariffs but should be related to customs, administration, and quotas, also. But it is going too far to say, as the staff of the Randall Commission says: "The trouble is that the computation itself is not relevant to the problem of determining the restrictiveness of tariff duties."[13] It is surprising that those who fought for the TAP for twenty years now tell us that they accomplished nothing. In some instances, as the Randall experts contend, the process was one of sloughing off excess tariffs, that is, protection not needed (e.g., the tariff on cigar-wrapper tobacco). Surely all would agree that tariffs have declined substantially in the last twenty years, even though one could not say that the reduction was 75 per cent.

Actually the history of trade restrictions abroad in the last twenty years suggests that whatever the philosophy of the TAP, the final outcome has been much greater restrictions on trade abroad than in this country. Crude rate comparisons suggest this, but much more important has been the introduction and spread of exchange controls, import quotas, state trading, exchange depreciation, multiple exchange rates, etc. Frequently foreign countries have followed an agreement under the

[13] *Randall Commission Staff Papers*, p. 296. Cf. pp. 277–279, 295–299.

TAP with a depreciation of their exchanges which makes foreign currencies more expensive, and thus restricts their imports, lowers prices of their exports on world markets, and thus stimulates their exports. The watch manufacturers in this country have complained bitterly of a depreciation in Switzerland following a prewar trade agreement with Switzerland. They contend that the depreciation on top of reductions in rates here further increases the competitive position of the watch manufacturers. Again, motorcycle manufacturers resent the willingness of the British to cut tariffs on motorcycles when, in fact, they refuse to allow any to come in. In the postwar period the British agreed to cut the rates on motorcycles from 33⅓ to 22½ per cent, while this country continued its 10 per cent rate. The Harley-Davidson Motor Company, manufacturers of motorcycles, put the issues as follows:[14]

The difference was that the British were able to ship motorcycles into the United States on the 10 per cent duty while without import permits the 10 per cent rate of duty into Great Britain would be absolutely valueless to American manufacturers. What actually happened was that the duty into England was reduced to 22½ per cent; and as we had surmised, that also was a very hollow gesture, a very poor example of reciprocity because since that time no import permits into England have been granted. . . .

Foreign Responsibility for Low Exports to the United States

Critics of American policy tend to overstress the tariff as an obstacle to trade. It is well to note that the failure to penetrate our or third markets is to be explained in large part by failures abroad (cf. Chapters 23 and 28). In replies to the European Cooperation Administration–Commerce Mission, foreign governments and representatives of the export trade noted that the fault lay to some extent with them: inadequate credit facilities for the export trade, unwillingness or incapacity to invest adequately for selling in the American market, poor selling organization, slow deliveries, poor marketing research, ignorance of the market, unrealistic rates of exchange, excessive red tape involved in exporting, more favorable prices for European sales.[15]

The official organ of Western European countries also comments on the serious effects on output, prices, distribution, etc., of high protectionism in France.[16]

---

[14] *Trade Agreements Extension Act,* Hearings before the Committee on Ways and Means, 1953, p. 57, also cf. U.S. Tariff Commission, *op. cit.,* Eighth Report, July, 1954, to June, 1955, chap. 6, for quantitative restrictions, exchange control, etc., against United States exports.

[15] See, especially, the French replies, *Report of the ECA-Commerce Mission,* pp. 154–159.

[16] Organization for European Economic Cooperation, *Progress and Problems of the European Economy,* 1954, pp. 95–96.

The basic source of France's difficulties is undoubtedly protection which surpasses that of any other Member countries. The first signs of a decline in the French economy appeared before 1914, shortly after the introduction of high customs tariffs. The existing French tariff protects both agriculture and a wide range of industry. The effects of this generally high tariff have been aggravated by the more radical results of import quotas. This protection extends to the rest of the franc area which, at the beginning of 1952 just as before the liberalisation of intra-European trade, received 90 per cent of its European imports from France.

Under cover of tariffs and quotas, a system of internal protection has developed. Vested interests have been formed and consolidated. A whole series of devices are used to maintain these privileged positions, which are considered by their beneficiaries as being their own inalienable property, without any regard for economic efficiency. The methods employed range from legally guaranteed prices and State subsidies to open or tacit cartels and fraud. Tax concessions and evasion, which vary in degree from sector to sector, add their effects to those deriving from internal features of the relatively unprogressive French taxation system.

The Nathan Commission, appointed by the French government in January, 1954, stated that the disparity between French and foreign prices "is widespread and most marked for domestically produced raw materials, agricultural products, and relatively highly fabricated industrial products." Aside from proposals for tax reform to get costs down, the Commission finds "an urgent need for reducing costs, for example, by the progressive removal of various restrictions on free competition and of measures permitting inefficient enterprises to live on more competitive enterprises. . . . The reliberalisation of trade with the O.E.E.C. countries is deemed a necessity for France."[17]

A senator comments as follows: "Furthermore, these nations make use of quota systems and manipulations of their money systems, all in order to prevent imports from the United States. In addition, they have exchange permits . . . it is practically impossible for the United States to export our goods to them unless we give them the money in advance to purchase our commodities. . . . "[18]

A congressman notes that "Great Britain, for example, permits only token imports of many American consumer products. As a result, under that quota one of the largest American manufacturers of electrical appliances was able to ship to England in 1953 exactly 1 dishwasher, 35 electric ranges, 25 deep freezers, 19 washers and dryers and 194 refrigerators."[19]

[17] International Monetary Fund, *International Financial News Survey,* Apr. 9, 1954.
[18] *Congressional Record,* May 20, 1954, p. 6540.
[19] *Ibid.,* May 21, 1954, p. A3766.

So much for the failures of the foreign exporters, but it should also be recognized that several of the European countries, particularly the United Kingdom, took special measures to stimulate exports to the United States. In other words, in the absence of interference, United States imports would have been much less than they actually were. The advantages given to exporters may well have offset the adverse effects of tariffs. Among the measures taken were the following: special treatment in the allocation of raw materials, power, and building permits; allocation of foreign exchange to help build export trade and to help expand export markets; expansion of consular service abroad; special research facilities for export production and sales; the privilege of retaining part of the dollar exchange received for exports as an incentive to export in dollar markets; special credits and export guarantees; limitation of sales to the domestic market (e.g., 25 per cent limit on British automobiles sold in the British market); and tax exemptions on export sales. In addition, monetary and fiscal measures were taken to prevent excessive purchases at home.[20]

Protectionism Abroad

The charge might easily be made that protectionism is the weapon of foreign countries much more than of the United States. How far foreign countries have gone in the direction of quotas, exchange controls, etc., is suggested by the following: Under the General Agreement on Tariffs and Trade (GATT) and the Organization for Trade Cooperation (OTC), contracting countries are allowed to maintain restrictions other than import duties in order to safeguard their balance of payments and external financial position. Discrimination is also allowed when warranted by the balance-of-payments position. Of the thirty-four contracting countries under the GATT, twenty-three resorted to the use of quantitative restrictions late in 1951. Aside from the United States, the countries not resorting to quantitative restrictions were the relatively small ones: Belgium, Canada, Cuba, the Dominican Republic, Haiti, Luxemburg, Nicaragua, and Peru. Included in the restrictive camp were the eight British Commonwealth countries, inclusive of the United Kingdom; twelve Continental European countries, inclusive of France, Germany, Italy, and Czechoslovakia; and also Brazil, Chile, and Indonesia. In addition, a number of countries not participating in the GATT but

[20] *Report of the ECA-Commerce Mission,* pp. 97–140; General Agreement on Tariffs and Trade, *International Trade,* 1953, pp. 92–93; International Monetary Fund, *op. cit.,* June 11, 1954, and Mar. 19, 1954. Export credit guarantees in 1953–1954 amounted to $4.1 billion annually, or 15 per cent of export trade. They covered 85 to 90 per cent of political risks and 75 to 85 per cent of economic risks.

having bilateral agreements with this country indulge in quantitative restrictions—notably Argentina.[21]

Of eighty-seven countries listed by the Department of Commerce, seventeen in the early fifties did not resort to import licenses and twenty-three did not require exchange permits (the latter does not include countries which require permits to import). The seventeen and twenty-three included in every instance, except for several American countries, were the small and unimportant countries.[22] Only fifteen countries, namely, smaller Latin American countries, required neither import licenses nor exchange permits.

In 1953 to 1955, restrictions were further reduced, though often within Europe, and hence reflected further discrimination against the dollar. But there was improvement vis-à-vis the dollar also, as we shall see later.

In its 1953 report, the GATT wrote: "Twenty-two governments stated that they were still exercising some degree of discrimination between sources of supply. The general tendency to intensify the restrictions had been first arrested and then reversed, and definite steps of relaxation had been taken by some countries whose balance of payments had improved."[23]

Restrictions of all kinds were used and often with discrimination against the United States. State trading not only made it possible to buy in the monopsonistic manner, thus cutting import prices received by foreign exporters, but also was an effective way of restricting the quantity of imports. Exchange control is an over-all mechanism for cutting demand for foreign currencies and especially for the dollar and hence for keeping dollar exports down. Import quotas and licensing have similar effects. So important are quotas that in the bargaining within the European Payments Union, at least until 1955, concessions made were in quotas, with underlying tariffs undisturbed. Multiple exchange rates, especially popular with Latin American countries, are a technique for discouraging imports by charging higher prices for purchases in dollar countries or for any currency used to purchase less essential imports (or else forcing the foreign exporter to depress the dollar price) and also a technique for raising prices of exports in great demand (the exporter receives few bolivianos, say, per dollar for exports of tin and hence is pressed to raise the dollar price). The great debate on coffee prices in the United States in 1954 is relevant here. The Brazilian government allowed coffee exporters a relatively small number of cruzeiros per dollar, and hence the pressure to increase dollar prices, especially since pro-

---

[21] U.S. Tariff Commission, *op. cit.*, July, 1951, to June, 1952, pp. 219–225, and July, 1954, to June, 1955; cf. *Foreign Economic Policy*, Hearings before the House Subcommittee of Committee on Foreign Affairs, 1953, pp. 171–175.

[22] *Randall Commission Staff Papers*, pp. 362–365.

[23] General Agreement on Tariffs and Trade, *op. cit.*, p. 124.

duction was low and demand high. Depreciation of the exchanges acts as a tariff in that the foreign currency becomes more expensive. In short, every diabolic device for cutting imports and giving less exports has been used.

One should not be misled by the increased liberalization of trade in Europe in the early fifties. Thus the House Ways and Means Committee notes that whereas in 1953 only three countries had any degree of freedom in importing goods from the dollar area, by early 1955 seven additional countries had liberalized their trade with dollar countries, and over-all liberalization had attained almost 60 per cent of the imports from dollar countries on the basis of 1953 imports.[24] But Western Europe was indeed cautious in its cutting of trade restrictions. The Economic Commission for Europe wrote:[25]

The process of dollar liberalization has generally been carried out in such a way as not to damage home industries: while permitting them to enjoy the same advantages as United States industry in the procurement of raw materials, intermediate products, and modern machinery, it has done little to give greater freedom in Europe to United States exporters of finished products. . . .

Another relevant matter is one that has been noted in Chapter 18, namely, that liberalization was especially important for trade among the European countries and therefore discrimination against the United States is reflected in the greater degree of relaxation among these countries than between them and the United States. In general, the tendency for the Western European countries was to make larger concessions in agricultural and mineral products rather than in fabricated ones. From Table 22-2 it will be noted that the degree of liberalization varied greatly, depending largely upon the availability of reserves[26] (see p. 377).

Another relevant aspect of this problem is that the increase in imports of Western European countries from overseas nondollar countries in the early fifties was largely in dollar commodities. The GATT notes that dollar commodities became of increasing importance in the production of European dependencies and also that whereas the prices of these commodities in the dollar area tended to fall, they rose in the dependencies—clearly a symptom of discrimination.[27] Mr. Fforde has shown reasons why this discrimination is likely to be found: " . . . given a

[24] *House Ways and Means Report 50 on H.R. 1*, pp. 37–44.

[25] *Economic Survey of Europe in 1954*, p. 101.

[26] F. Boyer and J. P. Salle, "The Liberalization of Intra-European Trade in the Framework of O.E.E.C.," *International Monetary Fund Staff Papers*, 1955, pp. 195, 208.

[27] General Agreement on Tariffs and Trade, "The Role in World Trade of the Dependent Overseas Territories," *Trade and Intelligence Paper* 2, October, 1954.

recognition of American domination—long and short-run fear of American competitive power—and international knowledge of the principles of scarce currency doctrine, then instability in international trade could produce a considerable amount of discrimination against the United States, even though no very effective payments arrangements are set up to facilitate it."[28]

One result of the shortage of dollars and the general breakdown of trade was an epidemic of bilateral agreements. A major objective of hundreds of bilateral agreements was to conserve dollars, but as the movement proceeded, many had to join in order to protect their trade. These agreements were from the primitive bilateral offset ones to the most advanced automatic transferability type (especially the Organization for European Economic Cooperation countries). The customs union was another approach to the problem of strengthening ties among non-dollar countries and discouraging imports from dollar countries. Professor Meade has discussed well the issues involved here and has pointed out that the gains are large when made by competitive countries which potentially are complementary economies.[29]

Peril Point and Escape Clauses

It is clear by now that something should be said about restrictions other than tariffs. Hence let us turn to the peril-point and escape clauses, which are frequently held to deter the development of the American market. These provisions stem from a fear that some industries may be injured seriously by tariff concessions; hence the peril-point provision requiring prior investigation and the escape-clause provision which corrects an *excessive* flow of imports following a trade concession. In the years 1944 to 1954, the opposition to the TAP increased, and this is evident in the peril-point amendment in the Trade Agreement Act of 1951, under which the Tariff Commission must suggest points beyond which concessions should not be made because such concessions might seriously damage domestic industries, and is also evident in the escape clause, which upon the finding of the Tariff Commission (subject to rejection by the President) may on similar grounds require a retraction of concessions (first used in 1943 and a required provision in all trade

[28] J. S. Fforde, "Cyclical Fluctuations and the Growth of Discriminatory Alignments in International Trade," *Economic Journal*, 1955, p. 50. For very useful surveys of bilateral arrangements almost everywhere, often reflecting discrimination against the United States, see R. F. Mikesell, *Foreign Exchange in the Postwar World*, 1954, chap. 13, and M. N. Trued and R. F. Mikesell, *Postwar Bilateral Payments Agreements*, 1955.

[29] Trued and Mikesell, *op. cit.*, and J. E. Meade, *The Theory of Customs Unions*, 1955, especially pp. 107–115.

agreements by executive order in 1947). Undoubtedly, these provisions influence to some extent the concessions made.

It is significant, however, that of nineteen investigations under the escape clause during the year ending June 30, 1952 (applications received as early as August, 1949), only one concession was made—for hatters' furs—and a concession was modified (though decisions had not been made in several cases). For jeweled watch movements containing seven but not more than seventeen jewels, the President rejected a recommendation of the Tariff Commission for increased protection, a decision that was reversed in 1954. Actually, the investigations did not cover a large amount of trade: motorcycles and parts, screws (usually called "wood screws"), spring clothespins, garlic, cherries (candied, crystallized, or glacé), bonito (canned in oil, etc.), tobacco pipes and tobacco pipe bowls of wood or root, pregnant mares' urine, dried figs.[30] By 1952, a concession was modified on dried figs by Presidential proclamation on August 16, effective August 30. In June, 1952, a Tariff Commission recommendation for modification in concession on garlic was denied by the President.[31]

In an article in the *American Economic Review*,[32] Professor Kravis covers a longer period. By the end of 1953, there were fifty-one escape-clause cases. The Tariff Commission had decided forty cases and recommended action to the President in eight cases, but the President invoked the escape clause in only three instances and requested further study in two cases. Only about 10 per cent of the imports in 1951 were involved in these cases—with whiskies and spirits, crude petroleum and its products, beef and veal, aluminum and its alloys, lead, and watches accounting for 9 per cent.[33]

In the year ending June 30, 1955, fourteen new escape-clause proceedings were instituted and thirteen were completed. Most of these cases did not cover important amounts of trade, e.g., alsike clover leaf, spring clothespins, coconuts, ground chicory, glue of animal origin, and red fescue seed. But hardwood plywood, lead and zinc, bicycles, watches, and fresh or frozen groundfish fillets were also included. The President approved increased restrictions in only two instances—alsike clover seed and bicycles—though not accepting the full measure proposed by the Tariff Commission. In another instance (lead and zinc), the President announced a program for accelerating domestic purchases. (Is this not a protective measure?) The Tariff Commission had proposed by a

[30] *Operations of the Trade Agreements Program*, Fifth Report, pp. 183–186.
[31] *Bell Report*, p. 63.
[32] I. B. Kravis, "The Trade Agreement Escape Clause," *The American Economic Review*, June, 1954, pp. 319–338.
[33] *Ibid.*, p. 323.

majority vote a rise of restrictions in five items and by a tie vote in two instances.[34]

Commissioners were divided on the issues. Difficulties of interpretation arose in large part because of disagreements on the base period to be chosen and the measurement of injury (e.g., the contribution of tariff concessions as against domestic factors toward reduced profits or rise of inventories, the significance to be attached to a decline in the share of a market, the relevance of gains in production of other commodities for multiproduct firms or industries).[35]

The relevant criteria are the following:[36]

If, as a result of unforeseen developments and of the effect of the obligations incurred by a contracting party under this Agreement, including tariff concessions, any product is being imported into the territory of that contracting party in such increased quantities and under such conditions as to cause or threaten serious injury to domestic producers in that territory of like or directly competitive products, the contracting party shall be free, in respect of such product, and to the extent and for such time as may be necessary to prevent or remedy such injury, to suspend the obligation in whole or in part or to withdraw or modify the concession.

In arriving at a determination in the foregoing procedure the Tariff Commission, without excluding other factors, shall take into consideration a downward trend of production, employment, prices, profits, or wages in the domestic industry concerned, or a decline in sales, an increase in imports, either actual or relative to domestic production, a higher or growing inventory, or a decline in the proportion of the domestic market supplied by domestic producers.

A moment's attention to one of the most important cases—that of watches—will bring out the important issues.[37]

In this instance the Tariff Commission was divided concerning the *present* threat, but a majority agreed that the American industry was threatened with serious injury in the future. What seemed to bother the majority was a rise of wages relative to Switzerland in the United States of two times since the war without a corresponding relative gain of productivity in this country, a serious matter with wages 80 per cent of costs, the large relative gains of the Swiss in the American market, the large inventories on hand in this country, the decline of employment in the production of pin-lever (relatively cheap) watches, and the failure of the market for American watches to grow with the national economy. The members of the Commission not especially concerned

[34] U.S. Tariff Commission, *Operation of the Trade Agreements Program,* July, 1954, to June, 1955, pp. 183–208.

[35] Kravis, *op. cit.,* pp. 325–335.

[36] *Randall Commission Staff Papers,* pp. 281–282.

[37] U.S. Tariff Commission, "Watches, Watch Movements, Watch Parts, and Watchcases," *Report* 176, 2d ser., 1953.

over this threat stressed the better selling job being done by distributors of imported watch movements, the shifts of taste with large rise of demand concentrated on the medium-priced watch (the watch built with Swiss movements), the gains of the American industry in the market for watches with more than seventeen jewels, and the adequate level of profits.

In refusing to accept the recommendations of the Commission, the President emphasized the high profits of the industry, the gains in sales of watches with more than seventeen jewels, the great harm that would be done to the Swiss economy with a heavy and localized concentration of the industry, and the large purchases of Switzerland from the United States. But the crucial passage was the repudiation of the share doctrine:[38]

One may well ask how, in this situation, three Commissioners found serious injury. The answer seems to lie almost entirely in the significance which they attached to the fact that the expansion of domestic jeweled watch production has not kept pace with expansion of imports, so that the industry today enjoys a smaller share of the larger market. Because of the dangerous precedent which would be involved in accepting this share doctrine as the determinant of serious injury, I should like to emphasize its far-reaching implications. Serious injury, by any definition, means a loss to someone. Declining production, lower employment, lower wages, lower returns or losses in capital invested—any of those things might indicate some degree of injury. But the share doctrine goes much further. In fact, it finds that serious injury exists when the domestic industry fails to gain something it never had, even though the industry may be prospering by all of the customary standards of levels of production, profits, wages and employment. This is the doctrine on which the claim of injury by three Commissioners appears to be based.

Whenever possible the President seemed disposed to reject the recommendations of the Tariff Commission for increased restriction under the escape clause. For example, in reply to a recommendation for the importation of domestic groundfish fillets the President (July 2, 1954) pointed out that with the great expansion of the fish-stick industry, which would increase greatly the consumption of groundfish fillets, it would be a great mistake to "hamper and limit the development of the market for the product and jeopardize present prospects for the increase in per capita consumption of fish which is the real solution of the industry's problem." In a decision of August 20, 1954, the President refused to accept a decision of the Tariff Commission to increase the duties on lead and zinc and instead agreed to purchase increased supplies at home for domestic stockpiles. (Incidentally this also might be

[38] *Ibid.,* p. 78.

considered a protectionist measure, certainly a subsidy.) In response to a divided vote by the Tariff Commission in respect to higher duties on hand-blown glassware the President held that "the fundamental cause of the difficulty of this industry lies in competition offered by machine-made glassware to both imported and domestic handmade ware." He refused to support a rise of duties.

Two notable cases should be presented here. The first is the reversal on Swiss watches. Here the President, basing himself on the defense argument on July 27, 1954, supported a substantial rise of duties on Swiss jeweled watches; otherwise, important skills would be lost. The President approved increased restrictions even though the domestic industry on the whole was very profitable, even though the Swiss watches were in a sense in a noncompetitive market (intermediate prices), and even though the domestic output was close to the amount presumably required to meet defense need.[39]

Finally, in a decision of August 19, 1955, the President announced an increase of 50 per cent in the duty on imported bicycles (or equivalent to about 10 per cent in the price of the imported bicycle). In this instance, given the law, the President could scarcely escape taking action. The industry was suffering greatly from the large and rapid importation of the lightweight bicycle. His support of a higher duty might be explained in part by the improved international economic position of the United Kingdom, the main exporter. "In my judgment of these developments [improving technology and meeting consumer tastes] rather than intervention by government, are the domestic industry's real hope for the future." His action "accords reasonable recognition in the interests of American consumers . . . assures to producers in friendly foreign lands an excellent competitive chance to share handsomely our large and growing market for bicycles . . . this nation's firmly rooted policy of seeking ever expanding levels of international trade and investment is in no respect altered by this decision."[40]

From the last, it is clear that the President was troubled over the conflicts raised by these rulings under the escape clause and the broader objectives of national policy. " . . . the President must take account of all relevant factors, including our national-defense requirements, requirements for carrying on successfully the foreign relations of the United States, and the necessity for maintaining and strengthening our domestic economy."

That the escape-clause and peril-point provisions are to be more troublesome to any administration favoring trade liberalization is supported by the revisions under H.R. 1 (the Trade Agreements Act of

---

[39] Cf. *Statement by a Committee for a National Trade Policy*, July 29, 1954.
[40] *The New York Times*, Aug. 20, 1955.

1955). In the future injury can be claimed when a segment of an industry is affected adversely by increased imports.

Sections 6 and 7 of the 1955 Act, as reported by the Senate Finance Committee, follow. In conference the words "have contributed materially, etc." in 7(*b*) were modified to "have contributed substantially towards causing or threatening serious injury." This provision seems to put more emphasis on the contribution of *imports* to the damage done. It was also made clear that injury could not be claimed on the basis of injury to one firm.[41]

In his first annual report on the *Operation of the Trade Agreements Extension Act of 1955* (February 11, 1957), the President discussed recent efforts to liberalize trade. Of seven escape clauses disposed of in 1956, the President granted increases in all but two (bicycles and linen toweling).

SECTION 6 OF THE TRADE AGREEMENTS EXTENSION ACT OF 1951

Sec. 6. (*a*) No reduction in any rate of duty, or binding of any existing customs or excise treatment, or other concession hereafter proclaimed under section 350 of the Tariff Act of 1930, as amended, shall be permitted to continue in effect when the product on which the concession has been granted is, as a result in whole or in part, of the duty or other customs treatment reflecting such concession, being imported into the United States in such increased quantities, either actual or relative, as to cause or threaten serious injury to the domestic industry producing like or directly competitive products.

(*b*) The President, as soon as practicable, shall take such action as may be necessary to bring trade agreements heretofore entered into under section 350 of the Tariff Act of 1930, as amended, into conformity with the policy established in subsection (*a*) of this section.

[On or before January 10, 1952, and every six months thereafter, the President shall report to the Congress on the action taken by him under this subsection.]

SECTION 7 OF THE TRADE AGREEMENTS EXTENSION ACT OF 1951

Sec. 7. (*a*) . . . [Within sixty days, or sooner if the President has taken action under subsection (*c*) of this section, the Tariff Commission shall transmit to the Committee on Finance of the Senate and the Committee on Ways and Means of the House of Representatives an exact copy of its report and recommendations to the President.][42] *The Tariff Commission shall immediately make public its findings and recommendations to the President, including any dissenting or separate findings and recommendations, and shall cause a summary thereof to be published in the Federal Register.*

[41] See Ways and Means Committee, *Trade Agreements Extension Act of 1955*, pp. 4–5; "The Trade Agreements Extension Act of 1955," *Senate Finance Report* 232, p. 14; and Committee on a National Trade Policy, *Trade Talk*, June 10, 1955.
[42] Bracketed material deleted.

(*b*) In arriving at a determination in the foregoing procedure the Tariff Commission, without excluding other factors, shall take into consideration a downward trend of production, employment, prices, profits, or wages in the domestic industry concerned, or a decline in sales, an increase in imports, either actual or relative to domestic production, a higher or growing inventory, or a decline in the proportion of the domestic market supplied by domestic producers. *Increased imports, either actual or relative, shall be considered as the cause or threat of serious injury to the domestic industry producing like or directly competitive products when the Commission finds that such increased imports have contributed materially to the serious injury or the threat of serious injury to such industry.*

(*e*) *As used in this Act, the terms "domestic industry producing like or directly competitive products" and "domestic industry producing like or directly competitive articles" mean that portion or subdivision of the producing organizations manufacturing, assembling, processing, extracting, growing, or otherwise producing like or directly competitive products or articles. Where a particular business enterprise is engaged in operations involving more than one industry, or more than one readily determinable segment of a single industry, the Commission shall, so far as practicable, distinguish or separate the respective operations of such business enterprise for the purpose of determining injury.*

In general, the pressure of protectionist groups, fearful of adverse effects of increased imports under the TAP, accounts for the peril-point amendments and the escape clause and also for the increased access to its use in the years beginning in 1955. As Professor Humphrey contends, the philosophy of the TAP has been not so much an extension of trade as a reduction of barriers when serious injury is not done to an American industry. Perhaps Humphrey overstates his case here, but the peril-point and escape clauses are evidence of this concern for protecting the weak industry and precluding serious losses of jobs. The use of the peril point, as Mr. Thorpe has pointed out, means concentration upon the effects on an industry without adequate attention to the broader issues of trade and political relations. A tendency to define industries narrowly, to take account of relative as well as absolute losses, and to consider the effects on individual products of multiproduct industries, irrespective of the general position—these tend to make the escape clause more restrictive.[43] The application of the flexible tariff, relevant when costs are high in less progressive industries competing with imports, also contributed to higher rates.

Quantitative Restrictions

Now we turn to another aspect of restrictions on trade.

In this country, quantitative restrictions are also invoked, though, in

[43] Cf. Humphrey, *op. cit.*, especially pp. 112–117, 126, 382–387.

general, restrictions of this type play a relatively small part in our over-all restrictionist programs. Quotas on sugar are used to protect our domestic producers. Other quotas are tied to our agricultural policy. Higher farm prices and income are the objectives of agricultural policy, with purchases and loans by the government and restrictions on output provided when inventories threaten to get too high. Obviously, unrestricted imports of agricultural products not only would increase the cost of the program (the government would purchase foreign supplies also) but would jeopardize its success (because of increased pressures on prices). Hence quotas on numerous agricultural commodities. It is not likely that these quotas would be abandoned as long as government intervention is necessary to maintain prices at a level reasonably close to parity. Should the government adopt the Brannan Plan, however, then prices could be depressed as supplies increase, and the pressure of imports would be less harmful to the program. At least consumers would gain as an offset to higher costs for the Treasury. (Under the Brannan Plan, farmers are not restricted in output but are compensated for the difference between market and a fair price.) Dr. D. Gale Johnson proposes that farm prices be allowed to respond to market forces; then the increased output in the United States would be reflected in reduced prices and increased consumption in our large market, and hence less pressure to dump abroad.[44]

In all, there were quotas on twelve products, all agricultural commodities. Suspension of tariffs on these products, according to Piquet, would have little effect. But should the quotas be suspended as well, then he estimates that imports would rise a minimum by $358 million, or 67 per cent, and a maximum by $833 million, or 156 per cent. The largest gains (maximum estimates) would be sugar, $387 million; butter, $215 million; live cattle and dressed beef, $73 million; linseed oil, $60 million.[45] It should be noted that except for butter, a rise of imports of which might solve Denmark's dollar problems, the net benefits of these increased imports would accrue primarily to the other Americas. The help would be especially important for Argentina, which in the years since the war has experienced serious trade problems.

Professor D. Gale Johnson has pointed out that in agriculture the strongly protected farm products (sugar, sheep, lambs, and wool) account for only 2.4 per cent of total agricultural employment; mildly protected products, 12.4 per cent; products mildly dependent on exports, 18.1 per cent; products strongly dependent on exports, 13.2 per cent.

[44] *Hearings by the Subcommittee of Joint Committee on the Economic Report on Foreign Economic Policy*, 1955, p. 358.

[45] H. S. Piquet, *Aid, Trade, and the Tariff*, p. 63; cf. U.S. Tariff Commission, *Investigation under S.22 of the Agricultural Adjustment Act*, Sept. 15, 1955.

Hence, he concludes that the removal of trade restrictions would not reduce employment; export employment would rise at least as much as import employment. Of course, the exports of industry may rise, not those of agriculture. I should say emphatically here what is said elsewhere, namely, that the general argument for free trade is not employment, but the most effective allocation of economic factors. In fact, the surest way of increasing employment is by excluding imports. I realize, however, that the economists who consider the employment aspects are induced to do so by the fear of the effects of trade liberalization on jobs. If jobs are our objective, then the correct approach is to introduce protectionism. In fact, at several points in this book I have contended that protectionism may be justified when the favorable effects on jobs are greater than adverse effects on costs. Should we, for example, raise tariffs and experience a loss of imports and of exports, the job situation would undoubtedly improve. (But income would fall unless there were adequate amounts of unemployment, real or disguised. The case for protectionism in underdeveloped countries rests largely on the grounds that they will gain more from increased employment than they will lose from misallocation of economic resources.) As far as agricultural employment is involved, even if it is assumed, as Johnson assumes, that employment in exports will rise more than it declines in the production of import-competing commodities (and thus a closer relation is assumed between imports and exports than actually exists), this is not the crucial problem. Protectionism is justified on the grounds of maintaining agricultural prices (and incomes) above world levels. Once a free market in agriculture becomes a national policy, then agricultural protectionism will have to find other supporting arguments.[46] As a lobbyist for the milk producers points out, United States prices are far above world prices. Unless imports are restricted, the support system is jeopardized and the costs of the program of supports greatly increased. Thus early in 1954, the price of butter in the United States was 67 cents; in Australia, 39 cents; in Denmark, 42 cents; in New Zealand, 39 cents.[47]

Professor Viner notes that employment should not be treated by tariffs. In his view, we should rely on fiscal and monetary instruments, but there are times when these tools will not be used or are inadequate.[48] Even Professor Haberler says that "deviations from the competitive ideal, or the existence of external economies, result in a deviation of the free trade position from the obtainable optimum in the sense explained. . . . If wages are rigid and workers become unemployed instead of ac-

[46] D. G. Johnson, *Trade and Agriculture*, 1950, pp. 50–53; cf. *House Hearings on Foreign Economic Policy*, 1953, p. 184, and C. Wilcox, letter to *The New York Times*, Apr. 4, 1954.
[47] *House Hearings on the Trade Agreements Extension Act of 1953*, pp. 305–312.
[48] *Hearings on Foreign Economic Policy*, 1955, p. 602.

cepting a wage cut or being transferred to other industries, the pre-requisites for free trade no longer exist."[49]

Customs Administration

A third aspect of restrictive policy other than published rates revolves around the administration of the tariff. For example, it is held that the methods of evaluation of a product tend to raise rates, that there are arbitrary methods of administration which introduce elements of un-certainty, and that there are long delays in the courts. An example of arbitrary valuations is the following case involving Canadian plywood:[50]

Of the producers' sales volume in the Canadian market 95 per cent was in quantities of more than 5,000 square feet subject to sizable discounts. The re-maining volume was sold in smaller lots at a higher price, but these sales accounted for a larger number of individual transactions. The Court ruled that the "usual" wholesale quantities price is that charged in the "greatest number of transactions," in this instance the price for 5 per cent of total volume of sales. . . .

Hence the tariff, applied to excessively high values, was therefore in-flated.

Here are some examples given by the Netherlands government:[51]

A Manufacturer wanted to export earthen ash-trays to the United States. He was not sure, however, whether the American customs officers would classify this article as a household article (15% duty), a smoking requisite (30% duty) or as luxury earthenware (50% duty).

An exporter of ladies' coats, who had obtained dollars for a three weeks' stay in the United States, was unable to clear his coats during this stay because the New York customs officers, after three weeks, still had not decided whether the import duty was to be imposed according to the material of which the coats were made or the buttons sewn on to them.

Netherlands carpets without a fringe are classed as carpets, rugs and mats (par. 116a up to 117c U.S. customs Tariff Act) subject to an import duty of 25 to 30%. If provided with a fringe they are classed as fringes and articles wholly or in part of fringes (par. 1529a U.S. customs Tariff Act) subject to an import duty of 45%.

An exporter wishes to ship young orchid plants to America. The American officer is afraid that he may be letting flower diseases into the country and he gives orders for the plants to be thoroughly fumigated. The result is that it will be two years before the plants flower again. This practice renders exports of orchid plants to America absolutely impossible.

[49] G. Haberler, *A Survey of International Trade Theory*, 1955, p. 16.
[50] *Bell Report*, p. 48.
[51] ERP, *Report of the ECA-Commerce Mission*, pp. 170–173.

The Customs Simplification Act of 1953 points up some of the problems:[52]

Since that time many changes have occurred in industry and commerce; and the Customs Simplification Act of 1953 will to a large extent modernize the administrative and procedural laws in accordance with the objective of giving improved service to the importing public at the least possible cost to the taxpayer.

The provisions which are most necessary to achieve these purposes are the following (the references are to sections of the Tariff Act of 1930): to simplify and make more equitable the formulae for appraising merchandise for assessment of ad valorem duties (sec. 402); to eliminate "special marking" requirements and to require only such marking as will indicate to the ultimate purchaser the country of origin of imported merchandise, with additional authority for relief in hardship cases; to authorize the institution of a modern program of internal audit (sec. 523); to eliminate time consuming and cumbersome procedures in connection with warehouse transfers (sec. 557 (*b*)); to repeal the provision for undervaluation penalties (sec. 489); to provide a more modern method for converting amounts in foreign currencies to amounts in United States currency (sec. 522); to permit correction by customs officers of admitted errors without appeal to the courts (sec. 502 (*c*)(1)); and a number of others of lesser individual importance, but cumulatively of major importance. The bill proposes no change in the tariff structure. Any change in amounts of duty payable under it will not be large.

Here are a few more oddities in classification:[53]

No man in a raincoat has the figure of a guardsman. Noting this, the makers of Burberrys inserted between the lining and the outer material a small length of elastic to draw their garments in across the small of the back. The customs man found it. Promptly, the Burberry ceased to be a raincoat, dutiable at ten per cent, and became liable to a forty-five per cent duty under Paragraph 1529 (*a*) governing "articles in part of braid."

The present tariff law dates from 1930. (It's been in effect longer than any other such law in U.S. history.) Since 1930, times have changed: A number of new products have appeared, and classification of the unknown has proved even more tortuous than classification of the known. Radar, until the Customs Court pointed out the nonsense, was classified as a clock. Nylon fiber yarn pays the duty rate for wool if it is crimped or curled, the duty rate for silk if smooth. Speedometers, even though they were in wide usage before 1930, are not classified as essential parts of cars but as measuring

[52] *Hearings of the Ways and Means Committee, H.R. 5106, on Customs Simplification,* 1953, pp. 15–16. Also cf. *Bell Report,* pp. 52–54, and *Report to the President on Foreign Economic Policies,* 1950, pp. 80–84.

[53] H. H. Miller, "Trade, Aid and the Shades of Smoot and Hawley," *The Reporter,* Mar. 31, 1953.

devices. If they were considered parts of cars, the tariff would be twelve and a half per cent. As measuring devices, the charge on them is sixty-five per cent, plus a specific duty of $4.50 if the value is more than ten dollars. Try those figures on an eleven-dollar speedometer, and after you've paid the customs man, see if you have enough left to settle the cop's ticket.

It has been charged also that administration is often performed in the interest of domestic producers. The 1953 Customs Simplification Act improved administration to some extent, though this was not a fundamental attack on the problems.

The major problems are customs classification and evaluation. Undoubtedly, as the staff of the Randall Commission claims, the tendency of the customs officials is to protect revenue and hence to help the protectionist cause. Also, there is little logic in the relationship of rates and especially of specific rates which are affected by movements in prices. There are complaints of excessively high valuation when commodities contain several materials, when they have to be classified as new commodities, or when customs evaluation is based on our domestic prices.[54]

One proposal is to eliminate foreign values as a source of evaluation, in part because of the delays involved in estimating foreign value. Witnesses on behalf of the domestic industries complain that the result of elimination of foreign value as a guide to value would be increased difficulty of imposing countervailing duties when the export value is less than foreign value.[55] One witness complimented the committee for not adhering to an earlier proposal to exclude the American selling price as a guide to evaluation and then added:[56]

The most important provision of H.R. 5106 is section 15 which establishes a new basis for ascertaining the value of imported merchandise. The duties which affect our industry are principally those provided in schedule 1 of the Tariff Act, the chemical schedule. Preponderantly they are ad valorem duties. The proponents of the customs simplification bill state that the bill does not alter the tariff rates which now afford protection to domestic industry and so they conclude that the bill does not in any way threaten our industries. Where ad valorem duties are concerned such a statement is naive and misleading. Ad valorem duties are the resultant of two components; the rate component and the value component. Each of these factors plays a significant part in the determination of the duty which must be paid by the importer. It is no answer to say that rates of duty are not being changed by the bill if the bill significantly changes the other equally important factor in duty determination—namely, the value component. . . .

Foreign value: Section 15 of the bill eliminates foreign value as a basis of

---

[54] *Randall Commission Staff Papers*, pp. 333–358.
[55] Cf. *Hearings on Customs Simplification*, 1953, pp. 22, 181–182; also see *Ways and Means Committee Hearings in Customs Simplification Act of 1955*, pp. 13–15.
[56] *Hearings on Customs Simplification*, 1953, pp. 152–154.

valuation. It creates a new concept known as comparative value as an alternative basis of valuation. It redesignates "cost of production" as constructed value. It redefines export value, United States value, the former cost of production value, and the American selling price. In addition, it defines certain terms used in those redrawn value provisions.

We object to the deletion of foreign value as one of the primary bases for valuation purposes. The present law requires that imported merchandise be valued on the basis of the foreign value or the export value, whichever is higher. It is our opinion that, in general, the use of foreign value results in a higher valuation than the use of export value. Consequently, the substitution of export value for foreign value as the primary basis of valuation will favor importers to the detriment of domestic industries. . . . Nearly $2 billion worth of other than coal tar products are manufactured annually by the chemical industry. The deletion of foreign value as a primary basis of valuation will have the effect of reducing the protection accorded our industry by the present tariff statutes by reducing the second or value factor in the equation which produces duties on chemical imports. The Tariff Commission reported to this committee when H.R. 1535 was under consideration that there is a general agreement among experts that the substitution of export value for foreign value will, as a rule, be more favorable to importers (Hearings, p. 230).

Bearing in mind that our foreign competition is largely cartelized, the proposed elimination of foreign value presents a further danger to our industry. . . . The accompanying definition of "freely sold or offered for sale" in the bill will make it possible for a sale to one or more selected purchasers, even though the sale is accompanied by restrictions, to qualify as value for the imported merchandise. It will thus be possible for European chemical producers to establish any selling price they please for exportations to the United States, including sales to exclusive distributors. The proposed bill makes it a simple matter for our foreign competition to arrange for the entry of chemical imports into this country at a landed cost which we cannot compete with.[57]

In general, there is a strong case for improved administration of customs and even for fair classification and evaluation. Administration should not be a device for providing a greater degree of protection than was intended by Congress, nor should the complicated procedures be a serious deterrent to trade. Who would deny that customs administration tends to discourage trade and also to keep rates higher than originally intended, though in part the effects result from legislation? A complete overhauling and simplification would undoubtedly increase trade, but obviously the protectionist could rightly claim that any concessions made should be considered as part of the general program of trade liberalization. If, for example, the effect is to increase trade by 5 to 10 per cent

[57] One official estimated that the substitution of export value for foreign-market value would reduce dutiable value by but 2½ per cent. Committee for National Trade Policy, *Trade Talk*, May 27, 1955.

(say, $1 billion), then he would fight more vigorously other approaches to increased imports.

In August, 1956, the President approved a new *Customs Simplification Act* which required valuation on export values only, not on *either* export or foreign domestic values. (See Senate Report 2560 on *Customs Simplification Act of 1956* and the *12th Annual Congressional Quarterly Almanac,* 1956, pp. 507–508.)

Effects of Reducing Restrictions

It is not easy to estimate the effects on imports of a more liberal trade program. Much depends on the reductions achieved. Economists may properly estimate the effects of a drastic cut in restrictions or even their complete removal, but when they are discussing issues of practical policy, their estimates should be restricted to practical measures toward free trade. Then the political economist must take account of the established industries, which will fight successfully against large or rapid declines in rates or removal of quotas; the weak industries, which will struggle even more against any measure tending to destroy them; the agricultural interests, which see in freer trade a destruction or at least weakening of their price-support program; the defense industries, which have a legitimate claim for protection; the regional interests, which have been subject to losses associated with Federal policies for many years—all these will narrow the range within which concessions may be made. Their opposition will be less in periods of exuberance than in periods of depression. In the latter, they will not merely oppose reductions. They will also seek higher restrictions.

Why is it held that the United States tariff is such an important factor? Here we may refer to a study made by Sir Donald MacDougall, in which he shows the differences in wage rates and man-hour output between the United Kingdom and the United States. What puzzles Mac-Dougall is that whereas on the basis of relative wages and man-hour output, United Kingdom sales abroad are large vis-à-vis American exports, British sales *to the United States* are surprisingly small compared with total British sales abroad. But MacDougall concentrates too much on wage costs and leaves out of account the importance of other costs. (See my discussion of the watchcase.) In discussing trade relations, he does allow, however, that imperfections of the market are very important. Might he not, just as he explains the large trade of the British with Commonwealth countries in terms of imperfections, also explain in part the small penetration of the British in the United States market in the same way?

Sir Donald MacDougall also finds that elasticity of substitution of British exports for United States exports was high in the prewar period;

that is, a *relative* reduction of British prices vis-à-vis American prices would result in a large gain of British sales against American sales. The last points, perhaps, to the importance of influencing third markets. On the issue of tariff reduction, the criticism to be made of MacDougall's results is the concentration on prewar and on labor costs.[58]

MacDougall's position has been well put by an anonymous author:[59]

The American industrial wage rate per hour is about 2½ times that in the United Kingdom (in terms of dollars). This means that for industries in which American productivity is less than 2½ times the British, British goods can be sold at a lower price than the American. For example, in the textile industries and footwear, American productivity before the war was only 1½ to 2 times the British. As a result British exporters were, in fact, able to compete most successfully with American exporters in third markets. They exported three times as many pairs of shoes, eight times as much cotton cloth, twenty times as much cotton yarn, over three hundred times as much woollen and worsted cloth, over ten times as much rayon yarn. These figures would be even more striking if American exports were compared not with British exports only, but with the exports of all Western European countries.

But though British and other European exporters competed so successfully with American exporters in third markets in these lines, they could make very little inroad in the American market itself. America's total imports of footwear (excluding rubber footwear) were only 0.6% of her total consumption. The corresponding figure for cotton cloth was 1.4%, for cotton yarn 0.05%, for woollen and worsted cloth 21.0%, for rayon yarn 0.5%. Judging by the figures of relative productivity and wages, Britain should have been able to undersell American goods in many lines by 20% to 30%. But apart from the cost of transport, the differing tastes of American and British consumers, and the general difficulties of selling goods in a foreign country, the American tariff largely ruled out the possibility of British sales in the American market. The American duty on footwear, for example, ranged from 10% to 35%, with an average rate of 21%. The duty on cotton cloth ranged from 7.75% to 57.5%, with an average rate of 31%. The average rate of duty on woollens and worsteds was equivalent to 75% ad valorem, that on rayon yarn to as much as 134%. Within each of these commodity groups, moreover, the tariff was finely graded so as to give higher protection to qualities for which higher protection was needed.

The United States Tariff Commission, in a post-war publication, recognized the restrictive effect of the American tariff in many of these lines. They reckoned, for example, that a reduction of 50% in the 1939 tariff might increase imports of woollens and worsteds three to ten times, and imports of rayon yarn thirty-five to one hundred times. Overall they estimated that a 50% reduction in American tariffs, as they existed in 1939, would increase American imports by about $0.75 billion. They were, however, reckoning in terms of

[58] G. D. A. MacDougall, "British and American Exports," *Economic Journal,* December, 1951, and September, 1952.
[59] ERP, *Report of the ECA-Commerce Mission,* pp. 195–196.

prices not much higher than in 1939. In current prices this would mean an increase of about $1.5 billion in American imports.

In replies to the European Cooperation Administration (ECA)–Commerce Mission, the Netherlands government gave the following examples of tariffs interfering with sales in the American market:[60]

Textiles. The general opinion of the firms who answered our questionnaire is that exports of textiles could reach a considerably bigger volume at a lower rate of import duty. The percentage with which the ultimate retail price exceeds the American market price practically always remains within the range of the import duty. . . .

Two firms report that, with the exception of newsprint which can be imported free of duty, the U.S. tariff is absolutely prohibitive with regard to the import of Netherlands paper into the U.S.A. . . .

Two manufacturers of bicycles report that several efforts have been made to sell to the U.S.A. but that until now their offers could not be materialized, partly due to the high tariff, partly in consequence of the high mark-up for the trade which reinforces the tariff rate.

Pottery. Several firms in this country have seriously tried to get a foothold in the American market. Some of them succeeded on a limited scale. The tariff of 50% ad valorem + 10¢ per dozen prevents larger volume trade. At a rate of 15–25% ad valorem a considerable expansion of the trade may be expected.

Optical instruments. A well-known firm in this country is keenly interested in the American market. Their main lines are microscopes, polarimeters and prism binoculars. The U.S. import tariff on these items is 45%, 60% and 20% respectively. Because of the very competitive prices and the high quality of the product a trade on a limited scale has been developed. A larger trade cannot be expected under this tariff while it is certainly absolutely prohibitive when larger advertising campaigns should be undertaken and greater allowances to the trade should be granted, *two conditions which should necessarily be fulfilled before making endeavors for a considerable larger and continent wide* trade. The performance of their microscope e.g. could in broad outline be compared with the model B.A. 8 of the American firm Bausch & Lomb, though there are some technical differences.

In response to a request of the ECA-Commerce Mission, the British government listed forty-five items sales of which would respond to tariff cuts in the United States. The rates on the relevant items varied from 10 to 70 per cent and included items as diverse as scientific instruments (generally United States tariffs 40, 45, and 60 per cent); silver-plated

[60] *Ibid.*, pp. 162–165.

candlestick (50); knitting machines for fully fashioned hosiery (40); chocolate-confectionery machinery (27½); herring, smoked, kippered, etc. (10); cotton cloth of counts exceeding 90 (mainly 27½); wool cloth weighing not more than 4 ounces per square yard (37½ cents per pound plus 25 per cent); rayon staple (20); and mechanical toys (70).[61]

What is especially important to note is the relation of the final price to the price received by the foreign exporter. Particularly in manufactured goods (and notably consumer goods), the price to the final buyer may well be several times that to the exporter. For example, the American Watch Association revealed that "the total value of final products of our industry, in 1947, was $322,619,000, of which only $48,607,000 or 15 per cent represented the cost of imported watch works; customs duty, $16,933,000; payroll, $14,679,000; wrist bands, $4,563,000; gift boxes, $4,906,000; and excise taxes, $35,485,000."[62] Distributive costs are especially important. Not only is the final product priced at six to seven times the cost of the imported materials, but note that if the tariff were cut by one-third, the gains to the consumer would be only 1 to 2 per cent. Note, further, that if the foreign seller reduced his price by 50 per cent, the gain to the American buyer would be only 8 per cent. (Throughout I assume that all reductions are passed on to the consumer.) This arithmetic points to one reason why it is difficult to expand sales to the American market. Not only are the distribution costs large compared with the export price, but in order to penetrate the rich market, large capital investments are required. European exporters are loath to make these investments as long as the market is an uncertain one.

Time well observes:[63]

Removing tariffs would certainly help foreign producers. But the main obstacle to big volume sales of foreign goods in the U.S. is the nature of the American market place itself.

A basic condition of selling in America is that goods must be sold in larger quantities than most foreign manufacturers are prepared to produce. The backbone of foreign industry is small and medium-sized plants, whose entire output would not warrant the large investment in promotion needed to sell in the U.S.

Foreign producers get another shock when they discover that the cost of distributing goods in the U.S. is considerably higher than in Europe. And because the American market is so big and active, the seller must make more noise with ads to be heard at all. Many foreign producers are reluctant even to whisper.

[61] *Ibid.*, pp. 141–142.
[62] *Ways and Means Committee Hearings on H.R. 4294, Trade Agreements Extension Act of 1953*, p. 1869.
[63] *Time*, Nov. 23, 1953, p. 106.

. . . While U.S. producers thrive on competition, most foreign businessmen shun it. Thus they tend to concentrate on basic commodities, semi-finished goods for special industrial use, or national specialties unlike any produced in the U.S.—Scotch whiskey, British woolens, French wines or Belgian lace.

. . . British textile weavers, accustomed to making cloth 36 inches wide, found that American patterns required it to be at least 39 inches wide. Some other sellers have made the necessary changes. But most foreign producers still see no reason why they should adapt their products to American wants, even if they could afford the expense. It is hard for them to accept the rule that in the American market place the buyer is king.

Foreign businessmen also feel that the American market is unpredictable and fickle. At home, customers are faithful to their traditional suppliers; the European producer is aghast at the casualness with which the American consumer is ready to leave one supplier for another who comes along with something brighter, cheaper—or better.

Thus, the American market seems treacherously unstable to foreigners. What is in demand one day may not be the next. Therefore, many foreign producers are reluctant to expand their sales in the U.S., even when there is a strong demand for their products. One Dutch manufacturer of tea sieves, whose products made a big hit with U.S. housewives, nevertheless refused to enlarge his production for fear the market might dry up. Many fail to expand because their sights are set lower than U.S. manufacturers, and the small market they already have seems big to them. Others, not without reason, believe that if they build up too sizable a market for their products, bigger American companies will start competing and squeeze them out—or pressure Congress to raise tariffs.

Actually, the fundamental reason why most foreign goods cannot compete successfully in the U.S. is that selling in the U.S. involves big stakes, and big stakes mean big risks. Few foreign producers are willing to take the gambles American producers accept as a matter of course. The constantly changing demands of the U.S. consumers can only be met by investment in new products and more efficient production methods that will lower prices. Foreign producers willing to meet such terms prosper, tariffs or no. British auto producers, for example, have shrewdly pushed sales of sport cars, something Americans wanted but did not have; last year they sold 31,243 cars in the U.S., far more than any other foreign country. The big lesson producers abroad must learn is that the main cause for failure to sell in the U.S. is not just high tariffs. It is the fact that foreign producers fail to study the market and use American methods to give the American consumer what he wants.

As Lubell puts it, "The data compiled by Humphrey, who is sympathetic with the liberal trade viewpoint, should lay to rest for good any notions that a reduction of American tariffs can bring about any spectacular increase in U.S. imports."[64] Over a period of fifty years Humphrey finds little association of imports and tariff rates, product by product; styling, ability to meet delivery dates, etc., are much more im-

[64] S. Lubell, *The Revolution in World Trade*, p. 87.

portant. In an excellent chapter, Humphrey comments on the institutional obstacles to a rise of imports, e.g., the failure of foreign manufacturers to advertise, the selling problems related to size of orders, and styling.[65] Tarshis stresses the significance of monopolistic elements and hence the importance of markups. What is more, the varying effects of markups in different industries generally affect the exportability of product A against that of product B.[66]

An examination of the tariff structure in the United States throws further light on these problems.[67]

In Table 22-2, it is revealed that as of 1949, dutiable imports were $2,695 million and the average rate as of January 1, 1952, was 13.3 per cent. With an average rate of 13 per cent, it seems dubious that the rate of itself (even admitting that there are many individual rates of 30, 40, 50, and more) can depress imports by large amounts compared with a dollar gap of, say, $4 billion to $8 billion. An estimate of the Tariff Commission reveals that only about $25 million of imports is subject to rates of 66 per cent or more. The amount is only a fraction of 1 per cent of imports. Of course, the amount excluded by these high rates may be several times the value of imports of the relevant items.[68]

Here is some relevant statistical material:

1. This breakdown is of some interest. The average rate is 5 per cent or less for imports of $238 million; 10 per cent or less, $786 million.

2. Again, note that items largely agricultural account for $1,237 million ($170 million already included in item 1). Reductions in these items would require a radical revision of agricultural policy, though, of course, the essentials of the price supports could still be maintained even though more imports were allowed, when foreign sources must provide the major supplies, e.g., wool.

3. Included in this table are important items for which the tariff is not required. In other words, even if the tariff were eliminated, imports in large quantities would not come in. This generalization applies largely to metals and manufactures ($338 million) and to some extent, of course, to all other categories.[69]

These three categories account for most of the dutiable imports. Allowing for tariffs so low that a removal would do little good, for agricultural tariffs tied up with agricultural policy and hence not reducible,

---

[65] Humphrey, *op. cit.*, chap. 10.

[66] L. Tarshis, *Introduction to International Trade and Finance,* 1955, pp. 128–129, 136–137.

[67] *Operations of the Trade Agreements Program,* Fifth Report, p. 164.

[68] *Hearings on Foreign Economic Policy,* 1953, pp. 198–200. Omitted from this calculation were cotton yarn, cotton gloves, leather gloves, handkerchiefs, and wool.

[69] Cf. Committee on Economic Development, *United States and Tariff Policy,* November, 1954, p. 3. (It is estimated that $3 billion of United States imports is subject to quotas and high tariffs.)

Table 22-2. United States Dutiable Imports (for Consumption) in 1949: Average Ad Valorem Equivalents of Rates of Duty in Effect on Specified Dates, by Tariff Schedules

	United States dutiable imports, 1949,* thousands of dollars	Average ad valorem equivalent based on rates in effect, %				% reduction in rates from	
		Before any agreements	On Jan. 1, 1945	On Jan. 1, 1951 (pre-Torquay)	On Jan. 1, 1952 (post-Torquay)†	Pre-agreement to Jan. 1, 1952	Jan. 1, 1945, to Jan. 1, 1952
1. Chemicals, oils, and paints......	78,451	22.4	16.7	12.9	10.9	51	34
2. Earths, earthenware, and glassware.........................	59,461	42.7	38.8	27.8	26.6	38	32
3. Metals and manufactures of.....	338,414	27.1	18.6	14.9	13.4	50	28
4. Wood and manufactures of.....	97,551	10.9	7.2	4.9	4.5	59	38
5. Sugar, molasses, and manufactures of‡.....................	345,179	29.9	15.5	10.8	10.8	64	31
6. Tobacco and manufactures of...	75,337	43.0	32.4	23.2	19.2	55	41
7. Agricultural products and provisions:							
Fishery products...........	72,615	14.5	11.8	9.4	9.0	38	24
Other.....................	412,278	19.3	14.3	11.4	11.2	42	22
Total or average..........	484,893	18.6	13.9	11.1	10.8	42	22
8. Spirits, wines, and other beverages................................	89,560	85.2	43.4	25.9	24.4	71	44
9. Cotton manufactures..........	22,649	35.6	28.7	22.7	22.4	37	22
10. Flax, hemp, jute, and manufactures of......................	141,755	11.4	8.6	5.0	5.0	56	42
11. Wool and manufactures of......	234,209	39.1	32.7	24.8	24.4	38	25
12. Silk manufactures.............	21,477	55.7	46.1	26.4	25.9	54	44
13. Manufactures of rayon or other synthetic textile...............	7,233	37.0	34.2	23.6	19.2	48	44
14. Papers and books.............	21,399	20.1	13.5	9.0	8.7	57	35
15. Sundries.....................	223,359	30.7	26.0	21.3	20.6	33	21
Free-list taxable..............	454,419	9.8	7.3	7.2	7.2	26	0.5
Total or average.............	2,695,346	25.8	18.3	13.9	13.3	49§	27§

* Preliminary.

† Assuming that all concessions negotiated at Torquay were in effect on Jan. 1, 1952.

‡ Chiefly cane sugar ($322 million), imports of which are regulated by quota.

§ If imports of cane sugar ($322 million), which are regulated by quota, were excluded from this calculation, the percentages of reduction would be 46 and 27 per cent, respectively, instead of 49 and 27 per cent.

SOURCE: Compiled from official statistics of the U.S. Department of Commerce.

for tariffs that are not protectionist because they are not needed, we draw the conclusion that tariff cuts or even removal of tariffs would not greatly increase imports, though admitting that there are many individual items where a reduction of the tariff from 10 to 70 per cent might greatly increase imports. (Cf. the British listing above.)

In this connection, the experience with a large rise in the tariff on Swiss watches in 1954 introduced by a Presidential order under the escape clause is of some interest. Apparently in the six months August, 1954, to January, 1955, the first six months after the rise of duties, Swiss exports of watches to the United States declined by 25 per cent from the total for the corresponding period in 1953–1954. But we should take into account the recession in 1954. With an imperfect market, as prevails for many imports of manufactured goods, the exporter may absorb all or a large part of the tariff and middlemen in the United States part of it. These factors may explain the fact that imports did not decline further.[70]

The most interesting study yet made on the effects of removal of tariffs and quotas is one by Dr. Piquet.[71] Above we have discussed individual cases where it is held that tariff concessions might be helpful. Now we turn to a composite estimate made up of individual markets.

On the assumption of a suspension of all tariffs for several years, Dr. Piquet finds that on the basis of conditions prevailing in 1951, the rise of imports would be from $800 million (minimum) to $1,800 million (maximum). With quotas also suspended, the totals would be $1,203 million minimum and $2,658 million maximum. A rise of imports of this amount would contribute substantially toward a solution of the dollar problem.

Unfortunately, however, a suspension of all tariffs and quotas is so far removed from practical economic policy that this approach is scarcely worth discussing. For example, as long as this country is determined to keep agricultural prices and incomes up, it is not likely that it will abandon protectionism, especially quotas.

Yet certain aspects of Piquet's study should be considered. First, he leaves out of account about 20 per cent of the total import trade, largely smaller items, as well as items not imported at all that might be imported should free trade prevail. (The conclusions reached from the study of 80 per cent are, however, applied to all items.) Second, the analysis is by items individually, without adequate consideration of their relationships. For example, if tariffs on woolens were removed and Western Europe captured our woolen industry, would a reduction in tariffs on raw wool raise wool imports? Or actually would not imports of wool disappear?

How Dr. Piquet obtains his estimate is not at all clear, except that we are informed that he consulted commodity experts. Obviously, he must estimate the response in each instance of export production abroad to the offer of a higher price to the foreign producer as tariffs are

[70] Cf. International Monetary Fund, *International Financial News Survey*, Feb. 25, 1955, p. 263.

[71] See H. S. Piquet, *Aid, Trade and the Tariff*, 1953; Conference Board Economic Forum, *The Economics of Tariffs*, 1953, especially pp. 48–67; and *Randall Commission Staff Papers*, pp. 298–311.

eliminated here, the extent to which foreign sellers will increase their profits in response to a more favorable competitive position rather than expand sales at the higher dollar prices available to foreign sellers in the United States market, the diversion from domestic consumption and sales in other markets (e.g., British sales in France) to the United States market (depending in part upon the elasticities of demand abroad (e.g., in the United Kingdom), the manner in which United States producers will respond to lower prices (divert production to other commodities, cut prices, or close up), the increase in sales accompanying lower prices in the United States (but higher prices for the foreign seller), etc.

We are not provided with any analysis of the relevant elasticities. Dr. Piquet tells us, for example, that the elasticity of demand for watches is high and for bicycles low. Here he does not seem to take into account the relationship of the export price and the price to the final consumer. How elastic is the demand for Swiss watch movements? A tariff suspension may well cut the price of the movement by $1 or perhaps one-third of the export price. It may then be assumed that the elasticity of demand would be high: a reduction of 33 per cent in price would increase sales greatly. But how high is the elasticity when actually the elimination of the tariff reduced the average $25 price of a Swiss watch (not the Swiss work) to the consumer by less than 5 per cent. In that context, elasticity of demand for the Swiss watchwork is low indeed, for it is given by the response of a reduction in price not from $3 to $2 but more nearly from $25 to $24.

Though the economists should be grateful to Dr. Piquet for his attempt to deal with a difficult problem, I am convinced that the results are necessarily the roughest kind of estimates and to gain widespread support would require much more analysis of elasticities than is evident in the material presented. It is an interesting fact that economists are divided on the issue of elasticity of demand for imported commodities. There are equally brilliant economists on either side of the fence.[72]

In a careful study of British export trade Mrs. Hutt comments as follows on the Piquet estimates:[73]

It is difficult to criticize Piquet's estimates as he gives no detailed account of the methods by which he made them, giving the impression that he used his knowledge of the particular commodities' demand and supply conditions and his experience at the Tariff Commission to make enlightened guesses. But in

---

[72] National Industrial Conference Board, *The Economics of Tariffs*, pp. 100–106; R. F. Harrod, "Imbalance of International Payments," *International Monetary Fund Staff Papers*, April, 1953, pp. 17–18; and Adler, Schlesinger, and van Westerberg, *The Pattern of United States Import Trade since 1923*, 1952 (reviewed by H. K. Zassenhaus, *Review of Economics and Statistics*, February, 1953, pp. 92–97).

[73] R. Hutt, "British Exports to the United States, 1948–1955," *Review of Economics and Statistics*, February, 1957.

the case of certain imports from the U.K. the estimates do not seem very probable and they are biassed in a particular direction. For instance, it is claimed that the suspension of the duty on bicycles would cause a substantial increase (i.e., 50–100%) in imports not only of the heavy and middle-weight type but also of lightweights. The duty at the time was only 7½% and even after the increase only 11¼%. Moreover, as the price is already considerably lower than that of the domestic lightweight and competitive with the heavier type it seems most unlikely that an increase of this magnitude would occur. Piquet also asserts that a moderate (i.e., 25–50%) rise in imports of cars would occur. As the duty is only 10% and design and performance are so much more important to the buyer than small price differentials, this too seems unlikely. Similar objections might be raised to the estimated increases in imports—woolens, china and other things—particularly as Piquet emphasizes the temporary nature of the suspension he is assuming. For these reasons I suspect that for U.K. goods the potential increases he asserts are over-estimates.

CHAPTER 23

Tariffs and the Dollar Gap: II

Appropriate Tariff Policy

What then is an appropriate tariff policy? The policy should be related to the size of the dollar gap and should not be designed to put the whole burden of the adjustment on imports. Of course, United States tariff policy has become a symbol of the willingness of the United States to cooperate with her friends. For this reason, it may be desirable to go beyond a point suggested by the purely economic considerations.

It is well at the outset to distinguish two problems, namely, the desirability of more trade and the dollar problem. The Trade Agreements Program (TAP) really stemmed from a desire to expand the total amount of trade. But since treatment of the dollar gap requires an expansion of imports without a corresponding rise of exports, the TAP, in theory at any rate, did not contribute toward a solution of the dollar gap. Even the Randall Commission erred in proposing that concessions in imports be countered by foreign concessions in favor of American exporters. Perhaps this proposal of the Randall Commission reflects the great influence of the exporters. In practice, the TAP contributed toward a solution of the dollar problem in so far as foreign negotiators outbargained the American negotiators or in so far as they imposed restraints on trade through quantitative controls or expanded their exports to the United States market through recourse to exchange depreciation and special aids. These are techniques not easily covered under the umbrella of the TAP. Is it not time that the objective of equal gains of exports and imports subsumed under the TAP was abandoned?

Even as late as 1955, authorities were making preposterous claims for the gains of trade under the TAP. Indeed trade with trade-agreement countries in some cases expanded by more than 1,000 per cent from 1937 to 1953. But nothing is said about the effects of these agreements upon trade with nonagreement countries, nor is any measure made of the contribution of the rise of income here and similar factors. In the same paragraph the powerful Ways and Means Committee comments on dollar shortage and the most practical way of treating it, namely, lowering tariffs, but no mention is made of how these agreements can solve the dollar problem.[1]

An appropriate tariff policy would take into account the need for balancing the dollar account, with increased imports contributing a fair share. It would also consider the relation of tariffs to other domestic policies. For example, tariff policy has to be reconciled with agricultural policy. Hence on the assumption that agricultural policy is not abandoned, it becomes necessary to continue restraints on imports of agricultural commodities.

Again, tariffs are an interference with the free-market system. In a world of free markets, the case against the tariff would be much stronger than it can be made out to be in the world of today, a world in which government redistributes income, provides social security, interferes with free markets in agriculture, and controls the rate of interest and, indirectly, of investment, both the amount and direction. In these circumstances, it becomes much more difficult to discard tariffs than under a free economy. For example, the Federal government bestows special favors upon industries in some regions, raises the prices of their agricultural products, and provides special tax concessions, all policies that jeopardize important industries in the North. In these circumstances, the case for maintaining certain industries of the developed regions is much greater than it would be in the absence of other forms of interference. One is sometimes puzzled by the fact that most economists favor protection for farmers against the vicissitudes of the market, but the economist who would protect, say, textile workers against free-market forces is a rarity indeed.[2]

It is often said that American industries do not need protection against foreign competitors any more than the old carriage industry needed protection against the automobile industry or Danbury hatters against the changing fashions of attire. The economy has not only survived but actually grown in the face of declining demand for some commodities or services provided by regions. In fact, the Randall Commission cites Danbury (hats); Danielson, Connecticut; Lawrence, Lowell, Massachusetts; Manchester, New Hampshire; Nashua, New Hampshire (textiles); Auburn, New York (International Harvester); Hornell, New

---

[1] Ways and Means Committee, *Hearings on the Trade Agreements Extension Act of 1955*, pp. 7, 62–63. At least the Committee on Economic Development suggests that the United States bargain tariff cuts for tariff cuts on behalf of third countries or for concessions to American investors abroad. *Ibid.*, p. 17.

[2] Cf. *Report of the New England Governors' Committee on the Textile Industry*, 1952; and S. E. Harris, "Interregional Competition," *American Economic Association Proceedings*, 1954.

York, and Altoona, Pennsylvania (shift from steam to diesel locomotives); and Scranton, Pennsylvania (coal), as examples of localities that adjusted to serious losses of industries and jobs.[3]

But on the basis of my experience in studying the textile situation, the Commission considerably underestimates the difficulties of the transition. Depression continued (and continues) for decades in the textile towns; workers do not move easily; new industries are not easily attracted when tax rates are high, labor-capital relations unsatisfactory (in part because of conditions in the older industries), the old mills scarcely suited for new enterprises, and their appearance a deterrent. Moreover the new industries attracted have too frequently been the exploitative, low-wage industries. From the survey of the Randall Commission staff, one would not suspect that Fall River, Lowell, and Manchester suffered large spells of unemployment even in the twenties, not to mention the thirties, or even that Lawrence was one of the most distressed towns in the country in the fifties. Textile towns in New England, coal towns in Pennsylvania, have been and continue to be problem towns.

In an interesting discussion of the problem of adjustment, members of the Fletcher school stress the ability to shift resources following a cut in tariffs: In motorcycles, the domestic industry shifted a large part of its production from heavy- to lightweight machines; in the case of garlic, to other vegetables and sugar-beet products; in watches, to those with more than seventeen jewels where protection was not reduced and the United States producers were particularly strong. In some instances the shift was to growing industries, as in response to increased demand for motorcycles.

Yet there are serious problems of adjustment, and they may easily be underestimated. Earlier in this discussion, I commented on the problems of adjustment in older regions. In a dissenting report on glacé cherries, minority commissioners wrote:[4]

More important . . . in our judgment, is the fallacy involved in the theory that producers of a particular product cannot be found to be seriously injured because of the possibility that they might cease the production of the item in question, and undertake increased production of other items or convert their operations to importing, thus retaining their markets, but abandoning their functions as producers of the product in question. . . . An interpretation of the escape clause which results in the elimination of many small industries on the uncertain ground that producers in these industries could shift to other lines of production, leaving the market in the United States to particular products under consideration to foreign producers, surely does violence to the intent of Congress.

[3] *Randall Commission Staff Papers*, pp. 411–426.
[4] *Hearings on Foreign Economic Policy*, 1953, pp. 185–187.

One congressman complains of the difficulties of adjusting to a decline in the tariff on daffodils.[5]

The two states of Washington and Oregon are the centers of the production of daffodils, iris, and tulips. . . . In my district alone, growers have produced some 30 million King Alfred daffodils annually—more than are grown in all of Holland. But now an excess of foreign bulbs is being dumped on the United States market at prices below the cost of domestic production, and many growers of the Northwest are facing bankruptcy. . . .

A representative of the plate-glass industry expressed the attitude of American workers toward mobility. (This may well be considered an untenable position, but it reflects attitudes that should not be dismissed too lightly.)[6]

The working men and women in this industry resent the ideas of being treated as robots who may be transferred from one job to another to satisfy the theories of foreign trade economists. . . . Many of them have worked in the glass industry all their lives, and are temperamentally and physically unfit except for the work they are doing. As individuals they have a right to a proper amount of protection against their displacement by foreign workers. . . .

Why do not economists say, not only that free trade prevails among regions to the great advantage of the nation and hence should prevail among countries, but also that the movement of industries from region to region may be too costly, that there is something to be said for slowing up the migration from North to South or East to West so that the transitional effects would be less costly? At any rate, all would agree that government should not take extreme measures, as it has in the past, to accelerate the rate of decline in the older regions and stimulate the rate of births in the new regions.

I am sympathetic with the proposals made by Mr. McDonald and elaborated in the *Randall Commission Staff Papers* to alleviate the distress caused by tariff reduction by providing aid to management and labor. In so far as such programs are practical and can be administered without serious abuses, there is much to be said for this approach. Clearly the case for tariff reduction is stronger in so far as protection against resultant distress is provided. But on the basis of past proposals and practices for aiding industries and regions in distress, I am skeptical that much will be done in this direction. The Randall Commission itself repudiated this approach.

Among the measures that might be taken are the following: liberalization of unemployment insurance, dismissal pay, retraining of workers, improved employment service, and payment of travel expenses to

[5] *Congressional Record*, May 21, 1954, p. A3767.

[6] *Hearings by the Senate Finance Committee on Trade Agreements Extension* (H.R. 1), 1955, p. 915.

workers moving to regions offering jobs. The Randall Commission staff estimates that the cost of a generous program per 100,000 displaced workers would be $140 million paid over several years.[7] This leaves out of account the problem of salvaging the investment and management involved. Here the proposals are limited to tax amortization, help in adapting capital to other uses, technical assistance, and loans on guarantees under the Small Business Administration.[8] It is obvious that management of industries vulnerable to foreign competition would not consider this adequate.

How much aid would be required depends in part upon the numbers that would be displaced. From this viewpoint also any tariff concessions are made with less damage in periods of growth than in periods of decline. Obviously, if the country adds 600,000 jobs a year, the problem is more easily solved than if the country loses a million or more jobs in a year.

The Commission staff put the total employment in foreign trade at 4,376,000. Here the assumption is that employment would suffer if trade were eliminated or drastically reduced. Actually there would be a loss of income and probably a rise of employment, since goods would be produced less efficiently. In some conditions, less trade might also mean higher incomes. It should be observed, however, that the 1,250,000 of employment related to processing and distribution of imports would largely, if not wholly, be transferred to servicing goods substituted for imports. Furthermore, some questions may be raised concerning the estimate of export employment. Does it follow, for example, that because 10 per cent of farm output is exported, 10 per cent of farm employment is the result of exports? Actually the disappearance of the export market would cut employment much less than 10 per cent.[9]

According to the Commission's staff, the number of United States workers providing goods "equivalent to the estimated increases in imports which would take place in the event of a temporary suspension of tariffs" would be as given in Table 23-1. (These "estimates take no account of probable increases in United States products or production techniques, or of the capacity of companies concerned to shift to other lines of production.")[10] The reader should note that these estimates deal only with the results of suspension of tariffs. Should quota suspension be included, then the increase of imports would be about 50 per cent more and hence presumably the number of jobs involved 50 per cent additional.

[7] *Randall Commission Staff Papers,* pp. 391–397.
[8] *Ibid., pp.* 387–388.
[9] *Ibid., pp.* 373–374.
[10] *Ibid., p.* 381.

According to this study the maximum number of jobs lost through a suspension of tariffs is estimated at 405,000; the minimum, at 189,000. More recently a congressional committee estimated that a 50 per cent cut in tariffs would threaten only 100,000 jobs.[11]

Table 23-1. Number of Workers Producing Goods Equivalent to Increases in Annual Imports after Temporary Tariff Suspension†

	No. of workers producing goods equivalent to					
Types of import increases in case of tariff suspension and area of employment	Estimated minimum import increase			Estimated maximum import increase		
	Total	Employed in		Total	Employed in	
		Nonagricultural industries	Agricultural industries‡		Nonagricultural industries	Agricultural industries‡
A. All commodities...............	189,090	57,360	131,730	404,990	135,040	269,950
1. Direct employment..........	109,040	40,060	68,980	237,820	97,540	140,280
2. Indirect employment§.......	80,050	17,300	62,750	167,170	37,500	129,670
B. Commodities in "area of maximum import competition"......	121,210	36,770	84,440	255,550	85,210	170,340
1. Direct employment..........	69,900	25,680	44,220	150,070	61,550	88,520
2. Indirect employment........	51,310	11,090	40,220	105,480	23,660	81,820
C. Commodities which would be likely to cause some displacement of domestic goods.........	96,240	23,870	72,370	202,650	57,640	145,010
1. Direct employment..........	59,660	18,280	41,380	127,730	44,960	82,770
2. Indirect employment........	36,580	5,590	30,990	74,920	12,680	62,240

† Based on estimated increases in imports in event of tariff suspension by Howard S. Piquet in *Aid, Trade and the Tariff.*
‡ Agricultural employment figures are based upon Bureau of Agricultural Economics data.
§ Includes estimates of offsetting employment in ocean transportation and insurance arising from assumed import increases.
SOURCE: U.S. Bureau of Labor Statistics, Branch of Interindustry Economics.

Let us assume that tariff reduction is required both on the grounds of improved political relations and as a contribution toward the solution of the dollar problem. Then how do we preceed?

1. The whole philosophy of the Trade Agreements Program should be discarded. The approach should be more imports, not more imports *and* more exports. In the past, the government has circumvented this problem by acquiescing when foreign countries imposed nontariff restrictions.

[11] *House Ways and Means Committee Report on Trade Agreements Extension Act of 1955,* p. 9.

2. In approving any cuts in tariffs, the government should consider the following:

   a. Past reductions.

   b. The vulnerability of the industry and the region.

   c. Related to *b* the reductions should be highly selective, taking into account the possibility of absorbing labor and capital displaced, allowing adequate time for adjustment, providing for suspension of scheduled declines in periods of economic deterioration, allowing special treatment and even increases and quotas where the defense argument could *legitimately* be used, termination of tariffs where this country clearly does not need this crutch (foreign competition is nonexistent at home and not serious abroad).

   d. Across-the-board cuts should be discouraged. The implication should not be that all industries should experience similar cuts. In fact, rates might rise in some instances and be eliminated in others.[12]

   e. Much has been made of the uncertainty of future American tariffs. I discuss this problem elsewhere (Chapter 22). Here I only observe that it is not possible to introduce complete certainty in trade policy either here or abroad. It would help greatly to simplify customs administration and introduce other reforms. The complete elimination of the escape clause is asking too much. Labor and industry should have some protection against unjustifiable agreements by United States negotiators. At least until 1955 the escape clause was not a serious deterrent to trade. Perhaps it would be less so if serious injury were not interpreted *inter alia* as a loss in the proportion of total output. Obviously, the serious injury should be related to an absolute loss of sales (quantities), or employment. Other criteria used (e.g., relation of costs and prices) should not be excluded.

       While discussing the problem of stability in trade restrictions, I am reminded of one objection which might be raised against the Randall proposals for a cut in tariffs by 5 per cent per year or any proposal for gradual attrition of tariffs. That is, though this might introduce an element of certainty, the net effect might be depressive. Industries vulnerable to foreign competition would be reminded that each year they were to taste an increased dose of foreign competition. Some might prefer a once-for-all substantial cut to a series of smaller cuts over many years. The transition would then be aggravated, but the crisis would be telescoped into

---

[12] Cf. *Randall Report,* p. 50; a sensible statement will be found in Council for Technological Advancement, *United States International Trade Policy,* December. 1953, pp. 16–18.

a shorter period. The choice is like the one between radical chest surgery or the orthodox treatment of tuberculosis through bed rest accompanied by crises over many years followed by recovery or death. This might, in truth, be an argument, not against moderate reductions at any one time, but rather against a *scheduled* decline over many years.

The Protectionist Case

Tariff reductions under a rigid formula are not supportable. I would emphasize especially the need of considering trade restrictions in relation to other government policies, and I would urge a distribution of the burden of trade relaxations in part on the basis of the costs of adjustment.

The Wage Argument

This, of course, does not mean that all arguments for protection advanced by protectionists should be accepted. The case is stronger for preservation of current restrictions than for a rise of restrictions, because large investments in plant and skills have been made on the basis of existing restrictions.

The major argument used by protectionists is that wages are higher in the United States than in other countries. For example, the American Tariff League compares hourly earnings for industrial workers in fourteen countries: The peak is $1.76 in the United States, and the minimum 19 cents in Japan; for Sweden, the figure is 75 cents; for the United Kingdom and France, 47 and 46 cents, respectively. The American Tariff League then contends that the wage differential puts the American producers at a disadvantage. Admitting that in some instances greater productivity is an offsetting factor, the Tariff League contends that protection is required when wage differentials are not offset by higher productivity. In support of its position, the League quotes the Secretary of Commerce, Sinclair Weeks:[13]

What I do suggest is that in the process of determination, when we come to those products where there exist radical differences in domestic and foreign labor costs not offset by greater productivity and where the output of this product is important to a substantial segment of the American economy, then we be guided in our tariff determination to the end that an adequate recognition of the labor standards of our workers in that industry be made.

Given this type of fair competition, I am entirely willing to place U.S. industry on its mettle as against any other industry anywhere in the world. Thereafter, let the man who makes the better mousetrap get the business.

[13] American Tariff League, *What about the Wage Gap?* p. 2.

This position is widely held by American businessmen. They genuinely believe that protection is appropriate in so far as wage differentials are not offset by higher productivity.

The President of the Kimberly-Clark Corporation had this to say (he emphasized the similarity of techniques and productivity here and abroad):[14]

I touched on the details of paper manufacture in my paper. We start with wood. That is the start of our whole operation—except for the trees themselves. From there on to the time that the wood gets to the mill, it is all labor. We pay about two and one half to three times as much to have that wood cut down and moved to the mill as they pay in Scandinavia. The next step is to have it ground in a grinder or digested in a digester. The size of the digester is practically the same here and abroad. True, there are some that are small, but generally speaking they are the same. Depending on the quality that we want to make, we have just so many "cooks" in twenty-four hours. We cook it six hours or eight hours or seven and one half hours, depending on the quality that we want to get. It is the same here and abroad for the same quality of pulp.

Then comes the stock preparation. We have just as many men on that and it takes just as long to mix our stock. No change. Then comes the paper machine; then the finishing room—and we have exactly the same kind of equipment when we rewind a roll, when we cut it up, when we package it.

Now comes distribution. The first thing is the cost of sending it from the mill to the market. Under normal circumstances, the cost of shipment from Scandinavia to New York or Baltimore or Savannah or New Orleans or San Francisco is less than the cost from Niagara Falls or Hamilton or Neenah, Wisconsin, to the same places or to other places where paper enters the open market. From there on, the paper is handled in exactly the same channels.

In presenting its case before the Ways and Means Committee, the representative of Bausch and Lomb Optical Company emphasized the point that hourly wages were $1.80 in this country, 45 to 71 cents in England, 30 to 40 cents in Germany, and 12 cents in Japan. Wages were a large part of total costs, and mechanization was limited.[15]

The manufacture of microscopes is largely a matter of handwork. At least 70 per cent of the manufacturing cost of a high-grade microscope, for instance, is represented by cost of labor. There is less mechanization in the manufacture of microscopes than is true of most products produced in the United States. Streamline assembly-line procedure is not possible because the quantities involved are not large enough to warrant the elaborate tooling and breakdown of individual operations as is true in the case of products made in large quantities such as automobiles, radios, refrigerators, and the like. . . . we estimated that, could we have adjusted our direct labor rates to the Japanese

[14] National Industrial Conference Board, *The Economics of Tariffs,* pp. 26–27.
[15] *Hearings on Trade Agreements Extension Act of 1953,* pp. 271–272.

level . . . we could have put out our 7 × 35 binocular in the dealer's hands at $23.50 as compared to the then Japanese price of $37.50, and our actual price of $108.50.

Time and again, almost identical complaints were presented to the Ways and Means Committee or to Congress directly. It is impossible to compete with foreign producers, it was held, when our wages are much higher and this differential is not offset by higher productivity. "Objection is voiced only when products made in countries in which 50 cents to $3 a day is paid for labor, such as is true in the sweat house labor areas of Europe, are allowed to enter in direct competition with products made in our country, where a much higher standard of living wages is in effect." This is the complaint of a congressman.[16] Representatives of the pin, clip, and fastener industry charged that wages were 50 per cent of production costs, wage rates much higher here and techniques of production similar, and imports were rising. The glove industry, it is claimed, also suffers from higher wages, while the French copy our techniques. In organic chemistry, the wage differential was considered too high for a non-mass-production industry.[17]

What makes the blow particularly hard to bear for American business is that the United States government goes out of its way to improve the productivity of European industry through a program under the European Cooperation Administration and also through a $100 million loan to the European Coal and Steel Community. The resultant gains of Europe, of course, cannot be subsumed as those related to comparative advantage in classical theory. A United States Senator complains bitterly of this help and then adds: " . . . no concrete support, or any other kind of support, has been given by this or the previous administration to the shriveling American coal industry. . . . "[18]

In a similar vein the minority report of the House Ways and Means Committee comments on relative costs at home and abroad. Foreigners can import our techniques, experience lower taxes, borrow at roughly similar rates, and yet pay much lower wages. Especially significant is the fact that in this country government sets minimum standards of working conditions, wages, social security, etc., to which other countries are not subject.[19]

Economists find it difficult to accept the high-wage argument for protection, for the fundamental basis of the theory of international trade is that each country concentrates on the production of commodities in which it has a comparative advantage. Hence the United States con-

---

[16] *Congressional Record*, May 20, 1954, p. 6539.
[17] *Hearings on Reciprocal Trade Agreements*, 1953, pp. 153, 173–175, 508.
[18] *Congressional Record*, May 20, 1954, p. 6540.
[19] *Hearings on the Trade Agreements Extension Act of 1955*, pp. 31–32.

centrates on industries where labor costs are a small part of total costs, where high wage rates are offset by high productivity, or where in the absence of high productivity, rich resources or subnormal wage rates are found.[20] This does not mean that current comparative costs are an infallible guide. Current costs may be too high but relative to foreign costs will be depressed as the industry matures (the infant-industry argument). Again, on the basis of present costs, a reallocation of resources may be suggested. But it is necessary to take account of the losses of capital and skills involved in the transfer, and the losses may be aggravated in so far as for economic or noneconomic reasons immobility prevails and the effect of exposing industries to foreign competition results in large losses from unemployment. In the examination of the readjustment experiences the staff of the Randall Commission is strangely silent concerning these heavy losses in coal and textile towns.[21] What I am trying to say here is that an allowance for these costs might well suggest a somewhat different rate of growth of new industries or decline of old than would otherwise be implied.

In proposing special tariff treatments when foreign wages are substandard, the Randall Commission seems to me to have entered a hornet's nest and to have accepted the validity of the high-wage theory in support of protectionism, for, after all, how is the government to decide when wages are substandard in the exporting nation except on the basis of relative wages abroad and in this country?[22]

The Defense Argument

I now turn to the defense argument, which is increasingly used to support protection of domestic industries. Even Adam Smith had recourse to defense as a justifiable reason for protection.

It is not easy to weight the defense argument properly. There is always the question of how much a nation is prepared to raise costs in peacetime in order to be prepared for an emergency. At present, the abandonment of large population centers and the creation of ribbon cities at distances of every twenty-five miles would provide a large measure of security against atomic warfare, but the resultant reduction of income by 90 per cent or more and the complete break with past associations suggest that the cost of increased security would be excessive.

Then how far can the defense argument be carried? All would agree that the country must have a minimum merchant marine even if this means large construction and operating subsidies and even preference

---

[20] Cf. W. Leontief in *Review of Economics and Statistics*, November, 1956, who concludes that capital is the scarce item in this country.

[21] *Randall Commission Staff Papers*, pp. 411–427.

[22] *Randall Report*, p. 62.

in shipments by the United States government. Some protection against a loss of foreign supplies of natural rubber is also required. Each case must be considered on its merits, but it is also necessary to add up the total costs.

In 1954, the government reviewed its subsidy shipping policy. Note that the government provides subsidies for construction and operation and also provides a controlled market for the shipowners.[23]

The declared shipping policy of the United States is to foster the development and encourage the maintenance of a privately owned and operated merchant marine adequate for the commercial and defense needs of the nation. In recognition of the disadvantage faced . . . the Merchant Marine Act, 1936, provides for assistance to the industry in the form of operating and construction subsidies. The basic principle of this assistance is parity; i.e., to grant subsidy when required to equate approximately American shipping companies' costs of construction and operation with those of their foreign competitors.

It is unfortunate that a large field of imports is closed because shipping is held to be an important defense industry. We should be certain that neither the subsidies nor the markets guaranteed are larger than they need be. Our comparative-cost disadvantage is unusually high in this industry. For example, on one typical trade route a representative wage cost was $20,000 for the United States, $5,200 for Norway, $8,310 for Belgium, and $4,700 for the United Kingdom. These high costs are not made up by great technical advances here.[24] The excess of United States over foreign seagoing labor costs was 57 per cent in 1947 and 71 per cent in 1951.[25]

Again, the domestic watch and clock industry has contended that the industry is indispensable for defense:[26]

Since the days of Adam Smith, economists have recognized the validity of the defense argument in support of tariffs for industries indispensable for the Military Establishment. The manifest essentiality of our industry to the national defense was entirely ignored in the Torquay negotiations, and was given only the most superficial consideration in President Truman's rejection of the Tariff Commission's recommendations in the escape-clause proceedings. . . .

For more than 3 years during World War II the clock and pin-lever watch industry was 100 per cent engaged in defense production. We manufactured some 25 million complete military items and some 3½ billion components and

---

[23] House Committee on Merchant Marine and Fisheries, *A Review of Maritime Subsidy Policy . . .* , 1954, p. 66.

[24] *Ibid.*, p. 43.

[25] House Committee on Merchant Marine and Fisheries, *Survey: The American Merchant Marine, Policies and Problems*, 1954, p. 7.

[26] *Hearings on the Trade Agreements Extension Act of 1953*, pp. 437–438.

parts, many involving almost incredible intricacy and accuracy considering the volume. . . .

Let me point out that the mechanical time fuse is the standard fuse, used by our armed services in immense quantities. Each such fuse contains a clockwork timepiece—equivalent in principle and function to a watch or small clock. This timepiece must be so ruggedly constructed that it will absorb without damage the shock of the blast which fires an artillery shell, yet will maintain such delicate accuracy that it will detonate the charge within a minute fraction of a second, as may be predetermined. The timepieces which control the detonation of by far the largest proportion of artillery shells of all kinds are made—and can be made—only by the horological industry. Other industries have attempted, but failed, in the effort to produce these mechanisms. Only one firm not actually engaged in manufacturing timepieces as such—but nevertheless a part of the horological industry—has succeeded in fuse-timer production.

I should add that the mechanical time fuse has not been displaced, and is not likely to be displaced, by the electronic or proximity fuse. Two reasons may be cited. The first is that the two fuses are designed to serve entirely different purposes. The second reason is that the use of proximity fuses actually increases the need for mechanical time fuses, since every proximity fuse is equipped with a mechanical time fuse which acts as a safety device.

President Eisenhower in 1954 allowed a substantial rise in the tariff on Swiss watches on the grounds that important skills required for defense were being lost. Serious differences of opinion were introduced in the course of the hearings and especially on the time required to train these workers, the availability of other industries to produce the necessary timepieces, the degree of decline of the watch industry, and the possibility of meeting war needs through stockpiling.[27]

The Assistant Secretary of Defense admitted that the "jeweled watch industry was uniquely qualified to produce jeweled watches and movements . . . on the other hand the mobilization requirements for jeweled movements for a 3-year mobilization period was found to be well within the capacity of the four companies to produce within a year's time."[28]

The report upon which the President acted was the following:[29]

The subcommittee received evidence to the effect that—

The Watch and clock industry has a unique pool of skilled workers, some of whom require up to 10 years of training and experience before they achieve professional proficiency in their precision crafts;

[27] See *Hearings before the Preparedness Subcommittee No. 6 of the Committee on Armed Services, United States Senate, on Essentiality to the National Defense of the Domestic Horological Industry,* July, 1954, especially pp. 32–34, 39–40, 163–183.

[28] *Ibid.,* p. 39.

[29] "Essentiality of the American Watch and Clock Industry," *Report of Preparedness Subcommittee No. 6 of the Committee on Armed Services, United States Senate,* S. Res. 86, 1954.

The Nation has historically called upon this skilled pool of workers from the watch and clock industry in time of war as its primary source of precision timepieces, military precision timing devices, and for the development and production of other essential miniature instruments;

In times of emergency, the Nation cannot safely rely on foreign precision timepieces, other precision timing devices, and jewel bearings, needed for defense requirements;

Unless the training and employment of this skilled pool of workers in the horological industry are continued, the pool of workers cannot be maintained intact. Their unique proficiencies and skills would deteriorate in industries requiring less highly developed skills and the particular skills required in time of war emergency would not be available.

An abundance of expert testimony was heard by the subcommittee. The testimony was in almost unanimous agreement that the pool of skilled workers of the American watch and clock industry is essential to the security of our country in time of war.

As stated above, the subcommittee has confined its study and confines its report to the precise question propounded by its charter—the essentiality of the industry to national defense.

On all the evidence, the subcommittee concludes:

1. Although the Nation was substantially self-sufficient in the production of precision instruments required for defense in World War II, it must be remembered that the Nation had over 2 years to prepare for war.

2. A future war may come swiftly and without advance notice. In such an event, there will be no time to provide training in the highly specialized and critical skills needed to produce the precision timing devices for defense requirements.

3. The highly skilled workers in the American watch and clock industry, who require long years of training and experience, and their unique ability to develop and produce, within the shortest time possible, precision instruments to minute tolerances, are essential to the national defense. Therefore, it is in the interest of national defense to keep this essential industry alive and vital.

In one Tariff Commission report, the importance of the defense arguments was minimized, but later official statements stressed the defense argument.[30] The issue seems to come down to the following: (1) In the contingency of large loss of capacity in the watch-clock industry and loss of skills, can nonwatch or -clock manufacturers produce the necessary military timepieces? (2) Can they do so within a reasonable period? (3) How large are the costs of protection? And how are they to be weighed against the gains from security? "Although a military need exists for a domestic watch industry, there is no way of determining at what level the industry should be maintained in peacetime in order to

---

[30] U.S. Tariff Commission, *Watches*, 1946, pp. 35–37.

make it possible for productive capacity to be quickly expanded to meet requirements in time of war."[31]

In many other industries where appeal is made to the defense argument, the case does not seem nearly so strong as in the instances just cited. The defense argument has been applied to textiles, to food, to metals, to oil, and to many other products. Obviously, it is helpful to have a large textile capacity in the midst of a major war, and the protection offered farmers through both quotas and subsidies facilitated the expansion of output in the war period. But the application of protection on the grounds of the defense argument to all industries providing necessary goods in wartime would greatly increase costs and reduce substantially our real income. With total war, virtually all industries become strategic. In many instances when it seems desirable to maintain capacity above the level given by competitive conditions, it might be best to pay subsidies outright for additional output rather than impose tariffs, which increase costs of *all* units.

The use of the defense argument is suggested by the following: First, consider petroleum, where the argument used is that foreign imports threaten the continuity of supplies at home.[32]

During World War II, and particularly in 1942 and 1943, the importing companies were unable to bring any substantial quantities of crude oil or its products into this country because of enemy submarines. This demonstrated clearly that there is no security in foreign oil for the defense of our own borders. Our excess domestic productive capacity of approximately 1 million barrels per day at the beginning of World War II made possible an adequate supply of petroleum products to enable ourselves and our allies to win that war. . . .

Since we cannot rely on petroleum from foreign lands for the protection of our own borders, we must consider whether there are adequate sources available in the United States.

Then in metals it is held that foreign competition results in closing of mines and therefore permanent losses of sources of supplies.[33]

Is it not true that the best way to destroy an enemy or the best way to keep him under your control is to destroy his sources of mineral resources or make him come to you for those mineral resources? We must admit that without metals we cannot long survive. And we must admit that when we have relied on outside sources for our supplies we have been compelled to pay all the traffic would bear when an emergency arose, or we have been compelled to do without. Suppose we look elsewhere and place our safety and security on

[31] *Ibid.*, p. 36.
[32] *Hearings on the Trade Agreements Extension Act of 1955*, pp. 1007–1008.
[33] *Ibid.*, pp. 152–153.

minerals located in faraway places where they must be transported to this country by ship . . . —is there not always the threat that these sources will be cut off when we most need them by the excessive operations of enemy submarines? Has this not been our experience? Look at the record.

Perhaps the most all-out case for protectionism and self-sufficiency is to be found in the reports of a Senate subcommittee headed by the most extreme of protectionists, Senator Malone. Malone would depend almost exclusively on Western Hemisphere supplies and through large depletion allowances and trade restrictions make this country self-sufficient in raw materials.[34]

The Tariff in Perspective

Exports in Third Markets. Obviously the way out is not primarily through a rise of imports stimulated by large cuts in tariffs and quotas. We must depend partly upon countries short of dollars capturing our markets abroad and partly on continued loans and grants.

In the longer run it is to be hoped that some progress will be made in squeezing American exporters out of third markets. Some improvement is noted for 1953 and 1954. It should be much easier for Europe to sell in Latin America or Asia than in the United States, where Europe is often at a locational disadvantage and the high selling costs are a great deterrent. Europe's prospects also improve with recovery and less dependence on loans from this country. Hence, though the results have been disappointing, they should improve.[35] It is well to remember also that trade among industrial countries is much less important than between industrial and nonindustrial countries. In 1951 to 1953, trade within and among three industrial groups of countries accounted for but 39 per cent of all exports.[36] Also, in the narrower context of Europe–United States competition it is well to recall the high elasticity of substitution of British for United States exports, as revealed in MacDougall's two excellent articles. In this connection, the distribution of trade is of some importance. The Continental European Payments Union countries sent but 9 per cent of their exports to the United States and Canada (1953), and the United Kingdom only 12 per cent (1952 to 1954). Western Europe could obtain $1 billion by winning 6 per cent of United States export markets *abroad*, but to gain equally through a rise of sales in the

[34] "Accessibility of Strategic and Critical Materials . . . for Our Expanding Economy," *Report of Subcommittee of the Minerals, Materials, and Fuel Economic Subcommittee*, 1954, especially pp. 3–33, 158–170.

[35] Cf. R. Harrod, "Importance of International Payments," *International Monetary Fund Staff Papers*, April, 1953, pp. 21, 26–29.

[36] General Agreement on Tariffs and Trade, *Tentative Estimates of the Composition of International Trade, 1951–1953*, July, 1954.

United States market, 35 to 40 per cent additional sales would be required.

How disappointing the European penetration of third markets at the expense of the United States has been is revealed by Table 23-2. The

Table 23-2. Percentage of Imports from Various Groups of Countries, 1937 and 1950 to 1954†

	1937	1950	1951	1952	1953	1954
Latin American imports from:						
United States and Canada..........	36	61	61	56	54	52
Continental EPU countries..........	34	15	18	20	20	22
United Kingdom...................	13	8	6	7	5	5
Other sterling area imports from:						
United States and Canada..........	14	14	16	17	12	12
Continental EPU countries..........	12	10	15	13	14	15
United Kingdom...................	35	40	34	32	35	35
Rest of world imports from:						
United States and Canada..........	25	28	30	30	30	29
Continental EPU countries..........	23	23	25	23	22	22
United Kingdom...................	8	10	8	8	7	7

† Figures for 1937 and 1952 to 1954 revised, International Monetary Fund, January, 1956.

SOURCE: Adapted from International Monetary Fund, *International Financial Statistics*.

three groups of countries listed account for three-quarters of the world imports, exclusive of trade of Western Europe and the United States and Canada. In the Latin American markets, it will be noted that Western Europe was still way behind its prewar position and had recovered to some extent by 1954, but the United Kingdom had lost additional ground from 1950 on. In the market of other sterling countries (exclusive of United Kingdom dependencies) there was again some improvement for the Continental EPU countries, bringing them above their prewar position, and by 1954 the United Kingdom's share in these markets was again at the 1937 level. Finally, in the markets of the rest of the world (exclusive of dependencies, Latin America, Western Europe, other sterling countries, and the United States and Canada), Continental EPU countries maintained their position relative to 1950 but the United Kingdom lost further. In 1954 and 1955, the nondollar countries seemed to make progress in capturing third markets.

United States Imports. In a later chapter, I comment on the contribution of loans and grants. I assume here that this country can afford to continue foreign aid and thus partially solve the dollar problem. I have no truck with the idea that we are on the verge of bankruptcy and hence cannot afford to continue foreign assistance. Surely rises of gross output of 190 per cent from 1933 to 1953, of *real* per capita disposable income (after taxes) of 99 per cent, of real gross private investment of 1,386 per cent, are not signs of bankruptcy, nor is the 26 per cent of gross national product (GNP) collected as taxes (in the three principal European countries the percentage was 31 to 34 per cent, and per capita incomes are only one-fourth to one-third as large as here), nor is the rise of the national debt a threat, for financing costs have risen by only 2 per cent of the rise of national income in the last twenty years and in 1953 the debt relative to income had fallen by 40 per cent vis-à-vis 1945.[37] In 1955, an additional rise of GNP (real) of about 7 per cent is to be noted after a drop of 3 per cent in 1954.

We turn, then, to the contribution of the United States import market toward a solution of the dollar problem. I do not assume a protectionist policy, but I do assume that tariff cuts will not play a large part.

Imports respond well to rising incomes in this country. Undoubtedly the greatest contribution that can be made to the solution of the dollar problem is continued prosperity here. Even if incomes rise only as rapidly as abroad, the dollar gap would be reduced. For United States imports are very sensitive to income fluctuations. Should incomes rise more rapidly (cf. the large reduction of the gap in 1951 to 1953), then the problem would probably vanish. Thus, from 1948 to 1953–1954 imports of manufactured goods into the United States rose $2,927 million, a rise in stable dollars of 44 per cent. In these same years, Western Europe more than doubled her total exports to the United States; of a gain of $1,100 million, $850 million were in manufactured goods. These figures do not exactly suggest highly restrictionist policies, and they do point to the great importance of American prosperity.[38]

But there are special reasons why, with an increase of income in this country, imports would increase greatly in the future. Thus, the Paley Committee estimated the rise of income in the years 1950 to 1975 at about 100 per cent; that in minerals required, at about 90 per cent. In 1950, the imports of selected crude and semimanufactured materials were estimated at $2.8 billion; by 1975, at $5.5 billion. In 1950, the deficit for materials (consumption minus production) was estimated at $860 million, or 9 per cent of consumption; in 1975, the projected deficit was estimated at $3 billion, or 20 per cent of consumption.[39]

[37] Cf. S. E. Harris, "The Bankruptcy Myth and National Security," *Washington Post and Times Herald*, Mar. 26, 1954.

[38] General Agreement on Tariffs and Trade, "Imports of Manufactured Goods into the United States," *Trade Intelligence Paper* 3, February, 1955, pp. 2–6.

[39] This material especially from the President's Materials Policy Commission, *Resources for Freedom: Foundations for Growth and Security*, vol. 1, 1952, and E. R. Schlesinger, "Long-run Outlook for U.S. Merchandise Imports," *International Monetary Fund Staff Papers*, February, 1954, pp. 387–415.

This growing dependence on foreign sources of materials points to one factor which is likely to narrow if not eliminate the gap. In an excellent article, Dr. Schlesinger deals fully with this problem. In general, he holds that imports of manufactures will rise more than all imports, though it should be noted that this conclusion rests on the assumption that Europe's competitive position will not continue to suffer vis-à-vis that of the United States.[40] (This is a bold assumption.)

Table 23-3. Estimated Percentage Increase from 1950 to 1975 in Value of United States Merchandise Imports, by Groups

	Imports, 1950		Estimated imports, 1975		Estimated percentage increase in value, 1950–1975
	Million 1950 U.S. dollars	Percentage distribution	Million 1920 U.S. dollars	Percentage distribution	
"Paley commodities"......	2,812.9	32	5,512.9	36	96
Other crude and semimanufactured materials.......	2,164.2	25	3,556.5	23	64
Foodstuffs...............	2,649.6	30	4,075.5	26	54
Finished manufactures.....	1,107.6	13	2,215.2	15	100
Total imports..........	8,734.3	100	15,360.1	100	76

In general, Schlesinger concludes that United States imports will rise sufficiently to yield a solution of the dollar problem for most countries. In the next ten years or so, there may still be difficulties because the rise of imports may not be adequate to offset the dollar gap that still prevailed in 1950, and besides, United States imports were at an unusually high level in 1950. (Since Schlesinger wrote, the situation seems to have improved to some extent.)

One of the troublesome aspects of the dollar problem is that gains will not be evenly distributed. For example, the independent sterling countries and the Continental Organization for European Economic Cooperation countries are likely to be confronted with difficulties because they will not benefit adequately from the rise of United States imports.[41]

Exports from these countries are not likely to expand so much as from all nondollar countries—a result associated with the nature of their exports. Hence, Dr. Schlesinger urges appropriate fiscal and monetary policies for Western Europe, increased sales to third markets by these countries, less reliance on imports from dollar countries, and possibly some foreign aid. In general, Dr. Schlesinger concludes, the outside

[40] Schlesinger, *op. cit.*, p. 389.
[41] *Ibid.*

world will be able to maintain its per capita nonmilitary imports from 1950 to 1975, though with some difficulties in the early years. But aside from the countries mentioned above, Latin America may be confronted with some difficulties, because large population rises are anticipated.[42]

In some respects, this survey may be overoptimistic. Western Europe may need not only appropriate monetary and fiscal policies, which are not easily achieved under modern democratic governments, but also a great

Table 23-4. Estimated Percentage Increase from 1950 to 1975 in Value of United States Merchandise Imports from Major Regions

	Imports, 1950, millions of 1950 U.S. dollars	Estimated imports, 1975, millions of 1950 U.S. dollars	Estimated percentage increase, 1950–1975
Sterling area	1,585.6	2,283.0	44
Continental OEEC countries and dependencies	1,170.1	1,966.9	68
Latin American republics	2,862.0	4,953.8	73
Canada	1,954.4	3,809.0	95
Other countries	1,162.2	2,347.4	102
All areas	8,734.3	15,360.1	76

advance in productivity. Furthermore, Schlesinger assumes that the decline in the ratio of United States imports to GNP is stopped. In view of the continued gains of services in national income and processing and fabrication costs relative to import costs, the increased emphasis on self-sufficiency related to the cold war, and the possibility that protectionism may increase, the improvement may not be so great as is assumed. On Schlesinger's assumptions, United States imports would rise by $6.5 billion from 1950 to 1975; on the assumption of a continued decline in the proportion of imports to GNP as from 1929 to 1950, the rise would be only $4 billion.[43] Against this, it should be noted that the pressure to utilize effectively foreign sources of materials (and conserve ours) may result in reductions and elimination of tariffs on raw materials. In some instances (e.g., mercury sold under monopolistic conditions), tariff reform would not greatly affect imports. But the tariffs on raw materials and on processed materials are not based on any consistent logic, and even though many imports are not affected by tariffs, some are.[44] The Paley Committee wisely seeks *"unilateral elimination* of im-

[42] *Ibid.*, p. 399.
[43] *Ibid.*, p. 396.
[44] Cf. *Resources for Freedom*, pp. 77–82, and *Randall Commission Staff Papers*, pp. 219–235.

port duty on any industrial material in either crude or refined form whenever it is determined that the United States is, or is expected to become, substantially dependent on the imports of the material and that such action is in accord with the national interest. . . . "[45]

Travel. But let us return to the shorter-run problem of dollar equilibrium, say, for the next five to ten years. Here also more can be said. For example, a frontal attack on tourism would contribute much toward the solution of the dollar problem. From 1922 to 1929, foreign-travel expenditures accounted for 0.68 per cent of national income; in the thirties, 0.66 per cent; but from 1946 to 1952, only 0.40 per cent (0.42 per cent in 1952). This is a low ratio, especially when allowance is made for the expected rise of rates of such expenditures with rising income.[46]

In 1953, travel accounted for $908 million of outlays, or 0.30 per cent of the national income of that year.[47] In 1929, the corresponding figure was 0.55 per cent and in 1937 to 1939 was 0.48 per cent. Should the proportion of travel outlays to national income return to that of 1929 (and with the much higher incomes of today this is not an optimistic projection), then travel outlays would rise to $1,705 million, or $800 million in excess of the total for 1953. Had these outlays risen from 1929 to 1952 as much as all consumption expenditures or all recreation outlays, the total would have been about $1,330 million, and had they risen as much as user-operated transportation (a gain of $13.2 billion), the rise would have been to $1,595 million.[48]

The difficulty is in part that the geographical distribution of these outlays has changed to the disadvantage of Europe. Here again Europe has suffered a loss in its competitive position, and again the burden on the adjustment process has increased. In 1929, Europe's receipts in United States travel exceeded $200 million, or 42 per cent of the total; in 1937, $100 million, or 28 per cent of the total of $360 million; in 1953, $292 million out of $908 million, or 32 per cent; in 1955, however, $401 million out of $1,095 million, or 36 per cent.[49]

What is the explanation of the disappointing rise of tourist outlays and especially in Europe? (Note improvements in 1954–1955, however.) Undoubtedly, the emergence of air travel and the great expansion in the

[45] *Ibid.*, p. 78; cf. D. D. Humphrey, *American Imports*, p. 37 and chap. 15. Here Humphrey suggests that imports may not rise so much as the Paley Committee estimated, for the Committee did not allow adequately for technical advances.

[46] *Randall Commission Staff Papers*, p. 463.

[47] *Survey of Current Business*, March, 1954, pp. 22–23. These figures differ from those published by the Randall Commission for various reasons. The latter seems to include payments made to American ships and hence not relevant as an import.

[48] Consumption figures from *Survey of Current Business*, July, 1953, and *National Income*, 1951, ed.

[49] Figures from *Survey of Current Business*, March, 1954, and *The United States and the World Economy*, pp. 73–77.

use of the automobile are relevant. They have opened up new areas outside Europe and especially made accessible to many cheap travel to Florida, California, Arizona, and other vacation points. But part of the explanation lies also in the failure of Europe and to some extent other parts of the world to provide the shipping and travel accommodations desired by Americans. Compare the great advances for provision of the requirements of multitudes in Florida and California with those in Europe. Perhaps the explanation in part is that Europe does not want vast tourist migrations. Undoubtedly, the capital investments involved have also been a deterrent. But all in all, a concerted campaign could surely increase travel abroad by $500 million, even at present income levels. In this competitive area, the United States, Canada, and the West Indies have forged far ahead of Europe.

Government Procurement. Now I turn to another area where imports might rise greatly. I have in mind government procurement. The tendency is for the United States to favor domestic producers and sellers. By various legislative acts and administrative practices, the government buys disproportionately from domestic sources.

The *Randall Commission Staff Papers* state:[50]

The "Buy American" Act of 1933 is the statute which applies most widely in this field. This Act provides that United States Government agencies, in procuring supplies for public use at home, must buy them from domestic sources if they are available from such sources, unless the domestic supplier's price is "unreasonable," or unless a domestic purchase would be "inconsistent with the public interest." Under the statute, United States Government agencies generally consider domestic prices as "unreasonable" only when they are 25 percent or more above foreign offers.

The Buy American Act is supplemented by other provisions of law which extend the principle to added fields. Funds loaned by the Public Housing Administration to municipal bodies must be spent by the latter in accordance with the Buy American Act. Borrowers from the Rural Electrification Administration must buy domestic materials with their borrowed funds unless the prices of such materials are "unreasonable." The Merchant Marine Act requires vessels benefiting from Federal construction subsidies to use domestic materials as far as practicable, and vessels benefiting from operating subsidies to use domestic supplies as far as practicable. The Post Office adds to these effects of these provisions by shipping overseas mail in American bottoms, even where this may have the effect of slowing up the movement of mail.

The 1954 Appropriations Act of the Defense Department has pushed Buy American preferences a step further. Under the Act, generally speaking, food and clothing must be bought from domestic sources; and the cotton or wool in clothing so purchased must also be of domestic origin.

[50] Especially pp. 315–320; also cf. *Resources for Freedom*, p. 79, and *ECA-Commerce Mission*, 1949, pp. 214–218.

When the original Buy American Act was introduced in 1933, the impact of the depression lent strong support to this legislation, but at that time Federal government purchases from business averaged about $1 billion as compared with $38 billion in 1953 and under considerably different economic conditions. (For all governments in the United States, the respective figures were $3 billion and $50 billion.) Even a small diversion of purchases from the present distribution could greatly ease the stringency in the dollar market. It is interesting that President Eisenhower, in 1955, related the price differential in favor of American sellers to the unemployment in depressed areas. Sellers in these areas might be preferred to foreign sellers when the price differential was not too great.

In the debate over the tariff, the great export interests have especially been vocal over the needs of free trade. It is not, therefore, to their credit that they have fought for protectionism when the issue of government contracts arose. They want the contracts even though their price bid is much higher than that of a foreign corporation. Thus in 1954 General Electric expressed great displeasure when the government accepted a bid to build generators for the McNary Dam in the Columbia River by a British concern which made a bid of $3,641,000, or 15 per cent below the General Electric bid of $4,293,000. The company's representative pointed out that this country would lose $1,159,000 in taxes (against $422,000 of import duties) and also 1 million hours of work and $2 million in wages. (The taxes lost are not entirely an irrelevant point.)[51] In fact, the allowance for taxes collected from domestic producers and sellers as against taxes collected if purchases are made abroad may justify large purchases in this country which otherwise could not be justified.

In congressional hearings, one congressman said: "Our United States productive units are carrying the burden of this extra armament and this extra purchase program abroad. Competing organizations in Europe are getting our aid, having the Government supply them the plant, and they keep the wages down by running the business by cartels."[52]

In 1955, the President cut the differential in favor of domestic sellers from 25 down to 6 to 10 per cent. A reservation was made, however, which provided depressed areas with a differential greater than 6 to 10 per cent. British bidders were denied contracts on the Chief Joseph Dam even though their successful competitors from Pittsburgh bid 17 per cent more for six generators and 18 per cent more for three transformers.[53]

---

[51] *The New York Times,* Jan. 6, 1954.

[52] *House Foreign Affairs Committee Hearings on H.R. 5710, Mutual Security Act Extension,* 1953, p. 479.

[53] National Committee on Trade Policy, *Trade Talks,* Sept. 16, 1955.

Conclusions

The general position taken in these chapters is that a solution of the dollar problem must stem not only from a rise of imports but also from *relative* losses of third markets by American exporters and by a continuance of loans and aid. Sacrifices should not be *concentrated* on industries vulnerable to foreign competition. This rise of imports, we emphasize, is more likely to be associated with the growth of the national income and the increased needs of raw materials from foreign sources than with a liberalization of trade practices.

This does not mean that liberalization of trade is not on the agenda, but we do stress the fact that practical considerations—such as the costs of adjustment (not offset by compensation), the relation of control by government of imports to other market controls (e.g., agriculture), the level of business activity, the past reductions in tariffs, the relative degree of trade restrictions here and abroad, the relevance of defense needs, the limited area in which tariff reduction is likely to be effective—limit the area of tariff reduction.

Furthermore, the problem is not merely one of tariff reduction, which, despite the denials of many who have fought for the Trade Agreements Program over twenty years and insisted on its gains, has been substantial. Indeed, some attention has been paid to injury done to American industries, and it is unrealistic to assume that no attention should be paid to this aspect of the problem. We agree that the escape clause may be abused, but at least until 1954 it was not abused, and properly limited (e.g., losses rather than failure to share a market's gain should be the criterion), the escape clause can be supported. There is, after all, a question of stimulating imports with minimum damage to domestic industries. But I hasten to add that the 1955 amendments may increase the protectionist effects of the escape and peril-point clauses.

The prospects for a decline in the dollar gap are good, especially if a new major war is not upon us. Particularly fruitful would be a rise of tourist outlays in relation to past proportions of this variable to income and a reduction of protectionism on the $50 billion of current government purchases from business, especially when sales are to growing and strong industries. Attacks along these lines, as well as the increasing needs of imports of raw materials and food, should contribute greatly toward the solution of the dollar problem. In so far as these are inadequate, losses of export markets of United States exporters, with exports greatly inflated in the past, should help solve the problem of dollar equilibrium. There are many reasons why this development has not obtained in recent years, but as both MacDougall and Harrod have shown, there are reasons to expect gains for Western Europe in third markets in the future, and in 1953–1954 there were some signs of improvement here. The failure to penetrate our market is much more the result of imperfections, inclusive of the high price of commodities to consumers as compared with that of the price of the export component, than it is of high-tariff policy in this country.

Especially important is the probable rise of imports of raw materials and food by the United States. According to one estimate, United States imports (in 1950 dollars) are estimated to rise from $8.7 billion in 1950 to $15.4 billion in 1975. According to another estimate, the increase would be $3.3 billion additional if allowance were made for the increase in *real* prices of imports.[54]

Against these potential gains, we should note that there are some trends which tend to cut trade: insecurity and hence emphasis on self-sufficiency; the tendency of services, largely nontraded, to grow more than income; the increased price of the final product relative to the import component (related to the growth of services); and finally the tendency of more and more countries to achieve markets at home large enough to ensure minimum costs—hence lesser gains from trade.

That we do not put excessive weight on the gains from liberalization of trade does not mean that we dispense with that approach completely. It has a place. We do not accept the high-wage or the "high wage when not offset by high productivity" arguments most frequently adduced by the protectionists. We regret that the Randall Commission has accepted this argument in a limited form. The defense argument has an element of strength, but it is important to weigh the costs against the gains of security, as well as the possibilities of alternative sources of supplies, and we must add up the costs of all these programs in terms of reduced income.

In the light of this discussion, we conclude that the various commissions that have reported on international economic policy have overstressed the importance of tariff policy or even trade policy generally; that the TAP can contribute little to the solution of the dollar problem unless its spirit is violated; that the TAP, however defensible in 1934 as an approach to more trade, is not acceptable today when what is required is not a balancing of imports and exports; that these commissions rightly stress other attacks (e.g., more tourism and an attack on buy-American legislation); that they all considerably underestimate what should appropriately be done through relative losses of export markets by the United States and United States aid and loans. Here they have been overimpressed by false theories of bankruptcy. None of these

[54] See *Resources for Freedom: Foundations for Growth and Security*, vol. I, 1952; Schlesinger, *op. cit.*, pp. 387–415; and an unpublished paper by H. G. Aubrey. For some reservations on these statistics, see S. E. Harris, Expansion of Latin American Trade," for the Rio de Janeiro Conference, 1954.

commissions, moreover, has faced up to the problem of the timing of liberalization of trade. Is a large cut now or five small cuts in the next five years the appropriate approach? Nor have they convinced the author that their estimates of the effect of liberalization on imports are even roughly accurate and, if accurate, adequate to solve our problems. Finally, the proposal to simplify tariff administration and correct abuses in classification and valuation is in order, but any resultant rise of imports must be considered as part of a general program for raising imports.

CHAPTER 24

The Contribution of Loans and Grants

In considering the issues raised in this chapter, the reader should recall the discussion in Chapter 19 on economic development. In particular the problems of saving, investments, the relation of these to inflation, controls, and the social culture are relevant.

Loans, Aid, and Offshore Procurement

Obviously the larger are loans and grants by the United States, the less the need for increased United States imports to solve the dollar problem, at least for the present, though one should not leave out of account the problem of considering the distribution of dollar gains by countries or regions against those originating in trade liberalization. In so far as loans are made, the cost of financing will rise from year to year and the time will come when financing costs will exceed new loans or loans plus grants. More on this later. But that time is far off, and should the costs of financing inclusive of repayment exceed new loans in, say, twenty-five years, the outside world and the United States would then have a considerable period of time to achieve the transition from an excess of United States exports to an excess of imports. For the present the impoverished world (especially Asia, Africa, and Latin America) would receive goods net rather than give them net. That would be an advantage.

It is worth mentioning that *total* loans do not have to be repaid, just as the total debt outstanding in this country is not repaid but tends to grow. By this we mean that foreign loans can be serviced: Loans becoming due can be repaid, and new loans made, or old loans extended. What is more, a large part of the profits made are reinvested abroad, and hence, to a considerable degree, the financing of the investment does not involve a transfer problem. Thus from 1946 to 1952, direct investment abroad by the United States was $4,431 million and reinvestment by subsidiaries, $3,810 million. The latter does not technically en-

ter into the balance-of-payments statistics, for the reinvestment by subsidiaries does not involve transfer of capital across national boundaries.
But this is in a sense a capital export and under a special accounting
system may be included (credit = capital yield received or paid and
offset by a debit-item capital export reinvested). For the years 1947 to
1952, earnings on United States investments abroad were $8,988 million
and reinvested earnings (raising no transfer problem), $3,510 million,
or 39 per cent.[1]

For the postwar years, the greatest importance is to be attached to
United States grants. (Figures do not balance in the last three years
largely because of omission of gold losses by the United States.)

Table 24-1. Balance on Goods and Services, Loans and Grants, 1946 to 1955
(In billions of dollars)

	1946–1952*	1953	1954	1955
A. Favorable balance on goods and service account..........................	43.4	4.7	5.0	4.2
B. Covered by				
1. Government loans................	8.9	0.2†	−0.2	
2. Government grants..............	26.9	6.2	4.8	4.1
3. Private short-term capital.........	4.0‡	−1.2	0.6	0.2
4. Private long-term capital..........	7.9	0.2	1.0	0.8
5. Private grants...................	....	0.5	0.5	0.5

* These figures include profits reinvested by foreign branches of United States
enterprises in accordance with Department of Commerce practice, but also included
are reinvestments by subsidiaries ($3.6 billion), not included by Department of
Commerce.

† Errors and omissions of $269 million should be added to short-term capital
inflow.

‡ Includes offset to $4.3 billion residual assumed to be a net short-term capital
inflow (43.4 = 8.9 + 26.9 + 4.0 + 7.9 − 4.3).

sources: United Nations, *The International Flow of Private Capital, 1946 to
1952*, pp. 2–3, and *Survey of Current Business*, March, 1955, pp. 8–9, and March,
1956, p. 6.

The United States government spends large sums of money on military operations abroad. These in a sense may be considered as additional imports, for the effects on the balance of payments are similar
to imports except that competition of United States producers is less
effective for purchases abroad than for imports generally. In a sense,
offshore purchases may be considered as government grants, since the

---

[1] Especially United Nations, *The International Flow of Capital, 1946–1952*, 1954,
pp. 1–9, and *Randall Commission Staff Papers*, pp. 80–81.

supplies and services purchased are made available for use by foreign governments.

Let us consider offshore procurement of military items. The objectives of purchases abroad (with payment in dollars) seem to be to reduce pressure on scarce markets in the United States and to strengthen our strategic position. ("To assure delivery in Europe of military items that will meet military requirements . . . to assure production in Europe of items such as ammunition and spare parts . . . to create a defense production base in Europe to meet minimum requirements."[2]) Another objective is to economize on the costs of military supplies and incidentally to help solve the dollar problem. (Foreign countries thus receive additional dollars.)

Offshore procurement raises many difficult problems. First, there is the complaint of American competitors. So far protests have been surprisingly infrequent; and according to the *Staff Papers,* only the shipbuilding industry has expressed disapproval. Second, there has been the problem of economical purchases. The Randall experts claim that purchases just below American prices point, in view of low labor costs abroad, to excessive pricing, but the House Committee, supporting the Defense Department, notes savings in general. Thus the United States buys a British model jet interceptor at $220,000, a French one at $291,-000, as compared with a comparable United States model, which costs $398,000.[3] Prices above 110 per cent of our prices are not allowed (10 per cent covers freight). Third, problems of parts and maintenance and continuance of programs become rather troublesome. Obsolescence alone may involve outlays of $1 billion yearly and be especially troublesome for foreign purchases. Fourth, the deterioration of economic conditions in the United States would greatly increase the pressure to purchase in this country. Despite all these problems, offshore procurement seems sensible, especially under high-employment conditions here and in the midst of a serious dollar problem. But in 1955 the government defended the program largely as a device for helping friendly countries to move ahead on procurement, with this country giving them a start.[4] Of course, in so far as the program brings inflationary pressures

[2] Report of House Committee on Foreign Affairs, *Mutual Security Act of 1953,* p. 16.

[3] *Ibid.,* p. 18.

[4] House Report on *Mutual Security Act of 1955,* pp. 12–13. The Senate Report of 1955 complains that the government had set up criteria for offshore purchases which brought the program to a virtual standstill. (One criterion was adverse "effect upon the economy of the United States, with special reference to any areas of labor surplus, or upon the industrial mobilization base, which outweigh the strategic and logistic advantages to the United States of procurement abroad.") "The Mutual Security Act of 1955," *Senate Report* 383, Report of the Committee on Foreign Relations, 1955, pp. 14–15.

in Europe and cuts its exports, the contribution toward the solution of the dollar problem is reduced, but the effects in this direction so far have not been serious.[5]

Offshore purchases are, however, only part of total military aid. In 1953, total government grants and credits were $6.4 billion and, in 1954, $4.7 billion; the respective totals for military grants were $2,681 million and $4,371 million, 53 to 68 per cent of the respective totals of all grants and credits.

In its December, 1955, report,[6] the government announced:

Deliveries from the production of foreign countries under offshore procurement contracts increased again last year, rising 25 percent over the 1954 total to comprise one-third of the mutual defense assistance annual transfers of material. The "offshore procurement" program affords an opportunity for a foreign country to earn dollars as well as maintain or increase its military production base. The resulting production is sometimes transferred as a military grant to the military services of the producing country, or is given by the United States Government to a third country.

Most of the offshore procurement contracts were placed in European countries from 1952 through 1954. In 1955 part of the offshore procurement for military grants was paid for with $26-million worth of foreign currencies the Government had acquired from the sale of surplus agricultural commodities.

Despite the rise of offshore procurement, however, the total of net grants and credits was down from $4,767 million in 1954 to $3,958 million in 1955. Military grants continued to decline, representing .56 per cent of net grants and credits in 1955 as compared with 68 per cent in 1954; the total was half the 1953 peak.[7]

---

[5] For criteria for recourse to offshore procurement, see *Randall Commission Staff Papers*, p. 62.

The amounts involved are large. For the fiscal years 1953 and 1954, the estimated procurement (the act of obtaining) is put at $1.5 billion each year. *Contracts placed* amounted to $600 million in fiscal year 1952, $1.6 billion in fiscal year 1953, and slightly more than $1 billion in fiscal year 1954. *Expenditures* (actual disbursements) would be $200 million, $800 million, and $1 billion or more in fiscal years 1953, 1954, and 1955. *Transfers* of materials, however, amounted only to $75 million in calendar year 1952 and $300 million in 1953. It is of some interest that of $2.264 billion of offshore contracts by July 18, 1953, France accounted for $1.075 billion, Italy $383 million, the United Kingdom $479 million. The relatively large totals for France point to the use of offshore procurement as an instrument for helping France solve her dollar problem, for in terms of investment capacity or even when allowing for strategic considerations, it is doubtful that allocations of more than twice as much for France as for the United Kingdom could be justified. *The Mutual Security Program for Fiscal Year 1954, Basic Data Supplied by the Executive Board*, p. 18; *Randall Commission Staff Papers*, pp. 64–65; and *Survey of Current Business*, April, 1954, p. 18.

[6] U.S. Department of Commerce, *Foreign Grants and Credits, December 1955 Quarter*, p. 1.

[7] *Ibid.*

A summary of foreign grants and credits by the United States Government from 1945 to the year 1955 is presented in Table 24-2 for both the period before the Korean invasion and afterward.

The total of grants and credits was $53 billion by December, 1955, or roughly $5 billion per year, in 1954 roughly $4.9 billion, and in 1955 $4.0 billion. Mutual security tended to become increasingly important after the invasion, and particularly military aid—with a downward tendency in 1954–1955. Economic and technical aid, whether included in mutual security or otherwise, became of declining relative importance from 1950 to 1953. In the years 1954 and 1955, a new trend seems to be developing in favor of economic rather than military aid.

In early 1956, the debate on foreign aid continues. The administration asks for somewhat more than $4 billion for fiscal year 1957, which would result in *outlays* at the same rate as fiscal year 1956. Military aid and defense-support aid (i.e., economic aid that makes possible an adequate military budget) still are the major items, but a modest rise in economic aid is also asked.

Actually the 1958 budget reveals that the government would spend $4.1 billion in fiscal year 1957 and wanted $4.4 billion in fiscal year 1958 (*The Budget 1958*, p. M-13). Even as I look over the proofs of this book on March 6, 1957, *The New York Times* gives the major findings of the *Report of the President's Advisory Committee on Foreign Aid*. The Committee recommends continuance of aid at the present level: $3.9 billion for military assistance, $1.7 billion for nonmilitary assistance, and $2.3 billion for expenditures abroad by our military forces and civilian agencies.

Some Details on Exports and Military Exports

I am indebted to Dr. Karl L. Anderson, Deputy Director of the Bureau of Foreign Commerce, and Carl Blackwell of the same bureau for the information in Table 24-3.

A letter from Karl Anderson to the author, January 24, 1954, states:

In your question as to "U.S. exports on military account . . . not entered technically as exports," I presume you refer to overseas transfers of military goods either acquired through offshore purchases or withdrawn from stocks of the U.S. military establishment abroad (not having been recorded as exports at the time of shipment from the U.S. for the account of our own armed forces). While it is true that these transfers are not covered in the basic merchandise export statistics compiled by the Census Bureau, they *are* included in the broader export totals utilized for balance-of-payments purposes.

Unfortunately, no direct record of these transfers is available. The more comprehensive military-aid totals entered in the balance of payments come from statistical sources independent of those on grant-aid military equip-

Table 24-2. Summary of Foreign Grants and Credits—by Program [Postwar
Period, July 1, 1945, through Mar. 31, 1955 (before and after Korean
Invasion, June 25, 1950); Calendar Year Ended Dec. 31, 1954
and 1955]
(In millions of dollars)

	Postwar period			Calendar year	
	Total	After Korean invasion	Before Korean invasion	1954 total	1955 total
Net grants and credits...........................	50,026	23,764	26,262	4,767	3,958
Net grants....................................	39,096	22,121	16,974	4,880	4,059
Gross new grants............................	42,833	23,728	19,105	4,950	4,128
Mutual security............................	29,177	22,106	7,071	4,784	3,862
Military aid:					
Military supplies and services.............	12,343	12,280	63	3,100	2,090
Multilateral-construction-program contribu-					
tions..................................	239	239	......	69	84
Other aid (economic and technical assistance)	16,595	9,586	7,008	1,615	1,689
Civilian supplies...........................	5,822	944	4,878	41	11
UNRRA, post-UNRRA, and interim aid.......	3,443	......	3,443		
Lend-lease.................................	1,906	......	1,906		
Greek-Turkish aid..........................	653	23	629		
Philippine rehabilitation....................	635	116	519	*	
Chinese stabilization........................	120	......	120		
Chinese military aid........................	120	4	116		
Military-equipment loans....................	220	220	......	69	52
Other......................................	739	316	424	56	102
Less prior grants converted into credits..........	2,256	1,000	1,256		
Less reverse grants and returns.................	1,481†	607†	874	70	69
Mutual-security counterpart funds:					
Military aid.............................	34	33	1	8	9
Other aid (economic and technical assistance)	766	433	333	61	61
Reverse lend-lease..........................	133	......	133		
Cash war-account settlements for lend-lease					
and other grants.........................	120	...	120		
Return of lend-lease ships...................	423	136	287	*	
Net credits....................................	10,931	1,643	9,288	−113	−101
New credits..................................	11,957	2,621	9,335	387	401
Export-Import Bank (for own account)........	4,390	1,739	2,651	276	207
Direct loans..............................	4,143	1,645	2,498	185	165
Loans through agent banks.................	248	94	153	91	43
British loan..............................	3,750	......	3,750		
Mutual security...........................	1,769	779	990	94	184
Surplus property (including merchant ships)....	1,487	3	1,484		
Lend-lease (excluding settlement credits).......	71	2	69		
Other......................................	490	99	390	17	10
Plus prior grants converted into credits..........	2,256	1,000	1,256		
Less principal collections......................	3,282	1,979	1,304	501	502

* Less than $500,000.
† Includes $5 million for return of civilian supplies and of military-equipment loans.
SOURCE: *Foreign Grants and Credits by the U.S. Government*, various issues (figures frequently revised).

ment and supplies earmarked as such when shipped from U.S. ports and so recorded by Census. Since the two series differ in timing and probably also in bases of valuation, as well as in substantive coverage, comparisons between them do not yield annual residuals reflecting satisfactorily the substantive difference in which you are interested. You may, nevertheless, find this residual sufficiently suggestive to be useful in connection with your inquiry. The enclosed tabulation, giving the two relevant series and the differences between them since 1947, is extracted from appendix table 4 (lines 28, 29, 30 and 45, 46 and 47) of the "Balance of Payments Supplement" to the *Survey of Current Business,* for the years 1947–1951, and from unpublished worksheets of the office of Business Economics for subsequent periods. To guide your interpretation of these data, I should add to the comments made above a more explicit observation regarding the timing discrepancies—i.e., that the Census record lags appreciably behind the corresponding component of the balance of payments entry.

Table 24-3. United States Government Exports under Military-aid Programs†
(In millions of dollars)

Year	As recorded for balance-of-payments purposes	As reported by Census Bureau in merchandise trade statistics	Difference‡
1947	40	27	13
1948	318	230	88
1949	189	147	42
1950	543	321	222
1951	1,394	1,072	322
1952	2,609	2,101	508
1953:			
First quarter..................	1,274	925	349
Second quarter...............	1,351	1,107	244
Third quarter................	815	910	−95

† Includes Greek-Turkish and Chinese military-aid programs as well as military grant aid under the Mutual Defense Assistance Program.

‡ Represents not only difference in coverage (the excess of first column is transfers of goods acquired through offshore purchase or withdrawn from stocks of United States military establishment abroad) but also discrepancies in timing and probably in valuation; see covering letter.

In the balance of payments of the United States, there are several items of importance related to the cold war. First, there are the military exports, which are financed by the United States taxpayer. Second, there are the military expenditures abroad by the United States military establishment, inclusive of purchases by military personnel. This type of expenditure provides dollars for foreign countries in the same manner as imports by the United States or grants. Third, stockpiling for military purposes is of some importance. Here again, dollars are made available in the same manner as when imports are increased. (It is estimated that through 1953, 80 per cent of stockpiling outlays were made abroad.)

A summary of these items is shown in Table 24-4.

Table 24-4. United States Trade and Items Related to Military Needs,
1950 to 1954
(In millions of dollars)

Year	Merchandise exports [exclusive of (2)]	Military exports*	U.S. merchandise imports	U.S. military expenditure abroad	Annual stockpile purchases abroad†	% (4) + (5) to imports
	(1)	(2)	(3)	(4)	(5)	(6)
1950	10,117	492	9,108	576	363	10.3
1951	14,123	1,388	11,202	1,270	591	16.6
1952	13,319	2,441	10,838	1,957	793	25.2
1953	12,383‡	4,096‡	10,954	2,496	597	28.3
1954	12,671	3,137	10,295	2,533§	?	?

* These figures differ from those in first column of last table probably because they represent revisions of the earlier figures given above.

† Total reduced by 20 per cent to allow for domestic purchases.

‡ Slightly modified in 1953.

§ Cf. the $2 billion estimate of the President's Advisory Committee on Foreign Aid for Fiscal Year 1956.

SOURCE: *Survey of Current Business; Reports of the Secretary of the Treasury on the State of the Finances,* and H. Schiller, *Review of Economics and Statistics,* p. 428.

Two points should be stressed. The first is that by 1953, foreign countries were receiving almost $3 billion from stockpile purchases and United States military expenditures abroad, or 28 per cent of merchandise imports. Presumably the stockpile purchases are included in imports, but the United States military *expenditures* abroad are not. The latter alone was providing $2.5 billion additional in dollars. The second point is that military *exports*, which were equal to 18 per cent of merchandise exports in 1952, 33 per cent in 1953, and 25 per cent in 1954, do not require payments in dollars.

In reply to a letter by the author, Dr. Karl Anderson wrote as follows (letter of May 18, 1954):[8]

U.S. military expenditures abroad, including the personal outlays of personnel stationed overseas, are much too large for omission from the balance of payments, and estimates of the relevant amounts are included (although not

[8] Also see *1951 Balance of Payments Supplement to the Survey of Current Business,* pp. 24, 66–67.

separately identified as such) in the regularly published balance-of-payments statistics. You might find it worthwhile to know that a rough guide to the magnitudes currently (or recently) involved can be gleaned from the routine quarterly statistics on the following basis: (*a*) The bulk of the difference between the item "imports of goods and services: merchandise, adjusted," in the standard balance-of-payments tables presented in the March, June, September, and December issues of the *Survey of Current Business,* on the one hand, and recorded merchandise imports as reported by the Census Bureau, on the other, consists of offshore purchases of goods by the U.S. Government (and mostly by military agencies). (*b*) Other components of the outlays in which you are interested comprise by far the greater part of the balance-of-payments item, "imports of goods and services: miscellaneous services: Government."

Actually, as far as the latest reports are concerned, you do not have to rely on inference from the published figures. Estimates of the relevant amounts for the third and fourth quarters of 1953 were cited in the text of the last quarterly *Survey* article on the balance of payments (March 1954 issue, page 20), which stated that "Military expenditures rose from $685 million in the third quarter [of 1953] to $744 million during the fourth"—i.e., to an annual rate of approximately $3 billion at the end of last year.

Deterrents to Investments Abroad

Why, it may be asked, have private investments abroad in the postwar period averaged but around $1 billion yearly even when $350 million of *reinvestment* of profits by subsidiaries is included? (The last, of course, does not make more dollars available, though the effect may be less pressure to buy dollars.)

Among the deterrents to foreign investment are the following: higher returns on capital at home;[9] the danger of confiscation; the danger of partial confiscation through discriminatory taxation, sales of needed domestic currencies (e.g., pesos) to investors abroad at high prices (few pesos for a dollar), conversion into dollars at high prices (many pesos for a dollar); restrictions on convertibility into dollars of profits and original investment, and forced revision of original contracts; and the obstacles to carrying on without interference, inclusive of demands for sharing ownership and management and providing employment for nationals. All these factors are not additive, e.g., the rate of return reflects unfavorable conversion rates of dollars into local currency and vice versa.

Time and again, studies have been made of the possible means of

[9] According to one estimate, the return on direct investments abroad in 1945, 1946, 1947, and 1948 *after foreign taxes* was 9.2, 12.2, 15.2, and 17.1 per cent and on similar investments at home *after United States taxes,* 7.7, 9.1, 12.0, and 13.8 per cent, a return substantially higher at home when allowance is made for taxes and risks. Also see later figures in this chapter.

increasing the flow of private capital, not only to solve the dollar problem but also to relieve the taxpayers of part of the burden of aid and
to help build up the economies of the underdeveloped nations. Among
the approaches used and suggested are the following:

First, the United States has fashioned treaties with foreign nations
which provide equal treatment for American investors, reciprocal concessions in taxation, and the like. Unfortunately, only limited advances
have been made under such treaties.

Second, the tax incentive has been suggested. The theory behind the
concessions is (1) that income invested abroad be taxed more lightly
than that invested at home, or at least that when taxes are lower abroad
on corporate income, then these corporations should not be taxed in the
United States on the difference between the United States rate and the
foreign rate, and (2) that any increase in foreign investment would
save the government money even if tax receipts were reduced, for in the
absence of additional private investment the government would have
to extend more aid. For example, under the House version of the new
Internal Revenue Code of 1954, corporations receiving certain income
from abroad were to receive tax credits of 14 per cent.[10] All kinds of proposals for tax preferential treatment are under consideration. It has even
been suggested that income from foreign investments be exempt from
taxation, the contention being that the government would lose only part
of the tax relinquished, for deductions are allowed for taxes paid abroad,
and also that there would then be an incentive for foreign countries to
reduce taxes as a means of attracting foreign capital. Aside from the
question of the propriety of exempting all incomes from a particular
source from taxation, the net effect of exempting this income would
be that a new and fruitful field of tax evasion for high-income groups
would be opened. Hence, for the proposal for full exemption, many substitute the suggestion to reduce rates on income from foreign investments.[11]

Among other suggestions for tax relief are the following: equal treatment of branches and subsidiaries, accelerated write-offs, and removal
of country and over-all limits which tend to restrict tax credits allowed
on taxes paid abroad.

A third approach for stimulating foreign investments is the guarantee
by government against certain contingencies upon payment of an insurance fee on investments abroad. So far, this program, which in a re-

[10] There are restrictions on the applicability of these credits, but the code also
provides several other concessions to encourage investment abroad. Ways and
Means Committee, *Internal Revenue Code of 1954*, pp. 73–78. The Finance Committee of the Senate, however, dropped the major concessions.

[11] Organization for European Economic Cooperation, *Private United States Investment in Europe and the Overseas Territories*, 1954, pp. 25–26.

stricted form is actually in operation, has not been a great success. Insurance against outright confiscation has some merit, but how does insurance protect against gradual or concealed confiscations? Furthermore, as the Minority Report of the Randall Committee said, guarantees tend to encourage confiscation: Why not confiscate as long as the United States government or an insurance program sponsored by the United States government will pay the bill? Finally, there is the danger that through a guarantee program, the government would, in fact, take the risks while private investment would obtain the profits.

In general, I am inclined toward the view that the government should consider concessions in taxes which would stimulate private investment, though questions of equity are raised which cannot be dismissed lightly. I am also convinced, as were some of the participants in the Princeton discussion of the *Randall Report,* that the net effect of practical measures in this field upon private investment abroad would not be great.[12]

It is not too clear that much can be done without a change of attitude on the part of both lenders and borrowers and an improvement in international relations. Maffry put forward interesting proposals, namely, that loans be made to domestic corporations that invest abroad and also that Western Europe, which has tended to make much more capital available to underdeveloped countries than the United States (he compares aid to India), should concentrate in this field and the United States, in turn, should lend to Western Europe. Another line of attack is suggested by foreign experience where much more is done to protect the investor against losses on foreign investments.[13]

One other aspect of private investment invites a brief comment. It is often said, and notably in the *Randall Staff Papers,* that investment by government or international agencies tends to discourage private investment, for foreign borrowers, alerted to the possibility of public loans or even grants at favorable terms, discourage loans from private sources. Undoubtedly, foreign borrowers prefer loans from public sources, and to some extent private loans are frowned upon. But it is not merely a preference for public sources per se; private investments are deficient in many respects. Thus, private investments fluctuate excessively and public authorities can introduce an element of stability. Again, public utilities receive most inadequate funds from private sources (in part, no doubt, owing to a careful scrutiny of rates charged), and in general what may be called overhead services, e.g., transportation, health, roads,

[12] *A Critique of the Randall Commission Report,* 1954, p. 45.

[13] A. Maffry, *Program for Increasing Private Investment in Foreign Countries,* 1952 (mimeographed); Organization for European Economic Cooperation, *op. cit.,* chap. 2; and Report of the Citizens Advisory Committee to the Senate Banking and Currency Committee, *Study of the Financial Aspects of the International Bank and of the Export-Import Bank and World Bank,* 1954, table opposite p. 30.

and education, receive little support from private lenders. Hence a need for nonprivate sources. As Nurkse has shown, the British in their period of heavy foreign investments concentrated much more on loans for utilities and other overhead than has this country in recent years.[14] The concentration in the postwar period has been large on exploitation of natural resources, and therefore the association is not between export of private capital and population but rather between the former and the availability of rich natural resources to exploit. Even manufacturing is neglected, though of late this country has shown an increasing interest in this field. It is therefore imperative that if capital is to flow on the basis of needs rather than as at present primarily on the basis of profitability, quick return on capital, and assurance of no serious problems of dollar convertibility, public investments and aid are required. The *Randall Report,* in the author's opinion, greatly underestimates the need of public intervention in this field. The experts of the Export-Import Bank are also fearful of public investments abroad and the effects on private lending.[15] But as Nurkse and Thorpe observe (and cf. Chapter 19), some way must be found to push investments in public utilities, social services, and the like—as the British did in the nineteenth century—if an adequate program is to be had.[16]

Evidence of distortions of United States investments after World War II is given in the following:

Of $14.1 billion of United States government investment abroad, Near Eastern, Asian, and Pacific countries profited from but $1.1 billion. These results may be justified by the great crisis in Europe and the low absorptive capacity of the underdeveloped countries. Even the International Bank for Reconstruction and Development as late as October, 1953, had granted but 13 per cent of its $1.76 billion of loans to Asia and the Middle East, though these areas had more than half the world's population, and by March, 1954, but 20 per cent of all disbursements were in these areas.[17] Again, the explanation is probably the doubts about absorption and capacity to repay. Of United States direct investments, Canada, with about ½ of 1 per cent of the world's population and about 2 per cent of the world's income, accounted for 31 per cent; Latin America, for 40 per cent; and Western Europe, for 15 per cent. This leaves little for Asia and Africa. Finally, from 1946 to 1951, United States direct investments in public utilities declined by 1½ per cent, rose in petroleum by 259 per cent (from $823 million to $2,957 million),

---

[14] See D. H. Robertson, *Britain in the World Economy,* 1954, p. 66.

[15] Report of the Citizens Advisory Committee . . . , *op. cit.,* pp. 9–11.

[16] R. Nurkse, "International Investment Today in the Light of the Nineteenth-century Experience," *Economic Journal,* 1954, pp., 748–755, and W. Thorpe, *Trade, Aid, or What?* 1954, pp. 175–176.

[17] International Monetary Fund, *International Financial Statistics.*

and rose in manufacturing by 91 per cent (from $2,261 million to $4,336 million).[18]

Capital Exports and National Income

The dollar problem would be greatly eased if capital exports from the United States increased by a few billion dollars annually. In so far as the proceeds of these loans were used to purchase commodities outside the United States, the contribution toward the solution of the dollar problem would be greater than if the loans were largely tied to United State exports. In so far as the loans were a source of additional exports from the United States, they would not contribute greatly to the elimination of the dollar gap directly, though the ultimate effects through exports or reduced imports of foreign countries might be favorable. Foreign loans and assistance raise imports of borrowing countries beyond their level in the absence of this financing, but let us note that this is one of the objectives of foreign borrowing.

Over a period of eight years (1946–1953), private capital exports from the United States were only $7.1 billion, or but $37/100$ of 1 per cent of the national income of close to $2 trillion during this period. In 1954 and 1955, capital exports were even less favorable. Had these exports been equal to the 7 per cent of income sent abroad by the British in the years of her great capital exportation, the total amount would have been $136 billion, or nineteen times the actual figure. (Even in the postwar period British private exports of capital are four times, relative to income, those of the United States.) Another estimate covering somewhat different periods and statistics points to a range of ten to fifteen times. Nurkse estimates that the application of the 4 per cent British figure of foreign investment to income (fifty years before World War I) would yield $10 billion for United States foreign investments per year in these eight years; the application of the 7 per cent ratio of 1905 to 1913 would

[18] Figures from *Randall Commission Staff Papers*, p. 86, and United Nations, *The International Flow of Private Capital*, 1954, pp. 46–52.

Useful discussions of the issues covered in this section are to be found in U.S. Department of Commerce, *Factors Limiting U.S. Investment Abroad*, pt. I, 1953; United Nations, *op. cit.*; The Report of the President's Material Policy Commission, *Resources for Freedom*, vol. I, pp. 63–72; *Randall Commission Staff Papers*, chaps. 2 and 3; *Report to the President on Foreign Economic Policy* (Gray Report), pp. 61–72; Commission on Foreign Economic Policy, *Report to the President and Congress*, 1954, especially pp. 16–27; House Committee on Foreign Affairs, *The Mutual Security Act and Overseas Private Investment*, Preliminary Report, June 3, 1953 (this, in turn, discusses the *Report of the President's Material Policy Commission*, the *Maffry*, the *Sawyer*, and the *Bell Reports*); Report to the Director for Mutual Security by the Advisory Committee on Underdeveloped Areas, *Economic Strength for a Free World*, 1953; The Mutual Security Program for Fiscal Year 1954, *Basic Data Supplied by the Executive Branch*, June 5, 1953; House Foreign Affairs Committee, *Mutual Security Act of 1953*; U.S. Department of State, *Point Four*, 1950.

yield a figure of $18 billion, or *about* twenty times the actual invest-ment.[19] Had private capital exports attained even the level relative to income of the twenties (1.4 per cent), they would have averaged $3.5 billion, or four times the actual figure. The drop of three-quarters meas-ures to some extent the deterioration of international economic rela-tions. Even the sum of all unilateral transfers (private and public) and loans (private and public) was only $52 billion in the years 1946 to 1953, or less than 3 per cent of United States national income during this period. It might be held that had exports of capital attained a few per cent of national income, then public grants could have been much smaller. On the basis of *per capita income*, which was surely at least six times as high in the United States in the postwar period as in the United Kingdom in pre-World War I, the United States could be as-sumed to be able to advance an amount in excess of 7 per cent of her income. From these statistics we do not draw the conclusion, however, that United States exports of capital should be running at the rate of $21 billion annually instead of the actual figure of $1 billion to $1½ bil-lion annually *in 1954 and 1955.*

It would be an oversimplification to base estimates of potential ex-ports of capital upon the British prewar experience, first, because the British profited more from exploiting foreign farms and mines with re-sultant cheaper foods and raw materials than this country would likely gain from capital movements on a similar scale, and, second, because exportation of capital at the rate of anything like 7 per cent of United States income would quickly saturate the markets for foreign capital abroad. Even by 1913–1914, the approximate value of long-term foreign investments outstanding of the major creditor countries was but $44 bil-lion ($18 billion for the United Kingdom).[20] Should the United States invest 7 per cent of its income abroad, within three to four years total *new* investments abroad would equal (allowing for price changes) all foreign investments outstanding in 1913.

Foreign investments *in* the United States helped us greatly; yet the amounts involved were not large. It is not long before a saturation point is reached. In 1866, the best available estimates put foreign investments in the United States at $600 million; in 1875, at $1.5 billion; in 1899, at $3.3 billion; in 1914, at $6.8 billion; in 1936, at $6.1 billion; in 1951, at $21.16 billion.[21] (The last, of course, reflected the inflow associated with uncertainties abroad and the faith in the dollar.)

A third reason is that the creditor nations in the pre-World War I

[19] Nurske, *op. cit.*, pp. 744–745.

[20] United Nations, *International Capital Movements during the Inter-war Period,* 1949, p. 2.

[21] U.S. Department of Commerce, *Foreign Investments in the United States,* 1937, pp. 22–23, 28; *Balance of Payments of the United States, 1949–51,* p. 162.

period did not have to contend with the serious transfer problems reflected in the widespread recourse to exchange control by debtors or with the strong nationalization movements and discrimination against foreign nations in debtor countries of recent years. Fourth (and related), the epidemic of defaults in the last generation has frightened the average investor away from foreign investments. Thus, as of December 31, 1946, the debt service on United States loans had been paid in full on $2,255 million of publicly offered dollar bonds, and interest was in default on $2,145 million. From 1920 to 1930, the United States had subscribed to more than $10 billion of foreign bonds (net). By 1930, the net portfolio was $7 billion. Sales of defaulted bonds and regular amortization of nondefaulted bonds had reduced the par value of such bonds held in this country by a few billion dollars.[22]

Fifth, the favorable prospects for investment in the United States which persisted throughout the first decade of the postwar period react against foreign investment. It has been estimated that earnings on capital invested in manufacturing in this country average around 15 per cent. In contrast, note the returns in Table 24-5 on foreign investments for 1952.[23]

Table 24-5. United States Investments Abroad and Income
from Investments, 1952

	Investment, billions of dollars (1)	Income, millions of dollars (2)	% (2) to (1)
Private............	23.1	1,584	6.9
Direct............	14.8	1,419	9.6
Other............	8.3	165	2.0
Government........	14.4	204	1.4

SOURCE: Calculated from *Randall Commission Staff Papers*, pp. 79, 83.

Sixth, the protectionist interests in this country militate against foreign investment, for the financing of foreign investments requires a steady rise of imports in payment for interest, profits, and amortization of past loans. Under the British condition of free trade in the generations before 1914, the required response of import trade did not encounter artificial barriers.

[22] U.S. Senate Committee on Finance, *Foreign Assets and Liabilities of the United States and Its Balance of International Transactions*, 1948, pp. 125–126.
[23] Cf., however, the author's earlier figures and also United Nations, *The International Flow of Private Capital, 1946–52*. The figure for 1950 is given as 15 per cent return on direct investment ($11.8 billion book value and $1.8 billion income after foreign taxes).

Cairncross and Nurkse have emphasized the fact that in the nineteenth century the situation was radically different from that in the years since the Great Depression: The British could gain much in cheaper imports and in larger relative returns of investment incomes and stimulation of their economy; the British exports of capital went primarily to relatively advanced countries and largely to countries with the same general background as the lending country; labor migrated with capital, and hence the whole program was an integrated one, whereas American investments move primarily to combine with cheap labor abroad (labor migration had been substantially cut); and finally the British investments were largely portfolio, appropriate when there was little fear of bankruptcies, national antagonisms, etc., prevalent more recently. (Indeed, Lederer notes that in the peculiar conditions of the post-World War II period there is much to be said for direct investments as a means of stabilizing capital flows.)[24]

More Capital Exports?

We should not conclude from this listing of the more conducive conditions for the exportation of capital in the century before World War I that a case cannot be made for private-capital exports from this country greatly exceeding the annual outflow of less than $1 billion in the postwar period. Even a contribution of 1 per cent of our national income would raise this figure to $3 billion to $4 billion a year in the next ten years. Capital exports at this level might well solve the dollar problem over the next decade. The alternative solutions are a rise of imports and/or a cut in exports. Elsewhere we discuss the difficulties of raising imports by several billion dollars through tariff policy. The maintenance of exports at the level of 1951 to 1956 could be greatly facilitated by a rise of capital exports. Hence, one argument for higher capital exports is that the rise could offer a solution of dollar shortage without cutting exports, with the understanding that over a long period the required transition to a substantial rise of imports to enable foreigners to finance their growing imports would be made.

Another important argument for enlarged capital exports is the need of foreign economic development as a condition for the acquisition by this country of required supplies of raw materials and food supplies. Crude materials and foodstuffs over the last one hundred years have become of increasing importance in our imports. In the future, this country will have to depend increasingly on foreign sources of supply

[24] Nurkse, *op. cit.*, pp. 745–746; A. K. Cairncross, *Home and Foreign Investment, 1870–1913*, pp. 188–191, 225–231; and W. Lederer, "Major Developments Affecting the United States Balance of International Payments," *Review of Economics and Statistics*, May, 1956.

of raw materials and foods. How could it be otherwise with the population rising by one-quarter in the next generation and real national income probably doubling? One of the serious problems of recent years has been the disproportionate rise of industrial output relative to the increase of mineral and agricultural production. In this country industrial production in 1953 was 139 per cent above the 1939 level and 135 per cent above the 1929 level, but mineral production has risen only by 71 and 71 per cent, respectively, and agricultural production, by 54 and 35 per cent, respectively. The world over, the increase in manufactured goods has been much greater than that of agricultural and mineral output. The pressure in the future is to be greater. For example, the President's Materials Policy Commission estimated that whereas in 1900 production of materials other than food and gold exceeded consumption in the country by 15 per cent, in 1950 there was a deficit of 9 per cent and in 1975 one of 20 per cent is expected or $3 billion (against $860 million in 1950). By 1970 to 1980, on the basis of reasonable assumptions, the United States demand for tin will rise by 18 per cent, of copper by 43 per cent, of iron ore by 54 per cent, of rubber by 87 per cent, of petroleum by 109 per cent, and of aluminum by 291 per cent.[25] Where are these resources to come from unless the United States and the United Kingdom (e.g., the Colombo Plan) pump considerable amounts of capital into the agricultural and mineral-producing nations and thus accelerate the development of these resources? In turn, these countries will finance their debts by increasing their exports of food and raw materials. The Paley Committee also suggests the use of the technique of long-term purchasing agreements to encourage exploitation of foreign sources of materials.

Capital Exports and Economic Conditions

These are not the only reasons for supporting a rise of capital exports. Another important consideration is the necessity of sustaining exports as a *stimulus* to the economy. Here I have in mind, in particular, the problem of deficiency of demand. In the thirties, unfortunately, this country imported rather than exported capital, with the result that capital movements were a depressant rather than a stimulus. In the years 1940 to 1955, with the growth of military outlays capital exports as a stimulus to our economy have not been needed except on occasion. In 1948–1949, industrial output declined by 8 per cent, but the drop in gross national product was much smaller. A higher level of capital exports might, however, have precluded a decline of imports of 7 per cent. Possibly the recession of 1953–1954 might also have largely been averted had capital exports been at a level of even $3 billion. Should political conditions become more normal, then deficiencies of demand may well

[25] *Resources for Freedom*, 1952, vol. I, pp. 2, 9.

plague us once more. Production would then decline, with later effects on imports. Under these conditions, a corrective exportation of capital would reduce the fluctuations in these variables. For example, Table 24-6 shows the fluctuation in seven recession periods. (I owe these figures to an unpublished paper of H. K. Zassenhaus, of the International Monetary Fund; also cf. Chapter 23.)

Table 24-6. Percentage Change in Employment, Production, GNP, and Imports, Five Recessions, United States

	1923–1924	1926–1927	1929–1932	1937–1938	1948–1949
Employment.................	.....	.....	−18.3	−4.5	−0.0
GNP (constant prices).......	−1.5	−1.9	−41.5	−6.1	−0.3*
Industrial production........	−6.8	−1.0	−47.3	−21.2	−8.3
Imports:					
Value....................	−4.8	−5.6	−69.9	−34.0	−7.1*
Volume..................	−2.3	+2.0	−40.5	−25.0	−2.4

* A UN group estimated the decline of United States national income and imports from the fourth quarter of 1948 and the second quarter of 1949 at 5 and 15 per cent, respectively. United Nations, *National and International Measures for Full Employment*, 1949, p. 30. (These figures have been adjusted on the basis of H. K. Zassenhaus, "Direct Effects of a United States Recession on Imports and Events," *Review of Economics and Statistics*, August, 1955.)

What is required in order to deal with these cyclical declines (and accompanying fall of imports and hence transmission of depression to other countries) is measures which would increase the funds available to pay for United States exports or other measures which might exclude depressions or contain them. In this connection, we should mention the Keynesian proposal that debtor countries be given drawing rights or a variant suggested by a UN commission that as United States imports decline, this country put dollars at the disposal of foreign countries, *pari passu,* thus enabling them to buy United States goods and at the same time stimulate the American economy with accompanying rise of United States imports.[26]

According to another survey the GNP from the last quarter of 1948 to the last quarter of 1949 declined by 3.2 per cent and by 3.8 per cent from the second quarter of 1953 to the first half of 1954. The drop of industrial production in these same two periods was 9 per cent in each instance, but the decline in the value of imports was only 10 per cent in the later recession as compared with 19½ per cent for the earlier period. The decline of imports of manufactured goods was much greater,

[26] See S. E. Harris (ed.), *The New Economics*, pp. 330–333, and United Nations, *National and International Measures for Full Employment*, pp. 59–61.

amounting to 23½ per cent in 1948–1949 and 20 per cent in 1953–1954. The loss of imports in the second period was concentrated on India and the countries designated "the rest of the world" (countries exclusive of Europe, the Americas, and sterling countries) and, in manufactured goods, on textiles. In the second recession the reduction in imports occurred mainly in primary products, and the industrial countries of Europe gained more in exports to the United States in nonmanufactures than they lost in manufactures.[27]

The capacity of Europe to insulate herself against a depression in the United States in 1953–1954 surprised most experts. There may be some factors at work that may increasingly stabilize international economic relations. Among these may be mentioned the increased importance of government outlays abroad by the most advanced countries which are tied more to political than to economic considerations, and these may increasingly also be countercyclical to ensure minimum economic conditions abroad and hence more political stability, and the increased importance of synthetics as substitutes for products formerly imported by the United States, which means that the foreign product (generally agricultural) is more flexible pricewise than the manufactured competitive item produced in large quantities in this country. Prices of these products are then adjusted abroad in response to a reduction of demand in the United States, and imports are not reduced so much as they otherwise would be. Again, the large American company operating abroad which suffers losses of imports into this country may react or be forced to react by foreign tax policies by bringing less funds back to this country, and thus the instability of sales by foreign countries is offset by saving for the foreign country of transfers of funds to this country.[28]

In this connection, the recent experience of Canada is of some interest. In the postwar period Canadian authorities demonstrated some capacity to neutralize the unstabilizing effects of influxes of capital by raising the price of the United States dollar as capital flowed in, thus making the inflow of capital more expensive, and, second, by paying for the inflow of gold and dollars with government balances, thus reducing the amount of reserves for the money market, or by offsetting inflationary effects of inward capital movements by the increase of government surpluses.[29]

Large capital exports from the United States might be justified, then, on the grounds of self-interest. It should be observed that capital exports

[27] General Agreement on Tariffs and Trade, "Imports of Manufactured Goods by the United States, 1948 to Mid-1954," *Trade Intelligence Paper* 3, 1955.

[28] See especially Lederer, *op. cit.*

[29] R. A. Radford, "Canada's Capital Inflows, 1946–53," *International Monetary Fund Staff Papers*, February, 1955, pp. 252–257.

supported by the need of exploiting foreign resources for our ultimate use would require a long-range program of capital exports, but capital exports as a preventive or cure of deficiency of demand would ordinarily fluctuate with economic conditions. The amount and timing of capital exports required for an ambitious development program would vary from the amounts and timing of a program to deal with depressions. Exports of capital for either or both of these reasons would help solve the dollar problem in the short run and, if wisely planned and administered, would dispose of the problem permanently. But obviously, if treatment of the dollar shortage were the only objective, flows and timing would vary from those required for all these objectives.

Help for Underdeveloped Countries[30]

In the world-wide struggle of ideologies, we find another support for a substantial capital-exporting program. The standard of living is low in the underdeveloped countries. According to the Rockefeller Report of 1951, the average annual income per person in underdeveloped areas was $80, or 5½ per cent of the average in the United States and 17 per cent of that for Western Europe. In Southeast Asia, the average figure was but $30.[31] According to one estimate, it is possible to increase the national income of the underdeveloped areas from $87 billion in 1950 to $372 billion by the year 2000, but the rise of per capita income of 180 per cent would not be nearly so large. Here the assumption is made that the program would be on an adequate scale to lick the population problem. Otherwise the gains would be absorbed in a rising population, with little or no improvement of standards. The analogy is with a rocket to the moon, which must move fast enough to escape the gravitational pull of the earth. This increase of per capita income would result from an industrialization of the underdeveloped areas with the percentage of gainfully employed workers in agriculture being reduced by 20 percentage points from 1950 to 2000 [from 57 to 37 per cent for Southern and Eastern Europe (exclusive of the U.S.S.R.), 73 to 53 per cent for Asia, 70 to 50 for Africa, and 65 to 45 per cent for Latin America]. This may be too optimistic an estimate, because it does not allow for the losses involved in shifting from agriculture to industry when the terms of trade are likely to improve for agriculture. The shift may also be excessive in view of the greater advantages of these countries in agriculture and especially in the face of improved demand. In many instances, there is evidence of uneconomic industrialization, that is, substitution of industry or the wrong kind of industry for agriculture.

[30] Cf. Chap. 19.
[31] *Partners in Progress: A Report to the President by the International Development Advisory Board,* March, 1951, p. 14.

But it is also possible that with these large inflows of capital and techniques a reduction of 27 to 35 per cent in the proportion of labor and agriculture may be consistent with a large rise in agricultural output and excess labor on farms and in mines, which would have to be diverted to other employments.[32]

In order to bring about a large-scale industrialization, improvement of agriculture, and a rise in the per capita national income of 2 per cent per year, or a doubling in thirty-five years, a UN committee has estimated that at least $10 billion annually of capital imports for underdeveloped countries would be required. An earlier and more modest estimate (though at a lower price level) had put the amount of external financing required by underdeveloped countries at but $3.9 billion (for other countries, $4.3 billion). But an estimate of the amounts of foreign capital required to move 20 per cent of the working population from agriculture is about $7 billion annually.[33]

The 1951 estimate of the United Nations group of experts is given in Table 24-7.[34]

The reader will note that the amount of investment required for 1.5 billion people with a national income of $96.6 billion is $19.1 billion, with about 80 per cent going to industry. Of the approximately 20 per cent of the income to be invested, domestic savings account for only $5.2 billion, and even when allowance is made for improvements in savings institutions of underdeveloped countries and a rise of savings with higher incomes, a deficit of $10 billion remains, which must come from abroad. The $19 billion investment program is about one-half of the United States net investment, though this country is highly developed and has but one-tenth the population of the underdeveloped areas.[35]

Undoubtedly, the underdeveloped countries might put $10 billion of foreign investments annually to good use and ultimately even to the advantage of the United States, but the view is widely held that they are not as yet prepared to use several billion dollars of foreign capital effectively. They need mature plans, which, in turn, require a highly competent administration, a large number of technicians, etc. The International Bank has been much impressed by the absence of mature plans.

---

[32] Cf. S. E. Harris, *Foreign Aid and Our Economy*, 1950, pp. 51–56; also Chap. 19 of this book on some reservations concerning industrialization and comparisons of income.

[33] *Ibid.*, pp. 38–41.

[34] United Nations, *Measures for the Economic Development of Under-developed Countries*, p. 76.

[35] On the difficulties of mobilizing domestic savings in underdeveloped countries, see United Nations Economic Commission for Asia and the Far East, *Mobilization of Domestic Capital: Reports and Documents of the Second Working Party of Experts*, 1953.

Table 24-7. Capital Required by Underdeveloped Areas Annually in Industry and Agriculture to Raise Their National Income Per Capita by 2 Per Cent Annually

Area	Population mid-1949, millions	Expected rate of annual population increase 1950–1960, %	National income, 1949, millions of dollars	Net domestic savings, 1949, millions of dollars	Needed for		Total needed, millions of dollars	Deficit [(7) − (4)], millions of dollars
					Industrialization, millions of dollars	Agriculture, millions of dollars		
	(1)	(2)	(3)	(4)	(5)	(6)	(7)	(8)
Latin America..........	158	2.25	24,000	1,990	1,580	960	2,540	550
Africa, excluding Egypt....	178	1.25	13,200	720	1,780	528	2,308	1,588
Middle East, including Egypt..........	94	1.50	9,000	540	940	360	1,300	760
South Central Asia*..........	436	1.50	24,000	1,200	4,360	960	5,320	4,120
Far East, excluding Japan†	661	0.75	26,400	790	6,610	1,056	7,666	6,876
Total..........	1,527	1.25	96,600	5,240	15,270	3,864	19,134	13,894

* Includes India, Pakistan, Ceylon, the Maldive Islands, and the adjacent areas of Nepal and Bhutan.
† Includes Burma, China (including Formosa), Korea, Mongolian People's Republic, Philippines, Thailand, British Borneo, Federation of Malaya, Hong Kong, Indonesia, Indochina, etc.

Before these countries can use billions effectively for an industrialization or development program, they need large outlays for education, for health, for transportation. For this reason, a UN group proposed a grant program of $3 billion yearly to finance the "overhead" of an industrialization program. "We therefore urge most strongly that some mechanism be created for transferring from the developed to the underdeveloped countries, by way of grants-in-aid, a sum of money which should increase rapidly, reaching eventually a level of about $3 billion a year."[36]

Not only lack of trained personnel but the whole pattern of culture may be a deterrent to economic development.[37] An advisory committee to the Director of Mutual Security has put well some of the noneconomic issues:[38]

The limitations on the rate at which a nation or a dependent area can achieve these objectives are set by its existing assets, its customs and institutions, and its underlying values and attitudes.

These limitations may be lifted if there can be obtained from domestic or foreign sources, additional capital investment, more people to contribute to production or greater productivity of existing people, improved technology, favorable changes in customs and institutions, or favorable changes in underlying values and attitudes.

Economic and technical programs cannot be limited to the international transfer of capital and technology, but must lay stress also on changes in customs and institutions and in underlying values and attitudes since such changes are often prerequisite to effective utilization of additional capital or improved technology.

Concern for the customs, institutions, underlying values and attitudes of other peoples must take into account (a) the sensitivity of other peoples about external interference, (b) the difficulty we often experience in making clear to the less developed areas the mutuality of our interests and theirs, and (c) the severe limits on our own understanding of the values and attitudes, customs and institutions most conducive to economic development of the kind serving our mutually agreed objectives.

Although our technical and economic aid programs in Asia and the overseas territories elsewhere must give increasing emphasis to changes in values and institutions, it is essential (a) to move slowly in deciding that particular changes must be brought about, (b) to limit proposals for change to those recognized and supported by competent and responsible persons in the participating country, and (c) not to emphasize American initiative in getting such changes considered and promoted, except where public recognition of American support for particular changes will itself serve overall U.S. objectives.

[36] United Nations, *Measures for the Economic Development of Under-developed Countries*, p. 84.

[37] Cf. *ibid.*, Chap. 3; also cf. Chap. 19 of this book for more extended treatment.

[38] *Economic Strength for the Free World: Principles of a United States Foreign Development Program*, 1953, pp. IV–V.

I do not believe that the underdeveloped countries could absorb even $7 billion of foreign capital annually in the fifties. According to the UN, the annual inflow into the underdeveloped countries in the twenties was not more than $500 million, and the current inflow, inclusive of grants, is nearer $1,000 million than $1,500 million. In view of the attitude of the American people, the attitude of debtor nations to private inflows, the great shortage of "overhead" capital (e.g., for public health and education), the pressures on the capital goods market of exporting nations (possibly relieved as recovery advances in Europe or with cyclical declines), the demands of the cold war on the exporting nations, the deficiencies of trained personnel, the lag in adequate planning—in view of all these, exportation of capital to underdeveloped countries in the 1950s at the rate of even $5 billion (1955 purchasing power) is out of the question.

Table 24-8. Projected Capital Outflow, Totals, Loans, and Grants for Overhead, Private Capital, 1956 to 1970
(Exclusive of military and related grants by United States government)

Year	Total,* billions of dollars	% of national income, United States, Canada, Western Europe	Of which public loans and grants, billions of dollars	Of which private capital, billions of dollars
1956	1.5	0.3	0.5	1.0
1957	2.0	0.4	1.0	1.0
1960	5.0	1.0	3.5	1.5
1970	10.0	1.5	7.0	3.0

* Three-quarters of the total from the United States.

The real issue is how much could be had from the Western nations (and it would have to be had primarily from government) and could be used effectively by these countries. Dependence primarily on private capital is out of the question. Foreign opposition is relevant, as is the unavailability of private capital for this purpose and the difficulty of adjusting private flows to foreign needs. Surely the schedule of capital flows would depend partly on economic conditions and partly on the state of the cold war. The greater the unemployment, the larger the gain for the industrial countries but also the greater the pressures to spend at home rather than abroad. It is not going to be easy to get appropriations from the United States government over and above about $4 billion to $5 billion now being made available largely for military aid. But in Table 24-8 is a schedule which reflects in 1956 attitudes of creditor nations, demands of the cold war, economic conditions, and growth of absorptive powers of the underdeveloped nations.

On this schedule, the average amounts made available would be $3+ billion from 1956 to 1960 and $7.5 billion in the 1960s. Should military tensions subside and the problems of adequacy of demand haunt the Western nations, then the amounts to be raised might be increased (with some flexibility according to cyclical conditions), and should the cold war become hotter, the outlays would have to rise more slowly. It should also be observed that the contribution of foreign countries should rise and, in fact, has been rising in recent years.[39]

In his interesting book, Mr. Myrdal objects to the abuse of foreign aid, especially the confused mixing of loans and grants. He would find ways of increasing the loans and provide for increased contributions by Western nations other than the United States. Myrdal is especially critical of the Western nations for having failed to assume the responsibility for providing the underdeveloped nations with adequate capital. In so far as capital comes in, then it becomes easier to bypass the stagnation phase in underdeveloped areas and introduce the required external economies, and the need for protectionism would be correspondingly reduced.[40]

Problems of Financing

Presumably a large part of the funds made available would be as grants, not loans. However, should the lending governments insist upon loans, either public or private, then it would be important that the rate of interest be kept down and, if amortization is required, that the period of amortization of public loans be extended over a long period. The Advisory Committee of the MSA suggested amortization in fifty to sixty years and delays in repayments for an initial period and rightly pointed out that repayment other than for individual projects was not required.[41] Whatever the appropriate policy for individual loans, the case for overall amortization of loans by any one country is weak. Just as the total debt and capital of this country have grown over long periods of time, so foreign capital and debts might be expected to grow.

Dr. Hinshaw has estimated the amount of new financing required to maintain $1 billion in excess of exports. The effects of higher rates of interest and amortization are evident.[42]

Conditions of loan	New financing required to maintain $1 billion excess of exports
2 per cent loan without amortization	$1.64 billion } in 25 years
2 per cent loan and 20-year amortization	4.41 billion }
8 per cent loan without amortization	46.9 billion in 50 years

[39] See United Nations, *The International Flow of Private Capital, 1946 to 1952*, p. 8
[40] G. Myrdal, *The International Economy*, 1956, chaps. 8 and 19.
[41] *Economic Strength for the Free World*, 1953, p. 31.
[42] S. E. Harris, *Foreign Aid and Our Economy*, p. 44.

On the assumption that $6.8 billion be made available annually in the fifties, $7.6 billion in the years 1960 to 1974, and $8.2 billion in the years 1975 to 1999 and assuming[43] (1) that all the investments shown in the last table were supplied by foreign investment, (2) that amortization at 3 per cent a year of the original amount started ten years after each loan was granted, and (3) that interest was charged at 3 per cent a year from the beginning, the total foreign investment, the amount remaining unpaid, and the cost for debt service as compared with incomes would run as shown in Table 24-9 in 1960, 1975, and 2000. (These fig-

Table 24-9. Estimated Debt Service and National Income, Underdeveloped Regions

Year	Total foreign investment to Jan. 1, billions of dollars	Unpaid balance to Jan. 1		Assumed debt service			National income, billions of dollars	Debt service as per cent of national income
		Total, billions of dollars	Subject to amortization in current year, billions of dollars	Interest on unpaid balance at 3%, billions of dollars	Amortization on amount subject to 3% charge, billions of dollars	Total for year, billions of dollars		
1960	68	68	6	2.04	0.18	2.22	124	1.8
1975	182	146	70	4.38	2.10	6.48	200	3.2
2000	387	213	131	6.39	3.93	10.32	372	2.8

ures are hypothetical and do not suggest foreign investments of these proportions, but they point to the practicability of financing on the assumptions of a large program and substantial growth.)

It is to be observed that even with a 3 per cent rate on loans, amortization over a period of forty-three years for each loan, and relatively large flows of capital abroad, the charge on the income of underdeveloped countries would rise to about 3 per cent and by the year 2000 the balance of imports due the United States would be $2.1 billion ($8.2 billion of new loans and $10.3 billion of debt service). This projection holds on the basis of various assumptions of growth, of relative peace, of wise investment policy, etc., which may not be realized. Should the national income of this country rise to $900 billion by the year 2000, as President Truman estimated (a lower rate of growth than in the past),

[43] *Ibid.*, pp. 40–43.

the excess of imports on account of this vast lending program would be but $\frac{2}{10}$ of 1 per cent of our national income.

Walter Salant wrote as follows:[44]

. . . let us assume that next year we invest five billion dollars abroad at an average return of 4 per cent a year. To avoid developing an import surplus, our net foreign investment would have to increase by 4 per cent a year. It would reach about $35 billion a year by the end of the century. However, if gross national product in money terms increased in the next 50 years at the same rate that Kuznets estimates a real national product rose from the decade of the 1870's to the 1920's, it would reach about 2 trillion dollars in 1948 prices by the end of the century. On that assumption, the $35 billion of net investment would be only 1¾ per cent of the gross national product.

Conclusion

On the basis of British experience or even our experience in the twenties, private-capital exports have been at a very low level in the postwar period. For various reasons, it is not to be expected that the British rate of capital exports would be appropriate for the United States in the fifties or sixties, but a higher rate than the present one is essential, though serious obstacles preclude a large rise in the near future.

The genuine problem is how much will be exported through private loans and through public grants and loans. The last two have played a much larger part than private loans in the postwar period and are likely to continue to be much more important. How much capital will go abroad in the next generation will depend upon the proportions between loans and grants and between public and private loans, as well as the rates of amortization and the level of interest charges, and upon our long-range commercial policy. It will be necessary to depend heavily upon public loans and grants in part because of the hostility of under-developed governments to private loans, in part because of the need for large "overhead" investments in which private capital is not interested, and in part because the appropriate flow can be determined primarily only by public authority. Difficult problems arise in determining the extent to which the flow and conditions should be determined by an international authority rather than by the countries providing the funds.

In view of the attitude of the American people and government, of the problems of need and capacity to absorb capital by underdeveloped nations, and of the pressures associated with the cold war, I suggest as a sort of rough program a capital outflow (exclusive of military grants) which would rise from $1.5 billion in 1956 to $5 billion in 1960 and $10 billion in 1970, or from 0.3 to 1.5 per cent of the income of this country, Canada, and Western Europe from 1956 to 1970. Public funds

[44] *Ibid.*, p. 45.

would account for one-third of the total in 1956, and private capital, two-thirds; by 1970, the respective proportions would be seven-tenths and three-tenths, respectively.

The solution of the dollar-shortage problem (of underdeveloped countries and indirectly of Western Europe through increased sales by Europe to these countries), of the problems of deficiency of demand that may arise in the Western countries in the future, of the important political and economic problems associated with distress in the under-developed countries, of the provisioning of required supplies of raw materials and food for this country—these are the problems to be solved by an adequate lending and grant program. But obviously the amounts and timing of capital flows will have to be integrated to serve the various objectives.

Problems of financing are not to be dismissed too lightly, but much depends on the period of amortization and the rate of interest charged (if any). Furthermore, the increasing part played by direct loans means that the United States corporations operating abroad seek to penetrate the United States market through sales of their products and thus help solve the transfer problem.

In this chapter, I have not discussed some issues reserved for consideration in earlier chapters on balance of payments, economic development, and institutions.[45] There the relevance of marginal propensity to import and consume; the allocation of resources and price movements among export, import-competing, and domestic industries associated with capital movements; the rate at which capital inflow rises or declines; the relation of trade to capital imports—the relevance of these variables for the transfer problems involved in capital imports is considered. Again one will find there a discussion of the reasons for limited help to underdeveloped countries by the International Bank for Reconstruction and Development. Many of the theoretical issues raised for the theory of international trade by economic development are considered elsewhere, e.g., the relevance of comparative costs and employment.

It is scarcely necessary to remind the reader that the foreign-aid program is tied to the dollar program as one approach to its solution but one which must be related to import and export policy. In a sense, increased foreign loans or aid, increased imports, or reduced exports by the United States are alternative solutions, though in detail one attack may achieve results that another fails to achieve. It should not be expected, whatever the global effects on dollar shortage, that each country's dollar account would be equally improved by an equal dollar con-

[45] See Chaps. 8, 18, 19.

tribution by any of the three alternative policies open to the United States.

I should perhaps conclude with a few words of criticism of the American aid program. Perhaps the authorities sometimes went too far in using aid as a means of achieving political objectives, the result then being a reduction of political gains. For example, the attempts to introduce or strengthen the private-enterprise system abroad in countries which were in no position to digest it frequently was harmful. Again, the excessive tying of the programs to the special interests of particular exporting groups, e.g., the farmers, the coal miners, the shipping interests, often aroused hostility and, of course, resulted in a confusion of the extent to which the program was one of helping foreign countries or special interests of this country. (The program of the Export-Import Bank is particularly vulnerable here.) The failure to integrate military and economic aid and the tying of aid to dollar deficits tended to result in malallocation of aid, for incentives to improve the dollar position were dulled. Finally, there has been much waste: " . . . when we draft a soldier, ship him to Europe, and then employ him full or part-time in the most ordinary of housekeeping duties, we are wasting some $5,000 annually in each such case."[46]

Point Four was a program proposed by the President in the early period of the recovery program for Europe. It was an attempt to "aid the efforts of the peoples of economically underdeveloped areas to develop their resources and improve their working and living conditions by encouraging the exchange of technical knowledge and skills and the flow of investment. . . . "

But as the government became increasingly conscious of the widespread desire to economize on aid, the emphasis was put increasingly upon technical assistance and less upon aid. Thus, in June, 1954, the President said: " . . . they should provide experts and know-how rather than large amounts of funds or goods, although they should not be allowed to fail due to lack of necessary teaching and demonstration equipment."[47] Hence in a period of five years only $488 million was appropriated for technical assistance.

[46] See especially W. A. Brown and R. Opie, *American Foreign Assistance*, 1953, especially chap. 21; S. E. Harris, *The European Recovery Program*, 1948, chap. 7 and introductory and concluding remarks; *Study of the Financial Aspects of International Trade and the Export-Import Bank and World Bank*, 1954, pp. 11–13; *Report on European Mission to Senate*, 1955, pp. 26–27, 42–43.

[47] For the evolution of the program see especially Senate Committee on Foreign Relations on *Development of Technical Programs, Background Information and Documents*, 1954.

CHAPTER 25

Exchange Rates and Dollar Shortage

This chapter is largely concerned with the repercussions of depreciation in the thirties and after World War II upon prices, exports, imports, employment and output, reserves and dollar shortage. It includes a brief discussion of multiple rates. In earlier chapters, we discussed the following subjects: the relation of excess issues of currency to exchange rates (Chapters 9 and 11), the relative effectiveness of exchange depreciation and other restrictive weapons on trade (Chapter 17), and the theory of the relation of exchange depreciation to output, prices, and external balance (Chapter 11). In the earlier chapters, the manner of reconciling the objectives of internal and external balance, the choice of restrictive policies among exchange depreciation and other measures, and the relevance of price and income adjustments in the analysis of devaluations also were discussed.

Effectiveness of Flexible Exchanges

In the *Freeman* on December 14, 1953, Professor Milton Friedman, of the University of Chicago, wrote as follows:

Yet its [dollar shortage] fundamental cause and cure are alike simple: the dollar shortage is a result of governmentally controlled and rigid exchange rates; if exchange rates were freed from control and allowed to find their own levels in a free market, as the Canadian dollar now does, the dollar shortage would evaporate overnight. . . .

Friedman is not alone in taking this position. In the years of the Marshall Plan great pressure was put upon European countries to introduce realistic exchange rates, by which was meant a reduced external value for their currencies consistent with an equilibrium in their balance of payments. In fact, the British devaluation of September, 1949, was undertaken in part as a result of pressure from this country. Obviously, if a country could balance its accounts by introducing realistic exchange rates, then foreign aid would not be necessary. The reason for pressing foreign authorities to correct their exchange rates is obvious. In fact, the International Monetary Fund operates on the same principle. The Fund may suggest to countries borrowing from the Fund that a more realistic exchange rate may avert further drains of the Fund's resources.

It is rather interesting that the same claims for exchange flexibility are being made now that used to be made for the gold standard: A loss of gold brings its own correction, it was said, through reductions in costs, in prices (and latterly in incomes), in higher rates and capital flows, in increased exports and reduced imports. But it is generally recognized now that the correctives are not forthcoming under gold. It is the theme of this chapter that even flexible exchange rates will not solve the dollar problem, though, as I contend in the chapter on convertibility, recourse to floating (as against flexible exchanges) would ease the transition to convertibility.

In a book published in 1936 (*Exchange Depreciation*), I contended that exchange flexibility not only was a *sine qua non* for an approach toward international equilibrium for European countries but also was a condition for freedom from the restrictionist monetary policies which were strangling domestic economies.

It is well to distinguish between the use of exchange flexibility in the Great Depression and its use in the postwar period. In the earlier period, there was a great reservoir of unused resources which could be the source of a higher national income. Indeed, exchange depreciation would tend to cut imports and raise exports and thus reduce the supply of goods accruing to the countries indulging in these unorthodox policies. But the argument in *Exchange Depreciation* was that incomes would rise because of the resultant rise of monetary supplies (possible once the requirement of conversion of money into gold at fixed price was abandoned), because of freer fiscal policies, higher prices, and accompanying gain of output. Furthermore, a reduction of imports and a rise of exports would tend to raise prices as would secondary effects of an increase of exports vis-à-vis imports. But with much unemployment, the rise of exports and reduced imports would not mean a corresponding cut in supplies; output would rise.

In the Great Depression, it was also assumed that countries indulging in a policy of exchange depreciation would improve their competitive position because costs and prices at home would not rise so much relative to costs and prices abroad as world currencies would rise in price in terms of their currencies. That this is exactly what happened in the thirties is evident from Table 25-1.[1]

This table shows that even after four years of depreciation the cost of living and wages of eight to eleven countries had adjusted not at all to the reduced external value of the currency and that after three

[1] S. E. Harris, *Exchange Depreciation*, 1936, p. 69.

Table 25-1. Percentage Adjustment to Exchange Depreciation of Wholesale Prices, Wages, Cost of Living, and Import and Export Prices

Index used	No. of countries	Amount of average adjustment up to and including year*			
		I†	II	III	IV
Wholesale prices‡	8	+25	+32	+40	+42
Wholesale prices§	8	+8	+23	+28	+36
Cost of living§	9	−4	+2	0	−1
Wages§	11	+1	+2	−2	−4
Import prices§	11	+68	+50	+56	
Export prices§	11	+60	+37	+37	

* Note that these figures are the quotients of the percentage change in the

$$\frac{\text{Country } X \text{ index}}{\text{French index}} \text{ (of prices, wages, etc.)}$$

divided by the index of *price* of francs, where negative adjustments occur, and divided by the percentage change in the index of the price of gold (francs) in the case of positive adjustments. It is thus possible to allow for all adjustments, whether positive or negative, without giving undue weight to negative adjustments (see text for fuller explanation).

† I is the first year (calendar) of depreciation.

‡ Compared with average of five gold-standard countries.

§ Compared with data for France.

sources: Wage indexes: *International Statistical Yearbook*, 1934–1935, p. 76. Wholesale prices: Bank of England *Statistical Summary*, March, 1935, and October, 1932, and *Statistisches Jahrbuch der Schweiz*. Import and export prices: *Review of World Trade*, 1934. Cost of living: *Wirtschaft und Statistik*, periodically.

years *relative* export prices in countries with depreciation had risen relative to prices in gold countries only 37 per cent as much as the foreign (gold) currencies had risen in price. In other words, exports had become much cheaper for the foreigner and sales much more profitable for the exporters of countries depreciating their currency, for export prices in the domestic currencies of the depreciating countries had risen and costs had responded scarcely at all.

In the postwar period, conditions have been different. With employment high, the major effect of depreciation was likely to be a reduced supply of goods resulting from a contraction of imports and expansion of exports. (Actually with close scrutiny of imports, the effects of depreciation on imports has not been great, for the volume of imports has largely been determined by other considerations. That is to say, restrictive practices, inclusive of exchange control, brought imports down to a level consistent with national policy, and hence the incidence of depreciation on imports was limited.) What is more, at a high level of employment there was the danger that costs (and hence prices) at home would quickly adjust to the foreign value of the currency. Continued gains of trade unionism and a greater awareness of the relation of prices and wages help to explain a quicker response and closer relation of price and wage movements to exchange movements than twenty years ago. With high employment, the offsetting effect (to losses through reduced imports and more exports) of increased supplies, it might be expected, would not weigh nearly so heavily as in the thirties, when output might rise greatly in response to depreciation. As exports rise and imports fall, less goods are available and hence prices tend to rise. As imports cost more in domestic currencies and exports are worth more in domestic currencies, the effects on domestic prices are inflationary, particularly with modern monetary elasticity, the prevalence of budgetary deficits providing part of the base for additional monetary supplies.

The immediate response to depreciation of 1949 was a drop in the dollar price of many British commodities. According to *The New York Times* "sellers of Dunhill pipes announced an immediate reduction of 30% in dollar prices; a large seller of English books, a cut of 10 to 20%; the sellers of the Hillman Minx British car, a drop of 20%; those of higher priced cars, 20% generally; and sellers of other cars, 15% to 20%." But it is well to point out that in the longer pull if the British are confronted with a loss of, say, $3 billion of goods through increased exports and reduced imports following a depreciation (not offset by a rise of output), then through monetary and fiscal policies the British should be induced to cut domestic consumption and investment by a corresponding amount. In so far as this is not achieved, the gains of depreciation are lost.[2]

In short, the gains of devaluation in the postwar period were not likely to be so great as in the thirties. Large unemployed resources and the absence of inflationary pressures point to larger gains in the earlier period. Depreciation was an antidepression as well as a balance-of-payments medicine in the early thirties but only a balance-of-payments tool in recent years—and in an inflationary milieu. I do not, as Harrod says in a provocative article, agree that "in the old days devaluation was regarded as a form of currency debauchery; this was a healthy view of it."[3]

In the post-World War II period there were large inflationary pressures. Exchange depreciation could not adequately treat these, and in

---

[2] S. E. Harris, "Devaluation of the Pound Sterling," *Harvard Business Review*, 1949, pp. 784–785.

[3] R. F. Harrod, "Imbalance of International Payments," *International Monetary Fund Staff Papers*, April, 1953, p. 25.

fact, these tendencies would reduce the advantage of depreciation directed toward an improvement of the competitive position. Again, though any gains of competitive position might balance to some extent losses resulting from structural maladjustments, these gains could not be held to be substitutes for reallocation of factors of production.

The Overvaluation of the Pound Sterling

In this discussion, I shall concentrate largely on the pound sterling, in part because of the interest in the British devaluation, which reduced the value of the pound sterling in September, 1949, from $4.02 to $2.80, or 30 per cent. Other pound-sterling countries followed the pound sterling downward though not all depreciated as much. A great many non-sterling countries also depreciated in 1949–1950, the continental non-sterling countries reacting in various ways: Italy and Switzerland did not depreciate at all, and in the Netherlands depreciation was roughly equal to the British. There were differences among sterling countries: Australian and South African movements were sympathetic with the British, but India's exchange declined only by 10 per cent and New Zealand's by 25 per cent (all in terms of dollars).

By an overvalued currency here, we mean an external value (and especially relative to an earlier period), which suggests that a country's exports have become less competitive, that is, they are more expensive vis-à-vis prices of competitors as compared with an earlier period. It should be noted that the deviation of exchange rates from an equilibrium level may be the result of monetary or real factors. When the deviation is mainly caused by the latter (e.g., loss of markets abroad because of the emergence of new industrial nations), the problem of correcting an overvaluation through changes in exchange rates may become formidable. The resultant loss of exports (and incidentally the rise of imports, since foreign currencies are cheap) accompanying an overvalued exchange brings losses of reserves or the imposition of abnormal restraints on trade (e.g., exchange control and quotas) or may bring even unemployment.[4]

I need scarcely say here that this is a simplified definition of overvaluation. Elsewhere I have noted many of the reservations, and some will be given here as we go along.[5] In fact, if the contention of this chapter —that at *no* value of a currency will there be equilibrium—is correct, then the concept of over- and undervaluation has a special meaning. A lower or a higher rate may reduce the deficit on international account

[4] All figures, unless otherwise noted, are the author's calculations based on statistics in International Monetary Fund, *International Financial Statistics.*

[5] *Exploration in Economics, Notes and Essays, Contributed in Honor of F. W. Taussig,* 1936, pp. 35–36; *Exchange Depreciation,* chap. 2; *The European Recovery Program; Foreign Economic Problems of the United States.*

but will not eliminate it. Surely, at no rate could the franc have brought a balancing of accounts in the early postwar period.

Cost, Price, and Exchanges, 1937 to 1952

First, let us consider the developments from 1937 to 1952 (the "pound" refers to the United Kingdom pound sterling throughout, and the "dollar" to the United States dollar):

a. Exchange Movements and Wholesale Prices. The pound in 1952 purchased (on the basis of the wholesale price index) one-third as much as in 1937.

The dollar purchased one-half as much in 1952 as in 1937.

Hence on the basis of wholesale price movements, the pound in 1952 was worth two-thirds as much as the dollar vis-à-vis 1937.

But the pound purchased 56 per cent as much in dollars as in 1937.

Hence, on this basis the pound was *undervalued* (cheap) in 1952. Against a 67 per cent *relative* value in the command over wholesale commodities, the pound had fallen to 56 per cent of its value in dollars. An American buyer could, therefore, purchase British goods at a bargain: his dollar gained more in purchasing pounds than it lost in value relatively in purchasing British goods. This argument assumes that wholesale prices are a good measure of the prices of export commodities.

b. Exchanges and Wage Rates. But what is the relation of pounds and dollars in the purchase of labor, the most important *cost?*

In labor, pounds = 45 per cent of the 1937 value, and dollars = 37 per cent of the 1937 value.

Hence, in 1952, the pound buys 122 per cent as much in labor relative to the dollar-pound purchasing power of labor in 1937.

However, not only is the pound more valuable in purchasing labor, but the pound is cheaper in dollars. In fact, the dollar purchases 83 per cent more in pounds (the equivalent of a 44 per cent drop in the dollar value of the pound). Hence, with each dollar buying 83 per cent more in pounds and each pound purchasing 22 per cent more in labor (relative to the United States and relative to 1937), the dollar buys 101 per cent more labor in 1952 in the United Kingdom than in 1937—again, relative to the United States–United Kingdom situation in 1937.

Here is a great advantage for the United Kingdom. One can draw the conclusion that the British have achieved a great competitive advantage in keeping their wage rise down and allowing the pound to depreciate in dollars. One might assume that there would be no dollar problem at all under these conditions.

In these fifteen years, British real wages changed very little (wages up to 222 per cent of 1937 and the cost of living 221 per cent). In the United States, the respective figures were 270 and 183, or a rise of real wages of 50 per cent. These differences confirm a tendency of money wages to rise much more than in the United Kingdom, but they also reflect a large rise of productivity in the United States not shared by the British. (In all these calculations, I leave out of account the effects of taxation on "real" wages except in so far as additional taxes are reflected in prices.)

That there still remains a dollar problem must be explained by all or some of the following:

1. A much larger rise in productivity in the United States is an important factor.

2. The wage figures relate to manufacturing, but manufacturing costs are much less than one-half of total costs of the final product, especially when purchased abroad. Hence the gains in reduced relative wage costs in the United Kingdom may be less for *all* wages than for manufacturing. This is aside from the fact that all costs are not labor costs.

3. The comparison may be misleading because of changes in the structure of employment. For example, it is possible that in this country the shift has been largely into more productive industries, and hence the gains of productivity may be even larger than might be suggested by a study of productivity on the basis of the employment pattern of the prewar period.

4. The strain on the British balance of payments related to the destructive effects of war inclusive of run-down plant, loss of invisible income, loss of markets, the heavy incidence of higher raw-material prices, etc., may mean that despite the improved competitive position of the pound sterling vis-à-vis unit costs as measured by wages, the situation is still serious. As a result of these untoward factors, the normal price relationship (here measured on a 1937 base) has been disturbed, and though compared with 1937 wage rates and foreign exchanges the British cost position seems greatly improved, actually a comparison with the reduced cost and price situation reflecting the deteriorated "normal" British position would show a much lower *base* price (and cost) than the 1937 one. Then (on the basis of a lower normal base) British costs would seem higher than in relation to the actual normal base of 1937.

In this connection, we should note that the competitive gain of Great Britain as measured by wholesale prices is much less than as measured by wage and exchange movements. Recall that the pound buys 67 per cent as much goods vis-à-vis the dollar but of dollars only 56 per cent. If the comparison is made of export price movements, the striking result is reached that the United Kingdom gained not at all, for her export prices rose by 244 per cent, whereas United States export prices rose by but 96 per cent. The *relative* drop of the pound in relation to these prices was 43 per cent, exactly equal to that in relation to the dollar. Somehow the large relative gain in command over labor of the pound was not transmitted to one over exports. Again, I must warn the reader that these results are subject to some reservations; for example, the structure of export trade changed to some extent.

The Devaluation of 1949

Second, we examine the price and cost movements of the years 1948 to 1952. (The pound devaluation occurred in September, 1949.) Was it a successful devaluation?

In wholesale prices, the gains of a 30 per cent devaluation had largely disappeared by 1952; prices in the United Kingdom were up by 49 per cent; in the United States, by 7 per cent. Hence the pound purchased relatively only 74 per cent as much as in 1948. With the pound purchasing 70 per cent as much in dollars as in 1948, the cheapening of British goods for purchasers in dollar countries was small indeed.

In export prices, the British position had improved somewhat. These prices had risen by but 31 per cent in the United Kingdom and 2 per cent in the United States. The pound had fallen by but 23 per cent relatively in export commodities and 30 per cent in the cost of dollars.

In costs as measured by wages, there was still a substantial gain. In fact, weekly wages in the United Kingdom had risen but 22 per cent, or half of the 43 per cent rise commensurate with a 30 per cent depreciation of the pound sterling. United States hourly wages had risen even more: by 24 per cent. Hence, Professor Hicks's statement in his admirable essay on the dollar shortage[6] that devaluation had failed because British labor had been unwilling to make the necessary sacrifice is not *wholly* justified. (In the United States real wages had risen by 13 per cent.)

In general, what was the net effect from 1948 to 1952? Depreciation was resorted to in order to improve the balance of payments. By 1949, reserves had fallen to a low figure of £1,752 million, but although they had jumped to £3,443 million in 1950, by 1952 they were down again to £1,958 million. (The rise to £2,798 million by December, 1954, was associated with other factors.) By 1951, an adverse balance of trade, which amounted to £448 million in 1949, had risen to £1,167 million and £756 million in 1951 and 1952, respectively. Even the large rise of reserves in 1950 should not be associated with an improvement in the British trade balance but rather with a return of capital which had fled in anticipation of the depreciation. These figures do not point to any great success for the devaluation, but the results would have been better had not the Korean War raised the prices of imports much more than exports (rises of 48 and 31 per cent, respectively, from 1948 to

[6] J. R. Hicks, "An Inaugural Lecture," *Oxford Economic Papers*, 1953, pp. 117–135.

1952). Devaluation probably contributed toward a rise of exports (volume) of 32 per cent in 1951 and 24 per cent in 1952, both over 1948. British goods were a bargain in these years compared with 1948, though by 1952 there was not a large net reduction relative to prices in the United States. One could also associate the improvement in British export trade with the boom caused by the Korean War, and notably in the United States, where output had risen more than 20 per cent. A striking point is that despite the fact that the dollar now cost 43 per cent more, British imports (in volume) rose to 22 per cent above 1948 in 1951, 12 per cent and 23 per cent above 1948 in 1952 and 1953. The failure of exports to rise more and imports to decline may be associated in part with the fact that sterling countries generally followed the pound downward, though not so much in every instance, and with the fact that other European countries and European dependencies and even some Latin American countries depreciated their exchanges, though to a lesser extent. One reason for the ineffectiveness of the British devaluation was that only 18 per cent of British exports in recent years has gone to the United States, Canada, and Latin America (partly depreciated) and 24 per cent of her import trade came from these countries. The remainder of her export and import trade was primarily with countries that depreciated, though not in every instance as much as the British.

A statistical summary (Table 25-2) points up the developments following the devaluation of September, 1949.

Surely the results have not been along expected lines. The gross

Table 25-2. Relevant Variables, 1949, and Annual Changes, 1949 to 1952, United Kingdom

	1949	1950	1951	1952
Gross national product, millions of pounds	10,926	+589	+1,161	+977
Gross national product, % change........	+7	+6	+10	+8
Real GNP, % change*.................	+4	+3	−2	−1
Excess of imports, millions of pounds.....	448	380	1,167	756
Export prices, % change (annual change)	+2	+4	+18	+5
Import prices, % change (annual change)	+2	+12	+33	−3
Exports, volume (annual change)........	+10	+16	+1	−5
Imports, volume (annual change)........	+9	No change	+12	−8
Cost of living (annual change)...........	+3	+3	+12	+9
Wholesale prices (annual change)........	+5	+14	+22	+2
Wage rates, % change (annual change)...	+2	+2	+9	+8
Monetary reserves, millions of pounds....	−257	+1,691	−1,069	−416

* Adjusted by Cost of Living Index.

SOURCE: International Monetary Fund, *International Financial Statistics.*

national product (real), as might have been expected, did not rise, for the total was roughly equal in 1949 and 1952. Exports did not rise relative to imports so much as might have been expected after a devaluation. Reserves increased only temporarily. That they did not fall drastically may be explained by the return flow of capital following a drastic devaluation.

A devaluation presumably raises the prices of exports at home as the domestic currency equivalent of the reduced foreign prices rises. How much the price rises at home depends on the various elasticities of supply and demand. In general, the more elastic supply and demand at home and the more inelastic supply and demand abroad, the more the world price will fall and hence the less domestic price will rise.[7]

In general, the downward pressure of the depreciation on world prices was not reflected in a substantial decline in world prices. The world-wide rise of income and demand constituted an inflationary force which neutralized those factors that tended to depress world prices of British (or sterling country) commodities following the depreciation as exports responded to a higher price obtainable in the more or less depreciated markets. Indeed, despite full employment there was some elasticity of supply, as is evident in the rise in the volume of exports—in fact, a high elasticity considering the high level of employment. (Elasticity for export markets was raised in a full-employment economy by recourse to subsidies, controls, etc.)[8]

Had the British alone devalued, elasticity of demand would have been higher than it actually was with a widespread recourse to devaluation. In any case, elasticity of demand for British exports would not be high, partly because the British accounted for a substantial part, i.e., 20 per cent of world exports; partly because the concessions in prices were also made by others; and partly because British exports are largely manufactured goods, the f.o.b. (export) prices of which are a relatively small part of the total price. A decline of 30 per cent in a price would not yield the expected response of demand because the gain of the consumer in the price of the finished product may be but 10 per cent. The restricted elasticity of demand undoubtedly contributed toward a depression of world prices, but here the rise of world income was a crucial factor, tending to raise world prices of British goods.[9]

What is especially striking is that import prices rose more than export prices. In the thirties one of the advantages of depreciation was

[7] The author has discussed this fully in his *Exchange Depreciation*, 1936, chap. 4. See also Chap. 11 of this book.

[8] Cf. the analysis by De Vries below.

[9] Cf. the discussion in the chapter on convertibility, where it is suggested that the elasticity of demand for British manufactures is high partly because they face intense competition.

supposed to be that in introducing depreciation, the British were able to force foreign sellers to reduce the world prices of commodities sold to Great Britain and thus prices of imports rose much less than those of export prices. Actually, the average annual rise of import prices in 1950 to 1952 was almost twice as much as that for exports.

Why, it may be asked, in response to a policy of depreciation (with restrictive effects) were the British unable to force foreigners to offer commodities at greatly reduced prices, as they had been in the early thirties? One explanation is undoubtedly that the British market was not nearly so important in 1950 to 1952 as in 1931, in part because the thirties were a period of depression and hence the only large free market was important to sellers, in part because, aside from depression, the British market had become much less important. Another factor of great importance was the outbreak of the Korean War, which greatly contributed to the rise of prices of imports. At any rate, the deterioration in the British terms of trade compounded of the depreciation and the increased pressure on raw-material markets resulting from the Korean War was marked. Yet an important offsetting factor was that unlike the thirties, inflationary pressures were strong, with the result that prices gradually rose in proportion to the increased price of the dollar.

Indeed, the volume of exports rose more than the volume of imports, as might be expected. But as a result of both volume and price changes, there was a net rise in the excess of imports (value) of £615 million in the years 1950 to 1952 (annual average) over 1949, or about one-third the rise of GNP in this period. Against a large rise in the excess of imports (value), we should note the substantial losses reflected in the relative increase in the *volume* of exports.

Intermediate Gains

Of course, the net results of the program of devaluation are not measured merely by the net change from 1948 to 1952. In 1949 and 1950, the United Kingdom gained a large competitive advantage vis-à-vis the dollar countries and others that did not experience a substantial depreciation. Thus in 1950 vis-à-vis 1948 the rise in British wages was but 4 per cent, in wholesale prices 20 per cent, in export prices but 8 per cent; the rise of exports by volume, 27 per cent, and of imports, 9 per cent. (The rises in prices aside from price movements in the United States corresponding to the depreciation should have been 43 per cent.) But against this we should note that United States export prices dropped by 10 per cent. Despite the fact that the adverse balance of *trade* was not affected, British reserves were up by £1,300 million, or 84 per cent.

By 1951, the position had deteriorated. Although British wages were up only by 13 per cent (again relative to 1948), wholesale prices had risen by 46 per cent and export prices by 26 per cent. Reserves dropped substantially, in part because of a large adverse balance for European Payments Union account, undoubtedly chiefly associated with heavy imports of other pound countries as they profited from a spectacular rise of their export prices. In this one year, however, British imports had risen by 20 per cent (pound value) and the volume of imports by 12 per cent, or twelve times as much as the volume of exports.

A Digression on Price Movements

In an interesting study of the problem of devaluation,[10] Mr. de Vries compared expected prices with actual prices. First, he compared (category 1) commodities primarily produced in sterling countries; second, he compared (category 2) commodities produced primarily in dollar countries and sold in relatively interconnected dollar and sterling markets; and third (category 3), he discussed *commodities, principally agricultural, many of which are in short supply in the sterling market, whose sterling prices differ from dollar prices.*

Table 25-3. Estimated Effects of Devaluation on Sterling Prices, Compared with Actual Price Changes, for Five Primary Commodities Supplied by the Sterling Area to the Dollar Area on Net Balance†
(Percentage increases over August, 1949, prices)

| Commodity | Estimated effects | Actual changes, August, 1949, to December, 1949 | | Nondollar area where price is quoted |
		United States	Nondollar area	
Category 1:				
Wool.........	14	18	18	United Kingdom
Tin...........	15	6	5	United Kingdom
Rubber........	21	52	40	Singapore
Cocoa.........	13	65	36	Gold Coast
Tea...........	2	29	19	Ceylon

† For notes and reservations, see original table.
source: B. A. de Vries, "Immediate Effects of Devaluation on Prices of Raw Materials," *International Monetary Fund Staff Papers*, September, 1950, p. 245.

It will be noted that in Table 25-3 the prices of wool rose about as much as was expected but tin substantially less and rubber, cocoa, and tea much more than expected. In Table 25-4, it is clear that prices rose (when comparisons are made) more than anticipated for copper, zinc,

[10] B. A. de Vries, "Immediate Effects of Devaluation on Prices of Raw Materials," *International Monetary Fund Staff Papers*, September, 1950, pp. 238–253.

Table 25-4. Postdevaluation Changes in Sterling Prices of Specified Categories of Commodities†

(Percentage increases over August, 1949, prices)

Commodity	Estimated effects	Actual changes, August, 1949, to January, 1950		Nondollar area where price is quoted
		United States	Nondollar area	
Category 2:				
Copper.........	29	51	43	United Kingdom
Lead..........	31	15	12	United Kingdom
Zinc..........	29	42	39	United Kingdom
Cotton.........	20	49	56	Egypt
Copra.........	...	54	22	Straits Settlements
Petroleum......	...	44	44	Iran
Category 3:				
Cotton.........	...	44	0	India
Cordage fibers..	...	62	31	British East Africa
Coconut oil.....	...	19	0	Ceylon
Sugar..........	...	42	0	United Kingdom
Wheat.........	...	56	35	United Kingdom
Bacon.........	...	27	1	United Kingdom
Butter.........	...	45	0	United Kingdom
Pig iron........	...	45	0	United Kingdom
Nitrate........	...	36	0	United Kingdom
Cocoa.........	...	73	59	Gold Coast
Rice..........	...	41	0	United Kingdom, India, Burma
Coffee.........	...	151	44	United Kingdom

† For notes and reservations, see original table.

SOURCE: B. A. de Vries, "Immediate Effects of Devaluation on Prices of Raw Materials," *International Monetary Fund Staff Papers*, September, 1950, p. 248.

and cotton but less for lead. In category 2, the rise in sterling prices is roughly equal in both sterling and dollar markets. (These are interconnected markets.) In category 3, the rises were substantial as compared with crude expectations (30 per cent devaluation suggests a 43 per cent rise in price), but note that in the nondollar area, the rise was zero or slight in eight out of eleven instances. Here the explanation is that prices were largely controlled by administrative decisions, subsidies, etc., in the United Kingdom and hence would not respond to a devaluation. In all instances, prices are subject to influences other than devaluation, and hence prices diverge from the expected level. For example, the marked relative rise in the price of rubber or copper may reflect the effects of the economic recovery.

A word about expected prices. Obviously, a devaluation of 30 per cent would involve a 43 per cent rise in sterling prices on the assumption that there is no effect on prices expressed in dollars. But it should be observed that other factors, such as changes in supply and demand, unrelated to devaluation will affect both dollar and sterling prices, and there are important reasons for expecting effects on dollar prices.[11]

De Vries's expected prices are suggested by the following:[12]

The question of the effect of devaluation on prices may be put in quantitative terms by asking how much sterling prices may be expected to rise and dollar prices to fall for each commodity. The answer will depend on the extent to which supply and demand in each market respond to the change in price. As the sterling price rises, supply in the sterling market will expand, and as the dollar price falls supply in the dollar market will contract. Similarly, under the assumption that incomes in each market are not much affected by devaluation, the demand in the sterling market will contract as sterling prices rise, and the short-run demand in the dollar market will expand as dollar prices fall. . . .

For many raw materials, the dollar and nondollar markets are not merged but are isolated from each other by obstacles and administrative controls. These hindrances prevent the free flow of goods and permit different prices and price movements in the two markets. Prices of commodities in this category behave differently from those which are formed by free market forces. A distinction should accordingly be made between commodity prices governed by the operation of free market forces in a world market and those in markets isolated from the prices quoted in other markets, either by exchange and import controls or by marketing arrangements including contractual agreements.

The immediate rise to be expected in the sterling price, and the associated fall in the dollar price as a result of the impact of devaluation, may be stated in simple terms for a commodity whose price is determined by economic forces and for which prices in dollar and sterling markets are so related that, costs of movement aside, they are equal at the official rate of exchange. In brief, the rise in sterling price must be such that the expansion of supply plus the contraction of demand in the sterling market induced by the rise in the sterling price is precisely equal to the contraction of supply plus the expansion of demand in the dollar market induced by the associated fall in the dollar price. The price changes in sterling and in dollars (in opposite directions) must equate the induced shifts in the inter-market trade in each commodity. This is the fundamental basis for determining the impact of devaluation on the prices of raw materials whose markets are not isolated.

According to the formula worked out below, the sterling price of a non-isolated commodity will rise more (and the dollar price will fall less), the less the share of the sterling market in total supply and total demand, and the more elastic the supply and demand in the dollar market and the less elastic the supply and demand in the sterling market. The common sense of

[11] Cf. S. E. Harris, *Exchange Depreciation*, 1936, chap. 2.
[12] De Vries, *op. cit.*, pp. 239–240.

this is readily apparent. In the first instance, the impact of sterling devaluation on the dollar price of a commodity cannot be large if the share of the sterling market in the total supply and the total demand is small. Under such conditions, the sterling market will simply follow the dollar market without affecting it very much. Given the share of the sterling market in total supply and total demand, then if a small fall in the dollar price brings a large expansion of demand and a large contraction of supply in the dollar market, the sterling price will be induced to rise considerably to meet the expanded demand and to replace the contracted supply of the dollar market. On the other hand, if the supply and demand are inelastic in the sterling market, supplies will not expand or be released for sale in dollar markets on a scale sufficient to induce a large fall in the dollar price.

Recently Mrs. Hutt, in a study of British export trade, threw further light on the effects of devaluation upon prices of classes of commodities.[13]

Table 25-5. Average Value of United Kingdom Exports to the United States by Commodity Groups, 1948 to 1954

Commodity	1948	Jan.–Aug., 1949	Sept.–Dec., 1949	1950	1951	1952	1953	1954
Foods...............	100	106	83	95	97	97	97	97
Raw materials........	100	72	55	69	93	77	78	74
Metals...............	100	132	100	97	139	176	132	148
Machinery...........	100	84	59	46	58	69	80	57
Vehicles.............	100	120	79	91	110	126	134	125
Textiles and clothing..	100	116	79	80	79	99	88	96
Other...............	100	110	84	83	94	99	87	88
Total*.............	100	107	78	83	94	104	100	99

* Individual groups were combined into a total by giving them the weights appropriate to the whole group even where coverage was limited.

It will be noted that in the last few months of 1949 following the devaluation British export prices declined by 27 per cent. The reduction in prices varied from 22 to 34 per cent for seven categories of exports. Volume of British exports to the United States rose by almost 40 per cent over that of the first eight months of 1949. By 1954, British exports to the United States were up by 61 per cent additional over those of late 1949 (91 per cent by 1955). By 1954, however, a substantial part of the advantage of the devaluation had been lost. British export prices were down only 8 per cent *in re* the predevaluation level, and prices in the United States were up 12 per cent. But whereas the price of textiles and clothing was down by 17 per cent vis-à-vis those of the predevalua-

[13] R. Hutt, "British Exports to the United States, 1948–1955," *Review of Economics and Statistics*, February, 1957.

tion level, the price of metals rose by 12 per cent and of vehicles by 4 per cent, suggesting, in part, variations in competitive position.

Some Conclusions on the 1949 Devaluation

In general, the results of this episode were considerably different from those of the thirties. The upward adjustment of costs and prices to exchange depreciation occurred much more quickly, partly because with a full-employment economy, it was much more difficult to prevent a response to cost and price movements. In one respect, the results were surprising. It might be assumed that with a full-employment economy, it would be difficult to increase exports, for a rise of exports must involve primarily transfers of factors; yet this was not the case. From 1948 to 1951, output rose by 6 to 7 per cent and exports rose by 28 per cent, and from 1949 to 1951 exports rose 17 per cent. (But the rise for exports from 1945 to 1948 had been almost 200 per cent and from 1946 to 1948 close to 40 per cent.) Compare this record from 1948 to 1951 with that of a 10 per cent rise of exports for the United Kingdom from 1931 to 1934, following the 1931 depreciation. The difference is undoubtedly explained by the abnormally low level of British exports in 1948, the prosperity after World War II, the depressed conditions in the thirties, and the effectiveness of special aids (government planning and controls) to the export industries in the years 1948 to 1951. Favorable income conditions abroad after the war counted for more than the expected inelasticity of supply conditions and the inflationary pressures. Undoubtedly, the net effects of the devaluation on the balance of payments could have been greater had not the Korean War raised prices of imports.

In view of the pound devaluation, it might be expected that sterling countries might have captured an increased part of the total world export trade, but this was not the case. The percentage of export trade to the world exports was as shown in Table 25-6.

Table 25-6

Area	1948	1949	1950	1951	1953
Sterling countries................	28	28	28	26	25
Continental EPU countries......	19	22	24	25	26

Thus, whereas sterling countries lost more than 10 per cent of their share of world trade, the Continental EPU countries gained 37 per cent. The relative decline of sterling countries occurred despite the high prices of raw materials and food sold by sterling countries. Aside from competitive gains by EPU countries, the grants of the United States and resultant exports contributed to a decline of the share of sterling countries. The relative gains for the Continental EPU countries, which are not primarily exporters of food and raw materials and which did not benefit from depreciation nearly so much as the sterling countries, suggest an improvement of the continental export position vis-à-vis the United Kingdom, associated in part with Germany's belated recovery.

Trade and Reserves

One other aspect of the trade balance should be noted. The net gains of reserves depend on the balance of *all* sterling countries, not merely on the United Kingdom balance. Table 25-7 shows a concise summary of developments from 1948 to 1953.

Table 25-7. Adverse Balance of Trade and Movements in Reserves,
Sterling Countries, 1938, 1948–1953
(In billions of dollars)

	1938	1948	1949	1950	1951	1952	1953
Excess of imports:							
All sterling countries.................	2.2	3.2	3.6	0.6	3.6	3.2	1.4
a. United Kingdom.................	1.9	1.8	1.7	1.1	3.3	2.1	1.8
b. United Kingdom dependencies.....	0.0	0.2	0.3	−0.6	−0.8	−0.3	0.4
c. Other sterling countries...........	0.3	1.2	1.7	0.2	1.0	1.4	−0.8
Gold and dollar reserves, United Kingdom (change)...............................	...	...	−0.3	+1.6	−0.7	−0.7	−0.7

SOURCE: All figures from *International Financial Statistics.*

This table reveals that in the postwar period the adverse balance of trade of sterling countries had been cut greatly. The average excess of imports was $2.62 billion in the years 1948 to 1953 as against $2.20 billion in 1938. On the basis of price and income changes, one would have expected at least twice as large a deficit in the postwar period as in 1938. This reduction from expected levels reflects undoubtedly the measures taken to moderate the flow of imports.

In 1950, the first large effects of devaluations are noted, with the excess of imports drastically reduced from $3.6 billion to $0.6 billion, with the United Kingdom showing the smallest relative and absolute improvement, other sterling countries cutting the excess down from $1.7 billion to $0.2 billion, and the dependencies converting a deficit of $0.3 billion to a credit of $0.6 billion. The rise of United Kingdom reserves was about one-half the gain of the trade balance for the sterling countries, suggesting some diversion of reserves and losses on other accounts, e.g., foreign aid. Thus, in 1950, credits, grants, and loans to the United Kingdom amounted to $750 million as compared with $1,148 million in 1949.[14]

In 1951 and 1952, there was a rebound, in part the result of the large rise in import prices (related to the Korean War) and in part the result of inflationary pressures which reduced the bounty on exports. The largest *absolute* rise in trade deficits was for the United Kingdom, and the largest relative rise for *other sterling countries*. United Kingdom reserves declined about 30 per cent as much as the increase in the trade deficit. Here, again, a large part of the explanation is that the trade deficit of the sterling countries is not reflected *pari passu* in a decline of United Kingdom reserves; e.g., there are increased debts to the EPU. In fact, the British account with the EPU was a credit of £80 million at the end of 1950, a debit of £166 million at the end of 1951 and of £218 million at the end of 1952.[15] Furthermore, it is well to remember that the increased deficit on trade account may be offset by a rise of credits in other items. (On current account, however, the United Kingdom balance deteriorated more than on trade balance.) In 1952, the trade balance improved somewhat. Reserves fell again. In this period, the British dependencies made a large contribution to balancing of accounts, but not so other sterling countries. In 1953–1954, the British balance improved greatly.

Notes on Prices of Individual Commodities

By scrutinizing dollar prices of international commodities one can visualize the effects of depreciation on individual commodities.

In cotton, the effects are not at all clear. Here, for example, United States authorities tend to meet foreign competition. Thus Egyptian cotton (Ashmouni) was about 40 per cent higher priced than United States cotton in 1949, and in 1951, despite the devaluation, was close to 80 per cent higher; in 1952, about 24 per cent higher.

The price of pulp dropped by 30 per cent in 1950 in Scandinavia (7 per cent in Canada), but the price in Scandinavia had risen from 91 per cent of the Canadian price in 1950 to 155 per cent of the Canadian price. (Scandinavian countries experienced a devaluation.)

Depreciation seemed to have a modest effect on relative prices of wheat. In 1949, Australian wheat was priced 12 per cent in excess of United States wheat; in 1951, United States wheat was 10 per cent higher and in 1952, 1 per cent lower.

[14] H. M. Stationery Office, *United Kingdom Balance of Payments, 1946 to 1953*, pp. 50–51.

[15] *Ibid.*, pp. 56–57.

Despite the pound depreciation, the price of Rhodesian copper rose relative to Canadian copper from 1948 to 1951, only 4 to 5 per cent less.

For cacao, British West African prices remained above Brazilian, but the excess was cut considerably.

By 1950, the price of British coal had fallen by 34 per cent, of United States coal only by 5 per cent, but from 1949 to 1952, the British price declined by 12 per cent and the United States price rose by 5 per cent.

One should not expect movements of these international commodities to be geared closely to exchange movements. For one thing, quality differentials are of some importance. In many of these markets, prices are manipulated by central authority. Thus, if the price of wheat from Australia were to fall by 30 per cent following a devaluation, the United States CCC may release wheat at a world price (in the absence of special agreements) competitive with Australian wheat. Or despite a depreciation, the African cacao cartel may maintain the dollar prices above the level given by the new exchange if the net effect were higher dollar receipts and higher profits.

In manufactured products, the evidence is mixed. For example, the prices of bicycles seemed to reflect the effects of the British devaluation. Thus, the United States importers' average prices to wholesalers for six leading models of British lightweight bicycles declined from $45 on September 30, 1948, to $36.62 on September 30, 1949, $36.40 on September 30, 1950, but the average increased to $38.86 and $40.06 in the next two years. Imports of all bicycles rose from an average of 17,000 in 1947 to 1949 to 68,000 in 1950 and 176,000 in 1951 (1, 3½, and 9 per cent of production in 1949, 1950, and 1951).[16]

In textiles, the response of British exports to devaluation was disappointing. In part, the explanation is that British textile exports are largely to countries which followed the British in the reduction of the value of their currencies. The volume of exports was lower in 1950 than in 1949. In 1950 and 1951, cotton piece goods exports were less than in 1949 and wool piece goods only slightly higher (5 per cent). In rayon, the rise was 25 per cent (average of 1950 and 1951 over 1949). It should be noted, however, that British prices declined substantially vis-à-vis United States export prices from 1949 to 1951. But the difficulty is that despite these gains, British prices for light cotton and rayon fabrics in 1951 still averaged almost 20 per cent above the United States export price in 1951. (For gray, unbleached, the figures were 202, 147, and 159 in 1949, 1950, and 1951, the United States price averaging 100.)[17]

---

[16] U.S. Tariff Commission, "Bicycles and Parts, Report of the Escape Clause Investigation," *Report* 184, 1953, pp. 5–11.

[17] G. Lovasy, "Rise of U.S. Share in World Textile Trade," *International Monetary Fund Staff Papers*, April, 1953, pp. 57–65.

Multiple Exchange Rates

Exchange depreciation has frequently been used in combination with multiple exchange rates as a means of achieving some form of international equilibrium or at least a balancing of accounts. Here the stress is put upon controls as against the market mechanism. Indeed, in the British experience of 1949, controls were part of the arsenal of weapons used, but in some countries the relative dependence on controls has greatly exceeded the British dependence. Where many rates are used, control of the markets is required to ensure that the various rates are applied to the appropriate transactions. This approach is attractive where a currency is overvalued and for various reasons a depreciation is not held advisable; e.g., a fall in the world price of exports would be confronted with an inelastic demand. Furthermore this approach is welcomed when a country seeks to maximize the returns on international transactions, for example, through paying out the minimum currencies for foreign currency received for exports, with inelastic domestic supply and foreign demand, and paying more in domestic currencies for exports, with elastic domestic supply and foreign demand. The result, instead of an across-the-board devaluation, is likely to be a *selective* devaluation, tending to devalue in the markets where it does some good. Furthermore, after the war, when controls became increasingly popular, this system has been used to protect domestic industries by setting high prices for foreign currencies used to purchase competing commodities and also through the relatively high prices paid in domestic currencies for the dollars, etc., received for exports, subsidizing certain exports. The span between the average buying and selling price for foreign currencies gives some indication of the protectionist trends as well as the possibilities of financing government. Thus in Brazil in May, 1955, the average import (selling) rate was 48 cruzeiros per dollar; the average export rate, 38.7 cruzeiros. Note that there is in this differential a discouragement of both exports and imports: importers pay more; exporters get less.

This kind of approach is especially popular in Latin America, and the gains are dependent in part upon the extent to which other countries use the same attack for maximizing receipts from foreign trade. The policies are more likely to succeed in small or medium-sized countries than in large countries. But the United Kingdom provided two rates early in World War II, applying the lower buying rate for foreign currencies received from the exports of such commodities as tin and Scotch, where domestic supply was inelastic and foreign demand inelastic.

Brazil has one of the most complicated and interesting of multiple-exchange-rate systems, and hence I discuss the Brazilian system in some detail. Thus, exporters are required to sell their exchange to the authorities, receiving 18.36 cruzeiros per United States dollar. Exporters of coffee receive a premium of 5 cruzeiros per dollar, and other exporters, 10 cruzeiros. (These are rates as of the early part of 1955.) It is clear that the government pays relatively little for currency received from foreign sales of coffee because of the strong position of coffee in foreign markets. The government groups imports into five categories, though, in fact, there are additional categories. In the five auction categories the potential importer must purchase a certificate, the price determined according to the classification of the import. In addition he pays the official price of 18.82 cruzeiros per dollar and generally an additional tax. In these five classes the certificate rate varied in late March, 1955, from 31 to 34 cruzeiros per dollar in category 1 to 130 in category 5. In category 1 were included such essential products as coal and fertilizers, and in category 4, for example, fresh fruits and office machinery. At present there are numerous *fixed* rates for newsprint, wheat, and petroleum products, the highest rate rising to 169 cruzeiros per dollar for import of premium gasoline.

By introducing an auction system for the five classes of imports, the government arrogated to the nation the windfalls that would otherwise have gone to the fortunate recipients of licenses. The authorities set minimum rates in each category, but the prices of certificates above the minimum are obviously determined by the demand for the imports in each category and the amount of each currency that is made available by the authorities for each category. Rates are kept down by releasing large amounts of the relevant currencies for the purchasers in any particular category. Naturally the authorities tend to release relatively large supplies of foreign currencies for categories 1 and 2, which cover more essential items. By setting fixed rates for some transactions, by determining the amount of exchange to be made available in each auction market, and by classifying commodities and even invisibles, e.g., capital imports, the government subsidizes some employments and hampers others, favors large against small enterprises, stimulates the output and sale of some items, and discourages others. The approach is that of control rather than dependence upon the functioning of the price system. However, once the decisions have been made relative to the fixed rates and/or minimum rates in each category, the classification of commodities, and the allocation of exchange, then the market has a supplementary job to do. As against the free-exchange system or even the limited-adjustment system as provided under Bretton Woods, this system has an appeal where foreign reserves strictly limit activities but where official plans for economic development are rather ambitious given the natural resources and other factors available; under these circumstances the government tends to assume large responsibilities, and therefore, selective depreciation has a stronger appeal than global depreciation.[18]

Summary

On the basis of postwar experience with devaluation, I am not inclined to be overly optimistic that in periods of high employment and inflationary pressures, exchange flexibility is a cure-all. The rise of exports from 1949 to 1953 was much larger than might have been expected in a full-employment economy, but it is not clear that the gains were *primarily* the result of a devaluation rather than the unexpected rise of income abroad. Other factors were also relevant in accounting for an improved balance, e.g., increased food production in Europe and greater restrictions on imports from the United States.[19] A large country like the United Kingdom is not likely to gain too much from devaluation, especially when she is joined by many other countries.[20] Against the resultant expansion of exports (the rise in volume greatly exceeded that in imports) we must put the increased deficit (in dollars) of the trade account. Here the crucial factor was the spectacular rise of prices of food and raw materials. The deterioration of the terms of trade reflected this rise, as well as the small depressive effect in world prices of exports accompanying devaluation.

Unfortunately, as compared with the 1930s, the British were not in a position to force sellers to make large concessions in prices on the British market as a result of the partial shutting of British markets associated with devaluation. But the main difference between the depreciation of the thirties and that of the 1949 to 1953 episode was that in the former the primary objective was an assault on the depression, with all inflationary pressures welcome, but in the later period, the primary objective was dollar balance and inflationary pressures were an obstacle.

The net results of depreciation from 1937 to 1952 or even 1949 to 1952 did not seem to be a gain of competitive power. Against the substantial cheapening of wage costs associated with both wage policy and the depreciation, the British seemed to lose heavily in productivity, in the relative gains involved in shifts to growing industries, and in general in a loss of appeal in world markets. However, the rise in prices of exports of goods and services from 1949 to 1955 was but 27 per cent as against a rise in the price of the dollar of 43 per cent. Hence British

[18] See *International Monetary Statistics*, May, 1955, pp. 58–59, for a description of the Brazilian system, and also see A. Kafka, "The Brazilian Exchange System," *Review of Economics and Statistics*, August, 1956.

[19] W. Thorpe, *Trade, Aid, or What?* 1954, p. 112.

[20] But cf. the interesting article by G. Orcutt, *Review of Economics and Statistics*, February, 1955.

exports had become cheaper, especially in view of the rise of export prices in the United States.[21]

Despite the fact that the excess of imports of sterling countries after the war was much reduced over the prewar period relative to the rise of prices, incomes, and trade, the sterling area continued to suffer from shortages of reserves. In these years and particularly in response to depreciation and to the Korean War, the British dependencies contributed toward a solution of the reserve problem (prices of their exports soared), but other sterling countries and also the United Kingdom tended to drain resources through excessive imports. Had it been possible for the United Kingdom and other sterling countries to expand exports greatly, the effects might have been more favorable. But the elasticity of demand for sterling exports is not high, and it would require a very high elasticity to raise exports to a level sufficient to offset a 30 per cent depreciation and provide a large inflow of dollars.

Harrod is quite right in his claim that even on the assumption of high elasticities of demand for manufactured goods, price concessions induced by devaluations would contribute only in a small way toward closing the dollar gap. He criticized the devaluation program effectively on other grounds also: the unwisdom of using it to close a gap in trade rather than as a mechanism for bringing costs in line with prices (though I suggest these may be related), the impotency of this weapon when the demand for imports of the country imposing it is highly inelastic and therefore results in no concession of dollar prices of imports, the adverse effects on the terms of trade, the difficulties of capturing third markets through devaluation, the bad timing of the devaluation which should have followed treatment of inflation, and the excessive degree of devaluation, which would have required a vast expansion of exports for its success.[22]

[21] H. M. Stationery Office, *The Economic Implications of Full Employment*, Cmd. 9725, 1956, p. 13.

[22] R. F. Harrod, "Imbalance of International Payments," *International Monetary Fund Staff Papers*, April, 1953, pp. 17–18, 24–28, and *The Dollar*, pp. 125–129.

CHAPTER 26

Adequacy of Reserves and the Price of Gold[1]

Introduction

One approach to the dollar shortage is to raise the price of gold. In an essay in the *International Monetary Fund Staff Papers*,[2] Mr. Harrod proposed a rise in the price of gold as a means of solving the problem of the dollar shortage. Estimating the dollar deficit at $2 billion for the average of years 1950–1951 and 1951–1952, he concluded that it is only necessary to raise the price of gold as much as prices of international commodities had risen since the prewar period ($1\frac{1}{3}$ times) in order to provide the required dollars. (As we have seen, the dollar deficit may well be much greater.)

Assuming that gold production were to have risen from 1936–1938 to 1954 about as much as world production and trade generally (about one-third) and that the price of gold were to have risen as much as the prices of international commodities did (representing an increase of $1\frac{1}{4}$ times), then the annual value of output outside the United States and the U.S.S.R. would have risen to $2,550 million and exactly balanced the annual surplus of goods and services exported by the United States of $2,462 million. Then the average balance of long-term capital exports from the United States of $851 million (1950 to 1952) would provide the required rise of reserves for the rest of the world. May I say at the outset that one can raise some objections to this analysis. First, would production have risen by one-third? Second, Mr. Harrod seems to leave out of account various leakages: diversion of gold to hoards and failure of gold countries to share their increased dollars with others, a point suggested by their tendency to increase imports from dollar countries. More on this later.[3]

---

[1] Reserves are also considered in the next chapter.
[2] R. F. Harrod, "Imbalance of International Payments," *International Monetary Fund Staff Papers*, April, 1953, especially pp. 10–12.
[3] Criticisms of Harrod's position arise in part, as we shall see, from the relevance of fiscal, monetary, exchange, and other policies; that is, the reserves required depend on the manner in which these policies are applied. The appropriate amount of

459

A rise in the price of gold has many appeals. In this manner, aid can be given to foreign countries without additional costs to the American taxpayer. Hence budgetary strain is relevant. It will be recalled that Ernest Bevin as Foreign Secretary once proposed that the United States make gold available to Europe as a means of alleviating the strain on the dollar market, hoping that aid not burdening the taxpayer would be welcome here. He had a poor press, however, and his proposal got nowhere.

A game might be played: Periodically the price of gold might be raised, or the excess gold received by this country turned back to the rest of the world. A variant of this program was suggested by a UN committee: A creditor country which, because of depressed conditions, cut its purchases should make foreign exchange (e.g., dollars or gold) available commensurate with its reduction of purchases. This proposal is not unrelated to Keynes's Bancor scheme, which put similar obligations on creditor countries. The effect of all these proposals would be to sustain demand for products of the economy subject to external strains.

Another advantage of a higher price for gold could be that gold would be revalued in this country, and hence (with, say, a 100 per cent rise) the United States government would obtain a windfall of $22 billion. The President's budgetary worries might well then be over for years. But should the government spend these $22 billion, the result would be a rise of bank reserves by more than 100 per cent. Hence it would be important that the inflationary effects of government spending of funds obtained through this windfall should be offset by restrictive operations. For example, the monetary authority might dispose of securities in the Reserve bank accounts and thus deprive the money market of resources. Indeed, the effects on the government security markets would have to be carefully watched. Further action might be through substantial increases in reserve requirements, which would require congressional action. Many would welcome an inflation in the United States as an approach to international equilibrium. Then sales of securities would not be required, for a greater rise of incomes and prices here would increase imports and reduce exports, thus helping to solve the dollar problem. As the expansion of the twenties showed, however, authorities here are not always prepared to subordinate monetary policy at home to the requirements of countries short of dollars.

But to return to the main theme. What is the case for a higher price for gold? First and foremost, dollar shortage could thus be treated. Second, and related, there is not enough gold available in the world.

reserves depends also on the definition of liquid assets, e.g., securities highly liquid in international markets. Cf. B. Goodman, "The Price of Gold and International Liquidity," *The Journal of Finance*, March, 1956, pp. 15–28.

How much gold is there actually in relation to needs? Let us deal with the second question first.

Gold, Prices, and Trade

One measure of the appropriate price for gold is the relation of the price of gold to other prices (Table 26-1).

On the basis of the relative movements of export prices, the price of gold should be raised from $35 to $69, for this relative increase equals that of export prices from 1937 to 1952. On the basis of all international prices, the rise should be to $82, but one might contend that the price of gold had been raised by 67 per cent by 1934 and yet wholesale prices

Table 26-1. Prices of Gold, of World Export Goods, and of
Wholesale Commodities

	1929	1937	1952	1953
Gold, dollars per ounce................	$20.67	$35.00	$35.00	$35.00
Export prices (1950 = 100)............	Not available	59*	116	116
Prices of wholesale commodities, United States (1948 = 100)................	60	54	107	106

* Note that Mr. Harrod's prices of international commodities rise by 1⅓ times (the source or manner of computation is not indicated); my figures here, by less than 100 per cent. But United States import prices rose by 167 per cent, and an average of United States export and import prices yield a figure (rise) of 133 per cent for the period 1937 to 1952.

SOURCE: *International Financial Statistics* and United Nations, *Yearbook of International Trade Statistics*, 1952.

and probably export prices were lower in 1937 than in 1929. Hence, why not relate gold prices to other prices of 1929? Should the relationships of 1929 and 1952 be the guide, then, since wholesale prices rose by 78 per cent, the dollar price of gold would rise from $21 (the 1929 price) to $38, not to $82 as suggested above. Another relevant factor should be noted. From 1928 to 1938, gold output rose by $9.6 billion (at $35 an ounce) but central gold reserves rose by $15.9 billion. In this manner (flow of gold to reserves out of banks and circulation) the reserves had been increased by about one-quarter.[4] Even if we assume that international prices had risen much more than wholesale prices, as suggested by the 1937 to 1952 movement, then the appropriate rise of gold prices for 1929 to 1952 would be from $21 to $43.

On the whole, the case seems stronger for adjustment in the price of gold according to developments from 1929 to 1952 than from 1934 to

[4] Figures before 1938 from Federal Reserve Board, *Monetary and Banking Statistics*, pp. 542ff.

1952, especially since the gold scarcity has been eased as a result of withdrawal of gold from circulation. (More on this later.)

We should note that total gold seemed adequate in 1928, though there were serious problems of maldistribution. In 1938, the supply of gold seemed more than adequate, though, of course, it was adequate in a world of large amounts of unemployment and reduced trade. Thus, from 1928 to 1938, world trade had fallen by $9 billion, or 30 per cent. In this period, wholesale prices had fallen but 10 per cent. *Real* trade had declined, and the large drop in dollars of trade itself reflected a scarcity of gold. At 1952 (or 1956) levels of trade, obviously more reserves would be needed than on the basis of 1938 trade.

A second basis for measuring the adequacy of gold is to compare gold reserves with world trade.

Table 26-2

	1928	1938	1952
1. World imports, billions of dollars................	30.6	21.4	68.9
2. World gold reserves...........................	9.8	25.9	35.5
3. % gold reserves to imports......................	32	121	52
4. % gold and foreign-exchange reserves to imports...	42	129	78

SOURCE: "The Adequacy of Monetary Reserves," *International Monetary Fund Staff Papers*, October, 1953. On the basis of figures in *International Financial Statistics* the figures would be 47 (row 3) and 74 (row 4) for 1953.

At least in relation to trade, reserves are much too low compared with 1938 but they are much larger in relation to 1928. An increase of $1\frac{1}{3}$ times in the price of gold would be required in order to bring reserves back to the 1938 relationship to trade. The shortage is much less on the basis of gold and foreign exchange, but it should be noted that foreign exchange is a claim on gold and really suggests a different distribution of reserves than on the basis of gold exclusively. Thus, the United States has much less relatively of the *world's* gold and foreign exchanges than of gold. It is also of interest that whereas foreign-exchange reserves were 31 per cent of gold reserves in 1928 and but 7 per cent in 1938, they were 50 per cent of gold in 1952.[5] At any rate, it is fair to say that the greater availability of foreign exchange tends to offset to some extent any scarcity of gold. But let me emphasize that both reduced trade and a higher price for gold suggest much higher relative reserves in 1938 than in 1928.

The adequacy of gold or reserves is a much more complicated problem than has so far been suggested. Obviously, a comparison with the

[5] The reader should compare the discussion of adequacy of reserves in the chapter on convertibility.

amount of trade throws some light on the matter, but many problems are involved.

Other Aspects of Adequacy

Are prices falling or rising? On this basis, the downward pressure on prices already evident in the later twenties points either to too little gold or to bad distribution. The corrective in the thirties operated through both an epidemic of devaluations (higher price of gold) and a reduction of prices, trade, and income—increased supply and reduced demands. In the forties, inflationary pressures point to a weakening of the argument for a higher price for gold. We have learned not to be too subservient to the availability of gold.

Are reserves being used effectively? As Keynes observed so well in his *Treatise*, tying up gold in minimum reserve requirements ties up gold unnecessarily. A tendency of some countries to hoard gold excessively embarrasses other countries suffering from maladjustments. The United States has often been charged with failing to use gold imported in the twenties to raise prices and in the thirties with failing to lend more freely. The criticisms in the twenties were overdone, and in the thirties the problem was not so much our failure to lend under chaotic conditions but Europe's refusal to keep liquid assets in Europe.

The adequacy of gold reserves depends also on the use of substitutes for gold (e.g., the use of sterling as a substitute for gold in adjusting balances), on the monetary and fiscal policies of countries (e.g., more gold is needed if countries are not prepared to take protective measures to prevent an inflation or if countries gaining reserves do not seek high-employment objectives), on the availability of commodity substitutes for gold (e.g., greater recourse to stockpiles reduces the need for imports and offers a source of exports as a substitute for gold losses), on the extent of movements in the terms of trade likely to be incurred, on exchange and trade policies (e.g., a greater dependence on exchange flexibility, exchange controls, or other restrictive practices makes it possible to get on with less gold), and on availability of long-term or short-term credits (or the possibility of aggravating movements of short-term capital).[6]

Perhaps we should also consider the change in the distribution of gold. Table 26-3 shows some relevant figures.

This table reveals the fact that the large gains in the reserves accrued to the United States and the large losses to Europe. Large relative gains

---

[6] Cf. the excellent article "The Adequacy of Monetary Reserves," *International Monetary Fund Staff Papers*, October, 1953, especially pp. 182–197.

Table 26-3

Area	% world gold reserves			% foreign exchange to all reserves		% world trade*			
						Exports		Imports	
	Avg 1937–1938	Avg 1950–1952	June, 1954	1937	1952	1937	Avg 1950–1952	1937	Avg 1950–1952
United States..........	54	69	65	...	...⎫	16	19	17	24
Canada...............	1	2	3	10	53⎬				
Latin America..........	3	5	5	18	34	6	10	9	10
Continental EPU.......	24	12	15	10	38	29	28	25	24
United Kingdom........	14	6	7	0	9	17	12	11	10
Other sterling countries..	2	2	2	63	99	9†	10†	10†	9†
Rest of world..........	3	3	2	48	81	17	14	19	12
All.................	100	100	100	8	28				

* Small omissions.
† Exclusive of United Kingdom dependencies = 4, 5, 5, 6.
SOURCE: Calculated from *International Financial Statistics*.

were also registered by Canada and Latin America. Gains of the United States are reduced when allowance is made for the increased importance of trade: Though the United States share of gold rose by more than 20 per cent from 1937–1938 to 1950–1952, the share of United States import trade rose by 41 per cent. Relative losses of reserves for Europe were much larger than the loss of trade. But recall the gains of reserves for Europe in 1953 to 1956.

To understand the relevance of these figures it is necessary to take account also of foreign-exchange reserves—primarily in United States dollars, British pounds, and European Payments Union credits. In 1952, net short-term liabilities of the United States were $7.8 billion, or $6.6 billion in excess of the 1937 figure. Liabilities to banks and to foreign governments amounted to $7.1 billion. The net figures (including other short-term liabilities and deducting short-term assets) would then be $6 billion. Against a rise of $10.5 billion in gold for the United States over the years 1937 to 1952, the short-term obligations to banks and official agencies had risen by $6 billion. From this viewpoint, the United States position seems less strong than from an inspection of gold figures. Thus of all reserves (gold and foreign exchange net), the United States share was 46 per cent in 1937 and in 1953. With United States imports up from 10.4 per cent in 1937 to 14.5 per cent by 1952, the ratio of her share of reserves of gold and foreign exchanges to her share of imports declined by almost 30 per cent.

Major changes of gold and dollar reserves are revealed by Table 26-4. It will be noted that Western Europe and Canada especially gained.[7]

From June, 1945, to June, 1954, the United States increased its supply of gold from $20.3 billion to $22 billion, or $1.7 billion; all others (except U.S.S.R.), from $13.3 billion to $15.1 billion, or $1.8 billion. But from 1948 to 1954, the United States lost $2.4 billion and all others gained $4.6 billion, the United States share dropping from 70 to 59 per cent (roughly its percentage in 1945).

The United Kingdom position is especially disturbing. Not only had her gold reserves declined from 14 to 6 per cent of world reserves,

Table 26-4
(In billions of dollars)

Area	Change, June, 1945, to March, 1948	March, 1948, to June, 1954
All areas.................	−3.7	+8.8
Europe...................	−2.4	+5.8
Latin America............	−0.7	+0.8
Asia and Oceania..........	−0.5	+0.7
Canada..................	−0.8	+1.7
Africa and other..........	−0.4	−0.1

but if short-term liabilities are deducted (with a rise of $5 billion to $6 billion from 1937 to 1952), then the reserves minus net short-term sterling liabilities are a negligible figure for 1937 and short-term liabilities exceeded reserves in 1952 by $8 billion. In 1953 and 1954, however, her gold reserves rose by $1,050 million and her foreign exchange declined by $210 million.[8] Her gold and dollar reserves were roughly equal in the middle of 1954 and of 1955. The net effect, allowing for the growth of exchange reserves, is a reduction of strength for the United Kingdom and the United States. In general, for the other groups of countries the relative gains in all reserves are about the same as in gold reserves. But whereas Continental EPU countries suffered a relative loss of gold reserves from 24 to 12 per cent, their loss of *all* reserves was but 25 to 16 per cent. Reserves of foreign exchanges are much less desirable now than in 1928 and 1938, for with the exception of dollar exchange, there are generally restrictions on use. The vast rise of dollar liabilities to foreign governments and banks stems in part from the free convertibility of dollars into gold.

[7] *Report of the National Advisory Council on International Monetary and Financial Problems*, 1955, pp. 11–13.
[8] The latter is a gross, not a net, figure.

The trends continued into 1956. In the year ending June 30, 1956, total reserves of the world (exclusive of the United States) rose $1.1 billion; those of the United States rose $138 million, but those of the United Kingdom declined by $309 million. For gold the respective figures were gains of $262 million and $138 million and a loss of $300 million.

In one respect the increase of short-term liabilities does not seem so troublesome for the British economy as it might at first appear. Though from 1937 to 1952 pound liabilities were up from $4 billion to $9.6 billion, the trade (imports) of sterling countries was up from $8 billion to $21 billion. Hence it may be assumed that the sterling short-term liabilities are not excessive relative to prewar. In fact, it has been held that present balances are a minimum, but as noted, external short-term liabilities are much larger relative to reserves than before the war.

In 1948, gross liabilities (foreign exchange) amounted to $13.3 billion: $2.9 billion in dollars and $11.5 billion in sterling. By 1952, $5.1 billion were in dollars and $6.5 billion in sterling. The sterling was held primarily by other sterling countries ($4.48 billion), rest of the world ($1.10 billion), and EPU countries ($899 million).[9]

Price of Gold and the Dollar Problem

I now turn to the second problem: the contribution of a higher price for gold to the solution of the dollar problem. Obviously, one effect would be to increase the dollar value of gold reserves. A doubling in the price of gold (end of 1954) would raise the dollar value of gold reserves by about $14.5 billion outside Canada and the United States. (I am discussing a doubling in the price of gold, since proposals have generally been for drastic revaluation, though I believe a more realistic approach would be a rise of about 50 per cent, a figure higher than suggested by the 1928 to 1952 relationship of prices but much lower than that suggested by 1938 to 1952 relations.) Inflationary trends are a relevant factor in suggesting moderation. In this manner, the problem of inadequate reserves, which is part of the dollar-shortage problem, would be largely solved for the time being. Should the rise bring about a large expansion in prices and incomes, then the solution may be only short-lived. But in view of the fact that a return to convertibility in 1954 was held to be hampered by a deficiency of about $3 billion in reserves, it can be seen that a rise of $14.5 billion would be a signal contribution. The gains would be especially important for Western Europe, which has lost reserves relatively to world reserves and relatively to trade.

The major objective of a rise in the price of gold would be to increase annually the dollar earnings of nondollar countries. How much reserves would rise would depend upon the effects on the output of gold, the

[9] "The Adequacy of Monetary Reserves," *International Monetary Fund Staff Papers*, October, 1953, p. 225; $1.1 billion allowance for errors and omissions.

proportion of current gold output used for the accumulation of gold reserves, and also the use made of additional dollars received.

It is not easy to estimate the rise in the output of gold in response to a doubling in the price of gold. One approach is to look backward and see how much the output rose after 1933 with a rise in the price of 67 per cent. From 1933 to 1936, output rose by 32 per cent and from 1933 to 1940, by 64 per cent.[10] Perhaps a 100 per cent rise would have as large an effect as the 67 per cent rise in the thirties. Effects per percentage rise in price would be less now both because, after twenty years of additional mining, less gold is available and because, with full employment, output would respond less to higher prices.

Another approach is to gauge the effects by the *reduction* in output as commodity prices rose by more than 100 per cent and the price of gold remained unchanged. The average output in 1950 to 1952 was one-third less than in 1937 to 1939. We might then assume that if the price of gold were brought into prewar relationship with United States wholesale prices, gold output would rise by 50 per cent (a decline of one-third corresponds to a rise of one-half).

Still another approach is to estimate output response on the basis of an estimated price elasticity for gold production. At present prices, a 10 per cent increase in the price of gold might produce an increase in the output of gold of 4 per cent. (This is based on an estimate of Professor Tinbergen of elasticity of supply of mining products.) Then, as price rises, output would continue to rise but at diminishing returns. At a price of $238 an ounce, the elasticity would be 0.52, and at $270, 0.50.[11]

One should not assume that all gold that is mined is added to gold reserves. The fact is that large amounts go into private hoards, especially in inflationary periods and uncertain times. For example, the comparison in Table 26-5 is of some interest.

According to figures provided by the International Monetary Fund, from 1947 to 1952, gold production was almost $5 billion but central reserves rose by only $1 billion. According to the Federal Reserve Board, private holdings of gold—outside the Soviet Union—rose by $4 billion from 1930 through 1953. In the years 1944 to 1953, private demand absorbed $3.7 billion of gold. Both inflationary pressures and the policy of South Africa begun early in 1949 of selling gold to private interests accounted in large part for the gains of hoards, and a decision of the IMF to liberalize its position on sales of gold tended to reduce private

---

[10] Calculated from Federal Reserve Board, *Banking and Monetary Statistics*, 1943, p. 542.

[11] I owe this to J. L. Enos, as presented in a paper, "The High Price of Gold," for the Haberler-Harris Seminar on International Economic Relations at the Graduate School of Public Administration, Harvard University. This paper has been published. The result of a 100 per cent rise in the price of gold would be an increase in output roughly of 40 to 50 per cent at different price levels.

Table 26-5
(In millions of dollars)

	Gold added to reserves	Gold output
1938	1,150	1,117
1950	350	845
1951	250	827
1952	350	851

SOURCE: *International Financial Statistics.*

sales.[12] Another estimate puts the ratio of additions of gold reserves to new output at one-half in 1946 to 1950, less than one-quarter in 1951 (possibly one-sixth), by 1953 roughly one-half, and by 1954 even higher.[13]

Relevant here is the price paid for gold in free markets. Bar gold converted at free exchange rates averaged $48 to $49 per ounce in four countries in 1948, $43 to $44 for seven countries in 1949, $40 to $41 in 1951, and (nine countries) $36 to $37 in October, 1953. It is clear that after the war the price of gold for a substantial part of sales was much above the $35 official figure.[14] The tendency of the price to decline suggests that the market for gold bars outside the monetary field was beginning to be saturated.

A rise in the price of gold does little good as far as the shortage of dollars is concerned if the resultant inflow of dollars is used to purchase more in dollar countries. In this connection, note that in 1950 through 1952 gold production in Canada and the United States averaged $223 million, or 27 per cent of the world total. Any gains in dollars accruing to the producers of these two countries would not contribute greatly to the solution of the dollar problem. It is also doubtful that the higher price for 7 per cent of gold production of Latin America would help solve the dollar problem, in part because Latin American reserves are adequate[15] and in part because any deficiencies are the result of prices not likely to be treated by a higher price of gold but especially because Latin America imports from the United States primarily and hence the gains of dollars would not accrue to others. (Small gains for

[12] *Federal Reserve Bulletin,* September, 1954.

[13] "Another Chapter in the Story of Gold," *Midland Bank Review,* February, 1955, p. 3.

[14] *Ibid.,* December, 1953, p. 16.

[15] On the basis of past relationships Latin American reserves are adequate, but on the basis of one study reserves would have to equal 90 to 100 per cent of imports in order to stabilize imports over a medium period. Then an addition of reserves of about $3 billion to $4 billion would be required. B. Brodevani, "Latin American Medium-term Import Stabilization Policies and the Adequacy of Reserves," *International Monetary Fund Staff Papers,* February, 1955, pp. 286–287.

other countries would follow in so far as the resultant higher incomes account for larger purchases by these countries from nondollar countries, but Canada's imports in 1952 were 74 per cent from the United States, and 61 per cent of Latin America's were from the United States and Canada.)

The major gold producer is, of course, the Union of South Africa, which accounted for almost half the world's gold production in 1950 to 1952. A higher price for South African gold would undoubtedly stimulate imports from the United States and Canada. In 1952, her imports from these countries were 25 per cent of her total imports. It is probable that of *additional* income, her imports would be an even larger percentage. The major gains of a higher price for gold, in part because sterling countries account for 60 per cent of gold output and in part because sterling countries trade primarily with other sterling countries, would accrue to sterling countries. Thus, South Africa imported 48 per cent of its goods from other sterling countries. All United Kingdom dependencies in 1952 exported and imported 46 per cent of their goods to and from other sterling countries. Other sterling countries exported 55 per cent and imported 52 per cent from other sterling countries,[16] but South Africa has balked at contributing dollars freely to the dollar pool.

In order to assess the rise of gold price required to solve a given dollar deficit, it is necessary to estimate the effects on gold output; the leakage of gold to hoards, reserves, etc.; and the use of gold to increase imports from dollar countries by gold-producing countries and also by other countries which profit from additional sales to gold-producing countries. When an estimate is made, it is found that very large rises in the price of gold are required and vast purchases by the United States, for which this country must in return give goods and services. For the major gold-producing countries the net result would be a great subsidy, a tremendous boom, and vast profits for gold-mining companies.[17]

In summary, what is or what is not an adequate reserve is a complicated problem, depending on many factors such as willingness to use monetary and fiscal policy to control inflation and deflation, the place of controls of foreign payments, the availability of substitutes for gold reserves, etc.

One way of increasing reserves is to raise the price of gold. But what is the appropriate increase? A comparison may be made with the rise in prices of international commodities, or the criterion may be the relation of present gold reserves to world import trade. In relation both to move-

[16] Figures from *International Financial Statistics.*
[17] Cf. J. L. Enos in *Public Administration Volume,* 1955.

ments of international prices and to world trade since the prewar period, an increase in the price of gold by more than 100 per cent would be required. Should the base period be the twenties or thirties? The case for a large rise in price is much less if the twenties rather than the thirties are considered the base period, for in the latter period, following a devaluation and a large drop in prices and trade, reserves were very high. This was the time when Graham and Whittlesey could write a book on the *Golden Avalanche*. Of course, in so far as an improved distribution of reserves can be effected, a rise in the price of gold may not be required. In this connection, it should be noted that the proportion of United States reserves of gold and foreign exchange (net) is but one-half as large relative to its proportion of world trade in 1952 as in the prewar period.

Against the use of a higher price of gold to solve the problem of inadequate gold reserves and the dollar shortage, the following arguments may be used: With a revaluation of the dollar price of gold, the resultant drain of goods from this country benefits foreign countries on the basis of the accidents of gold output and distribution rather than in accordance with political objectives. Again, it is easy to exaggerate the net improvement of the dollar position for the following reasons: First, gold output abroad may not respond greatly in a full-employment economy. Second, there will be leakages resulting from increased imports from dollar countries by the gold-producing countries and additions to their gold reserves and hoards. Third, the resultant inflation in gold countries will cut the exports in real terms. (Against this, note that the rise of imports and reduction of exports associated with inflation in the United States would help the outside world to solve its dollar problems. But note that the United States is not often prepared to determine domestic policy on the basis of international requirements of countries short of dollars.) Finally, the case for an upward revaluation of the price of gold loses strength when the world-wide problem is inflation and when total monetary supplies are not closely related to the amount of gold.

In short, one of the major arguments against a higher price for gold is that the gains would be concentrated on the gold-mining countries, though some of the gains would percolate to others. As a result of the unfavorable price of gold, world production in the early fifties was but two-thirds that of prewar, and this despite various subsidies by the gold-producing countries. In 1956, it seemed that the quest for uranium, a by-product of gold (or is it vice versa?), might stimulate gold production greatly in South Africa, where, it has been said, half of the world's potential supplies of uranium are to be found.[18]

[18] "Another Chapter in the Story of Gold," *Midland Bank Review*, February, 1955, pp. 1–5.

CHAPTER 27

Convertibility[1]

Inconvertibility and Convertibility

Before the Great Depression, owners of the pound sterling and many other currencies were free to exchange their currencies for other currencies, without interference, without permits, and therefore they were able to buy in the cheapest markets. Ordinarily they exchanged their currency for gold, which was acceptable to the foreign creditor. Even from 1931 to 1939, the holder of sterling could purchase foreign currencies freely, but prices of these currencies fluctuated to some extent.

With World War II begins the age of inconvertibility. Authority restricts the freedom to convert the pound sterling, say, into dollars. The restraints are exercised through the government itself providing for bulk purchases in nondollar areas, thus curbing the conversion of the pound sterling into dollars for some purposes; through the importation of certain commodities being subject to quotas and licenses (hence conversion of the pound sterling into dollars is discouraged); and through any request for dollars being subject to licensing. The inconvertibility of nondollar currencies into dollars, the most important expression of inconvertibility, was the common practice in most countries of importance during the first ten years after the war.

All this does not mean that convertibility is entirely absent. For example, the European Payments Union (EPU) provides a machinery for relatively free transferability of European currencies, subject to restraints on capital movements and the retention of quotas on imports,

[1] There is an increasing literature on this subject: see, for example, R. Harrod, *And So It Goes On*, 1951, and *The Dollar;* International Monetary Fund, *Fifth Annual Report on Exchange Restrictions*, 1954; *The Randall Report* and *Staff Papers;* L. Robbins, "The International Economic Problem," *Lloyd's Bank Review*, January, 1953; A. C. L. Day, "What Kind of Convertibility," *Lloyd's Bank Review*, April, 1953; A. C. L. Day, *The Future of £ Sterling*, 1954; R. Marjolin, "The European Trade and Payments System," *Lloyd's Bank Review*, January, 1954; D. H. Robertson, *Britain in the World Economy*, 1954, and "Internal and External Conditions of Convertibility," *International Chamber of Commerce*, May 20, 1953 (mimeographed); *The Economist* (frequent references); G. Haberler, *Currency Convertibility*, 1954.

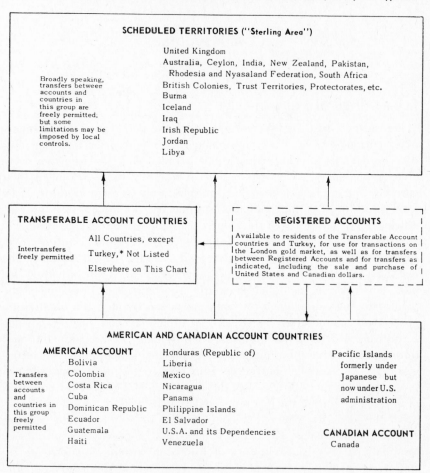

AMENDED JANUARY 20, 1955

UNITED KINGDOM EXCHANGE CONTROL REGULATIONS
OUTLINE OF PERMISSIBLE TRANSFERS

→ The arrow indicates direction of transfers, permitted without individual approval by the Control, between different categories of sterling accounts. All other transfers require separate approval.

SCHEDULED TERRITORIES ("Sterling Area")

Broadly speaking, transfers between accounts and countries in this group are freely permitted, but some limitations may be imposed by local controls.

United Kingdom
Australia, Ceylon, India, New Zealand, Pakistan,
    Rhodesia and Nyasaland Federation, South Africa
British Colonies, Trust Territories, Protectorates, etc.
Burma
Iceland
Iraq
Irish Republic
Jordan
Libya

TRANSFERABLE ACCOUNT COUNTRIES

Intertransfers freely permitted

All Countries, except

Turkey,* Not Listed

Elsewhere on This Chart

REGISTERED ACCOUNTS

Available to residents of the Transferable Account countries and Turkey, for use for transactions on the London gold market, as well as for transfers between Registered Accounts and for transfers as indicated, including the sale and purchase of United States and Canadian dollars.

AMERICAN AND CANADIAN ACCOUNT COUNTRIES

AMERICAN ACCOUNT

Transfers between accounts and countries in this group freely permitted

Bolivia
Colombia
Costa Rica
Cuba
Dominican Republic
Ecuador
Guatemala
Haiti

Honduras (Republic of)
Liberia
Mexico
Nicaragua
Panama
Philippine Islands
El Salvador
U.S.A. and its Dependencies
Venezuela

Pacific Islands formerly under Japanese but now under U.S. administration

CANADIAN ACCOUNT
Canada

* Payments with Turkey remain on a "bilateral" basis. All transfers require the specific approval of the United Kingdom Control, except transfers between Turkish accounts, from Turkish accounts to the accounts of residents of the sterling area, and from Registered Accounts to Turkish accounts.

adjusted to the deficits and surpluses of the members of the EPU. Thus in 1953 in the United Kingdom, exchange control was not imposed on transfers of pounds sterling belonging to accounts of other countries in the sterling area, but all payments to nonsterling countries required approval of exchange-control authorities. This privilege was granted automatically for licensed imports, contractual payments, and many types

Members of the European Payments Union†

United Kingdom and other scheduled territories (the "sterling area")	Iceland (member in its own right though also included in the scheduled territories)
Austria	Italian monetary area
Belgian monetary area	Netherlands monetary area
Denmark (including Faroe Islands and Greenland)	Norway
French franc area	Portuguese monetary area
Germany—West zones	Sweden
Greece	Switzerland and Liechtenstein
	Turkey (bilateral country)

† All of these, with the exceptions indicated, are transferable-account countries.

of noncontractual payments. "Payments to and receipts from countries in which the United Kingdom has negotiated monetary agreements, the American account area and Canada may be made either in sterling or in the currency of the paying/receiving country or monetary area. Payments to and from all other countries are predominately effected in sterling . . . ." The sterling accounts of nonresidents (residents outside the sterling area) are "available for payments in the sterling area and for transfers to residents in the same country or monetary area as the account holder." Privileges here vary according to whether the sterling is held by American accounts (which may even be transferred to dollars), transferable accounts, bilateral accounts, or residual groups.[2]

As of early 1955 the chart on page 472 indicates the transfers allowed under the British system.[3]

By the end of 1955, much progress had been made toward convertibility. With 25 per cent of world trade and 30 per cent of gold and foreign exchange, the sterling area is of special importance. Once sterling becomes convertible, the smaller countries will find it easier to introduce convertibility. By widening the transferable area, which in late 1955 included all countries outside the dollar and sterling area, the United Kingdom had moved far in the direction of multilateralism and convertibility, for transferable currency could be used for payments to and from all but dollar countries and could be converted into all currencies but dollars. It is significant that the discount of transferable sterling on the dollar market dropped from 20 per cent in 1949 to 1 per cent in late 1955.[4]

[2] See International Monetary Fund, *Fourth Annual Report on Exchange Restrictions*, 1953, pp. 286–288.

[3] *Midland Bank Review*, 1955.

[4] *Hearings of the Subcommittee of the Joint Committee on the Economic Report on Foreign Economic Policy*, 1955, pp. 183–187.

In short, by 1956 the major trading nations had advanced far toward convertibility. The lessons of 1946–1947, when the British dissipated large reserves as a result of a premature dash toward convertibility, had been learned. The relationship of internal monetary and fiscal policies and controls (see later discussion) to convertibility by 1956 was a matter of common knowledge. It was also known that no major country other than the United States could afford convertibility without pledges on the part of those sharing common reserves concerning the use of these central reserves. That the magnitude of reserves was a relevant condition not only was made clear by the 1947 experience, but was made doubly clear in 1955, when an inflationary boom in Great Britain resulted in substantial losses of reserves and increased caution in the advance toward convertibility. Complete convertibility of sterling could come only when the balance of the sterling countries had become sufficiently strong, given their reserves, to ensure reasonably stable exchanges. To do so without controls required a widely held confidence that the sterling countries would not be subject to large and continued strains. Economic strength and stability and a minimum of political instability were conditions for a successful convertibility.

By 1956, currency transferability prevailed for countries belonging to the EPU. In addition, preparation had been made to establish a $600 million European convertibility fund, available on evidence of willingness to cooperate on internal policies. The dollar was a convertible currency. As has been noted, sterling was convertible for dollar countries, transferable within the sterling countries, and intertransfers of sterling were freely permitted for transferable-account countries. In March, 1954, the large step had been taken of making the pound held by non-residents transferable: seventy-nine varieties of pound sterling had become one. But the dollar was available to sterling countries only within the limits made possible by dollar reserves. Ordinarily transfer-account countries could not convert sterling into dollars, though as free sterling markets grew outside, the possibility of converting sterling into dollars grew.[5]

One of the toughest problems confronting countries moving toward convertibility is that of relating it properly to trade and exchange policies. Obviously it is easier to introduce convertibility if artificial measures are taken to restrict imports or stimulate exports. Professor Triffin has shown as well as anyone the folly of combining convertibility and an excessive movement toward free trade. The restoration of a multilateral system of trade and payments must be accommodated to varying degrees of protection. What is required is the abandonment of discrimination, and equal access in third markets. A rapid removal of protection

[5] See especially the valuable volume, J. Polk, *Sterling: Its Meaning in World Finance*, 1956, especially pp. 43–45, 80–96, 110–115.

can only jeopardize convertibility. Not only are continued restrictions required, but convertibility must be accompanied by requests to other countries to restrain their demands on the convertible currency or convertibility will be short-lived.[6]

The Costs of Inconvertibility

Why, it may be asked, is there so much interest in the return to convertibility? The most usual explanation is that under inconvertibility, the disposition to buy in the cheapest market is impaired. If dollars are not available, the Italian importer will purchase machinery in France rather than in the United States, despite the fact that French machinery is substantially more expensive and is not exactly what he wants. Hence the gains of trade are greatly reduced. For example, late in 1953 the price of cotton was 32 cents per pound in the United States, 36 cents in Pakistan, and even much higher in Brazil. When dollars are scarce or unavailable, the British may have to buy in Brazil or Pakistan. Copper was priced at 31.02 cents per pound in Canada, 35.50 cents in Chile, and 33.47 cents in Rhodesia. Again, copra was 7 cents per pound in the Philippines and 10 cents in Indonesia in 1949. These are examples of the possibilities of increased costs associated with the pressure to buy in nondollar markets.[7] The reader is also referred to Chapter 28, where it is suggested that intra-Europe and intra-sterling-country trade was greater than might have been expected in view of the greater availability of United States commodities.

Yet it is easy to exaggerate the effects of diversion into more costly markets for the following reasons: First, the tendency will be to cut those imports from dollar countries which are relatively expensive in the dollar countries, that is, where costs are high or not much lower than elsewhere. Second, in fact the unavailability of dollars has been treated to some extent by special measures to make them available (e.g., under the Marshall Plan), and the result of thus inducing exports from dollar countries has often been higher prices for commodities from dollar countries (e.g., requirements for using American shipping). In fact, the availability of aid tends to increase purchases in dollar countries above what they otherwise would be, though not necessarily in excess of purchases in the absence of dollar shortage. What I am suggesting here is that the availability of aid tends to increase purchases in dollar countries because these purchases are subsidized. This is an offset to the increased purchases in nondollar countries.

Third, there is the possibility that trade blocs (e.g., the EPU) may result in a shift of tastes and an increased complementarity of output

[6] R. Triffin, "International Currency and Reserve Plans," in *Policies to Combat Depression*, 1956, pp. 377–404.
[7] Figures from International Monetary Fund, *International Monetary Statistics*.

and sales between, say, the United Kingdom and France, which may on this account increase the advantages of trade. In other words, diversions to a trade bloc may to some extent be an economic rather than a noneconomic diversion.[8]

Fourth, the trend of trade does not suggest large diversions due to lack of dollars and accompanying inconvertibility. Thus, the United States share of exports was up from 16 per cent in prewar to 19+ per cent in the years 1950 to 1953 and of imports from 17 to 24 per cent. Indeed, the export trade of Continental EPU countries to other Continental EPU countries rose from 43 to 45 per cent from the prewar period to 1950 to 1952. Indeed, this might be explained by the special facilities made available under the EPU, in turn related to the dollar shortage. Even the pattern of trade of the United Kingdom did not change greatly. With the EPU countries there was little relative change of British trade; with the United States, a decline of imports from 20 (prewar) to 17 per cent (1950 to 1953); with Latin America, from 10 to 7 per cent; with United Kingdom dependencies and other sterling countries, a rise of exports from 39 to 47 per cent and of imports from 31 to 39 per cent. These latter figures do suggest diversions.[9]

A comparison of the trade trends of Continental EPU countries and the United Kingdom points to greater losses for the latter from shifts of trade, the explanation certainly being to a substantial degree the unavailability of dollars. The shutting out of the products of hard-currency countries due to their currencies being unavailable not only meant purchase from high-cost sources to some extent but also reduced the stimulus of competition. In fact, many who have insisted on convertibility have argued that convertibility forces upon a country the appropriate domestic measures, inclusive of monetary and fiscal policies consistent with low costs, adequate exports, and deterrents to excessive imports.[10]

[8] Cf. Sir Dennis H. Robertson, *Britain in the World Economy*, chap. 4.

[9] Figures from International Monetary Fund, *International Trade Statistics*. In an able treatment of customs unions, Professor Meade notes that the promotion of customs unions may well add to economic welfare when the partners are competitive but might well become complementary. Also relevant is the fact that the countries joining are the major suppliers of one another. Then trade diversion will be less costly. In this connection the large intra-European trade means that the exclusion of imports from dollar countries is less costly than it otherwise would be, for diversions are relatively small. In addition to the figures above, note the following: About 70 per cent of Continental European (Western) trade is with other Western European countries and their overseas dependencies. The figure before the war was about 60 per cent. J. E. Meade, *The Theory of Customs Unions*, 1955, especially pp. 107–115, and International Monetary Fund, *International Financial Statistics*, June, 1956.

[10] Cf. R. Harrod, *And So It Goes On*, 1951, chap. 12; cf. also General Agreement on Tariffs and Trade, *International Trade*, 1953, pp. 19–22, where the increased importance of regionalization in trade is emphasized.

In a paper written for the International Monetary Fund, Mr. Harrod compiled some interesting figures which indicate the shifts of trade in the postwar period. The entire shift cannot be related to the dollar shortage and inconvertibility, but surely to some extent the explanation lies in this direction.[11]

First, consider United States imports. Here the largest rises are from countries exporting food and raw materials. Mr. Harrod estimated reported imports as a percentage of calculated imports. The latter are what imports would have been in 1950–1951 if they had increased in

Table 27-1. United States General Imports

	Rise, 1950–1951 avg., from 1936–1938 avg., millions of dollars	Reported imports, % of "calculated"
Latin American republics..............	+2,580	192
Canada.............................	+1,764	201
Continental OEEC...................	+797	103
France..........................	+132	101
Germany........................	+87	70
Italy...........................	+81	96
Switzerland......................	+98	169
U.S.S.R..........................	+8	44
United Kingdom....................	+226	77
Other sterling area.................	+1,116	133
Australia........................	+222	330
India, Burma, and Pakistan.........	+241	140
Malaya and Singapore..............	+193	70
Other countries....................	+925	79
Japan...........................	+25	38
Netherlands West Indies............	+140	293
All................................	+7,412	131

SOURCE: R. F. Harrod, "Imbalance of International Payments," *International Monetary Fund Staff Papers*, April, 1953, pp. 36–38.

the same proportion as world trade, i.e., prewar (1936 to 1938 average) trade multiplied by three.

The relatively poor record of parts of Western Europe and a fortiori of the United Kingdom may be related in some part to the increased facilities of trade with Europe and within the sterling area. (The United Kingdom suffered a double discouragement in that its exports to both Europe and sterling countries were favored by this double convertibility.) Another relevant consideration is, of course, that as a result of war the economic ties of the United States with the rest of the Americas

[11] R. F. Harrod, "Imbalance of International Payments," *International Monetary Fund Staff Papers*, April, 1953, especially pp. 36–46.

were greatly strengthened. United States imports from these countries increased from 36 per cent in 1936 to 1938 to 53 per cent in 1950–1951. Other sterling-area exports to the United States (reported United States imports as a percentage of calculated exports) equaled those of all countries and hence might have softened the impact of the changed pattern of United States imports. The improved export position of the Americas to the United States is to be contrasted with the weakened British and even Western European position.

But to understand the currents of trade, we have to consider further what was imported in the prewar and postwar periods. A consideration

Table 27-2

Imports	% reported imports to "calculated"	Rise of United States imports from 1936–1938 avg. to 1950–1951 avg., millions of dollars
Petroleum products..............	471	552
Wool, unmanufactured............	333	513
Machinery and vehicles...........	317	179
Coffee...........................	290	1,086
Metals and manufactures.........	203	1,092
Wood and paper.................	153	944
Animal products, edible...........	142	308
Other nonmetallic minerals........	132	258
Rubber, crude..................	118	455

SOURCE: R. F. Harrod, "Imbalance of International Payments," *International Monetary Fund Staff Papers*, April, 1953, p. 38.

of individual imports helps to account for the great expansion of exports to this country from Latin America (coffee, petroleum, and wool) and Canada (metals, wood, and paper). It will be noted that nine classes of commodities in Table 27-2 accounted for 72 per cent of all imports in 1950–1951. The largest gains were in raw materials and food.

An analysis of United States exports reveals similar trends: substantial relative losses of exports to Europe and gains to dollar countries. On the same basis as for imports, reported United States exports as a percentage of "calculated" exports were as follows: all, 132; Latin American republics, 214; Canada, 165; Continental Organization for European Economic Cooperation, 138; United Kingdom, 47; other sterling area, 121. The relative decline of imports of the United Kingdom from the United States was especially marked: a rise (in dollars) of 42 per cent from the average of 1936 to 1938 to the average of 1950–1951 as compared with an over-all rise of United States exports of 294 per cent. In contrast to a rise of United States exports of 245 per cent from 1938 to

1948–1951 for France, of 517 per cent for Germany, and of 617 per cent for Italy, that for the United Kingdom was but 32 per cent. Whereas there were large rises from 1938 to 1948–1951 in exports of United States manufactures of textiles, iron and steel mill products, machinery and vehicles, electrical and industrial machinery, automobiles, parts and accessories to OEEC countries, there was a marked decline to the United Kingdom or a slight rise. The tendency of the British to make sacrifices is especially evident in a decline in imports from dollar countries of manufactures of tobacco as against a rise of more than one-half for all OEEC countries. The tendency to shift from dollar markets, as well as loss of competitive power, is indicated by a rise in dollar purchases by the United Kingdom of raw cotton from the United States only one-half as great as for all OEEC countries.[12] It should be noted, however, that among the United States exports which increased greatly were coal, animal products, wheat and wheat flour, other vegetable products, and foodstuffs. The United Kingdom either was not greatly interested in these imports from the United States (e.g., coal) or else managed to get along without substantial increases in dollar value and (generally) decline in real value (e.g., foodstuffs).

In general, we may conclude that there was some diversion of trade into uneconomic channels and especially of United Kingdom trade, but the adverse effects are sometimes exaggerated.

The Return to Convertibility

At what rate should the movement toward convertibility proceed? Few would insist upon a sudden and complete resumption of convertibility. At first, convertibility might be limited to one or a few strong currencies, to nonresident accounts, and to current transactions. Of course, if all Western European countries returned simultaneously to convertibility, the chances of success might be increased. Should the United Kingdom return to convertibility alone, then there is the danger that the other EPU countries (and even sterling countries) and non-dollar Latin American countries would tend to increase their sales in the British market and restrict imports from the United Kingdom, thus tending to accumulate pounds sterling which might be converted into dollars. The Payments Union countries would pay through the EPU (the United Kingdom thus accumulating European currencies) and receive pounds sterling convertible into dollars. Obviously, a return to convertibility by the United Kingdom would require cooperation from those countries that might use their balances with the United Kingdom as an instrument for securing dollars. The dollar position of many coun-

[12] *Ibid.*, pp. 39–46.

tries might be so weak that convertibility would be an unwise risk. As is noted in the *Randall Commission Staff Papers,* imports of the sterling area from the rest of the world amount to about $12 billion, of which $3 billion are from dollar countries. The crucial issue becomes one of the extent to which the $9 billion of nondollar imports might be converted into dollars. This is aside from the possibility of converting sterling balances of £3.5 billion related to past transactions.[13]

A return to convertibility of smaller countries would raise even more serious problems than for Great Britain. Thus the authorities of the Netherlands note that only 15 per cent of their exports yield dollars. But should the gulden become convertible, *all* exporters to the Netherlands would be allowed to exchange guldens for dollars. The resulting pressure on the dollar and gold reserves of the Netherlands might well be imagined and especially if, as seems not unlikely, the result was increased restrictions on Netherlands exports as a means of replenishing dollar reserves of countries short of dollars. Under these conditions, the Netherlands might remain in the EPU and watch her reserves dwindle as other European countries obtain access to the dollar market through sales of gulden, or leave the EPU and watch European countries discriminate against her. Such considerations may well explain why, even as late as 1954, forty-seven out of fifty-seven countries retained their restrictions on transfers and payments on current account trade under Section II of Article 14 of the IMF charter: They were fearful that if they moved too fast in removing restrictions, they would become subject to pressures from other countries on their reserves. No one country dares get too far out of line. Even Great Britain must be sure of its competitive position, of the present and future balance, of adequate reserves to meet the demands of other countries for dollars through the pound market, and must have agreements with other countries not to discriminate against the British and unfairly penetrate their market. The British have had a foretaste of this kind of pressure: Frequently, when they freed the markets for raw materials, purchasers of dollar commodities with transferable sterling would under some conditions sell for soft currencies, thus involving the British in dollar losses, or many indulged in the "shunting" process; that is, they purchased transferable pounds sterling at a discount, used the proceeds to buy goods in sterling countries, and then would sell for dollars, thus depriving the British of potential dollar earnings. In order to discourage this process, the British authorities had to support transferable sterling.[14]

---

[13] *Randall Commission Staff Papers,* pp. 480–483.
[14] On these issues, see New York Reserve Bank, *Monthly Review,* May, 1955, pp. 54–56; *International Financial News Survey,* May 21, 1954, p. 360, and Oct. 8, 1954, pp. 117–119.

Other nondollar countries might greatly improve their dollar position by taking advantage of the British return to convertibility. From the British viewpoint, it would probably be better for the countries in an impoverished dollar position to make their currencies convertible at the same time as the British do. These countries would be more likely to take proper measures when the loss of dollars would be felt directly (e.g., an exchange of francs for dollars) than if the burden of dollar shortage could be shifted primarily to the United Kingdom. Of course, however, it would do the British little good if the European countries resumed convertibility before their international position was strong enough to ensure success. They would then be forced to introduce increased restrictions on trade as a means of maintaining convertibility in the face of declining reserves. It is scarcely necessary to add that Continental countries with some enthusiasm for convertibility, e.g., Germany and Switzerland, are even less able to undertake the task independently than are the British.

In 1954–1955, further progress was made toward convertibility, and that despite the British crisis. In preparation for convertibility the OEEC countries continued to remove or reduce discrimination against dollar imports, thus continuing the 1953–1954 trend. Austria, France, Norway, Portugal, and Turkey in the OEEC group alone maintained restrictions on *all* dollar imports. Switzerland's liberalization of dollar imports from Great Britain was 98 per cent; the Benelux countries, 86 per cent; and Western Germany, 60 per cent. But some quantitative restrictions inclusive of exchange control still prevailed in 1955 among the General Agreement on Tariffs and Trade countries, which accounted for 80 per cent of world trade. Of the thirty-three countries with which the United States maintained trade agreements under the GATT, twenty-two (and these generally the most important trading countries) imposed quantitative controls against dollar countries in early 1955. In addition, several countries not associated with the GATT, but tied to the United States through trade agreements, also imposed quantitative restrictions. As these restrictions are weakened or withdrawn, the pressure for increases in tariffs grows. The industries deprived of their protection are often not prepared for such large movements toward free trade. When, as in Latin America, much recourse is had to exchange control, multiple exchange rates, and quotas, the use of tariffs is greatly restricted.[15]

Convertibility is bound to be unsuccessful unless all nondollar countries are roughly in balance with the dollar countries, and, it should be noted, each country which is not in *over-all* balance is a potential drain

[15] U.S. Tariff Commission, "Operation of the Trade Agreements Program," *Eighth Report, July 1954–June 1955*, 1956, chap. 6.

on the dollar account. By over-all dollar balance I mean here that any dollar deficit on current account can be made up by capital movements (credit) and temporarily by use of reserves.

The Problem of Reserves

Even by 1953–1954 there were many who held that Europe was ready for convertibility; there were even those who held that reserves at the late 1953 level were adequate and that any further replenishment of reserves through loans would be wasteful in that it would remove the incentive for European countries to put themselves on a competitive basis. With $2.5 billion rise of reserves of gold and dollars in the year 1953 and $2 billion in 1954, the position of nondollar countries was further strengthened. From 1950 to 1955 non-Communist countries outside the United States added $10 billion in gold and dollar reserves.

It must be said at the outset that it is not easy to determine the precise amount of reserves that are required. The IMF had expressed the issues well:[16]

For such a country, what is an adequate level of reserves? Four standards, each more rigorous than the preceding, can be suggested:

1. Enough to enable a country in bad years, by resort to restrictions, to maintain its external debt payments and to purchase the goods and services necessary to avoid hardship to its population or dislocation to its economy and the possible emergence of an exchange crisis, i.e., to permit a reasonable distribution over *time* of the payments which it can afford to make over the entire cycle;

2. Enough to maintain currency convertibility, barring a severe depression, but with occasional necessity to resort to trade and exchange restrictions for balance of payments purposes;

3. Enough to maintain currency convertibility, barring a severe depression, but without the necessity for occasional resort to trade and exchange restrictions;

4. Enough to maintain currency convertibility, even through severe depressions (but not through prolonged periods of international deflation such as occurred in the thirties), without either the necessity for occasional resort to trade and exchange restrictions or the necessity for resorting to domestic deflationary policies for the purpose of restraining imports, even if this involves a substantial drain on reserves.

The nature of the problem is suggested by Table 27-3.

Actually, the nondollar countries would have to raise their gold reserves by $23.6 billion and their gold and dollar reserves by $22.1 billion in order to bring their reserves, relative to import trade, back to the 1938 level. Even if close to $4 billion in gold and convertible cur-

[16] "The Adequacy of Monetary Reserves," *International Monetary Fund Staff Papers*, October, 1953, p. 188.

rencies held by the international agencies were added, the deficit would be of the order of $18 billion to $19 billion. Whereas gold reserves equaled more than one-half of a year's import trade of nondollar countries and gold and dollar reserves almost two-thirds in 1938, the respective figures in 1953 (and 1954) were one-sixth and one-quarter.

A comparison of reserves (and trade of 1938 and 1952 or 1953 or even 1955) may, however, give a misleading view of the issues involved

Table 27-3. Reserves, Per Cent of Import Trade of All Nondollar Countries

Year	Gold	Gold and foreign exchange, dollars
1938	55	64
1953*	16	27

* Reserves, September, 1953; trade, 1953.

SOURCE: Calculated from International Monetary Fund, *International Trade Statistics* and *United States Treasury Bulletin.*

Table 27-4

	Ratio of gold reserves to imports			Ratio of gold plus foreign-exchange reserves to imports		
	1928	1938	1952	1928	1938	1952
1. All gold and reserves inclusive of international agencies	32	121	52	42	129	78
2. United States	85	592	202	85	592	202
3. United Kingdom	13	63	15	13	63	20
4. Continental EPU countries	25	78	20	45	32	36

SOURCE: "The Adequacy of Monetary Reserves," *International Monetary Fund Staff Papers*, October, 1953, pp. 206–207.

(with allowance for gains of more than $3 billion in reserves, 1953 to June, 1955). In 1938 reserves were high because of both the epidemic of devaluations in the thirties and the low level of trade and prices. A comparison of 1928 and 1952 suggests much smaller deficiencies than that of 1938 and 1952. This is evident from Table 27-4.

From this table we draw the conclusion that, as compared with 1928, reserves were more than adequate in 1952. The important exceptions are nondollar Latin American countries, with gold reserves down from 58 per cent in 1928 to 23 per cent in 1952 and all reserves down from 65 to 37 per cent, and Continental EPU countries, with gold reduced from 25 to 20 per cent of import trade and all reserves from

45 to 36 per cent. France and Italy, in particular, have suffered large losses.

Mr. Willis, of the United States Treasury Department, notes that Western Europe and its dependencies had gold and dollar reserves as of June, 1954, equal to 275 per cent of annual expenditures of the area in the United States for goods and services. In 1928 the corresponding figure was but 250 per cent. From 1949 to the middle of 1954, Willis observes that United States reserves of gold minus official foreign dollar balances held *here* had been reduced by $6 billion to $15.3 billion, a reduction more than equal to the $5 billion disinvestment of the United States abroad (excess of government net out-payments over net deliveries of goods and services). Foreign reserves of gold and dollars had increased by $9 billion in this period.[17]

Of course, we should not assume that reserves abroad were adequate in 1928. Europe had been suffering from severe monetary restrictions in the late twenties, and soon an economic catastrophe was to occur—related at least in part to the inadequacy and bad distribution of reserves. In the fifties, the world has to contend with volatile changes in import and export prices, political uncertainties, unpredictable attitudes toward foreign aid on the part of the United States, great structural changes in trade, reduced corrective movements of capital, possibilities of restrictions on movements of gold and desired currencies, and increased speculative influences—all these tend to increase the need of reserves.

But let us return to the 1938 reserves, recalling that this comparison exaggerates the deficiencies of today.

The problem is not only one of inadequate reserves relative to trade but also one of maldistribution. Below I present the ratio of reserves to trade for all EPU Continental countries, the United Kingdom, and four other EPU countries. Gold reserves were badly distributed in 1938, with a range of 32 to 208 per cent of import trade; in 1953, the range was from 14 per cent for France to 124 per cent for Switzerland, with an average of 23 per cent for Continental EPU countries. It is obvious that a return to convertibility would involve France and Italy, with gold reserves of 14 and 15 per cent of import trade, in much greater risks than Switzerland with 124 per cent. But France made substantial gains during the course of the next 1¾ years—a rise of more than 100 per cent. Incidentally, the United Kingdom gold reserves relative to import trade had declined from 111 to 28 per cent. (The decline is even greater if comparison is made with 1937. Gold reserves had fallen from $4.1 billion in 1937 to $2.9 billion in

[17] G. H. Willis, "Convertibility—The Current Approach," *The Journal of Finance,* 1955, pp. 160–161.

1938.) Note the large fluctuations of gold reserves, especially of the United Kingdom.

From 1952 to 1954, the distribution of reserves continued to improve. Whereas the United States lost 7 per cent of its reserves, the world gained 7 per cent. With imports down by 3 per cent in these two years,

Table 27-5. Gold Reserves (End of Year), 1938 to 1953
(In millions of dollars)

Year	All nondollar countries	United Kingdom	Continental EPU countries
1937	11,750	4,147	5,945
1938	10,992	2,877	6,060
1950	11,721	2,900	3,950
1951	10,491	2,200	4,125
1952	10,488	1,500	4,500
1955 (June)	12,939	2,400	5,825

SOURCE: International Monetary Fund, *International Financial Statistics.*

Table 27-6. Percentage of Reserves to Import Trade

Area	Gold		Gold and dollar balances (net)	
	1938	1953*	1938	1953†
United Kingdom...............	111	28	111	35
Continental EPU countries:	78	23	83	38
France......................	208	14	211	22
Italy.......................	32	15	33	28
Netherlands.................	124	30	129	40
Switzerland.................	193	124	210	168

* Reserves are for September, 1953, and trade for 1953.

† In 1953, the figures are for net short-term liabilities payable in dollars to foreign banks and official institutions, as reported by the United States Treasury.

SOURCE: Calculated from International Monetary Fund, *International Financial Statistics* and *United States Treasury Bulletin.*

the United Kingdom reserves rose by 43 per cent; for the Continental EPU countries trade imports rose by 8 per cent and reserves by 34 per cent. The trend continued in 1955, though the United Kingdom experienced serious losses.[18]

Convertibility and the British Crisis of 1954 to 1956

Since the problem of convertibility is so largely tied up with the reserve position of the United Kingdom, we should dwell on developments

[18] *International Financial Statistics,* January and February, 1956.

in the British position. Wright showed that in the years 1946 to 1952 the net contribution to the dollar pool by the United Kingdom was $417 million; by the United Kingdom colonies, $1,990 million; the drain of the other sterling area, $1,341 million; and the drain related to transactions with nondollar areas on the sterling-area account, $2,019 million; the total losses (all items not included here), $630 million. Pooling of dollar reserves brought economies, and savings were made as emphasis was increasingly put on dollar-saving exports by the other countries in the sterling area.[19]

In a later article, Mr. Stevens, distinguishing dollar-aid programs from other items, shows the history of the sterling-area balance over four periods from 1946 through 1954. In the first period (1946–1949), the adverse balance was $8.3 billion, inclusive of nondollar deficits of $1,430 million. In the second period, 1950 to June, 1951, with favorable effects associated with the outbreak of the Korean War, the gains on the balance of payments amounted to $1,193 million and reserves rose by $2,179 million, aid programs contributing substantially to the rise of reserves. From July, 1951, to June, 1952, raw-material prices fell, the adverse balance was $2,790 million, and loss of reserves, $2,182 million. In the final period through December, 1954, payments exclusive of aid were roughly in balance and reserves rose by more than $1 billion. Here the restriction of dollar imports, the prosperity in the United States, increased imports by this country, and the pressure to export goods by sterling countries in place of exports from dollar countries are all relevant.[20]

In the first half of 1954, the gold and dollar reserve position of the United Kingdom continued to improve (a rise of £179 million), but in the second half there was a decline of £92 million. In 1954 there had been a deficit on current balance including aid of £109 million with the nonsterling area and a credit with the sterling area of £269 million. Here was another instance where inconvertibility was costly. The gain was in soft currencies, the loss in dollars. The pressure on less developed countries was also evident in a reduction of reserves of other sterling countries of $1,180 million in 1954, or 25 per cent, as against a rise for the United Kingdom of £252 million, or 10 per cent.[21] In

---

[19] K. M. Wright, "Dollar Pooling in the Sterling Area, 1939–52," *American Economic Review,* September, 1954, pp. 568, 575.

[20] R. W. Stevens, "Some Notes on the Sterling Area's Postwar Balance of Payments," *Review of Economics and Statistics,* November, 1955, p. 358; cf. *United Kingdom Balance of Payments, 1946 to 1953,* table 10.

[21] *United Kingdom Balance of Payments, 1946 to 1954,* pp. 6–7, and *International Financial Statistics,* and cf. Ragnar Nurkse, "The Relation between Home Investment and External Balance in the Light of British Experience, 1945–1955," *Review of Economics and Statistics,* May, 1956; S. I. Katz, "The Future of Sterling," *The Journal of Finance,* January, 1955, pp. 430–441.

Table 27-7. The Sterling Area's Gold and Dollar Balance of Payments
and Its Financing, 1946 to 1954
(In millions of dollars)

	4 years 1946–1949	18 months 1950– June 1951	1 year July, 1951– June, 1952	2½ years July, 1952– December, 1954*
Net balance of payments:				
U.K. current-account balance....	−5,379	−511	−1,520	−1,010
U.K. capital account, net......	−309	+394	−313	+300
Net balance of overseas sterling area......................	−1,150	+1,197	−325	+690
Net settlements with nondollar areas......................	−1,430	+114	−631	+67
Whole sterling area, net........	−8,268	+1,193	−2,790	+47
Means of financing:				
U.S. and Canadian loans of 1946	4,864	45		
South African gold loan to U.K.	325			
IMF drawings by U.K........	300	....	....	−112†
ERP aid to U.K.‡.............	1,757	808	36	
Defense-support aid to U.K....	....	7	261	647
Net U.S. aid to overseas sterling area§......................	100	90	225	275
Net IMF, IBRD receipts by overseas sterling area........	135	35	85	220
Use of reserves (−, increase)...	788	−2,179	2,182	−1,077

Minor discrepancies due to rounding.

* In part provisional.

† Repurchase of IMF's remaining excess holdings of sterling, restoring the United Kingdom to its initial position.

‡ Includes grant aid, loan aid, and conditional aid, but not the United States share of the sterling counterpart of aid.

§ Estimates based on foreign-aid statistics published by the U.S. Department of Commerce.

SOURCES: United Kingdom—*Balance of Payments White Papers.* U.S. Department of Commerce balance of payments publications; International Monetary Fund, *International Financial Statistics.* Only a part of South Africa's gold and dollar transactions is included in these estimates for the periods prior to mid-1951.

1955–1956, the British faced a balance-of-payments problem requiring severe monetary measures and pressures to cut domestic and foreign investment. The bright prospects for convertibility in early 1954 were, therefore, rather dimmed in the next year.

Reserves and the British Experience of 1955–1956

A crisis in 1955 revealed the inadequate reserves held on behalf of sterling countries and in particular the vulnerable position of the United

Kingdom. In eighteen months, $900 million, or 30 per cent, of reserves was lost. From 1947 to 1953, the annual average fluctuations on current-account items for the United Kingdom was ±$943 million and of reserves, ±$678 million. The vulnerability is increased by the rise of short-term liabilities in pounds sterling, the reduction of overseas investment, and a decline of reserves relative to trade. In fact, reserves were equal to only three months of current debits in 1954–1955 as compared with six months in 1938.[22] The crucial changes are indicated in Table 27-8.

In the latter part of 1954 and through early 1956, the British experienced serious difficulties in their balance of payments, and the

Table 27-8. Aspects of Britain's International Capital Account
(In millions of pounds)

Position	December, 1938	June, 1955
United Kingdom liabilities:		
In sterling to countries.........................	598	3,860
In sterling to international bodies................	.....	479
Government debt to external currencies...........	.....	2,130*
United Kingdom assets:		
Gold and dollars (held for sterling area)..........	615	957†
Overseas investment............................	3,545	2,013‡
Subscription to IBRD and IMF.................	.....	557

* March, 1955.
† Pounds now devalued by more than 40 per cent.
‡ End of 1953.

results were to postpone indefinitely the final steps to sterling convertibility. There was evidence of inflation and an accompanying rise of imports unaccompanied by a corresponding growth of exports. Investment and consumer credit in particular had advanced too far. Not even a large and unexpected improvement in the budgetary position of the government was adequate to neutralize these inflationary trends. That the expansion was heavily concentrated in metals, engineering, and vehicles—a rise of 216,000 jobs in 1955 out of a total of 291,000, although this group accounted for only 20 per cent of total civilian jobs —tended to aggravate the inflation.[23]

Let us consider some of the relevant facts. The balance of payments had been a serious problem for years. Thus, from 1946 to 1953, the United Kingdom had an active balance of £1822 million with the rest of the sterling area (RSA). But against this she incurred debits of

[22] See J. Polk, *op. cit.*, pp. 116, 143, and "Sterling in the World Today," *Midland Bank Review*, February, 1956, pp. 1–7.
[23] See *Labor and Industry in Britain*, March, 1956, p. 7.

£2,295 million, roughly half accounted for by investments in the RSA and one-quarter in gold and dollar purchases. Net current balance over the years tended to be absorbed in capital exports, but increases of capital exports had to be scrutinized with resultant loss of international position. Thus in the first half of 1955, net capital exports to sterling countries dropped to 40 per cent of the average of 1952 to 1954. Approximately one-third (£473 million) of investments of the United Kingdom in RSA was absorbed in growth of pound balances in the United Kingdom. Against the £1,822 million current surplus of the United Kingdom with the RSA, the United Kingdom incurred a deficit of £2,136 million with the rest of the world.[24]

In 1954, the visible deficit of the United Kingdom in overseas trade was £599 million; in 1955, £862 million, a deterioration of £263 million; and the deterioration was £278 million with the United States and £172 million with Canada. It is not surprising, then, that from the first half of 1954 to the end of 1955 the sterling area lost $900 million of gold and dollar reserves, or a decline or 30 per cent.[25] There had also been serious losses in invisible earnings. Dr. Furth has also shown that the countries with the largest inflation in Western Europe experienced the largest adverse balance in the years 1953 to 1955. For the United Kingdom, prices rose to 103, 105, and 110 (1952 = 100) in successive years, 1953 to 1955, and the annual deficit was 19, 17, and 25 per cent of annual imports.[26]

It is of some interest that despite the large rise of prices in 1955, export prices rose by but 2 per cent. The crucial effects seem to have been in diverting goods from export to domestic markets. Although total consumer expenditures rose by but 3 per cent in 1955, the rise in private outlays on motoring and cycling was 26 per cent and on household goods, 5 per cent. Harrod has shown that what is more important than actual rise of outlays is the great expansion of orders—in the category of commercial-industrial, building starts rose as much as 80 per cent in one year. As excessive domestic demand is generated (a 30 per cent rise of output generated a 90 per cent growth of income in postwar Britain), the effects on exports are serious indeed. Hence Professor Nurkse suggests that the way out is not to sacrifice domestic investment to export needs but to stimulate savings so that a level of domestic investment sufficient to foster growth *and* of exports adequate to maintain international equilibrium would be possible.[27]

[24] J. Polk, *op. cit.*, pp. 129–130; *Midland Bank Review*, February, 1956, pp. 1–7.

[25] *Labor and Industry in Britain*, March, 1956, pp. 4, 17–19.

[26] J. H. Furth, "Indicators of Inflation in Western Europe," *Review of Economics and Statistics*, August, 1956.

[27] *British Record*, Mar. 30, 1956; R. Harrod, "The British Boom, 1954–55," *The Economic Journal*, March, 1956, especially pp. 1–10; and R. Nurkse, *op. cit.*, especially pp. 153–154.

In his *Are These Hardships Necessary?* (1947), Harrod had complained of the excessive investments in housing and other items not contributing to increased productivity. In a similar vein, Hutton in 1956 was critical of a policy of the wrong kind of investment as well as too little investment. Too much attention had been paid to the Keynesian relation of total savings and investment, according to Hutton, and not enough to the kinds of investment. After allowing for the rise of population and the increased export requirements, Hutton finds that only 12½ per cent of additional net disposable income was available in 1955 for additional domestic consumption and investment, yet the over-all consumption of the bulk of the population had increased by 20 to 30 per cent since 1938. Moreover, with heavy taxation of high income, savings were discouraged. Hence with inadequate savings, investments were inflationary and the more so since they were excessively the nonproductive type.[28]

In the British conditions of 1955, with overfull employment, with unfilled vacancies twice as high as unemployment, the generation of increased demand was likely to cause trouble. It is not clear that wage inflation has been a major cause of the inflation and deterioration of the balance of payments. Harrod, in fact, denied this, as is suggested by the continued undervaluation of the pound in 1955, though the government seemed to be concerned about wage inflation. Thus an official publication pointed to a rise of output per man-year of 4 per cent and of annual earnings in industry of 8 per cent.[29]

Official action to correct the inflationary trends has, indeed, been subject to severe criticism. The main points of criticism were excessive recourse to monetary policy in a period when its influence was not likely to be great, the failure to impose adequate restraints on consumption as a means of stimulating savings, the continuance of consumption subsidies, the inadequate rise of taxes and cut in government spending, and in general inadequate and retarded recourse to fiscal policy. The Bank of England did, however, raise rates from 3 to 5½ per cent, and the government put direct pressure on banks to reduce loans, increased the purchase tax and the tax on distributed profits, made purchases of goods on installment more difficult, reduced subsidies, cut expenditures, and restrained capital issues.[30]

British experience in 1954 to 1956 underlines the difficulties confronting the world in its trek toward convertibility. With large controls and trade barriers, the path was not an easy one in the years 1947 to 1952,

[28] G. Hutton, "The Capital Question," *Westminster Bank Review*, May, 1956, pp. 1–6.

[29] Cf. Harrod, *op. cit.*, p. 10, and *British Record*, Mar. 30, 1956.

[30] See previous items quoted and various issues of *The Economist* (especially Dec. 11, 1955) and *The Financial Times*.

but progress was made. In 1954 to 1956, with controls greatly reduced and freedom of transactions accelerated, the United Kingdom, entrusted with the reserves of the rest of the sterling area and financing half the world's trade, found that a modest amount of inflation (10 per cent in three years) might not only jeopardize the return to convertibility but also endanger the stability of sterling and the economy. A political crisis (e.g., Suez in 1956) aggravates the dangers.

What is more, the losses were concentrated on the United Kingdom, and hence the explanation could not be put primarily on dollar shortage. In 1955, Continental EPU countries gained $1 billion in gold reserves, or 16 per cent, even as the United Kingdom lost $500 million, or 20 per cent. The respective figures for gold and foreign exchange were a gain of $1.5 billion and a loss of $650 million. France and Germany experienced large gains, and no large country in Western Europe or the Americas experienced great losses.[31]

Conclusions on Reserves

I do not conclude from this presentation that convertibility should not proceed until gold reserves outside the dollar countries rise by about $20 billion, or less than twice gold reserves of 1953, and gold and dollar reserves by approximately $1\frac{1}{4}$ times the gold and dollar reserves of 1953. The general position is not that the ratio of the prewar period is sacred. In fact, as we noted, present reserves are adequate when comparison is made with the 1928 ratios, though we must allow for the changed situation since 1928.

Many reasons can be found for getting on with smaller reserves relative to trade than in 1938. First, most countries will continue to control capital movements to a greater degree than they did before the war. Second, the availability of emergency aid from the IMF (and, possibly, the United States) reduces the amount of reserves required to some extent. Third, as we shall note below, countries will be increasingly disposed to allow fluctuations in foreign exchanges to correct an adverse balance of payments. Fourth, most countries are more aware than before the war of the relation between internal policies and the balance of payments and are in a better position to correct policies that endanger the reserve position than in earlier years. Against these items we should weigh the factors tending to raise reserve requirements which we mentioned in the comparison of reserves—1928 and 1952— though the relevance of these factors is less when related to 1938 than when related to 1928.

Here we have, then, some reasons for not requiring a return to the ratio of reserves to import trade which existed just before the war, but

[31] International Monetary Fund, *International Financial Statistics,* June, 1956.

this does not mean that reserves in 1956 were adequate to ensure a return to convertibility. The general view in early 1954 and even in 1955 was that reserves were inadequate.[32] Recall the British convertibility fiasco of 1946–1947 and the crises of 1954 to 1956. Some will say that conditions were much improved in 1954–1955 and hence that the inflationary pressures which contributed to the failure of 1947 are not now present. But the 1946–1947 experience should not be dismissed too lightly. Furthermore, the large fluctuations of reserves of the United Kingdom in particular suggest the possibilities of large losses, which would bring reserves below the rock-bottom level. Unfortunately, de-

Table 27-9. Reserves: Nondollar Countries
(In millions of dollars)

	End 1951	End 1952	End 1954	End 1955
Gold..........................	9,261	10,433	13,819	14,409
Gold and short-term dollar assets*..	17,606	19,930	24,972	26,508

* These figures include liabilities to nonbanking and government accounts and also small amounts due in foreign currencies, but they give an accurate indication of trends.

SOURCE: *United States Treasury Bulletin, International Financial Statistics,* and *Federal Reserve Bulletin.*

spite the persistent teachings of Keynes, central banks still assume that a large part of reserves are not to be used. Again, a recession in the United States is a relevant consideration. Just as the boom in 1952–1953 in this country explains in no small part the rise of gold and dollar reserves of the nondollar countries, a recession may well cost the nondollar countries several billion dollars of reserves. However, the 1953–1954 recession, as is noted elsewhere, proved to be surprisingly innocuous. Again, even a deterioration of the terms of trade of but 10 per cent might cost Western Europe $3 billion in a single year, though some part might be made up by transfers of dollars by overseas countries. The pressure on the balance of payments of the United Kingdom from the middle of 1954 to the early part of 1956 reflects again the need of a large cushion of reserves if strong deflationary measures are not to be taken.

The striking gains of reserves from 1951 to 1955 outside the dollar countries are evident in Table 27-9. In four years, gold reserves were up by $5.1 billion and total gold and net short-term assets held in the United States by $8.9 billion.

The major gold and dollar reserves outside the dollar area belong to Western Europe ($15.8 billion in December, 1955). (About 60 per

[32] See *Randall Commission Staff Papers,* pp. 478–484.

cent is in gold.) A turn in the terms of trade such as occurred in 1949 to 1951 (21 per cent for the United Kingdom and 8 per cent for Continental EPU countries) would cost these countries about $3.5 billion in reserves, subject to any transfers of dollars from overseas countries gaining from higher prices for food and raw materials. (From 1950 to June, 1952, the United Kingdom lost $1,400 million of gold reserves and the EPU countries gained $550 million.) Certainly this experience does not point to a need of additional reserves which would bring reserves up to anything approaching their ratio to imports just before the war. Even if allowance is made for speculative movements, unexpected losses of exports and increases in the volume of imports, and (related) a substantial depression, the reserves of 1951 plus, say, a few billion dollars additional should be adequate. As is said elsewhere, correct internal policies should contain the loss of exports and rise of imports. That gold reserves are now concentrated in official coffers, that the IMF is available for help, that authorities are more prepared to use reserves and in emergencies impose restrictions—all these also reduce the amount of reserves required. Besides, *dollar* reserves are much higher than they were in the prewar period.

As a result of the experience of 1953–1954, when an American recession (which was, all things considered, greater than the 1949 recession) did not have a large effect on the European economic situation, there is less concern in the world about the damage likely to result from a United States depression. It should be noted, however, that though Europe suffered little and, in fact, the continued improvement in Europe seemed to help contain the decline in the United States, some of the raw-material-producing countries really felt the impact of this decline. Furthermore (see comments on Dr. Zassenhaus below), it is not clear that the external results of 1953–1954 were markedly out of line with experiences in earlier recessions.

In fact, this experience reminds us that it is important to make distinctions among the nondollar countries. Whereas Western Europe made large gains in 1953 and 1954, the experience of raw-material-producing and even to some extent food-producing countries was not equally fortunate. Europe gained in part because export prices of the agricultural countries declined. Europe's resilience in 1953–1954 is to be associated also with the elimination of inflationary forces, its improved competitive position, the moderate decline of income of Europe's customers, and the increased availability of supplies from nondollar countries. These were conditions which did not obtain in 1949, when a modest American recession in the United States had substantial effects on Europe.[33]

[33] Cf. *The Economist,* Apr. 24, 1954, and S. E. Harris, *Inter-American Trade:*

In this discussion we have concentrated largely on the relation of reserves to trade, but it is also important to consider reserves relative to nontrade liabilities. Here the British position is much weaker than it was before the war. Then, gold reserves were approximately equal to British short-term foreign liabilities. By contrast, in early 1954, short-term sterling liabilities amounted to £3.7 billion as against gold and dollar reserves of about £1 billion. All liabilities (short and long) were estimated at £5.9 billion as against gold and dollar reserves plus overseas investment of £4.8 billion.[34]

Our experience with reserves in the years 1946 to 1955 suggests that great improvements have occurred and especially since 1950, with reserves of nondollar countries up by $10 billion. But the crisis for the British in 1954 to 1956 points to the issue of the optimum distribution of reserves among nondollar countries. It still seems true (I write in June, 1956) that the British, entrusted with the responsibility for reserves of countries accounting for one-quarter of the world's trade, do not have adequate reserves and/or control of the policies of the sterling area to withstand even modest strains associated with a small relative expansion, inflation, and loss of capital. In the economic relations of 1956, a reserve for the United Kingdom of $4 billion instead of $2 billion to $3 billion and of the sterling area of $5 billion would be a long step toward convertibility. Even $5 billion would be only 25 per cent of the annual import trade of the sterling area.

Convertibility and Exchange-rate Policy

One condition of convertibility is an appropriate exchange-rate policy. In the prewar period, the use of flexible exchanges was not accepted, although a large depreciation occurred in most European and other countries. The preference seemed to be infrequent adjustments of exchange rates supplemented by controls and even by disguised adjustments of rates through reclassifying transactions among rates of exchange in use. In the postwar period under guidance from the IMF the practice has been one of adjustable pegs; that is, when a rate pegged through control of supply and demand of foreign exchange does not prevent large and sustained deficits in the balance of payments, even if corrected by available capital and foreign assistance, then the rate is allowed to fall.

Obviously, the reserves required would be smaller if adjustments in exchange could be made in response to a weakness in the international position. Under an ideal (and unattainable) system, no reserves at all

---

Measures for Expansion, September, 1954 (document for Rio de Janeiro Conference by Organization of American States).

[34] *The Economist*, Apr. 10, 1954; cf. *Midland Bank Review*, February, 1956.

would be required. Prices of currencies would be adjusted so that the market would clear all transactions at a price. The prewar adjustments were not so helpful as they might have been because they were infrequent and in some instances were not justified on grounds of international disequilibrium. The IMF has tended to discourage those exchange adjustments which might be interpreted as a form of economic warfare—exporting unemployment through an improved competitive position abroad by countries indulging in depreciation not justified by their international position. Even so, the French, despite IMF opposition, insisted on a substantial depreciation and a new cross-rate structure vis-à-vis the pound sterling and the dollar which tended to provide the French with dollars at the expense of the British.

Many people are not satisfied with the adjustable-peg system which has generally been in vogue following the war. Once a currency shows signs of weakness—as evidenced by the necessity of imposing additional restrictions, the loss of reserves, or a widening gap between the official and black-market rates—then speculators begin to operate on the currency, thus depressing it further. Even when exchange control prevails, the influence of speculation is felt: Many evade the regulations, those requiring other currencies anticipate their needs, and those requiring the weakened currency postpone purchases until the currency in distress reaches a low value. The result is a tendency to depress the currency below the appropriate level, and what is more, the monetary authority, in order to protect the currency against further assaults, is likely to choose a new rate on the low side. (In general, this has been the history of the British devaluation of September, 1949.)

What is also troublesome about the adjustable peg is that it is most difficult to choose the time and the appropriate percentage of devaluation. Again, a depreciation in the midst of inflationary pressures may well do little good, for the increased cheapness of the currency may soon be offset by a corresponding relative rise of costs and prices, especially when an economy is heavily dependent on imports, which now become more expensive with depreciation. Another point is that depreciation may well result in a reduction in the supply of dollars made available under certain market conditions. Thus, the British were slow to depreciate, in part because, in the early postwar years, supply-and-demand conditions were such that a reduction in the world price of British goods following depreciation would have meant a reduced supply of dollars. The British could sell all they could make available at existing world prices. By late 1949, they were prepared for a depreciation, for demand seemed to be receding and supply conditions had become more elastic. With elastic demand abroad and elastic supply at home, depreciation is more likely to pay. But they had not counted on the recovery early in 1950, the Korean War, and the spectacular rise in the price of imports. Hence with devaluation they profited less from improved demand conditions than they otherwise would have done. The devaluation was not a great success.

The issue is not merely one of timing. It is also one of measurement. As long as the practice is one of infrequent changes in the external value of a currency, the authorities are forced to estimate carefully the appropriate decline in value. Present and future costs, prices and markets at home and abroad, estimates of invisible accounts, expected capital movements, and the reactions of competitors to the devaluation, not only in the adjustments in their exchange rates but also in the imposition of tariffs and other trade restrictions to protect themselves against an improved competitive position of the countries depreciating—these are among the variables that have to be considered before a decision is made. The appropriate rate is the best rate for the next few years, not just for the time of decision.

For these and other reasons, there seems to be an increased interest in floating exchanges. By this we do not mean completely flexible exchanges as suggested by some British economists (but not by Keynes). Rather we mean a freedom of the exchanges to move within limits, not the few per cent suggested by Keynes as a deterrent to speculative capital movements, and *perhaps* even more than the 10 per cent fluctuation in the Canada–United States dollar rates since 1950. But the freedom to fluctuate within limits would relieve the authorities from having to make a once-for-all decision which is necessarily based on inadequate information. It is surely better to allow exchanges to reflect changing supply-and-demand conditions. This, in itself, would dampen the enthusiasm of speculators, for the possibility of fluctuations of several per cent (*both* up and down) would discourage those sales of currency which would occur should there be a virtual certainty that the currency would continue to fall. The possibility of a rise and hence losses on reconverting into the domestic currency would deter speculation. It would be possible to supplement the limited flexibility of exchange with a reserve or equalization fund to prevent fluctuations not justified by underlying conditions.

I am inclined to the view that floating exchanges as outlined above would ease the strain on reserves and hence would reduce the reserves required vis-à-vis imports as compared with the prewar period. This type of exchange adjustment would, of course, raise questions of competitive debasement and might well undermine the influence of the IMF, but the defense may well be made that one should not object to exchanges which fluctuate largely in response to supply-and-demand conditions. In view of the ever-increasing difficulties of adapting domestic costs to the requirements of the international competitive positions of a country, the weapon of limited flexible exchange rates should be used more broadly. Thus obstacles to once-for-all devaluations—the difficulty of deciding the correct extent and the correct time of the devaluation and the opposition of groups that anticipate reduced receipts for their products (e.g., a single country exporting one or a few raw materials or products for which demand is relatively inelastic)—strengthen the case for steady and numerous changes.

In the early fifties the IMF was criticized in many quarters for its rigid rate formula, that is, its emphasis on once-for-all changes in rates. The charge was frequently made that this prevented quick adjustment of exchange rates, say, to a large improvement in the United States balance of payments or a volatile movement of prices and costs elsewhere. It is, therefore, of some interest that in an address of May, 1954, the managing director of the Fund had this to say:[35]

The Fund stands for stability of rates and orderly changes in rates, but not for rigid rates that are to be permanently frozen. When a par value has become inappropriate because of changes in the economic position of a country, the Fund encourages a change to correct the fundamental disequilibrium that has come into being. Since the Fund was established, there has been a remarkable absence of friction in the economic relations of its members arising out of adjustments of exchange rates, and competitive devaluation of currencies has been avoided.

Even when countries have felt that they were no longer in a position to maintain fixed rates of exchange that move only within the narrow margins prescribed by the Fund's rules, they have consulted the Fund, and have explained in detail the difficulties that they face. The Fund has raised no objection to the fluctuating exchange rates of Canada and Peru. In fact, the relationship of Peru to the Fund is an outstanding example of this kind. Several years ago Peru abolished all exchange restrictions and virtually all of its import restrictions. As their monetary reserves were very limited, the Peruvian authorities believed that a policy of this kind could not be safely maintained unless the exchange rate was allowed to fluctuate. The Fund did not object.

In the early fifties the proposal for a flexible pound sterling gained many adherents, inclusive of the Randall Commission, but there has been much opposition. The view gained strength that flexible exchanges would be more costly in reserves than in the past and that flexible exchanges would result in a loss of confidence for the pound sterling. A flexible policy successful in the thirties was not likely in this view to be so in the 1950s.[36] The discussions of a floating rate, moreover, in pre-

---

[35] International Monetary Fund, *International Financial News Survey,* May 21, 1954; cf. *The Statist,* Dec. 13, 1952.

[36] Especially R. Harrod in *The Financial Times,* July 19, 1955.

liminary discussions of convertibility resulted in a fear of a disguised devaluation, which, in turn, brought forth from the Chancellor of the Exchequer the following on the value of the pound sterling: "I can give this policy [exchange rate] in one sentence: It has been and will continue to be the maintenance of exchange parity of $2.80 to the pound, either in existing circumstances or when sterling is convertible." In the crisis of 1955, the government relied not on flexible rates but on anti-inflationary monetary policies, control of investment, and other measures.

Convertibility and Trade Restrictions

I assume also that convertibility is not to be achieved by increasing trade restrictions. Obviously, since the major objective of convertibility is freedom to use currencies in the cheapest market, the attainment or maintenance of convertibility through an increase of restrictions is, indeed, a sham victory. Convertibility and the removal of restrictions and especially discriminatory restrictions are, in a sense, alternative approaches. There has been much controversy on the sequence of convertibility and the removal of restrictions. Convertibility, prematurely introduced, might induce an increase of restriction, and a removal of restrictions might prepare the way for convertibility. Indeed, Harrod contends that discrimination and maintenance of restrictions may be required as a temporary expedient in order to provide hard currencies. Harrod's position seems to be as follows: First, Europe must balance its accounts on a bilateral basis with dollar countries. Then she can make her currencies convertible. This implies support of discrimination against the dollar in trade to balance dollar accounts temporarily. Only if Western Europe can make her currency hard in relation to third countries will the triangular trade be possible which would solve Europe's dollar problems. Then third countries would accept European currencies, and hence, in the long run, Europe would balance its payments on a multilateral basis: sell more to third countries and use dollars obtained from these countries to liquidate balances with the Western Hemisphere.[37]

At present (1955–1956), trade is hampered by all kinds of restrictions and discriminations: high tariffs, troublesome customs procedures, quotas, subsidies on exports, shipping subsidies, preferential treatment of domestic bidders on public contracts, exchange control, state trading (discrimination against private traders), retention quotas (the seller in a hard-currency market is allowed to retain part of the proceeds of the hard currency and to get this privilege offers commodities at reduced prices in hard-currency countries), multiple exchange rates (the foreign-exchange authority sells dollars at varying prices according to priorities of imports and services, with sale price of dollars frequently including

[37] R. Harrod, *The Dollar*, 1954, pp. 146–150.

a tax), and dollars purchased at varying prices—for example, offering relatively few units of the domestic currency for dollars when the seller is in a strong position, as, for example, when supplies are inelastic and foreign demand inelastic, coffee being a good example, and offering many units of the domestic currency when supply conditions are elastic and foreign demand is elastic and hence when there is a gain to be had from a rise of output and foreign sales.[38] In this instance, there is an incentive to expand output; in the coffee case, there is not.

It is clear that even limited convertibility might put a strain on the balance of payments of most countries. This might well lead to increased restrictions, an unfortunate result. But even if increased restrictions were not imposed, a premature return to convertibility would result in a slowing up in the process of removing quotas, of returning purchases to foreign traders, of abandoning multiple rates, etc. It does little good to announce a return to convertibility if, through other kinds of restrictions, little freedom prevails to use a currency to purchase foreign goods in other markets. Fortunately by 1953, the authorities had recognized that convertibility was a means, not an end.

Professor Triffin has presented the classic view on the relation of restrictions and convertibility. He is rightly scornful of the United States Treasury view that all that was necessary was for Europe to set its house in order—stop inflation, readjust exchange rates, abolish trade and exchange controls, and require full gold or convertible-currency settlement for exports or other external transactions. In Triffin's view a restoration of a multilateral system of trade and payments must be accommodated to the varying degree of protection. All abnormal restraints should not be removed prematurely, or convertibility would be endangered. The immediate targets should be nondiscrimination and equal access in third markets.[39]

Mr. Butler, then Chancellor of the Exchequer, and others insisted that there should be gradual liberalization of trade as a preliminary to convertibility, but few believed that convertibility should follow the removal of all controls or that there should be a dash for convertibility. At the conclusion of the Commonwealth Conference of late 1952, British Labor party spokesmen strongly opposed hasty removal of restrictions in order to achieve convertibility. As *The Economist* expressed itself, one world in these matters was idealistic; in practice we would have to be content with $1\frac{1}{2}$ worlds, where there would be a large non-dollar world that would be relatively free of restrictions and prepared to

---

[38] See especially International Monetary Fund, *Fourth Annual Report of Exchange Restrictions*, 1953, for details on many of the restrictions. Also see the *Bell, Gray,* and *Randall Reports.*

[39] R. Triffin, *op. cit.,* pp. 379–384.

purchase from dollar countries in so far as dollars were available. Exchange controls and discrimination would not be wholly erased. As a preliminary to convertibility it was indeed necessary to remove at least some of the discrimination against the dollar—as had been done in the years 1953 to 1955 by European countries. It was, however, too much to expect that the world was ready for the abolition of quotas, exchange control, and licensing of imports. In 1953, the official British position had been that liberalization should not be sacrificed to convertibility. The Chancellor of the Exchequer in 1955 said: "First we should have a strong internal position; second we should have a degree of credit available; and third there should be wider trade policies, particularly between the dollar and the non-dollar world."[40] Butler did not say that Europe should at one stroke accept free competition with American goods through convertibility and removal of all other discriminations against the dollar, but there should be a gradual movement from the EPU and OEEC to wider systems of trade and payments.[41]

A view widely held is that convertibility cannot succeed as long as the United States remains a restrictionist country. But elsewhere we point out that trade restrictions in the United States have been greatly reduced, that they are not a serious deterrent to trade, that there has been a phenomenal rise of imports into this country, and that the greatest gains to be made in dollars are through capturing third markets at the expense of dollar countries. Nevertheless, I would not deny that an increase of imports into this country of $1 billion a year associated with reduced tariffs would contribute toward a successful convertibility. It is not, however, a *sine qua non* if restrictions in the countries returning to convertibility are not removed too quickly, if reserves can be replenished, if flexibility of exchanges is introduced, and if a number of other conditions are met which will be discussed presently.

Convertibility and the EPU

One aspect of the problem of restriction and discrimination relates to the operations of the EPU. The EPU is an organization which stimulates trade among Western European countries and their dependencies through provision of credits and multilateral balancing of accounts. In so far as this mechanism provides special facilities for trade among these countries, it, in fact, involves discrimination vis-à-vis other countries. Genuine convertibility might enlist the cooperation of the EPU countries

---

[40] *British Record,* July 29, 1955, p. 4; *The Economist,* Nov. 7, 1953, and Jan. 30, 1954.

[41] *International Financial News Survey,* July 23, 1954, p. 26, and *The Economist,* Nov. 6, 1954.

individually or as a unit to prevent these countries from putting an excessive burden on a few countries that introduce limited convertibility. The other EPU countries would have to restrain their enthusiasm for sales to the countries with convertible currencies and for restricting imports from these countries. The EPU countries not embarking on convertibility would also be fearful of the increased tendency of the countries with a penchant for convertibility to buy in hard-currency countries. Many EPU countries will find themselves deprived of a form of protectionism; yet they have officially announced their strong interest in convertibility and in 1955 proposed a cooperative program to support it.

However, one should not underestimate the contributions of the EPU. Aside from the successful pressures exerted to reduce quotas, the EPU, through its payments system and credits, has been able greatly to expand intra-European trade. The *real* gain of intra-European trade over the prewar period was almost 40 per cent and over 1948 almost 100 per cent, a large figure considering the effects of the war. Marjolin's estimate is total transactions of $70 billion to $80 billion for the first three years of its existence (ending June, 1953); of *bilateral deficits* and surpluses of $20 billion, of which $9 billion were settled by *multilateral* compensation and $6 billion by reversals through time of positions within the EPU, of $350 million by special grants of the United States, of $1 billion by initial credits granted by some countries and in other ways, of $2.1 billion by credits granted to the Union by creditors and by the Union to debtors, and $1.5 billion by net gold payments to and by the Union.[42] In 1956–1957 the advance toward a common market may well further increase European trade.

But under a convertible system the EPU would play a different role. Mr. Butler, Chancellor of the Exchequer, in June, 1955, remarked following a meeting on the EPU (reporting to the House of Commons on the recent Paris meeting of the OEEC):[43]

We have agreed that the EPU shall continue in principle for a year from 1st July with harder gold credit ratios, changing from 50/50 to 75/25, from 1st August, and with suitable arrangements for its termination in case of need. Also, in case there is to be a transition at some date at present unspecified to a wider system with convertibility of currencies, we made preparations for three things: first—and this was greatly to the relief of the European nations—assistance for countries in short term balance payments difficulties from the European Fund; secondly, a system of clearing of payments which

[42] R. Marjolin, "The European Trade and Payments System," *Lloyd's Bank Review,* January, 1954, pp. 2–3; and Organization for European Economic Cooperation, *Progress and Problems of the European Economy,* 1954, pp. 30–31; cf. *Fourth Annual Report of European Payments Union,* 1954, especially pt. II for transactions, 1950 to 1954.

[43] *British Record,* June 24, 1955, p. 4.

is being worked out in detail at present; and thirdly, assurances about continued trade liberalization in the period after any convertibility might be introduced.

In an official report, the EPU had this to say: [44]

It is the Board's hope that the arrangements which have been made for the renewal of the Union (which include a considerable simplification in its methods of operation) will enable it to continue usefully to function as an international payments mechanism as long as it may be needed. It has, however, been recognized from the beginning that the Union cannot be a perfect system and that its principal task must be to help Member countries during a transitional period, until they can conduct their international payments arrangements on a world-wide basis. Considerable progress in this direction has been made during the past year: the removal of trade restrictions, the extension of the transferability of some currencies, the establishment of international commodity markets, the removal of restrictions on current payments and capital movements, the narrowing of the spread between the free and official rates of exchange, are all evidence of the increasing strength of Member countries and of their approach to a situation in which convertibility on a world-wide basis can be envisaged.

During the past year, the Board has given considerable time to a study of the problems which the adoption of systems of convertibility by an important number of Member countries would pose for all Member countries and for the Union itself. From these studies, two major conclusions emerged. The first is that it would not be desirable for Member countries to adopt a system in which their currencies became convertible into dollars, unless such a system could be adopted in conditions which would make it possible for intra-European trade, and trade between Member countries and the rest of the world, to be maintained or increased. The second conclusion is that in modern conditions the maintenance of a successful system of convertibility will be possible for most Member countries only if they continue to work together with one another, and with the other principal trading nations of the world, to ensure that the conditions necessary for the sound development of international trade and finance, including long-term capital movements, under convertibility are maintained.

Convertibility and Competitive Position

Successful convertibility will not be achieved unless the countries embarking on such a program are competitive. Relevant are the monetary and fiscal policies, productivity, and wage policies. Flexibility of exchanges also would contribute toward attaining a competitive position. Inflationary monetary policies, unbalanced budgets, diversion of resources to domestic service industries (e.g., through social-welfare programs), relative losses in productivity, failure to offset *relative* price

---

[44] *Fourth Annual Report of European Payments Union,* 1954, pp. 112–113; cf. Chap. 18 for arrangements in 1955.

and/or income rises not related to productivity movements with exchange depreciation—all these would threaten the continuation of convertibility or even its establishment. The last sentence should not be interpreted as a criticism of welfare policies, investment programs, and the like, but rather that the contributions to these policies toward international disequilibrium should be given serious consideration.

It is important, however, to emphasize the fact that what is relevant are relative movements. Much inflation is compatible with a competitive position if this is more than matched elsewhere. A country that pursues a deflationary or noninflationary policy gains in its international economic relations, because other countries do not follow. The success of Western Germany in the years 1951 to 1955 would have been considerably less had other countries pursued equally austere policies. Much, of course, also depends on the relation of any income rise and the accompanying expansion of imports. When a rise of productivity and income is reflected in a gain of money income rather than in a decline in prices—the usual pattern in recent years—the unfavorable effects on the international balance of the lagging countries would be less than if greater relative rises in productivity were reflected primarily in price reductions.[45]

To many, the major argument for convertibility is that in its absence domestic producers are protected against many foreign competitors and thus government, monetary authorities, or the individual producer does not really pursue the policies which ensure minimum costs. Convertibility is the approach toward competitive costs.

Since so much has been said about the relevance of monetary, fiscal, and wage policies and so much of the responsibility for imbalance put upon those responsible for easy monetary policies, budgetary deficits, high-wage policies, and the like, I have put together Table 27-10, which includes the major variables over the several years for the United Kingdom, Germany, France, and the United States. Irresponsible policies undoubtedly contributed toward the dollar gap, though my view is that these were not as a rule a decisive factor. But just as inflationary policies, through their effect on competitive position, may increase the dollar shortage, so similar policies in the convertibility phase may endanger the maintenance of convertibility.

Table 27-10 shows that Germany's competitive position has improved, especially vis-à-vis France and also vis-à-vis the United Kingdom. Compare, for example, the large rise in the supply of money relative to that of industrial production and employment and of wages of France as against Germany and the smaller rise of prices for the latter. It is not surprising, then, that Germany has experienced a phenomenal rise of reserves whereas France and the United Kingdom experienced sub-

[45] Cf. Chap. 16.

Table 27-10. United Kingdom, Germany, France, and the United States:
Several Variables Relevant for a Study of Inflation and
Competitive Position, 1950 and 1953
(Percentage changes, 1950 to 1953)

	United Kingdom	Germany	France	United States
Monetary supplies.......	+1	+42	+50	+11
Wage (rates)............	+23	+32	+61	+20
Yield of long-term government bonds...........	+16	....	−17	+26
Budget, 1951–1953*......	Deficits = 7% of expenditures, 1951 and 1952	Net surplus, 1951 and 1952	Large deficits (20% of expenditures, 1951 and 1952)†	Surplus, 1951–1953
Prices:				
Wholesale............	+25	+16	+28	+6
Cost of living..........	+23	+7	+30	+11
Gold and foreign exchange	−24	+746	−35	−3

* Figures relate for the net balances for the two to three years considered together.
† The deficit relates primarily to nonordinary expenditures. Cf. Organization for European Economic Cooperation, *Progress and Problems of the European Recovery*, January, 1954, pp. 99–100.

SOURCE: Calculated from International Monetary Fund, *International Financial Statistics*.

stantial declines. There is also a contrast in the deficit spending of Germany, on the one hand, and France and the United Kingdom, on the other. This table might suggest why, early in 1954, the United Kingdom and France were in debt to the EPU whereas Germany was a creditor. Over a period of 3½ years under the EPU the United Kingdom had accumulated debts of $805 million ($551 million outstanding) and France, $845 million ($312 million outstanding). But Germany had advanced $918 million ($509 million outstanding).[46]

Europe's inability to equilibrate its dollar account is emphasized by an examination of the United States developments from 1950 to 1953 in contrast to those of the three major Western European countries. Note that monetary expansion was less (except vis-à-vis the United Kingdom), price rises in all but one of six instances substantially less, the wage inflations less in this country, and the rise of production and employment greater than that for the other countries with the exception of the United Kingdom. It might well be expected that our reserves would not fall greatly and our export balance rise.

[46] International Monetary Fund, *International Financial Statistics*.

From 1951 to 1953, the results are somewhat different. Here the greater expansion of income in the United States and the related off-shore-procurement program contributed to a great change in the balance of payments and the direction of movements of reserves.

From 1953 to 1955, however, the French position improved greatly, as evidenced by the stability of prices, the rise of wages and industrial production, and improvement of her international position. It is not clear, however, how long the favorable position of France can be sustained. With dollar grants cut in 1956, with excessive dependence on colonial trade and large (and hence unstable) agricultural exports, and with a precarious political and military situation, it is possible that the symptoms of relative price stability and gains of reserves and substantial gains of output may be misleading. In the meantime, the stability of prices in France and Germany and the United States (no significant change from 1952 to 1955) should be compared with the rise of 10 per cent in United Kingdom and 8 per cent in Italy from 1952 to 1955. In the three years 1952 to 1955, it might be noted that gross national product rose by 30 per cent in Western Germany, 13 per cent in France, 12 per cent in the United States, and 13 per cent in the United Kingdom. The 5 per cent rise in industrial output for the United Kingdom in 1955 is assumed to be for GNP.[47]

The Relevance of a Depression

Europe may not embark on convertibility in a serious way until she is reasonably sure that the United States is not beset by a depression. Europe is more fearful of a United States depression than of her tariff policy. As noted elsewhere, a depression of the order of 1937–1938 decline would, according to a UN committee, cost Europe $10 billion within two years. Not only would such losses mean great declines of sales in this market, but protective measures would exert a deflationary influence on European and other economies. Yet Europe is hopeful that this country will take necessary measures to prevent a recession and so has been assured by representatives of the United States government in 1953. "The United States Government has on many occasions declared its intention to preserve internal stability, and the United States representatives who have assisted in this preparation of the present report have repeated these assurances in the most forthright manner. . . ."[48]

How much imports are affected by a United States recession is suggested by the following illustration (see also Chapter 28): In 1929

---

[47] Figures from *International Monetary Statistics;* R. Nurkse, *op. cit.,* p. 129; *British Record,* Mar. 30, 1956; and H. Furth, *op. cit.*

[48] Organization for European Economic Cooperation, *Progress and Problems of the European Recovery,* January, 1954, p. 28.

to 1932, imports into the United States declined by 70 per cent, or equal to $1\frac{1}{2}$ times as much as industrial production and GNP. In 1937–1938, the decline of import value was 35 per cent, or six times the drop in GNP and equal to $1\frac{3}{5}$ times that in industrial output. As both Alder and Zassenhaus have shown, the decline tends to be greater for raw materials than for manufactured products and hence for regions producing the former.

Since writing the above, I have read an interesting paper presented by Dr. Zassenhaus[49] before the American Economic Association meeting in December, 1954, and subsequently published in the *Review of Economics and Statistics*. Zassenhaus notes that, as might be expected, import values (reflecting quantity and *price* movements) are more sensitive than import volume and also that the highest sensitivity is to be found in imports of crude materials and semimanufactured materials. He argues cogently that the effects of the 1953–1954 recession on imports were not markedly out of line with results in earlier recessions. In making this study, Zassenhaus adjusts the 1953–1954 imports for the change in the pattern of trade and hence, also, the expected changes in imports relative to production. He also points out that the substantial cut in imports was offset by a rise in supplies made available from other sources, that as in previous recessions output in nondollar countries rose while United States output declined, and in 1953–1954, in contrast to previous recessions, price stability prevailed in the United States. This stability tended to contain the price decline elsewhere. Hence Zassenhaus concludes that, all things considered, the external effects of the recession in 1953–1954 were about what was to be expected. Note that the rise of output in the nondollar world would tend to stimulate imports into the United States and thus contain the effects upon imports of a United States recession, and the stable prices in the United States would moderate the fall in the price of imports.[50]

In the literature on this subject, the view increasingly has been that the high correlation is between United States output (or income) and United States imports, not so much between prices of imports and the value of imports. But Dr. Adler and his colleagues in an important study stress the significance of a high price elasticity for manufactures, though not denying the importance of income elasticity.[51]

[49] "Direct Effects of a U.S. Recession on U.S. Imports—Expectation and Eventual," *Review of Economics and Statistics*, August, 1955.

[50] Cf. C. Chang, *Cyclical Movements in the Balance of Payments*, 1951, and L. Tarshis, *International Trade and Finance*, 1955, pp. 350–352, for a discussion of the greater response of imports of agricultural commodities and of agricultural countries to fluctuations of income than of imports of industrial commodities and countries.

[51] J. H. Adler, Schlesinger, and Van Westerborg, *The Pattern of United States Import Trade since 1923*, 1952.

The issue of whether price elasticity or income elasticity is more important—that is, is Europe's supply of dollars replenished more easily by introducing a competitive price or by relying on a high national income in this country?—is an important problem. Relying on new methods of comparing foreign and United States prices, Adler and associates found a higher price elasticity than is ordinarily to be had, but they also noted that price elasticities vary greatly according to the country of origin of the product and economic conditions in the United States. For the United Kingdom he found a high price elasticity (—5.2) and for Switzerland, a low price elasticity (—0.1 to —0.3). The difference is explained by the fact that British exports are highly competitive and hence a reduction in price as a means of capturing competitors' markets finds a large response but Swiss exports to the United States market (largely watches) are almost a monopoly.

However, Adler also finds that price elasticities were much lower in the twenties when income elasticities were higher (1.4) and much higher in the thirties when income elasticities were lower (1.0). In the thirties, prices moved much more violently than in the twenties, and generally the response is greater with a large price change as in the thirties than with a small price change as in the twenties. Moreover, in prosperity, high income will blunt the price effects and, in depression, low incomes intensify the influence of price movements as compared with the smaller sensitivity in prosperity.

Price elasticities are not easily dissociated from the effects of income. For example, a rise of income in the United States may, in itself, bring about an expansion of output abroad and sales in this market. Here an increase of sales may seem to be related to a price cut, but actually demand and supply are not independent, increased purchases being related to factors other than price cuts.[52]

In conclusion, striking changes of imports into the United States seem to be related especially to variations in total income,[53] but there is some evidence that by making their prices competitive, European exporters of manufactures who face strong competition may find a large response. It is not easy, however, to claim that the relation of the rise of purchases relative to the price decline is a measure only of price elasticity. This analysis, moreover, leaves out of account the extent to which elasticity of demand for the foreign component of the product is reduced in practice because the final price to the consumer in this country is a multiple of the import price. Finally, we should note that the present

[52] See *ibid.*, especially chaps. 5 and 6; H. K. Zassenhaus, "New Material on United States Imports," *Review of Economics and Statistics,* February, 1953, pp. 92–97; and G. Orcutt, "Measurement of Price Elasticities in International Trade," *Review of Economics and Statistics,* May, 1950, pp. 117–132.

[53] See W. Thorpe, *Aid, Trade or What?* and also Harrod in support of this view.

situation is more like that of the twenties, when price elasticities of exports to this country were much lower than in the thirties.

Trends of 1951 to 1956 and Some General Observations

Convertibility is a major issue of economic policy. No simple answer is available. A return to convertibility would not solve all our international economic problems. For example, the pressure of creditor nations that keep foreign goods out and fail to use their increased resources for lending abroad will plague the world as much under convertibility as under inconvertibility.

Even in early 1956 a return to universal convertibility was still out of the question. We can but look forward to the establishment of convertibility by certain European countries. Conditions for a widespread convertibility are adequate reserves, cooperation from creditor countries, sound monetary and fiscal policies by the countries returning to convertibility (unsound monetary and fiscal policies in the dollar countries may help, temporarily at least), continued gains in the competitive position of nondollar countries, and use of floating exchange rates.

Western European countries are in different stages of preparedness for convertibility. An examination of economic trends from 1950 to 1953 in the three largest Western European countries gives emphasis to this point, as does a study from 1952 to 1955.[54] For Germany, the large gains in output, the sound budgetary situation, the relative price stability, the marked improvement in reserve position—these are to be contrasted to some inflationary symptoms (despite price stability) in France, the moderate rise of production (40 per cent of Germany's), the unbalanced budget, and the unfortunate decline of savings. (Cf. earlier discussion of reserves in Chapter 26.

On the issue of convertibility, the position of the Randall Commission seems to the author to be essentially correct. The burden on Britain of a return to convertibility, since she finances 40 per cent or more of the world trade, would be great. The Commission favors "a gradual and controlled approach to full convertibility" and is aware (though inadequately) of the need of appropriate policies in Europe and in this country. The first step would be a commodity convertibility; that is, currencies obtained through current sales of commodities would be convertible.[55]

By 1954–1955, large advances had been made. Thus nonresidents in the United Kingdom have the right to convert sterling with the important exceptions of not being allowed to open American accounts

---

[54] Cf. Furth, *op. cit.*
[55] Commission on Foreign Economic Policy, *Report to the President and the Congress,* January, 1954, pp. 72–75.

which are transferable and to convert sterling arising from the sale of property and investment. Even by early 1954, currencies were consolidated into three types: dollar-account sterling available for any use open to those receiving dollar income, sterling belonging to any residents of the sterling area available within the sterling area but exchangeable for dollars only with permission, and finally, transferable sterling subject to no restrictions except nonuse in the dollar area. Nonresidents received preferential treatment over residents, who were subject to all kinds of restrictions on purchases of hard currencies; the nonresident was even beginning to receive privileges on capital as well as current transactions. In opening important commodity markets to unrestricted market forces, the British introduced a large element of commodity convertibility; that is, not only are goods purchased in the cheapest markets, but some commodities purchased with dollars may be paid for with sterling. Hence in this sense nonresident sterling is convertible.

By the latter part of 1954, Germany, Switzerland, and the Benelux countries had advanced far in the direction of making their currencies convertible. By this time these countries had virtually abandoned discrimination against the dollar. In Germany, with a strong export position, increased reserves, price stability, the deutsche mark a hard currency (97 marks = 100 Swiss francs), and the abandonment of many trade restrictions and subsidies for exporters, the movement toward convertibility had made great progress. Progress continued in 1955 and 1956.

In 1951 and 1952, when Europe was still experiencing a serious balance-of-payments problem, the discussion of convertibility centered around such issues as anti-inflationary policy and an improvement in the competitive position of Western Europe. By the end of 1952, enthusiasm for convertibility was on the increase, but there tended to develop an excessive emphasis on the shadow (convertibility) instead of on the substance (liberalization of trade). By 1953, the British in particular began to waver. They were concerned over the inadequacy of reserves, United States trade policy, the possibilities of a depression in the United States, and the problem of integrating policy with the Continental and even Latin American countries, which countries might drain dollars from the United Kingdom.

In 1953 to 1955 much progress was made in liberalizing trade, in particular in intra-European trade, but also in reducing discrimination against dollar imports. The stabilization of prices in some major countries, the provision for stand-by credits and the plans for a European Fund to help the weaker nations in Europe following convertibility, the slight effects of the American recession, the improved competitive position not only of the United Kingdom but of several Continental countries

—all these made possible both liberalization of trade and greater freedom to export capital and generally increased freedom to exchange currencies for dollars. By 1955, dollar convertibility was far advanced *de facto* though not *de jure*, but there were still strong voices shouting that too much emphasis was being put upon convertibility and the gains of income resulting from the return to a convertible currency and too little upon the effects of increased convertibility upon the output and employment of the major industries. Day and Austin Robinson, in particular, raised some questions here.[56]

In late 1956, there were still uncertainties. One commentator, late in 1954, announced that many countries seem to be on the verge of convertibility, standing there like the girl in the nursery rhyme:

> Mother, may I go to swim?
> Yes, my darling daughter!
> Hang your clothes on the hickory limb
> But don't go near the water!

But in 1955–1956, convertibility seemed as far off as in 1954. The balance-of-payments scare in Great Britain in 1954 to 1956 once more reminded the authorities that overexpansion was a constant threat to convertibility, either to its inception or to its continuance.[57] An increased fear that convertibility was premature as long as there was serious danger that with convertibility the current pound rate might have to be reduced or controls be reintroduced—this increased the caution. In other words, the support offered by floating exchange was beginning to be considered a mirage. Increased fears of protectionism in the United States, associated with the weak United States Trade Agreement Bill of 1955 and decisions by the President on the importation of Swiss watches and bicycles, also contributed toward a timorous attitude. An unwillingness of the Federal Reserve to contribute stand-by credits further suggests caution. Yet despite these reservations, much progress had been made: Inflation was under greater control than in the early fifties, and reserves were larger despite the reduction of trade barriers, and arrangements for temporary credits had been made.

On one issue there still was much disagreement: There were those who held that convertibility would increase the international services performed by the British economy, and this constituted an additional argument for convertibility, and there were others who feared that the

---

[56] The reader should consult especially *The Economist*, which over several years periodically published provocative articles on this subject. Also see A. C. L. Day, *The Future of Sterling*, 1954; "Recent Changes in Great Britain's Trade and Payments, Controls," *Federal Reserve Bank of New York Monthly Review*, January, 1954; and *Financial Times*, July 22, 1953, Jan. 27, 1954, and Sept. 27, 1954.

[57] *The Economist*, July 30, 1955.

effects of restrictive monetary and fiscal measures required to support convertibility would much more seriously affect the economy than the invisible income would improve it. (From 1950 to 1953 trade financed in sterling rose from £534 million to £1,493 million.[58])

In summary, the world in 1955–1956 was closer to convertibility than in 1950 to 1952, but there were still roadblocks, and caution is required lest the price of convertibility be reduced output and trade. International crises, such as the Suez crisis of 1956, further delay convertibility.

[58] *International Financial News Survey,* Aug. 6, 1954.

CHAPTER 28

Some Aspects of Trade and Dollar Shortage

General Comments

In earlier chapters we have considered various aspects of the dollar shortage. How much can trade policy contribute toward a solution of the problem of the dollar shortage? Flexibility of exchange rates? A change in the price of gold? Once the competitive position of the non-dollar countries improves sufficiently, in turn related to (1) the choice of appropriate exchange rates, (2) the resumption of a normal flow of capital from dollar countries, (3) the commercial policy of dollar countries, and following a removal of abnormal restrictions against dollar trade and cooperation in commercial policy among the nondollar countries (e.g., refraining from capturing dollars through special restrictions on trade from other nondollar countries), then convertibility of currency would be a recognition of the solution of the dollar problem.

I have reserved for the present chapter a study of the trends of trade in the postwar period. They are the barometer of the competitive rises of nondollar countries, of the choice of appropriate exchange rates, and they also reflect the relative advance toward convertibility of different countries and regions.

It is well to stress at the outset that even though all nondollar countries may be close to convertibility and there may be countries or regions strong enough to resume convertibility (on the assumption that other countries would not drain dollars from the minority returning to convertibility), there may also be others far below convertibility strength. In this connection the large gains of Europe (though even here in varying degrees) in the years 1953 to 1955 are to be contrasted to the losses of the raw-material countries and even food-producing areas. In fact, part of the increased strength of Western Europe was at the expense of these countries, which experienced a deterioration in their terms of trade. In 1954–1955 the losses of the United Kingdom vis-à-vis Continental Europe are also significant.

The shortage of dollars since 1913 has been attested by the large volume of grants and repudiated loans from the United States, the substantial inflow of gold into this country, and the imposition of unusual restraints on trade by nondollar countries. In the years 1913 to 1953 the gold stock of the country rose from $1.5 billion to $22 billion (the former at $20.67 an ounce, the latter at $35 an ounce). Indeed, one may contend that the gains of gold are not so large as they seem, since short-term external liabilities rose by $10.5 billion in these years.[1] These are a claim on our gold supplies. But it should be observed that the rise of external short-term liabilities reflects also the strength of the dollar and the gains of New York as the world's financial center. Large withdrawals are not likely. Large reserves of dollars by foreign countries are likely to be normal. The importation of this short-term capital reflects the strength of the American economy in the same sense that the importation of gold does.

On another issue we cannot be so certain. The existence of the dollar shortage has been attested in part by the large political grants of the last forty years. These are considered abnormal, unilateral grants. It may well be that in the uncertain and more closely knit world and under the pressures of the cold or hot wars, transfers from the strong countries to the weak may become a normal state of affairs. It would follow, therefore, that just as, say, normal private capital movements are not taken as a barometer of dollar shortage, political grants of $5 billion or even $10 billion per year may not be so considered.

If the nondollar countries are to achieve balance in their accounts, they must expand their exports to the dollar countries or reduce their imports. Of course, grants are a substitute for increased exports or reduced imports, and increased loans at least postpone the day of reckoning.

These adjustments may come as total trade rises, that is, through a gain of exports for nondollar countries vis-à-vis imports in a world with trade rising, or the adjustment may come primarily through a reduction of imports by nondollar countries as world trade tends to decline.

There are some misconceptions about trade trends. It is often said that trade has declined since the twenties. Actually there was a decline in the thirties, but a large rise since. Even in relation to national income, trade was higher in World War II and after than in the thirties. In part the explanation of the recovery is the large flow of political grants, but a major explanation of the gains is the rise of world income.

As was adumbrated earlier, there are many reasons for a downward trend in trade: increased trade restrictions in a nationalistic world, the

[1] Figures from *Historical Statistics of the United States, 1789–1945,* and *Survey of Current Business,* July, 1954.

greater importance of domestic commodities such as services, the substitution of synthetics for materials formerly imported, and (related) the
tendency to become self-sufficient in strategic items. Operating also to
reduce *international transactions* are such factors as reduced immigration (and hence less remittances and travel abroad) and institutional
obstacles to the exportation of capital. (Personal savings now go primarily to institutions which are to a substantial degree not allowed to
export capital. An offsetting factor is increased exports of capital out of
the increasingly important savings of corporations.)

Walther Lederer, of the Department of Commerce, has also pointed
out that there are factors which tend to increase the importance of trade
and especially United States imports. The exhaustion of raw materials
has been discussed earlier. He also mentions the increase in the proportion of imports which are competitive with domestic output (here the
marginal producer is held more likely to be in this country; the foreign
producer's supply is less elastic, as, for example, in rubber, and his price
flexibility greater; and hence in response to increased competition the
domestic seller is more likely to suffer); the growing proportion of imports produced abroad by American firms, which tend to favor their
own product and hence to import their products rather than purchase
at home (imports of American branches and subsidiaries amounted to
$2.2 billion in 1952); the declining sensitivity of imports to cyclical
declines (e.g., petroleum, foodstuffs). These are all factors that tend to
increase United States import trade. A greater disposition to grant credits or take advantage of higher rates of return abroad tends to stimulate
exports.[2]

*Allow me to present very briefly the major conclusions of this chapter
based on the dull statistics to be presented.*[3] The nondollar world has improved its international position more by increasing exports than by
reducing imports. Both the failure of the dependencies, Asia, and other
underdeveloped regions to provide the goods that might be substituted
for dollar goods and their failure to sell to the United States in excess
of purchase on the prewar model and thus provide dollars for Western
Europe have proved especially troublesome to Western Europe. Instead,
these countries accumulated large deficits and even deficits vis-à-vis the
dollar. But it should be noted that the rise of imports from the United
States of both Western Europe and other nondollar countries was associated with loans and grants in part and therefore was not so costly in

[2] W. Lederer, "Major Developments Affecting the United States Balance of
Payments," *Review of Economics and Statistics,* May, 1956, pp. 177–192.
[3] The reason for putting this chapter near the end is that it is not interesting reading. Some may prefer to read only this opening section.

pressure on reserves as they otherwise would have been. Another cause of the dollar problem was the great success of the United States in penetrating the markets of almost every region in competition with nondollar countries—again in part due to political grants and capital exports. Finally, observe that in 1952 to 1956 the dollar position of the nondollar world improved greatly, in part because of a gain of competitive prices in third markets, the increased availability of supplies from nondollar countries, and some gains in capital exports from the United States when they were especially needed. But the gains were unevenly divided between Western Europe and the others and between sterling countries (inclusive of the United Kingdom) and other non-European and non-American countries.

The main material in the statistical section is summarized more fully below (by sections).

1. The opening section deals with the relation of United States imports and national income, a subject touched on in other chapters also. A high association of imports and income, an explanation of the small volume of imports relative to gross national product for the United States, recent increases in the ratio of imports to income—these are main issues in this section.

2. *How can the dollar problem be solved?* Obviously, a rise of United States imports is one approach. A reduction of imports from dollar countries by nondollar countries is another. In section 2, it is made clear that the major shifts in the postwar period were not in a reduction of United States imports by nondollar countries but in an expansion of exports to the United States. This does not mean, of course, that even if Western European imports from the United States rose somewhat, strong measures were not taken to reduce imports from the United States. From 1946 to 1949, there was not a substantial change in the real value of European imports from the United States, but in the years 1950 to 1955, large increases occurred, despite the discrimination against dollar goods. Political grants largely explain these increases. From this section, it is apparent that the ratio of exports to and imports from the United States increased greatly from 1946 to 1951, though even in 1951 the ratio of exports to imports was only 40 per cent for Organization for European Economic Cooperation countries.

In 1952 and 1953, the Continental countries tended to rely less relatively on imports from the United States and Canada and to expand their exports relatively to the United States, but for the United Kingdom the improvement is not equally clear. The proportion of exports to the United States and Canada declined as did the proportion of imports from the United States. For other sterling countries there was a substantial relative loss of exports to the United States and Canada and a relative rise of imports for the two years together, but it should be observed that there was a large reduction for these countries in the excess of all imports over exports in 1952 and 1953.

In 1952, 1953, and 1954 (the figures in the text in section 2 generally go through 1951), there were significant changes in trade trends. Thus the United States excess of *exports* rose in these years and in 1955 declined. But there were large improvements for Continental European Payments Union countries. Their average excess of imports was down by about $800 million (average) in 1953 and 1954 over 1951, or almost 30 per cent. In 1955, however, there was a deterioration. For sterling countries the absolute and relative gains were even larger (a reduction of about one-half in the import deficit), with the United Kingdom accounting for the net gains and with the position of the sterling dependencies deteriorating and that of the other sterling countries improving. Again in 1955, a serious deterioration occurred.

General Agreement on Tariffs and Trade comments as follows on trade trends in 1952 and 1953:[4]

In the second period, from 1951 to the first half of 1953, the improvement in Europe's trade balance with the United States and Canada was primarily due to a decline by about $1,100 million in imports of primary products which was accompanied by a further substantial increase ($340 million) in the exports of manufactures in that region, while both Europe's exports of primaries to, and her imports of manufactured goods from, North America hardly changed. . . . Finally the ability of non-dollar suppliers to substitute their products for imports from North America was much greater in 1953 than in 1951, partly as a result of the delayed effect of the higher prices of 1951 upon output, but also owing to systematic efforts made by European countries to become less dependent on dollar imports through development of alternative sources of supply, both domestic and overseas.

3. In part the difficulties of Western Europe stemmed from her failure to find adequate substitutes for exports from dollar countries. This is the theme of section 3. But we should stress the point that as is noted earlier in this chapter and elsewhere, Western Europe had greater success after 1951 than before 1951 in finding alternative sources of supplies. It is necessary further to take account of the fact that the large dependence on United States exports was related to the large political grants made by the United States. Furthermore, as was stressed earlier, trade among regional groups of countries tended to rise in the postwar period. Hence, even if Western Europe could not cut her imports from the dollar countries adequately to solve the dollar problem, European

[4] General Agreement on Tariffs and Trade, *International Trade*, 1953, pp. 18–19.

countries were able to expand their trade with other nondollar countries and especially with dependencies and among themselves, and in view of the greater availability in the dollar countries, the trend toward regional trade was greater than the European Commission for Europe seemed to suggest.

4. In this section, we suggest some reasons why the United Kingdom has had special difficulties in export markets, but also relevant are the large gains of Western Europe inclusive of the United Kingdom in the years 1952 and 1953. In these years, though all United States imports of goods and services rose by but 9 per cent, Western Europe's sales in this market increased by 38 per cent. Again we note large gains for Europe but substantial losses for its dependencies. It is of some interest that from 1950 to 1953, Western Europe's sales of goods *and services in the United States market* rose from 22 to 29 per cent of all sales and to 31 per cent in 1954 but *all* sterling countries suffered a loss from 19 to 16 per cent and to 17 per cent in 1954. (Western Europe's proportion of sales of *merchandise,* 1950 to 1953, rose only from 12 to 20 per cent. From 1951 to 1953, however, the gains were especially large for services.) These gains should be associated with the large rise of exports generally. Thus the volume of all exports of Western Europe and the United Kingdom rose by 70 and 66 per cent, respectively, from 1938 to 1954, whereas imports were up by but 12 per cent and declined by 10 per cent, respectively.[5]

5. Relevant are statistics on the penetration of the United States in European markets. Though the United Kingdom seemed to gain ground on the Continental market, the United States gained even more. In the early 1950s, however, despite a gain of about $2 billion in exports of goods and services by the United States to Western Europe, the proportion of the United States command of Continental EPU trade markets seemed to be on the decline. (This was clearly the case for 1953 and 1954.)

6. In the sixth section of this chapter dealing with statistical matter, the major conclusions are as follows:

a. Western Europe suffered as a result of the large adverse balance of trade of a large group of countries. (In this category are included European dependencies, other sterling countries, *rest of the world,* and, on occasion, Latin America.) This adverse balance tended to rise absolutely and relatively in the postwar vis-à-vis the prewar period, but there was an improvement in 1953. Not so in 1954–1955, when Latin America, other sterling countries, and EPU dependencies all suffered a serious rise of imports vis-à-vis exports and British dependencies alone improved

[5] *The Economist,* Apr. 16, 1955; British Information Services, *Labor and Industry in Britain,* December, 1954, p. 164.

their position modestly vis-à-vis 1953. Here is part of the explanation of the deterioration of the British reserves and the modest gains of Continental Europe.

b. The availability of dollars earned by Asia, Africa, and Australia in the prewar period enabled Western Europe to balance its accounts with the United States, but instead of providing dollars, these countries were consumers of dollars in the postwar period, though, in part, the dollars were provided through loans and grants.

c. Large gains in exports from Western Europe to these regions, hence, did not yield the expected dollars or, until 1952–1953, many goods that might be substituted for dollar goods. In fact, European imports from these regions were roughly of the same proportions to total imports in 1953–1954 as in 1937.

d. Unrequited exports from Europe to these regions (e.g., grants or loans or withdrawals of balances) explain in part the failure to obtain goods in return.

7. *Trade and trends in reserves,* 1952 *to* 1955, varied greatly from earlier trends. In general the nondollar world gained in dollar balances and gold. In the years 1953 and 1954, the accretions seemed to amount to $4.5 billion. But the gains were unevenly divided, with Europe increasing its reserves substantially, Latin America moderately, and the other parts of the world (outside Europe, the Americas, and Iron Curtain countries) losing heavily. The favorable movement of reserves for nondollar countries was related to changes in the trade and service balance as well as to capital movements. In 1955, gains for nondollar countries were moderate (about $1 billion), with the United Kingdom in difficulties.

8. *A loss of competitive power in third markets* is part of the explanation of the dollar problem for Western Europe. A comparison of the penetration of the United States as against competitors in various markets shows substantial gains for this country. (In 1937, United States and Canada accounted for 17 per cent of world imports; in 1952 to 1954, for 24 per cent.) Only in the United Kingdom and other sterling countries did the United States (and Canada) lose ground in 1952 to 1954 compared with the prewar period, and here the explanation was in part discrimination. On the European Continent, in Latin America, in Canada, in other sterling countries, and in the *rest of the world,* the relative gains of this country were substantial. In part, the explanation lies, of course, in loans and especially grants of the United States.

9. A similar picture is revealed when the analysis is based on British rather than United States statistics.

10. A final problem is the relation of exports to prices of export commodities. Here the smaller rise of prices of commodities exported by the

United States and Western Europe is relevant, but despite the favorable price history of the underdeveloped countries, they suffered a deterioration in their international position.

1. *United States and Imports*

It is commonplace that imports into the United States are closely related to national income in this country. The level of income has been a much more important factor in the last generation than changes in commercial policy. From the years 1933 to 1939, for example, imports into the United States rose by $900 million. This was a period during which large cuts were made in tariffs and national income rose by $35 billion. But from 1939 to 1953, when tariffs were cut as they had been in the earlier period, imports rose by $9.6 billion. In this period, gross product had risen by $278 billion. In the later period, the increase of imports was ten to eleven times that of the earlier period and of income, eight times.

The relation is also given clearly by Table 28-1.

Table 28-1. Gross National Product and Imports, Dollar and Percentage Movements, 1920 to 1939, Various Years

Years	Billions of dollars		Per cent	
	GNP	Imports	GNP	Imports
1920–1921	−16.7	−2.81	−19	−52
1921–1929	+30.0	+1.89	+41	+74
1929–1932	−45.5	−3.12	−43	−70
1932–1939	+32.1	+1.07	+55	+79

SOURCE: *European Cooperation Administration Commerce Mission*, table I (the author's calculations).

It is clear from these figures that in periods of great change, imports fluctuate with income, though more than income. Perhaps this helps to explain the European fears of an American depression. These fears are not based merely on Marxist theory. A decline of income on the 1920–1921 model might reduce imports by $5 billion to $6 billion. In addition, there would be losses resulting from reduced aid and loans. Inclusive of secondary effects of reduced exports on United States income (the export multiplier) the effects on the rest of the world might be serious indeed. The 1953–1954 experience was reassuring, however, though this relates only to a modest decline.

As a general rule, imports rise with income and fall with income. Over the years 1919 to 1953, a total of thirty-five years, the relative movements failed to be in the same direction only in three years (Table 28-2).

Table 28-2

Year	% change in income	% change in imports
1928	+2	−3
1933	−4	+12
1952	+5	−2

SOURCE: *European Cooperation Administration Commerce Mission,* table 1, and International Monetary Fund, *International Financial Statistics.* Note that the latter gives import figures on an f.o.b. basis and for 1946 also shows inverse movements.

An examination of annual relative changes of GNP and United States imports reveals a fairly persistent tendency of imports to rise or fall relatively more than GNP. There are, of course, some exceptions.

This same tendency prevails even when the relative change in imports and GNP is put in real terms (corrected for prices).

Table 28-3 reveals the trends of United States imports of manufactured goods from 1948 to 1954. It will be noted that from 1948 to 1953–1954 there was a rise of imports of manufactured goods of 44 per cent.[6]

Table 28-3. Changes in Value, Volume, and Price (Unit Value) of United States Imports of Manufactures

	Millions of dollars	Index numbers (1936–1938 = 100)		
		Value	Volume	Unit value*
Value, 1948.....................	2,927	298	126	237
Change:				
1948–1949.....................	−264	−27	−4	−13
1949–mid-1950.................	+460	+47	+36	−23
Mid-1950–mid-1951.............	+1,221	+125	+26	+40
Mid-1951–mid-1953.............	+305	+31	−5	+24
1951–1953–mid-1954............	−142	−15	+2	−11
Value, 1953–1954................	4,507	459	181	254

* The unit-value index has been determined by dividing the volume index into the value index. As shown in the table, it slightly differs from the official figures.

From the last quarter of 1948 to the last quarter of 1949, GNP and industrial production in the United States fell almost identical percentages as from the second quarter of 1953 to the first half of 1954. But total imports declined by 19½ per cent in the first recession and only 10 per cent in the second, whereas imports of manufactured goods

[6] General Agreement on Tariffs and Trade, "Imports of Manufactured Goods by the United States, 1948 to Mid-1954," *Trade Intelligence Paper* 3, pp. 1–6.

dropped by 23½ and 20 per cent, respectively. The drop in the value of total imports was about twice as great in the earlier recession, though the drop started from a lower level. An upward trend in sales to the United States by Western Europe ($1,100 million from 1948 to 1953–1954, of which $850 million was in manufactured goods) concealed the cyclical movements: During the first postwar recession imports from Western Europe dropped by $100 million, but during the second they rose by $100 million.[7]

The Economic Commission for Europe notes that the 1953–1954 recession was unusual. Imports into the United States dropped by 5 per cent in value and from Western Europe by $223 million. (The period covered varies somewhat from the above, for the comparison is of the first three quarters of 1953 and the corresponding period for 1954.) But against this decline Western Europe's sales to overseas countries rose by $800 million and to Eastern Europe by $175 million. Overseas countries sold $400 million more to Europe and were prepared to sacrifice reserves. Hence the small effects of the recession—not to mention the upward trend of output and trade in Western Europe.[8]

The complaint is frequently made that imports into the United States are small. To some extent, this position can be supported by facts. With about two-fifths to one-half of the world's income, this country accounts for about one-sixth of the world's import trade, or about 30 per cent of the proportion of its income. Compare, for example, Canada, which with 6 per cent of the United States income has an import trade 40 per cent as large (seven times as large relatively as United States imports). A comparison of United States and Canadian import trade and national income points toward excessive restrictionism in this country, but this seems to me to be only one explanation. A much more important one is the fact that this country, like the U.S.S.R. (which used to import a value equal to about 1 per cent of its income), is relatively self-sufficient. In the last generation, the magic of chemistry, the need of defense protectionism (e.g., shipping, synthetics, rubber), the spread of industrialization, and increased servicing at home tended to cut trade further. When the economies of scale can be attained by many more countries (hence the differences in unit costs are reduced and the case for trade weakened) or synthetics can make imports dispensable, then trade tends to fall.

It is an interesting fact, however, that despite these developments, United States import trade has expanded greatly in recent years, both absolutely and relatively. For example, whereas its import trade in 1938

---

[7] *Ibid.*

[8] Economic Commission for Europe, *Economic Survey of Europe in 1954*, pp. 84–86.

was 10+ per cent of the world's, by 1948 it was 13+ per cent and for 1952 to 1954, 15— per cent, a net relative gain of almost 50 per cent. Even as a percentage of GNP, our import trade rose from 1948 to 1953, as it did from 1938 to 1953, though not to the predepression level. The record is even better than it seems if allowance is made for the fact that, as compared with the twenties, this country tends to spend much more on services relatively speaking and therefore for this reason imports are discouraged: Services are primarily a domestic product (Table 28-4).

Table 28-4. Percentage of Imports to GNP

1919–1920 = 5.4	1934–1939 = 3.0	1953 = 3.0
1921–1929 = 4.3	1946–1948 = 2.7	1954 = 2.9
1930–1933 = 2.8	1949–1952 = 3.2	

SOURCE: European Cooperation Administration Commerce Mission and International Monetary Fund, *International Financial Statistics*. (1952 IMF figure for imports adjusted to Department of Commerce Series.)

Of interest is the point that if imports were as large relative to income as in the twenties, then United States imports would be $4 billion larger. But it should also be noted that the current tariff on dutiable imports is one-third that of the Fordney-McCumber Law operative in the twenties.[9]

Inclusive of imports of military services and goods, the rise has been as shown in Table 28-5.

Table 28-5. Number of Times

	Rise of imports	Rise of GNP
1953 vis-à-vis 1939.........	5	4
1953 vis-à-vis 1947.........	2	1½

SOURCE: *Economic Report of the President*, 1953.

2. *Trends in Trade*

While on the subject of trade, it is worth pointing out that there have been large changes in the proportion of trade by different areas. In general, the United States, Canada, and Latin America have gained, and the United Kingdom and Continental EPU countries have suffered large losses. The sterling area, other than the United Kingdom, has held its relative position, and the dependencies have even improved their position.

Perhaps of more significance for our present problem is the movement of trade vis-à-vis the United States. It is to be recalled that many coun-

[9] Cf. *European Cooperation Administration Commerce Mission*, p. 194.

Table 28-6. Percentage of World Exports and Imports

Area	Exports				Imports			
	1938	1948	1952	1953	1938	1948	1952	1953
United States....................................	14.9	23.5	20.6	21.1	10.4	13.4	14.5	15.5
Canada..	4.4	6.2	6.4	6.1	3.3	5.0	5.8	6.3
Latin America.................................	7.8	12.3	9.5	10.2	6.6	10.0	8.8	8.5
Continental EPU countries................	31.3	18.6	25.9	26.0	32.9	27.4	27.5	27.9
Continental dependencies.................	3.6	3.6	3.9	3.9	3.3	4.5	5.5	5.2
Sterling area.	27.6	27.9	25.3	24.7	33.5	30.5	27.5	26.1
United Kingdom...........................	13.1	12.1	10.3	10.1	19.4	14.7	12.2	12.2
United Kingdom dependencies..........	4.6	5.3	4.9	4.3	4.2	5.1	4.7	4.7
Other sterling countries................	9.9	10.4	10.0	10.3	9.9	11.3	10.5	9.2
Rest of world...................................	10.8	8.0	8.7	8.1	10.1	9.2	10.5	10.5

SOURCE: Calculated from International Monetary Fund, *International Trade Statistics.*

tries, especially in Western Europe, took special measures to restrict imports from and expand exports to the United States. Relevant figures are shown in Table 28-7.

This table reveals that the ratio of exports to the United States to imports from the United States improved substantially in 1948 and 1951 over 1946 in all the classifications. [The OEEC (Western European) countries did not improve their position by 1948.] Apparently the largest relative improvement vis-à-vis the United States was made by *other* Europe (here the discouragement of trade with the Iron Curtain countries is relevant, with a saving by the United States of an excess of exports of $700 million to $800 million), by OEEC dependencies, and by *all other* countries (especially Asia and Africa), OEEC countries, Canada, and Latin America, in that order.

The above figures are for exports and imports. The balance of goods and *services* gives a somewhat different result. Against a reduction in the adverse trade balance of $402 million for OEEC countries from 1946 to 1951 shown in Table 28-7, the total balance is improved by $1,079 million; there is no net dollar improvement for Canada under the broader balance. The Latin American countries show a deterioration of $409 million (against a deterioration of $3 million in the trade balance above), and the gain of all others is cut from $627 to $439 million.

In general, the dollar imbalance on commodity account was reduced greatly. Latin America's slightly more adverse balance should be noted, a development related in part to the increase in total Latin American–United States trade. The improvement of about $400 million, or 12 per cent, was disappointing for the OEEC countries (for the entire current

Table 28-7. Excess of Imports from the United States Percentage of Exports to and Imports from the United States, 1946, 1948, and 1951

	OEEC countries*			OEEC dependencies			Other Europe			Canada			Latin America			All other		
	1946	1948	1951	1946	1948	1951	1946	1948	1951	1946	1948	1951	1946	1948	1951	1946	1948	1951
Excess of imports from, over exports to, U.S., millions of dollars	3,411	3,518	3,009	180	30	−556†	810	21	70	569	323	386	266	511	269	1,277	1,167	650
% exports to U.S. to imports from U.S..............	26	26	40	64	96	211	21	90	76	61	83	85	88	84	93	44	55	79

* Marshall Plan countries (OEEC = Organization for European Economic Cooperation).
† Excess of exports to United States.
SOURCE: Economic Commission for Europe.

balance, $1,079 million). In view of their rise of prices and national income, which ordinarily lead to a relative expansion of imports, the gains (i.e., reduction of adverse balance) were substantially larger than is suggested by these figures. Of course, to some extent the rise of income and prices was treated by a devaluation.

An examination of these figures will also reveal that the largest adjustments were made not by cutting imports from the United States (with the exception of *other* Europe, where political considerations were decisive) but by expanding exports to the United States (see Table 28-8). This does not mean, of course, that imports from the United States were not kept down drastically by restrictions but merely that the

Table 28-8. United States Trade—Percentage Change of Exports and Imports, 1946 to 1951

Area	Exports of U.S. to	Imports of U.S. from
OEEC countries.............	+17	+142
OEEC dependencies..........	No change	+230
Other Europe...............	−72	+3
Canada.....................	+83	+155
Latin America..............	+77	+96
All other..................	+37	+152

SOURCE: Economic Commission for Europe, *op. cit.*, *passim.*

improvement in the trade balance was related primarily to an expansion of exports. There is an especially striking contrast in the results for the OEEC countries and dependencies and *other* Europe, on the one hand, and Canada, Latin America, and all other countries, on the other. The latter three experienced a *large* rise of imports *from* the United States as well as a large expansion of exports to the United States (see Table 28-8).

It should be observed, however, that Latin America, with an abnormally large contribution to United States imports in 1946 (36 per cent), reduced its share to 30 per cent by 1951 and raised its share of exports to the United States from 18 to 25. In this connection, note the large changes in the relative position of OEEC, OEEC dependencies, and other Europe as against the three other groups: The first three suffered a decline of their imports from 50 to 38 per cent of total United States exports, while the rise for the others brought their percentage up from 50 to 62 per cent, their position thus rising by 60 to 65 per cent relative to Europe and its dependencies. In the proportion of exports to the United States, the two groups retained their relative position in 1951 vis-à-vis 1946. In general, then, Europe and its dependencies cut imports drastically and reduced their share of United States exports, as well as the proportion of United States exports to their national income, but they also greatly expanded their exports to the United States. It should be noted, however, that in 1951 exports of raw materials to the United States were on an unusually high level.

Perhaps a somewhat later trend should be observed. What follows is derived from official United States figures. By 1954, the excess of exports of the United States was as shown in Table 28-9.

Table 28-9. United States Trade, 1954
(In millions of dollars)

Region	Excess of exports of U.S. to regions (excess of imports of regions)	% U.S. imports from each area to U.S. exports to each region
Western Europe....................	2,313	68 (40)
Western Europe dependencies.......	−381	154 (211)
Canada...........................	796	79 (85)
Latin America....................	617	87 (93)
All other........................	1,641	62 (79)
Sterling area....................	119	96 (92)
United Kingdom.................	−100	108 (71)

SOURCE: Computed from *Survey of Current Business*, July, 1954, p. 21, and June, 1955, pp. 8ff.

In general, improvement (that is, a rise of United States imports from these regions vis-à-vis exports to these regions) continued notably for Western Europe and the sterling area (especially the United Kingdom). Other areas suffered a deterioration. (The 1951 figures are in parentheses in the last column.) Again we note the setback in 1955 and especially for sterling countries.

Improvement in the Western European situation and notably after 1951 was related to the greater dependence on nondollar sources for supplies. The overseas territories expanded their exports in the markets of metropolitan countries and notably in dollar commodities, that is, commodities otherwise available only in dollar countries. Hence Western Europe substituted imports from nondollar for those from dollar countries. Thus between 1951 and 1953, the imports of dollar commodities for four Western European countries (Belgium, France, Portugal, and the United Kingdom) from overseas dependencies rose by $331 million, or 38 per cent, and from dollar countries declined by $443 million, or 25 per cent.[10] All imports of Western Europe from outside declined from 1951–

[10] General Agreement on Tariffs and Trade, "The Role in World Trade of the Dependent Overseas Territories," *Trade Intelligence Paper* 2, 1954, pp. 1–5.

1952 to 1953–1954 by $148 million (2 per cent) and from the dollar area by $784 million (23 per cent).[11]

3. *Alternative Sources of Imports for Europe*

In one important objective, Western Europe failed in the *early* post-war period, namely, in finding sources of imports to take the place of those from the United States. The following is relevant:[12]

a. In 1948 dollars, Western European imports, in 1938, amounted to $19,400 million and $16,600 million, $16,050 million, and $17,350 million in 1948, 1950, and 1951, respectively. Imports were down by more than $3 billion in 1950 and more than $2 billion in 1951, or reductions of 17 and 11 per cent from the 1938 level.

b. However, imports from the dollar area were down by but $300 million in 1950, or 6 per cent, and up by $1,500 million, or 29 per cent, by 1951. The dollar area accounted for 27 per cent of Western European imports in 1938, 31 per cent in 1950, and 39 per cent in 1951 (all figures in 1948 dollars).

c. Under the impact of a balance-of-payments crisis in 1952, Western Europe cut its imports from $4,997 million (current dollars and quarterly rate) in 1951 to $4,165 million in the third quarter of 1952, but there was an insignificant change in the proportion of imports from the dollar areas.

In short, the improvement came largely from restrictions on imports, not from finding alternative sources of imports. But the reader should also keep in mind the point made earlier, namely, that there have been large gains of exports to the dollar countries.

d. The OEEC had planned, in 1948, to cut imports to $14,950 million by 1952–1953. Actual imports were $14,000 million in 1951–1952. But actual imports from Central and North America were $1,500 million above the programmed amount of $3,800 million, and the total imports were $950 million less.

e. A significant fact is that in 1948 dollars, imports from Eastern Europe were reduced from $3,150 million in 1938 to $1,000 million and $850 million in 1950 and 1951, an indication of the seriousness of the decline of East-West trade.

f. Finally, as observed earlier, there was an improvement for Western Europe from 1951 to 1954. United States exports to Western Europe rose by $730 million, but United States imports from Western Europe increased by $1,462 million. The improvement is also evident in Table 28-10.[13] (But cf. 1953 and 1954.)

[11] Economic Commission for Europe, *Economic Survey of Europe in 1954*, p. 102.
[12] Based on *ibid.*
[13] All figures from Economic Commission for Europe, *Economic Survey of Europe since the War*, pp. 86–87; *Survey of Current Business*, July, 1954, and June, 1955; and also International Monetary Fund, *International Statistics*.

Table 28-10

	Export trade to U.S. and Canada, %			Import trade from U.S. and Canada, %		
	1951	1953	1954	1951	1953	1954
Continental EPU countries......	8	9	7	16	12	12
United Kingdom...............	11	12	11	16	17	16

4. *Western European Exports to the United States*

An analysis of exports from Western Europe to the United States further clarifies the picture. Total exports to the United States f.o.b. amounted to $1,205 million in 1928, $508 million in 1938, $1,027 million in 1948, $1,349 million in 1950, and $2,006 million in 1951.

On the basis of a comparison of the percentage for the average of the years 1950 and 1951 vis-à-vis the average of 1928 and 1938, the United Kingdom's share dropped from 26 to 24 per cent. The only other major changes were Germany (all), 13½ to 9½ per cent; Switzerland, 4 to 7½ per cent; Belgium and Luxemburg, 7 to 10½ per cent. By 1953 and the third quarter of 1954, the British share of the United States market had dropped to 7 and 6 per cent, respectively (9 per cent in 1937). For Continental EPU countries the decline was from 14 to 12 and 11 per cent, respectively.[14]

An examination of United States import statistics reveals that from 1951 to 1953 Western Europe made important gains in the United States markets. This is especially evident in the fact that whereas total imports of goods and *services* of the United States had risen by only $1,356 million and of merchandise declined by $248 million, Western Europe's exports to the United States rose by $1,342 million and $329 million, respectively.[15] Table 28-11 also stresses another point, namely, that the gains for Western Europe (especially large for export services) were offset by losses of dependencies and other underdeveloped areas. The other Americas, however, continued to gain in the market of the United States.[16]

In 1954, similar trends prevailed. United States imports of goods and

[14] From International Monetary Fund, *International Trade Statistics.*

[15] But note that 1951 gives OEEC countries and 1952 and 1953, Western Europe, the latter of which includes Finland, Spain, and Yugoslavia. Hence the rise is overestimated to some extent.

[16] Cf. International Monetary Fund, *International Monetary Statistics*, February, 1955, p. 32.

Table 28-11. Percentage Change of United States Imports, 1951 to 1953

Area or country of origin (except 1)	All goods and services	Merchandise adjusted exclusive of military expenditures
1. All United States imports.............	+9	−2
2. Western Europe*.....................	+38	+17
3. Western Europe dependencies*.........	−3	−8
4. Sterling area.......................	−8	−22
5. United Kingdom.....................	+28	+16
6. All others (exclusive of above and other Americas)........................	−6	−22

* 1951 = OEEC; 1953 = Western Europe.
SOURCE: Calculated from *Survey of Current Business*, July, 1954.

services declined by 3½ per cent; of imports from Canada, 4 per cent; and from Latin America, 4 per cent; but from Western Europe there was a rise of 2 per cent and from the United Kingdom of 8 per cent. *All* sterling countries maintained their relative position.

For the early postwar period and even for later years Table 28-12 is of some interest. A country tends to lose ground in export markets be-

Table 28-12. Western Europe's Exports to the United States by Commodities and United Kingdom's Share†

Commodity	Western Europe, % total export trade by commodities			United Kingdom, % total		
	1928	1938	1951	1928	1938	1951
a. Metals and machinery.........	6	6	24	33	19	9
b. Food........................	14	11	10	18	7	7
c. Textiles and manufactures......	21	14	15	42	42	39
d. Leather, fur and manufactures..	11	4	3	33	35	34
e. Beverages....................	....	9	10	..	70	68
f. Precious stones and metals......	6	5	7	22	13	47
g. Chemicals and related products	7	9	9	14	14	19
h. Machinery....................	2	3	3	19	23	31
i. Vehicles and parts.............	⅙ of 1%	⅕ of 1%	2	0	0	90
j. Tobacco, clocks and watches, and wood, cork, and manufactures.....................	10	21	12	6	2	2
k. Others.....................	18	19	9	43	26	25

† Totals do not add up to 100.
SOURCE: Calculated from materials in *Economic Survey of Europe since the War*, p. 279.

cause its exports are either less in demand in general or in increased competition from similar exports of other countries.

I have singled out the United Kingdom for special treatment because her balance-of-payments problems have been especially troublesome.

In the table, items *a* to *d* and *k* are the most troublesome ones for the United Kingdom, either because her share of exports to the United States has been drastically reduced (metals and machinery,[17] food, and all other) or because commodities in which the British are vitally interested account for a declining part of trade (food and all other). Not only is food less important as a means of earning dollars in the United States, but the British participation has fallen greatly. In beverages, there is little change in the importance of British contributions. Precious stones, chemicals, machinery, and vehicles and parts are all industries which have become more important, and the British competitive position has improved, but they are not nearly so important in Europe's exports as industries *a* to *e*. Under *j*, we include three industries tending to grow in importance in which British participation is small.

In one respect, the British situation is more vulnerable than it seems here, for Germany is a serious threat in the fifties, and in chemicals (Germany's share down from 46 to 18 per cent), in vehicles and parts (Germany's share down from 100 to 5), in machinery (Germany's share down from 52 to 22 per cent), her competition is especially threatening as she seeks to recover her prewar position. It should also be noted that Switzerland, in staying out of the war, was able to improve its competitive position greatly, especially in leather, furs and manufactures, precious stones, and metals and machinery.

The trade history of the later fifties may reflect this increased competition. In rereading the last paragraph, I check with the latest figures. From 1951 to 1954, the rise of exports was as follows:[18]

Germany, Federal Republic . . . .   +51%
Continental EPU countries . . . .   +11%
United Kingdom . . . .   +2%

Recent gains in third markets vis-à-vis the United States and also of Germany and even France vis-à-vis the United Kingdom are evident in Table 28-13.

5. *Sales of United Kingdom, Western Europe, and United States by Categories to Western Europe and Other Areas, 1938 and 1951, and 1951 and 1953*

Another approach to an appraisal of British competitive power is to compare exports of the United Kingdom and other European countries

---

[17] France and Belgium made remarkable relative gains.
[18] International Monetary Fund, *International Financial Statistics.*

Table 28-13. Exports to Overseas Countries Outside the Dollar Area: First Half of 1952 to First Half of 1954

	United Kingdom	France	Western Germany	7 Western European Countries	United States
1st half 1952, millions of dollars..................	308	127	177	959	1,176
1st half 1954, millions of dollars..................	225	152	272	951	988
% change................	−27	+20	+54	−1	−16

SOURCE: Computed from *Economic Survey of Europe in 1954*, p. 97.

to Western Europe and other areas. The comparison is between 1938 and 1951, and all the figures are in dollars of 1948 purchasing power.[19]

United Kingdom exports of *food and raw materials* to Western Europe were way down (by almost 45 per cent) and to other areas were up by about 15 per cent. All of Western Europe increased exports of these items to Western Europe, and the gain of Western Europe in these exports to other areas exceeded that of the United Kingdom to these areas.

In textiles and miscellaneous industries, United Kingdom exports to Western Europe rose by about one-half and somewhat less to other areas. Her record was better than that of the rest of Western Europe.

Britain's success in increasing exports within the categories of engineering, metals, and chemicals is impressive, showing a rise of $2\frac{1}{2}$ times from 1938 to 1951 to Western Europe and $1\frac{1}{2}$ times to other areas. Again the record is much better than for Western Europe.

For all items considered together the United Kingdom's export gains exceeded those of Western Europe by about two-thirds for trade to Western Europe and less than one-third to the other areas. In relation to most important Western European countries, the United Kingdom gained in exports to Western Europe. (Denmark's position improved a little more, and Italy and the Netherlands equally, but in relation to exports to other areas, France gained much more and Switzerland and Denmark also gained more.)

In the Western European market, the relative gains of the United States exceeded those of the United Kingdom and, by an even greater margin, those of Western Europe, especially in the food and raw-material category. In textiles, the United States lost ground in the Western European markets to Western Europe and the United Kingdom and in engineering to the United Kingdom. In other areas, the United States

[19] The original material upon which this analysis is based is in Economic Commission for Europe, *op. cit.*, p. 102.

improvement greatly exceeded that of Western Europe and the United Kingdom, especially in food and raw materials.

Another classification[20] shows that the United Kingdom gained vis-à-vis the United States and Germany in exports to Western Europe (1948 prices) of machinery and chemicals and gained even more in other manufactures (rise of 115 per cent for the United Kingdom, 14 per cent for the United States, and 9 per cent for Western Germany vis-à-vis all of Germany in 1938).

An examination of exports of the United States from 1950 to 1953 reveals an increase both absolutely and relatively to Western Europe. Whereas in 1950 United States exports of goods *and services* amounted to $14.4 billion and exports to Western Europe $4.5 billion, or 32 per cent of the total, by 1953 the total was $21.3 billion, with Western Europe accounting for $7.7 billion, or 37 per cent. Again these figures point to failure despite discrimination to curb the inflow of United States imports, but the trend seems less disappointing when attention is directed toward the percentage of *merchandise* imports into Europe. In Continental EPU countries, the United States share of imports declined from 1950 to 1953 and the share of Continental EPU countries increased, but the gains for the United States in the British market are supported even by British import figures.[21]

6. *Failure to Cash In on Overseas Exports*

We have stressed above the large rise of overseas exports, more so for Western Europe generally than for the United Kingdom. In no small part the dollar problem became more acute because the increased sales to third countries did not yield dollars they had before the war when these countries sold to the dollar area and used part of the proceeds to buy from Western Europe, which in turn thus obtained the dollars required to liquidate their debt to the Western Hemisphere.

In this connection, it should be stressed at the outset that the trade balance of the third countries (this category includes all countries but Western Europe, United States, Canada, and Iron Curtain countries) was much less satisfactory in the early fifties than before the war. The following figures are germane: These countries had an adverse balance of $350 million in 1938, a favorable balance of $1,042 million in 1950, and an adverse balance of $5,305 million in 1952, $1,673 million in 1953, and $1,877 million in 1954. The adverse balance was 5 per cent of $7.6 billion of export trade of these countries in 1938, 20 per cent of the $27 billion in 1952, 6 per cent of $27 billion in 1953, and 7 per cent of $29

[20] See *ibid.*, p. 94, for source materials.
[21] Figures from *Survey of Current Business*, July, 1954, and International Monetary Fund, *International Financial Statistics*.

billion in 1954. By the last year sterling countries (other than the United Kingdom) were roughly in balance on trade, and Latin America had a credit balance, but EPU dependencies and the "rest of the world" had an adverse balance of about $2.5 billion.[22] The deterioration in balance of overseas countries puts a much greater burden on Western Europe, either in financing the larger dollar value of imports or in the loss of dollars that otherwise would have been available.

Western Europe's failure to divert more of its exports to the dollar area is also reflected in its large exports to other areas. By 1951, Western Europe's exports were up (in 1948 dollars) by more than 40 per cent over exports of 1938 ($10 billion to $14.15 billion) and by 63 per cent over the volume of 1948. Exports to the dollar area were up by two-thirds over the 1938 level and close to double the 1948 level. Unfortunately, it was the large gains in exports to the overseas sterling area and dependent territories which failed to yield the required dollars. These exports rose by 93 per cent from 1938 to 1951, as against 41 per cent for all exports.[23]

These increased sales overseas would have helped solve the dollar problem had these countries provided supplies that could have been substituted for those drawn from the dollar area or had they provided dollars, but they did neither in adequate quantities. (But note the increased supplies from these countries in 1952 and 1953.) In fact, the overseas countries do not provide a larger part of Western Europe's imports than in 1938. From 1937 to 1953, imports of Continental EPU countries from the European dependencies, rest of world, and other sterling countries declined from 46 to 37 per cent; the United Kingdom imports from these countries increased, however, from 58 to 64 per cent.[24]

There are various explanations of these failures. First, much of the exports was unrequited. Thus over a postwar period that lasted 5½ years, India, Pakistan, Iraq, and Ceylon paid for imports by drawing down their balances by £300 million, a value equal to one-third of their imports from the United Kingdom. Again, during the 6½ years ending June, 1952, private capital of £1 billion went to British Dominions or colonies, or one-fifth of the British exports to this area. From 1949 through 1954, the British advanced £1,224 million.[25] Second (and related to the above), the capital exports did not yield the imports to European countries as anticipated—in the French case because the capital outlays yield goods for export from the underdeveloped coun-

---

[22] Calculated from *International Financial Statistics.*
[23] Economic Commission for Europe, *op. cit.,* p. 100.
[24] *International Financial Statistics.*
[25] *United Kingdom Balance of Payments, 1946–1954,* pp. 10–11.

tries only after a long interval, in the British case because the independent British countries have embarked on large industrialization programs
and require an increased proportion of food and raw materials for their
own use. Third, the overseas countries tend to increase their imports
from the dollar area, and thus the dollars are consumed before they
become available to Western Europe.[26] Indeed, the British dependencies
increased their export balance to the United States and Canada from
$171 million in 1937–1938 to $411 million and $500 million, respectively,
in 1950 and 1951, but the deficit of the independent overseas sterling
countries rose from $93 million to an average deficit of $177 million in
the years 1948 to 1951. In fact, the Economic Commission for Europe
notes that the overseas sterling countries increased their exports to the
dollar area in real terms by 40 per cent from 1937–1938 to 1948–1951.
But the rise of imports by three-quarters from the dollar area and the
fall in the purchasing power of gold more than offset the rise of exports
and the improved terms of trade for the sterling countries. Over the
years 1946 to 1952 (first half of 1952 at annual rate), the overseas franc
and sterling area had a net deficit with the dollar area of $363 million.[27]

An over-all examination of other sterling countries reveals that they
tended to drain the dollar resources of the United Kingdom, but we
should distinguish between the independent sterling countries and the
British colonies, the latter on the whole tending to improve the dollar
position of the sterling countries. In general the pressure to withhold
dollars from the sterling pool (e.g., South Africa) and failure to restrain
adequately the consumption of dollar balances helped bring about periodic crises. Inflationary policies in the sterling countries tended to aggravate the situation. From 1946 to 1952, there was a reduction of $630
million in the drawings from the sterling-area dollar pool. Among the
important contributions were $417 million by the United Kingdom and
$1,990 million by the United Kingdom colonies; other sterling countries
drained $1,341 million, with the drawings of India, Pakistan, Australia,
and Ireland especially large. In 1953 and 1954 (provisional), the United
Kingdom colonies contributed $562 million and the other sterling coun-
tries withdrew $243 million.[28]

United States trade statistics suggest burdens on Europe's reserves
associated with the large adverse balance on merchandise and service
account for the underdeveloped countries. The adverse balance of

[26] Cf. G. Haberler, "The Foreign Trade of Western Europe: Accomplishments and
Prospects," *The Academy of Political Science*, 1953, p. 83.
[27] All figures from Economic Commission for Europe, *op. cit.*, pp. 100–103, 111–
120.
[28] *United Kingdom Balance of Payments, 1946–1954*, no. 2, table 9; K. M. Wright,
"Dollar Pooling in Sterling Area, 1939–52," *American Economic Review*, 1954, pp.
559–576; and E. Zupnick, "The Sterling Area's Central System," *Quarterly Journal
of Economics*, February, 1955, pp. 71–84. Cf. pp. 486–491 of this book.

OEEC dependencies, the sterling countries (exclusive of the United Kingdom), and *all other* countries (exclusive of the above, Europe, Canada, Latin America, and Iron Curtain countries) was as shown in Table 28-14. (In 1954, the adverse balance was in excess of $1,200 million.)

In general, what is significant is the substantial size of the deficits and the tendency of these countries to increase their imports when their exports rise; note the changes for 1951. This excess of imports puts a burden upon the reserves of Western Europe, but also it reflects capital imports and grants from the United States. It should be noted that on

Table 28-14. United States Trade with Underdeveloped Countries,
1949 to 1953
(In millions of dollars)

	1949	1950	1951	1952	1953
United States imports from these under-developed countries.................	3,204	4,527	6,199	5,685	5,461
United States exports to these countries	5,443	4,046	6,472	6,402	6,244
Total balance vis-à-vis United States...	−2,239	+481	−273	−717	−783

SOURCE: Calculated from *Survey of Current Business*, July, 1954.

the whole the British countries (and notably the colonies) were in a stronger position vis-à-vis the United States than the other countries included in this table. But in contrast to the prewar period, these countries did not accumulate an excess of credits vis-à-vis the United States.

It should also be noted that Western Europe encountered difficulties in coping with United States competition in overseas areas, in part because exports were often tied to United States aid or loans and in part because some countries (e.g., Japan) required commodities that could be provided by the United States and not by Western Europe.[29]

7. *Trade and Reserve Trends, 1952–1955*

In the two years 1952 and 1953, the position of the outside world improved vis-à-vis the United States. This is especially evident in a contrast of the figures for 1951 and 1953:[30]

a. A reduction took place for the outside world in the adverse balance of payments on goods and services of $455 million, or 9 per cent. (This occurred despite the rise of United States merchandise exports of $952 million and of imports of but $236 million.)

b. While the United States gained $53 million of gold in 1951, it lost $1,163 million in 1953.

c. Whereas this country exported $734 million of capital in 1951, there

[29] Economic Commission for Europe, *op. cit.*, pp. 111–112.
[30] U.S. Department of Commerce figures in *Survey of Current Business*, July, 1954.

was a net inflow in 1953 of $721 million, explained in no small part by a net importation of short-term capital of $1,038 million. In other words, for the outside world gains of gold and exports of short-term dollar capital in 1953 were $1,884 million (a small part not reserves) as compared with losses of gold and an inflow of short-term capital of $84 million in 1951. Moreover, the exportation of United States capital to Canada and Latin America in 1953 amounted to $547 million as compared with a net inflow into the United States in all of $721 million—again suggesting large gains for the nondollar countries.

But against these unusual gains of almost $2 billion in 1953 and more than $3 billion vis-à-vis 1951 for the nondollar countries, we should note that unilateral transfers for the United States were $1,771 million higher in 1953 than in 1951.

In 1953 as compared with 1951, countries trading with the United States used their resources primarily, not to increase purchases from the United States, but to build up their gold and dollar resources.

A word about relations among regions. *Western Europe* absorbed most of the *rise* (over 1951) of unilateral transfers ($1,482 million), of gold ($1,026 million), and of capital exports to the United States ($1,355 million). For the year, unilateral transfers exceeded the remainder of the adverse balance of payments by about $2 billion, the difference being absorbed in accretions of gold and dollar balances *by nondollar countries*.

The United Kingdom and the sterling countries showed a different pattern from that of Western Europe. The sterling countries reduced imports from the United States more than they expanded exports. [In fact, exports of all sterling countries to the United States were less than in 1951 (but more for the United Kingdom).] The sterling countries greatly improved their balance of goods and services with the United States. Western Europe, exclusive of the United Kingdom, suffered a deterioration in its balance. The gains of gold at the expense of the United States, however, were largely concentrated on Continental EPU countries. The sterling countries did not greatly increase their dollar assets, and an explanation of this fact is that unilateral transfers were greatly reduced (for the United Kingdom they were $254 million in 1951 and −$44 million in 1953—a return flow to the United States).

For the other regions the significant changes vis-à-vis the United States, 1951 to 1953, were as follows:

Latin America: A large drop of United States exports to Latin America —$725 million, or 19 per cent—and a drop in the adverse balance on merchandise and service account from $1,033 million to $193 million.

All other countries (primarily Asia, Africa, the Near East, exclusive of sterling and European dependencies): A rise of unilateral transfers of about $530 million and an adverse balance of merchandise and serv-ices of $418 million.

Preliminary figures point to a similar trend in 1954, though the trend in the second half of 1954 was not favorable. The United Kingdom and the Continental EPU countries continued to gain reserves for the two years 1953 and 1954 as a whole. In fact, the whole nondollar world seemed to add $4.5 billion additional of gold and exchange in 1953 and 1954 and $1 billion in 1955. The reserve position of Latin America improved (and primarily in foreign exchange), and the sterling countries (other than United Kingdom) suffered large losses in these two years.

In 1954, Western Europe's balance with the United States on goods and service account improved by almost $600 million, but that of sterling countries deteriorated by $239 million and the United Kingdom by $78 million. In 1955 there was a further improvement of $600 million for Western Europe; but in the second and third quarters of 1956 there was a deterioration of $500 million vis-à-vis the same period in 1955.

8. *The European Dollar Problem and Competition in Third Markets*

We have noted above that the United States had gained ground not only in its share of total export trade but also in its share of Western European markets. Here it may be helpful to survey more carefully the competitive position of the United States and Western Europe in third markets, for much is made of the point that penetration of third markets held by dollar countries can greatly ease the dollar problem.

In the United Kingdom market, the share of the United States, Canada, and Latin America was substantially less in 1950 to 1953 than in 1937; the Continental EPU countries had increased their share some-what in this market, and other sterling countries and dependencies sub-stantially (for the last, 31 per cent in 1937, 38⅓ per cent in 1950 to 1952, and 43 per cent in 1953). These movements reflect discrimination against dollar countries and the effects of sterling convertibility in encouraging trade among sterling countries and of the EPU in stimulating trade among Western European countries. In view of the greater availability of supplies in the dollar countries, the conclusion may be drawn that the effect of inconvertibility and dollar shortage was a tendency for trade to move in uneconomic channels.

In the markets of United Kingdom dependencies, the same trends are apparent, though the relative gains of the United Kingdom and Conti-nental EPU countries are in part at the expense of other sterling coun-tries and the *rest of the world*.[31] But if Europe improved its position somewhat in these countries, in the markets of other sterling countries it lost to the United States and Canada and other sterling countries. In

[31] As defined by the IMF.

the markets designated *rest of the world,* the United States gained heavily with Europe's position roughly unchanged (a decline in 1953). In part, the large gains for the United States in these countries (notably Asia) are associated with military operations and government unilateral grants. The competitive position obviously improves when exports are given away.

In Latin America and Canada, the failures of European countries to reestablish their position are especially evident. Thus the United States' share in Latin American import trade rose from 44 per cent in 1937 to 60 to 61 per cent in 1950 to 1953, whereas the share of Continental EPU countries dropped from 26 to 18 per cent (to 15 per cent in the latter part of 1953), and the United Kingdom's share was down from 13 to 8 per cent in 1950 to 1952 (7 per cent in the latter part of 1953). Movements in Canada are roughly in the same proportions, with the EPU countries losing less relatively, with the United Kingdom's proportion dropping from 18 to 10+ per cent and other sterling countries suffering even larger losses (11 to 6⅔ per cent in 1950 to 1952 and to 2½ per cent in the latter part of 1953). This failure of other sterling countries to maintain their position in the dollar markets was, of course, also costly in terms of the European dollar position.

Finally, we return to the markets of Continental EPU countries. Unlike the trends in the United Kingdom, the United States' share rose greatly, much more than the share of other Continental EPU countries. The United Kingdom roughly maintained its position, other sterling countries gained, and the rest of the world lost (the last in part because of the effects of war). By 1953–1954, the United States seemed to be losing ground and other European countries gaining.[32]

In general, the trends from 1937 to 1953 continued into 1954. From 1953 to 1955, however, there were some signs of improvement. In Latin America, imports from Continental European Payments Union countries rose from 20 to 23 per cent, while those from the United States and Canada dropped from 54 to 49 per cent. The Continental European Payments Union countries increased their share of the market in the United States and Canada from 11 to 12 per cent. But the penetration of Continental European Payments Union countries by the United States and Canada increased; and in all these instances the sterling-area countries and the United Kingdom either maintained their position or lost.

9. *Structure of Trade of Sterling Countries*

How does the structure of trade seem viewed from the angle of United Kingdom *total* trade? Relative exports to the United States and Canada

---

[32] Statistics based on material in International Monetary Fund, *International Financial Statistics,* March, 1954.

declined somewhat from 1937 to an average of 1950 to 1954 (12 to 11.6), and imports from these countries (1937 to 1950–1954 average) were down from 20 to 16 per cent. This suggests the greater significance of restrictions on dollar imports than expansion of dollar exports. Allowance should be made for the large rise of United States imports. As might be expected from earlier discussions, United Kingdom trade with other EPU countries changed relatively little and with Latin America declined. Her export trade to United Kingdom dependencies rose from 9 to 14.75 per cent and import trade from 7 to 16 per cent, suggesting great advance in this trade. (These figures are for the years 1937 to 1950–1953.) In contrast, relative exports to other sterling countries rose much less, and imports were 24 per cent of the total in 1937 and 1950 to 1953. Exports and imports both declined substantially in relation to the *rest of the world.*

A rise of exports of other sterling countries to the United States and Canada (10 per cent in 1937 to 12½ per cent for 1950–1953 of all exports) suggests the favorable interpretation of large dollar earnings for British dependencies, but the rise of imports for these countries from 15 to 16½ per cent was less fortunate. Again the failure of these countries to maintain exports to the United Kingdom (a decline from 45 per cent of all exports in 1937 to 36.75 per cent for 1950–1953) points to the slow response of exports or substitutes for commodities from dollar countries.

10. *Commodity Prices and Trade*

In part, the explanation of the dollar shortage may be the price movement of important materials. In Table 28-15 I list items as well as the countries exporting the largest proportion.

Table 28-15 should be considered in relation to the rise of export trade and terms of trade for important countries and areas. Comparing an average of 1937–1938 and 1950–1952, we find that the largest rise in export prices and improvement in terms of trade obtained for Latin America and the United Kingdom dependencies and the least satisfactory results for the United States and the United Kingdom.

For Latin America the spectacular rise in the price of coffee and large rises for wool, zinc, lead, sugar, and copper are relevant. But note also the small rise for beef. The United Kingdom dependencies profited especially from the large rise in the prices of copper. For other sterling countries the substantial rises in the price of rice, jute, cotton, wool, and lead are especially relevant but also the small rise for butter and mutton and lamb.

On the whole, the Continental EPU countries, the United Kingdom, and the United States did not fare too well. Especially germane for

Table 28-15

Commodity	Price rise, avg. of 1950–1952 over avg. of 1937–1938, %	Rise (+) or fall (−), 1953 over 1950–1952	Main countries of export (% of world exports in parentheses for 1950)
1. Coffee.................	762	+	Brazil(55), Colombia(20)
2. Rice..................	443	+	Thailand(32), Burma(27), United States (19)
3. Jute...............	384	−	Pakistan(60)
4. Cotton..............	374	−	United States(44), Egypt(21)
5. Wool...............	366(Australia)*	−	Australia(49), New Zealand(15), Union of South Africa(12), Uruguay(11)
6. Zinc...............	362	− −	Canada(39), Mexico(18)
7. Lead...............	326	−	Mexico(26), Australia(19), Canada(16)
8. Sugar..............	298	+	Cuba(71), Philippines(6)
9. Pulp and newsprint.....	298	−	Canada(53), Scandinavia(46)
10. Copper..............	287	+	Chile(34), Northern Rhodesia(26), Canada(18)
11. Newsprint............	281	+	Canada(53), Sweden(27)
12. Coal................	254†	+	Germany(39), United States(34), United Kingdom(21)
13. Rubber..............	247	− −	Malaya(53), Indonesia(30), Ceylon(7)
14. Tin.................	245	−	Malaya(44), Bolivia(21), Indonesia(16)
15. Wheat...............	234	−	United States(40), Canada(32), Australia(16)
16. Petroleum and products	224	−	Venezuela(41), Iran(23), Saudi Arabia (14)
17. Tobacco.............	221	No change	United States(47), Turkey(11)
18. Beef...............	193	+	Argentina(48), Canada(20), Uruguay(12)
19. Tea................	171	+	India(46), Ceylon(45)
20. Butter..............	155	+	Denmark(33), New Zealand(25), Netherlands(18), Australia(15)
21. Bacon and ham........	148	+	Denmark(61)
22. Mutton and lamb.......	105	+	New Zealand(72), Australia(19)

* U.S. = 224.
† U.S. = 208.
SOURCE: Original materials in International Monetary Fund, *International Financial Statistics*, December, 1953. 1953 figures based generally on first eight to ten months. − − = large decline.

these countries is the relatively small rise in the prices of manufactured goods, but it should also be noted that except for cotton and rice (of special interest to the United States) and coal (of interest to the United States, Germany, and Great Britain), these countries did not share in the gains resulting from large rises in the prices of raw materials.

Another classification (Table 28-17) gives the index of export prices and quantities—again 1937–1938 to 1950–1952 (1937–1938 = 100).

Again the greater rise of export prices for underdeveloped regions is to be noted, but here we should also stress the varying rate of expansion of exports. Against the more favorable price history of the *rest of the world* (exclusive of above and Communist countries) is to be put a gain of but 6 per cent in exports. The rise for the United States and

Table 28-16. Prices of Exports and Terms of Trade for the United States, United Kingdom, and Several Areas, 1950 to 1952 (1937 and 1938 = 100)

Area	Export prices	Terms of trade (export indices divided by import)
United Kingdom dependencies.............	273	143
Latin America........................	240	166
Other sterling countries..................	237	116
Continental EPU countries...............	209	95
United States........................	196	79
United Kingdom......................	172	72

SOURCE: Calculated from materials in International Monetary Fund, *International Financial Statistics*, December, 1952.

Table 28-17. Export Prices

Area	Export prices	Exports— quantum index
World............................	241	134
World, exclusive of U.S.............	251	132
Europe...........................	204	135
Canada and U.S...................	201	204
Rest of world*....................	276	106

* Exclusive of Communist countries.

SOURCE: Calculated from United Nations, *Yearbook of International Statistics*, 1952, p. 18.

Canada was seventeen times as great and for Europe six times as great. In 1953–1954 (average) the terms of trade of the United States improved slightly and of Latin America, of the United Kingdom, and of other sterling countries, substantially.

At the end of this chapter (summary is to be found at the beginning) we ought to say again that trade, despite its restrictions or perhaps because of rising incomes and removals of restrictions, continued to gain. By the second half of 1955, world trade (annual rate) had risen to $86 billion [the figure in 1950 was $57 and in 1954 (second half) $78 billion]. World trade had risen by 34 per cent in volume from 1950 to the second half of 1955, as compared with 33 per cent for the gains of industrial output. A striking aspect of recent gains has been the increased percentage of trade for industrial countries, related in large part to the tendency of industrial countries to get along with smaller quantities of raw materials and to rely increasingly on manufactured raw materials.

From 25 per cent in 1938, the ratio between the consumption of raw materials and fuels and the gross value of manufacturing production, had in the industrial areas fallen to 19 per cent in 1952. By 1955, it had further dropped to 17½ per cent. Or in other words, for each unit of raw materials and energy consumed, the quantity of manufactures produced in the industrial countries in 1952 was 32 per cent larger than in 1938; by 1955, the gain had further grown to 42 per cent above pre-war.

Not only economies in raw materials but also the increased impor-1tance of synthetic raw materials is relevant in explaining the reduced trade of nonindustrial countries. By 1955, the consumption of *manufactured* raw materials in industrial areas rose (in 1950 dollars) from $820 million in 1938 to $3.5 billion in 1950 and $6.4 billion in 1955.[33]

[33] See General Agreement on Tariffs and Trade, *International Trade*, 1955, 1956, pp. 1–11.

CHAPTER 29

Some General Observations

Over the last forty years periods of international disequilibrium have become much more important than they had been in the nineteenth century, which had witnessed the evolution of the classical theory of international trade. The explanation of these years of strong imbalances lies partly in the great political upheavals since 1914, with their accompanying revolutions and wars. But also relevant, and not entirely independent of the above, were two other factors: the emergence of institutional factors that interfered with the adjustments assumed under classical economics, and the rapid emergence of the United States as the dominant economic power. The latter is of particular significance for various reasons, but notably because with its growth the United States tended to absorb excessive supplies of gold which are supposed to be available for the adjustment process, and, related, for the economic isolationism in this country, which over a considerable part of the last generation or two brought high tariffs and the failure to assume the responsibilities of a great creditor country in the manner of Great Britain in the preceding 100 years.

It is not surprising that the theory of comparative costs is not the vital cog in international economics that it was in the system constructed with such brilliance by Ricardo. Aside from its relevance it should be noted that the theory itself in its present form is a much more complicated theory than the labor-cost theory which Ricardo first presented. For example, to explain the great advantages of the United States in the automobile industry would require an analysis not merely of labor costs but of many other variables, which might explain why an industrial giant like General Motors, producing 4 million cars a year, can achieve market control and also why the British or the Germans can obtain the largest segment of foreign markets by catering to the special tastes of the smaller foreign markets.

But there are special reasons why the comparative-cost doctrine is less relevant than it used to be. First, the pricing system upon which it is

543

based has become a less important factor in most economies. The dependence is much more upon planning, the allocation of resources by authority. In part the introduction of national objectives by authority may mean encouragement of industries or employment not supportable on comparative-cost principles. For example, underdeveloped countries —at least in part for noneconomic reasons and in part because a longer view and government intervention yield a different optimum structure of employment than one based on free pricing in the *current* state of the economy—depart from employments suggested by comparative costs. But it should also be allowed that often the intervention of government has resulted from the failure of the expected adjustments to function; e.g., the outflow of gold does not bring the expected decline of prices and the rise of exports. Then it may be necessary to introduce exchange control in order to ensure the minimum imports required to provide the food and raw materials for the workers to process.

The failure of the gold standard to operate satisfactorily brought new approaches to the treatment of international disequilibrium. Exchange flexibility is one approach which is consistent with the free market, especially where the rates are determined by free-market forces, with the monetary authority intervening only to protect the currency against unhealthy speculation. It is a significant fact that in the 1930s the outstanding classical economists who should have welcomed this approach were as a rule most critical of the epidemic of devaluations, which they considered most unorthodox. By the late 1940s, however, having been confronted with the alternative of exchange control, they envisaged exchange flexibility as the ideal approach, that is, consistent with free-market principles.

After World War II the introduction of numerous international institutions was an acknowledgment that the automatic forces needed some reinforcements. It was necessary to provide temporary reserves and capital to meet the needs of reconstruction and economic development and to introduce some impairment of sovereignty through control of exchange rates, restrictions on quantitative controls, and on discrimination. These and similar measures were directed toward limiting the area of economic warfare and raising the level of trade in order to increase greatly the range of trade within which adjustments might be made. But aside from the international agencies, governments participate in an increasing degree in the process of balancing international accounts.

That the disequilibrium problem continues to harass the authorities is in some respects surprising, since the managers now have available the powerful weapon of fiscal policy as well as the older weapon of monetary policy. Indeed, over the years the authorities have failed to make the most effective use of monetary policy, in part because of lack of courage and in part because of failure to understand the issues but also in part because the weapons available to the monetary managers were rather blunted. Surely the managers of the system might have been expected to do better once the more modern weapons of open-market operations, changes in reserve requirements, and qualitative controls became available. That these weapons continued to be relatively ineffective may be associated with the availability of other controls and the tough assignment to monetary authorities in an economic milieu of intense depression or one in which the pressure on limited resources was unusually great. In the early fifties there seems to be an increased interest and faith in the monetary weapon.

Undoubtedly the increased attention paid to domestic objectives and in particular full employment increased the difficulties of the monetary authorities. Whereas the earlier objectives of maintaining a fixed price for gold or even the later one of accommodating trade raised tough problems for them, that of reconciling the international with the new domestic objectives increased the difficulties for the authorities, especially since the attainment of one objective might jeopardize the other and also since a division of authority among those responsible for monetary policy, fiscal policy, and direct controls further complicated matters.

Dollar shortage over the years has come to be a symbol of the disequilibrium, but it is not the only expression of the disequilibrium. Shortages of German marks and Belgian and Swiss francs for the British and the French; quotas, exchange control, and discrimination against dollar countries; export subsidies and the increased recourse to intra-area trade—all these were also signs of disequilibrium.[1] Inconvertibility was also an expression of lack of balance, and the freedom to convert into dollars was not the only freedom abrogated by inconvertibility.

No one can say how long these periods of marked disequilibrium will continue. In the fifties, there were reassuring signs, not the least of which were the gains in third markets by nondollar countries, large relative gains of imports from nondollar countries (reflecting in part protectionism),[2] and the more skillful use of monetary and fiscal policies by nondollar countries. That the United States responded to her rapid gains of productivity by increasing incomes rather than passing the gains on in lower prices helped ease the dollar problem as did trade liberalization since the passage of the Reciprocal Trade Act in 1934. Discrimination against the dollar and the highly protectionist policies of the nondollar world also helped, though this was more like an

---

[1] On the last, see General Agreement on Tariffs and Trade, *International Trade*, 1954, pp. 9–10.

[2] *Ibid.*, p. 16. Imports for nine European countries of primary products from dollar countries dropped from 27 per cent in 1948 and 1949 to 18 and 17 per cent in 1953 and 1954.

aspirin treatment than the surgery required. By taking measures of this kind the nondollar world moved toward a balanced dollar account but only by reducing the total gains of trade. By the mid 1950s, as noted, there were reassuring signs.

How much longer the problems of international disequilibrium will trouble the world will depend especially upon the trends in the cold and hot wars. But many other factors are also relevant: the manner in which the United States takes its gains of increased productivity and similarly for the nondollar world; the trade policies of both the United States and other countries; the extent to which the day of reckoning can be put off by long-term loans and grants by the large creditor countries; the use made of these resources by the borrowing countries; the extent to which the increased need for raw materials and food by the United States over the next generation will increase the prices and the value of her imports; the skill and courage with which all countries will use both fiscal and monetary policy to contract and expand as the situation requires, taking into account both domestic and international objectives; and finally the success of the nondollar countries in capturing third markets from the United States, in turn related to skills in reallocating resources, increasing productivity, depressing relative prices, etc.   •

It is not likely that these problems are going to be solved overnight, though they may well give us less trouble than they did in the first postwar decade, in part because the imbalance in the early postwar years was related to the damage caused by the war. We can also be reasonably sure that the world in the next ten to twenty-five years will not be one with the dependence upon free-market forces that classical economics assumed. Automatic responses will not balance accounts, and it will be necessary to depend upon many overt actions by responsible authorities. That the objectives of economic policy include full employment, economic growth, and the telescoping of economic development into a relatively short time and not merely the optimum allocation of factors of production as assumed in classical economics greatly strengthens the need for planning, inclusive of central determination of savings, investments, and the use of taxes and public expenditures to help achieve these objectives. In so far as imbalance persists in the international accounts, then special treatment is required to bring about some kind of international balance. Excessive dependence on the pricing mechanism is likely to be rejected in part because these responses may be too slow, just as they are in wartimes.

At the end of a decade following World War II, world trade had recovered in a rather remarkable manner: The volume of trade in 1954–

1955 was about 50 per cent above the prewar volume, a rise not far out of line with that in output. However, as compared with the pre-World War I period, trade relative to output was still at a low level. Much progress had been made in the fifties in removing obstacles to trade, but it can also be said that though impediments remained much more important than in the prewar period, trade had rebounded satisfactorily.

However, the structure and distribution of trade had undergone significant changes which seem to have long-run relevance. Trade within industrial areas and also within regions (e.g., Western Europe, North America) and within associated countries (e.g., the sterling area) seems to be more important relatively than in the pre-World War II years. With great shortages in raw materials and/or increased economies in their use, trade in raw materials has declined. The industrial countries seem to use about one-half the input of raw materials, power, etc., per unit of value added as compared with nonindustrial countries. This means that the former process much more. Greater gains of output in underdeveloped countries then tend to be more costly in materials.

With population rising more rapidly in nonindustrial countries, their relative contribution of food exports tends to decline and the production and exports of food by industrial countries to rise. It is not surprising, then, that food prices were almost 40 per cent higher in 1954 (second half) than in 1950; raw materials, 15 per cent higher; and all traded commodities, only 10 per cent higher. The shift from agriculture to industry in part associated with development and rising income is relevant here.

It is clear that trade has recovered in a satisfactory fashion, but it is also clear that the structure of trade has changed. For example, between industrial and nonindustrial countries trade in raw materials has become much less important relatively (an 8 per cent decline in volume from 1938 to 1952); in food and manufactured goods, much more important, with respective rises of 46 and 82 per cent.

In part the trends point to uneconomic changes, e.g., the larger rise of factory output in nonindustrial than in industrial countries. There is also some evidence, e.g., in the much larger rise of textile prices in non-industrial than in industrial countries, that excessive protectionism may have been invoked. The great relative increases of regional trade may also point to some extent in the same direction, but some of these realignments are quite consistent with comparative-cost principles. For example, with much larger population increases in nonindustrialized countries and greater technical advances in industrialized countries it might be expected that the industrialized countries would produce and export more food.

Those who are convinced that the forces at work bringing on disequilibrium are rather intractable support the trend toward regional trade and protectionist devices, especially against dollar commodities. In the longer run they may seek supranational organizations. But surely the experience with the Iron and Steel Community in Europe and other existing international organizations does not support high hopes that such institutions would be favored and would achieve desired objectives in the next generation.

Perhaps in the light of the history of the first postwar decade, what may be expected would be retention of some of the abnormal controls for some time, with gradual relaxation and dependence on regional trade agreements and international organizations as the world moves back further toward a prewar pattern of trade. Surely, however, there are many changes in these patterns which are likely to be permanent or semipermanent. Estimates of the abnormal strength of the dollar, both in degree and in durability, are still uncertain elements.

A glance at the long-run trends since 1875 underlines some of the reasons for the maladjustments of the last ten years and also points toward causes at work for long periods of time. The explanation of disequilibrium is not only war and its aftermath. Europe, in particular, has experienced serious losses in the years since 1913. Trade in general has not expanded as it had from 1876 to 1913. Europe's relative position quite consistently deteriorated in the total picture and that of the large European countries and the United Kingdom especially. Europe's overseas trade and her intra-European trade became relatively less important. Europe was slow to respond to the increased competition of the United States and to the large losses suffered by textiles by turning to the products (e.g., engineering products) increasingly wanted. By responding through monetary and wage policies Europe might (and did to some extent) solve her balance-of-payments problems but through a relative deterioration in her standard of living. By importing capital and new techniques she might contribute toward higher standards and international equilibrium.[3]

Let us finally contrast the pre-World War I, the interwar, and the post-World War II periods. In the first of these three periods, say from 1850 to 1914, international economic problems were relatively simple. The United Kingdom assumed the leadership in the administration of a

[3] On the issues of the last few paragraphs, see especially General Agreement on Tariffs and Trade, *International Trade, 1954*, 1955; F. Altschul et al., *The Political Economy of American Foreign Policy* (W. Y. Elliott, ed.), 1955; and United Nations, *Growth and Stagnation in the European Economy*, 1954 (by I. Svennilson); D. C. Bok, "The First Three Years of the Schuman Plan," *Princeton Studies in International Finance*, 1955.

gold standard that worked tolerably well, though not so well as is often assumed. New gold discoveries and new techniques for manufacturing money contributed greatly to the workability of the standard. The British serving their interests, namely, a profitable outlet for savings and cheaper food and raw materials, provided large supplies of capital for external use. The combination of peace, monetary expansion, widely diffused and sustained growth, and British leadership was adequate to prevent long periods of serious international disequilibrium. The only weapon at hand was monetary policy, and that largely concentrated in Great Britain. With sustained growth, optimism prevailed, and the growth neutralized any adverse effects of excessive orthodoxy.

World War I ushered in a period of international disequilibrium. Economic collapse and inflation hit Central Europe after the war. The unfortunate return to prewar parity injured the British economy; the agricultural countries began to experience a deterioration in their position by the later twenties. With the weakening of the British money market, the United States and France shared a responsibility for leadership, but they tended to hold on to large supplies of gold, which reflected to some extent increased economic strength. Pessimism began to prevail, and the authorities, enslaved by nineteenth-century economics, continued to rely on therapy that fitted an earlier period and which did not take into account new institutions and older ones now undergoing change.

But the troublesome problems began with the Great Depression. As in the previous period (the twenties), the authorities tended to lean excessively on monetary policy. The response to structural change, for example, the change in reciprocal supply and demand for traded commodities, was slow. The major countries relied on deflationary policies which brought losses and unemployment or, with a lag, on devaluations, which allowed greater scope for monetary expansion. Competitive debasement spread, and often the debasement was introduced not only to correct a price-cost disparity but also to deal with structural problems which could not be effectively treated by monetary policy.

Many of the smaller countries, unable to contend with world-wide forces as the larger countries could to some extent through tariffs (e.g., the United Kingdom) or devaluation (e.g., the United Kingdom and the United States), had recourse to controls, multiple exchange rates, commodity agreements inclusive of restriction of output, and exports. These countries often continued their long-run trend of depreciation of their currencies. They provided part of their needed savings through the inflationary process, which, in turn, was reflected in depreciation of currencies, and one result of the expansion of money and the loss of exports was a steady depreciation of the currency.

In general, the thirties could be described as a period of disappointment. Under the pressure of declining demand, the tendency was to counter deflationary forces by restrictive measures, both of output and of trade; but there was a failure to introduce expansive policies which had begun to be urged by thoughtful economists. By the end of the thirties, output in the United States and Western Europe, despite gains of productivity and population, was roughly at the 1929 level.[4]

With World War II, the problems of balancing international accounts became more serious. The war itself was a disruptive influence, to say the least. But the war also showed that fiscal policy had large potentialities, for overnight the unemployment problem was licked as deficit financing provided the additional cash required to turn out war supplies. In the postwar era, the backlog of demand for consumption goods inclusive of housing, the great advances of consumer credit, the quest for economic development, the accompanying expansion of investment, the large tasks entrusted to government both to defend against the Iron Curtain countries and to underwrite welfare programs—all these increased inflationary pressures. Limited resources could not meet these demands without either rising prices or central allocation of demands and resources. These pressures were held in check to some extent through controls, with a tendency to relax controls in democratic countries as production recovered and exceeded prewar levels. There was much less opposition to an increased role of government to underwrite demand than in the thirties.

After World War II inflation was the threat just as deflation concerned the authorities in the thirties. Where the upward pressure was greatest, and notably in the countries damaged directly by war, the need for rehabilitation, accelerating investment, and raising standards of living tended not only to inflate the economy but also to weaken international positions. The recourse to monetary policy was often delayed. Confronted with inflationary forces, the authorities in Western European countries relied primarily on controls, but as their recovery proceeded and gains over prewar conditions were made, they began to use fiscal policy (i.e., increased taxes and reduced public expenditures) and continued to rely on increased imports to soften the inflationary flows.

In the smaller countries, e.g., Latin America, inflation proceeded much more rapidly than in the United States and even more than in Western Europe. The pressure for economic development quickened the inflationary pace, and the unprecedented demands for raw materials and food in Europe and North America brought gains of reserves for these countries and a conversion of reserves into local currencies. As incomes rose in response to increased exports and reserves, the defense mobilized against adverse balances of payments was largely one of import controls,

[4] Cf. the excellent treatment by A. H. Hansen, *The American Economy*, 1957.

export controls, multiple exchange rates, and the like. There seems to be little hope for moderating the inflationary movement in these countries other than a deflation of plans and/or increased savings and/or a large rise of capital imports.

In general, the contrast between the post-World War I and post-World War II periods is striking. Above all the attention now is concentrated on objectives of full employment, growth, and stability. In the great British crisis of 1955–1956, the difficulties lay not in inadequate output or even consumption—in fact, the gains in almost all of Western Europe since 1948 have been phenomenal—but rather in the external position. Whereas in the interwar period the internal decline induced international disequilibrium, the latter in turn further depressing output, in the post-World War II period the achievement of full employment, growth, and relative internal stability in most countries often brought problems of external equilibrium. At least the most important objectives have been achieved. The problem of continued economic advance at home will not be sacrificed to external equilibrium; convertibility is a means to an end, not an end. The crucial problem of the next ten years, in the absence of a major war, will be to reconcile full employment and growth, accompanied by the minimum amount of inflation in periods of full employment, with external stability. That does not, of course, mean that a substantial amount of inflation resulting from excessive demand, given available resources, should not be registered in pressure on the exchanges and deterioration of the international position. This pressure is a useful barometer for those responsible for internal policies.

The British crisis of 1955–1956 underlines the issues raised. In a period of nine years (1946–1955), the home costs per unit of output rose by 44 per cent, of exports of goods and services by 55 per cent. It is interesting that in the years 1953 to 1955, the respective rises were only 4 and 0 per cent, and yet a crisis developed. What is more, wholesale prices in this country rose as much as British prices in these nine years. This rise of British prices may have been excessive in a period during which national output rose by 30 per cent and industrial output by 56 per cent, though the largest part of the rise may be associated with the aftermath of war. In pointing to the rise of prices, brought on only to the extent of 20 per cent of the total by the increases in import prices, the government stresses the increase of incomes, primarily wages and secondarily profits, as factors tending to increase costs. Concerned over the substantial loss of the British share of exports of manufactured goods, the government urges moderation in income demands, continued rise of productivity, and increased savings. Inflation of costs and prices will make it difficult to pay for the necessary imports.[5]

[5] See especially *The Economic Implications of Full Employment*, Cmd. 9725, 1956,

Here, indeed, the conflict involved in achieving the national objective of high employment and growth and international equilibrium is clearly revealed. For Great Britain this is a problem of first-rate importance— and not yet solved. Somehow exports must be increased adequately out of the rising output and imports reduced relatively. Can the free market accomplish this? However, the major problem of domestic activity is close to a solution.

Name Index

Adler, J. H., 202, 506–507
Alexander, S. S., 130
Anderson, Karl L., 411, 414
Aubrey, G., 299

Bagehot, Walter, 107
Balogh, T., 141, 217–218, 233, 236
Baster, J., 287
Bean, L., 189, 287, 295
Beckerman, W., 58
Bernstein, E., 212–213, 225, 231, 236
Beveridge, Sir William, 222
Bloomfield, H. I., 141
Bohr, K. A., 306
Buchanan, N. S., 288, 295, 297, 302
Butler, R. A., 499, 501

Cairncross, A. K., 71, 74, 422
Cairnes, J. E., 4, 20, 23, 24
Cassel, G., 122–123
Chenery, H. B., 290, 291
Clark, Colin, 174, 189
Crosland, C. A. R., 233

Day, A. C. L., 510
De Scitovsky, T., 290, 310–311
De Vries, B. A., 447–450

Edgeworth, F. Y., 6, 50–51
Ellis, H. S., 247, 288, 295, 302
Enos, J. L., 467n.

Fforde, J. S., 357
Fisher, Irving, 135
Frankel, S. H., 288, 314–316

Friedman, Milton, 198–199, 230–231, 436
Fullarton, John, 89, 100, 115
Furth, J. H., 489

Goldenweiser, E. A., 160
Goschen, V., 138
Graham, F., 56, 223, 230

Haberler, Gottfried, 5, 7, 52n., 56n., 63–64, 161, 211, 230–231, 235–236, 366
(See also Subject Index)
Hagen, E. E., 291
Hansen, Alvin, 260
Harris, C. D., 168–169
Harrod, Roy, 210–211, 235–236, 332, 404, 458–459, 477, 489–490, 498
Hawtrey, R. G., 83, 102
Heckscher, E. F., 53–54, 62, 257
Hicks, J. R., 201, 218–220, 232–233, 236, 443
Hinshaw, R., 431
Hirschman, A. O., 245n.
Hoover, E. M., 167
Hume, David, 82–83, 113–114, 222
Humphrey, D. D., 347, 376
Hutt, R., 379, 450
Hutton, Graham, 29–30, 62, 490

Isard, W., 57–58, 170–171

Jevons, W. S., 100
Johnson, D. Gale, 365–366
Johnson, Harry, 213–214, 231, 236

553

Subject Index